'C' EDITION

The CELTIC fake Book

ISBN 978-0-634-01727-8

HAL•LEONARD® CORPORATION

7777 W. BLUEMOUND RD. P.O. BOX 13819 MILWAUKEE, WI 53213

Visit Hal Leonard Online at
www.halleonard.com

What Is Celtic?

What is meant by the term "Celtic"? Ireland, Scotland, Wales, the Hebrides Islands, Brittany (a region of France), and Galicia (a region of Spain) were inhabited for many hundreds of years by a group of peoples known as the Celts. Over the last 1,000 years the Celts ceased to exist as an identifiable race. However, their culture still survives in scattered parts of the British Isles and western France. Of the six languages spoken by the ancient Celts (Irish, Scottish Gaelic, Manx, Welsh, Cornish and Breton), all but Manx and Cornish are used to this day by native speakers. In modern context, the popular use of the term "Celtic music" is quite loosely defined. In many circles it is simply a synonym for "Irish"; in others it is applied heedlessly to any music (folk, new-age, even classical!) with an Irish or Scottish flavor.

This book presents a unique and diverse collection of "Celtic music." A significant attempt was made to locate and include the ancient traditional music of the Celtic countries, particularly the British Isles. There are many tunes, now otherwise lost, which were collected from native speakers in Ireland, Scotland, and the Hebrides Islands around the turn of the 20th century. More than eighty of the songs include native language other than English.

Beyond authentic Celtic music this book gives particular attention to Irish musical culture. As a bonus, we have included a considerable number of "popular" Irish songs which arose in the 19th and early 20th centuries, such as those made famous by Thomas Moore, various American Tin Pan Alley composers, and other entertainers (from the Emerald Isle and elsewhere) who were influenced by the Irish.

—The Editors

Contents

Song Index by Nationality

Folksongs from the Hebrides

Though the Hebrides Islands are now part of Scotland, they have a unique musical culture.

WELSH FOLKSONGS

IRISH POPULAR SONGS

Most date from the 19th and early 20th centuries and were composed to fit a particular popular genre. Many are American Tin Pan Alley songs, but others come from Ireland, England, Scotland and elsewhere.

SONGS IN GAELIC

'Gaelic' refers generically to the Celtic languages which are native to Ireland, Scotland and Wales. These include Irish, Scottish Gaelic, Manx, Cornish and others.

INTRODUCTORY GAELIC PRONUNCIATION GUIDE

Many of the songs in this book are presented in their native Gaelic tongue, the language of the Celts, Irish, Picts, Scots, and Welsh. While the dialects vary, they do share one common trait: the spoken Gaelic language is as beautiful and majestic as its homeland—especially in song.

Gaelic has a unique spelling system quite different from English, but don't let that intimidate you. As with any language, it takes time and practice to become accustomed to new sounds and spellings.

The following pronunciation summary is meant only as an introductory guide to help you through the lyrics. The English sounds used to describe the Gaelic pronunciation are sometimes only approximate—especially considering dialectical differences—but always reasonably close.

Foghraíocht (Pronunciation)

from John Gleeson, Coordinator of Irish Studies, University of Wisconsin-Milwaukee

Gaelic	English	Gaelic	English
a	like "a" in *father* (but not quite)	í	like "ee" in *bee*
á	like "a" in *call*	j	j
ae	like "a" in *lay*	l	l
ao	like "a" in *lay* or "ee" in *bee*, depending on dialect	m	m
		mh	v
b	b	mb	m
bh	v	n	n
bp	b	ng	n
c	k	o	like "u" in *hug*
ch	like "ch" in *J.S. Bach* (American Pronunciation)	ó	like "o" in *crow*
d	d	p	p
dh	no equivalent in English, voiced like "ch"	ph	f
		r	r
e	like "e" in *check*	s	like "s" in *song* when preceded or followed by "a," "o," or "u"; like "s" in *sugar* when preceded or followed by "e" or "i"; never like "s" in *as*
é	like "a" in *case*		
ea	like "a" in *cat*		
eo	like "o" in *hole*	t	t
f	f	t	like "ch" in *chin* when followed by "e" or "i"
fh	usually silent		
g	g	th	h
gh	no equivalent in English, voiced like "ch"	u	like "u" in *hug*
		ú	like "oo" in *zoo*
h	h (except when following another consonant)	v	v
i	like "i" in *fit*		

ABDUL ABULBUL AMIR

Words and Music by
William Percy French

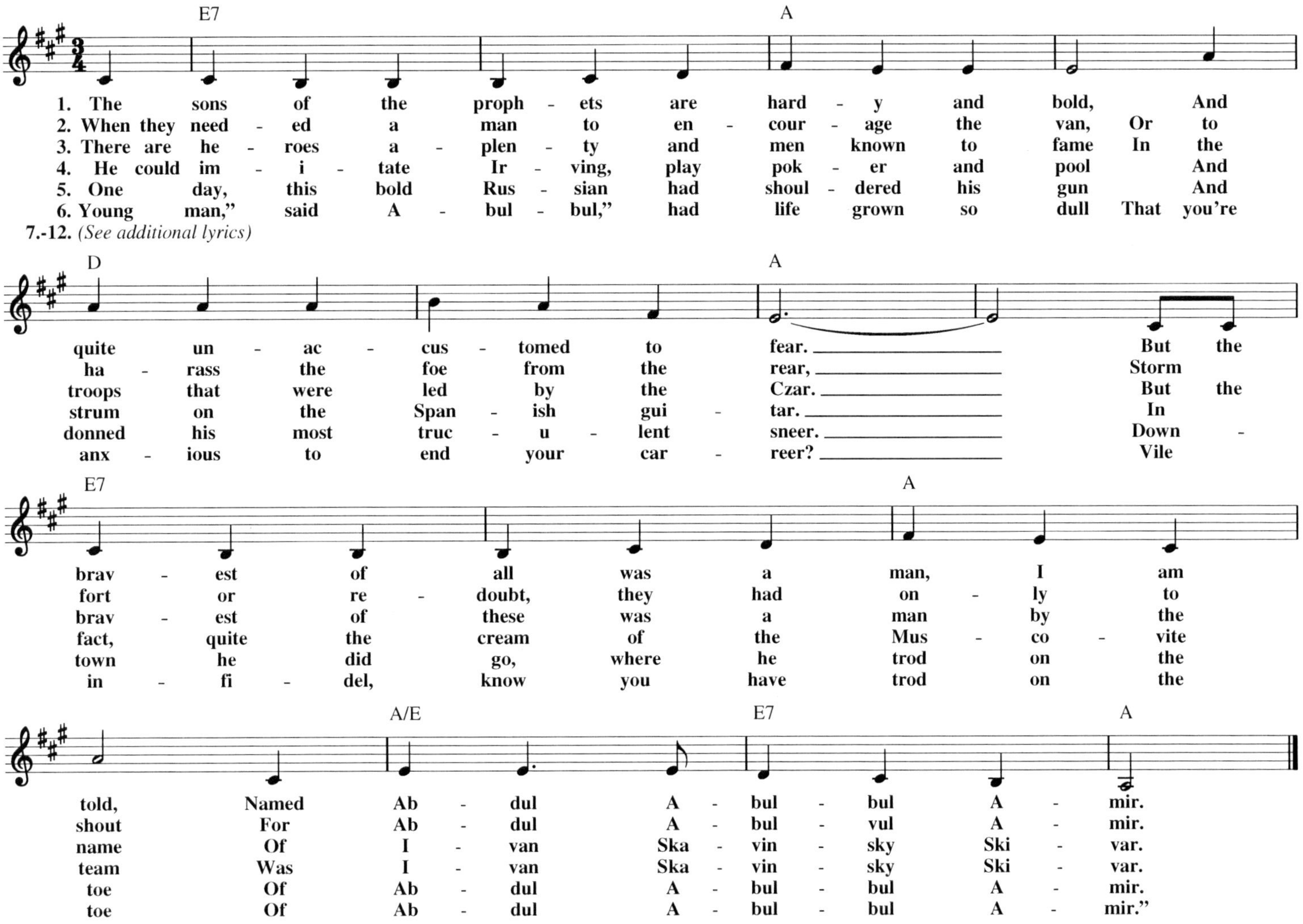

1. The sons of the proph-ets are hard-y and bold, And the brav-est of all was a man, I am told, Named Ab-dul A-bul-bul A-mir.
2. When they need-ed a man to en-cour-age the van, Or to ha-rass the foe from the rear, For Ab-dul A-bul-vul A-mir.
3. There are he-roes a-plen-ty and men known to fame In the troops that were led by the Czar. Of I-van Ska-vin-sky Ski-var.
4. He could im-i-tate Ir-ving, play pok-er and pool And strum on the Span-ish gui-tar. Was I-van Ska-vin-sky Ski-var.
5. One day, this bold Rus-sian had shoul-dered his gun And donned his most truc-u-lent sneer. Of Ab-dul A-bul-bul A-mir.
6. Young man," said A-bul-bul," had life grown so dull That you're anx-ious to end your car-reer? Of Ab-dul A-bul-bul A-mir."

7.-12. *(See additional lyrics)*

Additional Lyrics

7. Quoth Ivan, "My friend, your remarks, in the end,
Will avail you but little, I fear,
For you ne'er will survive to repeat them alive,
Mr. Abdul Abulbul Amir!"

8. They fought all that night, 'neath the pale yellow moon;
The din, it was heard from afar;
And great multitudes came, so great was the fame
of Abdul and Ivan Skivar.

9. As Abdul's long knife was extracting the life -
In fact, he was shouting "Huzzah!"
He felt himself struck by that wily Kalmuck,
Count Ivan Skavinsky Skivar.

10. The sultan drove by in his red-breasted fly,
Expecting the victor to cheer;
But he only drew nigh to hear the last sigh
Of Abdul Abulbul Amir.

11. There's a tomb rises up where the blue Danube flows;
Engraved there in characters clear;
"Ah stranger, when passing, please pray for the soul
Of Abdul Abulbul Amir."

12. A Muscovite maiden her lone vigil keeps,
'Neath the light of the pale polar star;
And the name that she murmurs as oft as she weeps
Is Ivan Skavinsky Skivar.

AIGNISH ON THE MACHAIR

Folksong from the Hebrides

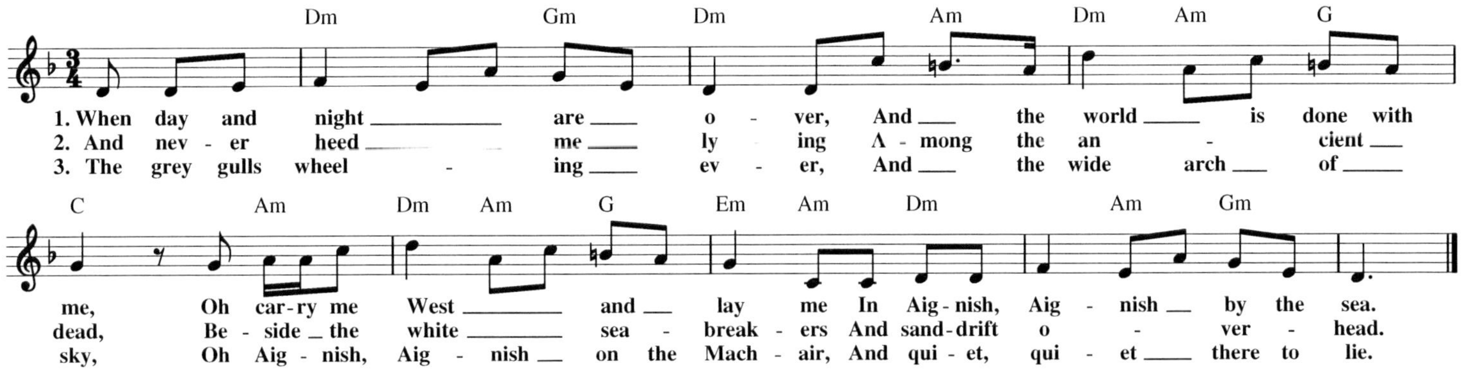

1. When day and night are o-ver, And the world is done with me, Oh car-ry me West and lay me In Aig-nish, Aig-nish by the sea.
2. And nev-er heed me ly-ing A-mong the an-cient dead, Be-side the white sea-break-ers And sand-drift o-ver-head.
3. The grey gulls wheel-ing ev-er, And the wide arch of sky, Oh Aig-nish, Aig-nish on the Mach-air, And qui-et, qui-et there to lie.

ACROSS THE WESTERN OCEAN

Irish folksong

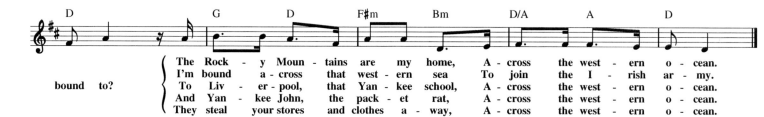

1. Oh, the times are hard and the wag - es low,
2. Oh the land of prom - ise ___ there you'll see,
3. And to Liv - er - pool I'll ___ take my way,
4. There's _ Liv - er - pool Pat, with his tar - p'lin hat,
5. Be - ware the pack - et ___ ships, I say,

A - me - lia, where you bound to?

The Rock - y Moun - tains are my home, A - cross the west - ern o - cean.
I'm bound a - cross that west - ern sea To join the I - rish ar - my.
To Liv - er - pool, that Yan - kee school, A - cross the west - ern o - cean.
And Yan - kee John, the pack - et rat, A - cross the west - ern o - cean.
They steal your stores and clothes a - way, A - cross the west - ern o - cean.

AILLTE

Folksong from the Hebrides

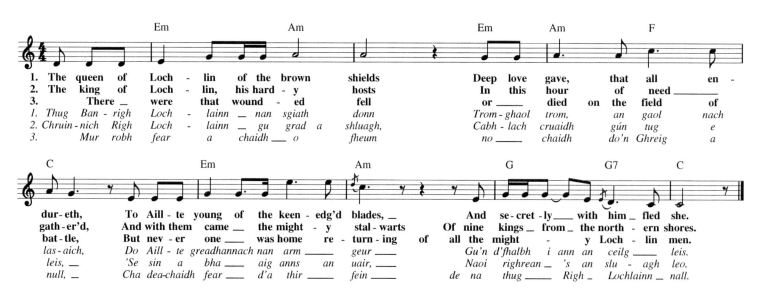

1. The queen of Loch - lin of the brown shields Deep love gave, that all en -
2. The king of Loch - lin, his hard - y hosts In this hour of need ___
3.   There _ were that wound - ed fell or ___ died on the field of

1. Thug Ban - righ Loch - lainn _ nan sgiath donn Trom - ghaol trom, an gaol nach
2. Chruin - nich Righ Loch - lainn _ gu grad a shluagh, Cabh - lach cruaidh gún tug e
3.   Mur robh fear a chaidh ___ o fheum no ___ chaidh do'n Ghreig a

dur - eth, To Aill - te young of the keen - edg'd blades, _ And se - cret - ly ___ with him _ fled she.
gath - er'd, And with them came _ the might - y stal - warts Of nine kings _ from _ the north - ern shores.
bat - tle, But nev - er one ___ was home re - turn - ing of all the might - y Loch - lin men.

las - aich, Do Aill - te greadhannach nan arm ___ geur ___ Gu'n d'fhalbh i ann an ceilg ___ leis.
leis, _ 'Se sin a bha ___ aig anns an uair, ___ Naoi righrean _ 's an slu - agh leo.
null, _ Cha dea - chaidh fear ___ d'a thir ___ fein _ de na thug ___ Righ _ Lochlainn _ nall.

ALL THROUGH THE NIGHT

Welsh folksong

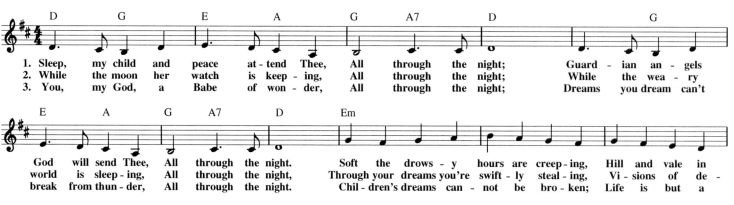

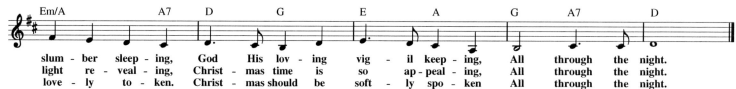

1. Sleep, my child and peace at - tend Thee, All through the night; Guard - ian an - gels
2. While the moon her watch is keep - ing, All through the night; While the wea - ry
3. You, my God, a Babe of won - der, All through the night; Dreams you dream can't

God will send Thee, All through the night. Soft the drows - y hours are creep - ing, Hill and vale in
world is sleep - ing, All through the night, Through your dreams you're swift - ly steal - ing, Vi - sions of de -
break from thun - der, All through the night. Chil - dren's dreams can - not be bro - ken; Life is but a

slum - ber sleep - ing, God His lov - ing vig - il keep - ing, All through the night.
light re - veal - ing, Christ - mas time is so ap - peal - ing, All through the night.
love - ly to - ken. Christ - mas should be soft - ly spo - ken All through the night.

ALISTER, SON OF COLL THE SPLENDID
(Alasdair Mac Colla)

Folksong from the Hebrides

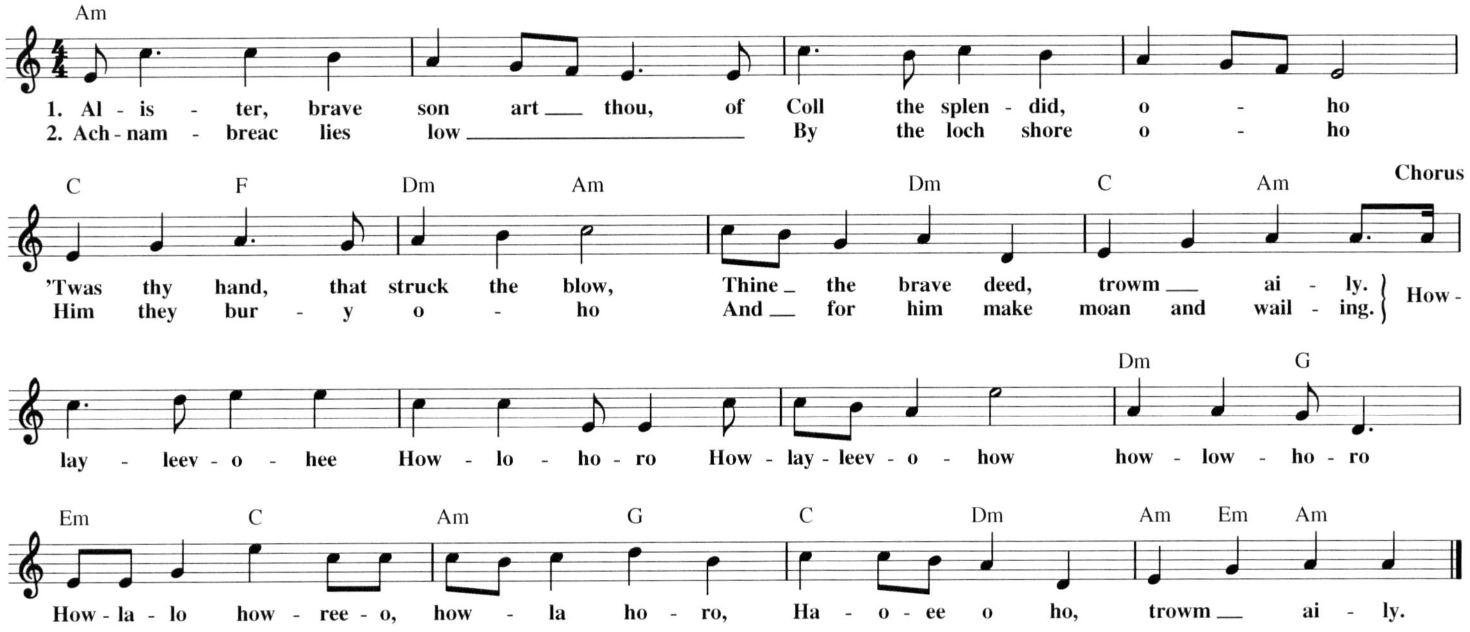

1. Al - is - ter, brave son art ___ thou, of Coll the splen - did, o - ho
2. Ach - nam - breac lies low ____ By the loch shore o - ho

'Twas thy hand, that struck the blow, Thine _ the brave deed, trowm ___ ai - ly. } How -
Him they bur - y o - ho And _ for him make moan and wail - ing.

lay - leev - o - hee How - lo - ho - ro How - lay - leev - o - how how - low - ho - ro

How - la - lo how - ree - o, how - la ho - ro, Ha - o - ee o ho, trowm ___ ai - ly.

Gaelic Lyrics

1. Alasdair Mhic o-hó
   Chòlla ghasda, o-hó
   As do laimh gu'n o-hó
   Earbainn tapadh trom eile.

   Chorus

2. Chall eilibh o hi chall o ho ro
   Ehall eilibh ohao chall o ho ro
   Chall a lo hao rio chall a ho ro
   Hao i o ho trom eile.

AR FOL LOL LOL O

Irish folksong

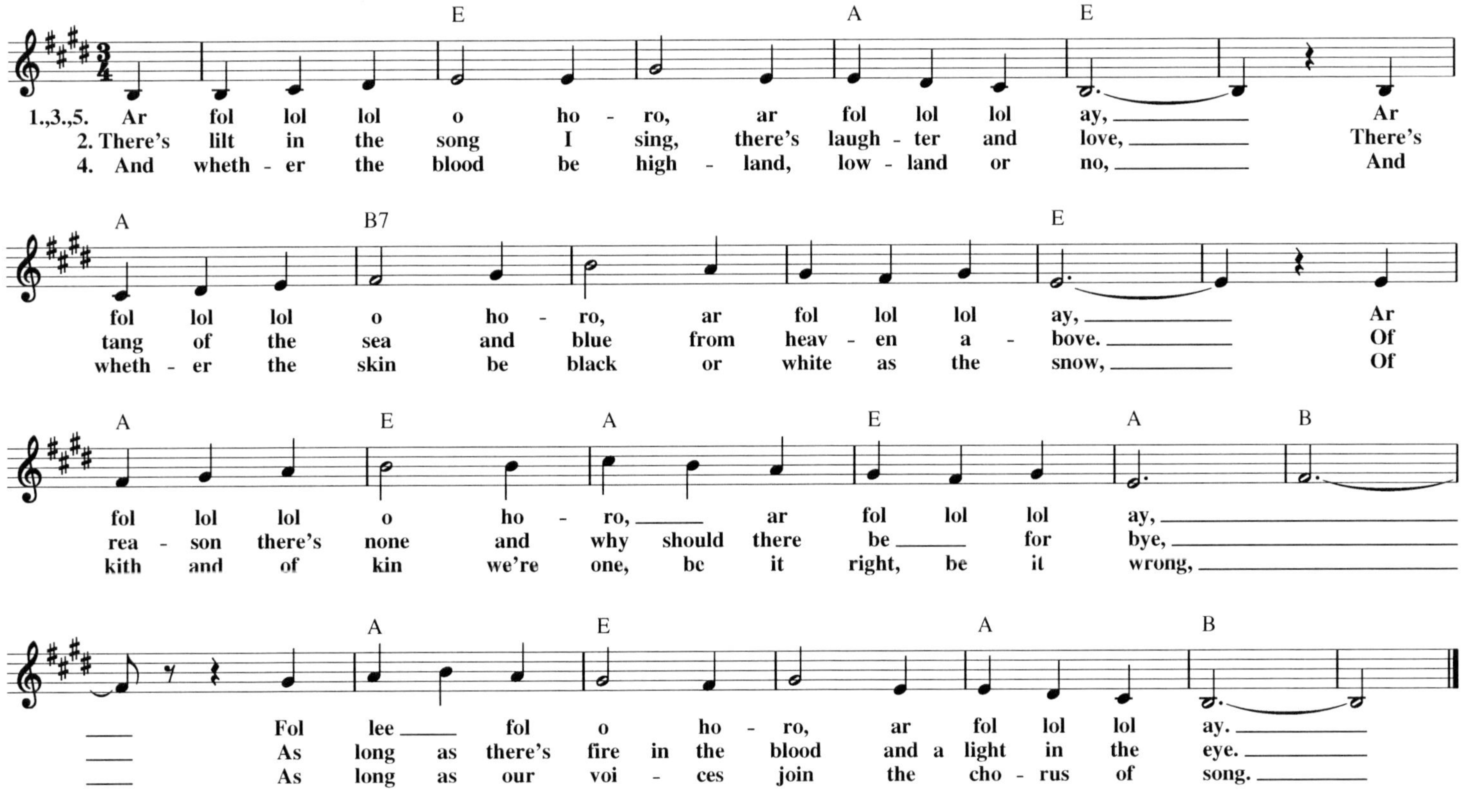

1.,3.,5. Ar fol lol lol o ho - ro, ar fol lol lol ay, ____ Ar
2. There's lilt in the song I sing, there's laugh - ter and love, ____ There's
4. And wheth - er the blood be high - land, low - land or no, ____ And

fol lol lol o ho - ro, ar fol lol lol ay, ____ Ar
tang of the sea and blue from heav - en a - bove. ____ Of
wheth - er the skin be black or white as the snow, ____ Of

fol lol lol o ho - ro, ____ ar fol lol lol ay, ____ Ar
rea - son there's none and why should there be ___ for bye, ____ Of
kith and of kin we're one, be it right, be it wrong, ____

____ Fol lee ___ fol o ho - ro, ar fol lol lol ay.
As long as there's fire in the blood and a light in the eye. ____
As long as our voi - ces join the cho - rus of song. ____

14

ALONG WITH MY LOVE I'LL GO

Copyright © 2001 by HAL LEONARD CORPORATION

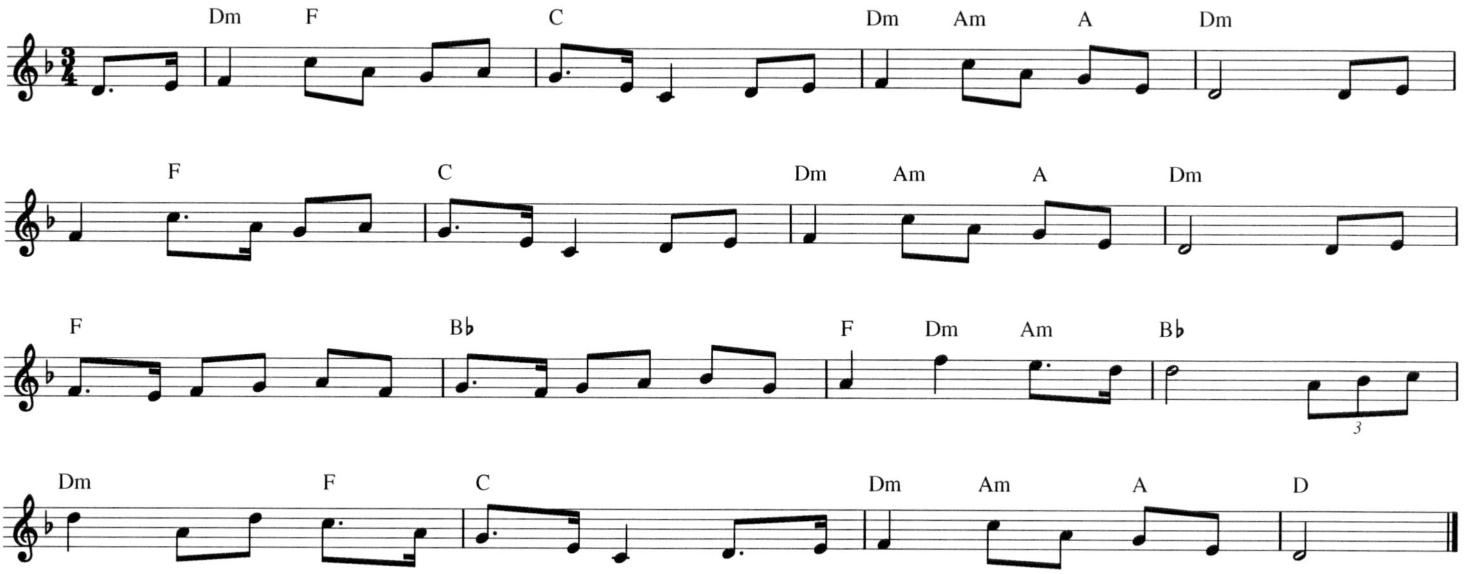

ALTAR ISLE O' THE SEA
(Donull nan Donull)

Copyright © 2001 by HAL LEONARD CORPORATION

Folksong from the Hebrides

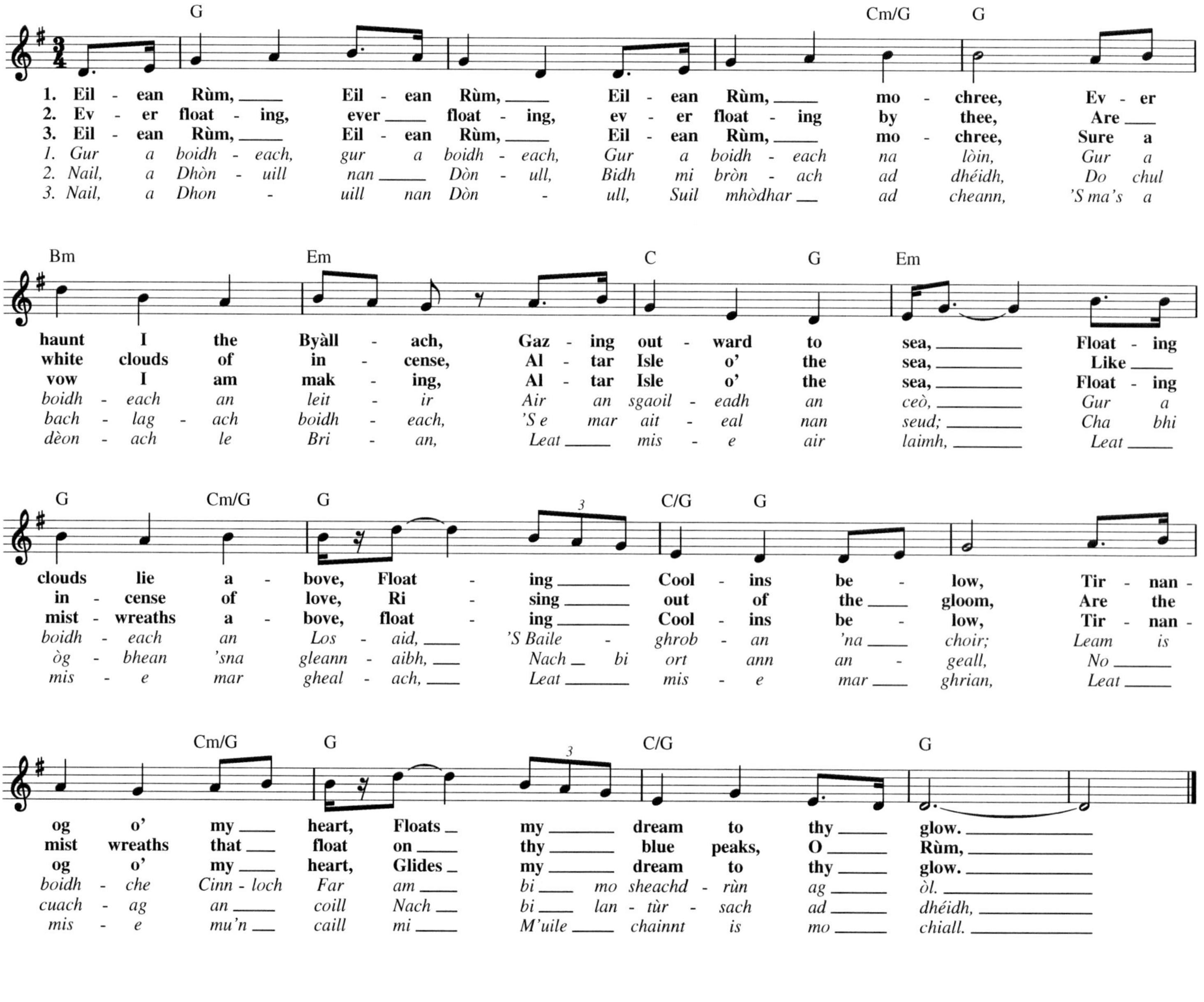

"ARE YOU THERE, MO-RI-AR-I-TY?"

Irish folksong

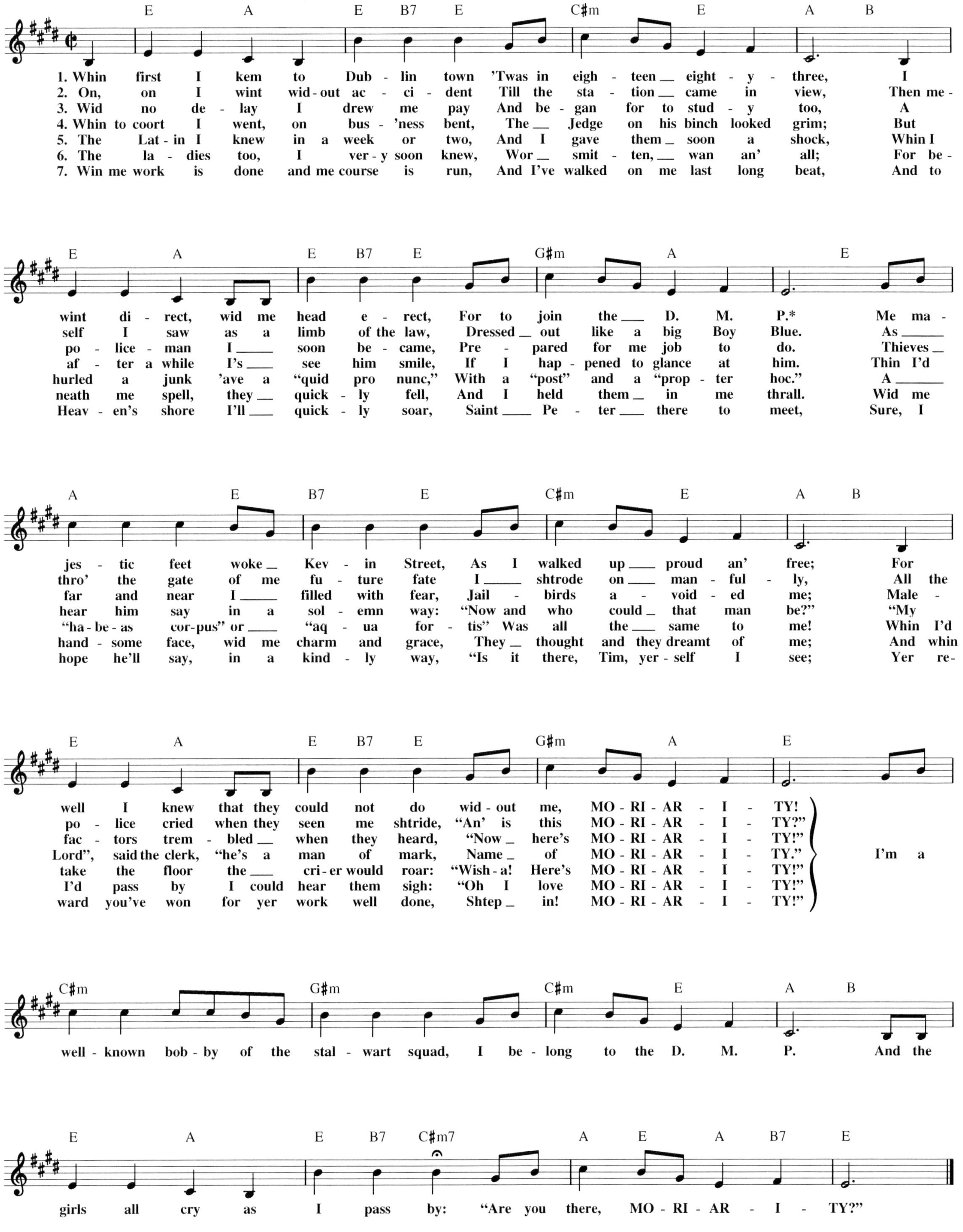

*Dublin Metropolitan Police

16

ARTHUR McBRIDE

Copyright © 2001 by HAL LEONARD CORPORATION

Irish folksong

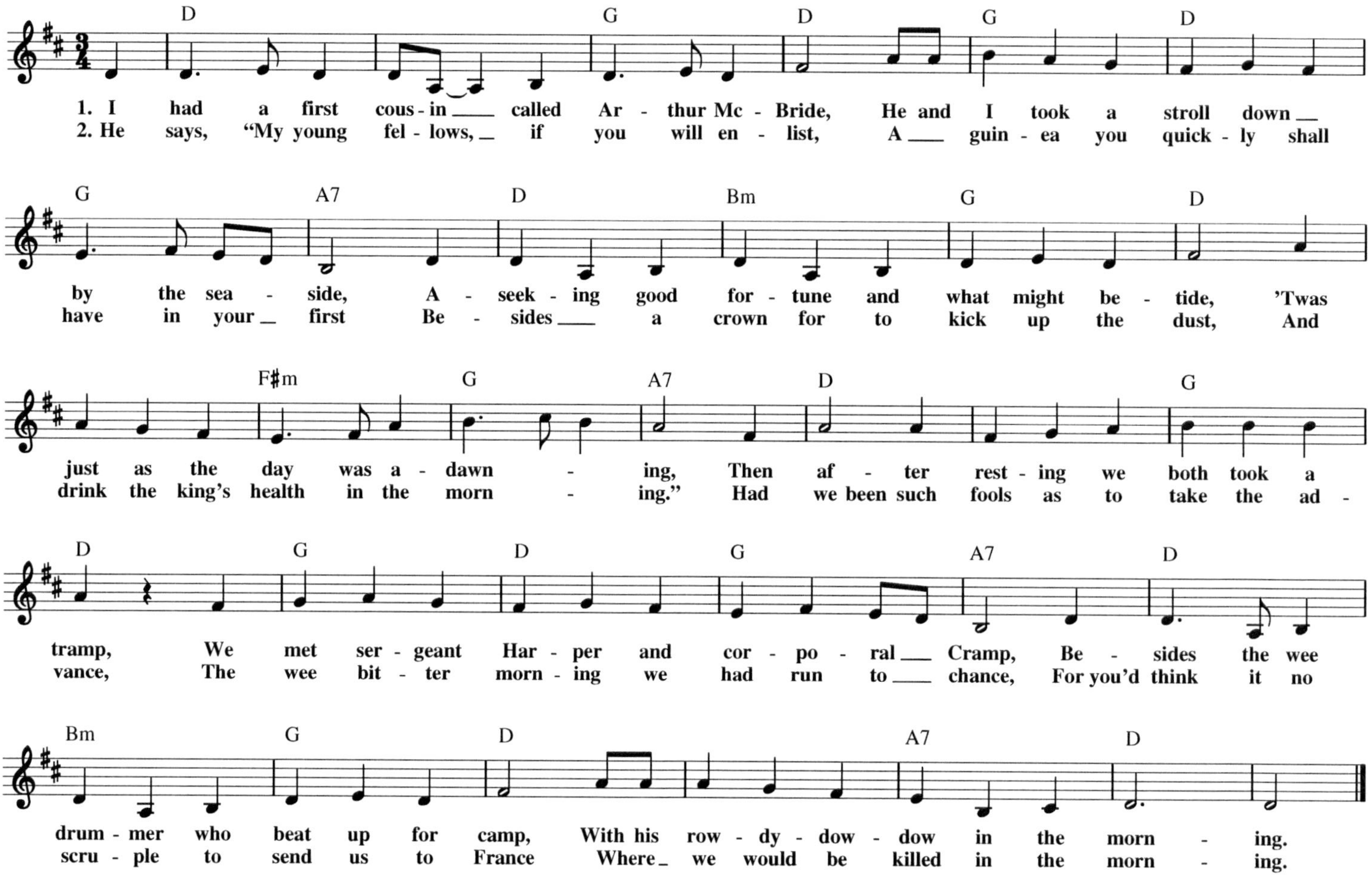

AS I ROVED OUT (I)

Copyright © 2001 by HAL LEONARD CORPORATION

Irish folksong

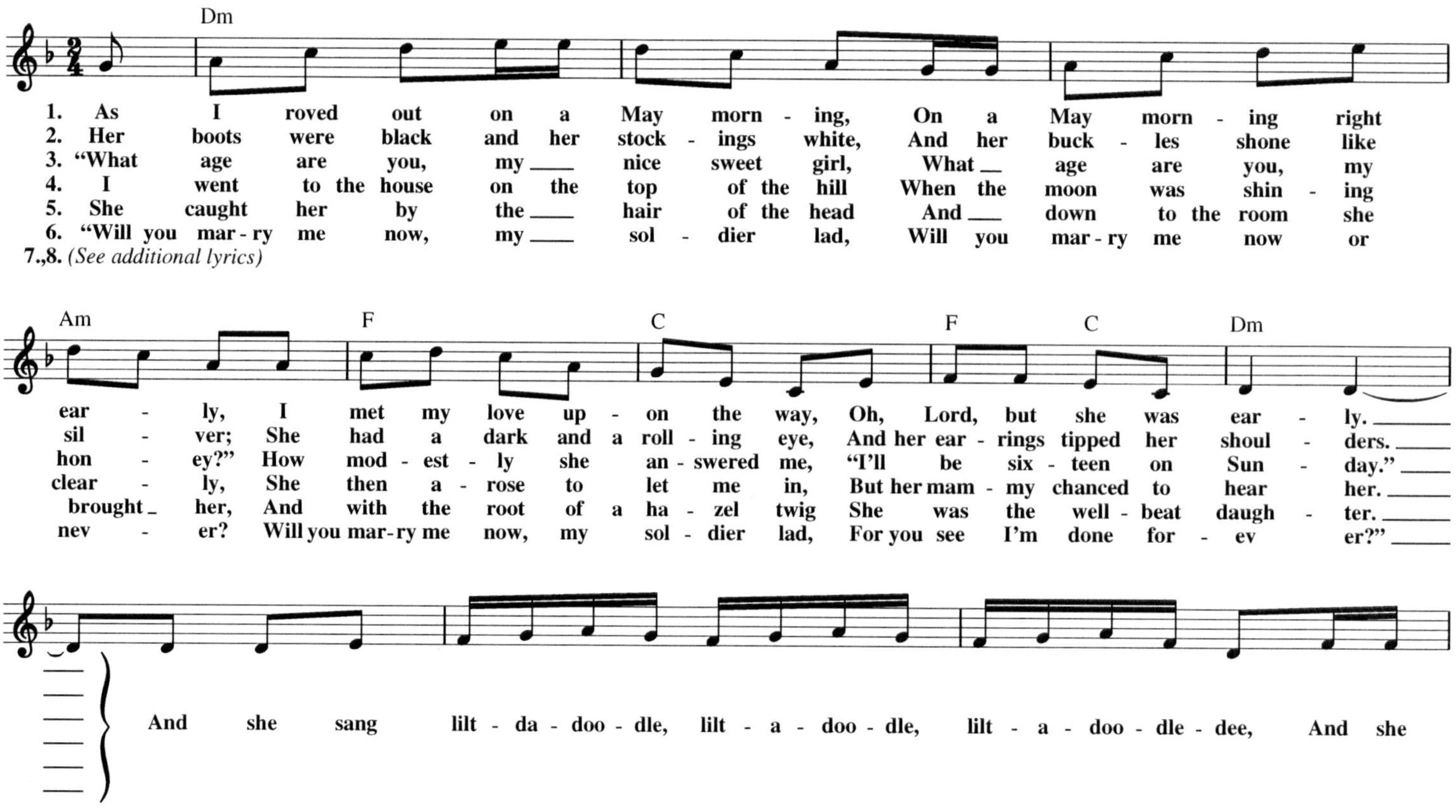

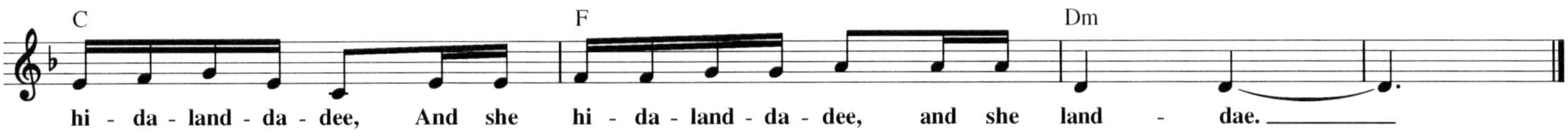

hi - da - land - da - dee, And she hi - da - land - da - dee, and she land - dae. _____

Additional Lyrics

7. "No, I won't marry you, my bonny wee girl,
I won't marry you, my honey,
For I have got a wife at home,
And how could I disown her?"
Chorus

8. A pint a night is my delight,
And a gallon in the morning;
The old women are my heartbreak,
But the young ones is my darling.
Chorus

AS I ROVED OUT (II)

Irish folksong

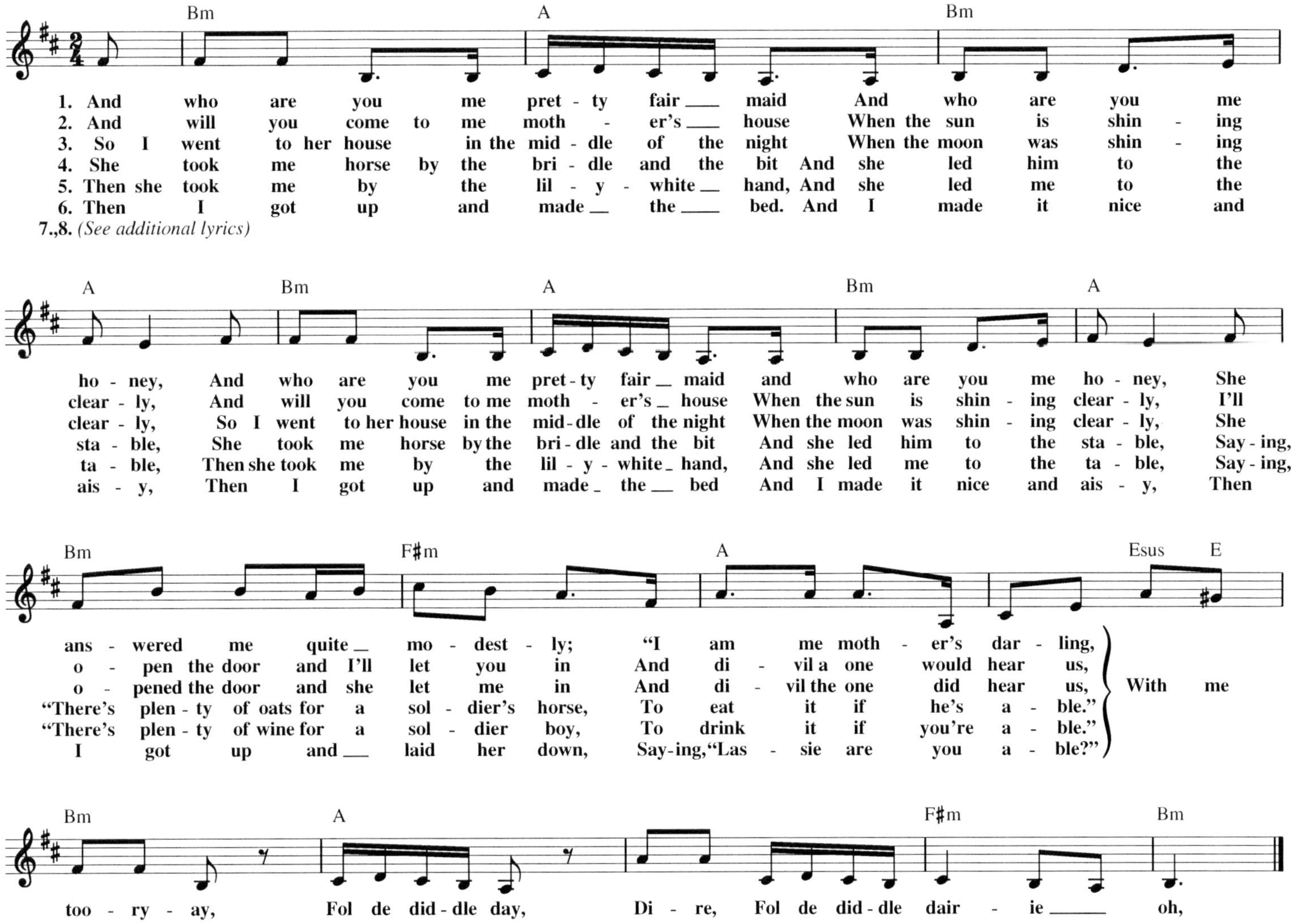

1. And who are you me pret - ty fair __ maid And who are you me
2. And will you come to me moth - er's __ house When the sun is shin - ing
3. So I went to her house in the mid - dle of the night When the moon was shin - ing
4. She took me horse by the bri - dle and the bit And she led him to the
5. Then she took me by the lil - y - white __ hand, And she led me to the
6. Then I got up and made __ the __ bed. And I made it nice and

7., 8. *(See additional lyrics)*

ho - ney, And who are you me pret - ty fair __ maid and who are you me ho - ney, She
clear - ly, And will you come to me moth - er's __ house When the sun is shin - ing clear - ly, I'll
clear - ly, So I went to her house in the mid - dle of the night When the moon was shin - ing clear - ly, She
sta - ble, She took me horse by the bri - dle and the bit And she led him to the sta - ble, Say - ing
ta - ble, Then she took me by the lil - y - white __ hand, And she led me to the ta - ble, Say - ing,
ais - y, Then I got up and made __ the __ bed And I made it nice and ais - y, Then

ans - wered me quite __ mo - dest - ly; "I am me moth - er's dar - ling,
o - pen the door and I'll let you in And di - vil a one would hear us,
o - pened the door and she let me in And di - vil the one did hear us, } With me
"There's plen - ty of oats for a sol - dier's horse, To eat it if he's a - ble."
"There's plen - ty of wine for a sol - dier boy, To drink it if you're a - ble."
I got up and __ laid her down, Say - ing, "Las - sie are you a - ble?" }

too - ry - ay, Fol de did - dle day, Di - re, Fol de did - dle dair - ie _____ oh,

Additional Lyrics

7. And there we lay till the break of day,
And divil a one did hear us (repeat)
Then I arose and put on me clothes,
Saying, "Lassie, I must leave you."

8. And when will you return again
And when will we get married (repeat)
When broken shells make Christmas bells
We might well get married.

AT THE WAVE MOUTH
(Aig Beul nan Tonn)

Folksong from the Hebrides

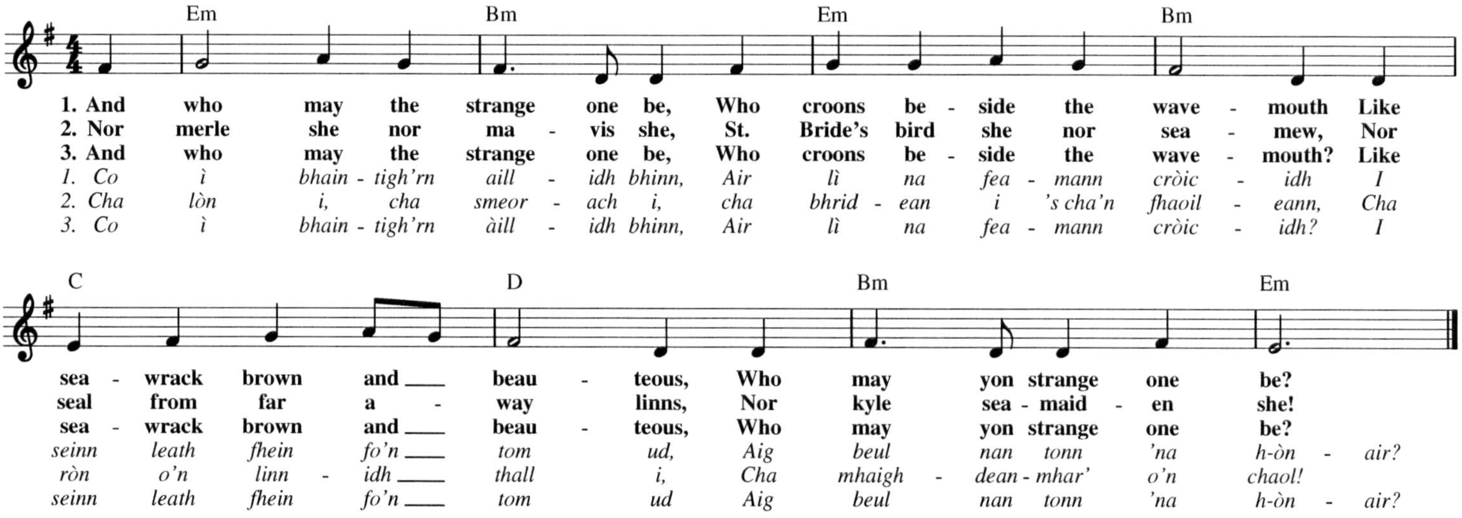

1. And who may the strange one be, Who croons be-side the wave-mouth Like
2. Nor merle she nor ma-vis she, St. Bride's bird she nor sea-mew, Nor
3. And who may the strange one be, Who croons be-side the wave-mouth? Like

1. Co ì bhain-tigh'rn aill-idh bhinn, Air lì na fea-mann cròic-idh I
2. Cha lòn i, cha smeor-ach i, cha bhrid-ean i 's cha'n fhaoil-eann, Cha
3. Co ì bhain-tigh'rn àill-idh bhinn, Air lì na fea-mann cròic-idh? I

sea-wrack brown and ____ beau-teous, Who may yon strange one be?
seal from far a-way linns, Nor kyle sea-maid-en she!
sea-wrack brown and ____ beau-teous, Who may yon strange one be?

seinn leath fhein fo'n ____ tom ud, Aig beul nan tonn 'na h-òn-air?
ròn o'n linn-idh ____ thall i, Cha mhaigh-dean-mhar' o'n chaol!
seinn leath fhein fo'n ____ tom ud Aig beul nan tonn 'na h-òn-air?

AULD LANG SYNE

Scottish folksong
Words by Robert Burns

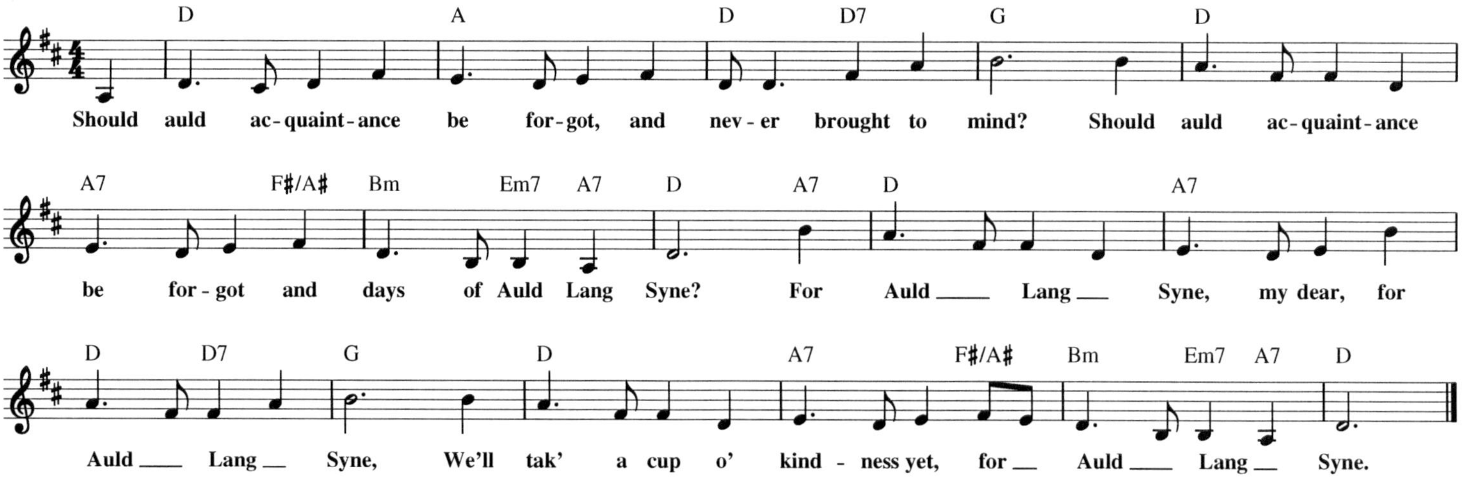

Should auld ac-quaint-ance be for-got, and nev-er brought to mind? Should auld ac-quaint-ance

be for-got and days of Auld Lang Syne? For Auld ____ Lang ____ Syne, my dear, for

Auld ____ Lang ____ Syne, We'll tak' a cup o' kind-ness yet, for ____ Auld ____ Lang ____ Syne.

AS I WAS GOING TO BALLYNURE

Irish folksong

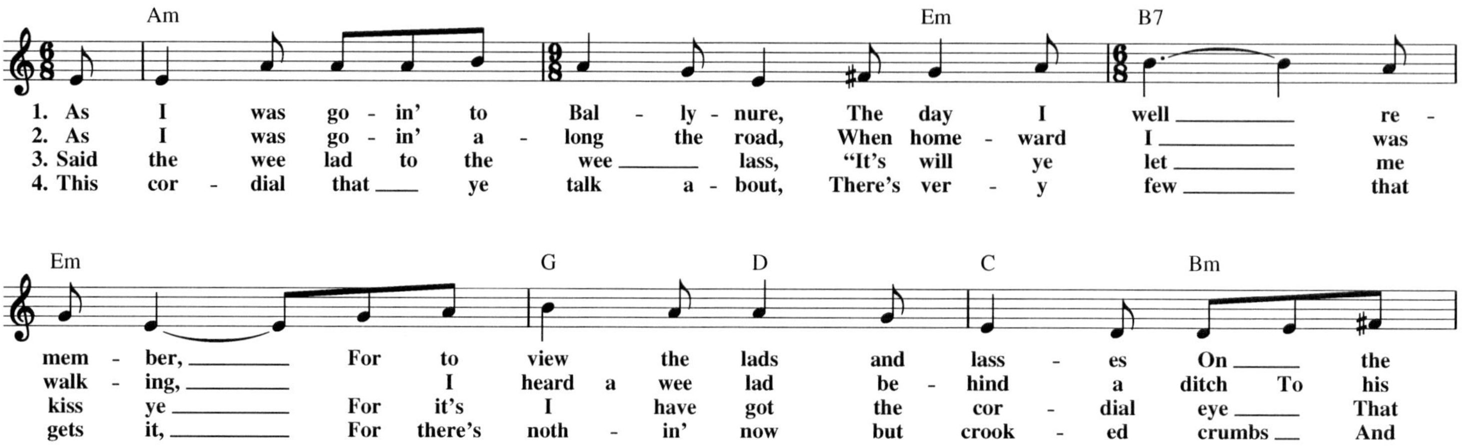

1. As I was go-in' to Bal-ly-nure, The day I well ____ re-
2. As I was go-in' a-long the road, When home-ward I ____ was
3. Said the wee lad to the wee ____ lass, "It's will ye let ____ me
4. This cor-dial that ____ ye talk a-bout, There's ver-y few ____ that

mem-ber, ____ For to view the lads and lass-es On ____ the
walk-ing, ____ I heard a wee lad be-hind a ditch To his
kiss ye, ____ For it's I have got the cor-dial eye ____ That
gets it, ____ For there's noth-in' now but crook-ed crumbs ____ And

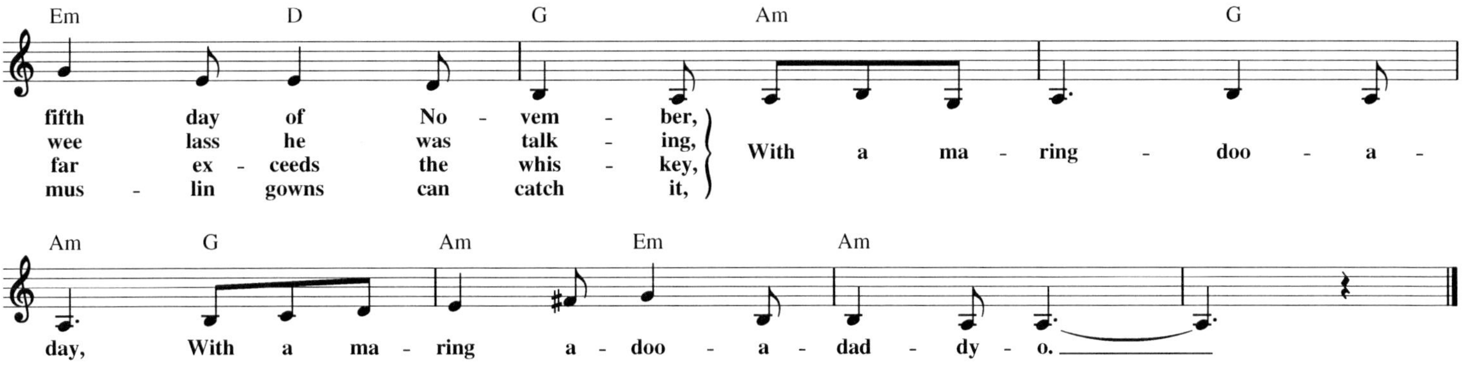
Em D G Am G
fifth day of No - vem - ber,
wee lass he was talk - ing,
far ex - ceeds the whis - key,
mus - lin gowns can catch it,
With a ma - ring - doo - a -
Am G Am Em Am
day, With a ma - ring a - doo - a - dad - dy - o.

THE ASH GROVE
(Llwyn On)

Welsh folksong

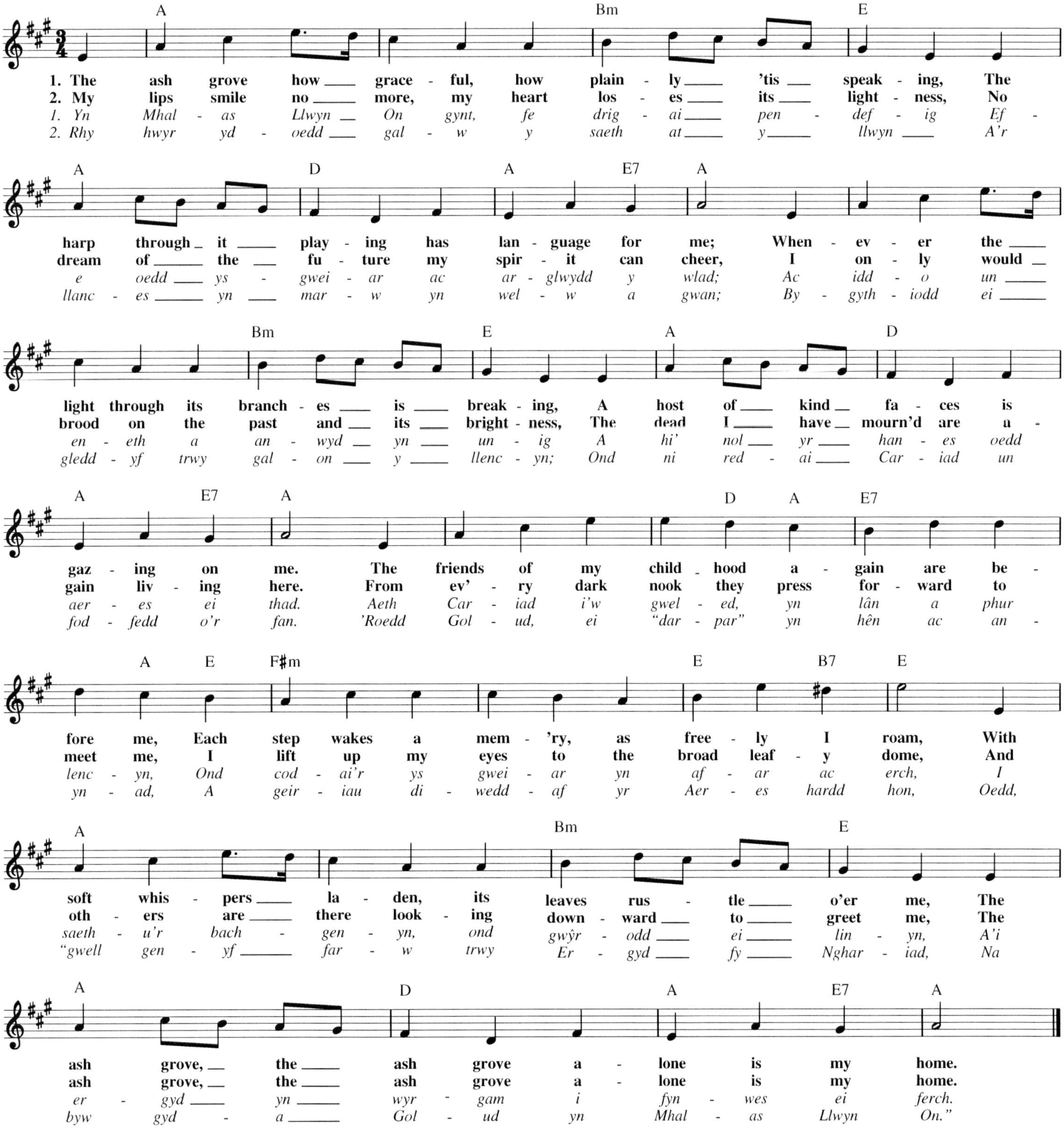
1. The ash grove how grace - ful, how plain - ly 'tis speak - ing, The
2. My lips smile no more, my heart los - es its light - ness, No
1. Yn Mhal - as Llwyn On gynt, fe drig - ai pen - def - ig Ef -
2. Rhy hwyr yd - oedd gal - w y saeth at y llwyn A'r
harp through it play - ing has lan - guage for me; When - ev - er the
dream of the fu - ture my spir - it can cheer, I on - ly would
e oedd ys - gwei - ar ac ar - glwydd y wlad; Ac idd - o un
llanc - es yn mar - w yn wel - w a gwan; By - gyth - iodd ei
light through its branch - es is break - ing, A host of kind fa - ces is
brood on the past and its bright - ness, The dead I have mourn'd are a -
en - eth a an - wyd yn un - ig A hi' nol yr han - es oedd
gledd - yf trwy gal - on y llenc - yn; Ond ni red - ai Car - iad un
gaz - ing on me. The friends of my child - hood a - gain are be -
gain liv - ing here. From ev' - ry dark nook they press for - ward to
aer - es ei thad. Aeth Car - iad i'w gwel - ed, yn lân a phur
fod - fedd o'r fan. 'Roedd Gol - ud, ei "dar - par" yn hên ac an -
fore me, Each step wakes a mem - 'ry, as free - ly I roam, With
meet me, I lift up my eyes to the broad leaf - y dome, And
lenc - yn, Ond cod - ai'r ys gwei - ar yn af - ar ac erch, I
yn - ad, A geir - iau di - wedd - af yr Aer - es hardd hon, Oedd,
soft whis - pers la - den, its leaves rus - tle o'er me, The
oth - ers are there look - ing down - ward to greet me, The
saeth - u'r bach - gen - yn, ond gwŷr - odd ei lin - yn, A'i
"gwell gen - yf far - w trwy Er - gyd fy Nghar - iad, Na
ash grove, the ash grove a - lone is my home.
ash grove, the ash grove a - lone is my home.
er - gyd yn wyr - gam i fyn - wes ei ferch.
byw gyd - a Gol - ud yn Mhal - as Llwyn On."

AVONDALE

Irish folksong

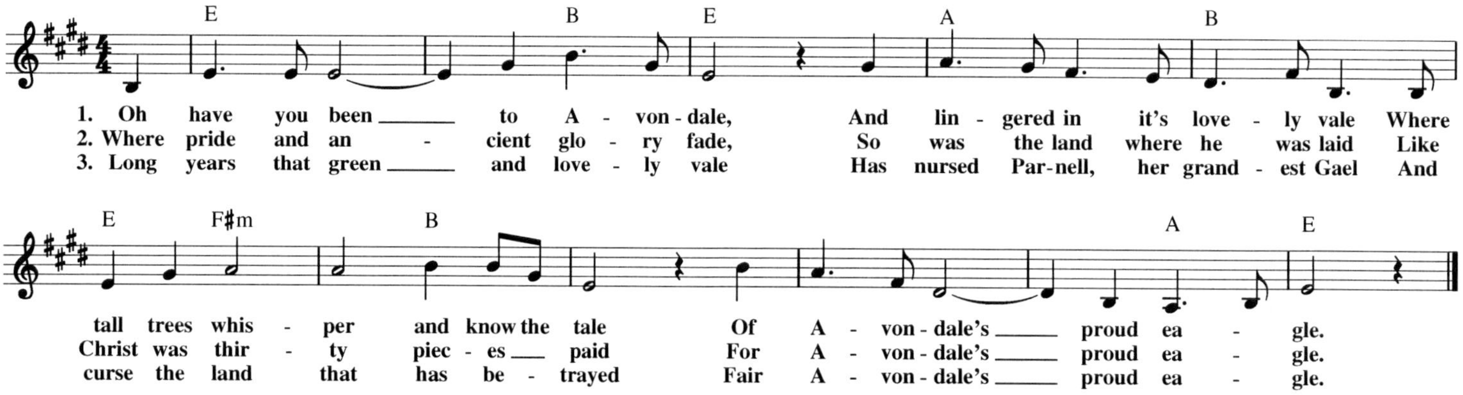

1. Oh have you been _____ to A - von - dale, And lin - gered in it's love - ly vale Where
2. Where pride and an - cient glo - ry fade, So was the land where he was laid Like
3. Long years that green _____ and love - ly vale Has nursed Par-nell, her grand - est Gael And

tall trees whis - per and know the tale Of A - von - dale's _____ proud ea - gle.
Christ was thir - ty piec - es _____ paid For A - von - dale's _____ proud ea - gle.
curse the land that has be - trayed Fair A - von - dale's _____ proud ea - gle.

BALOO BALEERIE

Scottish folksong

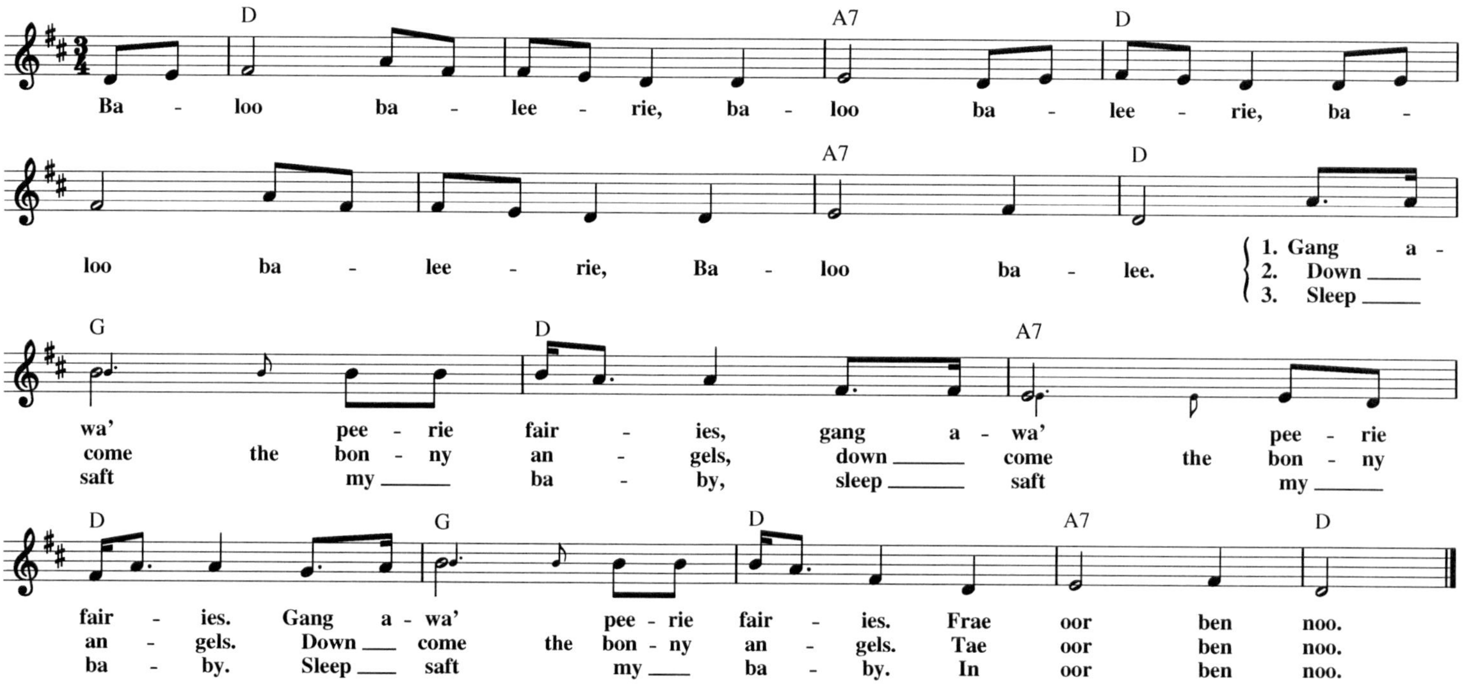

Ba - loo ba - lee - rie, ba - loo ba - lee - rie, ba -

loo ba - lee - rie, Ba - loo ba - lee.

1. Gang a -
2. Down _____
3. Sleep _____

wa' pee - rie fair - ies, gang a - wa' pee - rie
come the bon - ny an - gels, down _____ come the bon - ny
saft my _____ ba - by, sleep _____ saft my _____

fair - ies. Gang a - wa' pee - rie fair - ies. Frae oor ben noo.
an - gels. Down _____ come the bon - ny an - gels. Tae oor ben noo.
ba - by. Sleep _____ saft my _____ ba - by. In oor ben noo.

BALOO, LAMMY

Scottish folksong

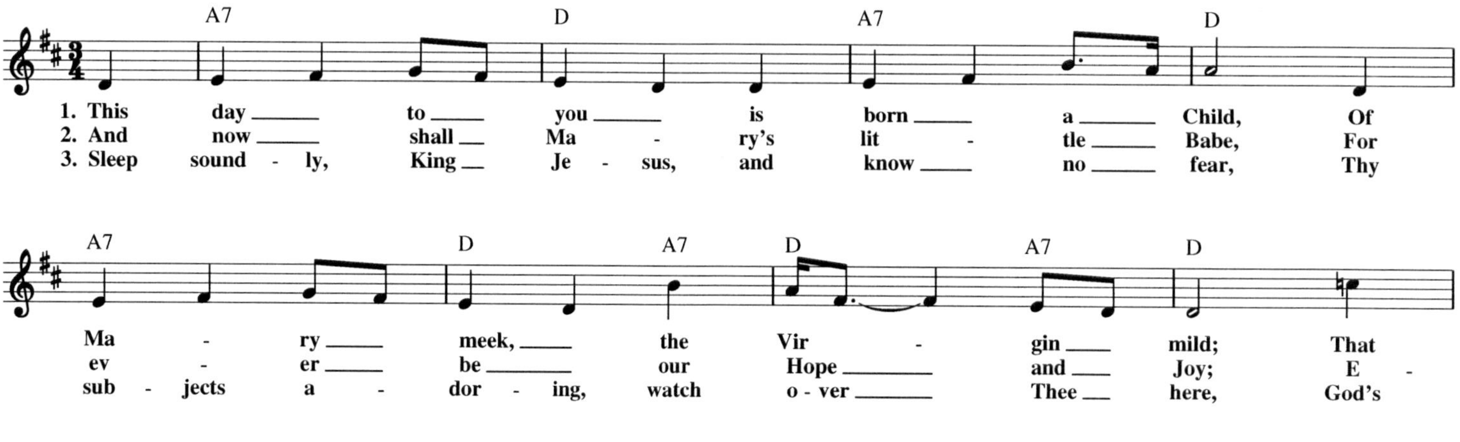

1. This day _____ to _____ you _____ is born _____ a _____ Child, Of
2. And now _____ shall _____ Ma - ry's lit - tle _____ Babe, For
3. Sleep sound - ly, King _____ Je - sus, and know _____ no _____ fear, Thy

Ma - ry _____ meek, _____ the Vir - gin _____ mild; That
ev - er _____ be _____ our Hope _____ and _____ Joy; E -
sub - jects a - dor - ing, watch o - ver _____ Thee _____ here, God's

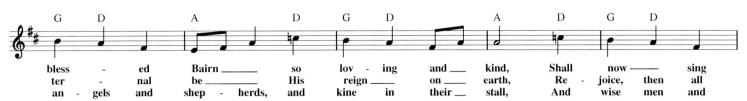

THE BAND PLAYED ON

Words by John F. Palmer
Music by Charles B. Ward

THE BANKS OF THE SUIR

Irish folksong

THE BANTRY GIRLS' LAMENT

Irish folksong

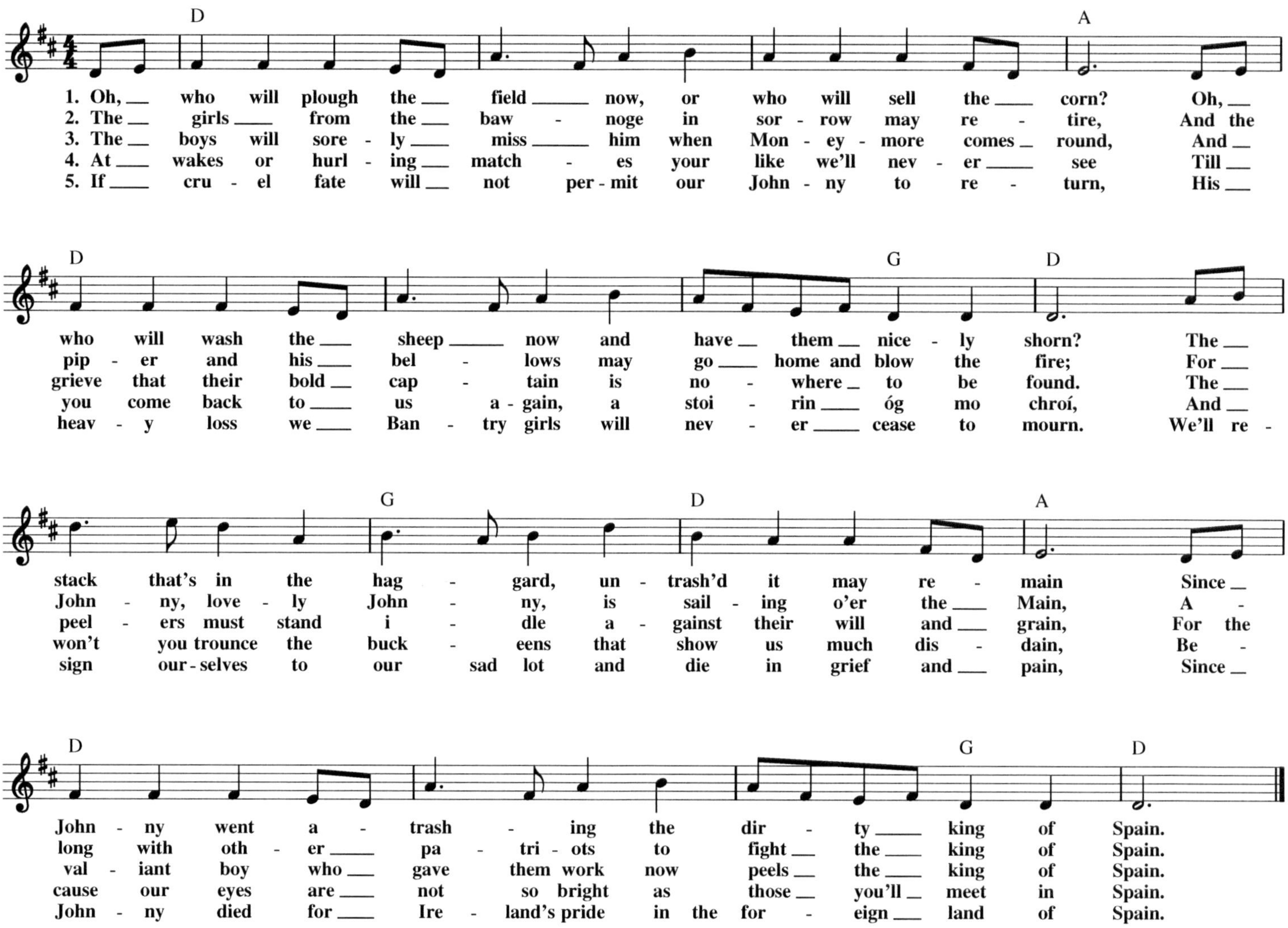

1. Oh, who will plough the field now, or who will sell the corn? Oh,
2. The girls from the bawnoge in sorrow may re-tire, And the
3. The boys will sore-ly miss him when Mon-ey-more comes round, And
4. At wakes or hurl-ing match-es your like we'll nev-er see Till
5. If cru-el fate will not per-mit our John-ny to re-turn, His

who will wash the sheep now and have them nice-ly shorn? The
pip-er and his bel-lows may go home and blow the fire; For
grieve that their bold cap-tain is no-where to be found. The
you come back to us a-gain, a stoi-rin óg mo chroí, And
heav-y loss we Ban-try girls will nev-er cease to mourn. We'll re-

stack that's in the hag-gard, un-trash'd it may re-main, Since
John-ny, love-ly John-ny, is sail-ing o'er the Main, A-
peel-ers must stand i-dle a-gainst their will and grain, For the
won't you trounce the buck-eens that show us much dis-dain, Be-
sign our-selves to our sad lot and die in grief and pain, Since

John-ny went a-trash-ing the dir-ty king of Spain.
long with oth-er pa-tri-ots to fight the king of Spain.
val-iant boy who gave them work now peels the king of Spain.
cause our eyes are not so bright as those you'll meet in Spain.
John-ny died for Ire-land's pride in the for-eign land of Spain.

BARBARA ALLEN

Scottish folksong

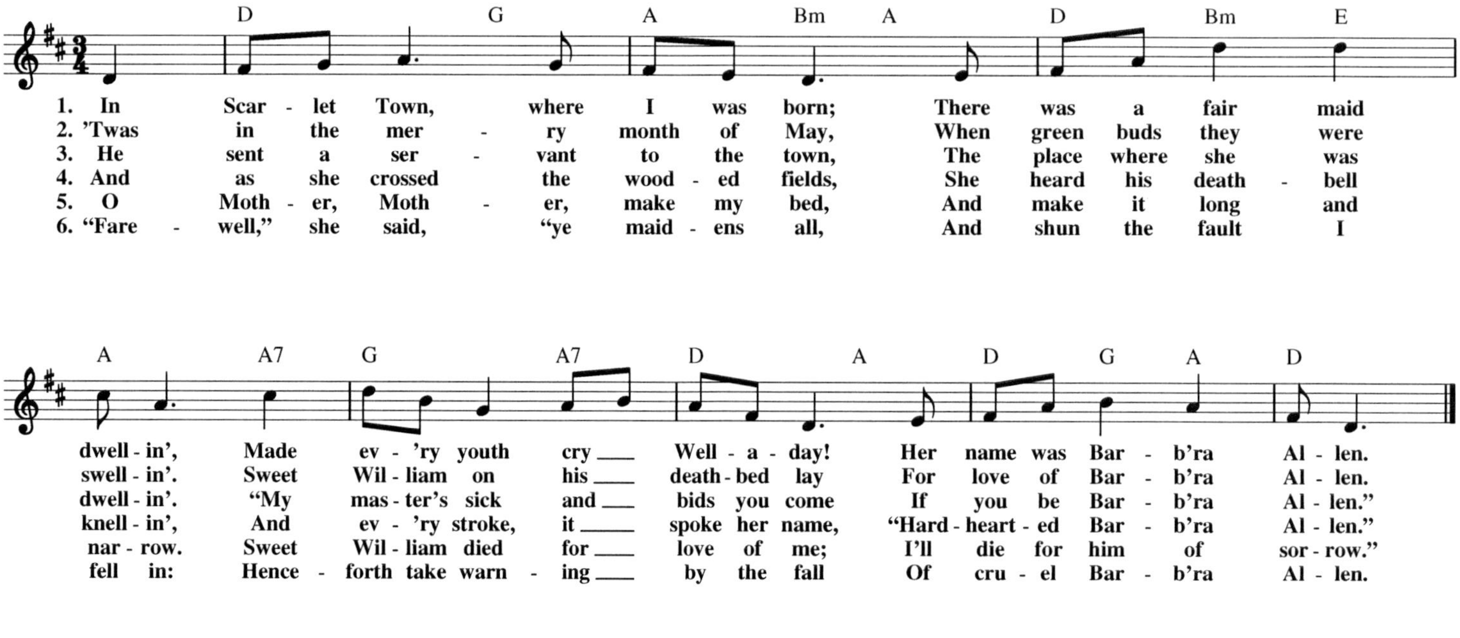

1. In Scar-let Town, where I was born; There was a fair maid
2. 'Twas in the mer-ry month of May, When green buds they were
3. He sent a ser-vant to the town, The place where she was
4. And as she crossed the wood-ed fields, She heard his death-bell
5. O Moth-er, Moth-er, make my bed, And make it long and
6. "Fare-well," she said, "ye maid-ens all, And shun the fault I

dwell-in', Made ev-'ry youth cry Well-a-day! Her name was Bar-b'ra Al-len.
swell-in'. Sweet Wil-liam on his death-bed lay For love of Bar-b'ra Al-len.
dwell-in'. "My mas-ter's sick and bids you come If you be Bar-b'ra Al-len."
knell-in', And ev-'ry stroke, it spoke her name, "Hard-heart-ed Bar-b'ra Al-len."
nar-row. Sweet Wil-liam died for love of me; I'll die for him of sor-row."
fell in: Hence-forth take warn-ing by the fall Of cru-el Bar-b'ra Al-len.

THE BARNYARDS OF DELGATY

Scottish folksong

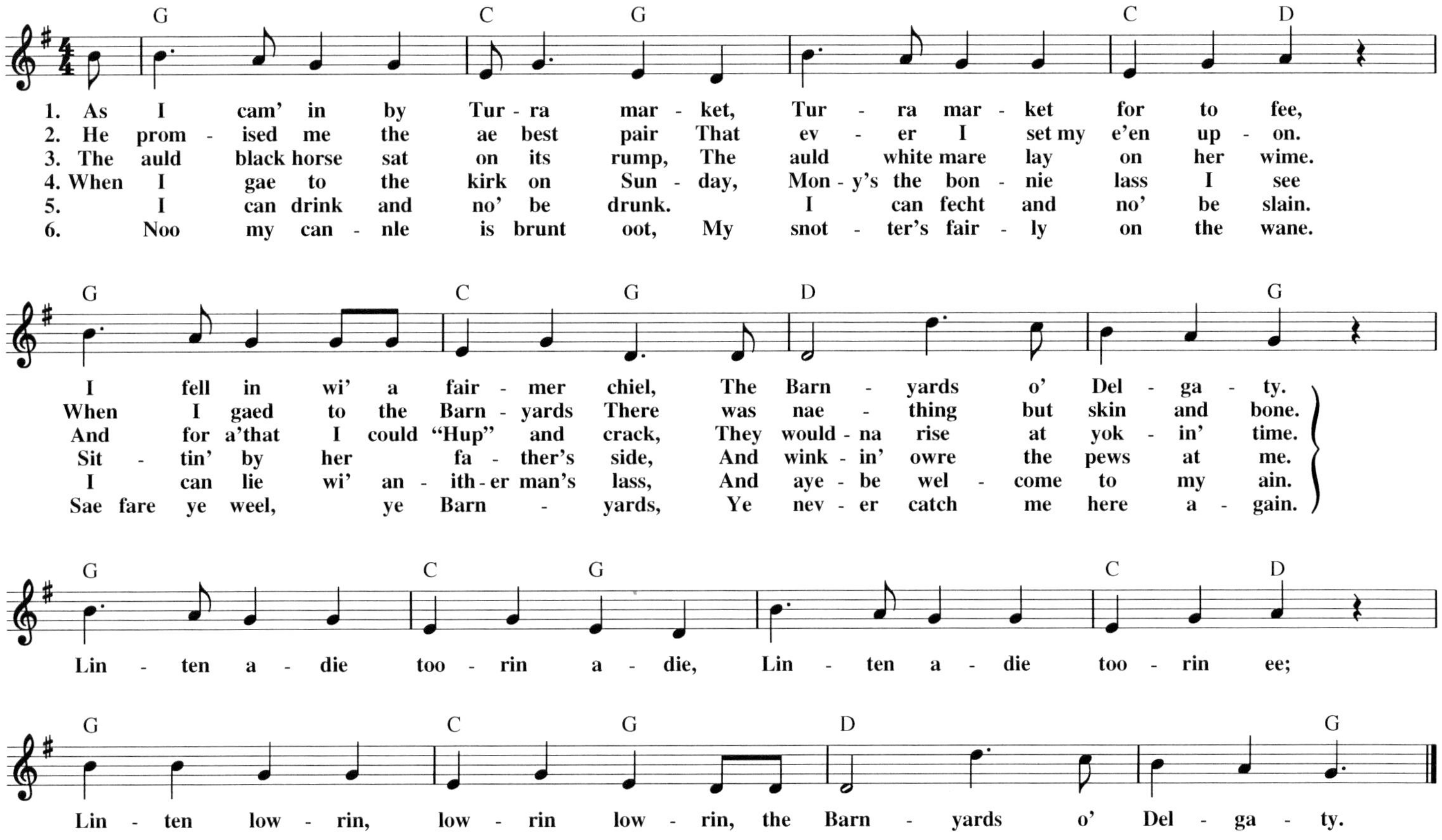

1. As I cam' in by Tur - ra mar - ket, Tur - ra mar - ket for to fee,
2. He prom - ised me the ae best pair That ev - er I set my e'en up - on.
3. The auld black horse sat on its rump, The auld white mare lay on her wime.
4. When I gae to the kirk on Sun - day, Mon - y's the bon - nie lass I see
5. I can drink and no' be drunk. I can fecht and no' be slain.
6. Noo my can - nle is brunt oot, My snot - ter's fair - ly on the wane.

I fell in wi' a fair - mer chiel, The Barn - yards o' Del - ga - ty.
When I gaed to the Barn - yards There was nae - thing but skin and bone.
And for a'that I could "Hup" and crack, They would - na rise at yok - in' time.
Sit - tin' by her fa - ther's side, And wink - in' owre the pews at me.
I can lie wi' an - ith - er man's lass, And aye be wel - come to my ain.
Sae fare ye weel, ye Barn - yards, Ye nev - er catch me here a - gain.

Lin - ten a - die too - rin a - die, Lin - ten a - die too - rin ee;

Lin - ten low - rin, low - rin low - rin, the Barn - yards o' Del - ga - ty.

BE THOU MY VISION

Irish folksong
Ancient Irish poem
Translation by Mary E. Byrne

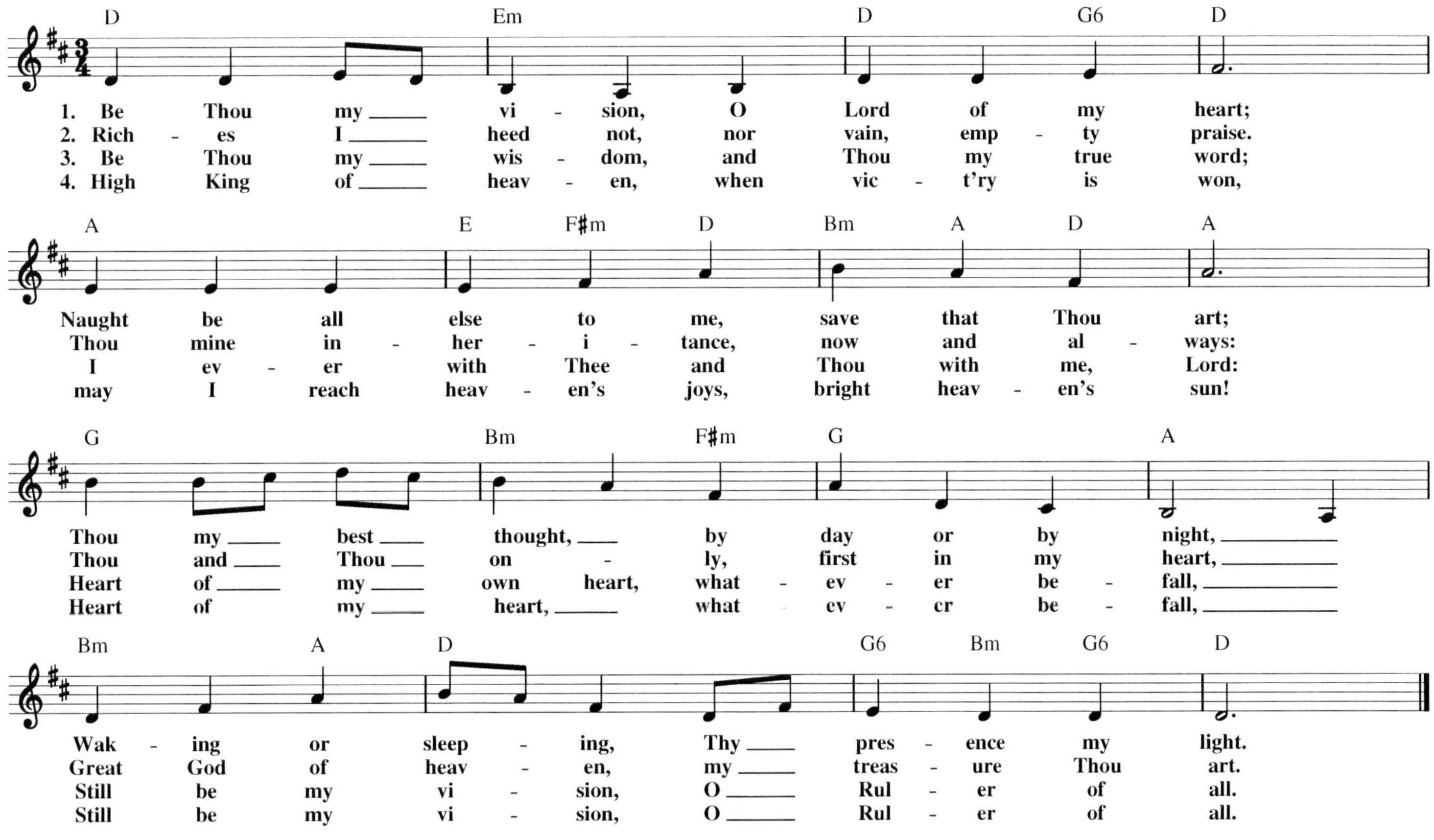

1. Be Thou my vi - sion, O Lord of my heart;
2. Rich - es I heed not, nor vain, emp - ty praise.
3. Be Thou my wis - dom, and Thou my true word;
4. High King of heav - en, when vic - t'ry is won,

Naught be all else to me, save that Thou art;
Thou mine in - her - i - tance, now and al - ways:
I ev - er with Thee and Thou with me, Lord:
may I reach heav - en's joys, bright heav - en's sun!

Thou my best thought, by day or by night,
Thou and Thou on - ly, first in my heart,
Heart of my own heart, what - ev - er be - fall,
Heart of my heart, what ev - cr be - fall,

Wak - ing or sleep - ing, Thy pres - ence my light.
Great God of heav - en, my treas - ure Thou art.
Still be my vi - sion, O Rul - er of all.
Still be my vi - sion, O Rul - er of all.

THE BARD OF ARMAGH

Irish folksong

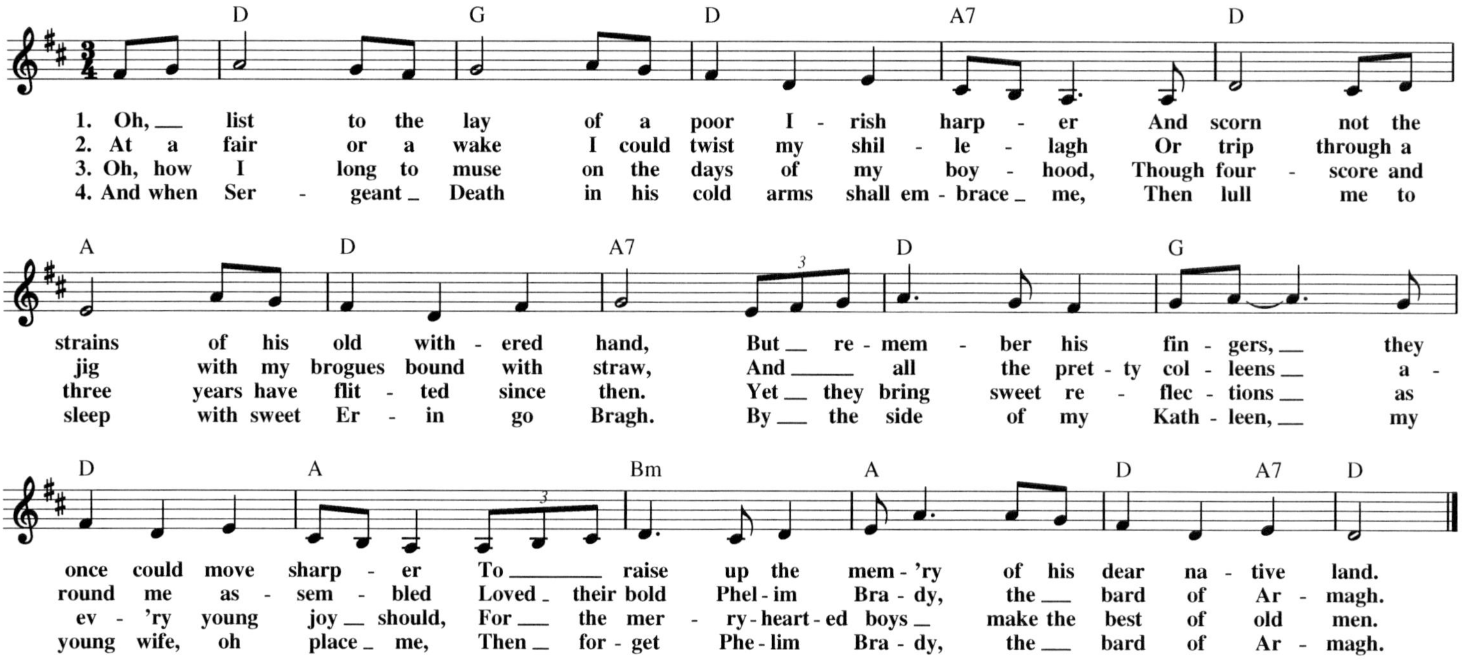

1. Oh, __ list to the lay of a poor I - rish harp - er And scorn not the
2. At a fair or a wake I could twist my shil - le - lagh Or trip through a
3. Oh, how I long to muse on the days of my boy - hood, Though four - score and
4. And when Ser - geant Death in his cold arms shall em - brace __ me, Then lull me to

strains of his old with - ered hand, But __ re - mem - ber his fin - gers, __ they
jig with my brogues bound with straw, And _____ all the pret - ty col - leens __ a -
three years have flit - ted since then. Yet __ they bring sweet re - flec - tions __ as
sleep with sweet Er - in go Bragh. By __ the side of my Kath - leen, __ my

once could move sharp - er To _____ raise up the mem - 'ry of his dear na - tive land.
round me as - sem - bled Loved _ their bold Phel - im Bra - dy, the __ bard of Ar - magh.
ev - 'ry young joy _ should, For __ the mer - ry - heart - ed boys _ make the best of old men.
young wife, oh place _ me, Then __ for - get Phe - lim Bra - dy, the __ bard of Ar - magh.

A BARRA LOVE LILT

Folksong from the Hebrides

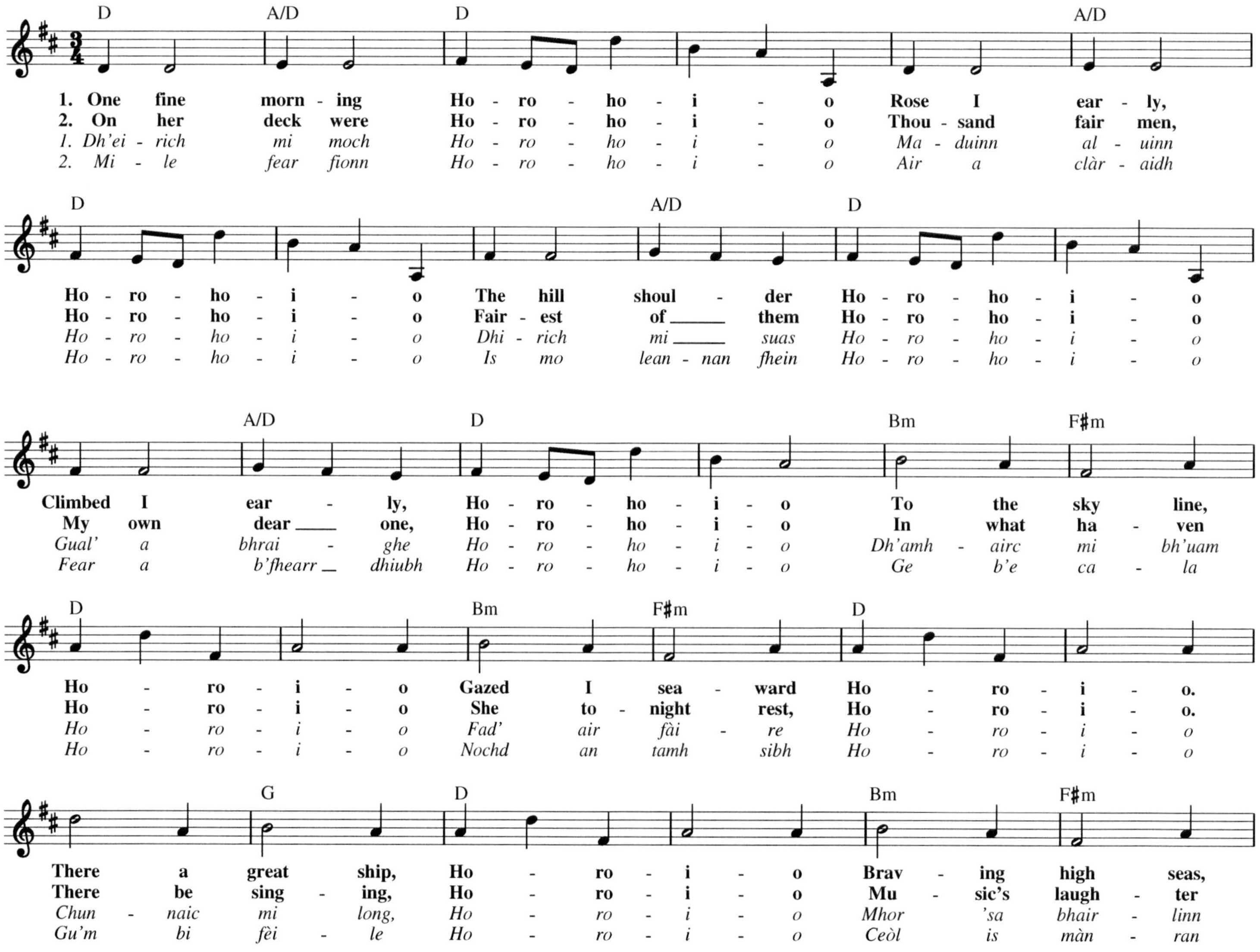

1. One fine morn - ing Ho - ro - ho - i - o Rose I ear - ly,
2. On her deck were Ho - ro - ho - i - o Thou - sand fair men,
1. Dh'ei - rich mi moch Ho - ro - ho - i - o Ma - duinn al - uinn
2. Mi - le fear fionn Ho - ro - ho - i - o Air a clàr - aidh

Ho - ro - ho - i - o The hill shoul - der Ho - ro - ho - i - o
Ho - ro - ho - i - o Fair - est of _____ them Ho - ro - ho - i - o
Ho - ro - ho - i - o Dhi - rich mi _____ suas Ho - ro - ho - i - o
Ho - ro - ho - i - o Is mo lean - nan fhein Ho - ro - ho - i - o

Climbed I ear - ly, Ho - ro - ho - i - o To the sky line,
My own dear _____ one, Ho - ro - ho - i - o In what ha - ven
Gual' a bhrai - ghe Ho - ro - ho - i - o Dh'amh - airc mi bh'uam
Fear a b'fhearr _ dhiubh Ho - ro - ho - i - o Ge b'e ca - la

Ho - ro - i - o Gazed I sea - ward Ho - ro - i - o.
Ho - ro - i - o She to - night rest, Ho - ro - i - o.
Ho - ro - i - o Fad' air fài - re Ho - ro - i - o
Ho - ro - i - o Nochd an tamh sibh Ho - ro - i - o

There a great ship, Ho - ro - i - o Brav - ing high seas,
There be sing - ing, Ho - ro - i - o Mu - sic's laugh - ter
Chun - naic mi long, Ho - ro - i - o Mhor 'sa bhair - linn
Gu'm bi fèi - le Ho - ro - i - o Ceòl is màn - ran

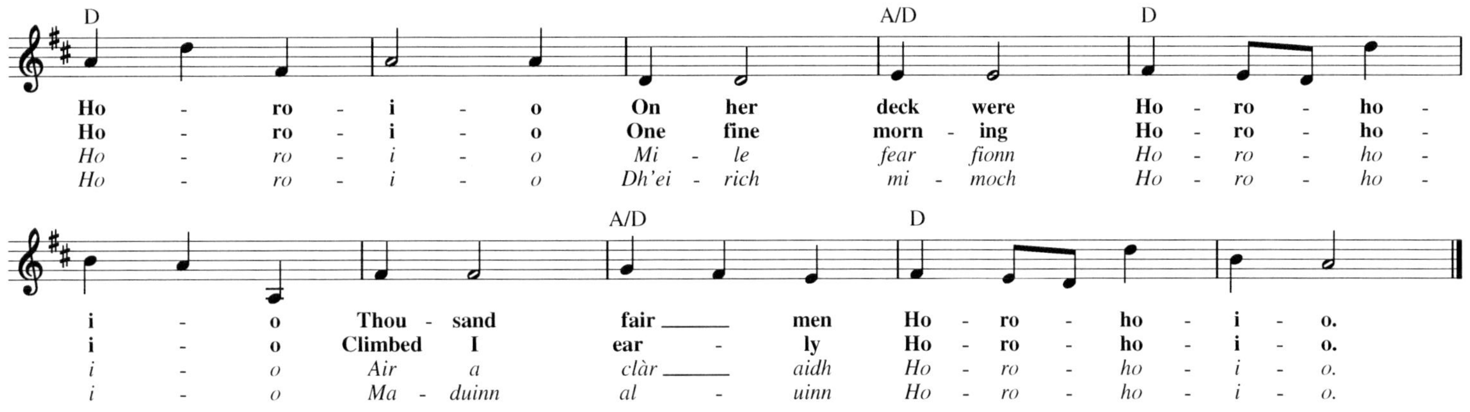

BATCHELOR'S WALK

Irish popular song

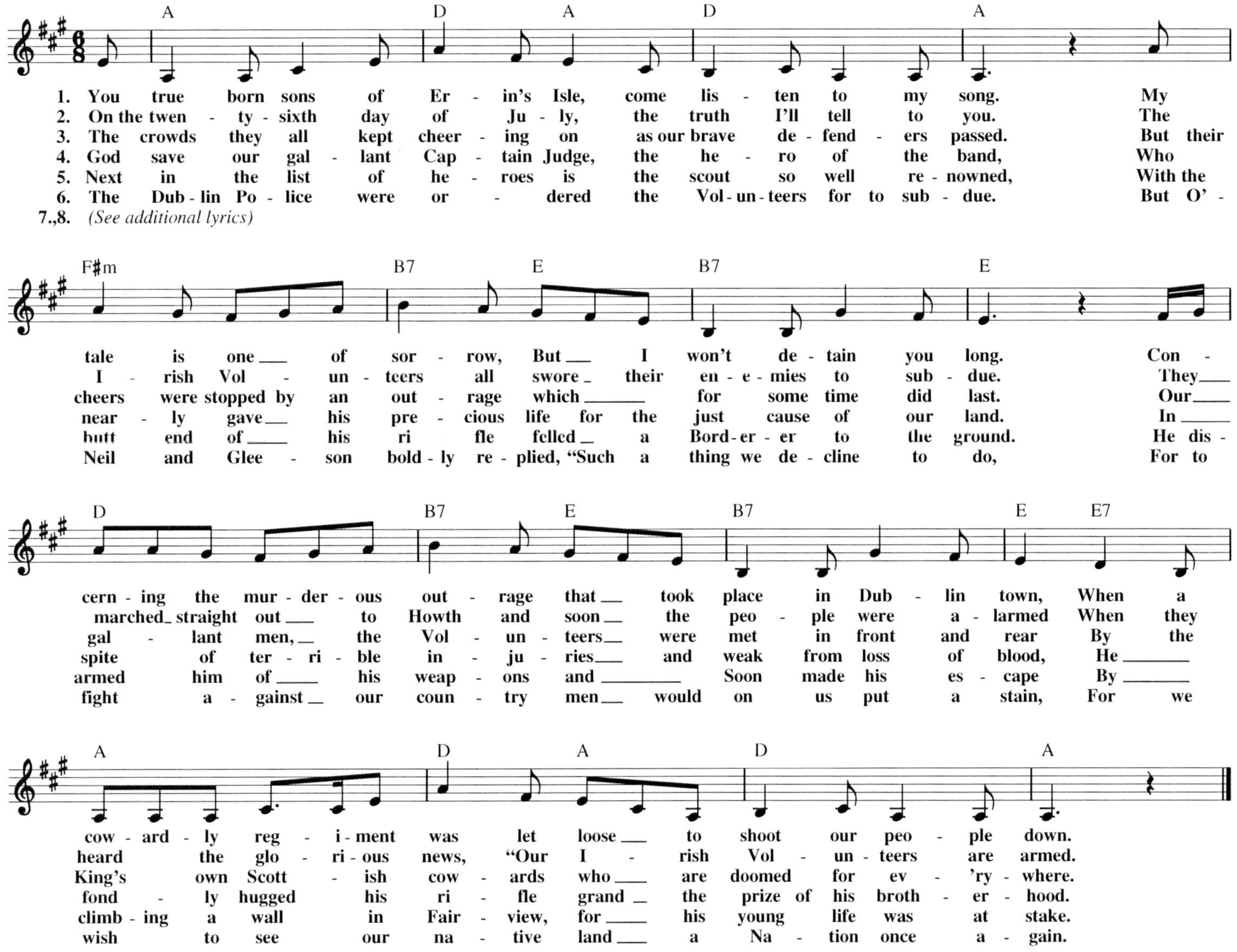

Additional Lyrics

7. On Batchelor's Walk a scene took place, which I'm sure had just been planned,
For the cowardly Scottish Borderers turned and fired without command.
With bayonets fixed they charged the crowd and left them in their gore,
But their deeds will be remembered in Irish hearts for evermore.

8. God rest the souls of those who sleep apart from earthly sin,
Including Mrs. Duffy, James Brennan and Patrick Quinn;
But we will yet avenge them and the time will surely come,
That we'll make the Scottish Borderers pay for the cowardly deeds they done.

THE BEGGARMAN

Irish folksong

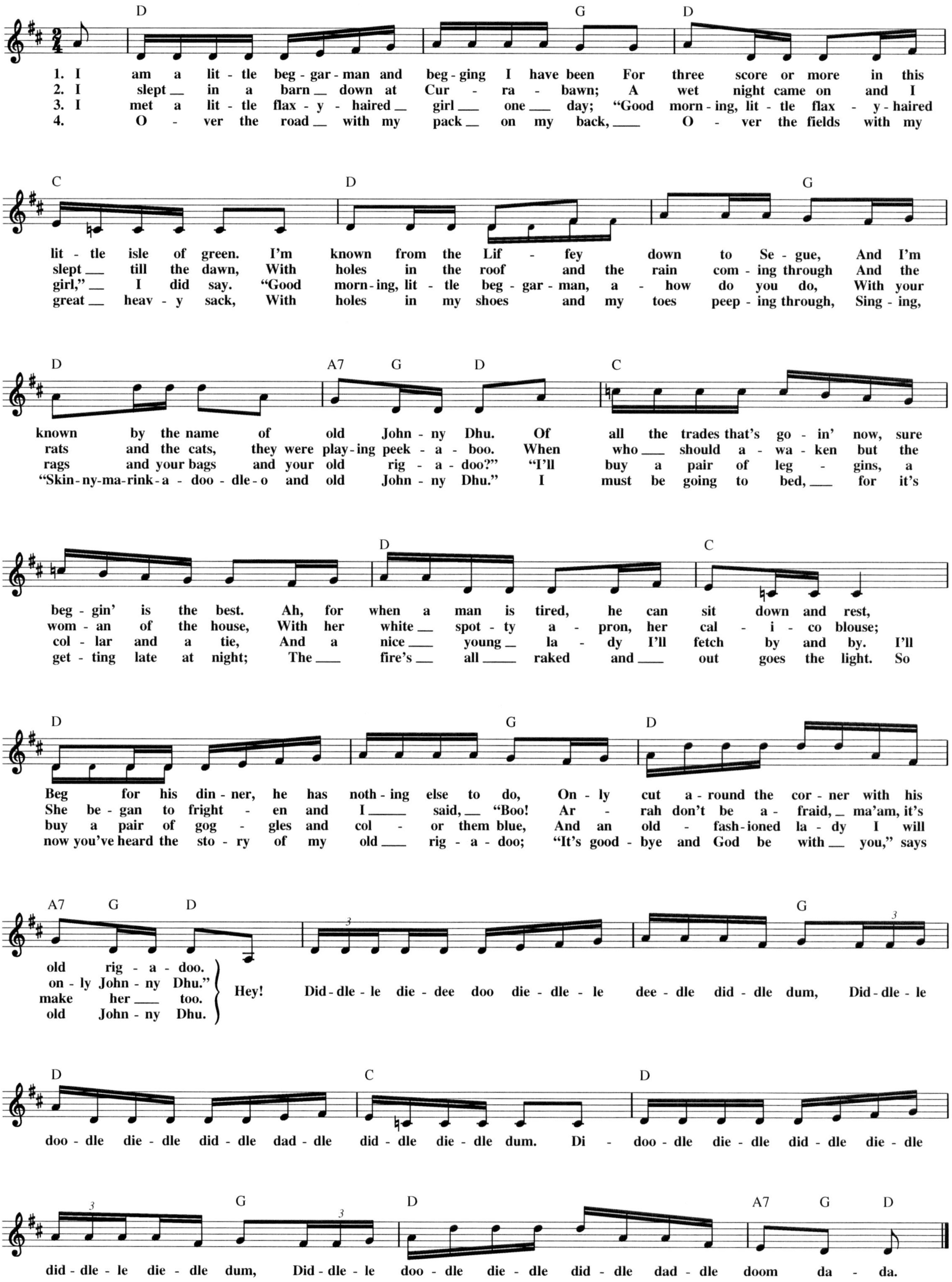
D G D
1. I am a lit - tle beg - gar - man and beg - ging I have been For three score or more in this
2. I slept in a barn down at Cur - ra - bawn; A wet night came on and I
3. I met a lit - tle flax - y - haired girl one day; "Good morn - ing, lit - tle flax - y - haired
4. O - ver the road with my pack on my back, O - ver the fields with my
C D G
lit - tle isle of green. I'm known from the Lif - fey down to Se - gue, And I'm
slept till the dawn, With holes in the roof and the rain com - ing through And the
girl," I did say. "Good morn - ing, lit - tle beg - gar - man, a - how do you do, With your
great heav - y sack, With holes in my shoes and my toes peep - ing through, Sing - ing,
D A7 G D C
known by the name of old John - ny Dhu. Of all the trades that's go - in' now, sure
rats and the cats, they were play - ing peek - a - boo. When who should a - wa - ken but the
rags and your bags and your old rig - a - doo?" "I'll buy a pair of leg - gins, a
"Skin - ny - ma - rink - a - doo - dle - o and old John - ny Dhu." I must be going to bed, for it's
D C
beg - gin' is the best. Ah, for when a man is tired, he can sit down and rest,
wom - an of the house, With her white spot - ty a - pron, her cal - i - co blouse;
col - lar and a tie, And a nice young la - dy I'll fetch by and by. I'll
get - ting late at night; The fire's all raked and out goes the light. So
D G D
Beg for his din - ner, he has noth - ing else to do, On - ly cut a - round the cor - ner with his
She be - gan to fright - en and I said, "Boo! Ar - rah don't be a - fraid, ma'am, it's
buy a pair of gog - gles and col - or them blue, And an old - fash - ioned la - dy I will
now you've heard the sto - ry of my old rig - a - doo; "It's good - bye and God be with you," says
A7 G D G
old rig - a - doo.
on - ly John - ny Dhu."
make her too.
old John - ny Dhu.
Hey! Did - dle - le die - dee doo die - dle - le dee - dle did - dle dum, Did - dle - le
D C D
doo - dle die - dle did - dle dad - dle did - dle die - dle dum. Di - doo - dle die - dle did - dle die - dle
G D A7 G D
did - dle - le die - dle dum, Did - dle - le doo - dle die - dle did - dle dad - dle doom da - da.

BELIEVE ME, IF ALL THOSE ENDEARING YOUNG CHARMS

Irish popular song
Words by Thomas Moore

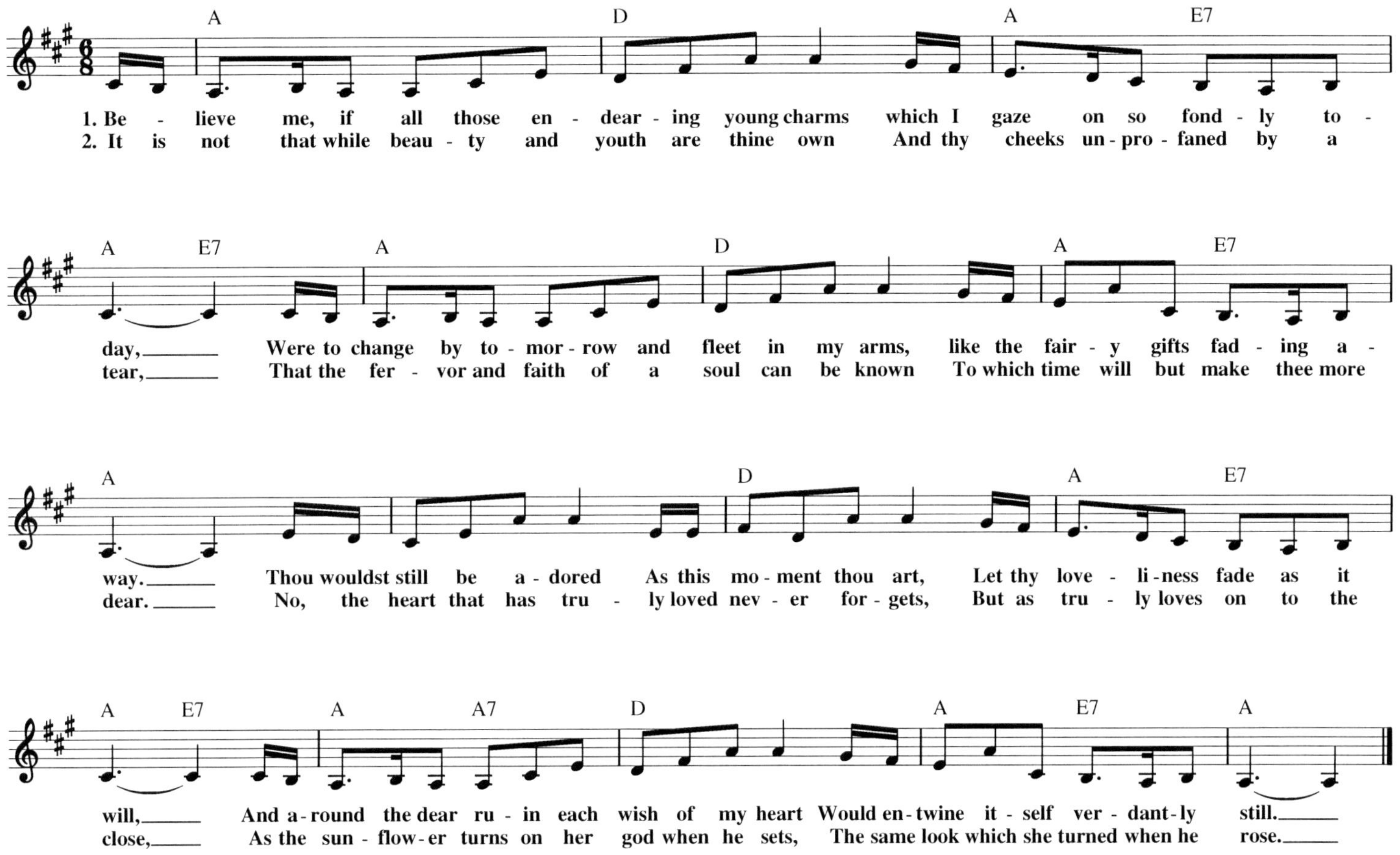

1. Be - lieve me, if all those en - dear - ing young charms which I gaze on so fond - ly to -
2. It is not that while beau - ty and youth are thine own And thy cheeks un - pro - faned by a

day,_____ Were to change by to - mor - row and fleet in my arms, like the fair - y gifts fad - ing a -
tear,_____ That the fer - vor and faith of a soul can be known To which time will but make thee more

way._____ Thou wouldst still be a - dored As this mo - ment thou art, Let thy love - li - ness fade as it
dear._____ No, the heart that has tru - ly loved nev - er for - gets, But as tru - ly loves on to the

will,_____ And a - round the dear ru - in each wish of my heart Would en - twine it - self ver - dant - ly still._____
close,_____ As the sun - flow - er turns on her god when he sets, The same look which she turned when he rose._____

THE BELLS OF SHANDON

Irish folksong

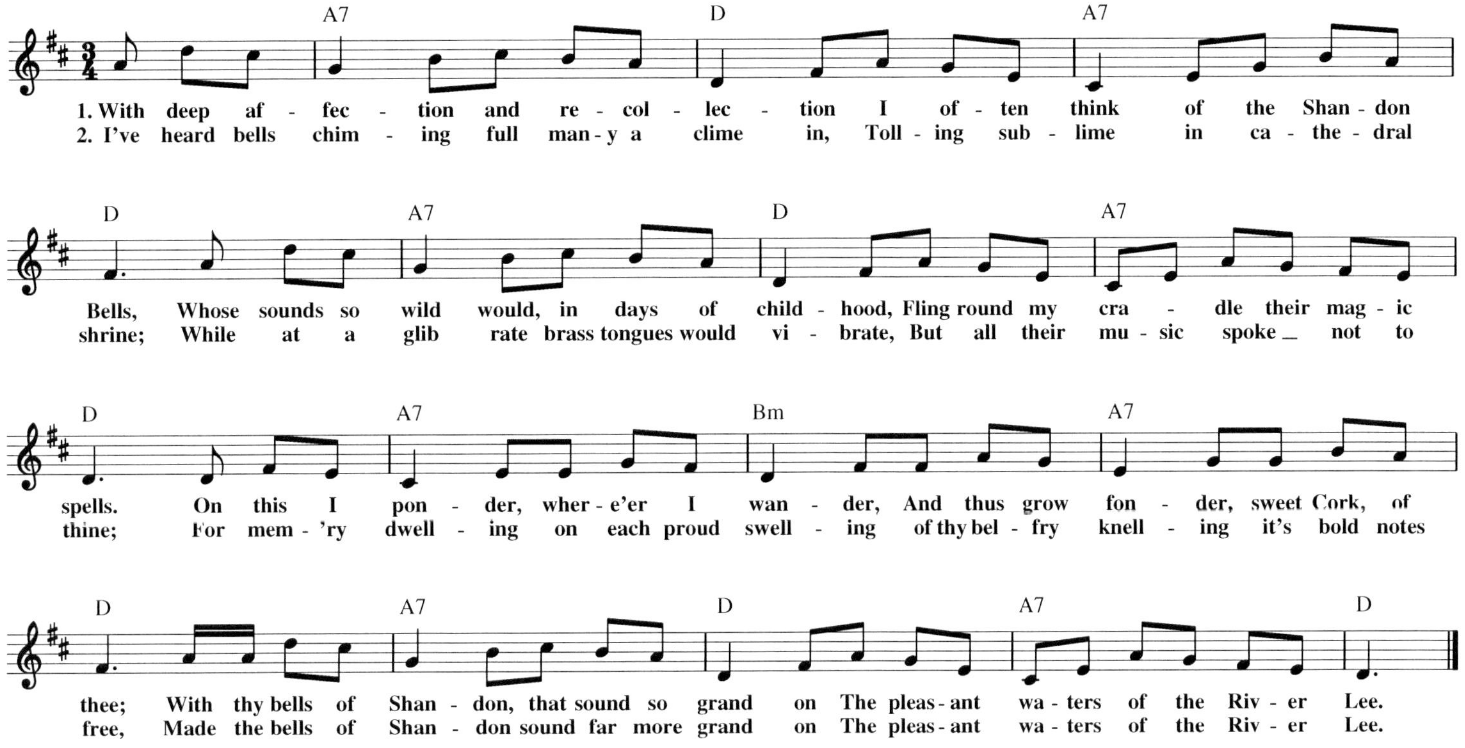

1. With deep af - fec - tion and re - col - lec - tion I of - ten think of the Shan - don
2. I've heard bells chim - ing full man - y a clime in, Toll - ing sub - lime in ca - the - dral

Bells, Whose sounds so wild would, in days of child - hood, Fling round my cra - dle their mag - ic
shrine; While at a glib rate brass tongues would vi - brate, But all their mu - sic spoke_ not to

spells. On this I pon - der, wher - e'er I wan - der, And thus grow fon - der, sweet Cork, of
thine; For mem - 'ry dwell - ing on each proud swell - ing of thy bel - fry knell - ing it's bold notes

thee; With thy bells of Shan - don, that sound so grand on The pleas - ant wa - ters of the Riv - er Lee.
free, Made the bells of Shan - don sound far more grand on The pleas - ant wa - ters of the Riv - er Lee.

BENDEMEER'S STREAM

Irish popular song
Words by Thomas Moore

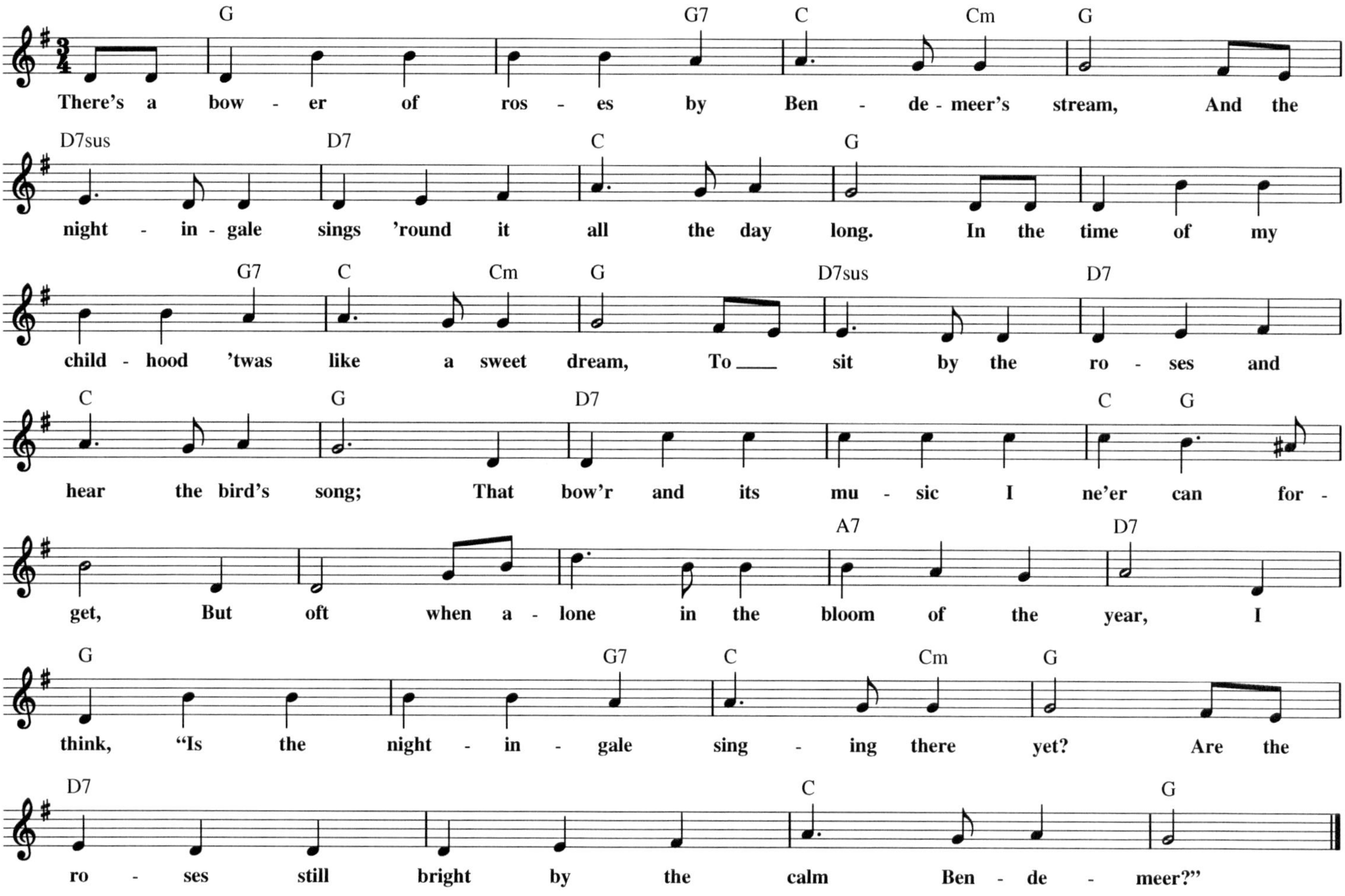

BESIDE THE RIVER LOUNE

Irish folksong

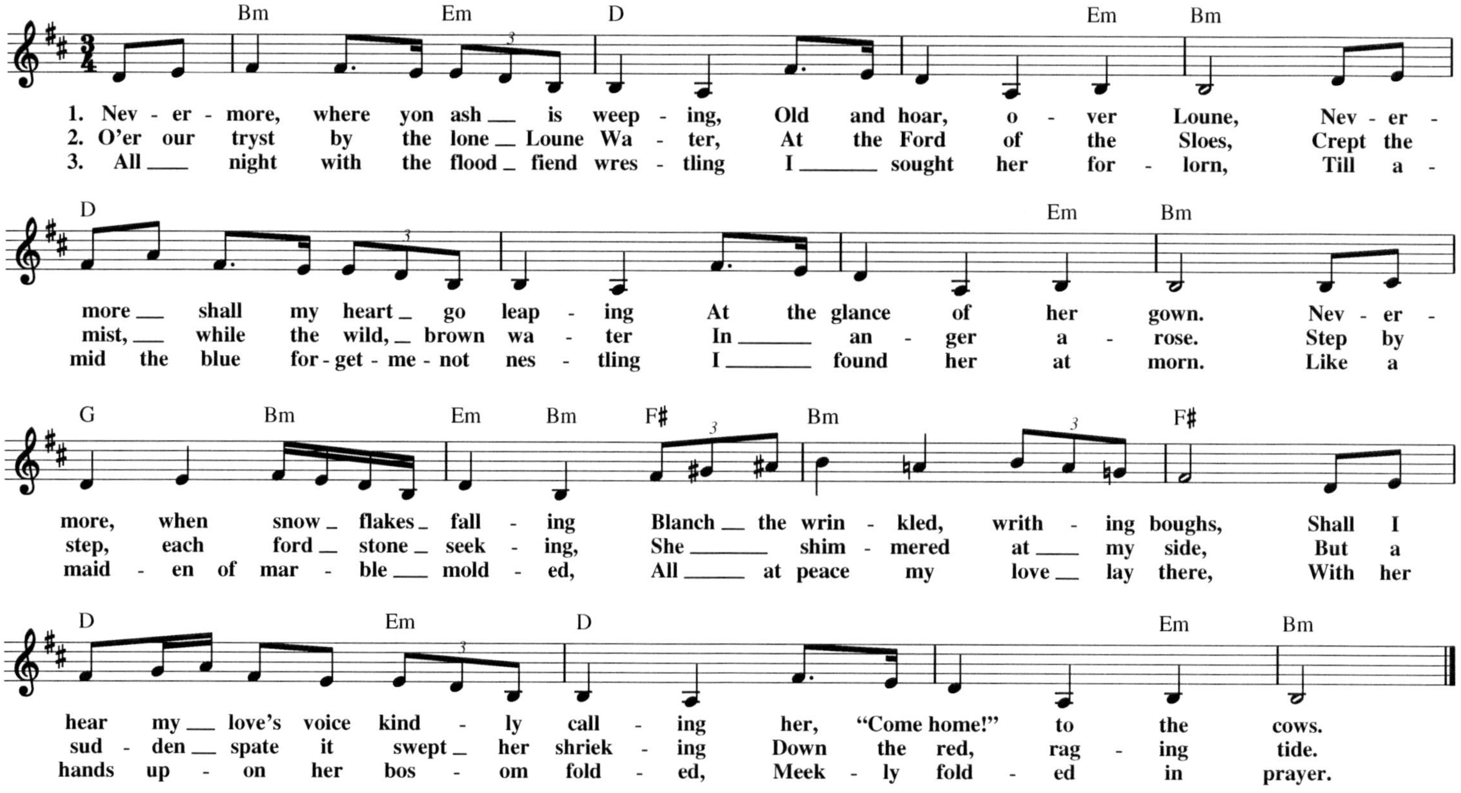

BIRDS AT THE FAIRY FULLING

Folksong from the Hebrides

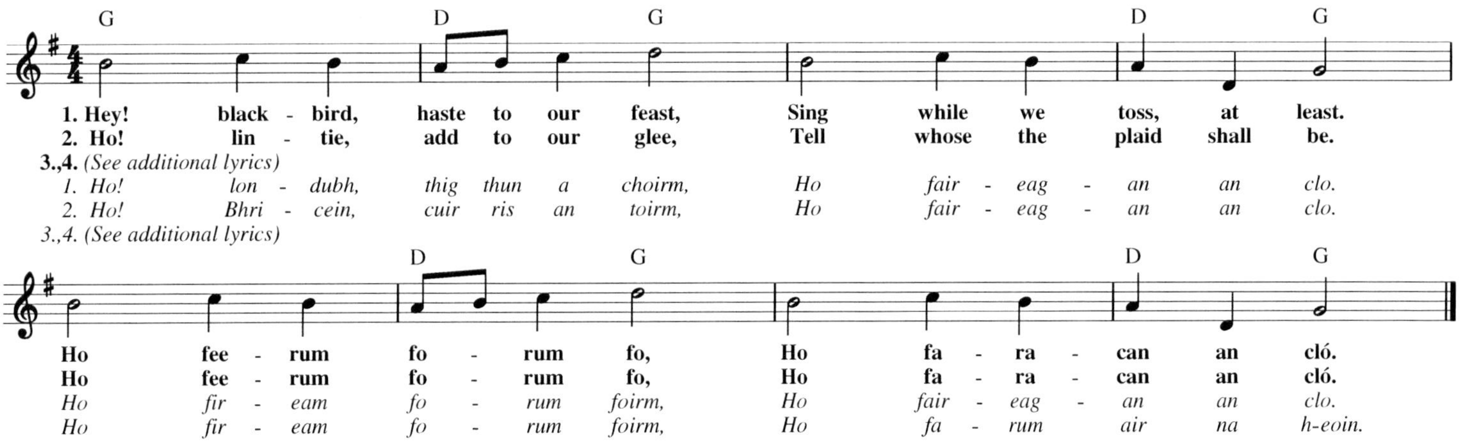

Additional Lyrics

3. Ho! mavie,* whistle and call
   To whom the plaid may fall.
   Ho, wing and feather and song,
   Toss till the web is strong.

4. Ho feerum forum fo,
   Ho faracan an cló.
   Heart's love to Benakshee,**
   Well knows she whose 'twill be!

3. Ho! smeorach, ceileir is gairm
   Ho faireagan an clo.
   Ho, sgiath is iteag is gairm,
   Ho faireagan an clo.

4. Ho fiream forum foirm,
   Ho faireagan an clo.
   Gradh air a' bheanag shith,
   Ho beannachd air na h-eoin!

* *Thrush, lowland Scots*
** *Little fairy woman.*

THE BLACK CAVALRY

Irish folksong

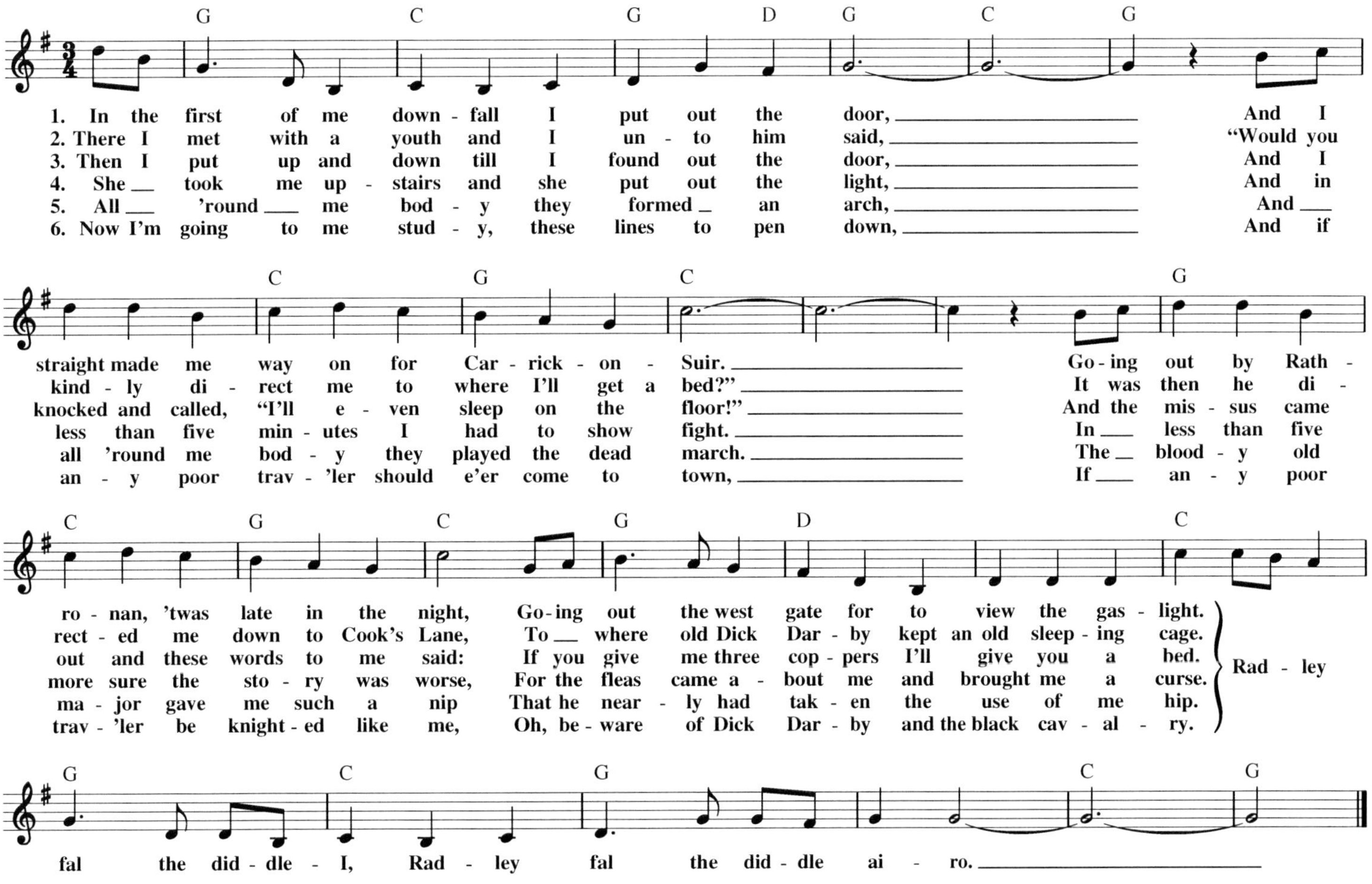

THE BLACKBERRY BLOSSOM

Irish folksong

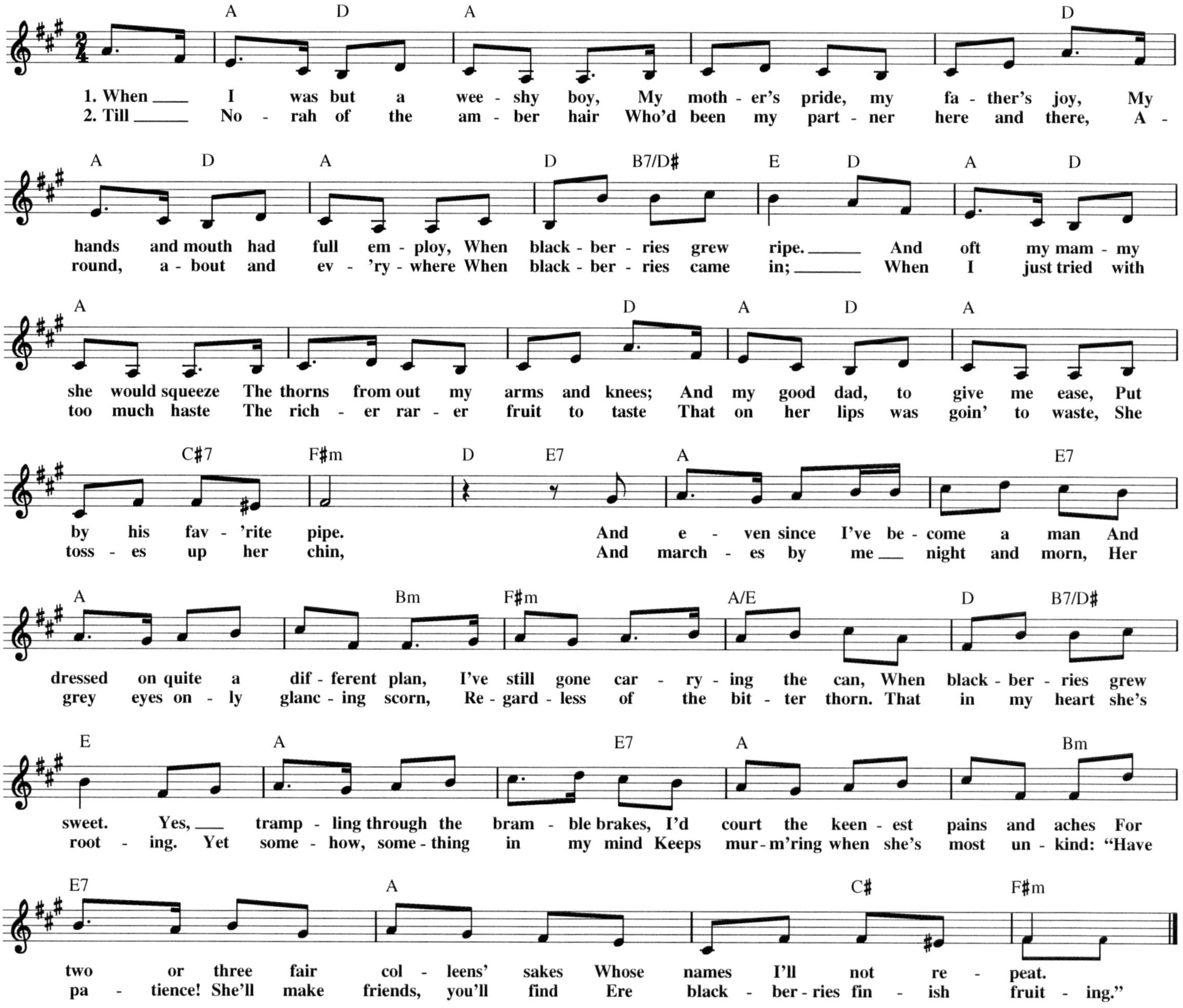

BLACKWATER SIDE

Irish folksong

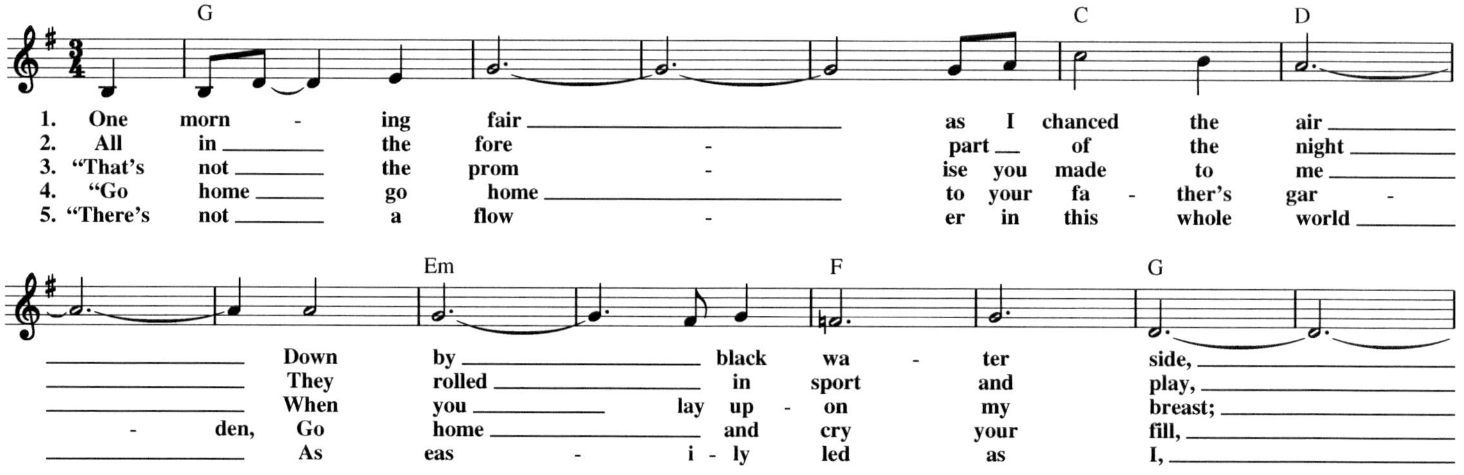

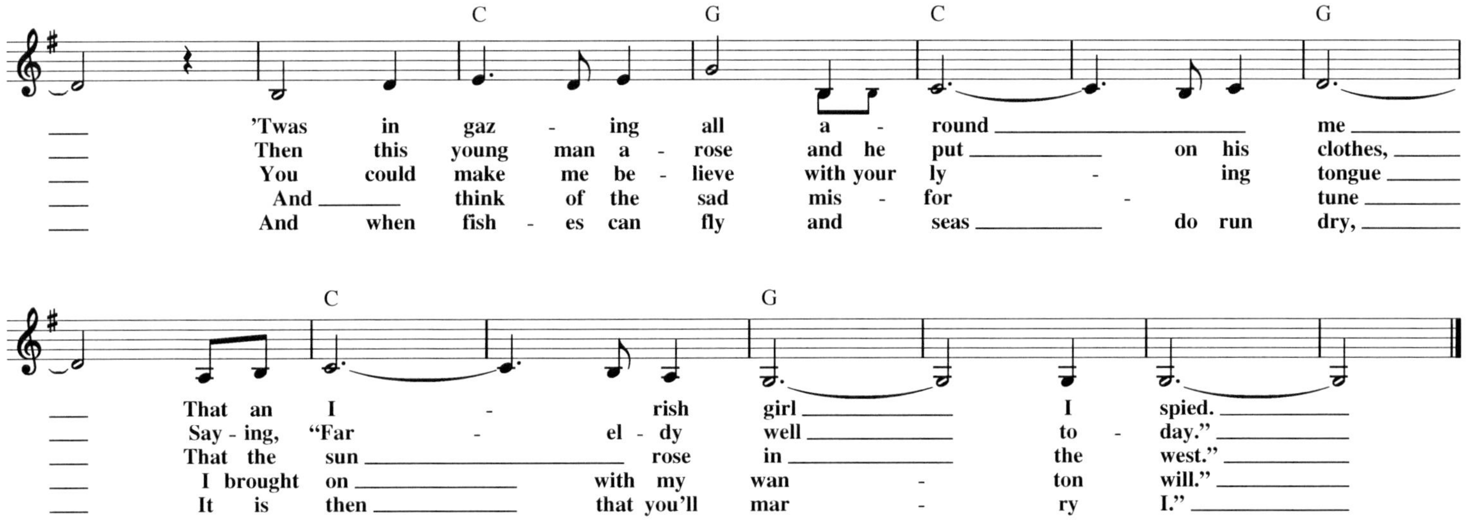
C G C G
'Twas in gaz - ing all a - round me
Then this young man a - rose and he put on his clothes,
You could make me be - lieve with your ly - ing tongue
And think of the sad mis - for - tune
And when fish - es can fly and seas do run dry,
C G
That an I - rish girl I spied.
Say - ing, "Far - el - dy well to - day."
That the sun rose in the west."
I brought on with my wan - ton will."
It is then that you'll mar - ry I."

THE BLUE BELLS OF SCOTLAND

Scottish folksong

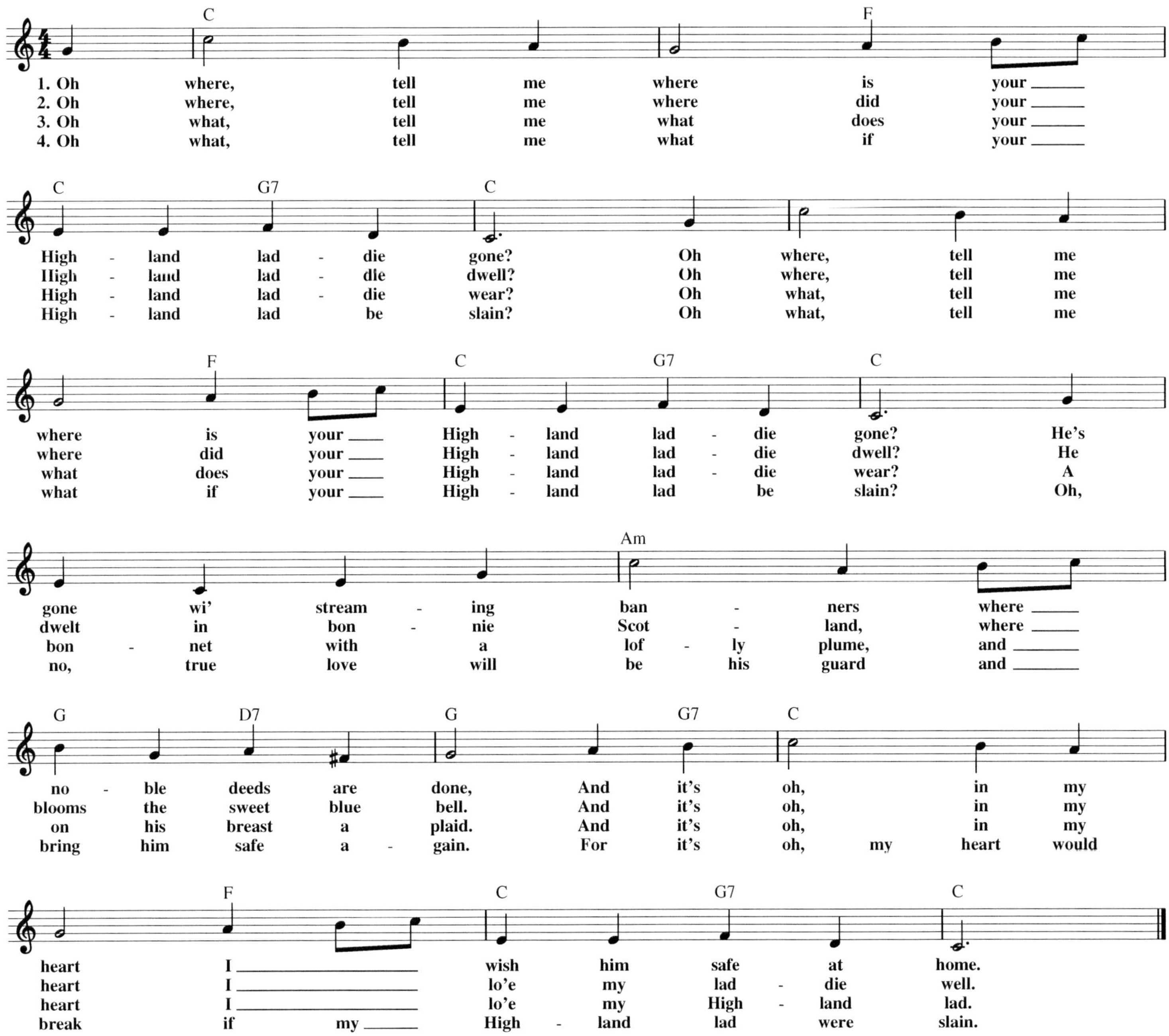
C F
1. Oh where, tell me where is your
2. Oh where, tell me where did your
3. Oh what, tell me what does your
4. Oh what, tell me what if your
C G7 C
High - land lad - die gone? Oh where, tell me
High - land lad - die dwell? Oh where, tell me
High - land lad - die wear? Oh what, tell me
High - land lad be slain? Oh what, tell me
F C G7 C
where is your High - land lad - die gone? He's
where did your High - land lad - die dwell? He
what does your High - land lad - die wear? A
what if your High - land lad be slain? Oh,
Am
gone wi' stream - ing ban - ners where
dwelt in bon - nie Scot - land, where
bon - net with a lof - ly plume, and
no, true love will be his guard and
G D7 G G7 C
no - ble deeds are done, And it's oh, in my
blooms the sweet blue bell. And it's oh, in my
on his breast a plaid. And it's oh, in my
bring him safe a - gain. For it's oh, my heart would
F C G7 C
heart I wish him safe at home.
heart I lo'e my lad - die well.
heart I lo'e my High - land lad.
break if my High - land lad were slain.

BLESSING OF THE ROAD
(Duan an Rathaid)

Folksong from the Hebrides

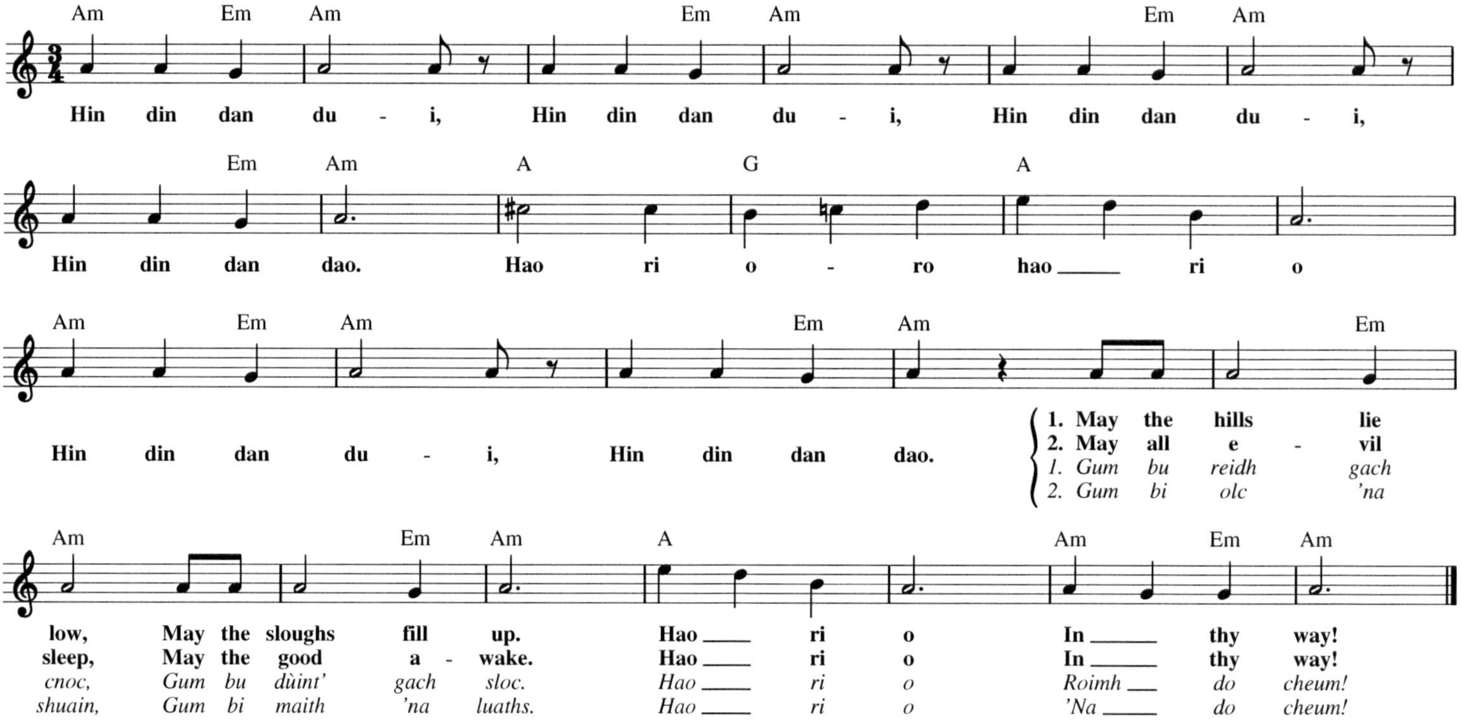

THE BOLD FENIAN MEN

Irish popular song
Words by Michael Scanlan

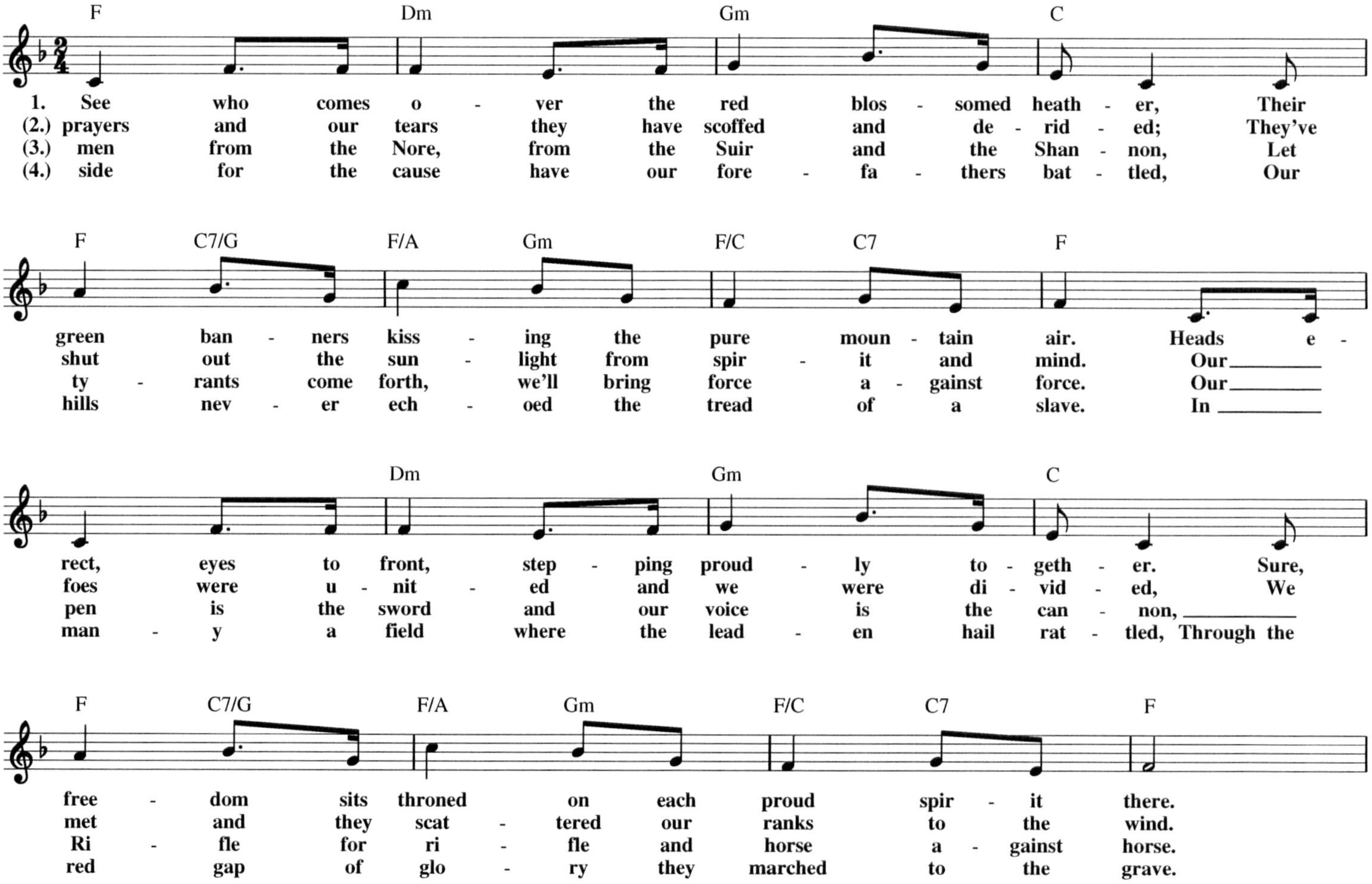

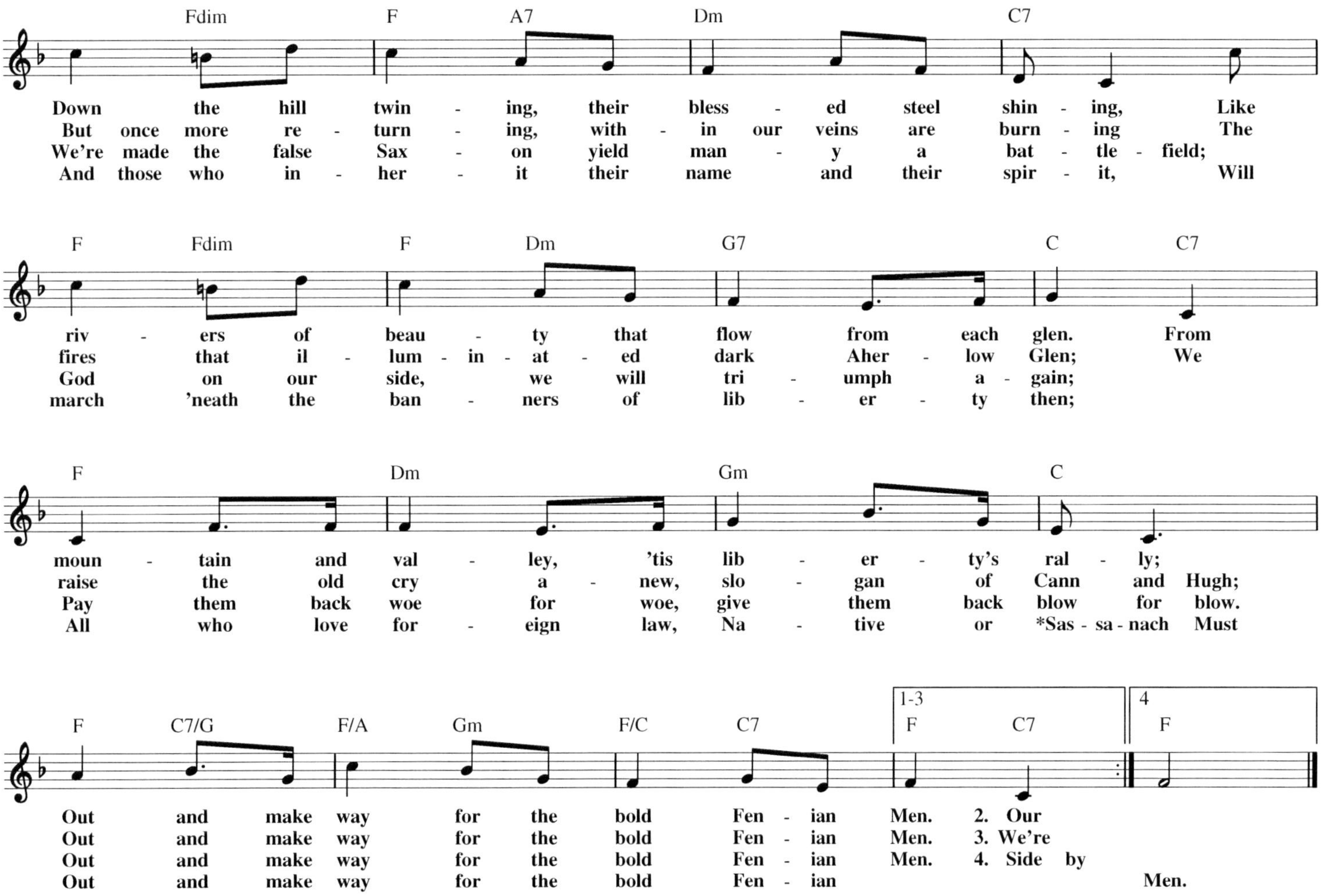

Down the hill twin - ing, their bless - ed steel shin - ing, Like
But once more re - turn - ing, with - in our veins are burn - ing The
We're made the false Sax - on yield man - y a bat - tle - field;
And those who in - her - it their name and their spir - it, Will

riv - ers of beau - ty that flow from each glen. From
fires that il - lum - in - at - ed dark Aher - low Glen; We
God on our side, we will tri - umph a - gain;
march 'neath the ban - ners of lib - er - ty then;

moun - tain and val - ley, 'tis lib - er - ty's ral - ly;
raise the old cry a - new, slo - gan of Cann and Hugh;
Pay them back woe for woe, give them back blow for blow.
All who love for - eign law, Na - tive or *Sas - sa - nach Must

Out and make way for the bold Fen - ian Men. 2. Our
Out and make way for the bold Fen - ian Men. 3. We're
Out and make way for the bold Fen - ian Men. 4. Side by
Out and make way for the bold Fen - ian Men.

derogatory term for the English

BONEY WAS A WARRIOR

Irish folksong

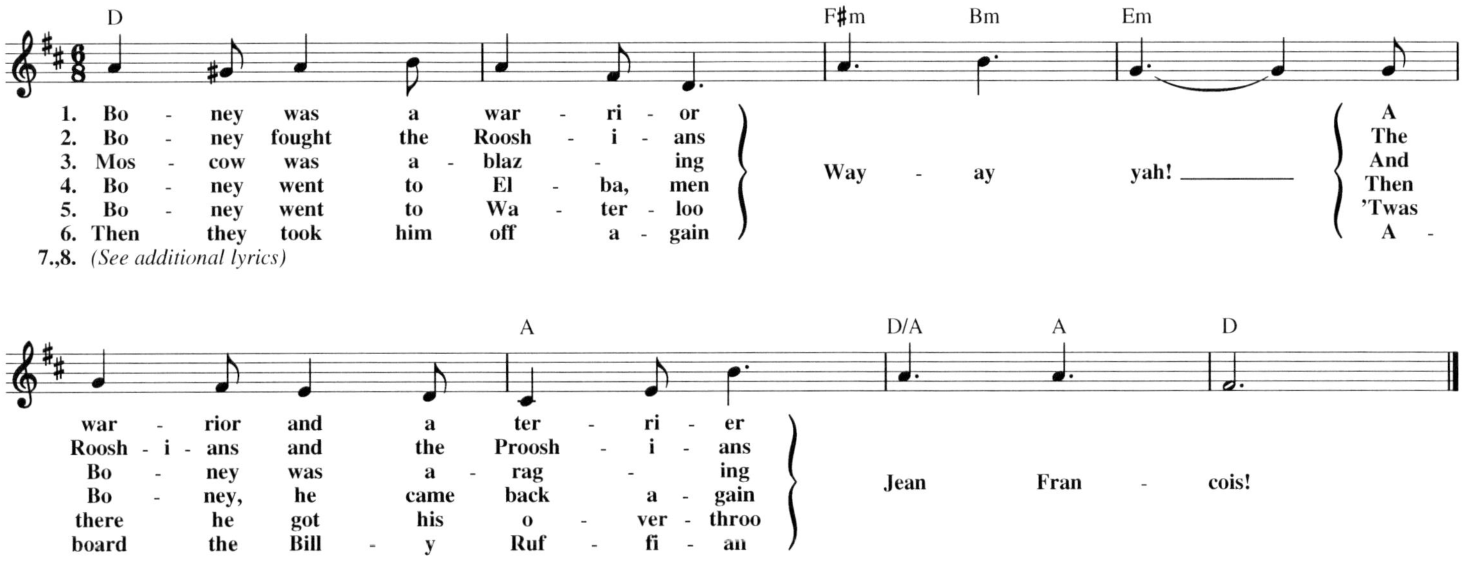

1. Bo - ney was a war - ri - or   Way - ay yah! ____ A
2. Bo - ney fought the Roosh - i - ans   The
3. Mos - cow was a - blaz - ing   And
4. Bo - ney went to El - ba, men   Then
5. Bo - ney went to Wa - ter - loo   'Twas
6. Then they took him off a - gain   A -

7.,8. *(See additional lyrics)*

war - rior and a ter - ri - er   Jean Fran - cois!
Roosh - i - ans and the Proosh - i - ans
Bo - ney was a - rag - ing
Bo - ney, he came back a - gain
there he got his o - ver - throo
board the Bill - y Ruf - fi - an

Additional Lyrics

7. He went to Saint Helena
    Way-ay yah!
    There he was a prisona
    Jean Francois!

8. Boney broke his heart and died
    Way-ay yah!
    Away off in Saint Helena
    Jean Francois!

THE BOLD TENANT FARMER

Irish folksong

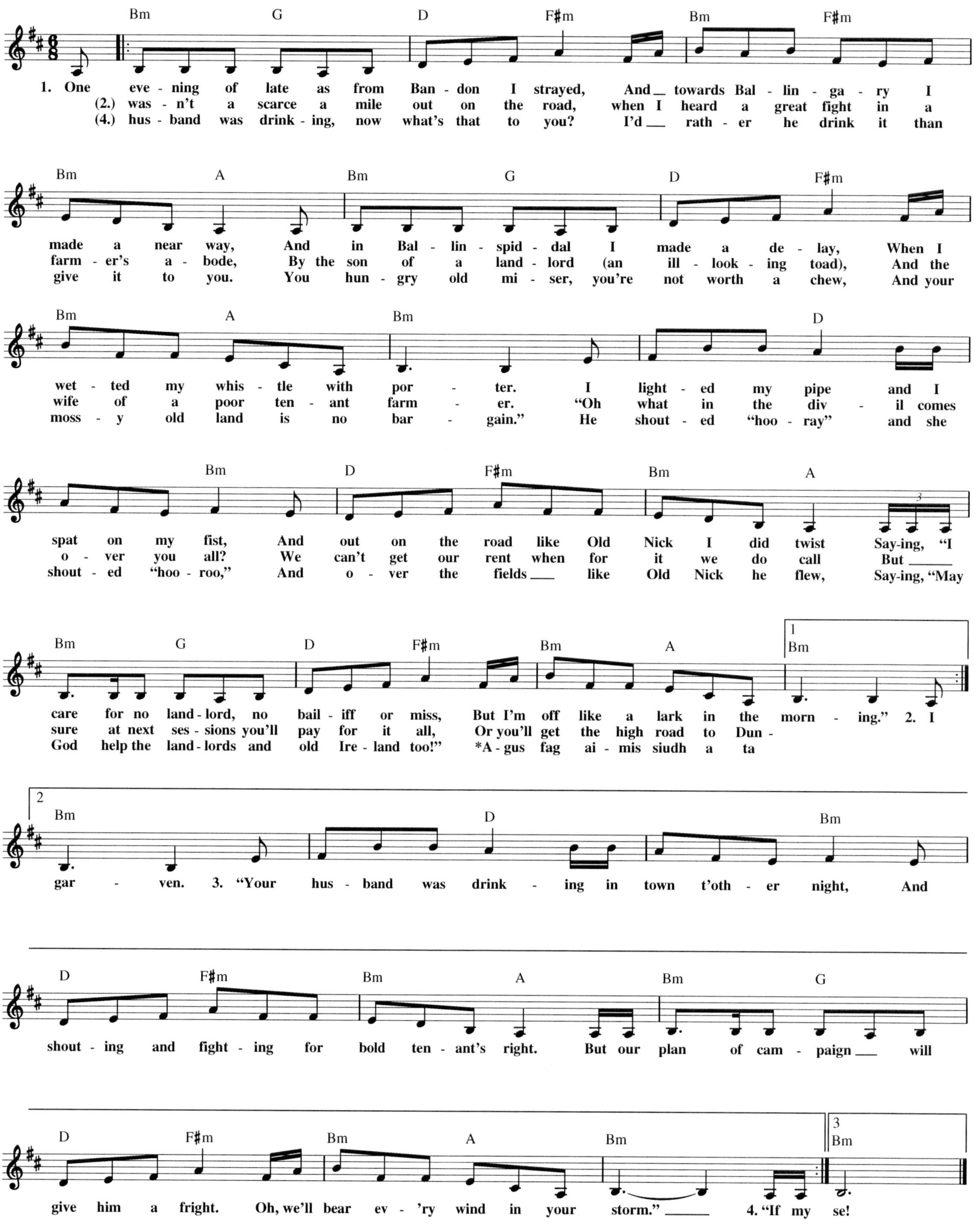

Let us leave that as it is.

BOLD THADY QUILL

Irish folksong

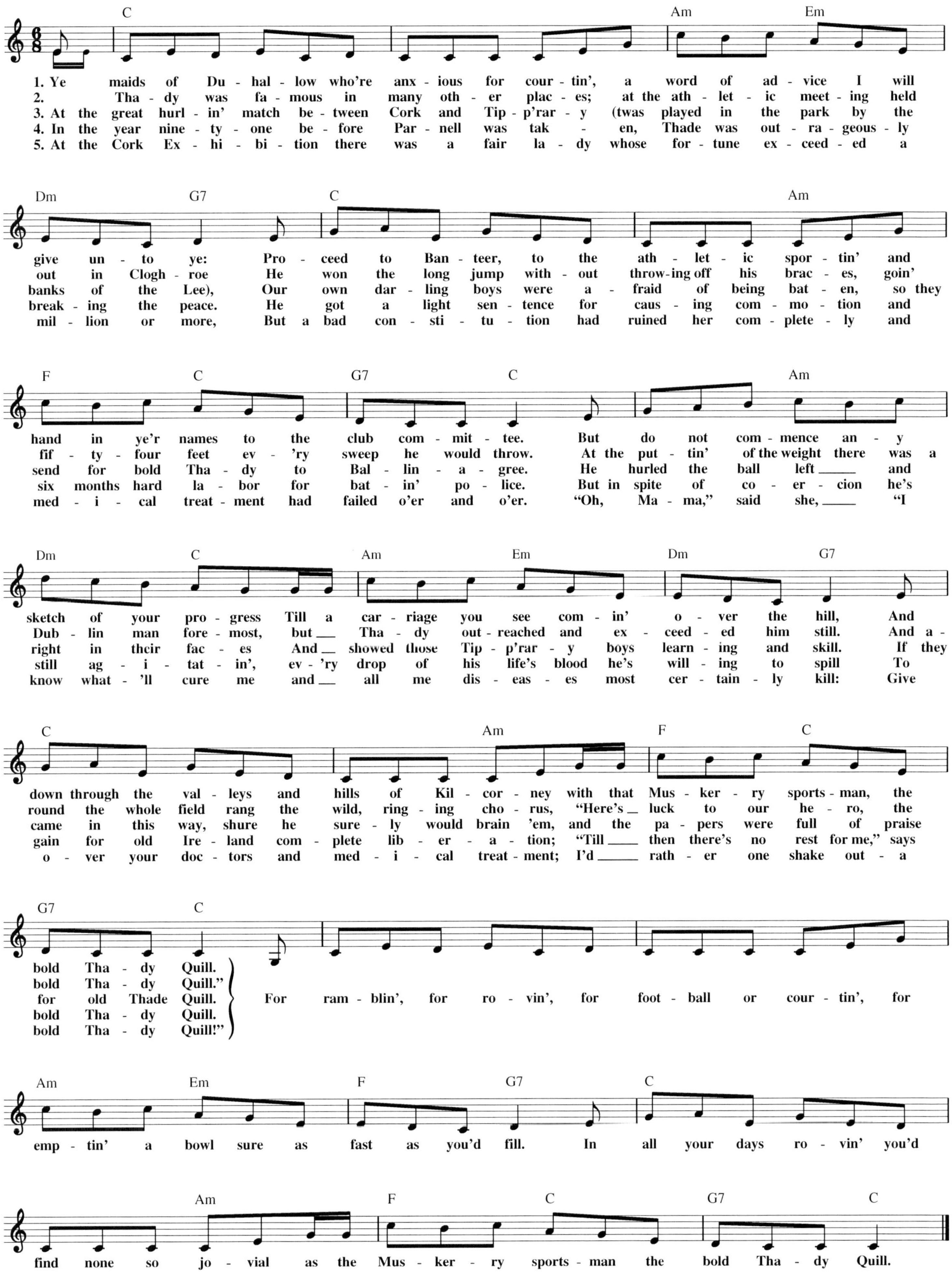

C Am Em
1. Ye maids of Du - hal - low who're anx - ious for cour - tin', a word of ad - vice I will
2. Tha - dy was fa - mous in many oth - er plac - es; at the ath - let - ic meet - ing held
3. At the great hurl - in' match be - tween Cork and Tip - p'rar - y (twas played in the park by the
4. In the year nine - ty - one be - fore Par - nell was tak - en, Thade was out - ra - geous - ly
5. At the Cork Ex - hi - bi - tion there was a fair la - dy whose for - tune ex - ceed - ed a
Dm G7 C Am
give un - to ye: Pro - ceed to Ban - teer, to the ath - let - ic spor - tin' and
out in Clogh - roe He won the long jump with - out throw-ing off his brac - es, goin'
banks of the Lee), Our own dar - ling boys were a - fraid of being bat - en, so they
break - ing the peace. He got a light sen - tence for caus - ing com - mo - tion and
mil - lion or more, But a bad con - sti - tu - tion had ruined her com - plete - ly and
F C G7 C Am
hand in ye'r names to the club com - mit - tee. But do not com - mence an - y
fif - ty - four feet ev - 'ry sweep he would throw. At the put - tin' of the weight there was a
send for bold Tha - dy to Bal - lin - a - gree. He hurled the ball left and
six months hard la - bor for bat - in' po - lice. But in spite of co - er - cion he's
med - i - cal treat - ment had failed o'er and o'er. "Oh, Ma - ma," said she, "I
Dm C Am Em Dm G7
sketch of your pro - gress Till a car - riage you see com - in' o - ver the hill, And
Dub - lin man fore - most, but Tha - dy out - reached and ex - ceed - ed him still. And a -
right in their fac - es And showed those Tip - p'rar - y boys learn - ing and skill. If they
still ag - i - tat - in', ev - 'ry drop of his life's blood he's will - ing to spill To
know what - 'll cure me and all me dis - eas - es most cer - tain - ly kill: Give
C Am F C
down through the val - leys and hills of Kil - cor - ney with that Mus - ker - ry sports - man, the
round the whole field rang the wild, ring - ing cho - rus, "Here's luck to our he - ro, the
came in this way, shure he sure - ly would brain 'em, and the pa - pers were full of praise
gain for old Ire - land com - plete lib - er - a - tion; "Till then there's no rest for me," says
o - ver your doc - tors and med - i - cal treat - ment; I'd rath - er one shake out - a
G7 C
bold Tha - dy Quill.
bold Tha - dy Quill."
for old Thade Quill.
bold Tha - dy Quill.
bold Tha - dy Quill!"
For ram - blin', for ro - vin', for foot - ball or cour - tin', for
Am Em F G7 C
emp - tin' a bowl sure as fast as you'd fill. In all your days ro - vin' you'd
Am F C G7 C
find none so jo - vial as the Mus - ker - ry sports - man the bold Tha - dy Quill.

THE BONNY EARL OF MURRAY

Scottish folksong

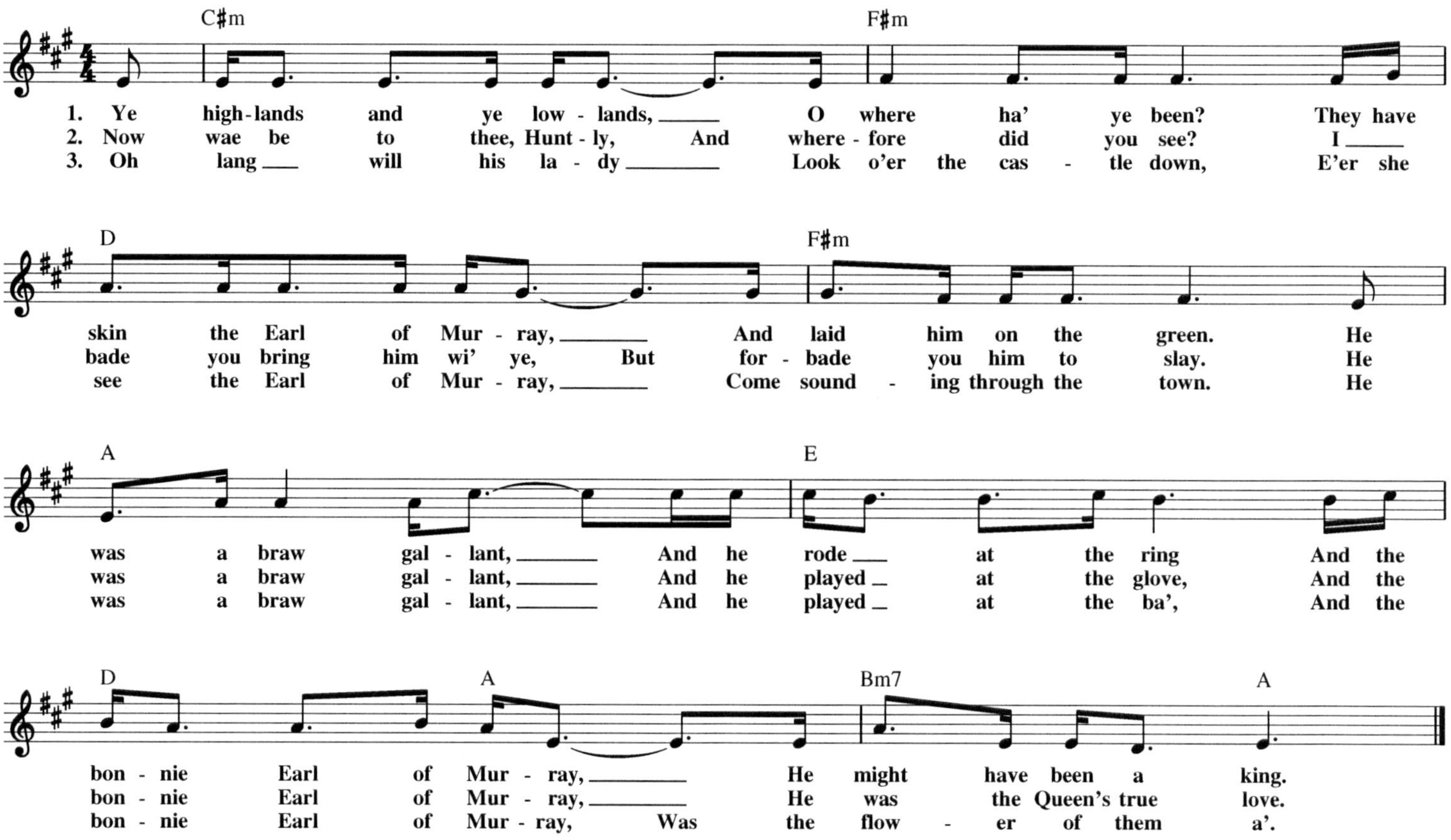

1. Ye high-lands and ye low-lands, O where ha' ye been? They have
2. Now wae be to thee, Hunt-ly, And where-fore did you see? I
3. Oh lang ___ will his la-dy ___ Look o'er the cas-tle down, E'er she

skin the Earl of Mur - ray, ___ And laid him on the green. He
bade you bring him wi' ye, But for-bade you him to slay. He
see the Earl of Mur-ray, ___ Come sound - ing through the town. He

was a braw gal - lant, ___ And he rode ___ at the ring And the
was a braw gal - lant, ___ And he played _ at the glove, And the
was a braw gal - lant, ___ And he played _ at the ba', And the

bon - nie Earl of Mur - ray, ___ He might have been a king.
bon - nie Earl of Mur - ray, ___ He was the Queen's true love.
bon - nie Earl of Mur - ray, Was the flow - er of them a'.

BOSTON BURGLAR

Irish popular song

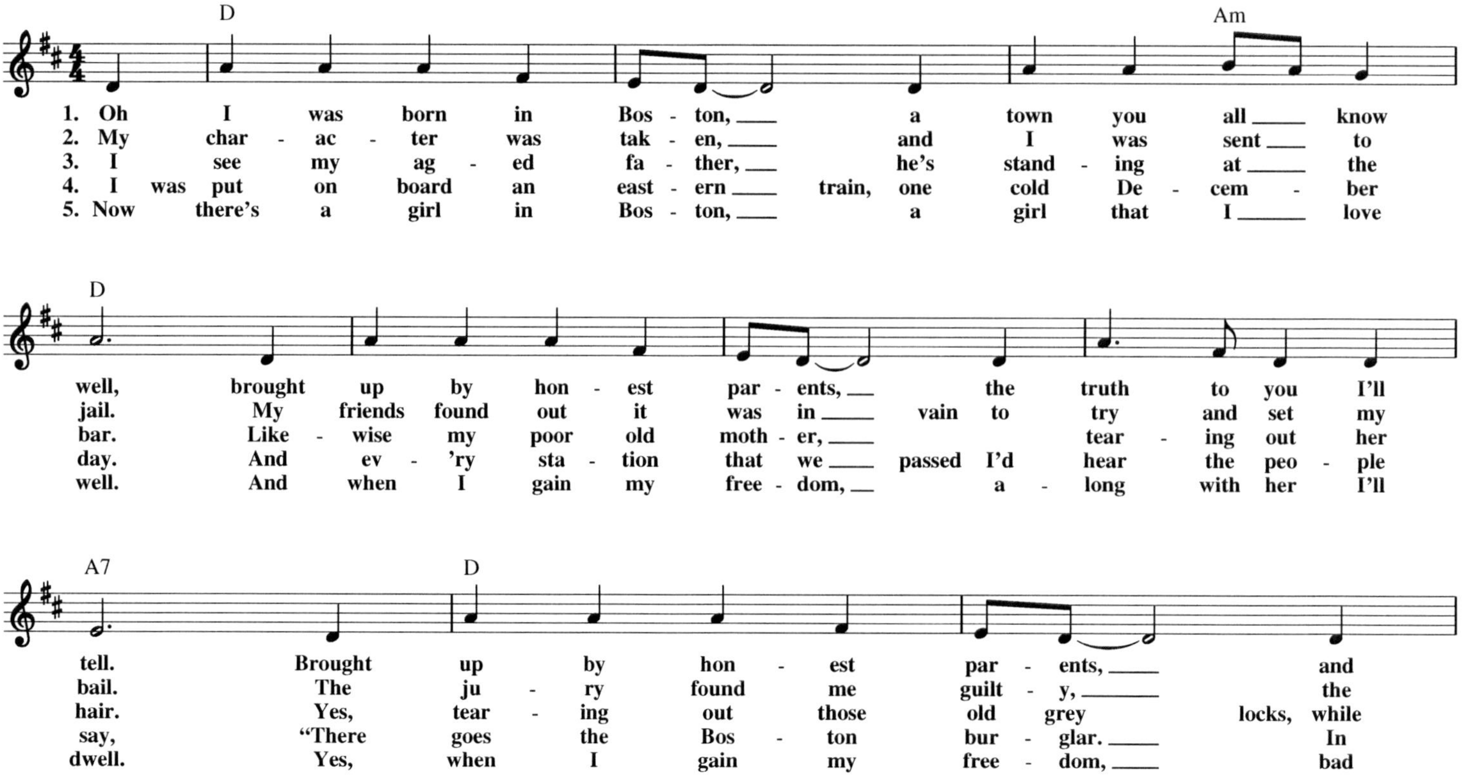

1. Oh I was born in Bos - ton, ___ a town you all ___ know
2. My char - ac - ter was tak - en, ___ and I was sent ___ to
3. I see my ag - ed fa - ther, ___ he's stand - ing at ___ the
4. I was put on board an east - ern ___ train, one cold De - cem - ber
5. Now there's a girl in Bos - ton, ___ a girl that I ___ love

well, brought up by hon - est par - ents, ___ the truth to you I'll
jail. My friends found out it was in ___ vain to try and set my
bar. Like - wise my poor old moth - er, ___ tear - ing out her
day. And ev - 'ry sta - tion that we ___ passed I'd hear the peo - ple
well. And when I gain my free - dom, ___ a - long with her I'll

tell. Brought up by hon - est par - ents, ___ and
bail. The ju - ry found me guilt - y, ___ the
hair. Yes, tear - ing out those old grey locks, while
say, "There goes the Bos - ton bur - glar." ___ In
dwell. Yes, when I gain my free - dom, ___ bad

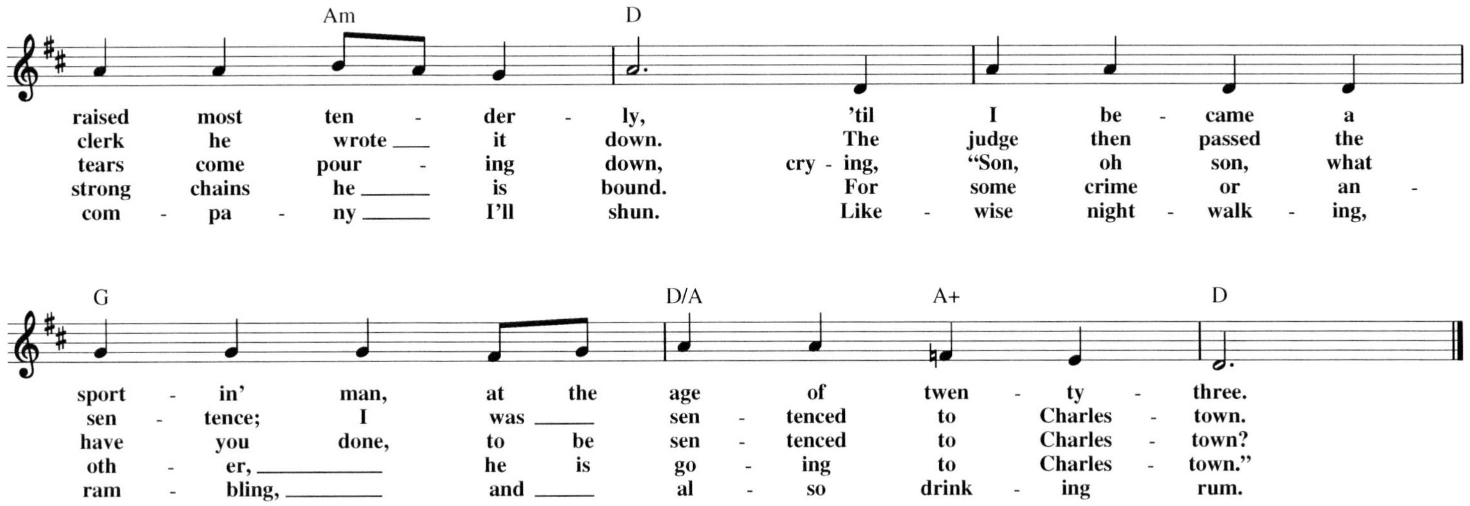

raised most ten - der - ly, 'til I be - came a
clerk he wrote ___ it down. The judge then passed the
tears come pour - ing down, cry - ing, "Son, oh son, what
strong chains he ___ is bound. For some crime or an -
com - pa - ny ___ I'll shun. Like - wise night - walk - ing,

sport - in' man, at the age of twen - ty - three.
sen - tence; I was ___ sen - tenced to Charles - town.
have you done, to be sen - tenced to Charles - town?
oth - er, ___ he is go - ing to Charles - town."
ram - bling, ___ and ___ al - so drink - ing rum.

THE BONNIEST LASS

Scottish folksong
Based on a poem by Robert Burns

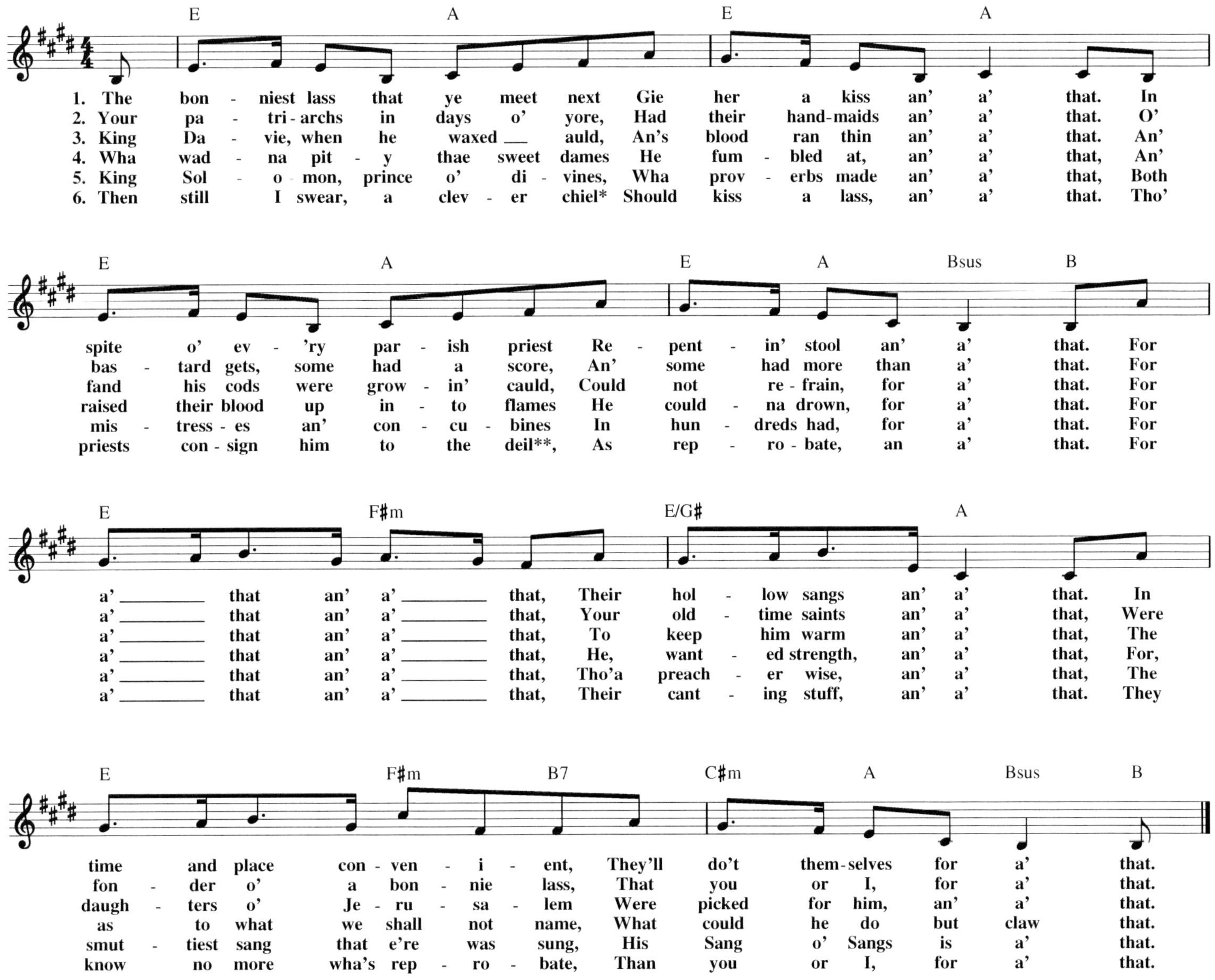

1. The bon - niest lass that ye meet next Gie her a kiss an' a' that. In
2. Your pa - tri - archs in days o' yore, Had their hand-maids an' a' that. O'
3. King Da - vie, when he waxed ___ auld, An's blood ran thin an' a' that. An'
4. Wha wad - na pit - y thae sweet dames He fum - bled at, an' a' that, An'
5. King Sol - o - mon, prince o' di - vines, Wha prov - erbs made an' a' that, Both
6. Then still I swear, a clev - er chiel* Should kiss a lass, an' a' that. Tho'

spite o' ev - 'ry par - ish priest Re - pent - in' stool an' a' that. For
bas - tard gets, some had a score, An' some had more than a' that. For
fand his cods were grow - in' cauld, Could not re - frain, for a' that. For
raised their blood up in - to flames He could - na drown, for a' that. For
mis - tress - es an' con - cu - bines In hun - dreds had, for a' that. For
priests con - sign him to the deil**, As rep - ro - bate, an a' that. For

a' ___ that an' a' ___ that, Their hol - low sangs an' a' that. In
a' ___ that an' a' ___ that, Your old - time saints an' a' that, Were
a' ___ that an' a' ___ that, To keep him warm an' a' that, The
a' ___ that an' a' ___ that, He, want - ed strength, an' a' that, For,
a' ___ that an' a' ___ that, Tho'a preach - er wise, an' a' that, The
a' ___ that an' a' ___ that, Their cant - ing stuff, an' a' that. They

time and place con - ven - i - ent, They'll do't them-selves for a' that.
fon - der o' a bon - nie lass, That you or I, for a' that.
daugh - ters o' Je - ru - sa - lem Were picked for him, an' a' that.
as to what we shall not name, What could he do but claw that.
smut - tiest sang that e're was sung, His Sang o' Sangs is a' that.
know no more wha's rep - ro - bate, Than you or I, for a' that.

young man
**devil*

THE BONNY BUNCH OF ROSES

Irish folksong

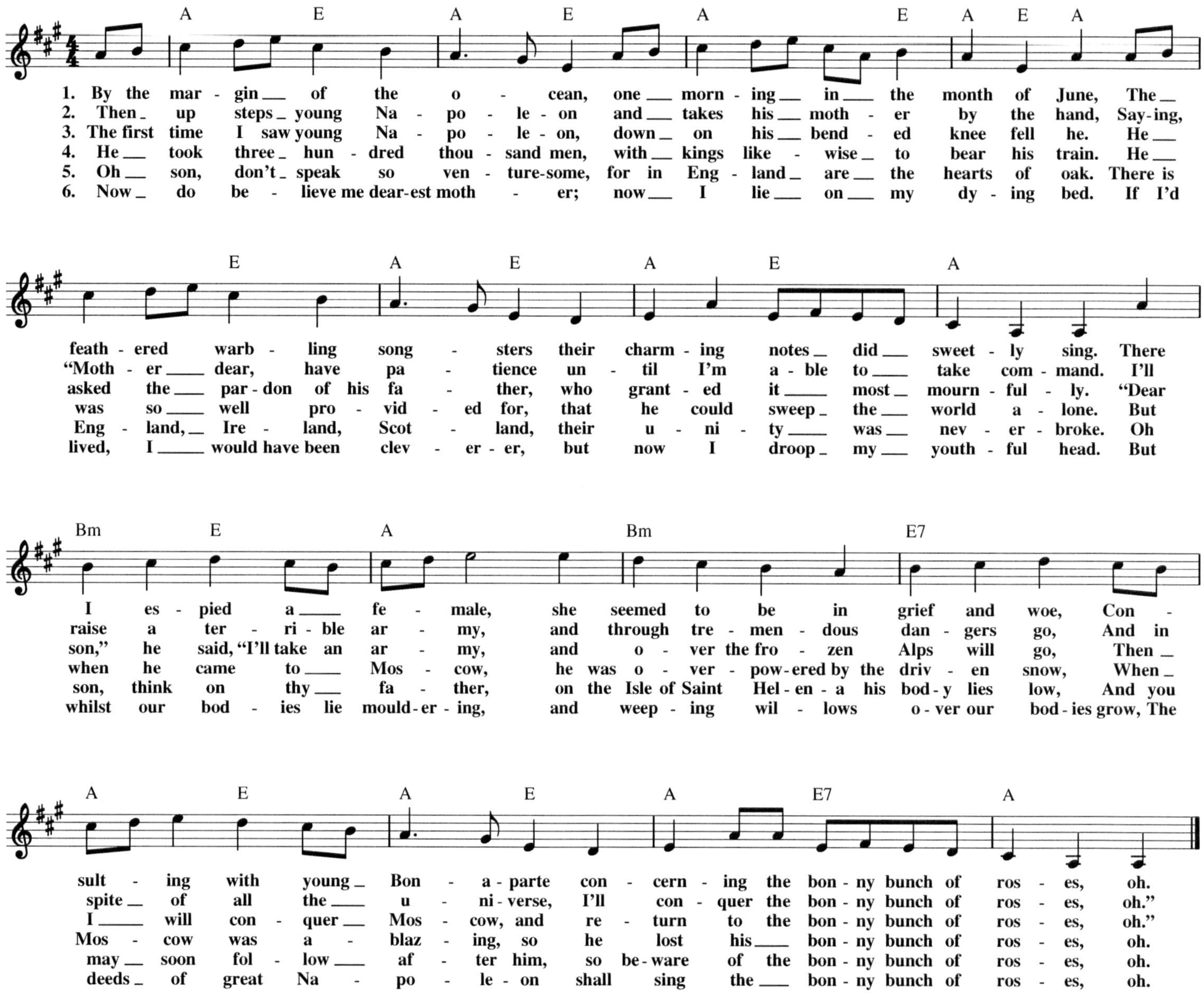

THE BONNY SHIP THE DIAMOND

Scottish folksong

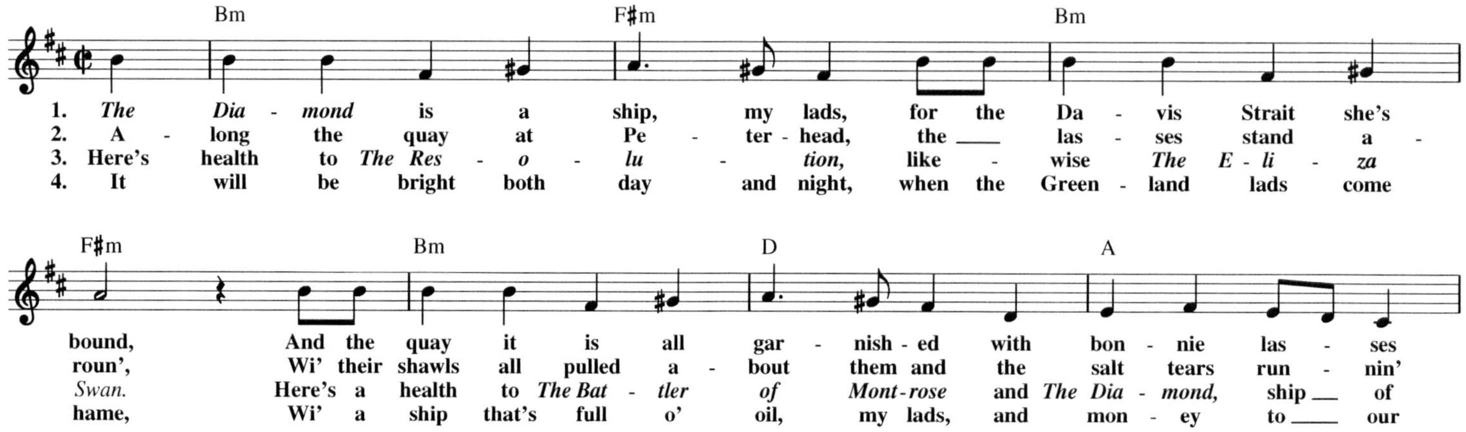

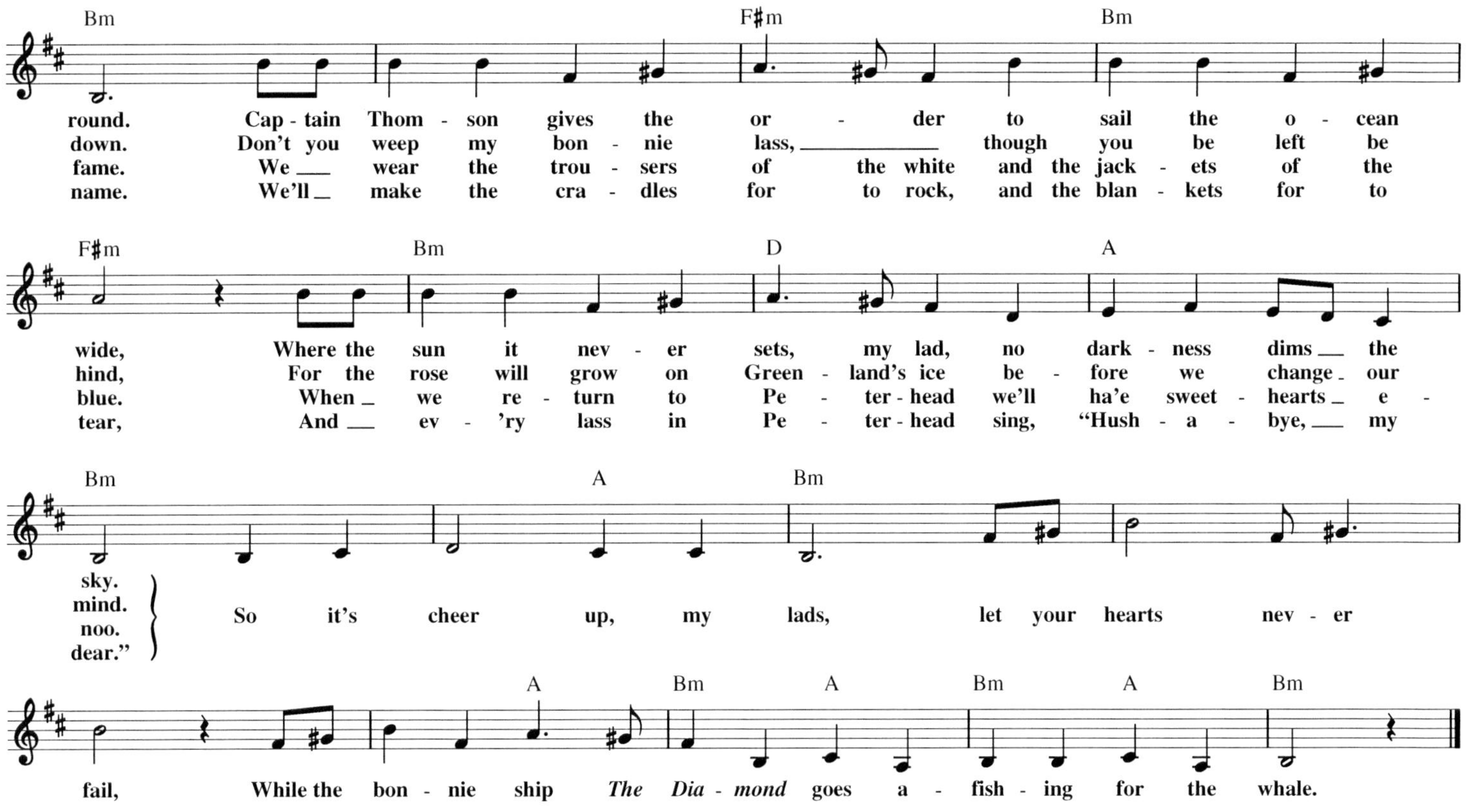

round. Cap-tain Thom-son gives the or - der to sail the o - cean
down. Don't you weep my bon-nie lass, _____ though you be left be-
fame. We __ wear the trou-sers of the white and the jack-ets of the
name. We'll __ make the cra-dles for to rock, and the blan-kets for to

wide, Where the sun it nev-er sets, my lad, no dark-ness dims __ the
hind, For the rose will grow on Green-land's ice be-fore we change our
blue. When __ we re-turn to Pe - ter-head we'll ha'e sweet-hearts __ e-
tear, And __ ev-'ry lass in Pe - ter-head sing, "Hush-a - bye, __ my

sky.
mind.
noo.
dear." So it's cheer up, my lads, let your hearts nev-er

fail, While the bon-nie ship *The Dia-mond* goes a - fish-ing for the whale.

BOULAVOGUE

Irish folksong
By P.J. McCall

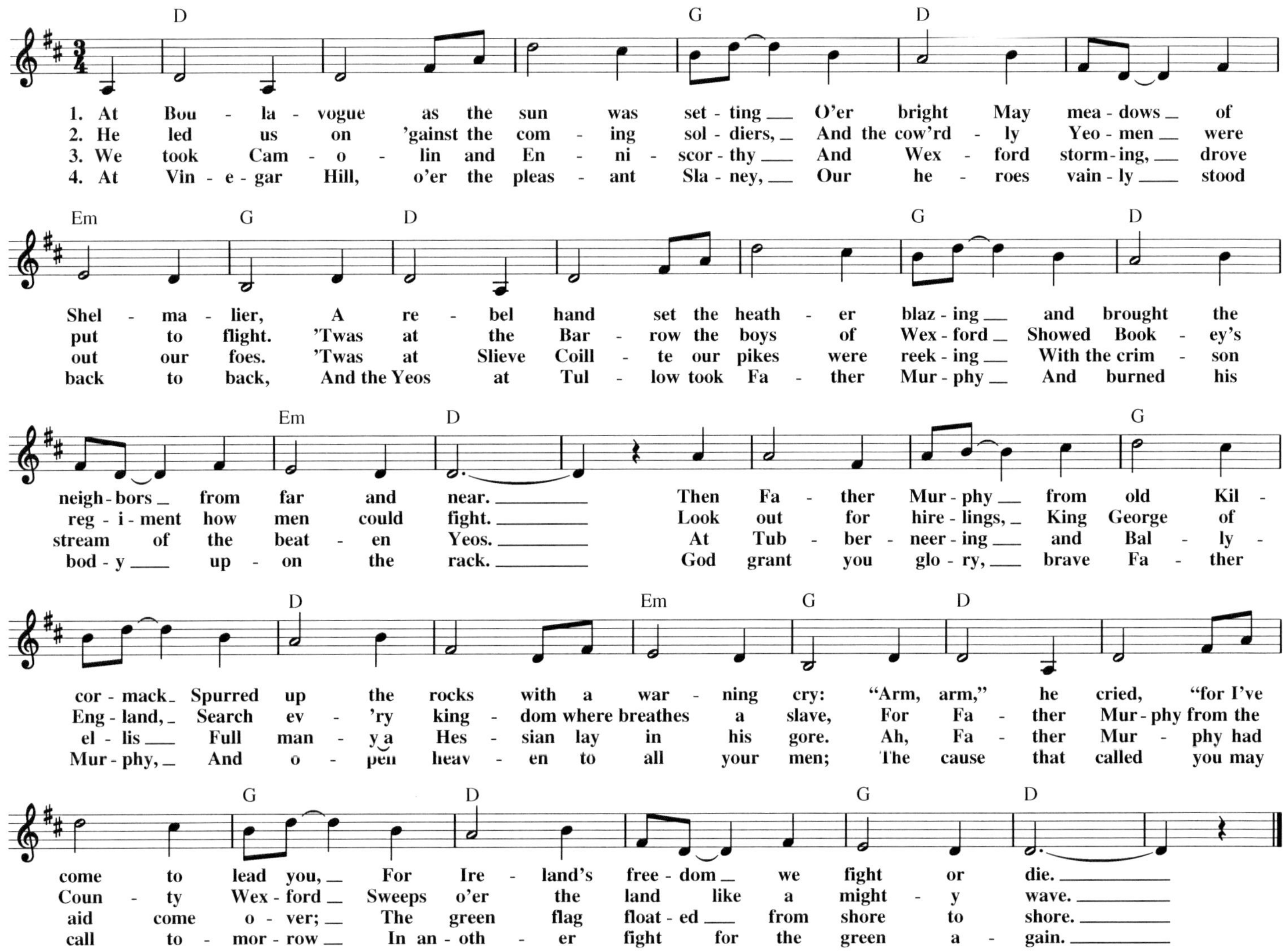

1. At Bou-la-vogue as the sun was set-ting __ O'er bright May mea-dows __ of
2. He led us on 'gainst the com-ing sol-diers, __ And the cow'rd-ly Yeo-men __ were
3. We took Cam-o-lin and En-ni-scor-thy __ And Wex-ford storm-ing, __ drove
4. At Vin-e-gar Hill, o'er the pleas-ant Sla-ney, __ Our he-roes vain-ly __ stood

Shel-ma-lier, A re-bel hand set the heath-er blaz-ing __ and brought the
put to flight. 'Twas at the Bar-row the boys of Wex-ford __ Showed Book-ey's
out our foes. 'Twas at Slieve Coill-te our pikes were reek-ing __ With the crim-son
back to back, And the Yeos at Tul-low took Fa-ther Mur-phy __ And burned his

neigh-bors __ from far and near. _____ Then Fa-ther Mur-phy __ from old Kil-
reg-i-ment how men could fight. _____ Look out for hire-lings, __ King George of
stream of the beat-en Yeos. _____ At Tub-ber-neer-ing __ and Bal-ly-
bod-y __ up-on the rack. _____ God grant you glo-ry, __ brave Fa-ther

cor-mack __ Spurred up the rocks with a war-ning cry: "Arm, arm," he cried, "for I've
Eng-land, __ Search ev-'ry king-dom where breathes a slave, For Fa-ther Mur-phy from the
el-lis __ Full man-y a Hes-sian lay in his gore. Ah, Fa-ther Mur-phy had
Mur-phy, __ And o-pen heav-en to all your men; The cause that called you may

come to lead you, __ For Ire-land's free-dom we fight or die. _____
Coun-ty Wex-ford __ Sweeps o'er the land like a might-y wave. _____
aid come o-ver; __ The green flag float-ed __ from shore to shore. _____
call to-mor-row __ In an-oth-er fight for the green a - gain. _____

THE BRAVE IRISH LAD

Irish folksong

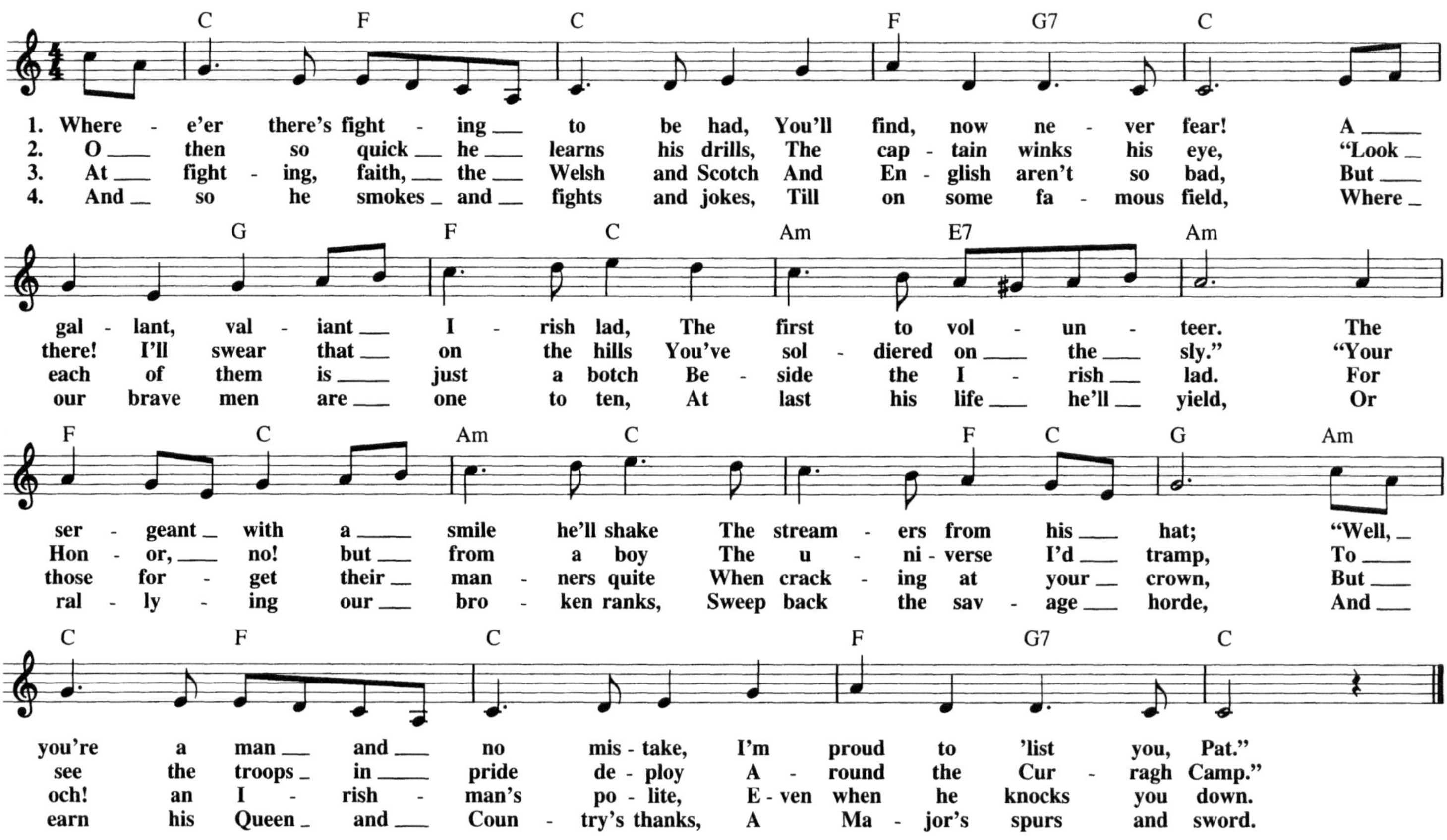

1. Where - e'er there's fight - ing ___ to be had, You'll find, now ne - ver fear! A ___
2. O ___ then so quick ___ he ___ learns his drills, The cap - tain winks his eye, "Look ___
3. At ___ fight - ing, faith, ___ the ___ Welsh and Scotch And En - glish aren't so bad, But ___
4. And ___ so he smokes ___ and ___ fights and jokes, Till on some fa - mous field, Where ___

gal - lant, val - iant ___ I - rish lad, The first to vol - un - teer. The
there! I'll swear that ___ on the hills You've sol - diered on ___ the ___ sly." "Your
each of them is ___ just a botch Be - side the I - rish ___ lad. For
our brave men are ___ one to ten, At last his life ___ he'll ___ yield, Or

ser - geant ___ with a ___ smile he'll shake The stream - ers from his ___ hat; "Well,
Hon - or, ___ no! but ___ from a boy The u - ni - verse I'd ___ tramp, To
those for - get their ___ man - ners quite When crack - ing at your ___ crown, But
ral - ly - ing our ___ bro - ken ranks, Sweep back the sav - age ___ horde, And

you're a man ___ and ___ no mis - take, I'm proud to 'list you, Pat."
see the troops ___ in ___ pride de - ploy A - round the Cur - ragh Camp."
och! an I - rish - man's po - lite, E - ven when he knocks you down.
earn his Queen ___ and ___ Coun - try's thanks, A Ma - jor's spurs and sword.

BRENNAN ON THE MOOR

Irish folksong

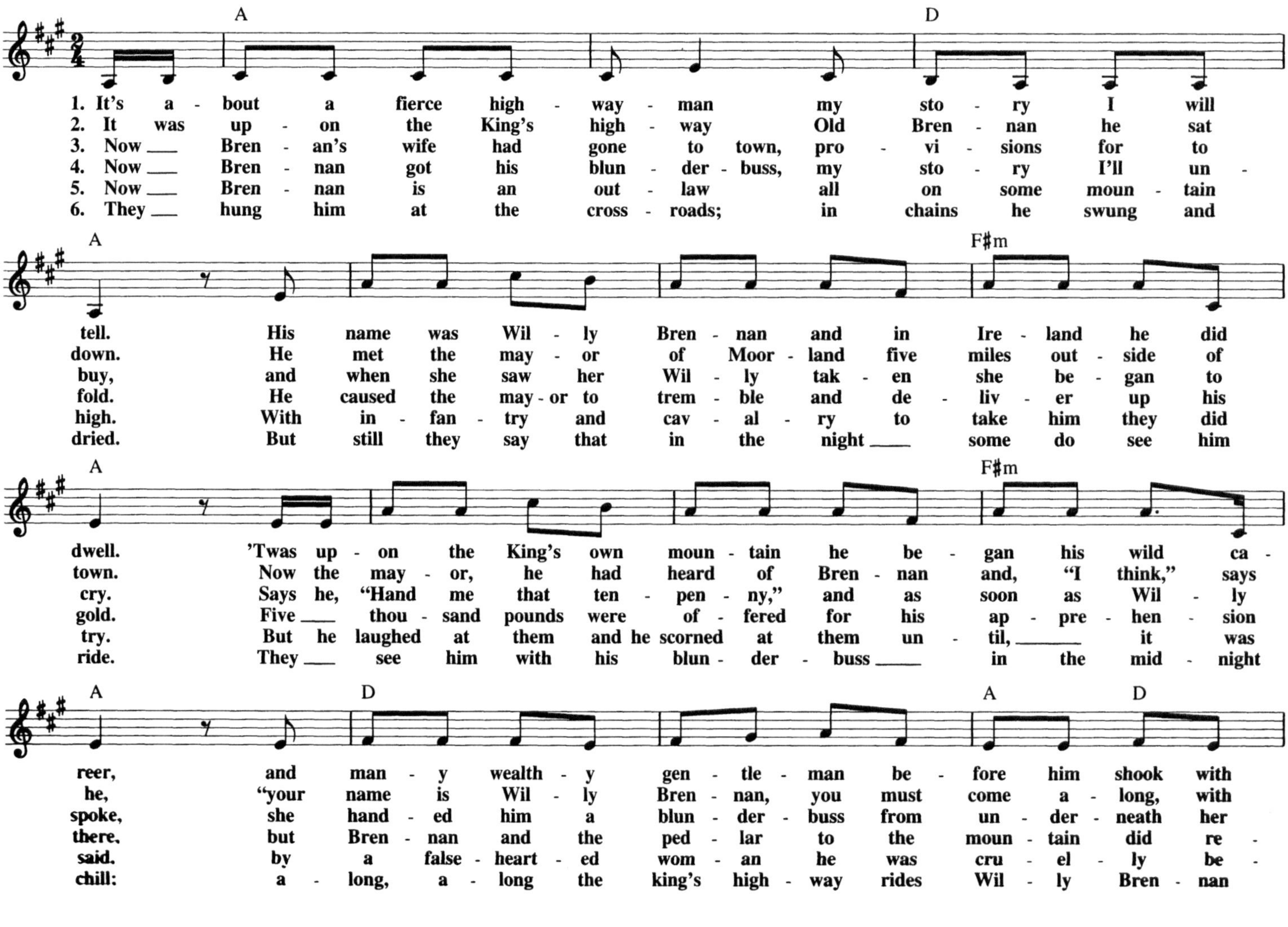

1. It's a - bout a fierce high - way - man my sto - ry I will
2. It was up - on the King's high - way Old Bren - nan he sat
3. Now ___ Bren - an's wife had gone to town, pro - vi - sions for to
4. Now ___ Bren - nan got his blun - der - buss, my sto - ry I'll un -
5. Now ___ Bren - nan is an out - law all on some moun - tain
6. They ___ hung him at the cross - roads; in chains he swung and

tell. His name was Wil - ly Bren - nan and in Ire - land he did
down. He met the may - or of Moor - land five miles out - side of
buy, and when she saw her Wil - ly tak - en she be - gan to
fold. He caused the may - or to trem - ble and de - liv - er up his
high. With in - fan - try and cav - al - ry to take him they did
dried. But still they say that in the night ___ some do see him

dwell. 'Twas up - on the King's own moun - tain he be - gan his wild ca -
town. Now the may - or, he had heard of Bren - nan and, "I think," says
cry. Says he, "Hand me that ten - pen - ny," and as soon as Wil - ly
gold. Five ___ thou - sand pounds were of - fered for his ap - pre - hen - sion
try. But he laughed at them and he scorned at them un - til, ___ it was
ride. They ___ see him with his blun - der - buss ___ in the mid - night

reer, and man - y wealth - y gen - tle - man be - fore him shook with
he, "your name is Wil - ly Bren - nan, you must come a - long, with
spoke, she hand - ed him a blun - der - buss from un - der - neath her
there, but Bren - nan and the ped - lar to the moun - tain did re -
said. by a false - heart - ed wom - an he was cru - el - ly be -
chill: a - long, a - long the king's high - way rides Wil - ly Bren - nan

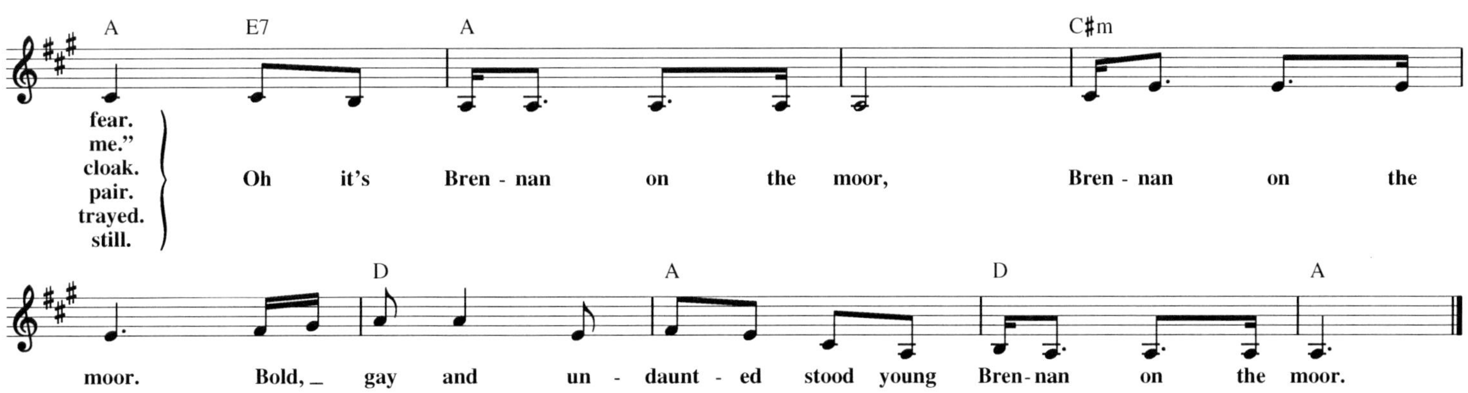

fear.
me." cloak.
pair.
trayed.
still.

Oh it's Bren - nan on the moor, Bren - nan on the moor. Bold, _ gay and un - daunt - ed stood young Bren - nan on the moor.

BOLD ROBERT EMMET

Irish folksong

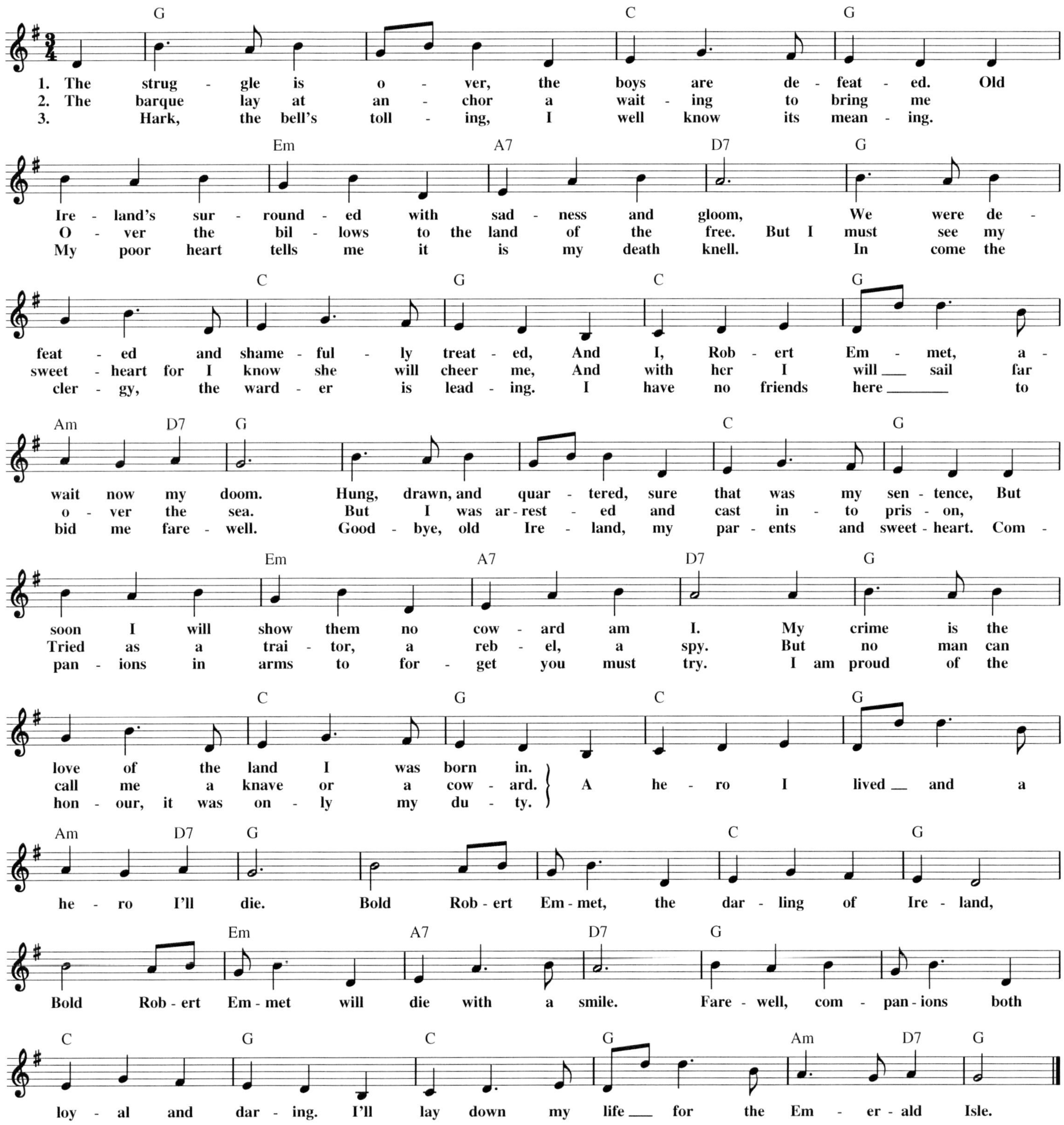

1. The strug - gle is o - ver, the boys are de - feat - ed. Old Ire - land's sur - round - ed with sad - ness and gloom, We were de - feat - ed and shame - ful - ly treat - ed, And I, Rob - ert Em - met, a - wait now my doom. Hung, drawn, and quar - tered, sure that was my sen - tence, But soon I will show them no cow - ard am I. My crime is the love of the land I was born in. A he - ro I lived _ and a he - ro I'll die. Bold Rob - ert Em - met, the dar - ling of Ire - land, Bold Rob - ert Em - met will die with a smile. Fare - well, com - pan - ions both loy - al and dar - ing. I'll lay down my life _ for the Em - er - ald Isle.

2. The barque lay at an - chor a wait - ing to bring me O - ver the bil - lows to the land of the free. But I must see my sweet - heart for I know she will cheer me, And with her I will _ sail far o - ver the sea. But I was ar - rest - ed and cast in - to pris - on, Tried as a trai - tor, a reb - el, a spy. But no man can call me a knave or a cow - ard.

3. Hark, the bell's toll - ing, I well know its mean - ing. My poor heart tells me it is my death knell. In come the cler - gy, the ward - er is lead - ing. I have no friends here _ to bid me fare - well. Good - bye, old Ire - land, my par - ents and sweet - heart. Com - pan - ions in arms to for - get you must try. I am proud of the hon - our, it was on - ly my du - ty.

BROKEN-HEARTED I'LL WANDER

Irish folksong

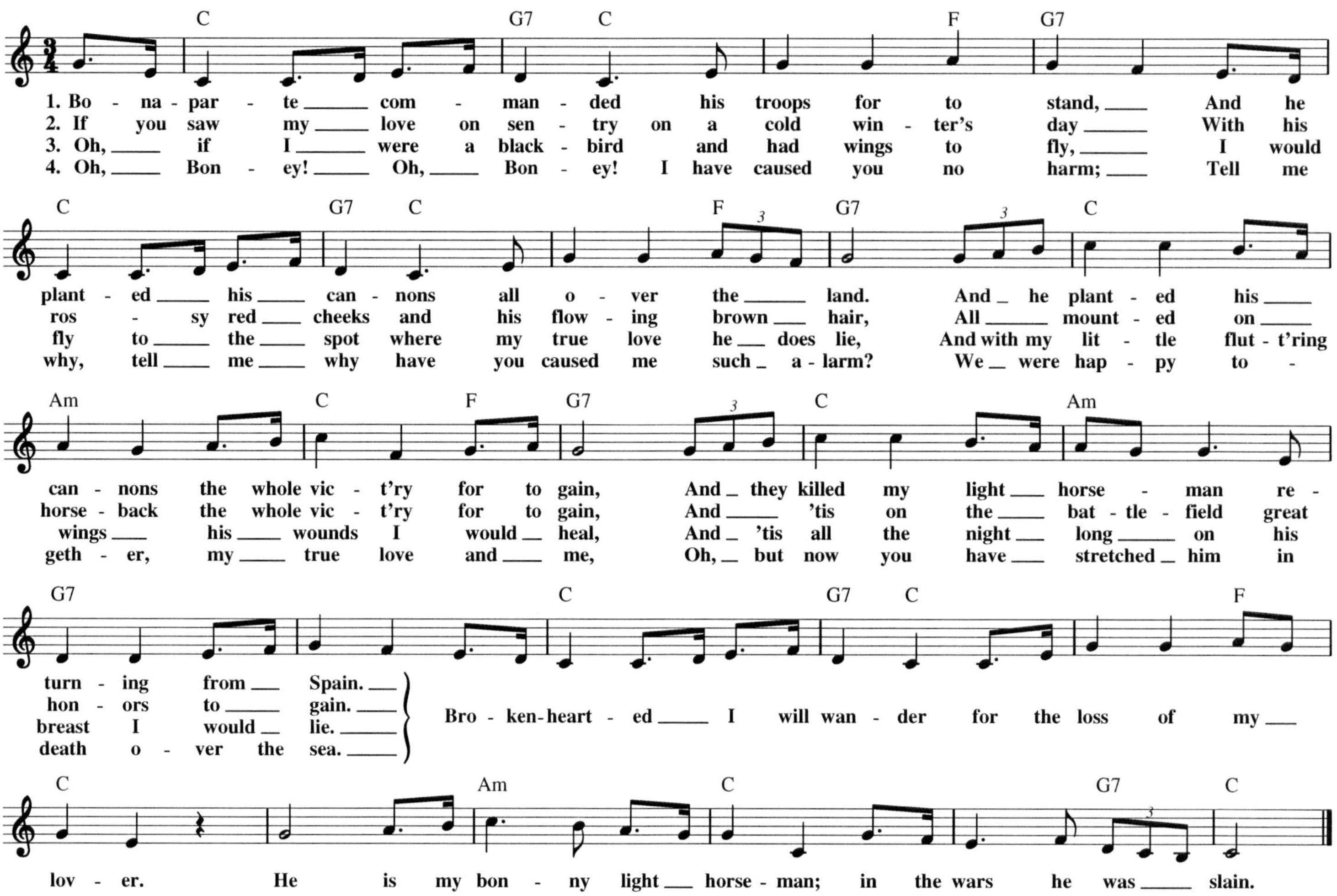

THE BUTCHER BOY

Irish folksong

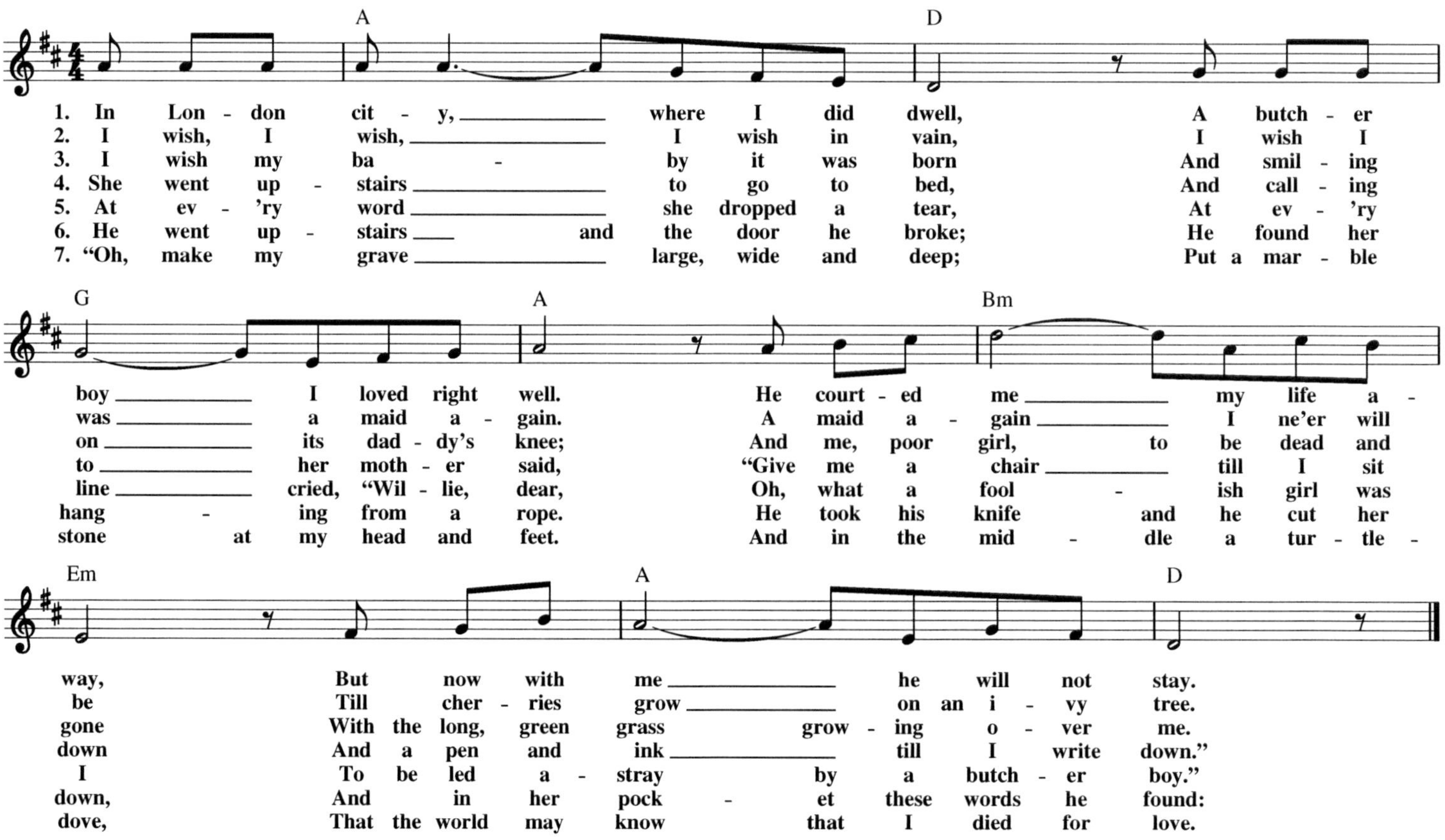

BUNGLE RYE

Irish folksong

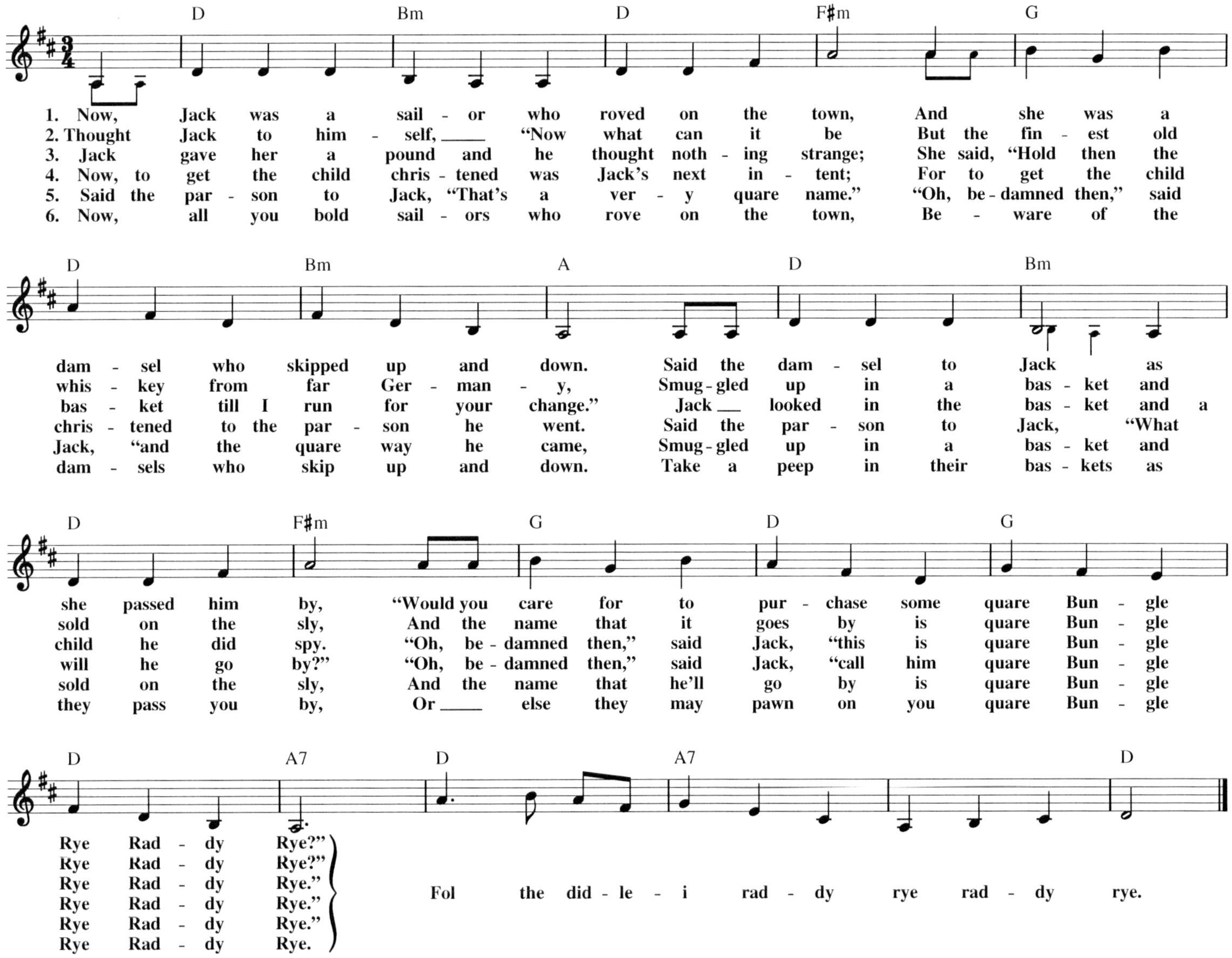

1. Now, Jack was a sail - or who roved on the town, And she was a
2. Thought Jack to him - self, ____ "Now what can it be But the fin - est old
3. Jack gave her a pound and he thought noth - ing strange; She said, "Hold then the
4. Now, to get the child chris - tened was Jack's next in - tent; For to get the child
5. Said the par - son to Jack, "That's a ver - y quare name." "Oh, be - damned then," said
6. Now, all you bold sail - ors who rove on the town, Be - ware of the

dam - sel who skipped up and down. Said the dam - sel to Jack as
whis - key from far Ger - man - y, Smug - gled up in a bas - ket and
bas - ket till I run for your change." Jack looked in the bas - ket and a
chris - tened to the par - son he went. Said the par - son to Jack, "What
Jack, "and the quare way he came, Smug - gled up in a bas - ket and
dam - sels who skip up and down. Take a peep in their bas - kets as

she passed him by, "Would you care for to pur - chase some quare Bun - gle
sold on the sly, And the name that it goes by is quare Bun - gle
child he did spy. "Oh, be - damned then," said Jack, "this is quare Bun - gle
will he go by?" "Oh, be - damned then," said Jack, "call him quare Bun - gle
sold on the sly, And the name that he'll go by is quare Bun - gle
they pass you by, Or ____ else they may pawn on you quare Bun - gle

Rye Rad - dy Rye?"
Rye Rad - dy Rye?"
Rye Rad - dy Rye."
Rye Rad - dy Rye."   Fol the did - le - i rad - dy rye rad - dy rye.
Rye Rad - dy Rye."
Rye Rad - dy Rye.

BYKER HILL

Irish folksong

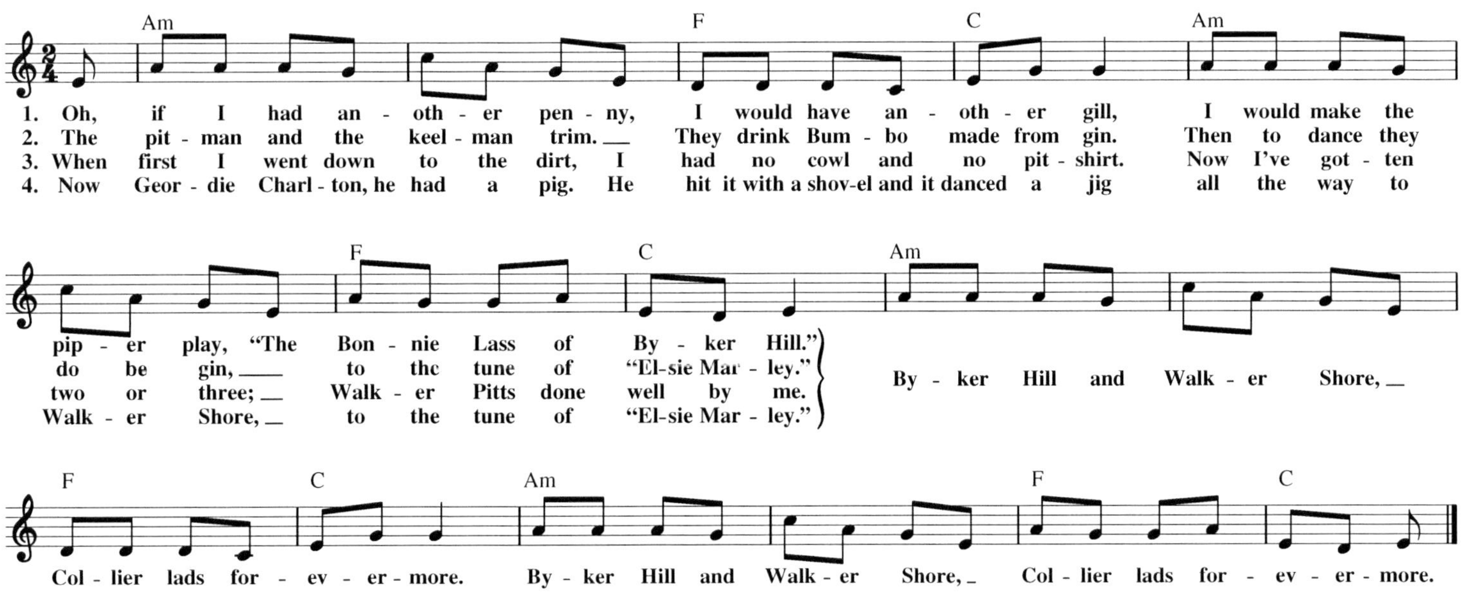

1. Oh, if I had an - oth - er pen - ny, I would have an - oth - er gill, I would make the
2. The pit - man and the keel - man trim. ____ They drink Bum - bo made from gin. Then to dance they
3. When first I went down to the dirt, I had no cowl and no pit - shirt. Now I've got - ten
4. Now Geor - die Charl - ton, he had a pig. He hit it with a shov - el and it danced a jig all the way to

pip - er play, "The Bon - nie Lass of By - ker Hill."
do be - gin, ____ to the tune of "El - sie Mar - ley."
two or three; ____ Walk - er Pitts done well by me.   By - ker Hill and Walk - er Shore, ____
Walk - er Shore, ____ to the tune of "El - sie Mar - ley."

Col - lier lads for - ev - er - more. By - ker Hill and Walk - er Shore, ____ Col - lier lads for - ev - er - more.

A BUNCH OF THYME

Irish folksong

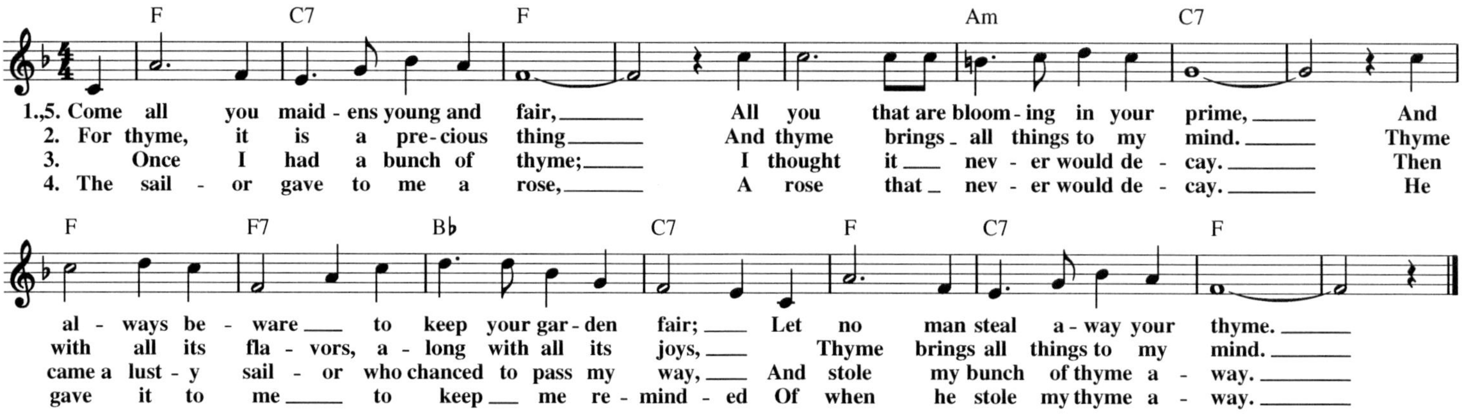

1.,5. Come all you maid-ens young and fair, All you that are bloom-ing in your prime, And
2. For thyme, it is a pre-cious thing____ And thyme brings all things to my mind.____ Thyme
3. Once I had a bunch of thyme;____ I thought it ___ nev-er would de-cay.____ Then
4. The sail-or gave to me a rose, A rose that ___ nev-er would de-cay.____ He

al-ways be-ware ___ to keep your gar-den fair; ___ Let no man steal a-way your thyme.____
with all its fla-vors, a-long with all its joys, ___ Thyme brings all things to my mind.____
came a lust-y sail-or who chanced to pass my way, ___ And stole my bunch of thyme a-way.____
gave it to me____ to keep ___ me re-mind-ed Of when he stole my thyme a-way.____

THE CALTON WEAVER

Scottish folksong

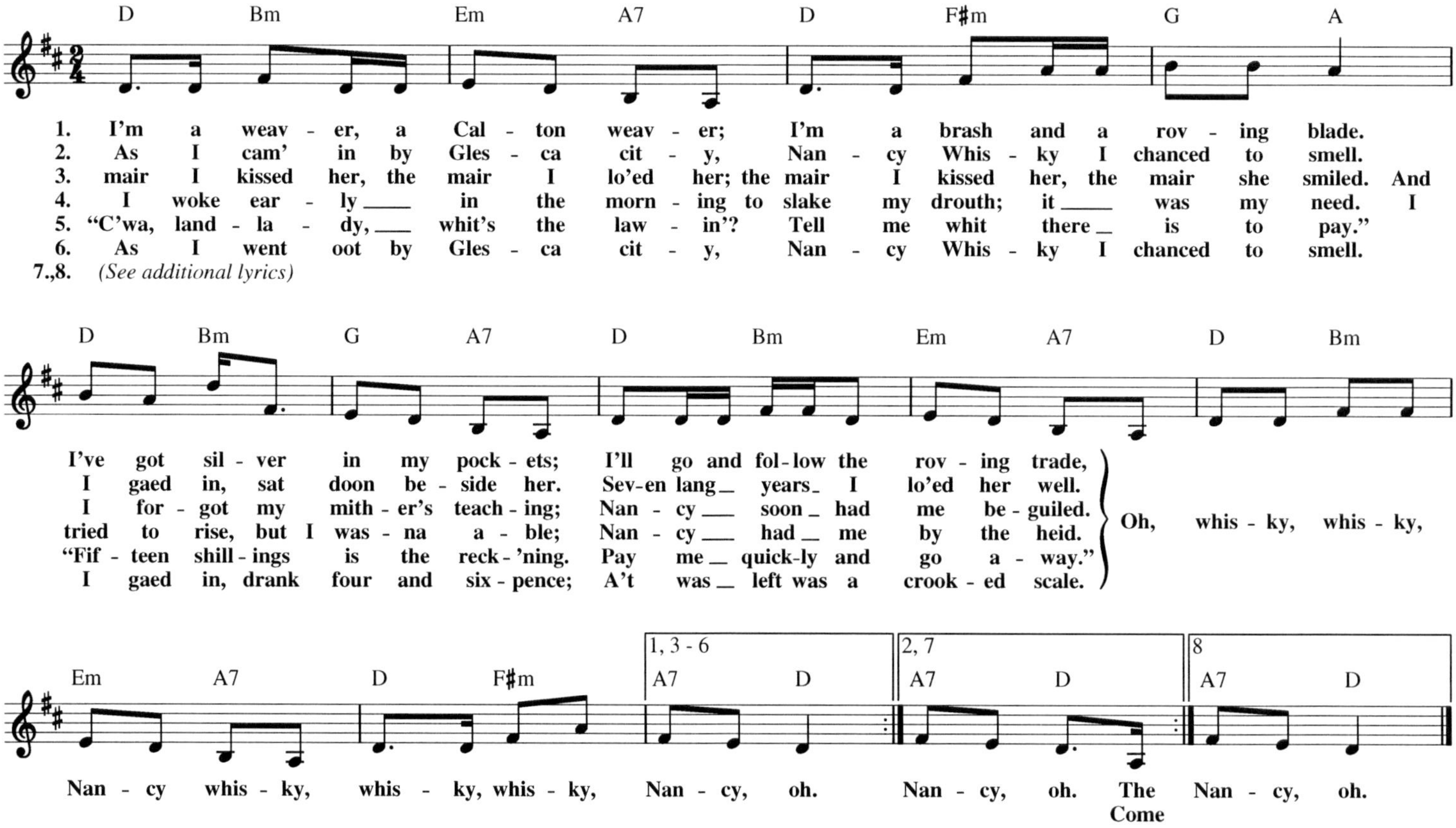

1. I'm a weav-er, a Cal-ton weav-er; I'm a brash and a rov-ing blade.
2. As I cam' in by Gles-ca cit-y, Nan-cy Whis-ky I chanced to smell.
3. mair I kissed her, the mair I lo'ed her; the mair I kissed her, the mair she smiled. And
4. I woke ear-ly____ in the morn-ing to slake my drouth; it____ was my need. I
5. "C'wa, land-la-dy, ___ whit's the law-in'? Tell me whit there ___ is to pay."
6. As I went oot by Gles-ca cit-y, Nan-cy Whis-ky I chanced to smell.
7.,8. *(See additional lyrics)*

I've got sil-ver in my pock-ets; I'll go and fol-low the rov-ing trade,
I gaed in, sat doon be-side her. Sev-en lang years____ I lo'ed her well.
I for-got my mith-er's teach-ing; Nan-cy ___ soon had me be-guiled.
tried to rise, but I was-na a-ble; Nan-cy ___ had ___ me by the heid.
"Fif-teen shill-ings is the reck-'ning. Pay me ___ quick-ly and go a-way."
I gaed in, drank four and six-pence; A't was ___ left was a crook-ed scale.
} Oh, whis-ky, whis-ky,

Nan-cy whis-ky, whis-ky, whis-ky, Nan-cy, oh.
[1, 3 - 6] Nan-cy, oh. The
[2, 7] Nan-cy, oh. Come
[8]

Additional Lyrics

7. I'll gang back to the Calton weaving;
I'll surely mak' the shuttles fly.
I'll mak' mair at the Calton weaving.
Than ever I did in a roving way.

8. Come, all ye weavers, Calton weavers,
A' ye weavers where'er ye be.
Beware of whisky, Nancy whisky;
She'll ruin you as she ruined me.

CAPTAIN MacDONALD'S FAVOURITE JIG

Irish folksong

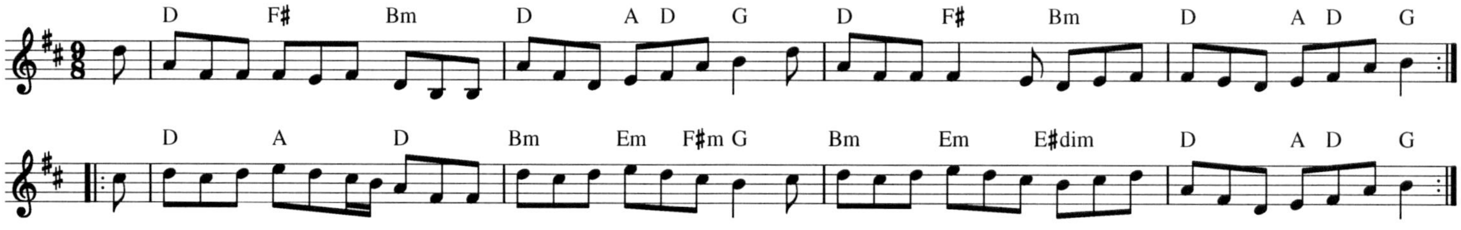

THE CAMPBELLS ARE COMING

Scottish folksong

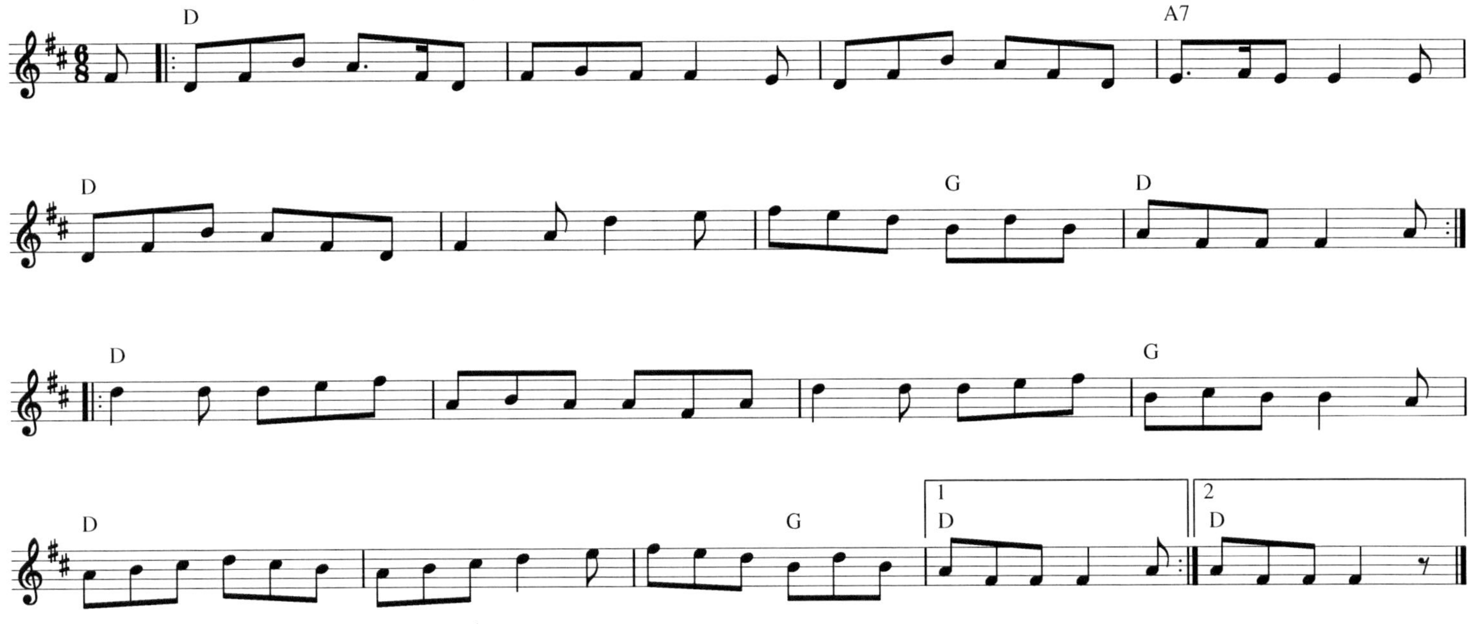

CARRICKFERGUS

Irish folksong

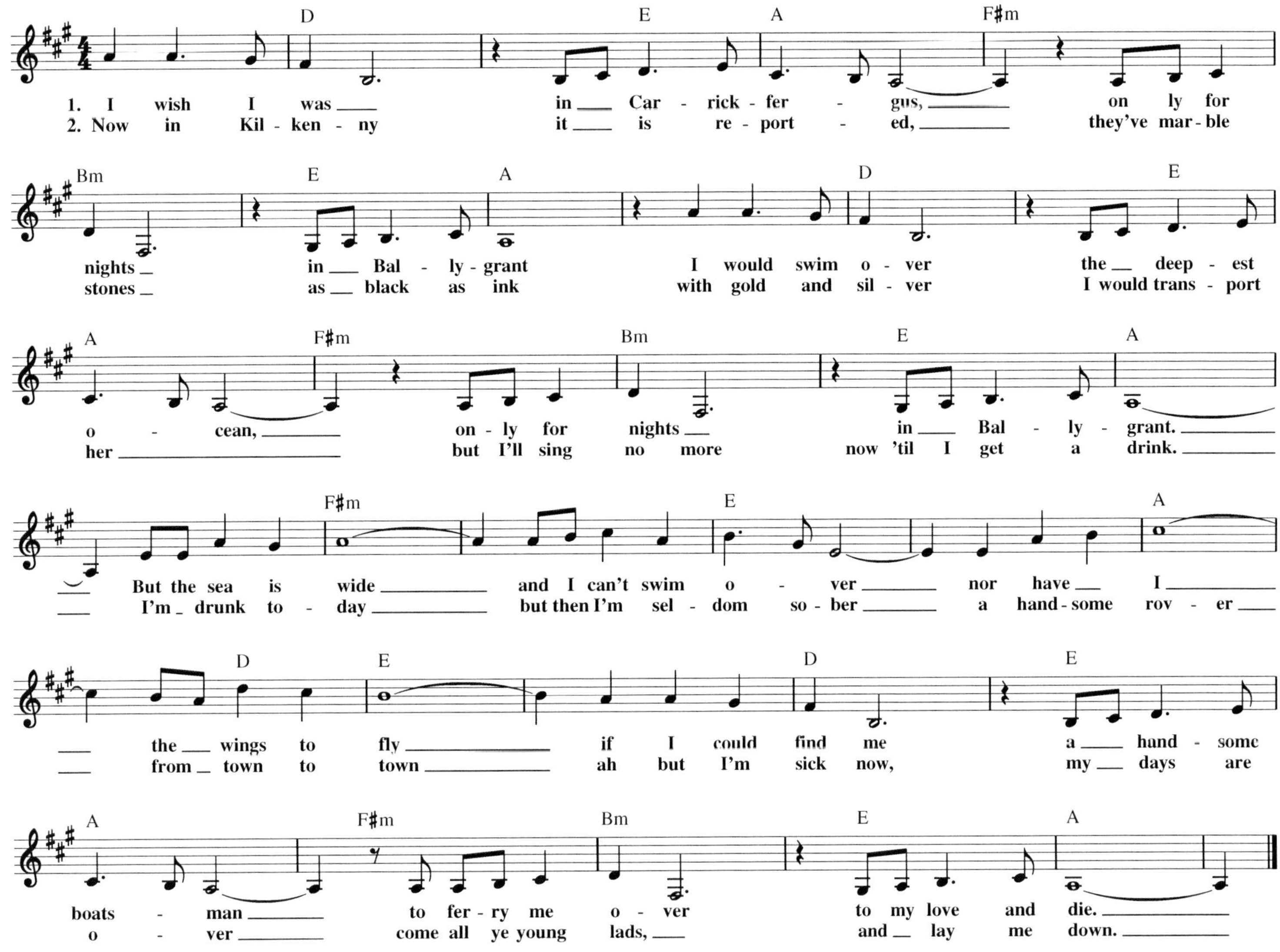

1. I wish I was ____ in ____ Car - rick - fer - gus, ____ on - ly for
2. Now in Kil - ken - ny it ____ is re - port - ed, ____ they've mar - ble

nights ____ in ____ Bal - ly - grant I would swim o - ver the ____ deep - est
stones ____ as ____ black as ink with gold and sil - ver I would trans - port

o - cean, ____ on - ly for nights ____ in ____ Bal - ly - grant. ____
her ____ but I'll sing no more now 'til I get a drink. ____

But the sea is wide ____ and I can't swim o - ver ____ nor have ____ I
I'm drunk to - day ____ but then I'm sel - dom so - ber ____ a hand - some rov - er

the ____ wings to fly ____ if I could find me a ____ hand - some
from ____ town to town ____ ah but I'm sick now, my ____ days are

boats - man to fer - ry me o - ver to my love and die. ____
o - ver ____ come all ye young lads, ____ and ____ lay me down. ____

CARISTIONA

Folksong from the Hebrides

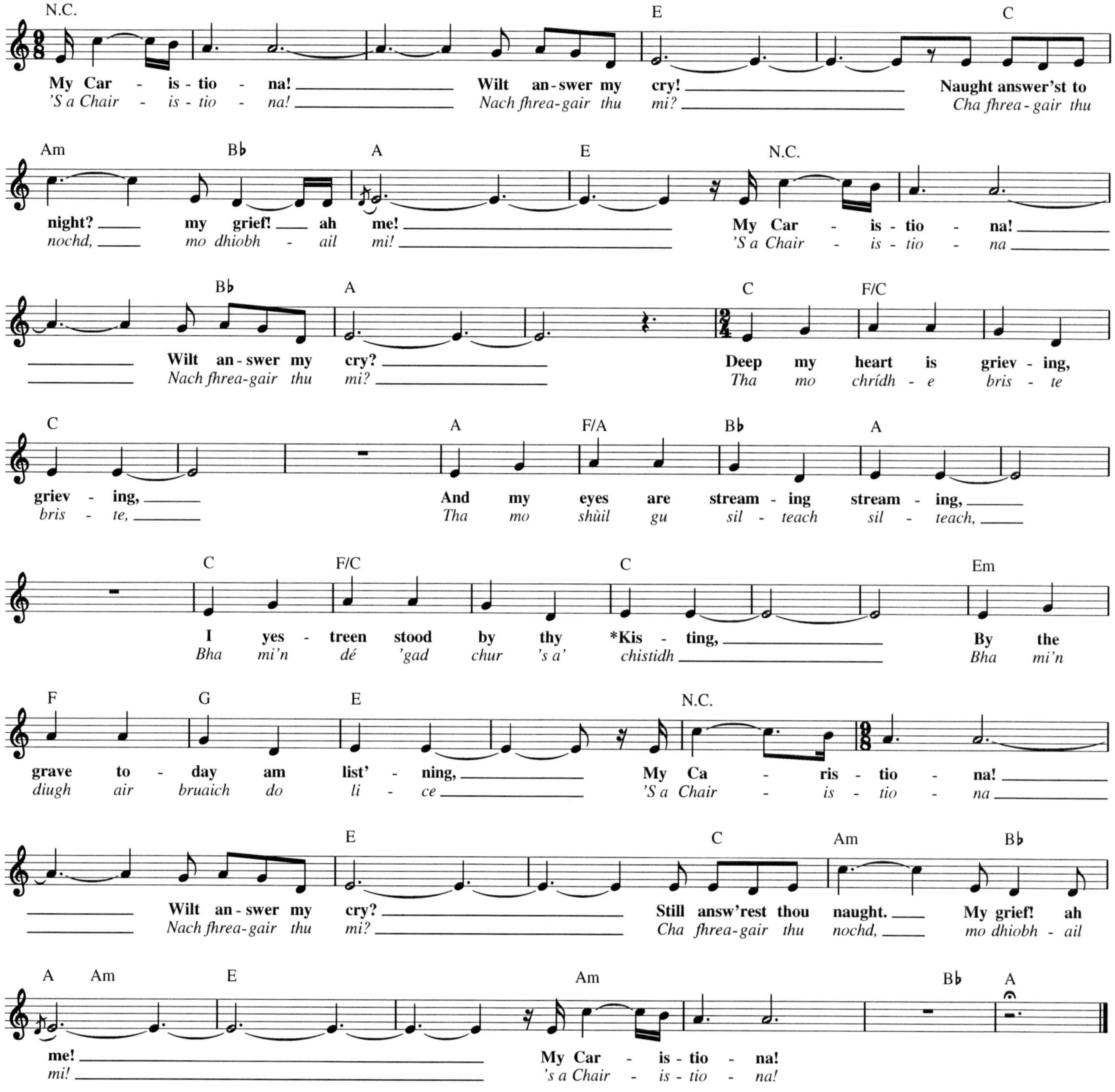

*Kisting = laying in the Kist or coffin

THE CHANTY THAT BEGUILED THE WITCH

Folksong from the Hebrides

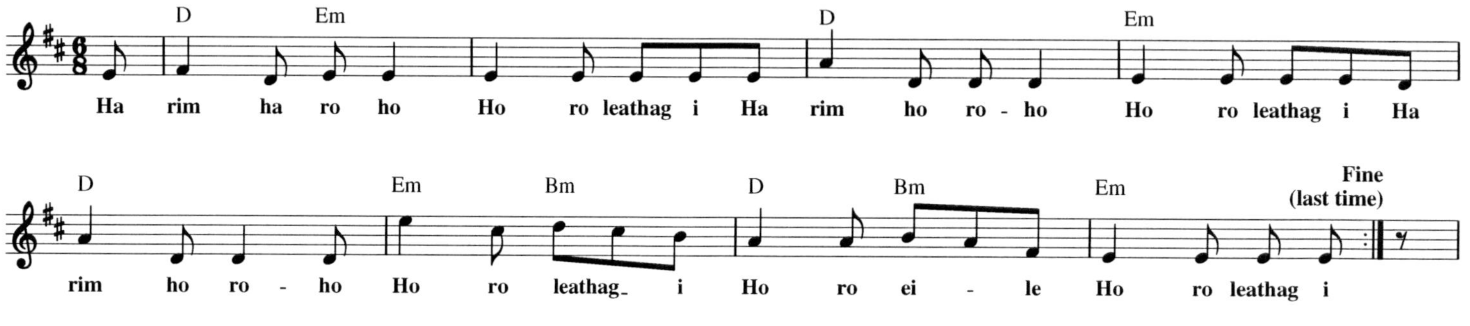

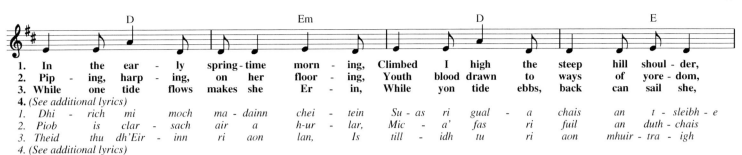

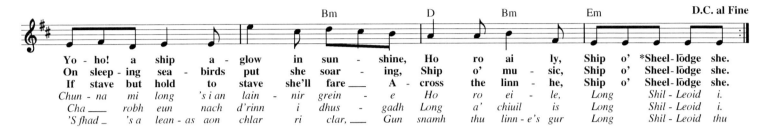

Additional Lyrics

4. Never a wind but fears the strain
Of filling thy sail when under way.
I lose e'en the Coolins behind yon sail
Yo ho ro aily, Ship o' Sheellōdge she.

4. Gur deuchainn air gach gaoth a sheideas
Do shiuil bhana lionadh glelan thug thu 'n
Ciulinn mor speur diom
Ho ro eile long ShilLeoid thu

*Sil Leod = the seed or Clan of Macleod

CHARLIE IS MY DARLING

Scottish folksong

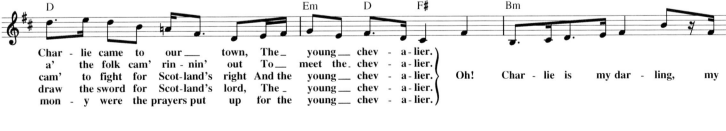

THE CHRIST-CHILD'S LULLABY
(Taladh Chriosta)

Folksong from the Hebrides

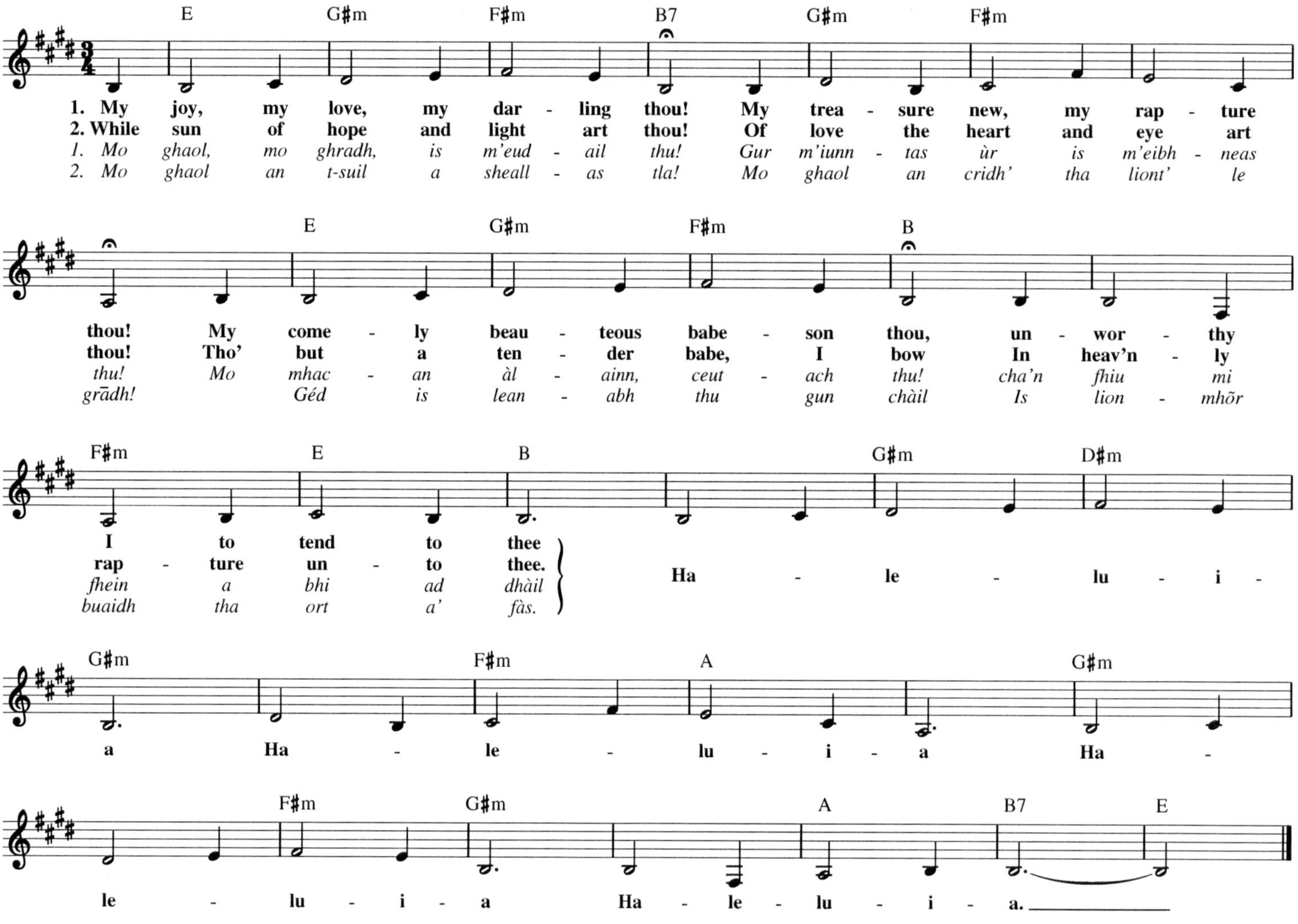

1. My joy, my love, my dar - ling thou! My trea - sure new, my rap - ture
2. While sun of hope and light art thou! Of love the heart and eye art
1. Mo ghaol, mo ghradh, is m'eud - ail thu! Gur m'iunn - tas ùr is m'eibh - neas
2. Mo ghaol an t-suil a sheall - as tla! Mo ghaol an cridh' tha liont' le

thou! My come - ly beau - teous babe - son thou, un - wor - thy
thou! Tho' but a ten - der babe, I bow In heav'n - ly
thu! Mo mhac - an àl - ainn, ceut - ach thu! cha'n fhiu mi
grādh! Géd is lean - abh thu gun chàil Is lion - mhōr

I to tend to thee }
rap - ture un - to thee. } Ha - le - lu - i -
fhein a bhi ad dhàil }
buaidh tha ort a' fàs. }

a Ha - le - lu - i - a Ha -

le - lu - i - a Ha - le - lu - i - a. _____

A CHURNING LILT

Folksong from the Hebrides

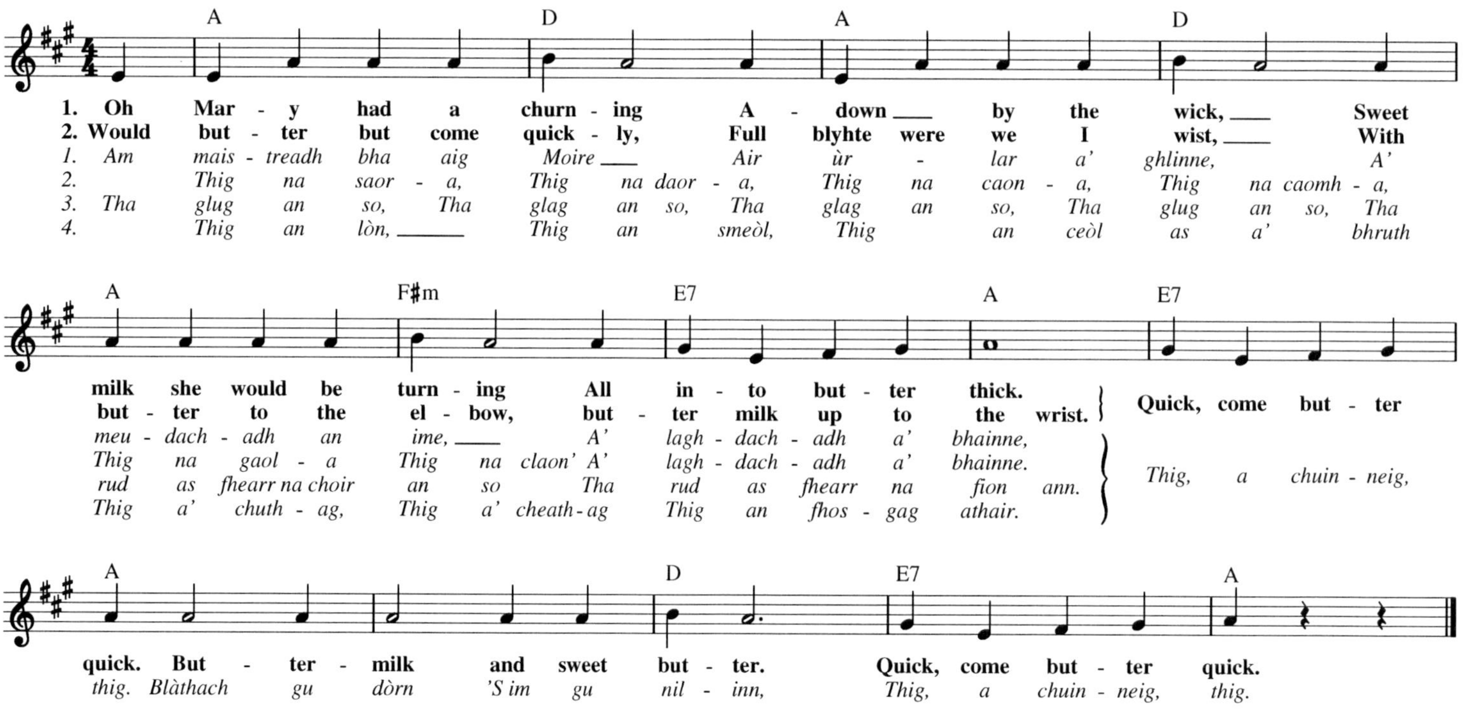

1. Oh Mar - y had a churn - ing A - down _____ by the wick, _____ Sweet
2. Would but - ter but come quick - ly, Full blythe were we I wist, _____ With
1. Am mais - treadh bha aig Moire Air ùr - lar a' ghlinne, A'
2. Thig na saor - a, Thig na daor - a, Thig na caon - a, Thig na caomh - a,
3. Tha glug an so, Tha glag an so, Tha glag an so, Tha glug an so, Tha
4. Thig an lòn, _____ Thig an smeòl, Thig an ceòl as a' bhruth

milk she would be turn - ing All in - to but - ter thick. }
but - ter to the el - bow, but - ter milk up to the wrist. } Quick, come but - ter
meu - dach - adh an ime, _____ A' lagh - dach - adh a' bhainne, }
Thig na gaol - a Thig na claon' A' lagh - dach - adh a' bhainne. } Thig, a chuin - neig,
rud as fhearr na choir an so Tha rud as fhearr na fion ann. }
Thig a' chuth - ag, Thig a' cheath - ag Thig an fhos - gag athair. }

quick. But - ter - milk and sweet but - ter. Quick, come but - ter quick.
thig. Blàthach gu dòrn 'S im gu nil - inn, Thig, a chuin - neig, thig.

CHRISTMAS DUANAG
(Duan Nollaig)

Folksong from the Hebrides

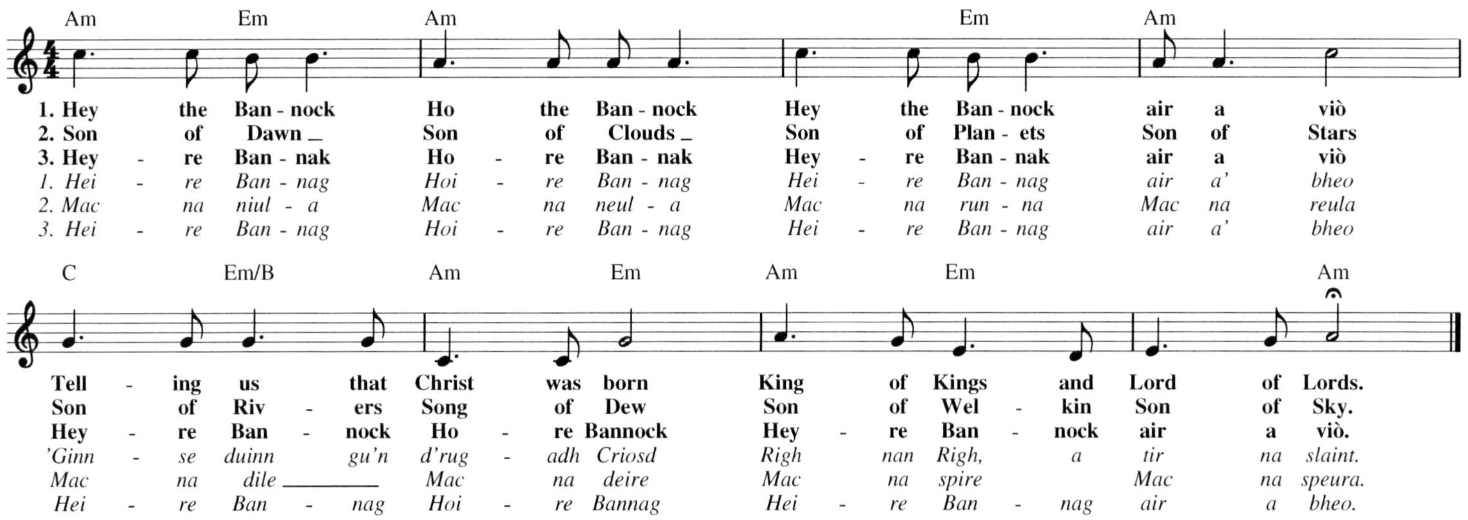

CLANRANALD'S PARTING SONG

Folksong from the Hebrides

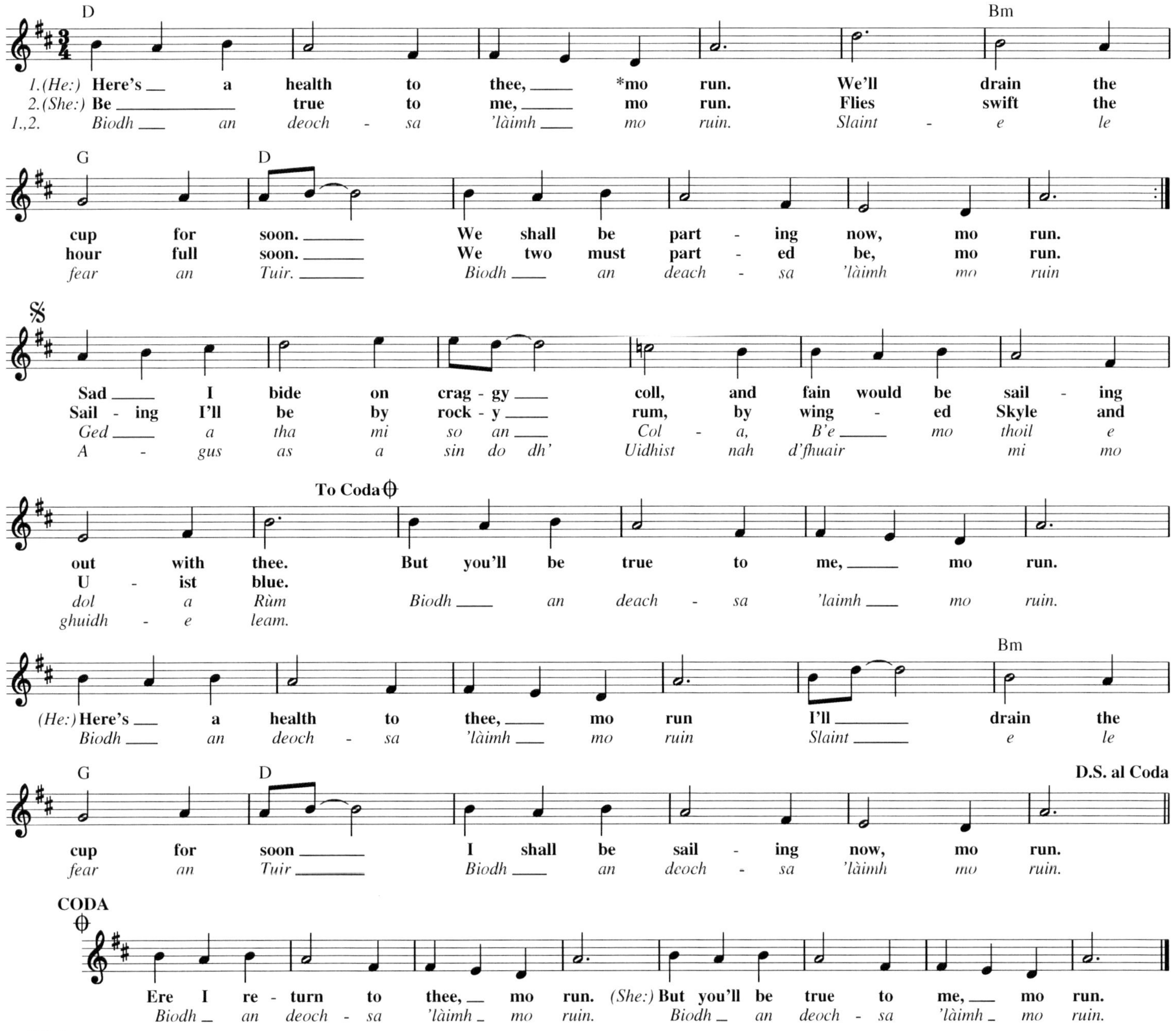

*My love

CLARE'S DRAGOONS

Irish folksong

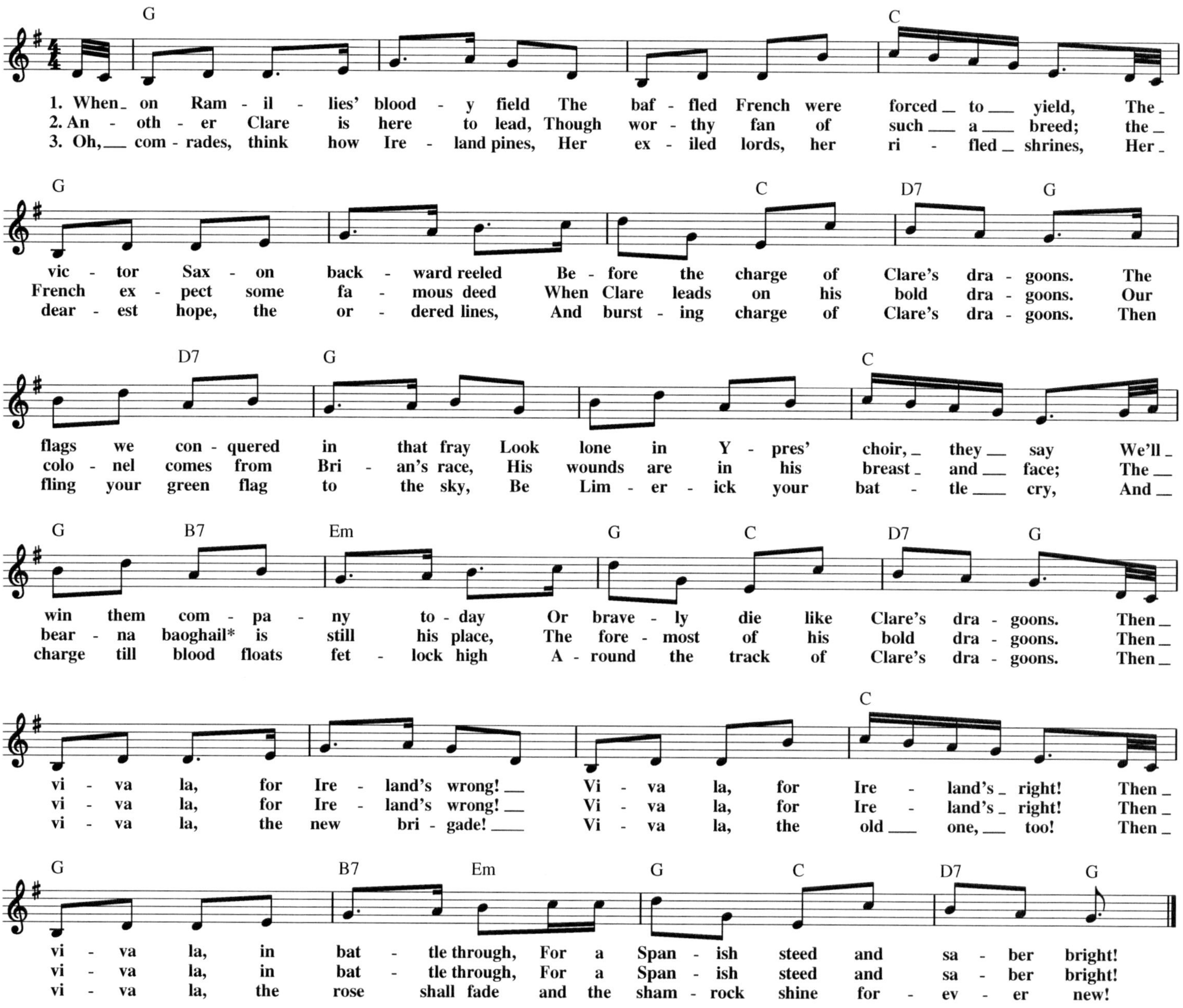

1. When on Ram - il - lies' blood - y field The baf - fled French were forced to yield, The
2. An - oth - er Clare is here to lead, Though wor - thy fan of such a breed; the
3. Oh, com - rades, think how Ire - land pines, Her ex - iled lords, her ri - fled shrines, Her

vic - tor Sax - on back - ward reeled Be - fore the charge of Clare's dra - goons. The
French ex - pect some fa - mous deed When Clare leads on his bold dra - goons. Our
dear - est hope, the or - dered lines, And burst - ing charge of Clare's dra - goons. Then

flags we con - quered in that fray Look lone in Y - pres' choir, they say We'll
colo - nel comes from Bri - an's race, His wounds are in his breast and face; The
fling your green flag to the sky, Be Lim - er - ick your bat - tle cry, And

win them com - pa - ny to - day Or brave - ly die like Clare's dra - goons. Then
bear - na baoghail* is still his place, The fore - most of his bold dra - goons. Then
charge till blood floats fet - lock high A - round the track of Clare's dra - goons. Then

vi - va la, for Ire - land's wrong! Vi - va la, for Ire - land's right! Then
vi - va la, for Ire - land's wrong! Vi - va la, for Ire - land's right! Then
vi - va la, the new bri - gade! Vi - va la, the old one, too! Then

vi - va la, in bat - tle through, For a Span - ish steed and sa - ber bright!
vi - va la, in bat - tle through, For a Span - ish steed and sa - ber bright!
vi - va la, the rose shall fade and the sham - rock shine for - ev - er new!

* *bearna baoghail: wherever there is danger*

THE COCKIES OF BUNGAREE

Irish folksong

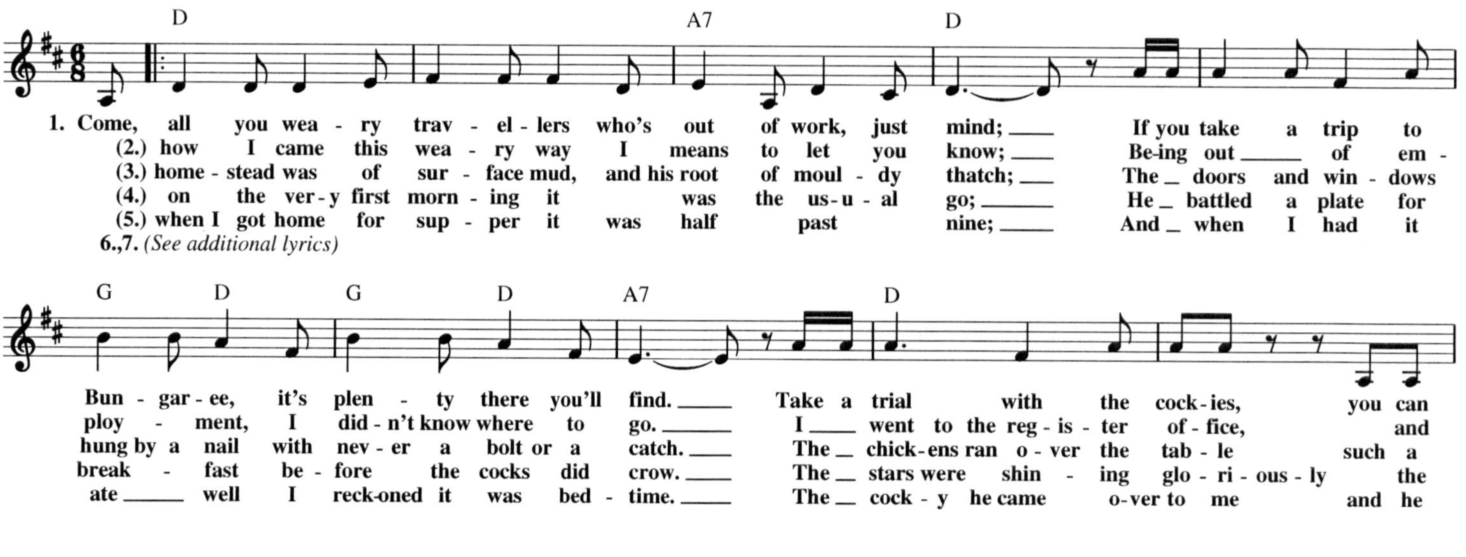

1. Come, all you wea - ry trav - el - ers who's out of work, just mind; If you take a trip to
(2.) how I came this wea - ry way I means to let you know; Be - ing out of em -
(3.) home - stead was of sur - face mud, and his root of moul - dy thatch; The doors and win - dows
(4.) on the ver - y first morn - ing it was the us - u - al go; He bat - tled a plate for
(5.) when I got home for sup - per it was half past nine; And when I had it
6., 7. (See additional lyrics)

Bun - gar - ee, it's plen - ty there you'll find. Take a trial with the cock - ies, you can
ploy - ment, I did - n't know where to go. I went to the reg - is - ter of - fice, and
hung by a nail with nev - er a bolt or a catch. The chick - ens ran o - ver the tab - le such a
break - fast be - fore the cocks did crow. The stars were shin - ing glo - ri - ous - ly the
ate well I reck - oned it was bed - time. The cock - y he came o - ver to me and he

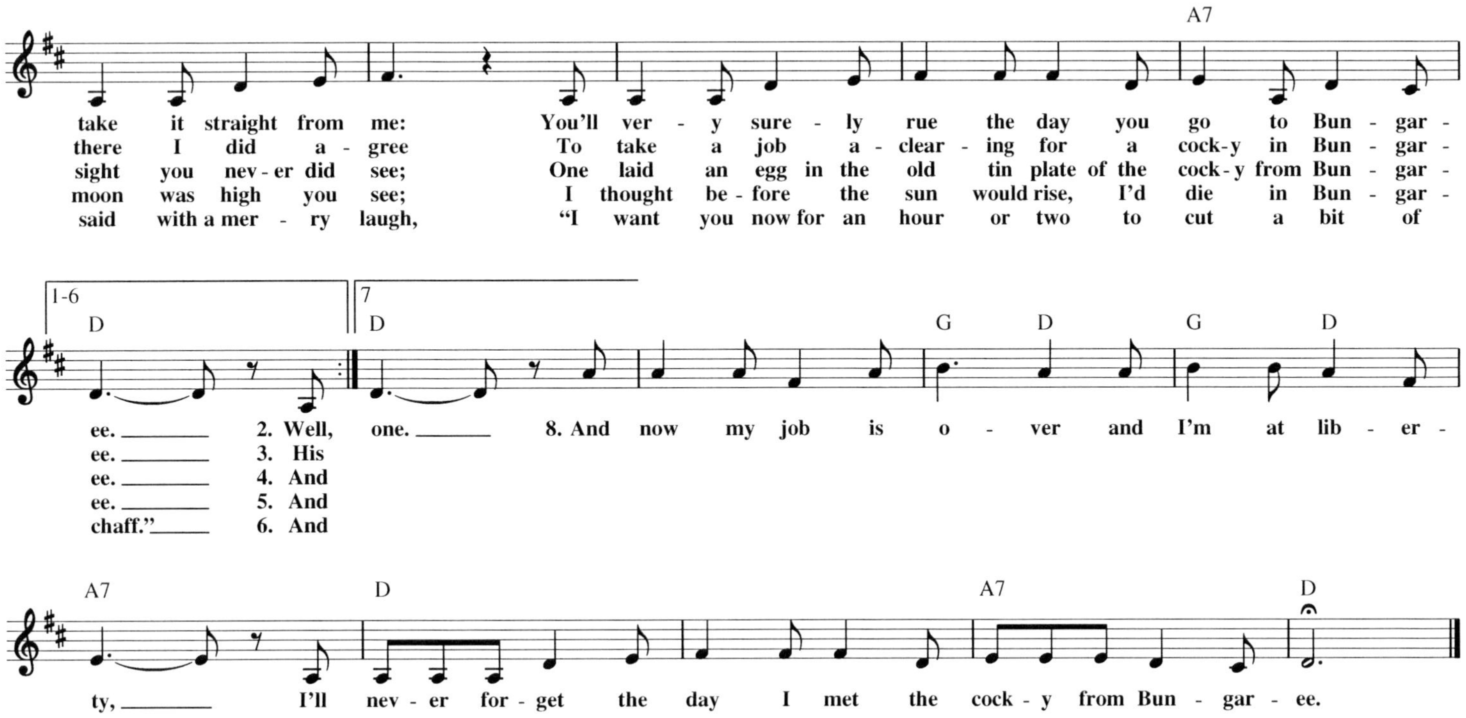

take it straight from me: You'll ver - y sure - ly rue the day you go to Bun - gar -
there I did a - gree To take a job a - clear - ing for a cock - y in Bun - gar -
sight you nev - er did see; One laid an egg in the old tin plate of the cock - y from Bun - gar -
moon was high you see; I thought be - fore the sun would rise, I'd die in Bun - gar -
said with a mer - ry laugh, "I want you now for an hour or two to cut a bit of

ee. _____ 2. Well, one. _____ 8. And now my job is o - ver and I'm at lib - er -
ee. _____ 3. His
ee. _____ 4. And
ee. _____ 5. And
chaff." _____ 6. And

ty, _____ I'll nev - er for - get the day I met the cock - y from Bun - gar - ee.

Additional Lyrics

6. And when I had it finished, I'd to nurse the youngest child;
   Whenever I said a joking word, the missus she would smile.
   The old fellow got jealous, looked like he'd murder me;
   And there he sat and whipped the cat, the cocky from Bungaree.

7. Well, when I had my first week done, I reckoned I'd had enough;
   I walked up to the cocky, and I asked him for my stuff.
   I went down in to Ballarat, and it didn't last me long;
   I went straight in to Sayer's Hotel, and I blew my one pound one.

COME TO THE HILLS

Irish folksong

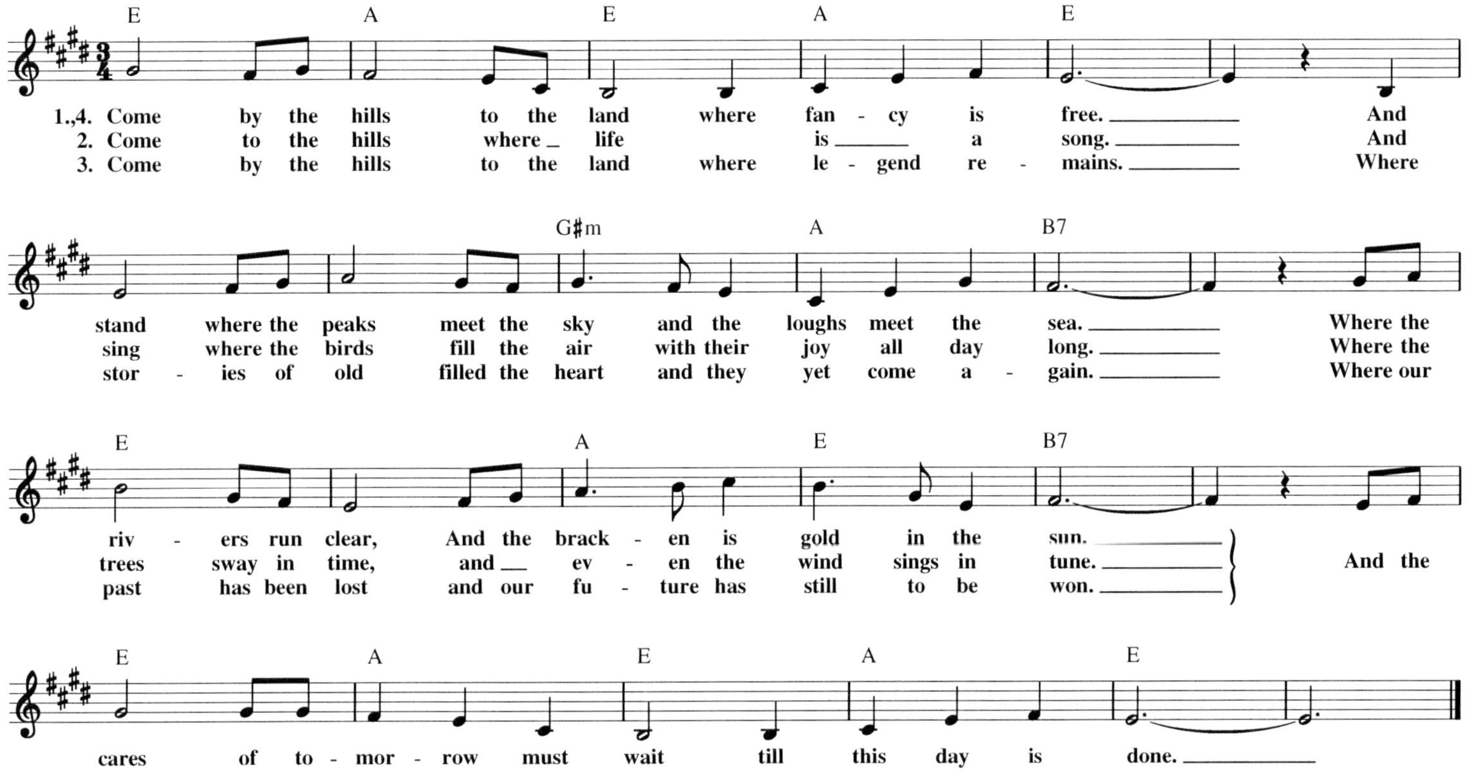

1.,4. Come by the hills to the land where fan - cy is free. _____ And
2. Come to the hills where life is a song. _____ And
3. Come by the hills to the land where le - gend re - mains. _____ Where

stand where the peaks meet the sky and the loughs meet the sea. _____ Where the
sing where the birds fill the air with their joy all day long. _____ Where the
stor - ies of old filled the heart and they yet come a - gain. _____ Where our

riv - ers run clear, And the brack - en is gold in the sun. _____ And the
trees sway in time, and ev - en the wind sings in tune. _____
past has been lost and our fu - ture has still to be won. _____

cares of to - mor - row must wait till this day is done. _____

THE COCKLE GATHERER
('S trusaidh mi na Coilleagan)

Folksong from the Hebrides

COLL NURSE'S LILT
(Shibeag, Shibeag)

Folksong from the Hebrides

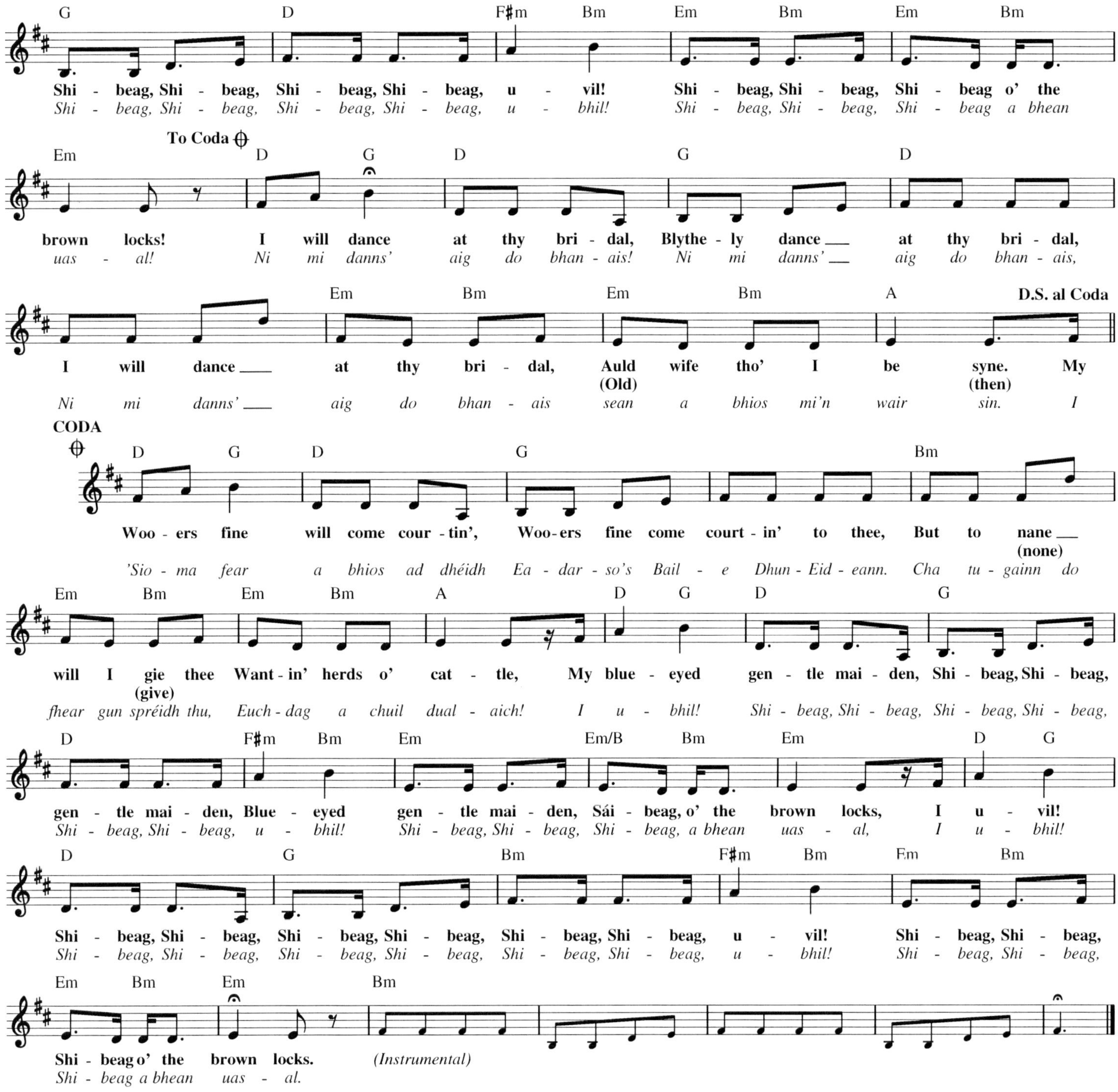

*A child's name, pronounced eepak

COOLEY'S REEL

Irish folksong

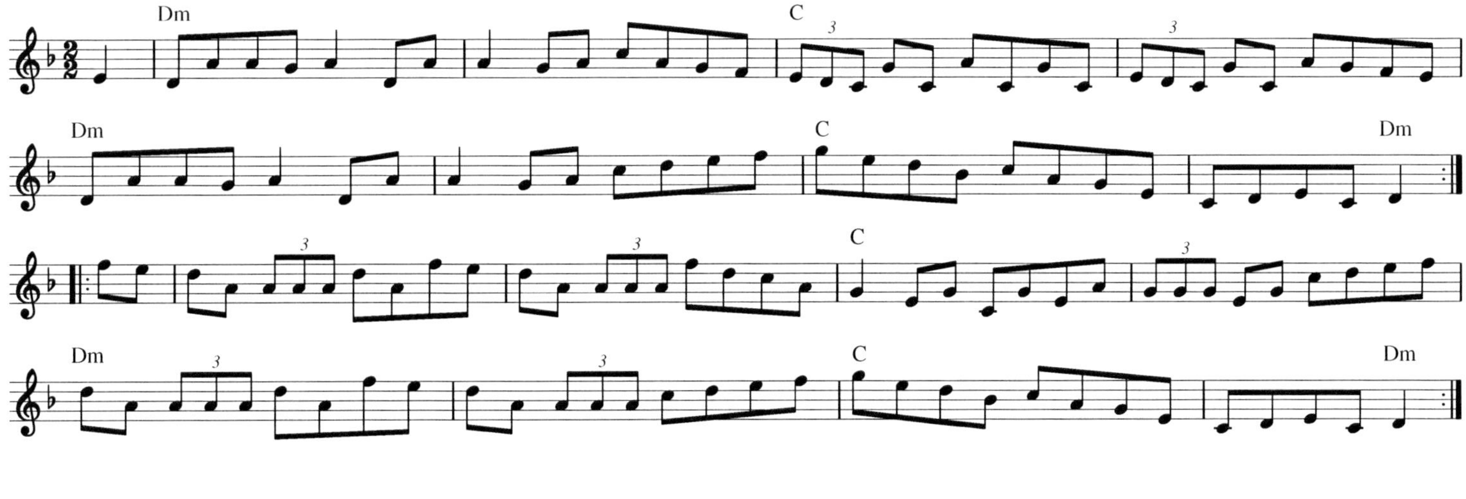

COME SIT DOWN BESIDE ME

Irish folksong

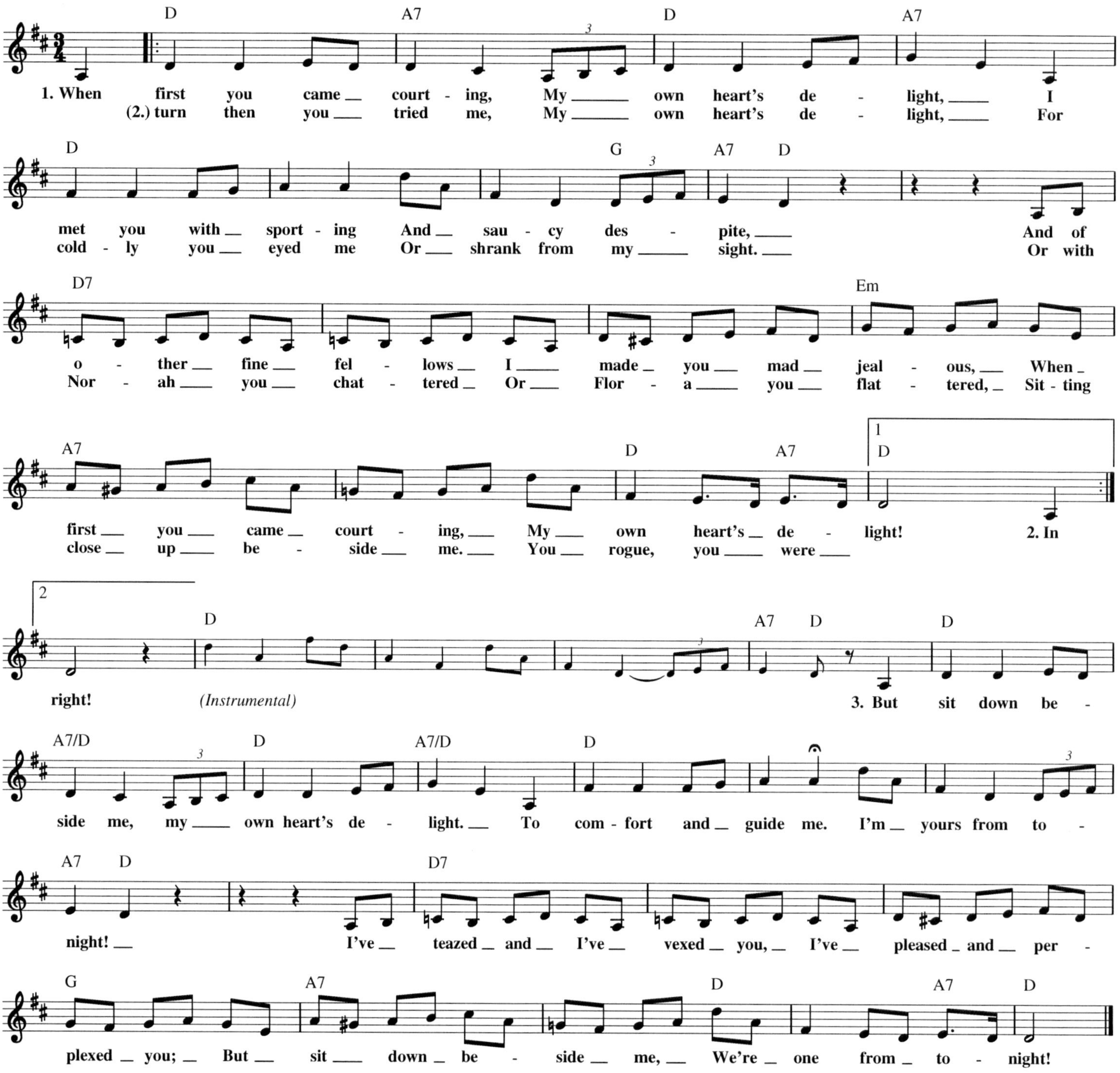

1. When first you came __ court - ing, My __ own heart's de - light, __ I
(2.) turn then you __ tried me, My __ own heart's de - light, __ For

met you with __ sport - ing And __ sau - cy des - pite, __ And of
cold - ly you __ eyed me Or __ shrank from my __ sight. __ Or with

o - ther __ fine __ fel - lows __ I __ made __ you __ mad jeal - ous, __ When __
Nor - ah __ you __ chat - tered __ Or __ Flor - a __ you __ flat - tered, __ Sit - ting

first __ you __ came __ court - ing, __ My __ own heart's __ de - light! __ 2. In
close __ up __ be - side __ me. __ You __ rogue, you __ were __

right! __ *(Instrumental)* __ 3. But sit down be -

side me, my __ own heart's de - light. __ To com - fort and __ guide me. I'm __ yours from to -

night! __ I've __ teazed __ and __ I've __ vexed __ you, __ I've __ pleased __ and __ per -

plexed __ you; __ But __ sit __ down __ be - side __ me, __ We're __ one from __ to - night!

COME BACK TO ERIN

Irish folksong

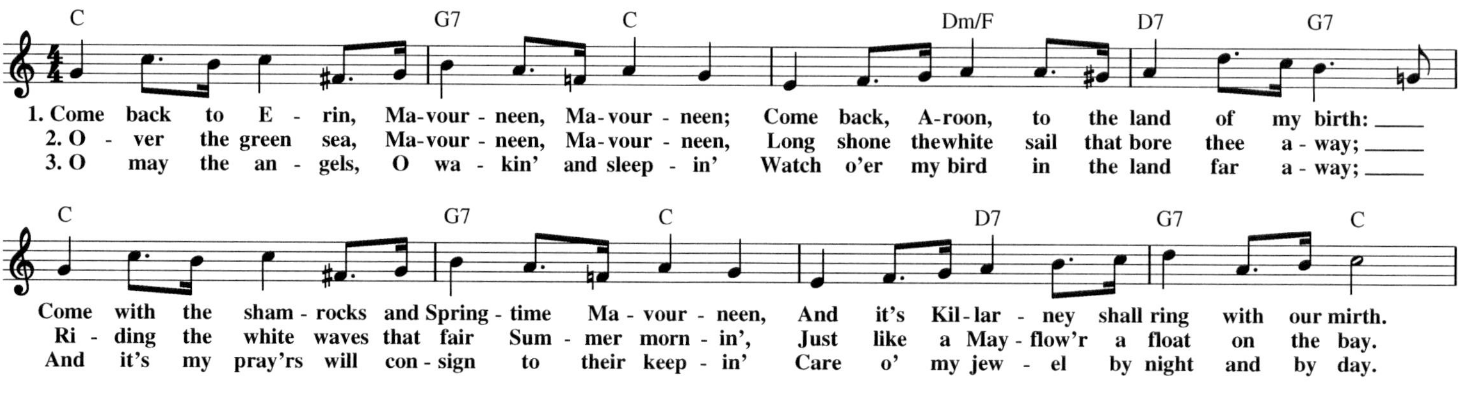

1. Come back to E - rin, Ma-vour - neen, Ma-vour - neen; Come back, A-roon, to the land of my birth: __
2. O - ver the green sea, Ma-vour - neen, Ma-vour - neen, Long shone the white sail that bore thee a - way; __
3. O may the an - gels, O wa - kin' and sleep - in' Watch o'er my bird in the land far a - way; __

Come with the sham - rocks and Spring - time Ma-vour - neen, And it's Kil - lar - ney shall ring with our mirth.
Ri - ding the white waves that fair Sum - mer morn - in', Just like a May - flow'r a float on the bay.
And it's my pray'rs will con - sign to their keep - in' Care o' my jew - el by night and by day.

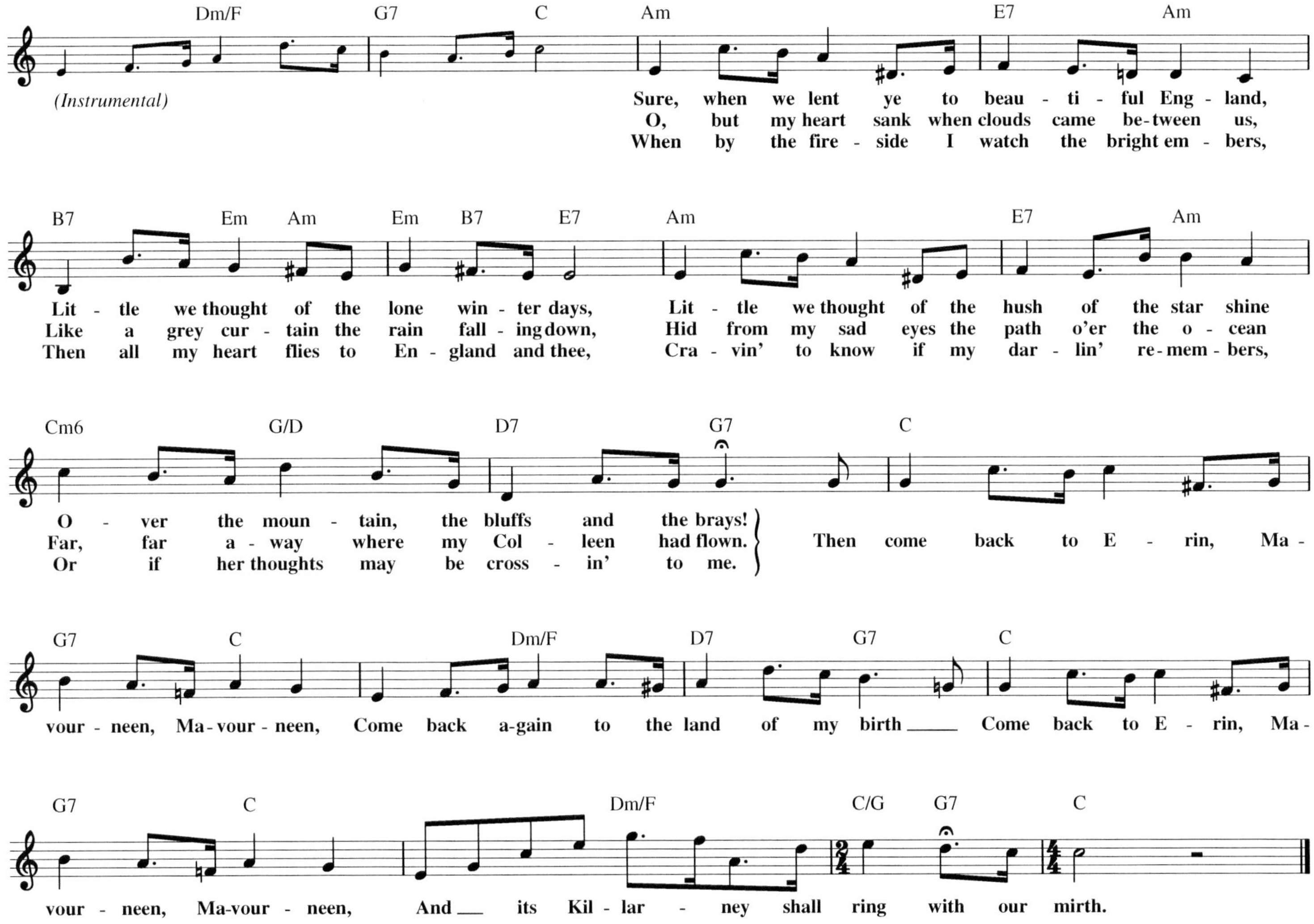
Dm/F G7 C Am E7 Am
(Instrumental)
Sure, when we lent ye to beau - ti - ful Eng - land,
O, but my heart sank when clouds came be - tween us,
When by the fire - side I watch the bright em - bers,
B7 Em Am Em B7 E7 Am E7 Am
Lit - tle we thought of the lone win - ter days, Lit - tle we thought of the hush of the star shine
Like a grey cur - tain the rain fall - ing down, Hid from my sad eyes the path o'er the o - cean
Then all my heart flies to En - gland and thee, Cra - vin' to know if my dar - lin' re - mem - bers,
Cm6 G/D D7 G7 C
O - ver the moun - tain, the bluffs and the brays!
Far, far a - way where my Col - leen had flown.
Or if her thoughts may be cross - in' to me.
Then come back to E - rin, Ma -
G7 C Dm/F D7 G7 C
vour - neen, Ma - vour - neen, Come back a - gain to the land of my birth Come back to E - rin, Ma -
G7 C Dm/F C/G G7 C
vour - neen, Ma - vour - neen, And its Kil - lar - ney shall ring with our mirth.

CONVICT OF CLONMEL

Irish folksong

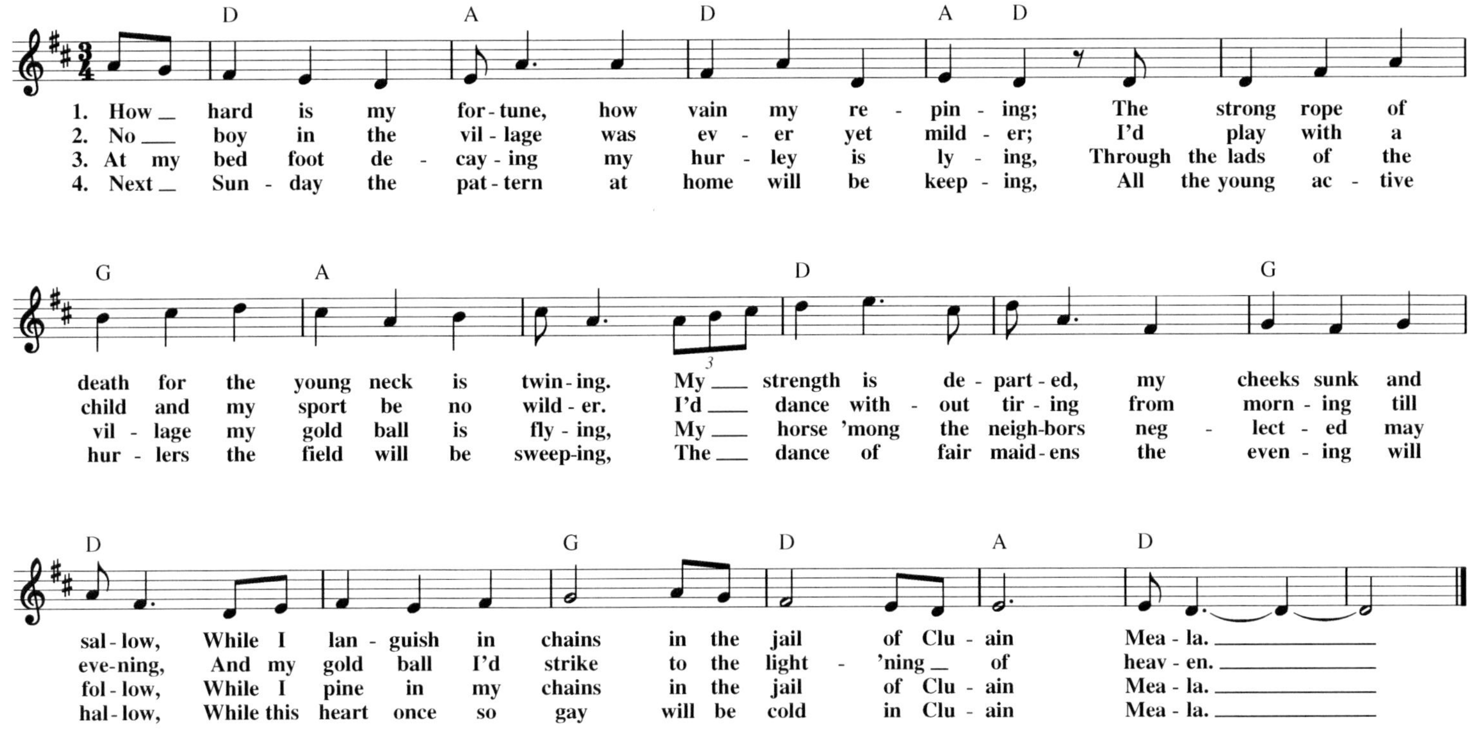
D A D A D
1. How hard is my for - tune, how vain my re - pin - ing; The strong rope of
2. No boy in the vil - lage was ev - er yet mild - er; I'd play with a
3. At my bed foot de - cay - ing my hur - ley is ly - ing, Through the lads of the
4. Next Sun - day the pat - tern at home will be keep - ing, All the young ac - tive
G A D G
death for the young neck is twin - ing. My strength is de - part - ed, my cheeks sunk and
child and my sport be no wild - er. I'd dance with - out tir - ing from morn - ing till
vil - lage my gold ball is fly - ing, My horse 'mong the neigh - bors neg - lect - ed may
hur - lers the field will be sweep - ing, The dance of fair maid - ens the even - ing will
D G D A D
sal - low, While I lan - guish in chains in the jail of Clu - ain Mea - la.
eve - ning, And my gold ball I'd strike to the light - 'ning of heav - en.
fol - low, While I pine in my chains in the jail of Clu - ain Mea - la.
hal - low, While this heart once so gay will be cold in Clu - ain Mea - la.

COLUMBUS WAS AN IRISHMAN
(In Ireland He Was Born)

Irish folksong

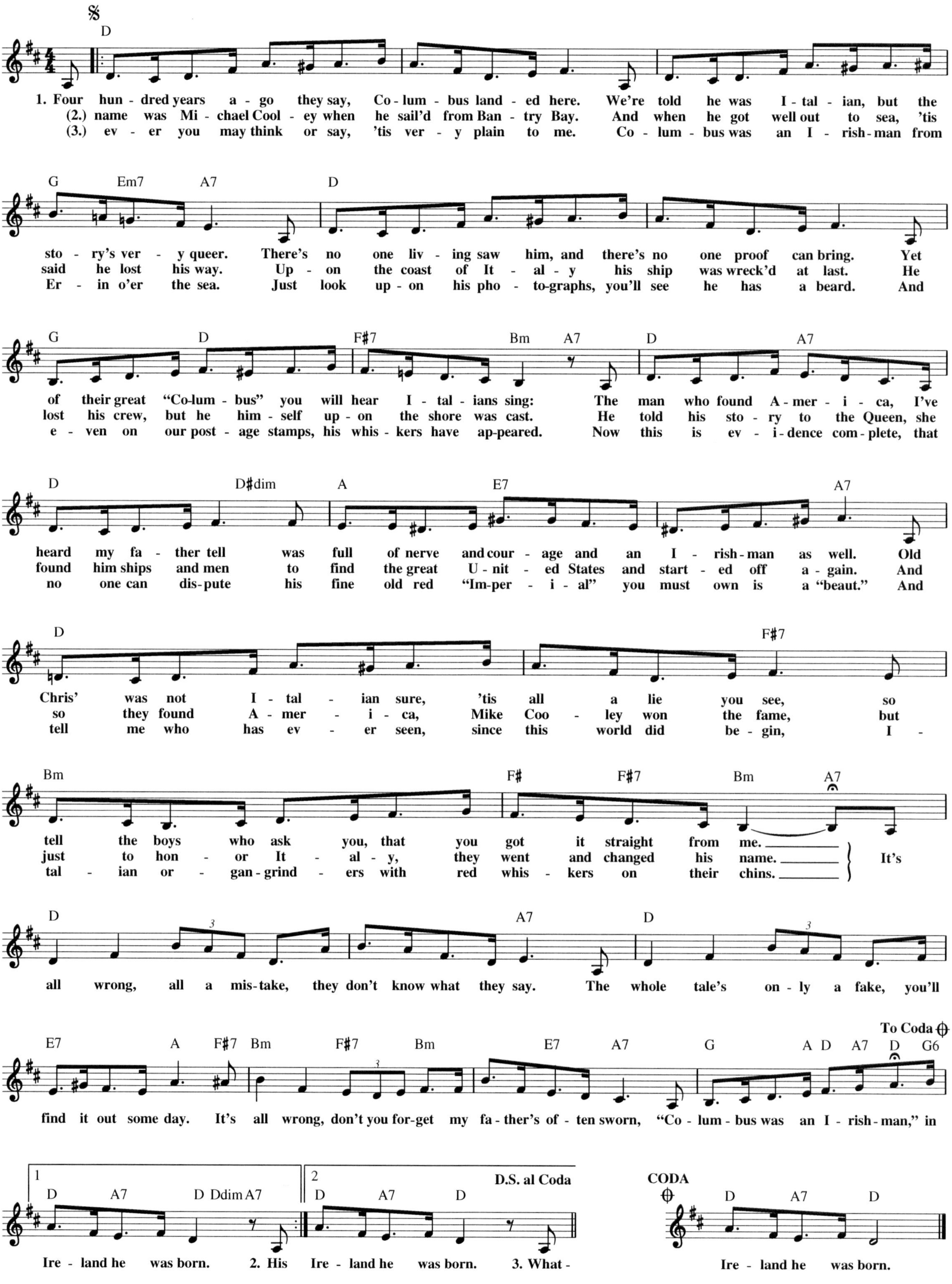

COMIN' THROUGH THE RYE

Scottish folksong
Words and Music by
Robert Burns

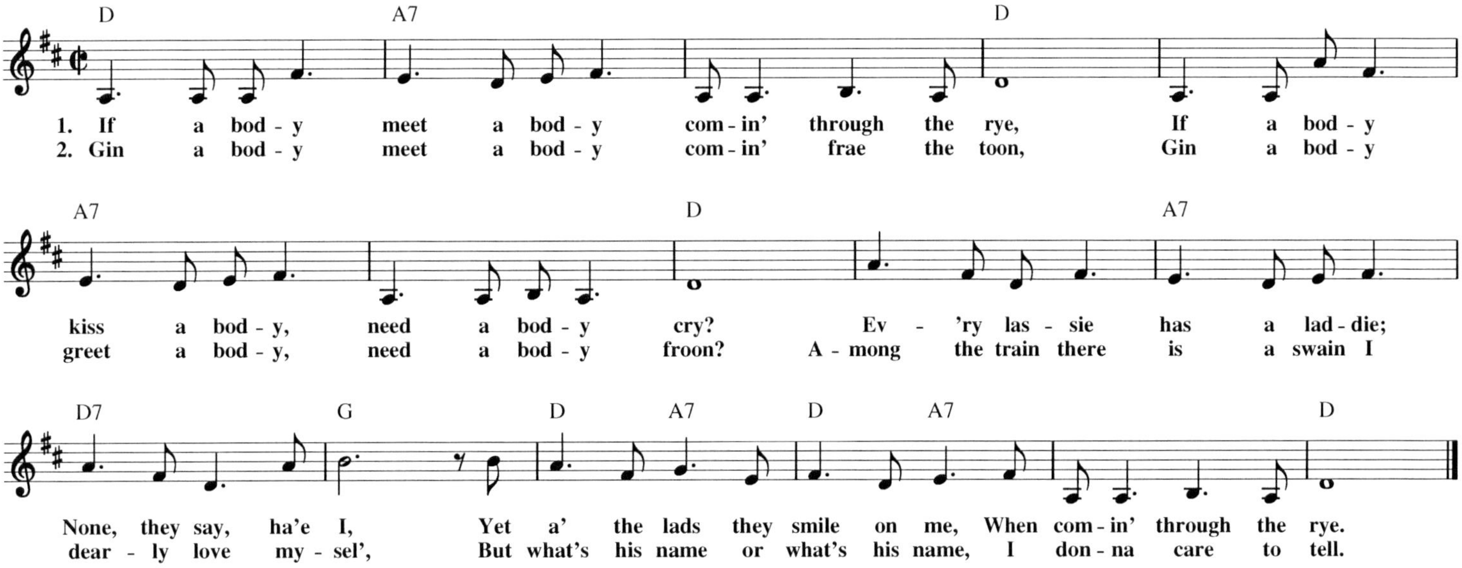

1. If a bod-y meet a bod-y com-in' through the rye, If a bod-y
2. Gin a bod-y meet a bod-y com-in' frae the toon, Gin a bod-y

kiss a bod-y, need a bod-y cry? Ev-'ry las-sie has a lad-die;
greet a bod-y, need a bod-y froon? A-mong the train there is a swain I

None, they say, ha'e I, Yet a' the lads they smile on me, When com-in' through the rye.
dear-ly love my-sel', But what's his name or what's his name, I don-na care to tell.

THE CORK LEG

Irish folksong

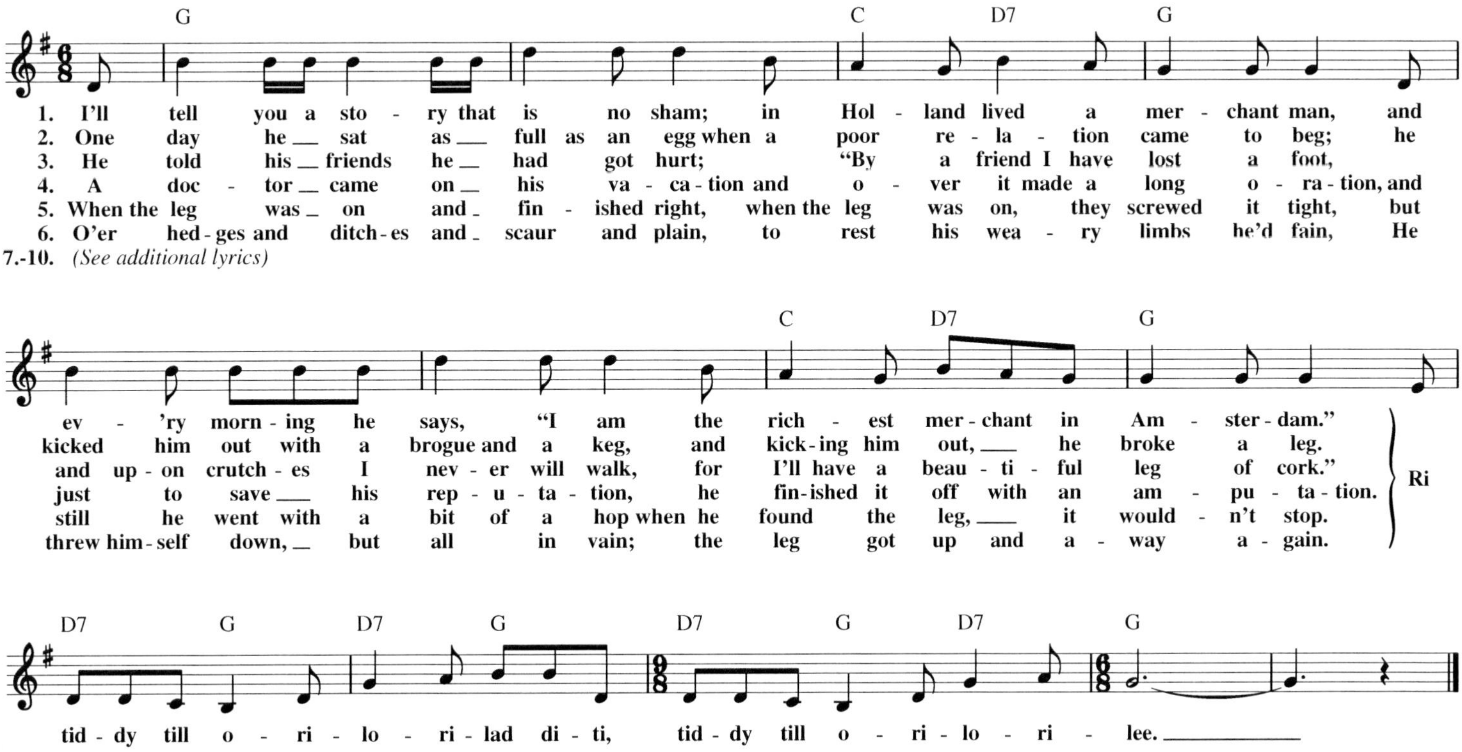

1. I'll tell you a sto-ry that is no sham; in Hol-land lived a mer-chant man, and
2. One day he sat as full as an egg when a poor re-la-tion came to beg; he
3. He told his friends he had got hurt; "By a friend I have lost a foot,
4. A doc-tor came on his va-ca-tion and o-ver it made a long o-ra-tion, and
5. When the leg was on and fin-ished right, when the leg was on, they screwed it tight, but
6. O'er hed-ges and ditch-es and scaur and plain, to rest his wea-ry limbs he'd fain, He

7.-10. *(See additional lyrics)*

ev-'ry morn-ing he says, "I am the rich-est mer-chant in Am-ster-dam."
kicked him out with a brogue and a keg, and kick-ing him out, he broke a leg.
and up-on crutch-es I nev-er will walk, for I'll have a beau-ti-ful leg of cork."
just to save his rep-u-ta-tion, he fin-ished it off with an am-pu-ta-tion.
still he went with a bit of a hop when he found the leg, it would-n't stop.
threw him-self down, but all in vain; the leg got up and a-way a-gain.

Ri

tid-dy till o-ri-lo-ri-lad di-ti, tid-dy till o-ri-lo-ri-lee. _____

Additional Lyrics

7. He called to them that were in sight,
"Stop me or I'm wounded quite."
Although their aid he did invite,
In less than a minute he was out of sight.

8. And he kept running from place to place;
The people thought he was running a race.
He clung to a post for to stop the pace,
But the leg, it still kept up the chase.

9. Over hedges and ditches and plain and scaur,
And Europe he has travelled o'er.
Although he's dead and is no more,
The leg goes on as it did before.

10. So often you see in broad daylight
A skeleton on a cork leg tight.
Although the artist did him invite,
He never was paid, and it served him right.

COSHER BAILEY'S ENGINE

Welsh folksong

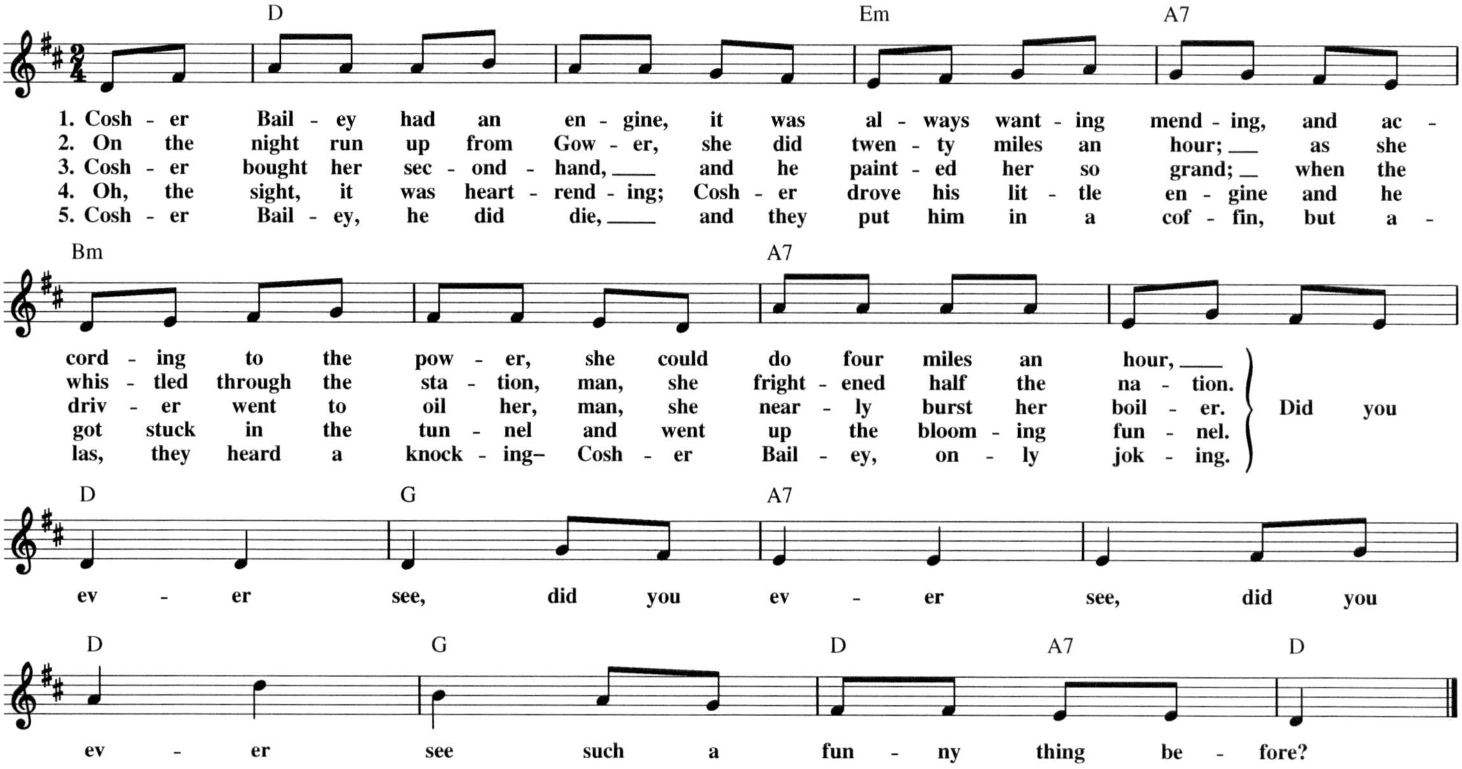

1. Cosh - er Bail - ey had an en - gine, it was al - ways want - ing mend - ing, and ac -
2. On the night run up from Gow - er, she did twen - ty miles an hour; ___ as she
3. Cosh - er bought her sec - ond - hand, ___ and he paint - ed her so grand; ___ when the
4. Oh, the sight, it was heart - rend - ing; Cosh - er drove his lit - tle en - gine and he
5. Cosh - er Bail - ey, he did die, ___ and they put him in a cof - fin, but a -

cord - ing to the pow - er, she could do four miles an hour, ___
whis - tled through the sta - tion, man, she fright - ened half the na - tion.
driv - er went to oil her, man, she near - ly burst her boil - er. ⎞ Did you
got stuck in the tun - nel and went up the bloom - ing fun - nel. ⎟
las, they heard a knock - ing– Cosh - er Bail - ey, on - ly jok - ing. ⎠

ev - er see, did you ev - er see, did you

ev - er see such a fun - ny thing be - fore?

THE COUNTY OF MAYO

Irish folksong
Words by Thomas La Nelle

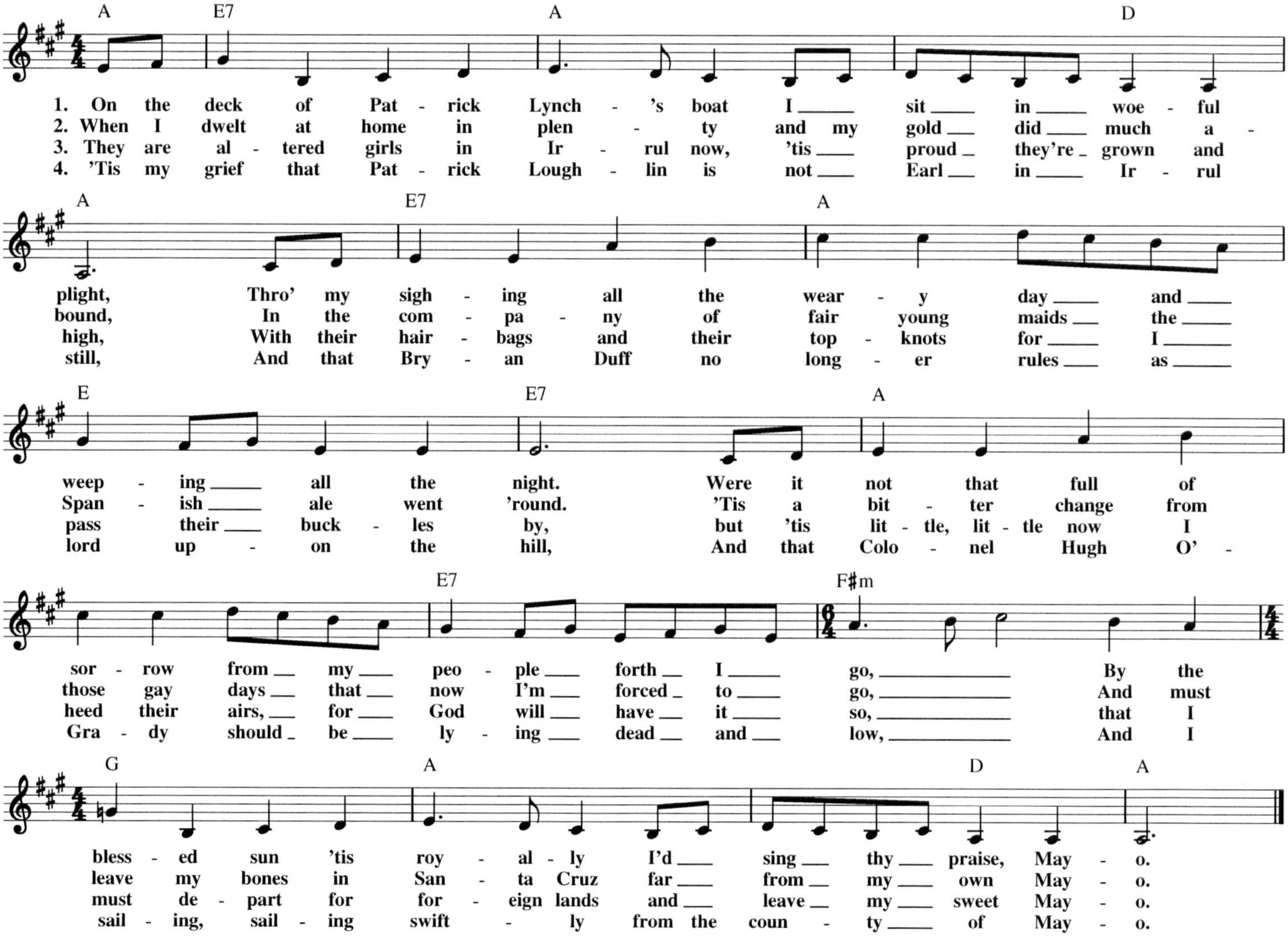

1. On the deck of Pat - rick Lynch - 's boat I ___ sit ___ in ___ woe - ful
2. When I dwelt at home in plen - ty and my gold ___ did ___ much a -
3. They are al - tered girls in Ir - rul now, 'tis ___ proud _ they're _ grown and
4. 'Tis my grief that Pat - rick Lough - lin is not ___ Earl ___ in ___ Ir - rul

plight, Thro' my sigh - ing all the wear - y day ___ and ___
bound, In the com - pa - ny of fair young maids ___ the ___
high, With their hair - bags and their top - knots for ___ I ___
still, And that Bry - an Duff no long - er rules ___ as ___

weep - ing ___ all the night. Were it not that full of
Span - ish ___ ale went 'round. 'Tis a bit - ter change from
pass their ___ buck - les by, but 'tis lit - tle, lit - tle now I
lord up - on the hill, And that Colo - nel Hugh O' -

sor - row from ___ my ___ peo - ple ___ forth ___ I ___ go, ___ By the
those gay days ___ that ___ now I'm ___ forced _ to ___ go, ___ And must
heed their airs, ___ for ___ God will ___ have ___ it ___ so, ___ that I
Gra - dy should _ be ___ ly - ing ___ dead ___ and ___ low, ___ And I

bless - ed sun 'tis roy - al - ly I'd ___ sing ___ thy ___ praise, May - o.
leave my bones in San - ta Cruz far ___ from ___ my ___ own May - o.
must de - part for for - eign lands and ___ leave ___ my sweet May - o.
sail - ing, sail - ing swift - ly from the coun - ty ___ of May - o.

CRADLE SPELL OF DUNVEGAN
(Taladh an Leinibh Leoidich)

Folksong from the Hebrides

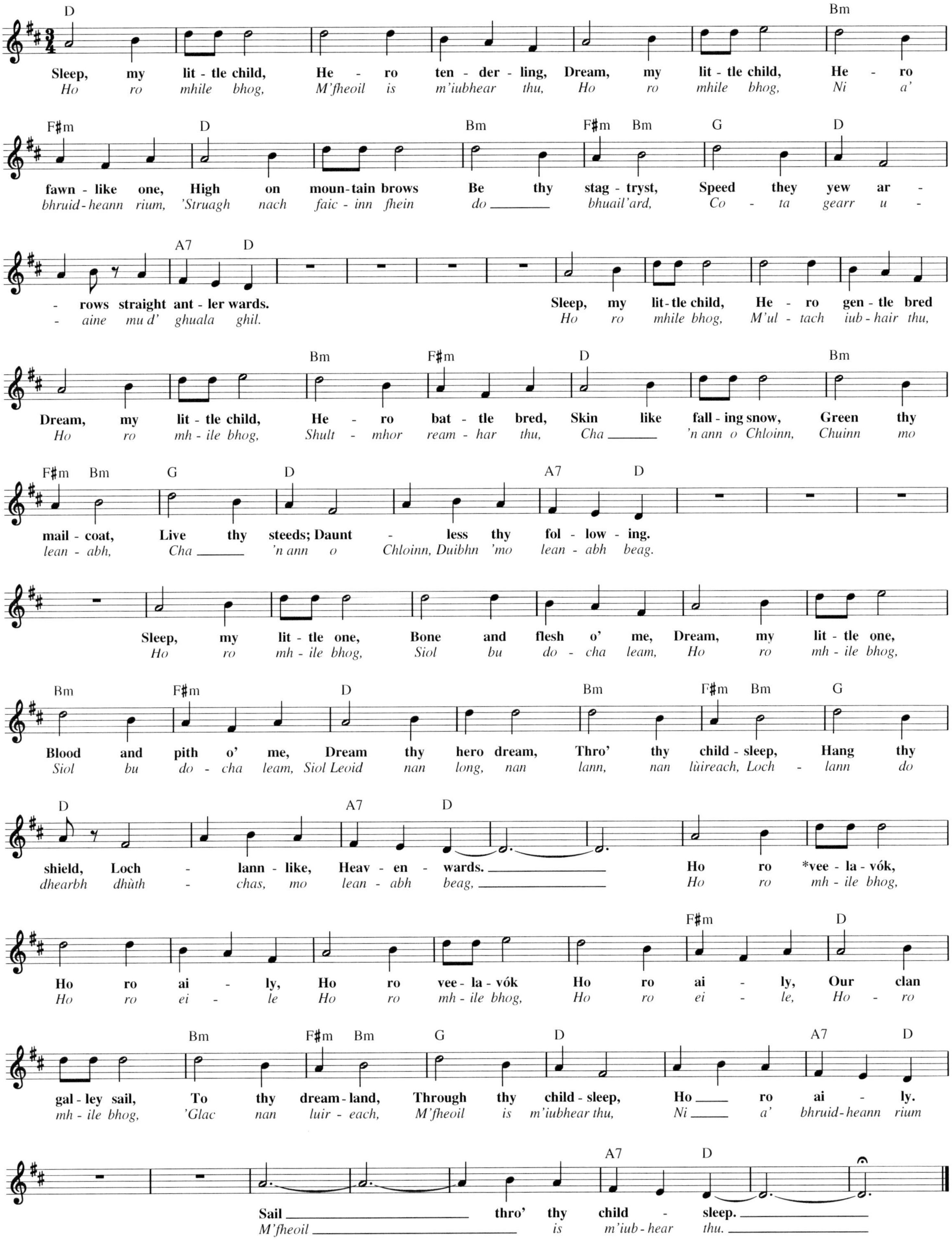

*Honey love

THE COURTING OF THE KING OF ERIN'S DAUGHTER
(Nighean Righ Eireann)

Folksong from the Hebrides

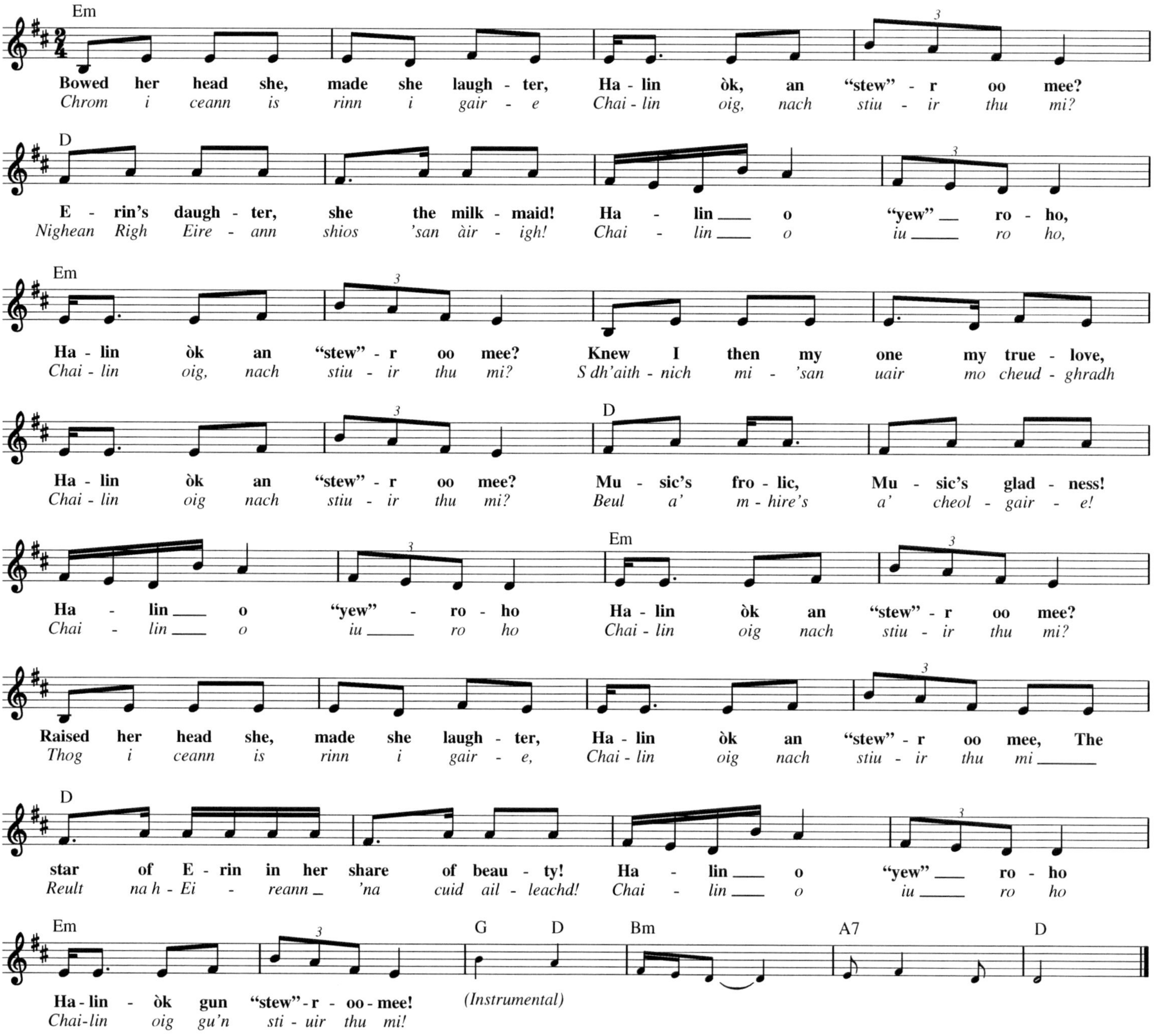

CREDHE'S LAMENT FOR CAIL

Irish folksong

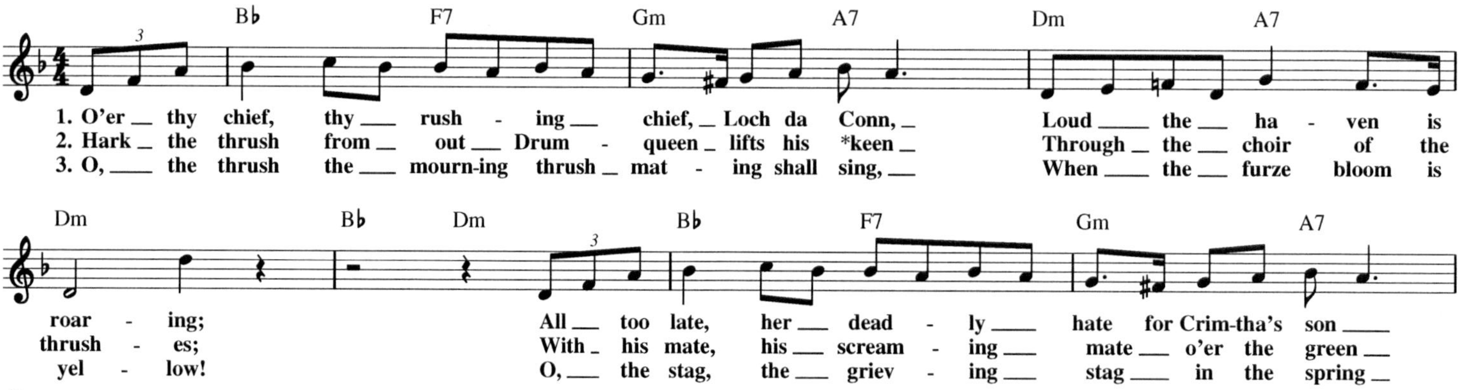

*Lament

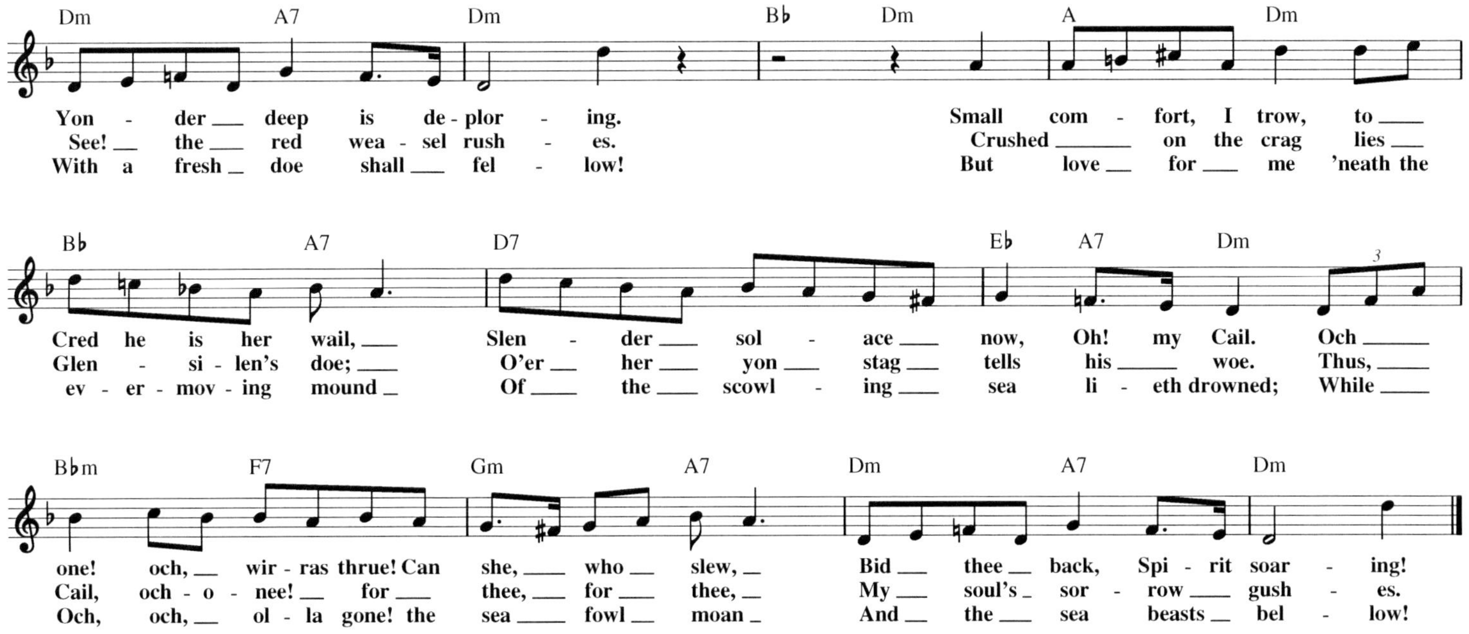
Yon - der deep is de - plor - ing. Small com - fort, I trow, to
See! the red wea - sel rush - es. Crushed on the crag lies
With a fresh doe shall fel - low! But love for me 'neath the
Cred he is her wail, Slen - der sol - ace now, Oh! my Cail. Och
Glen - si - len's doe; O'er her yon stag tells his woe. Thus,
ev - er - mov - ing mound Of the scowl - ing sea li - eth drowned; While
one! och, wir - ras thrue! Can she, who slew, Bid thee back, Spi - rit soar - ing!
Cail, och - o - nee! for thee, for thee, My soul's sor - row gush - es.
Och, och, ol - la gone! the sea fowl moan And the sea beasts bel - low!

THE CRUISKEEN LAWN

(Cruiscín Lán)

Irish folksong

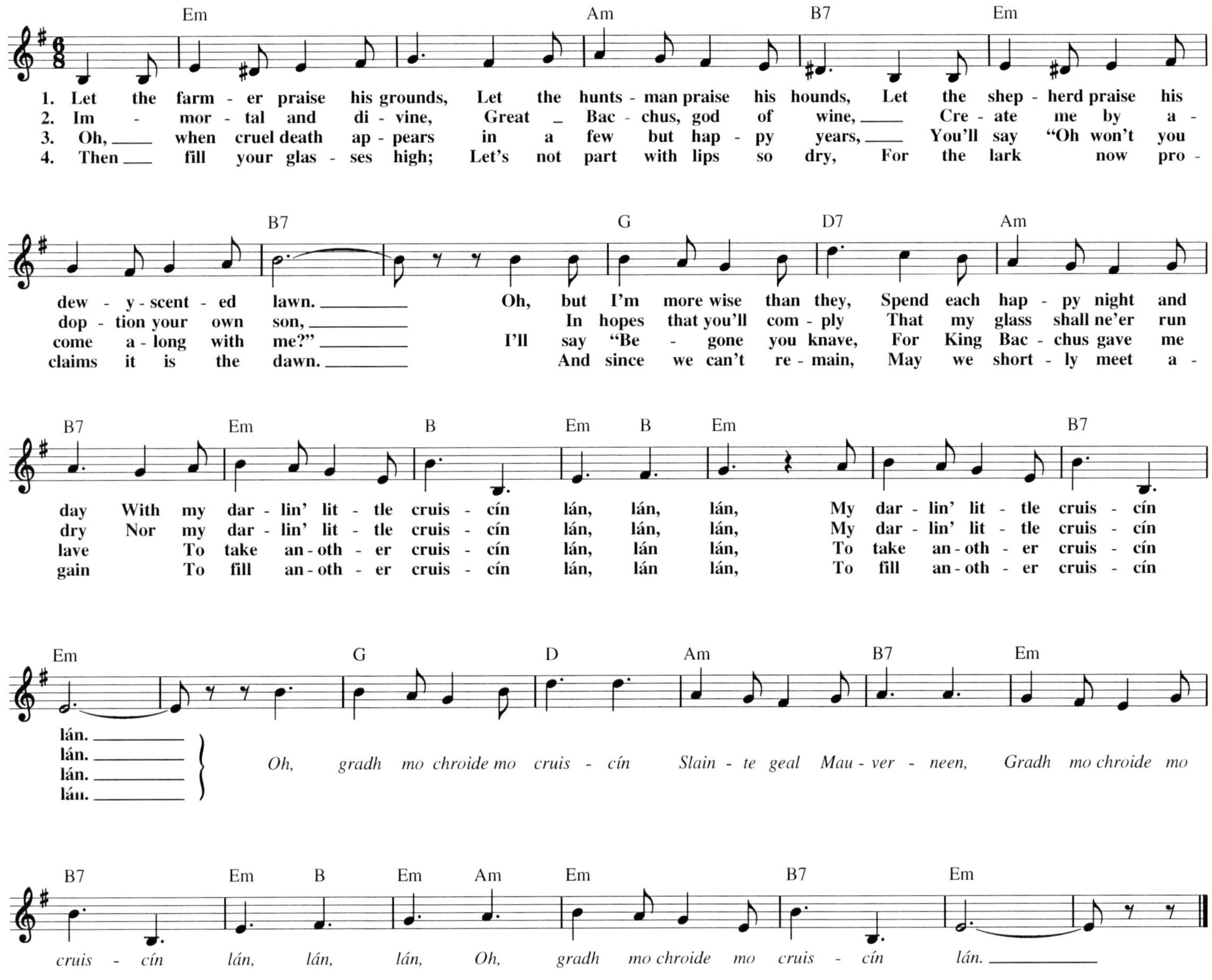
1. Let the farm - er praise his grounds, Let the hunts - man praise his hounds, Let the shep - herd praise his
2. Im - mor - tal and di - vine, Great Bac - chus, god of wine, Cre - ate me by a -
3. Oh, when cruel death ap - pears in a few but hap - py years, You'll say "Oh won't you
4. Then fill your glas - ses high; Let's not part with lips so dry, For the lark now pro -
dew - y - scent - ed lawn. Oh, but I'm more wise than they, Spend each hap - py night and
dop - tion your own son, In hopes that you'll com - ply That my glass shall ne'er run
come a - long with me?" I'll say "Be - gone you knave, For King Bac - chus gave me
claims it is the dawn. And since we can't re - main, May we short - ly meet a -
day With my dar - lin' lit - tle cruis - cín lán, lán, lán, My dar - lin' lit - tle cruis - cín
dry Nor my dar - lin' lit - tle cruis - cín lán, lán, lán, My dar - lin' lit - tle cruis - cín
lave To take an - oth - er cruis - cín lán, lán lán, To take an - oth - er cruis - cín
gain To fill an - oth - er cruis - cín lán, lán lán, To fill an - oth - er cruis - cín
lán.
lán.
lán.
lán.
Oh, gradh mo chroide mo cruis - cín Slain - te geal Mau - ver - neen, Gradh mo chroide mo
cruis - cín lán, lán, lán, Oh, gradh mo chroide mo cruis - cín lán.

THE CROPPY BOY

Irish folksong

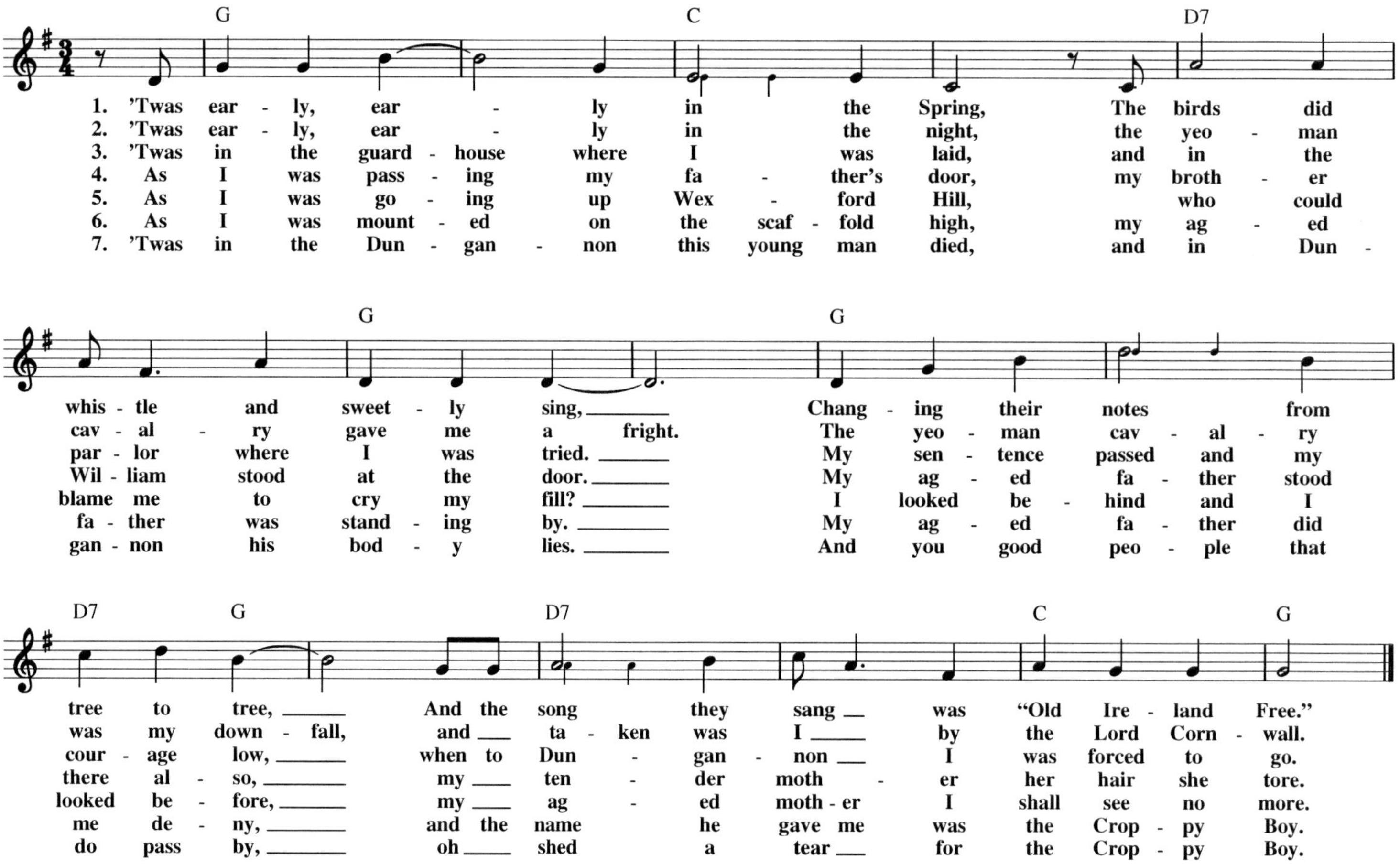

1. 'Twas ear - ly, ear - ly in the Spring, The birds did
2. 'Twas ear - ly, ear - ly in the night, the yeo - man
3. 'Twas in the guard - house where I was laid, and in the
4. As I was pass - ing my fa - ther's door, my broth - er
5. As I was go - ing up Wex - ford Hill, who could
6. As I was mount - ed on the scaf - fold high, my ag - ed
7. 'Twas in the Dun - gan - non this young man died, and in Dun -

whis - tle and sweet - ly sing, Chang - ing their notes from
cav - al - ry gave me a fright. The yeo - man cav - al - ry
par - lor where I was tried. My sen - tence passed and my
Wil - liam stood at the door. I looked be - hind and I
blame me to cry my fill? My ag - ed fa - ther stood
fa - ther was stand - ing by. My ag - ed fa - ther did
gan - non his bod - y lies. And you good peo - ple that

tree to tree, And the song they sang was "Old Ire - land Free."
was my down - fall, and ta - ken was I by the Lord Corn - wall.
cour - age low, when to Dun - gan - non I was forced to go.
there al - so, my ten - der moth - er her hair she tore.
looked be - fore, my ag - ed moth - er I shall see no more.
me de - ny, and the name he gave me was the Crop - py Boy.
do pass by, oh shed a tear for the Crop - py Boy.

CUCHULLAN'S LAMENT FOR HIS SON
(Cuchulann 's a Mhac)

Folksong from the Hebrides

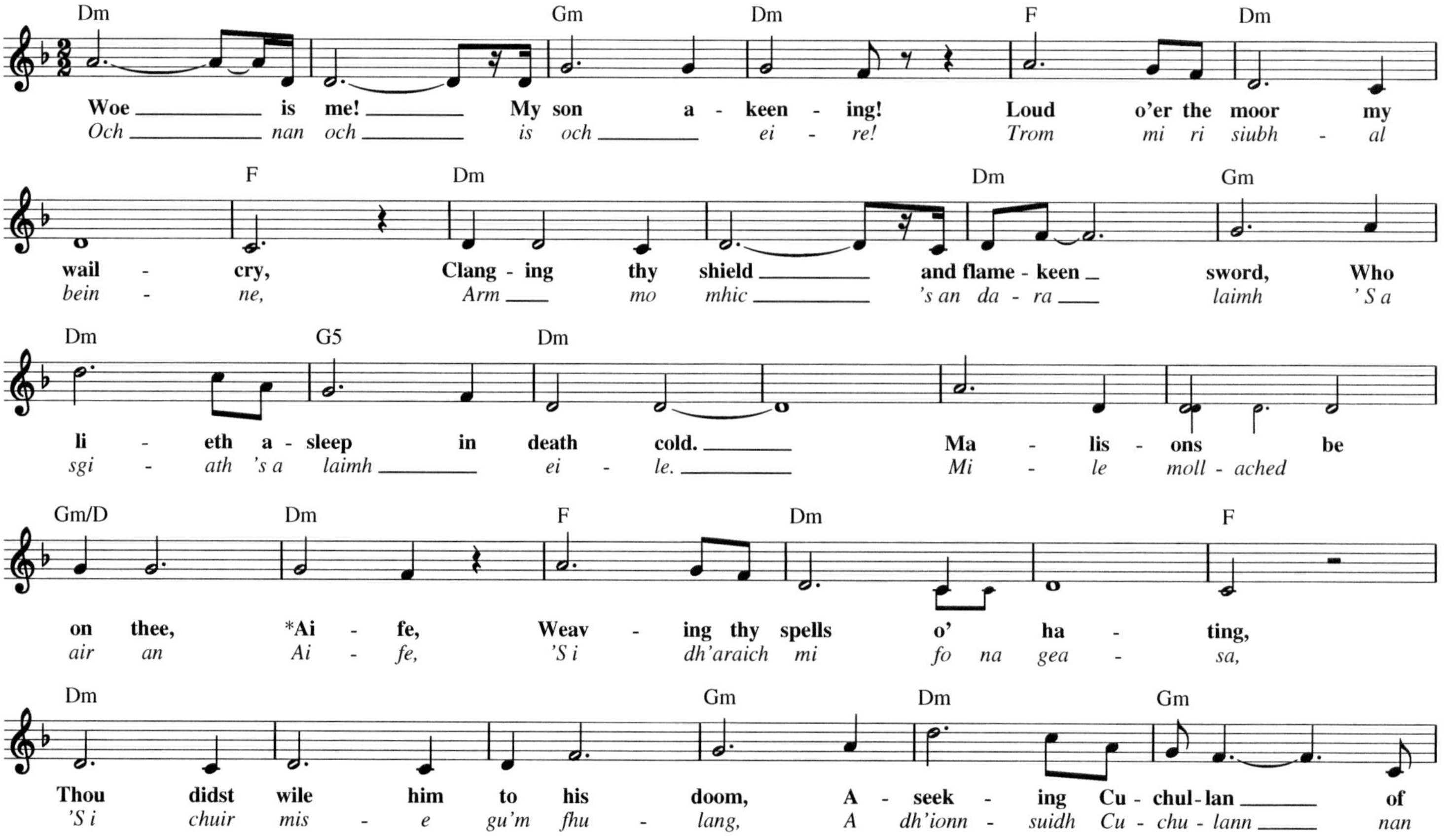

Woe is me! My son a - keen - ing! Loud o'er the moor my
Och nan och is och ei - re! Trom mi ri siubh - al

wail - cry, Clang - ing thy shield and flame - keen _ sword, Who
bein - ne, Arm mo mhic 's an da - ra laimh 'S a

li - eth a - sleep in death cold. Ma - lis - ons be
sgi - ath 's a laimh ei - le. Mi - le moll - ached

on thee, *Ai - fe, Weav - ing thy spells o' ha - ting,
air an Ai - fe, 'S i dh'araich mi fo na gea - sa,

Thou didst wile him to his doom, A - seek - ing Cu - chul - lan of
'S i chuir mis - e gu'm fhu - lang, A dh'ionn - suidh Cu - chu - lann nan

The wife of Curhullan, Pronounced I-fa

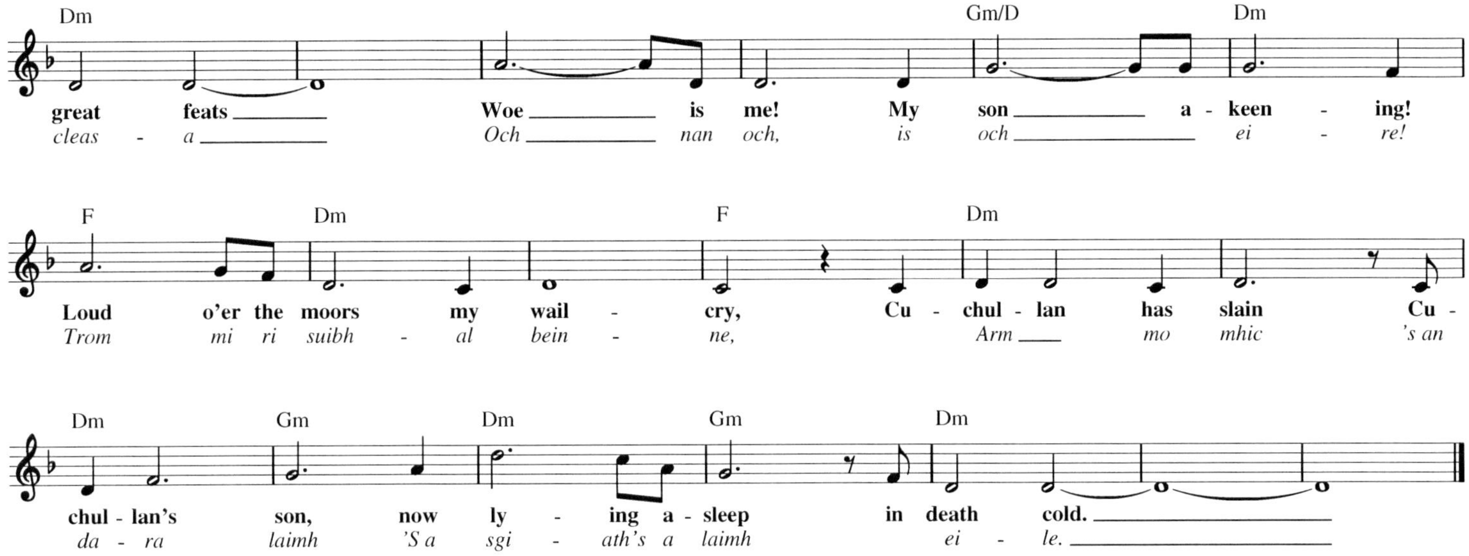

great feats _____ Woe _____ is me! My son _____ a-keen-ing!
cleas - a _____ Och _____ nan och, is och _____ ei - re!

Loud o'er the moors my wail - cry, Cu - chul - lan has slain Cu-
Trom mi ri suibh - al bein - ne, Arm _____ mo mhic 's an

chul - lan's son, now ly - ing a - sleep in death cold. _____
da - ra laimh 'S a sgi - ath's a laimh ei - le. _____

THE CUCKOO MADRIGAL

Irish folksong

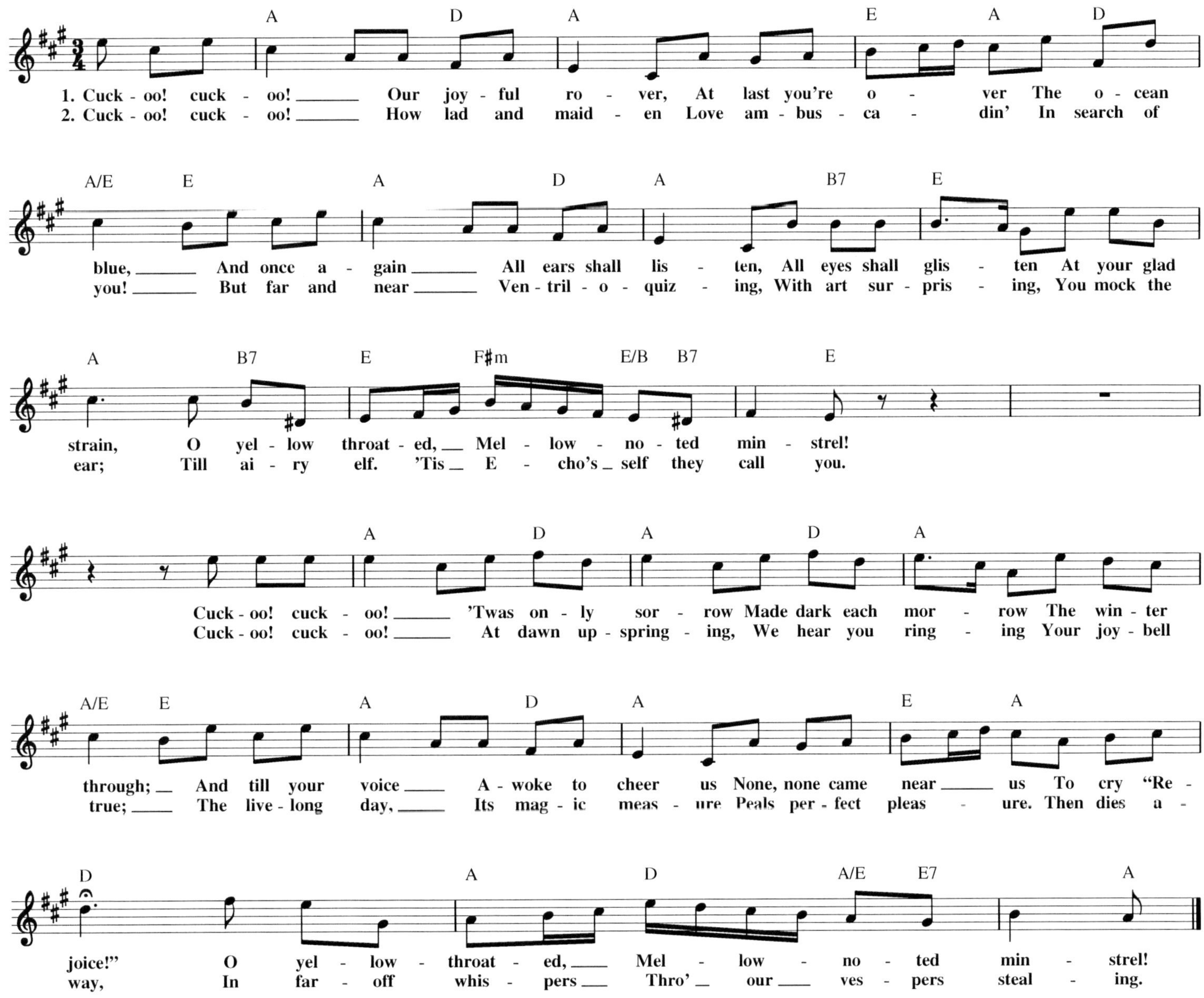

1. Cuck - oo! cuck - oo! _____ Our joy - ful ro - ver, At last you're o - ver The o - cean
2. Cuck - oo! cuck - oo! _____ How lad and maid - en Love am - bus - ca - din' In search of

blue, _____ And once a - gain _____ All ears shall lis - ten, All eyes shall glis - ten At your glad
you! _____ But far and near _____ Ven - tril - o - quiz - ing, With art sur - pris - ing, You mock the

strain, O yel - low throat - ed, _____ Mel - low - no - ted min - strel!
ear; Till ai - ry elf. 'Tis _____ E - cho's _____ self they call you.

Cuck - oo! cuck - oo! _____ 'Twas on - ly sor - row Made dark each mor - row The win - ter
Cuck - oo! cuck - oo! _____ At dawn up - spring - ing, We hear you ring - ing Your joy - bell

through; _____ And till your voice _____ A - woke to cheer us None, none came near _____ us To cry "Re -
true; _____ The live - long day, _____ Its mag - ic meas - ure Peals per - fect pleas - ure. Then dies a -

joice!" O yel - low - throat - ed, _____ Mel - low - no - ted min - strel!
way, In far - off whis - pers _____ Thro' our _____ ves - pers steal - ing.

THE CURRAGH OF KILDARE

Irish folksong

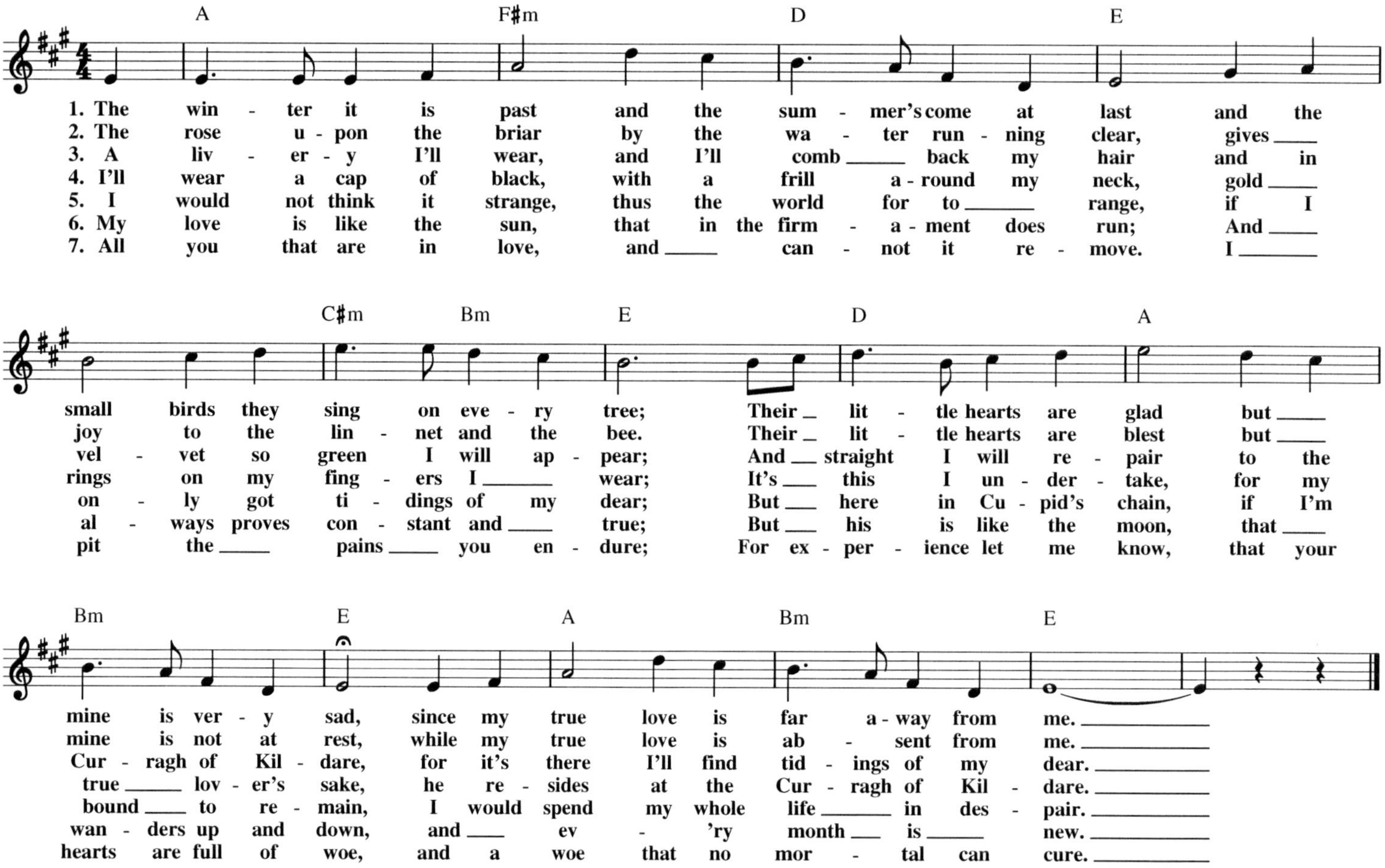

1. The win - ter it is past and the sum - mer's come at last and the
2. The rose u - pon the briar by the wa - ter run - ning clear, gives ____
3. A liv - e - ry I'll wear, and I'll comb ____ back my hair and in
4. I'll wear a cap of black, with a frill a - round my neck, gold ____
5. I would not think it strange, thus the world for to range, if I
6. My love is like the sun, that in the firm - a - ment does run; And I
7. All you that are in love, and ____ can - not it re - move. I ____

small birds they sing on eve - ry tree; Their _ lit - tle hearts are glad but ____
joy to the lin - net and the bee. Their _ lit - tle hearts are blest but ____
vel - vet so green I will ap - pear; And _ straight I will re - pair to the
rings on my fing - ers I ____ wear; It's ____ this I un - der - take, for my
on - ly got ti - dings of my dear; But ____ here in Cu - pid's chain, if I'm
al - ways proves con - stant and ____ true; But ____ his is like the moon, that ____
pit the ____ pains ____ you en - dure; For ex - per - ience let me know, that your

mine is ver - y sad, since my true love is far a - way from me. ____
mine is not at rest, while my true love is ab - sent from me. ____
Cur - ragh of Kil - dare, for it's there I'll find tid - ings of my dear. ____
true ____ lov - er's sake, he re - sides at the Cur - ragh of Kil - dare. ____
bound ____ to re - main, I would spend my whole life ____ in des - pair. ____
wan - ders up and down, and ____ ev - 'ry month ____ is ____ new. ____
hearts are full of woe, and a woe that no mor - tal can cure. ____

CURSE OF THE ASPEN TREE
(An Crithionn Cruaidh)

Folksong from the Hebrides

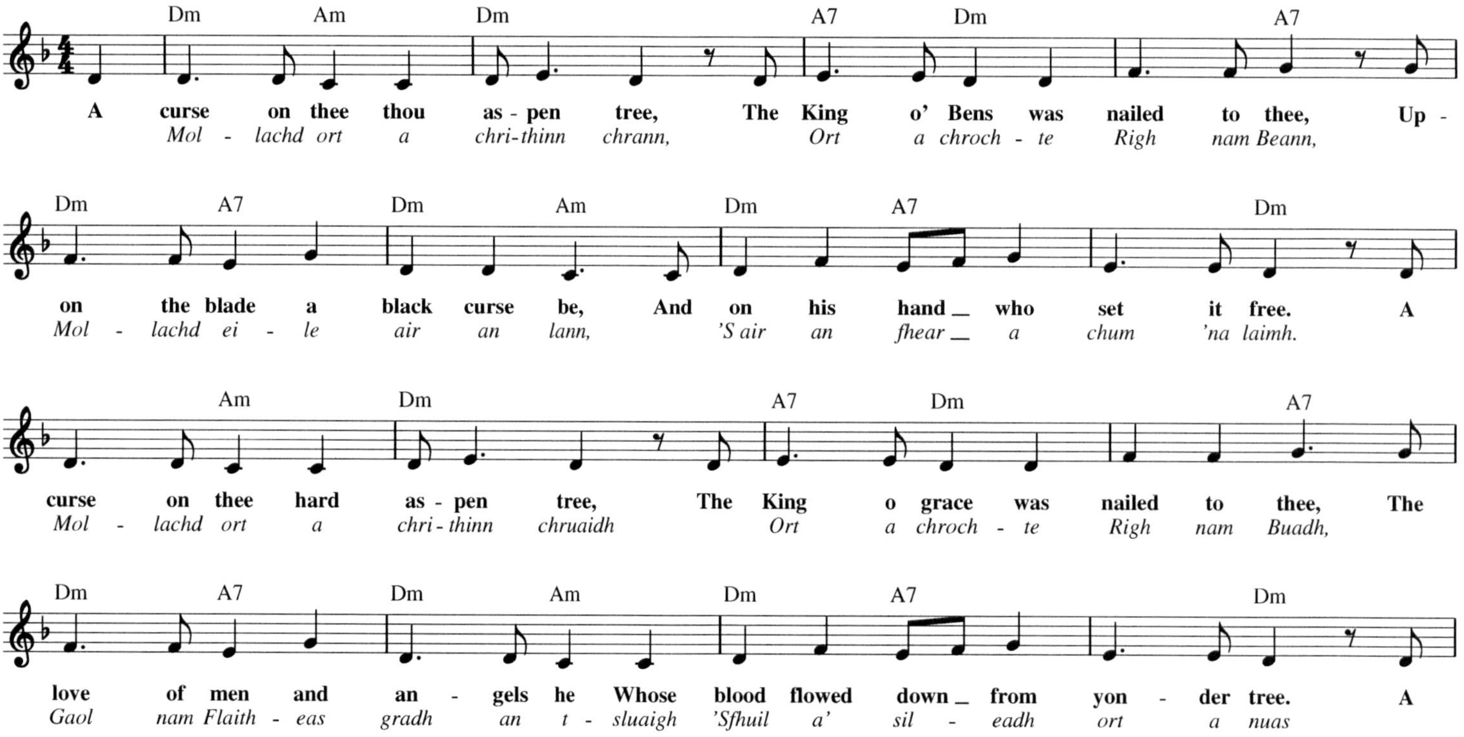

A curse on thee thou as - pen tree, The King o' Bens was nailed to thee, Up -
Mol - lachd ort a chri - thinn chrann, Ort a chroch - te Righ nam Beann,

on the blade a black curse be, And on his hand ____ who set it free. A
Mol - lachd ei - le air an lann, 'S air an fhear ____ a chum 'na laimh.

curse on thee hard as - pen tree, The King o grace was nailed to thee, The
Mol - lachd ort a chri - thinn chruaidh Ort a chroch - te Righ nam Buadh,

love of men and an - gels he Whose blood flowed down ____ from yon - der tree. A
Gaol nam Flaith - eas gradh an t - sluaigh 'Sfhuil a' sil - eadh ort a nuas

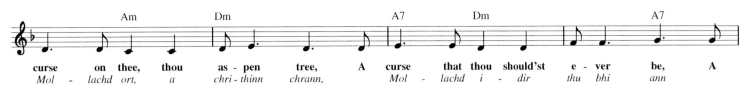

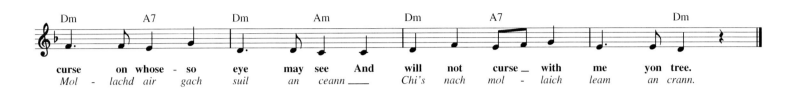

DANNY BOY

Irish folksong
Words by Frederick Edward Weatherly

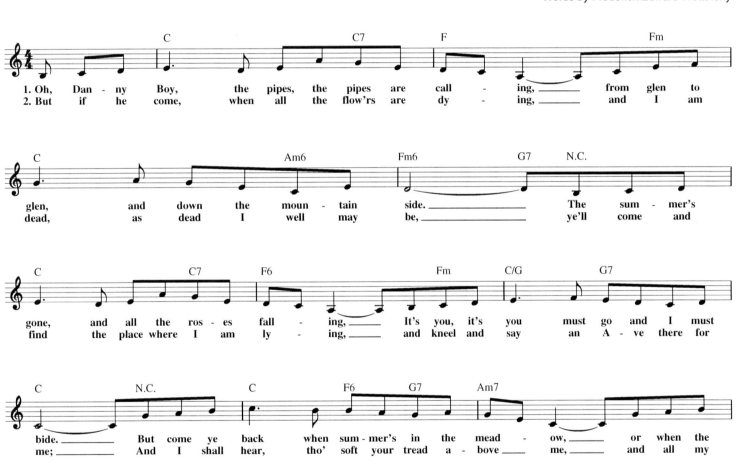

DANCE TO YOUR SHADOW
(Bando Ribinnean)

Folksong from the Hebrides

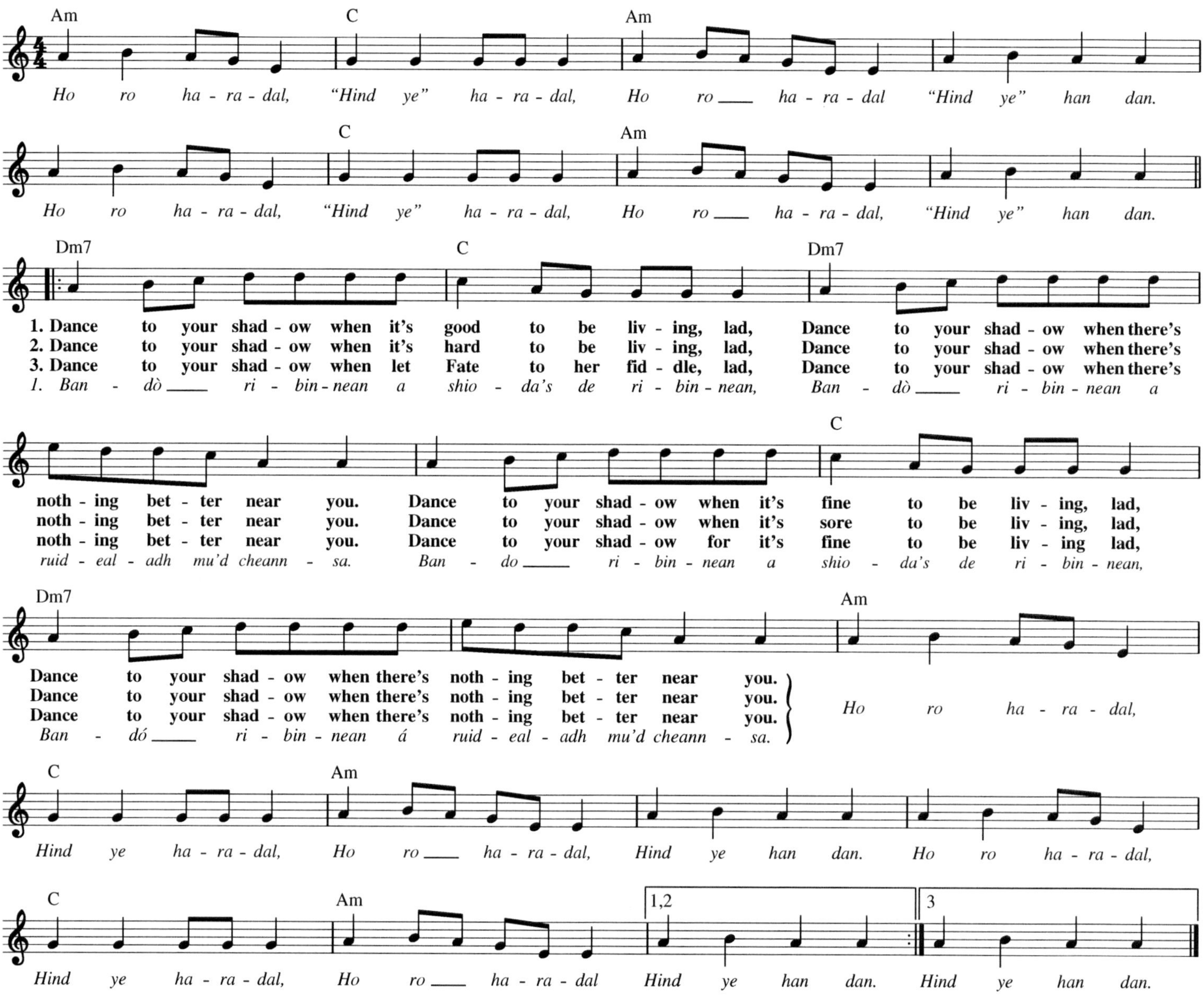

DARBY KELLY

Irish folksong

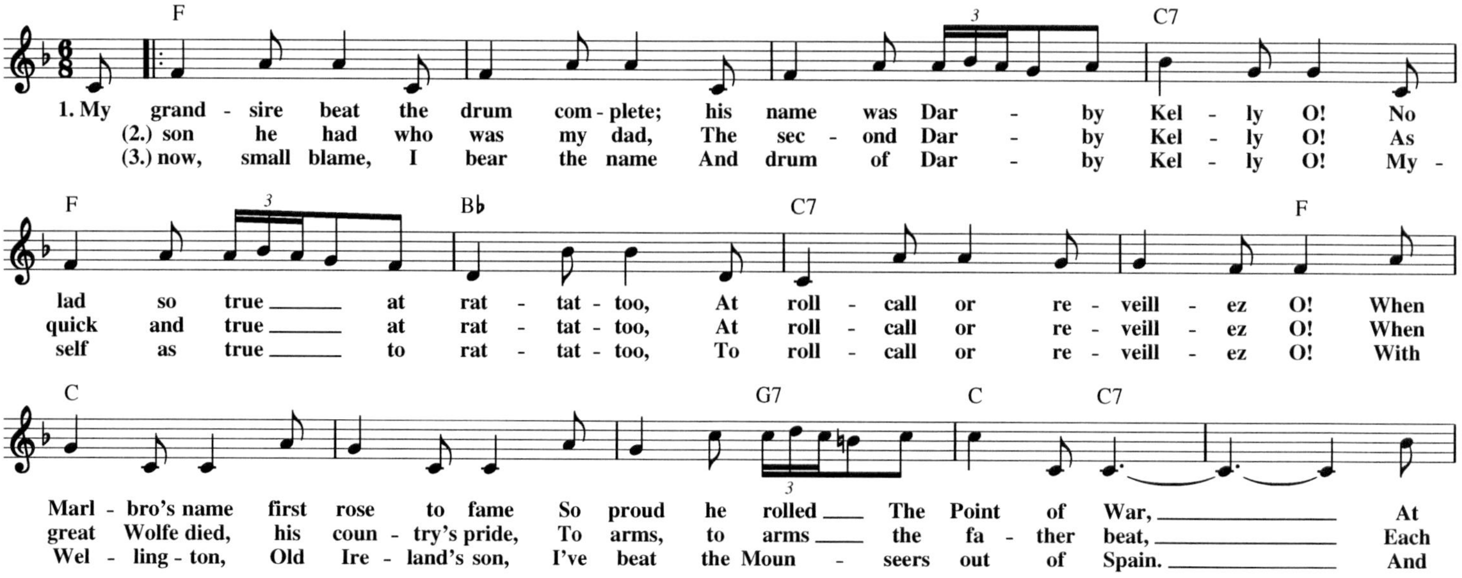

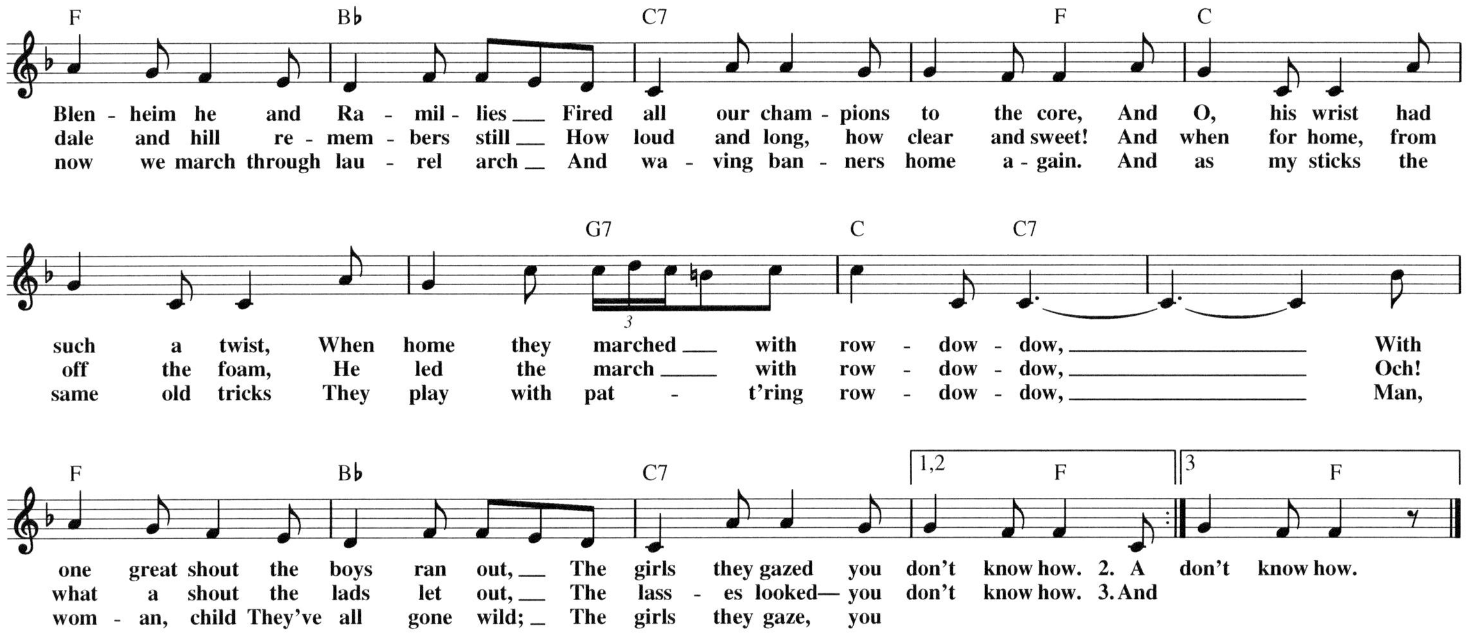

Blen - heim he and Ra - mil - lies ___ Fired all our cham - pions to the core, And O, his wrist had
dale and hill re - mem - bers still ___ How loud and long, how clear and sweet! And when for home, from
now we march through lau - rel arch And wa - ving ban - ners home a - gain. And as my sticks the

such a twist, When home they marched ___ with row - dow - dow, _____ With
off the foam, He led the march _____ with row - dow - dow, _____ Och!
same old tricks They play with pat - t'ring row - dow - dow, _____ Man,

one great shout the boys ran out, ___ The girls they gazed you don't know how. 2. A don't know how.
what a shout the lads let out, ___ The lass - es looked— you don't know how. 3. And
wom - an, child They've all gone wild; _ The girls they gaze, you

THE DEAR LITTLE SHAMROCK

Irish folksong

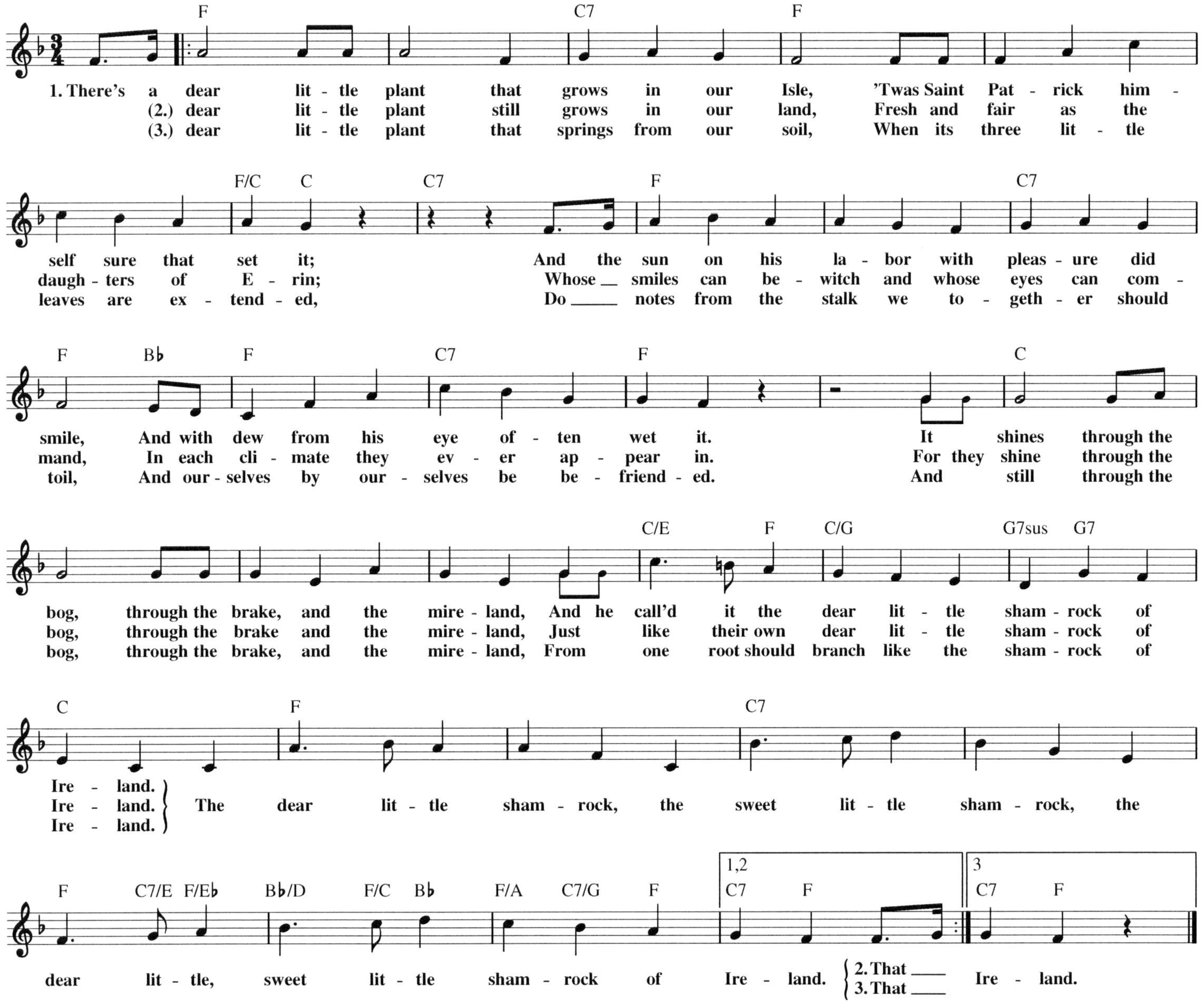

1. There's a dear lit - tle plant that grows in our Isle, 'Twas Saint Pat - rick him -
(2.) dear lit - tle plant still grows in our land, Fresh and fair as the
(3.) dear lit - tle plant that springs from our soil, When its three lit - tle

self sure that set it; And the sun on his la - bor with pleas - ure did
daugh - ters of E - rin; Whose _ smiles can be - witch and whose eyes can com -
leaves are ex - tend - ed, Do _____ notes from the stalk we to - geth - er should

smile, And with dew from his eye of - ten wet it. It shines through the
mand, In each cli - mate they ev - er ap - pear in. For they shine through the
toil, And our - selves by our - selves be be - friend - ed. And still through the

bog, through the brake, and the mire - land, And he call'd it the dear lit - tle sham - rock of
bog, through the brake and the mire - land, Just like their own dear lit - tle sham - rock of
bog, through the brake, and the mire - land, From one root should branch like the sham - rock of

Ire - land. The dear lit - tle sham - rock, the sweet lit - tle sham - rock, the
Ire - land.
Ire - land.

dear lit - tle, sweet lit - tle sham - rock of Ire - land. 2. That _____ Ire - land.
3. That _____

DICK DARBY

Irish folksong

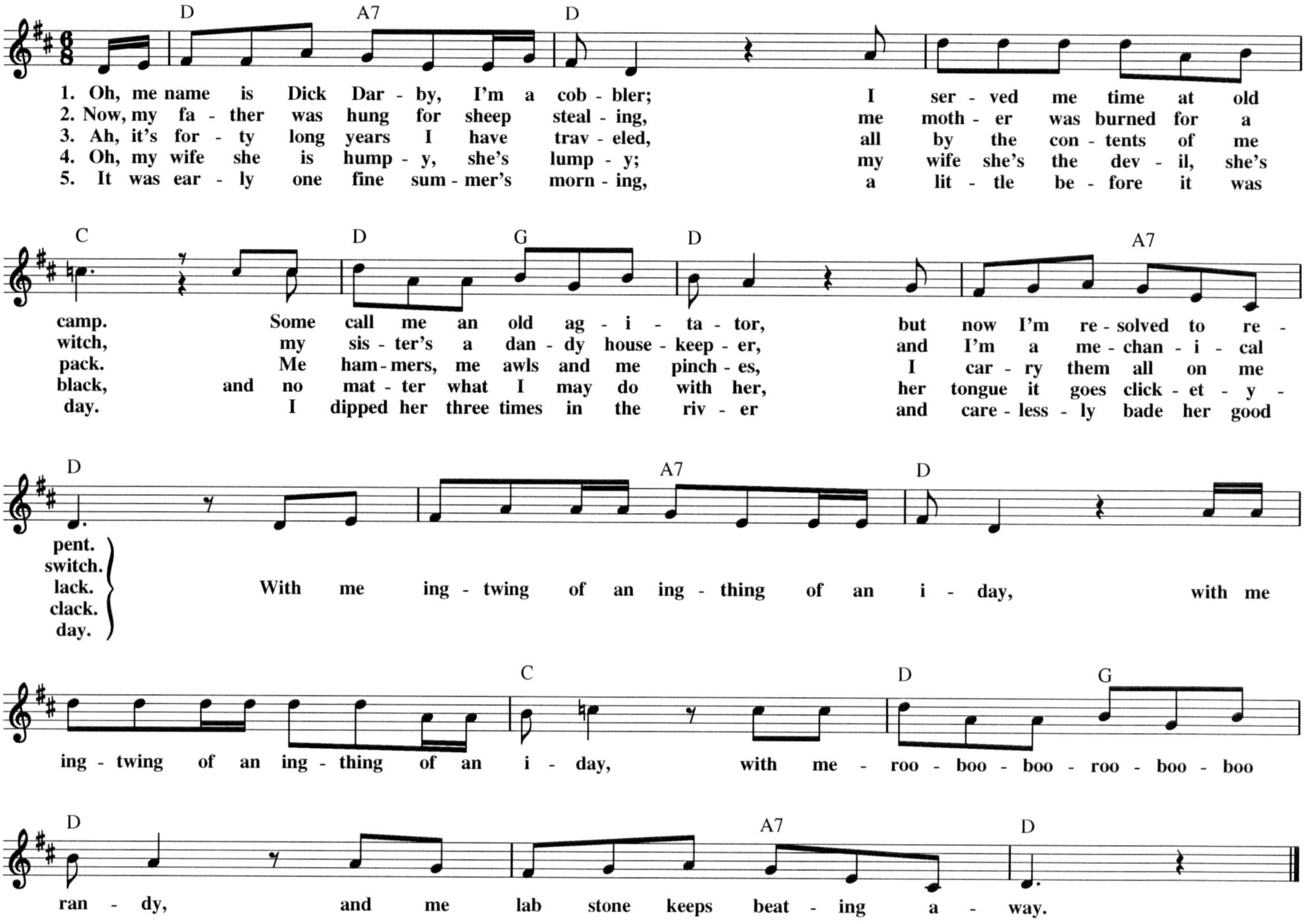

1. Oh, me name is Dick Dar - by, I'm a cob - bler; I ser - ved me time at old
2. Now, my fa - ther was hung for sheep steal - ing, me moth - er was burned for a
3. Ah, it's for - ty long years I have trav - eled, all by the con - tents of me
4. Oh, my wife she is hump - y, she's lump - y; my wife she's the dev - il, she's
5. It was ear - ly one fine sum - mer's morn - ing, a lit - tle be - fore it was

camp. Some call me an old ag - i - ta - tor, but now I'm re - solved to re -
witch, my sis - ter's a dan - dy house - keep - er, and I'm a me - chan - i - cal
pack. Me ham - mers, me awls and me pinch - es, I car - ry them all on me
black, and no mat - ter what I may do with her, her tongue it goes click - et - y -
day. I dipped her three times in the riv - er and care - less - ly bade her good

pent.
switch.
lack.   } With me ing - twing of an ing - thing of an i - day,   with me
clack.
day.

ing - twing of an ing - thing of an i - day,   with me - roo - boo - boo - roo - boo - boo

ran - dy,   and me lab stone keeps beat - ing a - way.

THE DOON

Irish folksong

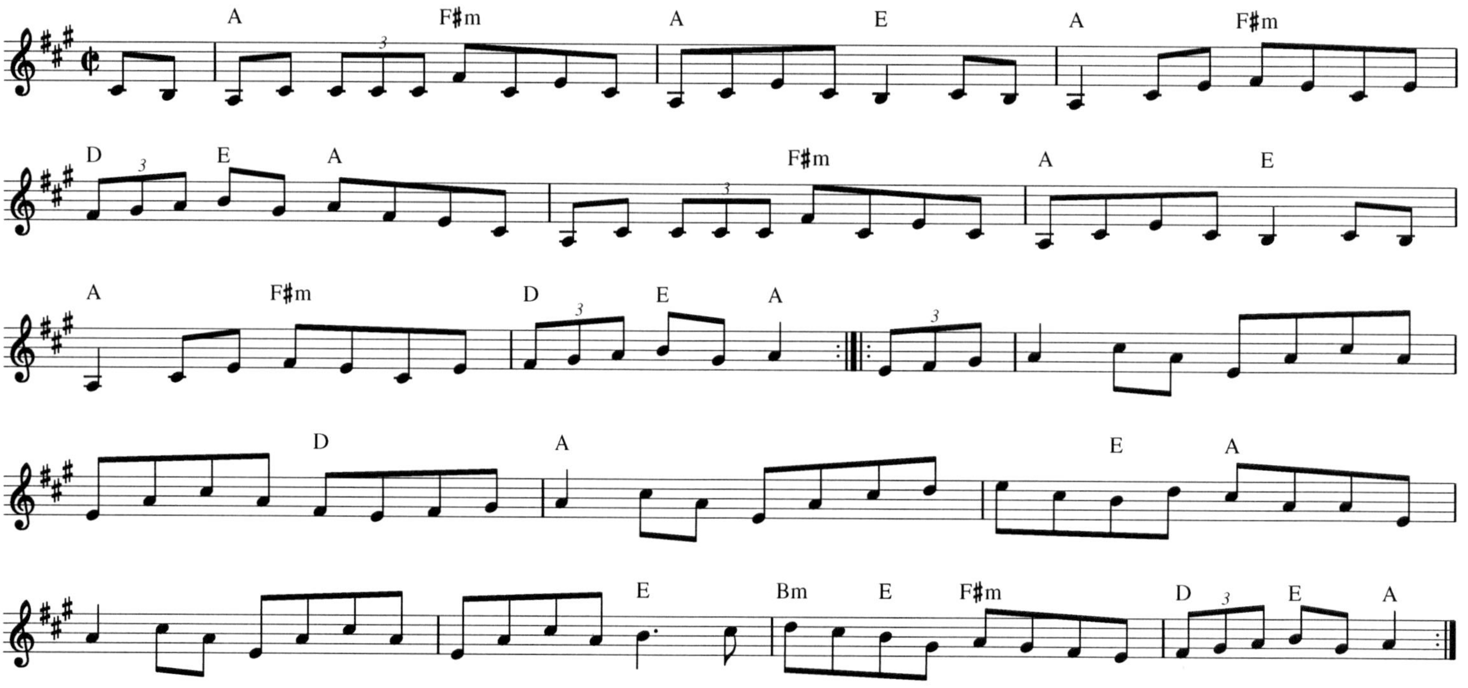

THE DINGLE PUCK GOAT

Irish folksong

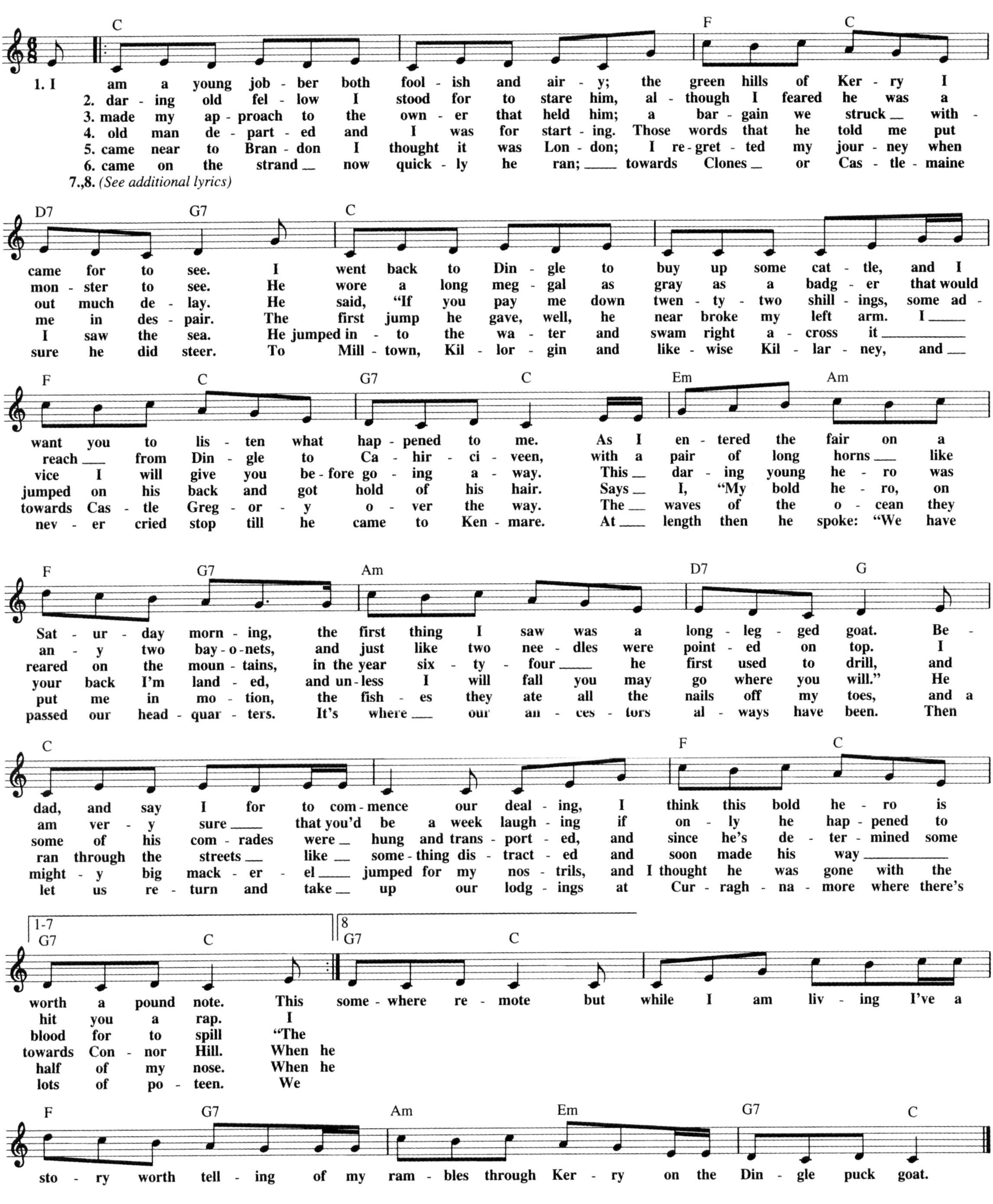

Additional Lyrics

7. We done our returns and stopped there till morning;
   It's during the night I sat up on his back.
   As the day it was dawning he jumped from the corner,
   And t'wards Castle Island he went in a crack.
   To the town of Tralee we next took our rambles.
   I think he was anxious to see some more sport.
   Outside of the town we met some Highlanders.
   He up with his horns and he tore all their clothes.

8. The Highlanders shouted and bawled, "Meela murder!
   Send for the polis and get him to jail."
   But the louder they shouted the faster my goat ran,
   And over the Basin he gave them legbail.
   On crossing the Basin I fell on the footway;
   Away went the goat and I saw him no more.
   Sure if he's in Ireland he's in Camp or in Brandon,
   Or away in the mountains somewhere remote.

DON'T YOU WEEP AFTER ME

Irish folksong

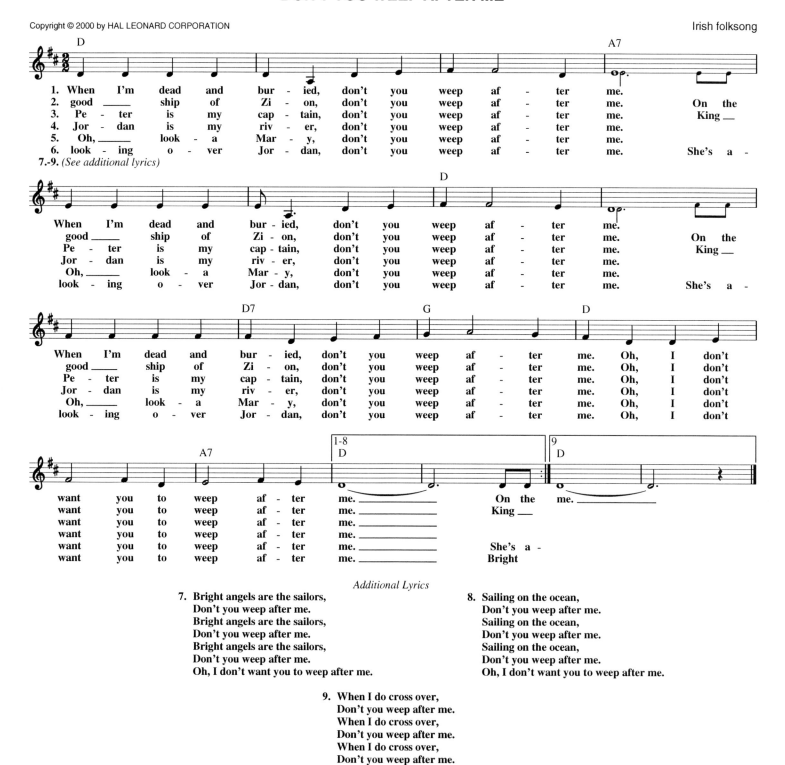

Additional Lyrics

7. Bright angels are the sailors,
Don't you weep after me.
Bright angels are the sailors,
Don't you weep after me.
Bright angels are the sailors,
Don't you weep after me.
Oh, I don't want you to weep after me.

8. Sailing on the ocean,
Don't you weep after me.
Sailing on the ocean,
Don't you weep after me.
Sailing on the ocean,
Don't you weep after me.
Oh, I don't want you to weep after me.

9. When I do cross over,
Don't you weep after me.
When I do cross over,
Don't you weep after me.
When I do cross over,
Don't you weep after me.
Oh, I don't want you to weep after me.

DOWN BY THE SALLEY GARDENS

Irish folksong
Words by William Butler Yeats

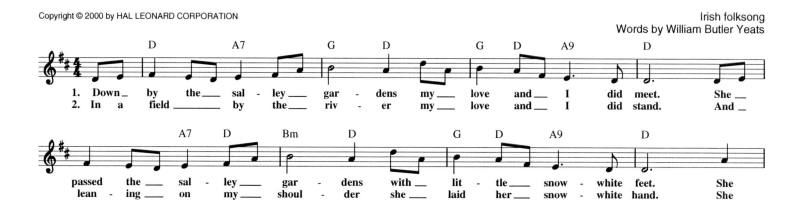

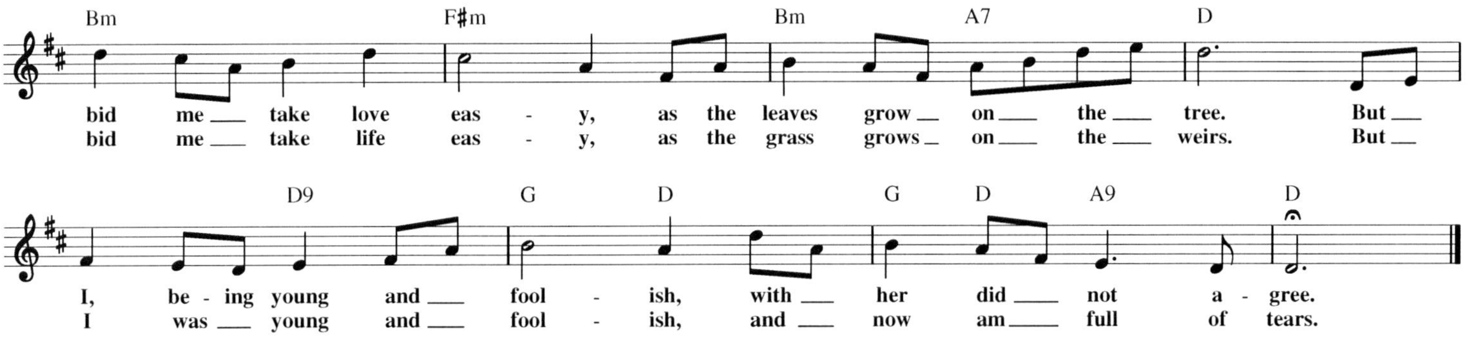

bid me __ take love eas - y, as the leaves grow __ on __ the __ tree. But __
bid me __ take life eas - y, as the grass grows __ on __ the __ weirs. But __

I, be - ing young and __ fool - ish, with __ her did __ not a - gree.
I was __ young and __ fool - ish, and now am __ full of tears.

THE DOWERLESS MAIDEN
(Gun Chrodh, Gun Aighean)

Folksong from the Hebrides

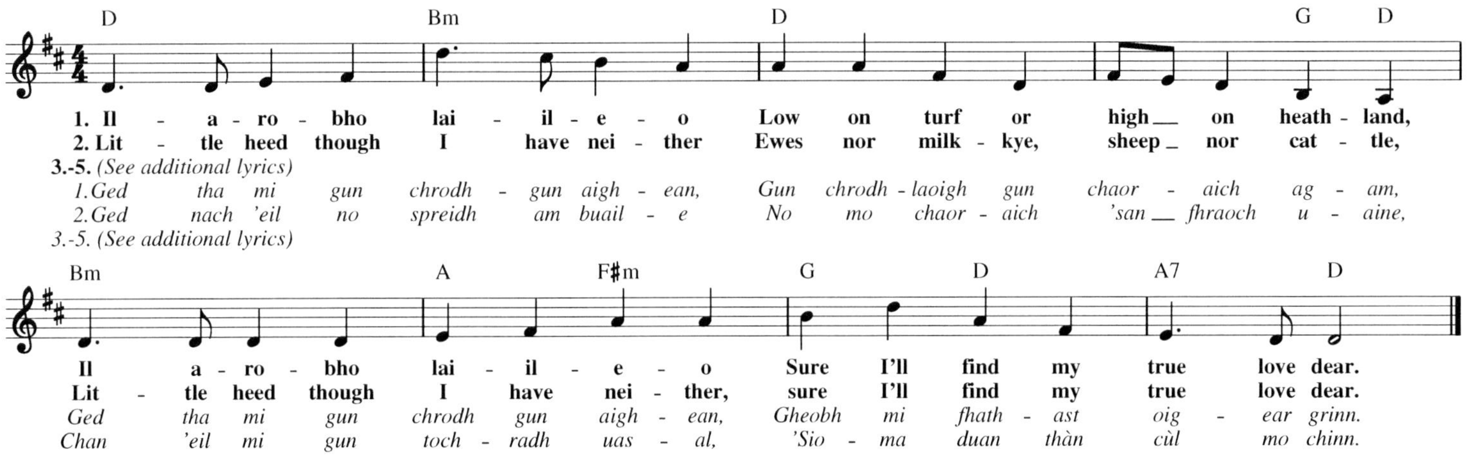

1. Il - a - ro - bho lai - il - e - o Low on turf or high __ on heath - land,
2. Lit - tle heed though I have nei - ther Ewes nor milk - kye, sheep __ nor cat - tle,

1. Ged tha mi gun chrodh - gun aigh - ean, Gun chrodh - laoigh gun chaor - aich ag - am,
2. Ged nach 'eil no spreidh am buail - e No mo chaor - aich 'san __ fhraoch u - aine,

3.-5. *(See additional lyrics)*

Il a - ro - bho lai - il - e - o Sure I'll find my true love dear.
Lit - tle heed though I have nei - ther, sure I'll find my true love dear.

Ged tha mi gun chrodh gun aigh - ean, Gheobh mi fhath - ast oig - ear grinn.
Chan 'eil mi gun toch - radh uas - al, 'Sio - ma duan thàn cùl mo chinn.

3.-5. *(See additional lyrics)*

Additional Lyrics

3. **Ilarabho laiileo**
   High on crag or low on moorland
   I larabho laiileo
   Sure I'll find my true love dear.

4. **Ne'er was wealth o'kine on upland,**
   Sheep or goat on rock or shoreland,
   Aught to me, and my own dear one
   Far away on stormy seas

5. **Ilarobho laiileo**
   High on cragland low on moorland
   Silarobho laiileo
   Sure I'll find my true love dear.

3. *Ged tha mi gun chrodh gun aighean*
   Gun chrodhlaoigh gun chaoraich agam
   Ged tha mi gun chrodh gun aighean
   Gheobh mi fhathast òigear grinn.

4. *Fhir a dh'imicheas thar cuantan,*
   Giulain mile beannachd uamsa,
   Dh'ionnsuidh oigear a'chuil dualaich,
   Ged nach d'fhuair mi e dhomh fhin.

5. *Ged tha mi gun chrodh gun aighean*
   Gun chrodhlaoigh gun chaoraich agam
   Ged tha mi gun chrodh gun aighean,
   Gheobb mi fhathast òigear grinn.

DROWSY MAGGIE

Irish folksong

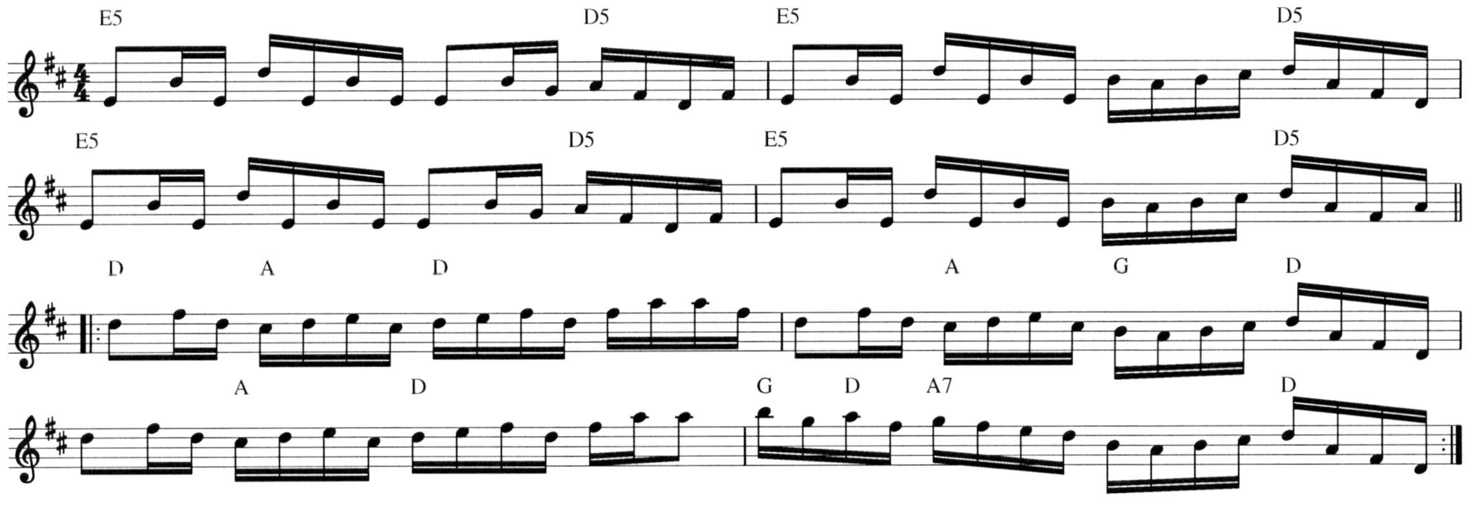

DOWN WENT McGINTY

Words and Music by
Joseph Flynn

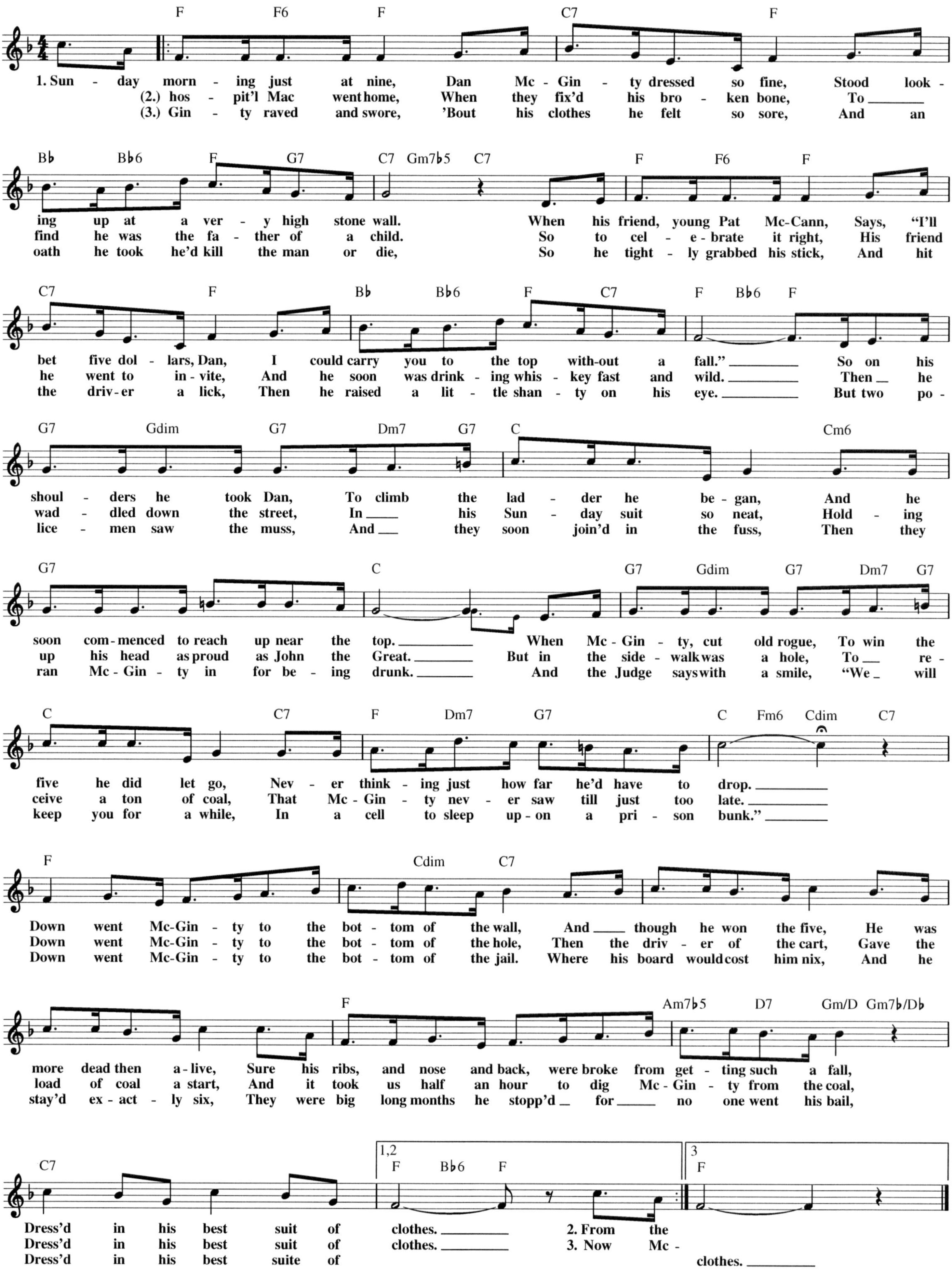

THE DOWIE DENS OF YARROW

Scottish folksong

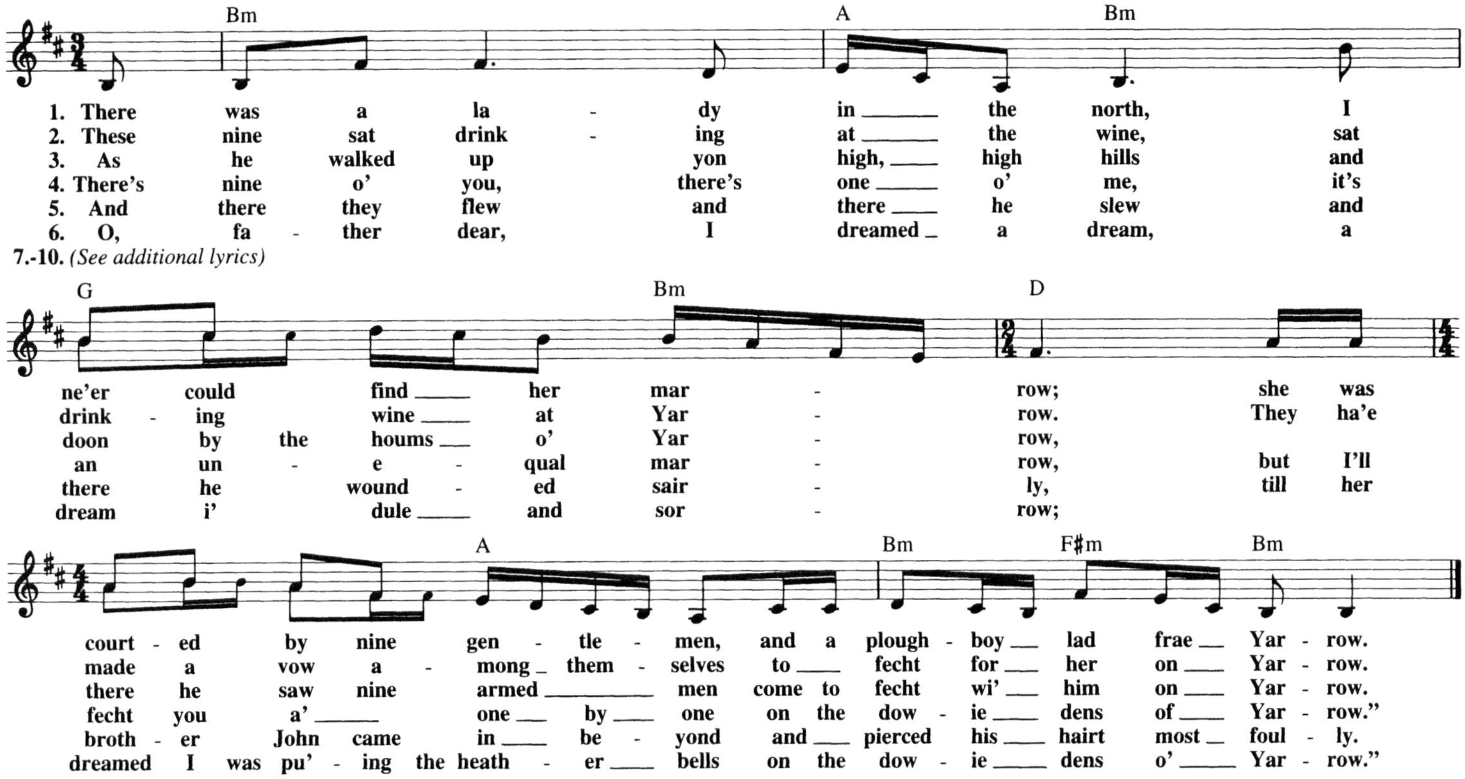

1. There was a la - dy in ____ the north, I
2. These nine sat drink - ing at ____ the wine, sat
3. As he walked up yon high, ____ high hills and
4. There's nine o' you, there's one ____ o' me, it's
5. And there they flew and there ____ he slew and
6. O, fa - ther dear, I dreamed __ a dream, a

7.-10. *(See additional lyrics)*

ne'er could find ____ her mar - row; she was
drink - ing wine ____ at Yar - row. They ha'e
doon by the houms ___ o' Yar - row,
an un - e - qual mar - row, but I'll
there he wound - ed sair - ly, till her
dream i' dule ____ and sor - row;

court - ed by nine gen - tle - men, and a plough - boy __ lad frae ____ Yar - row.
made a vow a - mong __ them - selves to ____ fecht for ____ her on ____ Yar - row.
there he saw nine armed _____ men come to fecht wi' ____ him on ____ Yar - row.
fecht you a' ____ one by ____ one on the dow - ie ____ dens of ____ Yar - row."
broth - er John came in ____ be - yond and ____ pierced his ____ hairt most __ foul - ly.
dreamed I was pu' - ing the heath - er ____ bells on the dow - ie ____ dens o' ____ Yar - row."

Additional Lyrics

7. "O, dochter dear, I read your dream,
   I doubt it will bring sorrow,
   For your lover John lies pale and wan
   On the dowie dens o' Yarrow."

8. As she walked up yon high, high hill
   And doon by the houms o' Yarrow,
   There she saw her lover dear
   Lying pale and wan on yarrow.

9. Her hair it being three-quarters long,
   The colour it was yellow,
   She wrappit it roond his middle sae sma'
   And bore him doon to Yarrow.

10. "O, father dear, ye've seiven sons,
    Ye may wed them a tomorrow,
    But the fairest flooer amang them a'
    Was the lad I wooed on Yarrow."

A DRUID OF THE ISLES

Folksong from the Hebrides

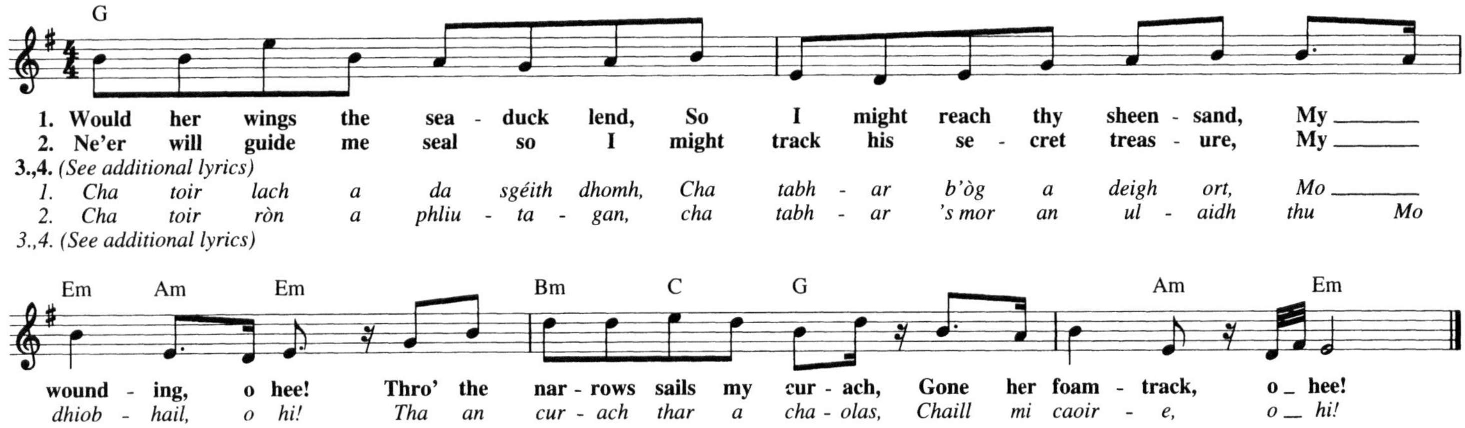

1. Would her wings the sea - duck lend, So I might reach thy sheen - sand, My ____
2. Ne'er will guide me seal so I might track his se - cret treas - ure, My ____

3.,4. *(See additional lyrics)*

1. Cha toir lach a da sgéith dhomh, Cha tabh - ar b'òg a deigh ort, Mo ____
2. Cha toir ròn a phliu - ta - gan, cha tabh - ar 's mor an ul - aidh thu Mo

3.,4. *(See additional lyrics)*

wound - ing, o hee! Thro' the nar - rows sails my cur - ach, Gone her foam - track, o __ hee!
dhiob - hail, o hi! Tha an cur - ach thar a cha - olas, Chaill mi caoir - e, o __ hi!

Additional Lyrics

3. Water gat I from thy cool streams,
   Cresses sweet from Odhran.
   My wounding, o hee!
   Thro' the narrows sails my curach,
   Gone her foam-track, o hee!

4. Pith and strength from Carnan gat I,
   Music sweet from Trah-Bàn.
   Thro' the narrows sails my curach,
   Gone her foam-track, o hee!

*3. Thug an tobair fuar burn domh,
   'S Odhran biolair ur domh.
   Mo dhiobhail, o hi!
   Tha an curach thara chaolas,
   Chaill mi caoire, o hi!*

*4. Thug an Carnan li is luth dhomh,
   Rinn an Traigh-Bàn nuall domh
   Mo dhiobhail, o hi!
   Tha an curach thar a chaolas,
   Chaill mi caoir-e, o hi!*

THE DUBLIN STAGE

Irish folksong

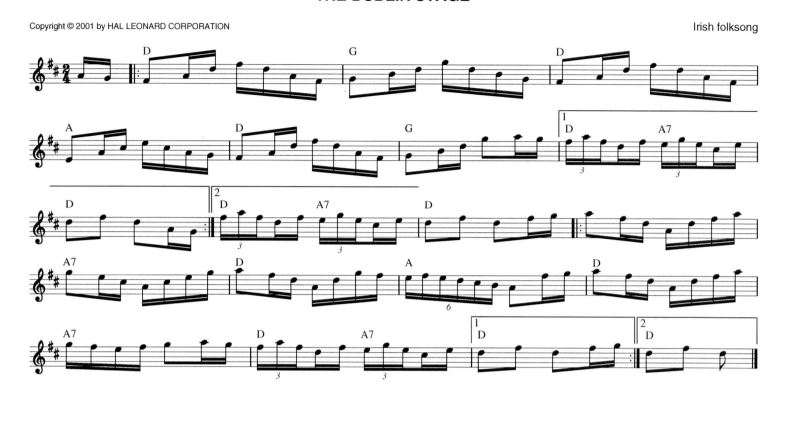

A DUNVEGAN DIRGE
(Cha tig Mór)

Folksong from the Hebrides

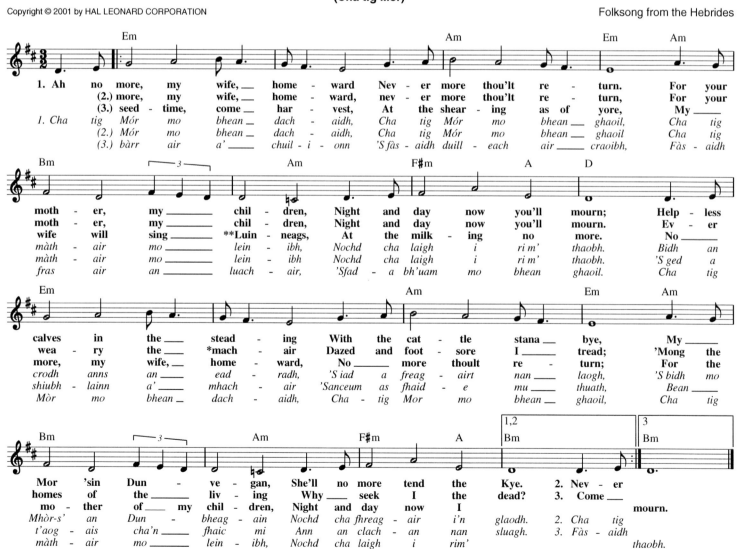

Machair - wide stretch of sandy shore.

**Luinneag - a ditty*

DUFFY'S BLUNDERS

Words and Music by
Joseph Flynn

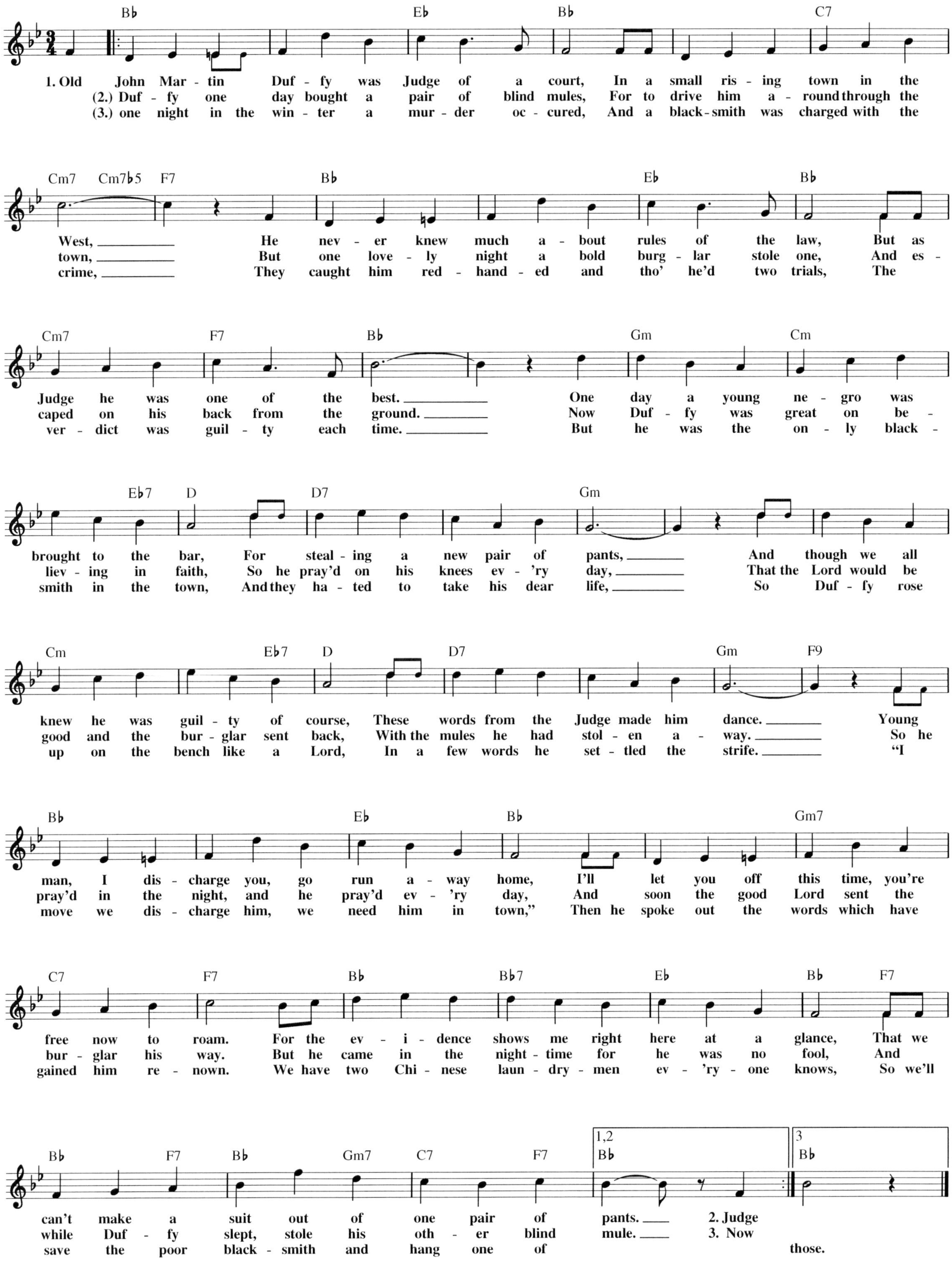
B♭ E♭ B♭ C7
1. Old John Mar - tin Duf - fy was Judge of a court, In a small ris - ing town in the
(2.) Duf - fy one day bought a pair of blind mules, For to drive him a - round through the
(3.) one night in the win - ter a mur - der oc - cured, And a black - smith was charged with the
Cm7 Cm7♭5 F7 B♭ E♭ B♭
West, He nev - er knew much a - bout rules of the law, But as
town, But one love - ly night a bold burg - lar stole one, And es -
crime, They caught him red - hand - ed and tho' he'd two trials, The
Cm7 F7 B♭ Gm Cm
Judge he was one of the best. One day a young ne - gro was
caped on his back from the ground. Now Duf - fy was great on be -
ver - dict was guil - ty each time. But he was the on - ly black -
E♭7 D D7 Gm
brought to the bar, For steal - ing a new pair of pants, And though we all
liev - ing in faith, So he pray'd on his knees ev - 'ry day, That the Lord would be
smith in the town, And they ha - ted to take his dear life, So Duf - fy rose
Cm E♭7 D D7 Gm F9
knew he was guil - ty of course, These words from the Judge made him dance. Young
good and the bur - glar sent back, With the mules he had stol - en a - way. So he
up on the bench like a Lord, In a few words he set - tled the strife. "I
B♭ E♭ B♭ Gm7
man, I dis - charge you, go run a - way home, I'll let you off this time, you're
pray'd in the night, and he pray'd ev - 'ry day, And soon the good Lord sent the
move we dis - charge him, we need him in town," Then he spoke out the words which have
C7 F7 B♭ B♭7 E♭ B♭ F7
free now to roam. For the ev - i - dence shows me right here at a glance, That we
bur - glar his way. But he came in the night - time for he was no fool, And
gained him re - nown. We have two Chi - nese laun - dry - men ev - 'ry - one knows, So we'll
B♭ F7 B♭ Gm7 C7 F7 1,2 B♭ 3 B♭
can't make a suit out of one pair of pants. 2. Judge
while Duf - fy slept, stole his oth - er blind mule. 3. Now
save the poor black - smith and hang one of those.

DUMBARTON'S DRUMS

Scottish folksong

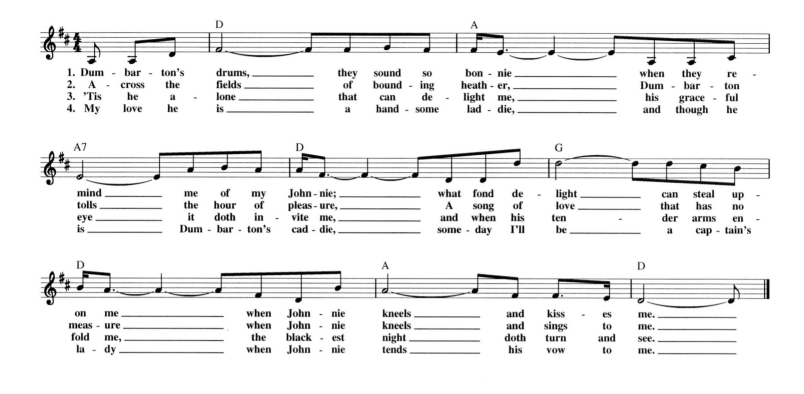

1. Dum - bar - ton's drums, _____ they sound so bon - nie _____ when they re -
2. A - cross the fields _____ of bound - ing heath - er, _____ Dum - bar - ton
3. 'Tis he a - lone _____ that can de - light me, _____ his grace - ful
4. My love he is _____ a hand - some lad - die, _____ and though he

mind _____ me of my John - nie; _____ what fond de - light _____ can steal up -
tolls _____ the hour of pleas - ure, _____ A song of love _____ that has no
eye _____ it doth in - vite me, _____ and when his ten - der arms en -
is _____ Dum - bar - ton's cad - die, _____ some - day I'll be _____ a cap - tain's

on me _____ when John - nie kneels _____ and kiss - es me. _____
meas - ure _____ when John - nie kneels _____ and sings to me. _____
fold me, _____ the black - est night _____ doth turn and see. _____
la - dy _____ when John - nie tends _____ his vow to me. _____

ÉAMANN AN CHNOIC

Irish folksong

1. Cé _ hé sin a - muigh, A bhfuil faobhar ar a ghuth, Ag réa - bahd mo dhor - ais _ dhún -
2. (See additional lyrics)

ta? Mi - se Éam - ann a' Chnoic A - tá bái - te fuar fliuch Ó _ shior - shiúl _ shébh - te s' gleann -

ta! A lao dhil s'a chuid Cad a dhéanfa - inn - se dhuit, Mu - na gcuirf - inn ort be - inn de m'

ghú - ne, 'S go bhfuil pú - dar go tiubh, Dá _ shior-shéi-deadh leat 'S go mbeim-is a - raon _ múch - ta.

Additional Lyrics

2. Is fada mise amuigh
   Faoi shneachta is faoi shioc
   'S gan dánacht agam ar aon neach;
   Mo sheireach gan scor,
   Mo bhranar gan chur,
   Is gan iad agam ar aon chor!
   Níl caraid agam
   Is danaid liom san,
   Do ghlacfadh mé moch ná déanach,
   'S go gcaithfidh mé dul
   That farraige soir
   Ó is ann ná fuil aon de m' ghaoltaibh.

THE EARL OF MORAY

Irish folksong

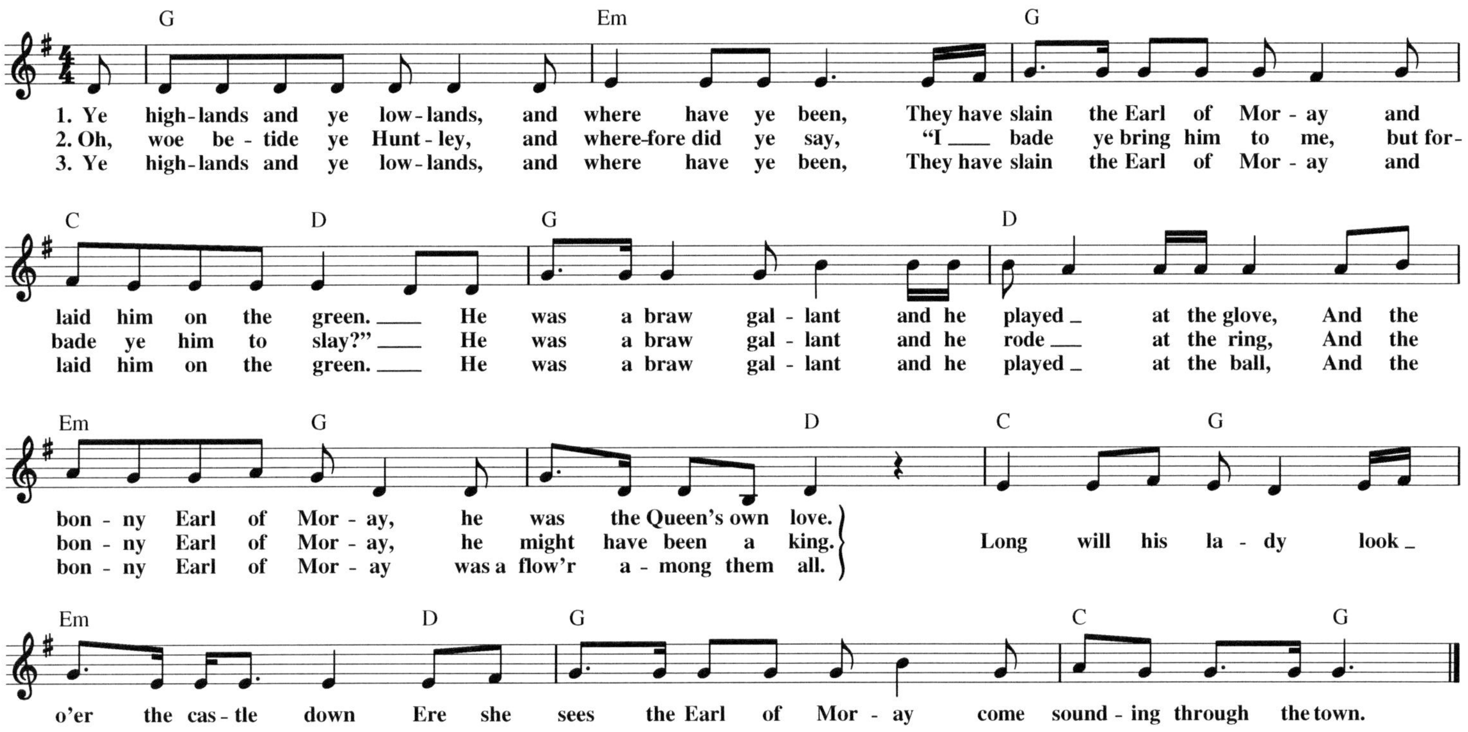

1. Ye high-lands and ye low-lands, and where have ye been, They have slain the Earl of Mor-ay and
2. Oh, woe be-tide ye Hunt-ley, and where-fore did ye say, "I __ bade ye bring him to me, but for-
3. Ye high-lands and ye low-lands, and where have ye been, They have slain the Earl of Mor-ay and

laid him on the green. __ He was a braw gal-lant and he played __ at the glove, And the
bade ye him to slay?" __ He was a braw gal-lant and he rode __ at the ring, And the
laid him on the green. __ He was a braw gal-lant and he played __ at the ball, And the

bon-ny Earl of Mor-ay, he was the Queen's own love.) Long will his la-dy look __
bon-ny Earl of Mor-ay, he might have been a king.}
bon-ny Earl of Mor-ay was a flow'r a-mong them all.)

o'er the cas-tle down Ere she sees the Earl of Mor-ay come sound-ing through the town.

ERIN! OH ERIN!

Irish popular song
Words by Thomas Moore

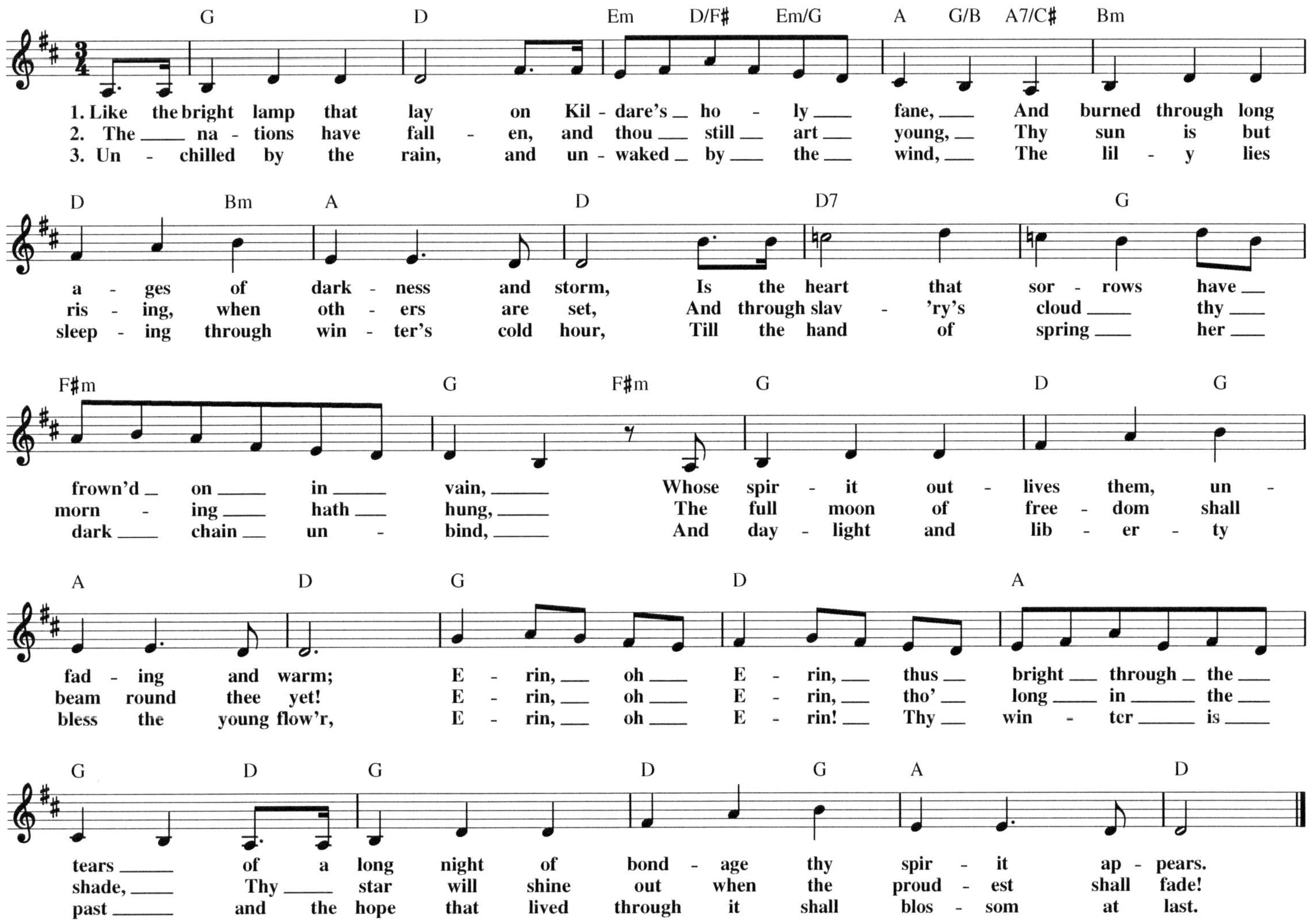

1. Like the bright lamp that lay on Kil-dare's __ ho - ly __ fane, __ And burned through long
2. The __ na - tions have fall - en, and thou __ still __ art __ young, __ Thy sun is but
3. Un - chilled by the rain, and un - waked __ by __ the __ wind, __ The lil - y lies

a - ges of dark - ness and storm, Is the heart that sor - rows have __
ris - ing, when oth - ers are set, And through slav - 'ry's cloud __ thy __
sleep - ing through win - ter's cold hour, Till the hand of spring __ her __

frown'd __ on __ in __ vain, __ Whose spir - it out - lives them, un -
morn - ing __ hath __ hung, __ The full moon of free - dom shall
dark __ chain un - bind, __ And day - light and lib - er - ty

fad - ing and warm; E - rin, __ oh __ E - rin, __ thus __ bright __ through __ the
beam round thee yet! E - rin, __ oh __ E - rin, __ tho' __ long __ in __ the
bless the young flow'r, E - rin, __ oh __ E - rin! __ Thy __ win - ter __ is

tears __ of a long night of bond - age thy spir - it ap - pears.
shade, __ Thy __ star will shine out when the proud - est shall fade!
past __ and the hope that lived through it shall blos - som at last.

THE EASTER REBELLION

Irish folksong

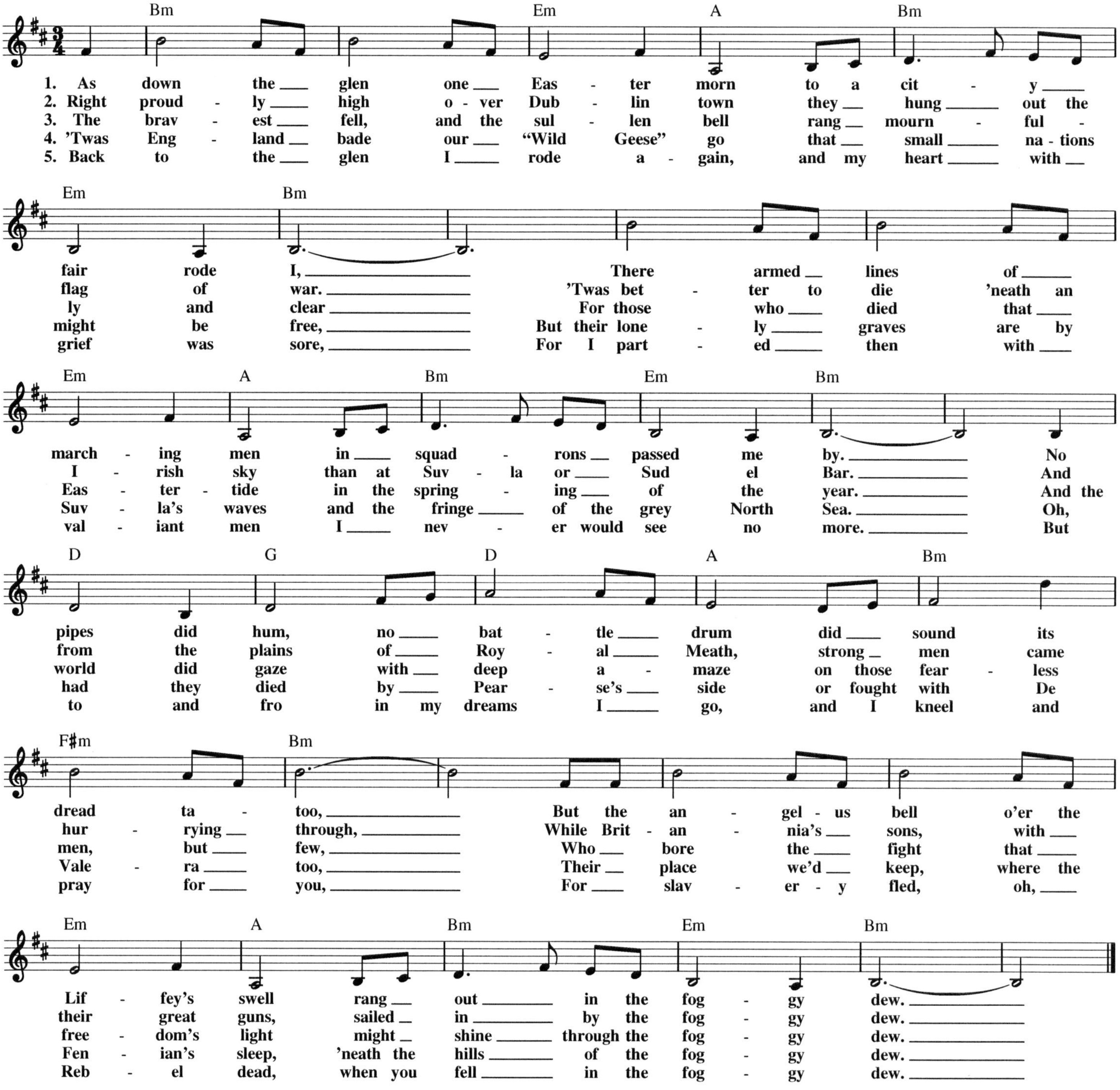

1. As down the ___ glen one ___ Eas - ter morn to a cit - y ___
2. Right proud - ly high o - ver Dub - lin town they ___ hung _____ out the
3. The brav - est ___ fell, and the sul - len bell rang ___ mourn - ful -
4. 'Twas Eng - land ___ bade our ___ "Wild Geese" go that ___ small na - tions
5. Back to the ___ glen I ___ rode a - gain, and my heart _____ with ___

fair rode I, _____ There armed ___ lines of _____
flag of war. _____ 'Twas bet - ter to die 'neath an
ly and clear _____ For those who ___ died that ___
might be free, _____ But their lone - ly ___ graves are by
grief was sore, _____ For I part - ed ___ then with ___

march - ing men in ___ squad - rons ___ passed me by. _____ No
I - rish sky than at Suv - la or ___ Sud el Bar. _____ And
Eas - ter - tide in the spring - ing of the year. _____ And the
Suv - la's waves and the fringe _____ of the grey North Sea. _____ Oh,
val - iant men I ___ nev - er would see no more. _____ But

pipes did hum, no ___ bat - tle ___ drum did ___ sound its
from the plains of ___ Roy - al ___ Meath, strong ___ men came
world did gaze with ___ deep a - maze on those fear - less
had they died by ___ Pear - se's ___ side or fought with De
to and fro in my dreams I ___ go, and I kneel and

dread ta - too, _____ But the an - gel - us bell o'er the
hur - rying ___ through, _____ While Brit - an - nia's sons, with
Vale - ra ___ too, _____ Their ___ place we'd ___ keep, where the
pray for ___ you, _____ For ___ slav - er - y fled, oh,
Reb - el dead, when you fell _____ in the

Lif - fey's swell rang ___ out _____ in the fog - gy dew. _____
their great guns, sailed ___ in _____ by the fog - gy dew. _____
free - dom's light might ___ shine _____ through the fog - gy dew. _____
Fen - ian's sleep, 'neath the hills _____ of the fog - gy dew. _____
Reb - el dead, when you fell _____ in the fog - gy dew. _____

EILEEN OGE

Irish folksong
Words by Percy French

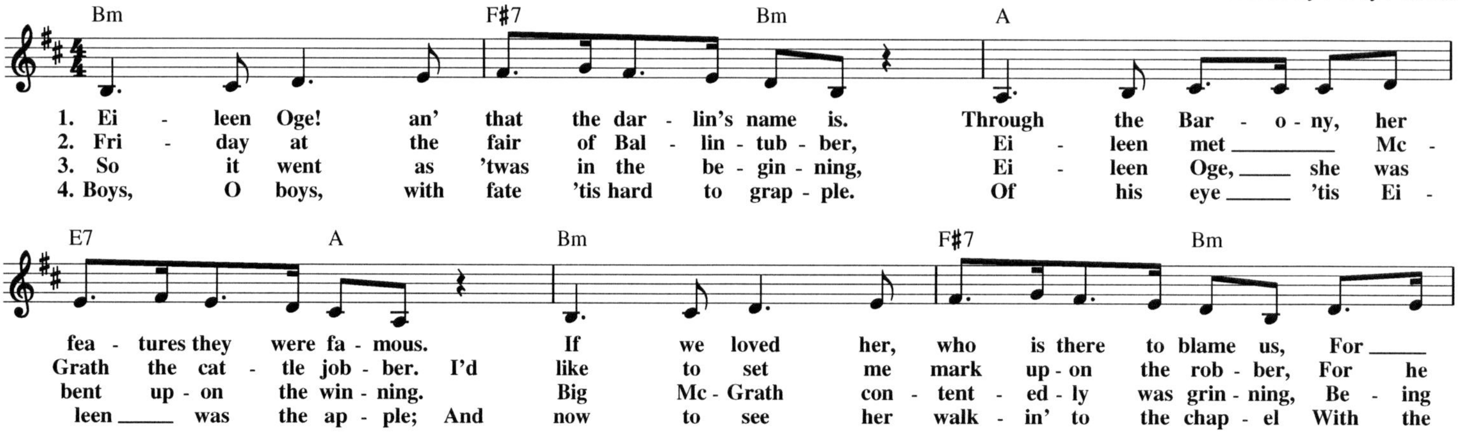

1. Ei - leen Oge! an' that the dar - lin's name is. Through the Bar - o - ny, her
2. Fri - day at the fair of Bal - lin - tub - ber, Ei - leen met Mc
3. So it went as 'twas in the be - gin - ning, Ei - leen Oge, ___ she was
4. Boys, O boys, with fate 'tis hard to grap - ple. Of his eye ___ 'tis Ei

fea - tures they were fa - mous. If we loved her, who is there to blame us, For ___
Grath the cat - tle job - ber. I'd like to set me mark up - on the rob - ber, For he
bent up - on the win - ning. Big Mc - Grath con - tent - ed - ly was grin - ning, Be - ing
leen ___ was the ap - ple; And now to see her walk - in' to the chap - el With the

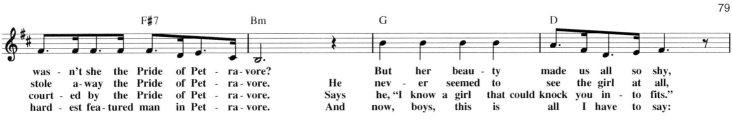

was - n't she the Pride of Pet - ra - vore? But her beau - ty made us all so shy,
stole a - way the Pride of Pet - ra - vore. He nev - er seemed to see the girl at all,
court - ed by the Pride of Pet - ra - vore. Says he, "I know a girl that could knock you in - to fits."
hard - est fea - tured man in Pet - ra - vore. And now, boys, this is all I have to say:

Not a man could look her in the eye. Boys, O boys! sure that's the rea - son why We're in
E - ven when she o-gled him un - der-neath her shawl. Look - in' big and mas-ter - ful when she was look - in' small, Most pro -
At that, Ei - leen near - ly lost her wits. The up - shot of the ruc-tion was that now the rob - ber sits With his
When you do your court - in', don't make a dis - play. If you want them to run af - ter you, just walk the oth - er way, For they're

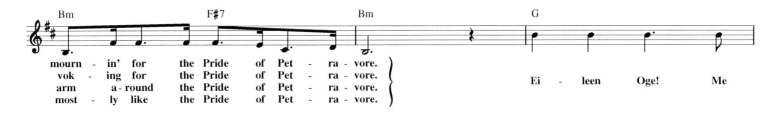

mourn - in' for the Pride of Pet - ra - vore.
vok - ing for the Pride of Pet - ra - vore.
arm a - round the Pride of Pet - ra - vore.
most - ly like the Pride of Pet - ra - vore. Ei - leen Oge! Me

heart is grow - in' grey, Ev - er since the day you wan - dered far a - way.

Ei - leen Oge! There's good fish in the say, But there's no one like the Pride of Pet - ra - vore.

EILEEN AROON

Irish folksong

1. I know a val - ley fair,
2. Who in the song so sweet,
3. Were she no long - er true,
4. Youth will in time de - cay,
Ei - leen __ A - roon;
I know a cot - tage there
Who in the dance so fleet,
What would her lov - er do,
Beau - ty must fade a - way
Ei -

leen __ A - roon,
Far in the val - ley shade
Dear are her charms to me,
Fly with a bro - ken chain,
Cas - tles are sacked in war,
I know a ten - der
dear - er her laugh - ter
far o'er the sound - ing
chief - tains are scat - tered

maid, Flow'r of __ the __ ha - zel glade,
free, Dear - est __ her __ con - stan - cy,
main, Nev - er __ to __ love a - gain,
far, Truth is __ a __ fixed __ star,
Ei - leen __ A - roon.

AN ERISKAY LOVE LILT
(Gradh Geal mo chridh)

Folksong from the Hebrides

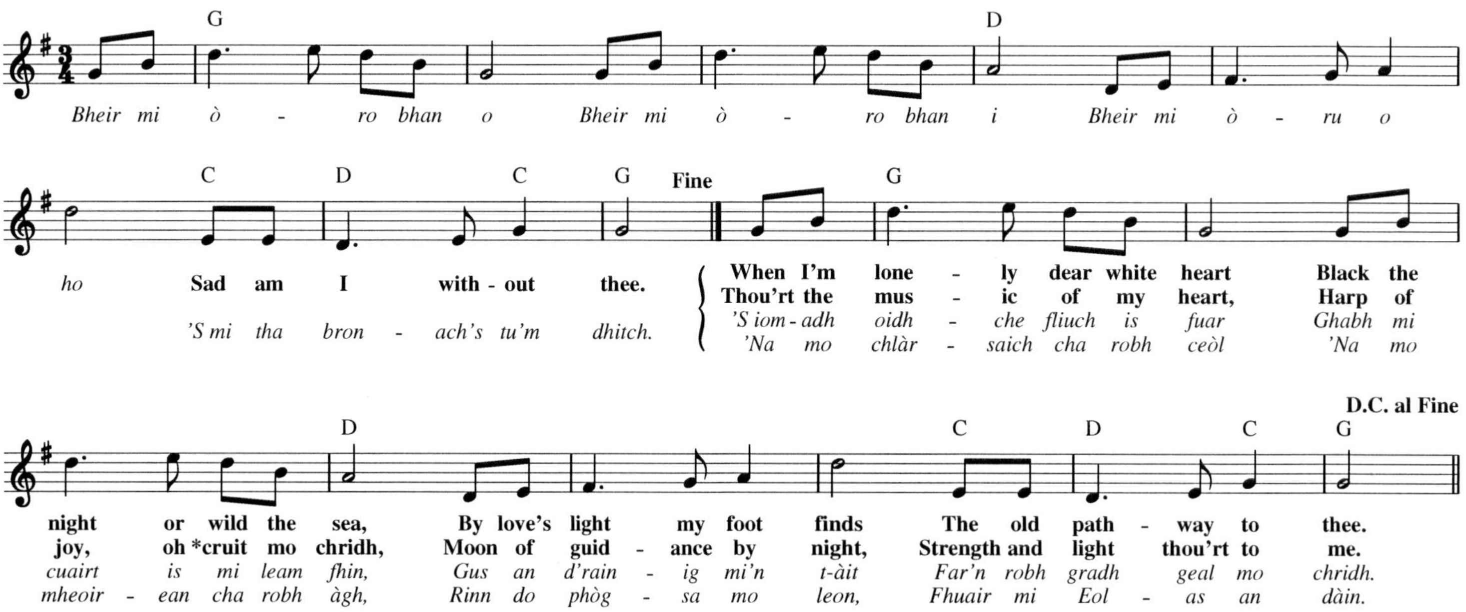

Bheir mi ò - ro bhan o Bheir mi ò - ro bhan i Bheir mi ò - ru o

ho Sad am I with - out thee.
'S mi tha bron - ach's tu'm dhitch.

When I'm lone - ly dear white heart
Thou'rt the mus - ic of my heart,
'S iom - adh oidh - che fliuch is fuar
'Na mo chlàr - saich cha robh ceòl

Black the
Harp of
Ghabh mi
'Na mo

D.C. al Fine

night or wild the sea, By love's light my foot finds The old path - way to thee.
joy, oh *cruit mo chridh, Moon of guid - ance by night, Strength and light thou'rt to me.
cuairt is mi leam fhin, Gus an d'rain - ig mi'n t-àit Far'n robh gradh geal mo chridh.
mheoir - ean cha robh àgh, Rinn do phòg - sa mo leon, Fhuair mi Eol - as an dàin.

*"Harp of my heart," pronounced "crootch mo chree."

AN ERISKAY LULLABY
(The Mermaid's Song)

Folksong from the Hebrides

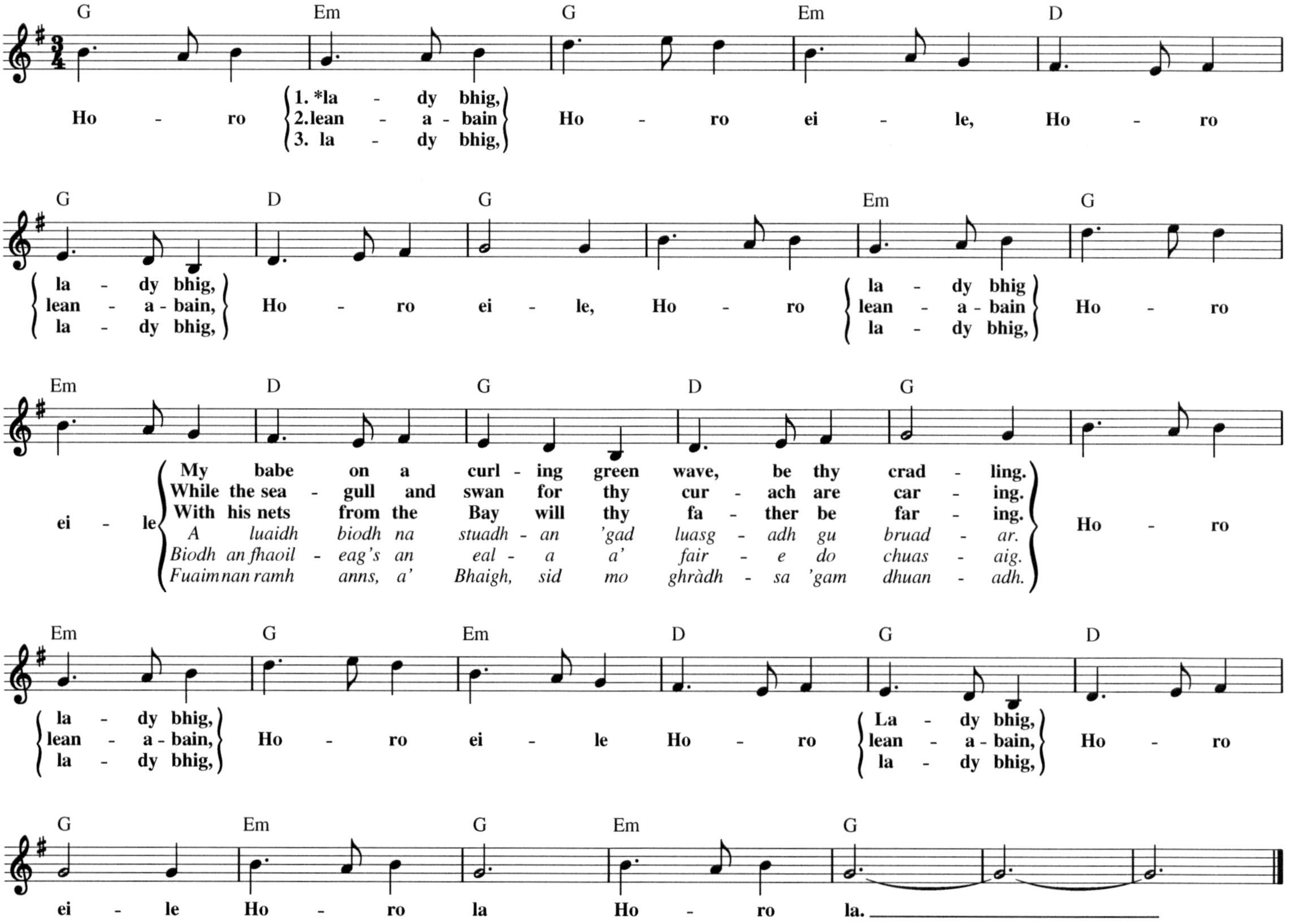

Ho - ro
1. *la - dy bhig,
2. lean - a - bain
3. la - dy bhig,
Ho - ro ei - le, Ho - ro

la - dy bhig,
lean - a - bain,
la - dy bhig,
Ho - ro ei - le, Ho - ro
la - dy bhig
lean - a - bain
la - dy bhig,
Ho - ro

ei - le
My babe on a curl - ing green wave, be thy crad - ling.
While the sea - gull and swan for thy cur - ach are car - ing.
With his nets from the Bay will thy fa - ther be far - ing.
A luaidh biodh na stuadh - an 'gad luasg - adh gu bruad - ar.
Biodh an fhaoil - eag's an eal - a a' fair - e do chuas - aig.
Fuaim nan ramh anns, a' Bhaigh, sid mo ghràdh - sa 'gam dhuan - adh.
Ho - ro

la - dy bhig,
lean - a - bain,
la - dy bhig,
Ho - ro ei - le Ho - ro
La - dy bhig,
lean - a - bain,
la - dy bhig,
Ho - ro

ei - le Ho - ro la Ho - ro la.

*"lady bhig" means "lady wee"; "leanabain" means "little child"

ETHNE'S CROON TO HER CHILD COLUMBA

Folksong from the Hebrides

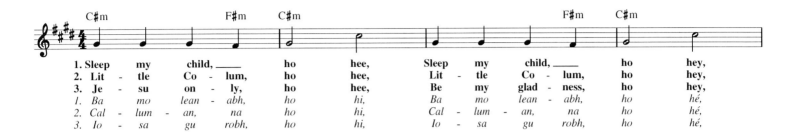

FAIR HARVARD

Irish folksong
Words by Samuel Gilman

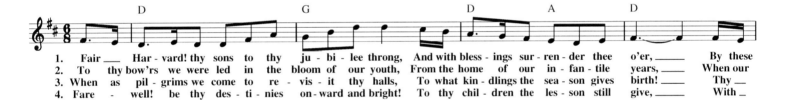

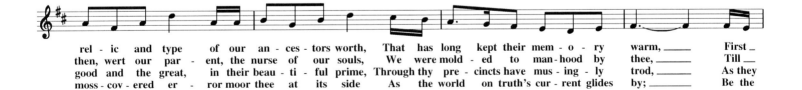

THE FAIR HILLS OF ÉIRE O!

Irish folksong

1. Take a bless-ing from my heart ___ to the land of my birth, And the
2. The ___ soil is rich and soft, ___ the ___ air is mild and bland Of the
3. A ___ fruit-ful clime is Éire's, ___ through ___ val-ley, mead-ow, plane, And the

fair ___ hills of Éir - e ___ O! And to all that sur-vive ___ of ___
fair ___ hills of Éir - e ___ O! Her ___ bar-est rock is green-er to
fair ___ hills of Éir - e ___ O! The ___ ver-y bread of life ___ is ___

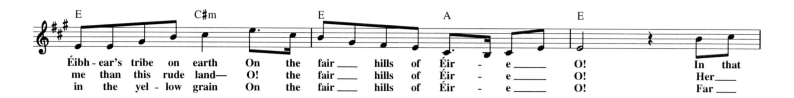

Éibh-ear's tribe on earth On the fair ___ hills of Éir - e ___ O! In that
me than this rude land— O! the fair ___ hills of Éir - e ___ O! Her ___
in the yel-low grain On the fair ___ hills of Éir - e ___ O! Far ___

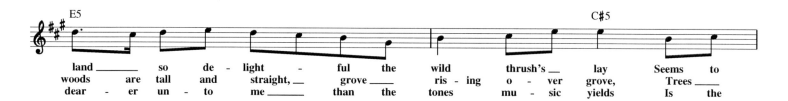

land ___ so de-light-ful the wild thrush's ___ lay Seems to
woods are tall and straight, ___ grove ___ ris-ing o-ver grove, Trees ___
dear-er un-to me ___ than the tones mu-sic yields Is the

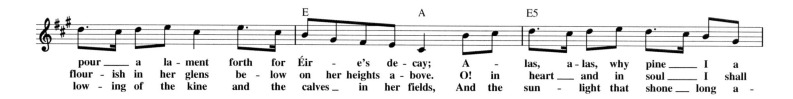

pour ___ a la-ment forth for Éir-e's de-cay; A - las, a-las, why pine ___ I a
flour-ish in her glens be-low on her heights a-bove. O! in heart ___ and in soul ___ I shall
low-ing of the kine and the calves ___ in her fields, And the sun-light that shone ___ long a -

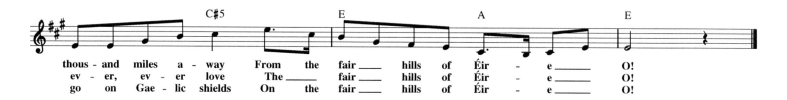

thous-and miles a-way From the fair ___ hills of Éir - e ___ O!
ev-er, ev-er love The ___ fair ___ hills of Éir - e ___ O!
go on Gae-lic shields On the fair ___ hills of Éir - e ___ O!

Gaelic Lyrics

1. *Beir beannacht óm chroí go tír na h-Éireann, Bán-chnuic Éireann Ó!*
Chun a maireann de shólra Ír is Éibhir Ar bhán-chnuic Éireann Ó!
An áit úd 'n-ar bh'aoibhinn binn-ghuth éan
Mar shámb-chruit chaoin a'caoine Gaodhal;
'Sé mo chás bheith míle míl' i gcéin Ó bhán-chnuic Éireann Ó!

2. *Bionn barr bog slím ar chaoin-chnuic Éireann, Bán-chnuic Éireann Ó!*
'S is fearr ná'n tír seo diogha gach sléibh'ann, Bán-chnuic Éireann Ó!
Dob árd a coillte 's ba dhíreach réidh,
'S a mbláth mar aol ar mhaoilinn géag,
Tá grá am chroi im inntinn féin Do bhán-chnuic Éireann Ó!

3. *Is osgailte fáilteach an áit sin Éire, Bán-chnuic Éireann Ó!*
'Gus tora na sláinte i mbarr na déise I mbán-chnuic Éireann Ó!
Ba bhinne ná méar' ar théadaibh ceóil
Seinm is géimre a laogh 's a mbó
Agus taithnemh na gréine orra, aosda 's óg, Ar bhán-chnuic Éireann Ó!

A FAIRY PLAINT
(Ceol-brutha)

Folksong from the Hebrides

1. I am sad, O lit - tle sis - ter;
2. Low my hut is low ____ and nar - row, } O hi O hu ____ O ho.

3.,4. *(See additional lyrics)*

1. Nach truagh leat fhein phiùth - rag a phiuth - ar
2. 'S mi - se bhean bhochd chian - ail dhub - hach } *O hi O hu ____ O ho.*

3.,4. *(See additional lyrics)*

Pi - ty me, O lit - tle sis - ter.
Want - ing wisp o' thatch ____ or heath - rope. } O hi O hu ____ O ho.

Nach truagh leat fhein nochd ____ mo chumh - a
Mi'm both - an beag io - sal cumh - ann } *O hi O hu ____ O ho.*

Additional Lyrics

3. The hill waters streamsweep through it,
   O hi O hu O ho.
   Cold hill waters streamsweep through it,
   O hi O hu O ho.

4. But not that my cause of sorrow,
   O hi O hu O ho.
   'Tis not that my cause of sorrow,
   O hi O hu O ho.

3. *Gun lùb siomain gun sop tughaibh*
   O hi O hu O ho.
   Uisge nam beann sios 'na shruth leis
   O hi O hu O ho.

4. *Ged's oil leam sin cha'n e chreach mi*
   O hi O hu O ho.
   Cha'n e chuir mi cha'n e fhras mi.
   O hi O hu O ho.

A FAIRY'S LOVE SONG
(Tha mi sgith)

Folksong from the Hebrides

Why should I sit and sigh, Pu - in' brack - en, pu - in' brack - en, Why should I sit and sigh
Tha mi sgith 's mi leam fhin Buain a rain - ich, buain a rain - ich Tha mi sgith 's mi leam fhin

On the hill - side drea - ry? When I see the plov - er ris - ing Or the cur - lew wheel - ing,
Buain a rain - ich daonn - an. Cul an tom - ain braigh an tom - ain Cul an tom - ain bhoidh - ich

Then I trow my mor - tal lov - er Back to me is steal - ing. Why should I sit and sigh,
Cul an tom - ain braigh an tom - ain H-uil - e lath - a m'òn - ar. Tha mi sgith 's mi leam fhin

Pu - in' brack - en, pu - in' brack - en, Why should I sit and sigh All a - lone and wea - ry?
Buain a rain - ich buain a rain - ich, Tha mi sgith 'smi leam fhin Buain a rain - ich daonn - an.

FAREWELL, NANCY

Irish folksong

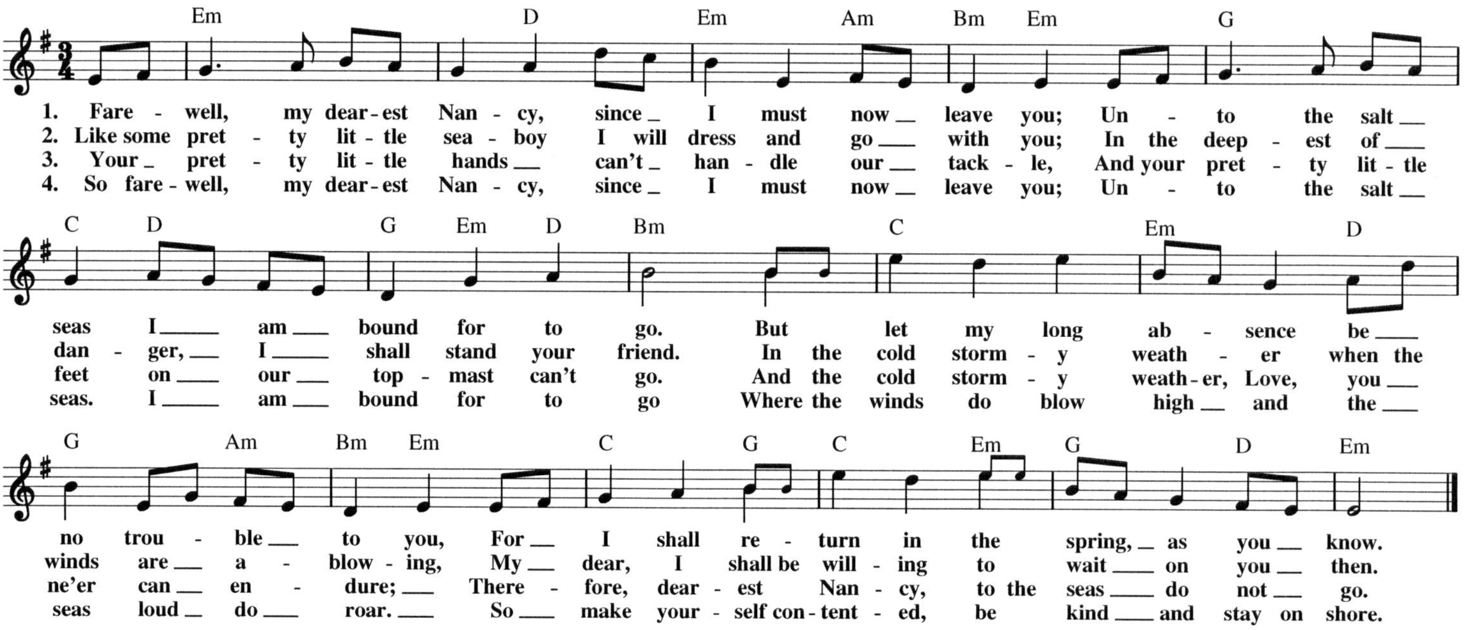

THE FATE CROON

Folksong from the Hebrides

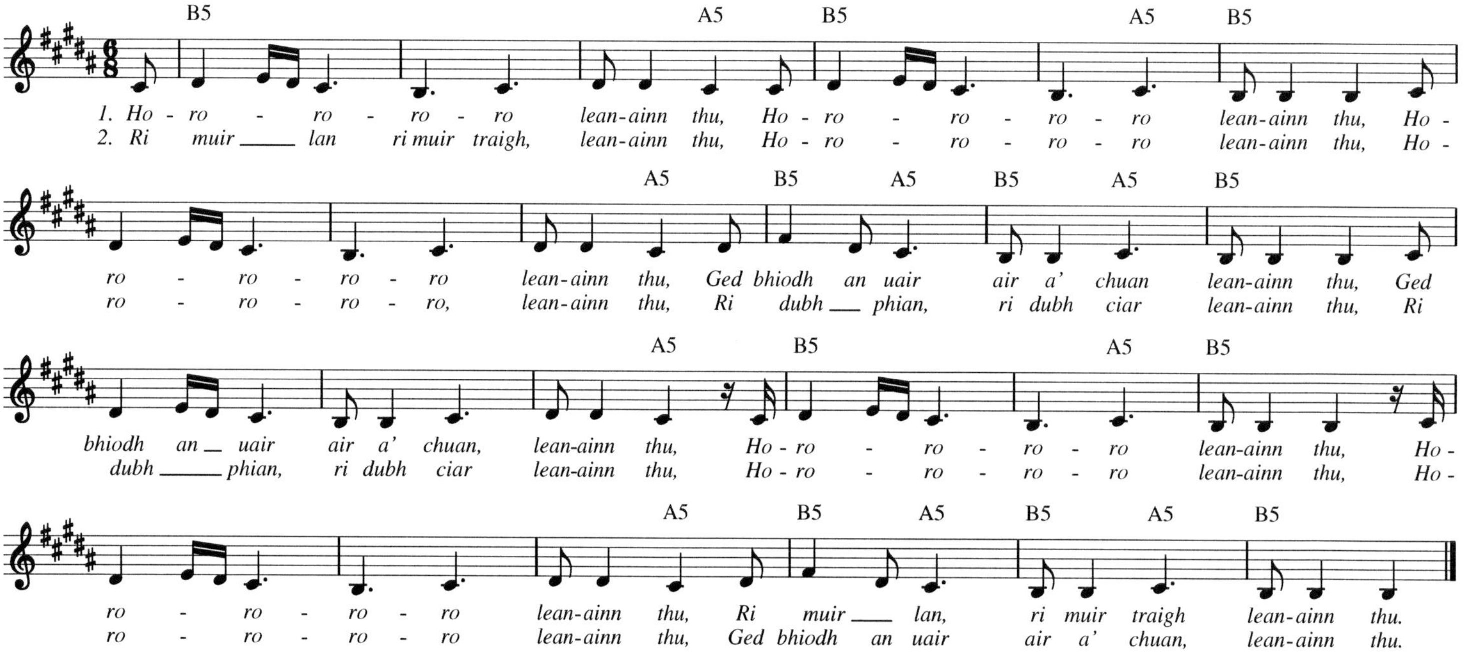

FAREWELL TO THE MAIGUE

Irish folksong

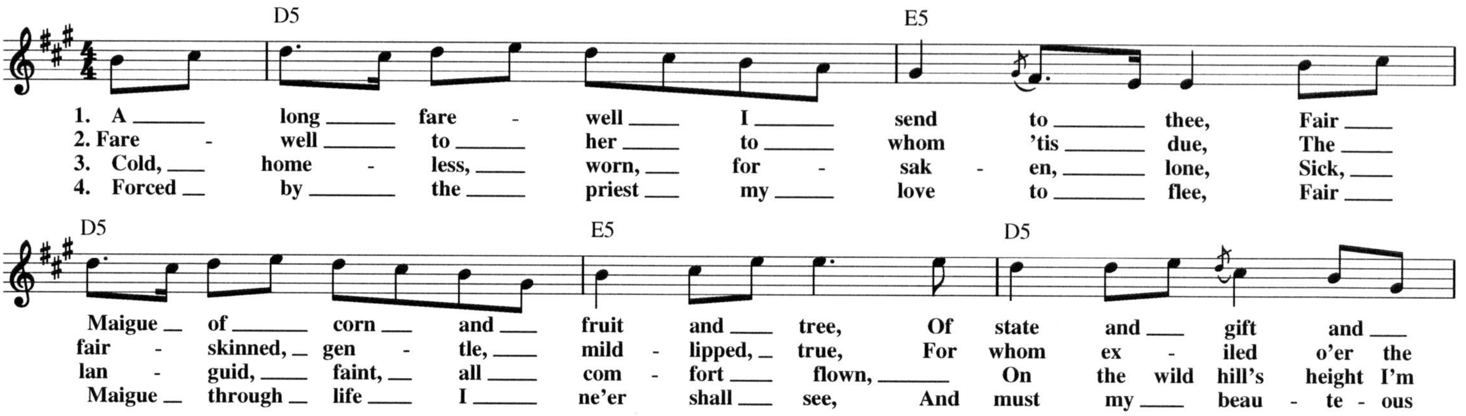

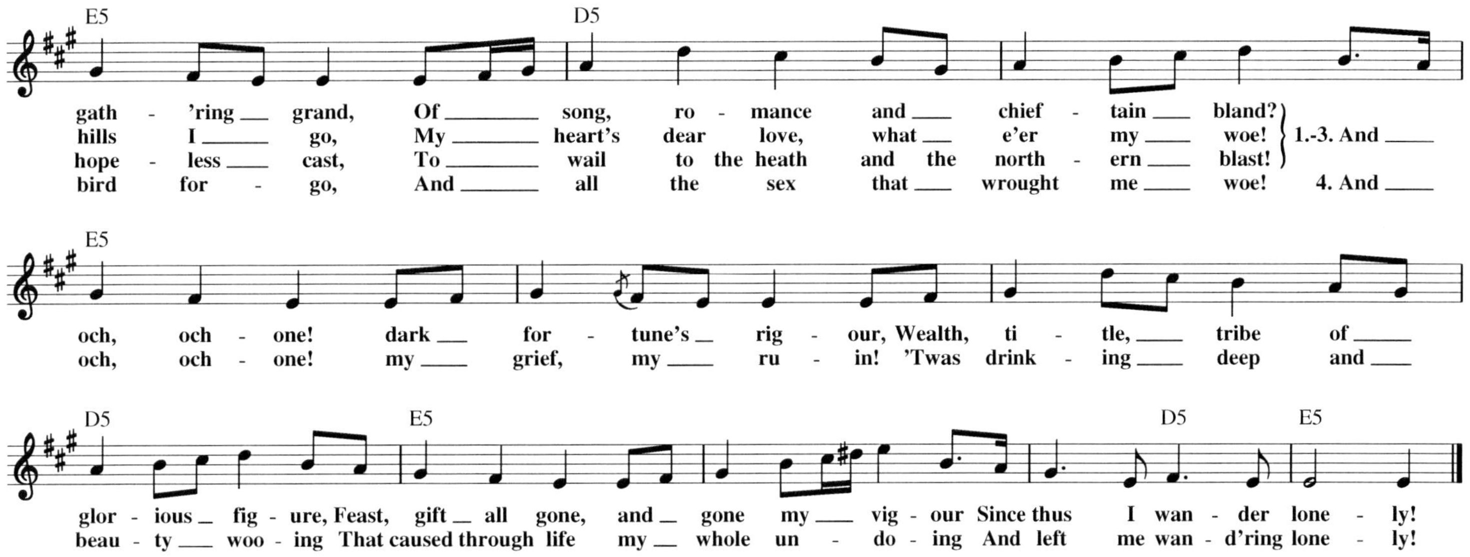

Additional Lyrics

1. Ó! slán is céad ón dtaobh so uaim
Cois Máighe na gcaor, na gcraobh, na gcruach,
Na stáid, na séad, na saor, na slua,
Na ndán, na ndréacht, na dtréan gan ghruaim!

Chorus: Is och, ochón! is breóite mise,
Gan chuid, gan chóir, gan chóip, gan chisde,
Gan sult, gan seód, gan spórt, gan spionna,
O seóladh me chun uaignis!

2. Slán tar aon don té dar dual,
An bháinchnis bhéasach, bhéaltais, bhuadhach,
Chuir tráth chun sléi me i gcéin am ruaig,
'Si grá mo chéibh, bé 'n-Eirinn cuach!
(Chorus)

3. Is fánach faon mé, is fraochmhar fuar,
Is támh-lag tréith, 's is taomach trua,
I mbarr an tsléi gan aon, mo nuar!
Am páirt ach fraoch is gaoth adtuaidh!
(Chorus)

4. Ó dháil an chléir dham céile nua,
Cois Máighe go h-éag ní h-é mo chuairt,
Go bráth lem ré táim réidh lem chuaich,
Le mnáibh an tsaol chuir me ar buairt.

(Final Chorus)
Is och, ochón! mo bhrón, mo mhille!
Iomarca an óil is póga bruinneall
Chuir mise lem laethibh gan fód, gan fuithin,
Fós gan lomad fuadair!

FELIX, THE SOLDIER

Irish folksong

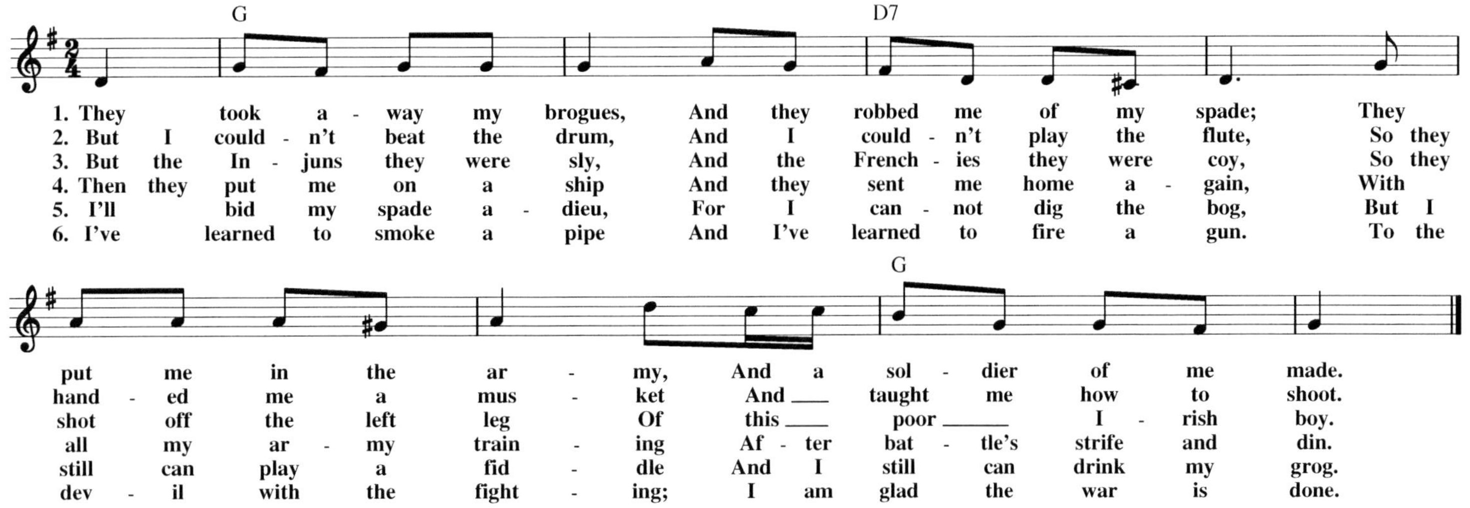

FATHER MURPHY

Irish folksong

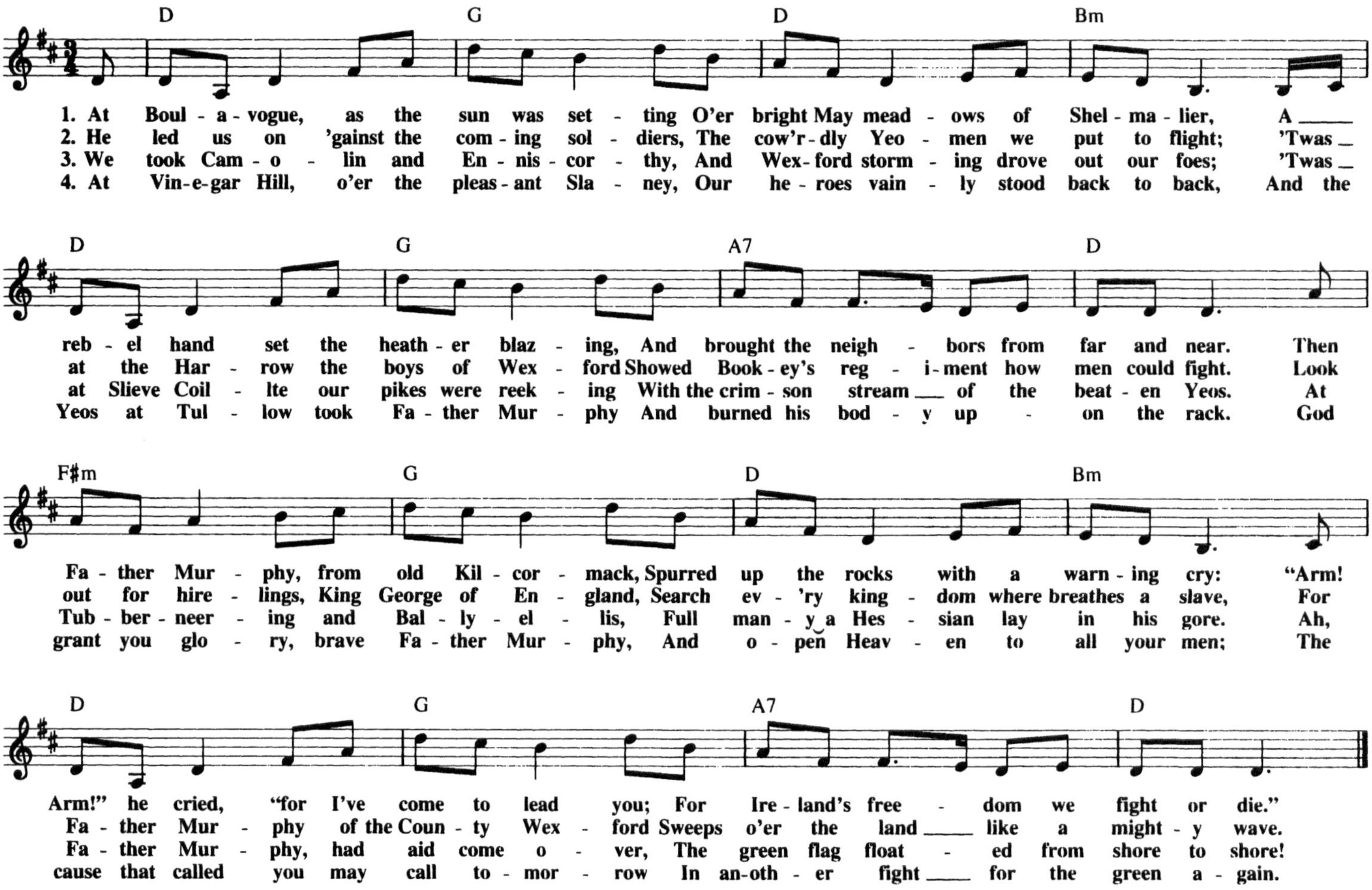

THE FENIAN MAN O' WAR

Irish folksong

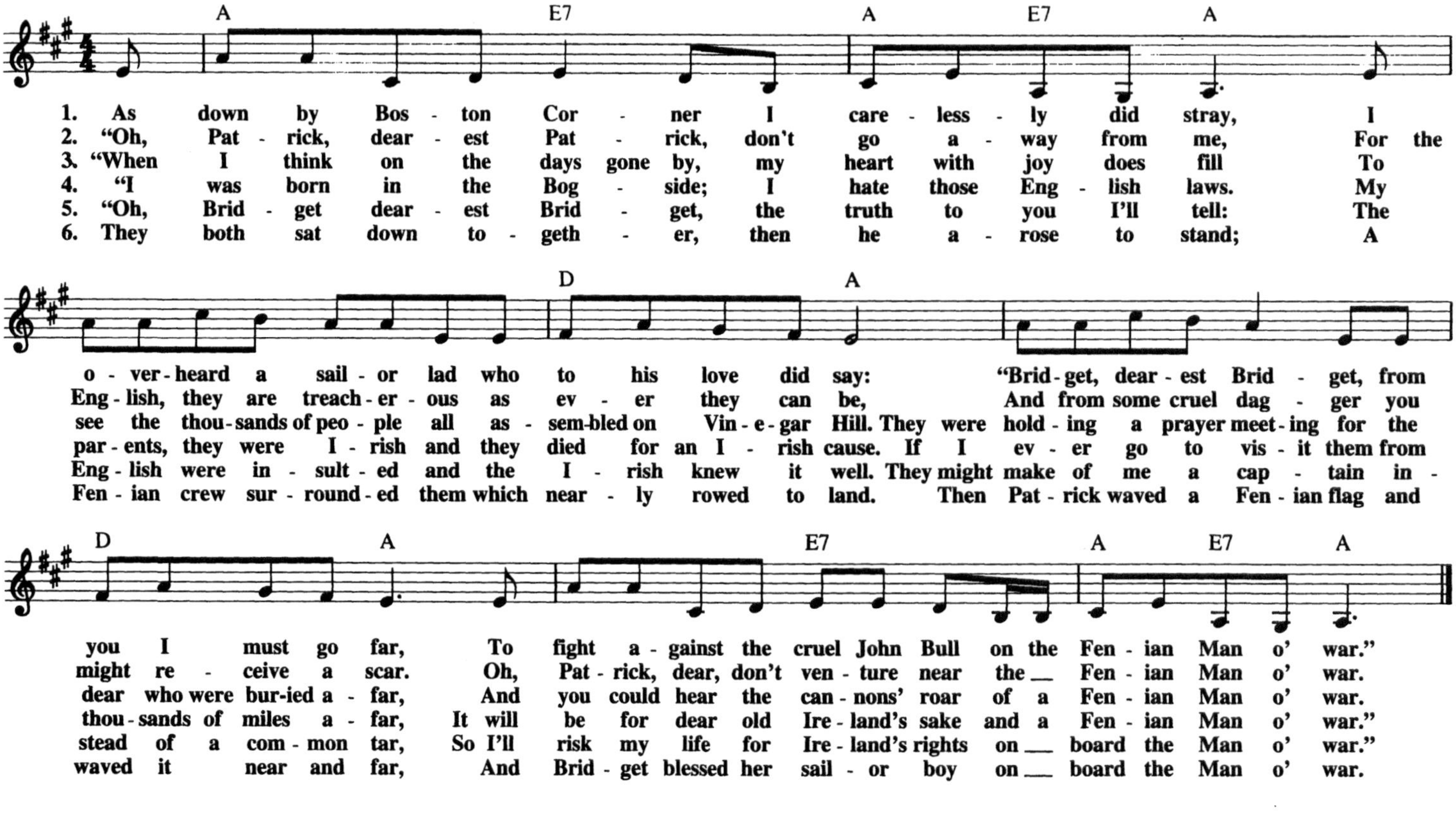

THE FENIANS OF CAHIRCIVEEN

Irish folksong

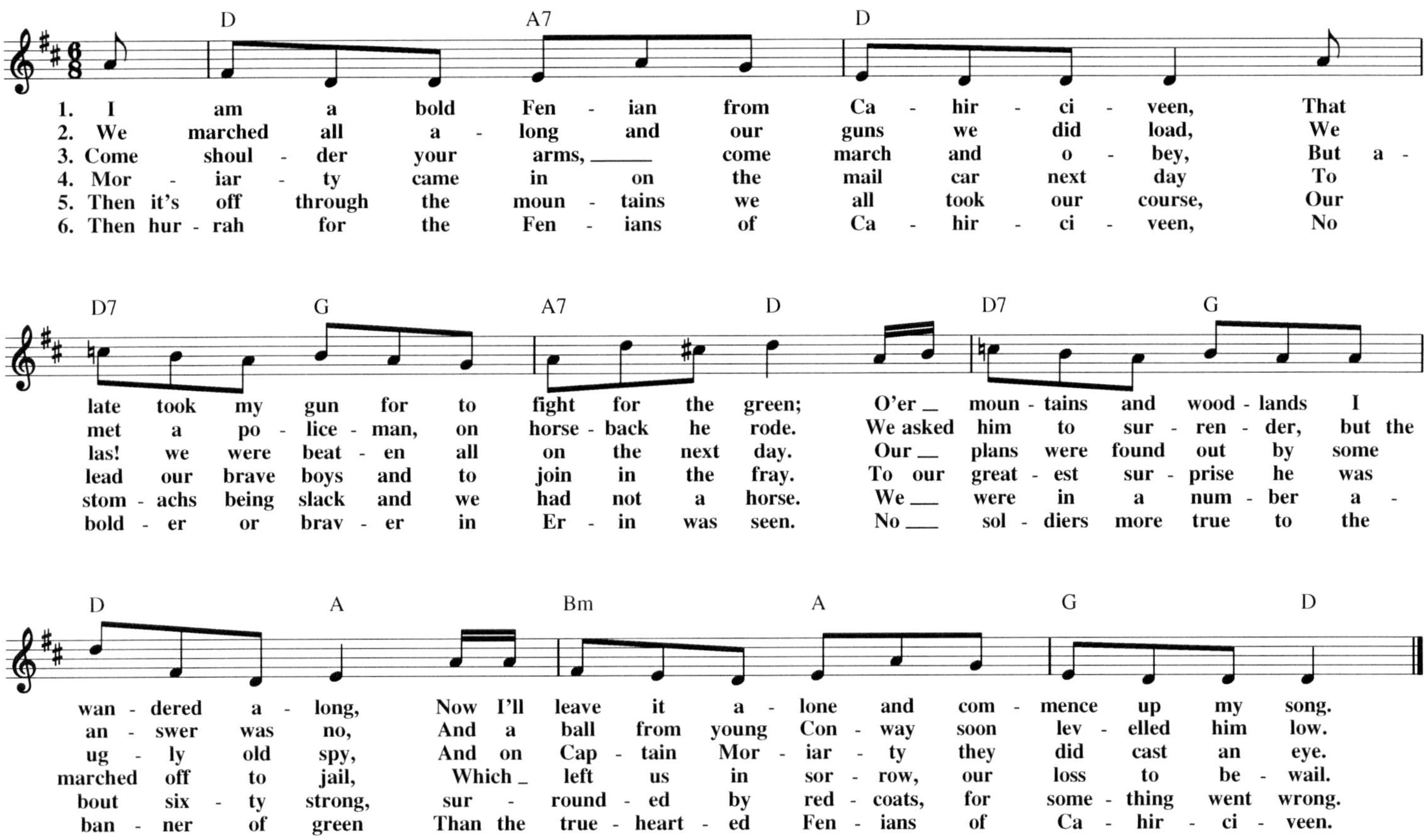

1. I am a bold Fen - ian from Ca - hir - ci - veen, That
2. We marched all a - long and our guns we did load, We
3. Come shoul - der your arms, _____ come march and o - bey, But a -
4. Mor - iar - ty came in on the mail car next day To
5. Then it's off through the moun - tains we all took our course, Our
6. Then hur - rah for the Fen - ians of Ca - hir - ci - veen, No

late took my gun for to fight for the green; O'er _ moun - tains and wood - lands I
met a po - lice - man, on horse - back he rode. We asked him to sur - ren - der, but the
las! we were beat - en all on the next day. Our _ plans were found out by some
lead our brave boys and to join in the fray. To our great - est sur - prise he was
stom - achs being slack and we had not a horse. We _ were in a num - ber a -
bold - er or brav - er in Er - in was seen. No _ sol - diers more true to the

wan - dered a - long, Now I'll leave it a - lone and com - mence up my song.
an - swer was no, And a ball from young Con - way soon lev - elled him low.
ug - ly old spy, And on Cap - tain Mor - iar - ty they did cast an eye.
marched off to jail, Which _ left us in sor - row, our loss to be - wail.
bout six - ty strong, sur - round - ed by red - coats, for some - thing went wrong.
ban - ner of green Than the true - heart - ed Fen - ians of Ca - hir - ci - veen.

FILIMIOORIOORIAY

Irish popular song

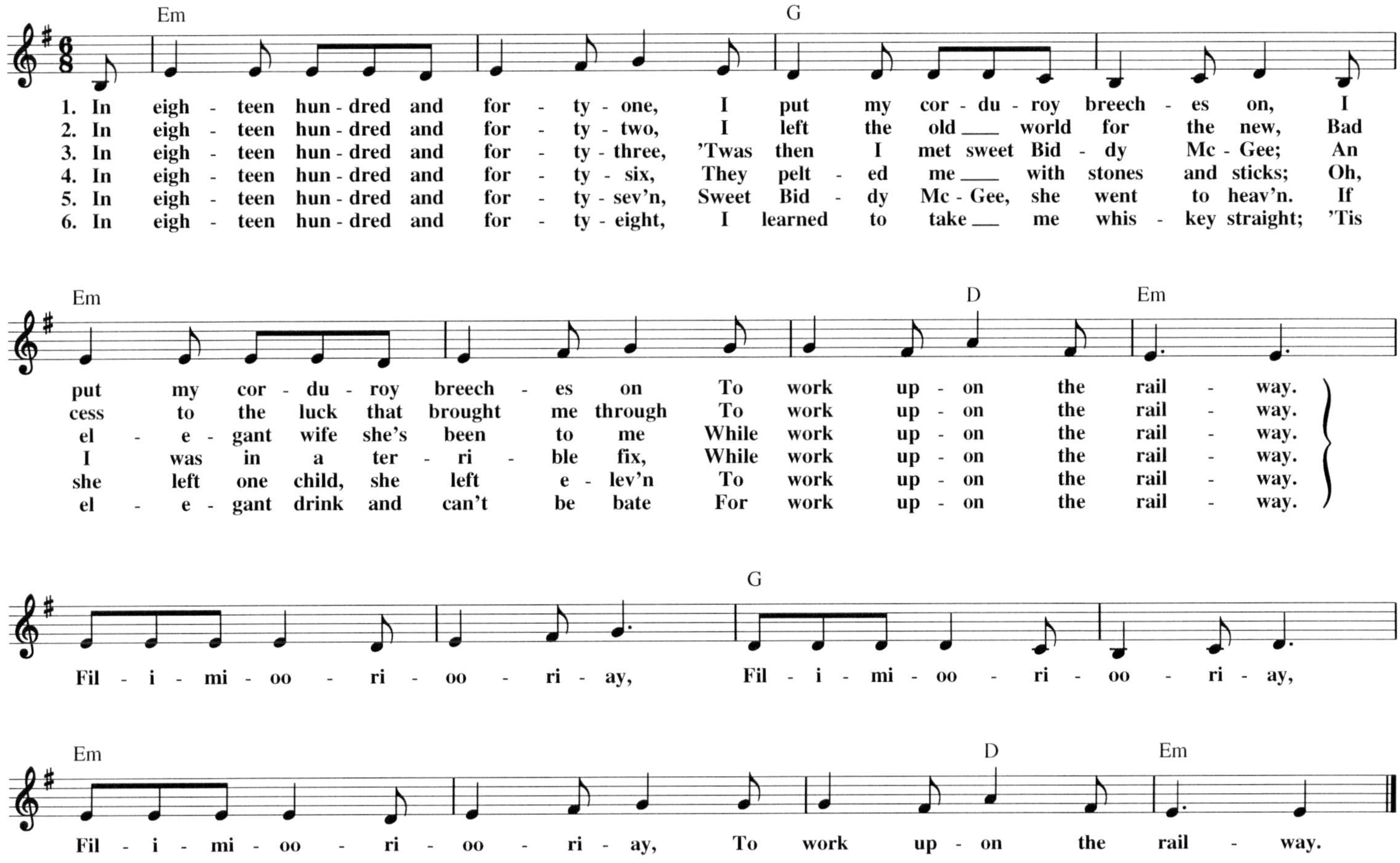

1. In eigh - teen hun - dred and for - ty - one, I put my cor - du - roy breech - es on, I
2. In eigh - teen hun - dred and for - ty - two, I left the old _ world for the new, Bad
3. In eigh - teen hun - dred and for - ty - three, 'Twas then I met sweet Bid - dy Mc - Gee; An
4. In eigh - teen hun - dred and for - ty - six, They pelt - ed me _ with stones and sticks; Oh,
5. In eigh - teen hun - dred and for - ty - sev'n, Sweet Bid - dy Mc - Gee, she went to heav'n. If
6. In eigh - teen hun - dred and for - ty - eight, I learned to take _ me whis - key straight; 'Tis

put my cor - du - roy breech - es on To work up - on the rail - way.
cess to the luck that brought me through To work up - on the rail - way.
el - e - gant wife she's been to me While work up - on the rail - way.
I was in a ter - ri - ble fix, While work up - on the rail - way.
she left one child, she left e - lev'n To work up - on the rail - way.
el - e - gant drink and can't be bate For work up - on the rail - way.

Fil - i - mi - oo - ri - oo - ri - ay, Fil - i - mi - oo - ri - oo - ri - ay,

Fil - i - mi - oo - ri - oo - ri - ay, To work up - on the rail - way.

FINNEGAN'S WAKE

Irish folksong

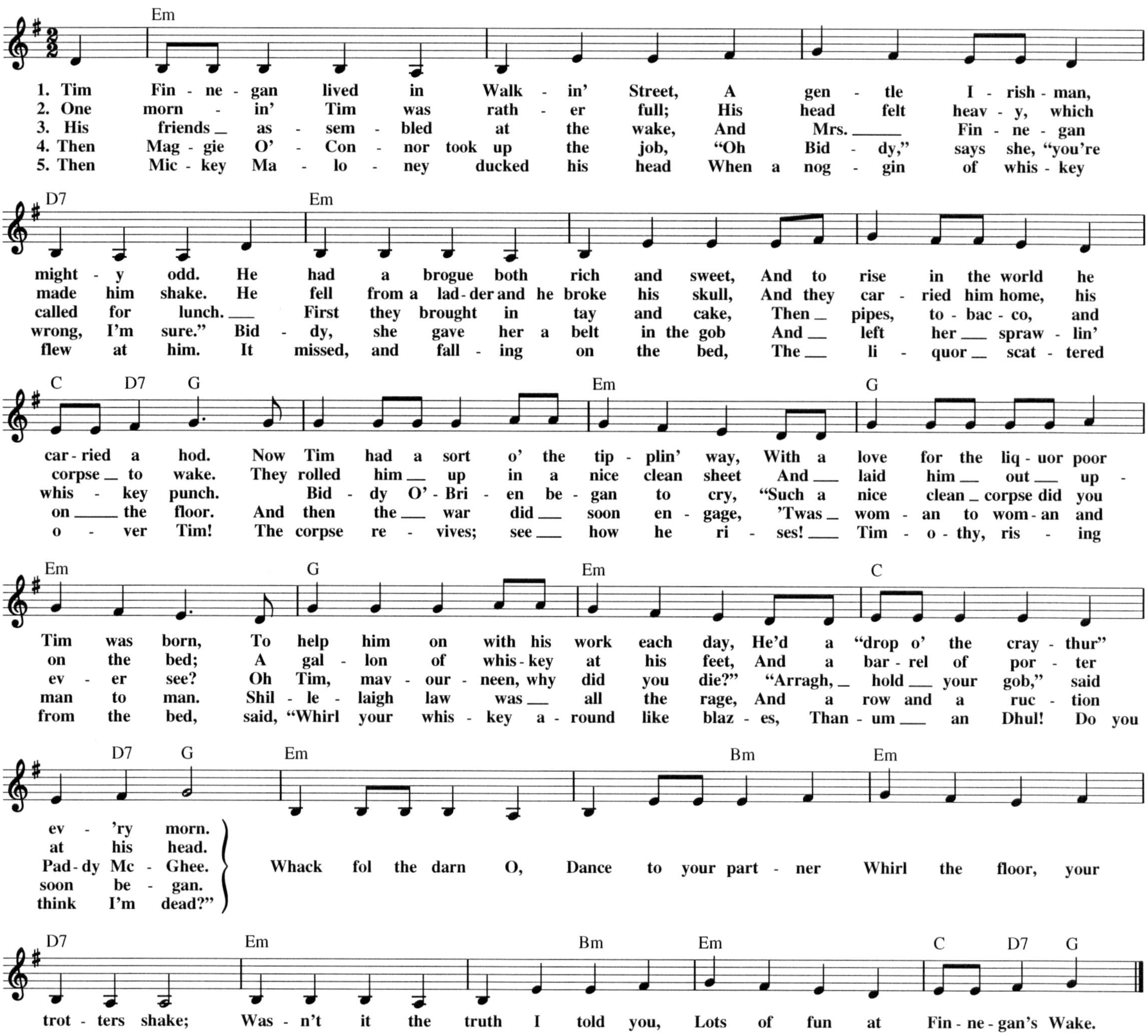

THE FIRST SWALLOW

Irish popular song
Words by C. Barnard

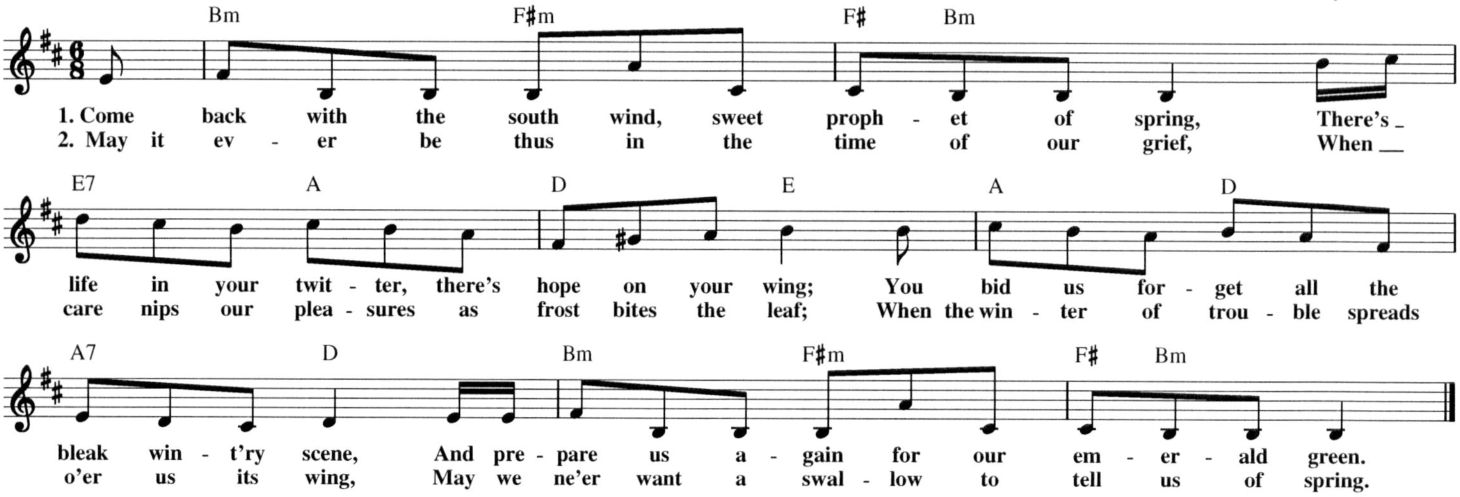

FLORA MACDONALD'S LOVE SONG

Folksong from the Hebrides

Al - lan __ would __ that thou could'st hear me! Ho Ho fa li _____

Ail - ein __ duinn __ nach till thu'n taobh - sa? Ho Ho fa li _____

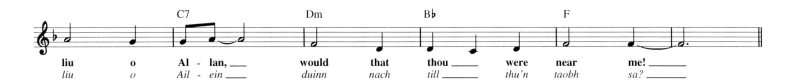

liu o Al - lan, ___ would that thou ___ were near me! _____

liu o Ail - ein ___ duinn nach till _____ thu'n taobh sa? _____

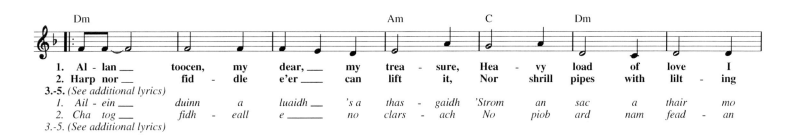

1. Al - lan __ tooen, my dear, ___ my trea - sure, Hea - vy load of love I
2. Harp nor __ fid - dle e'er ___ can lift it, Nor shrill pipes with lilt - ing

3.-5. *(See additional lyrics)*

1. Ail - ein __ duinn a luaidh __ 's a thas - gaidh 'Strom an sac a thair mo
2. Cha tog __ fidh - eall e _____ no clars - ach No piob ard nam fead - an

3.-5. *(See additional lyrics)*

car - ry. }
chan - ter. } Al - lan __ would __ that thou wert near me! Ho Ho fa

ghiul - an }
siubh - lach } *Ail - ein __ duinn, __ nach till thu'n taobh - sa. Ho Ho fa*

li _____ liu o Al - lan __ would that thou ___ were near me. _____

li _____ liu o Ail - ein __ duinn nach till _____ thu'n taobh - sa. _____

Additional Lyrics

3. Sad each day, for thee I'm longing
   Gone with thee all joy and gladness.
   Allan would that thou were near me.
   Ho Ho fa li liu o
   Allan would that thou were near me.

4. In deep groves and leafy woodlands
   Fain would I with thee be wand'ring.
   Allan would that thou were near me.
   Ho Ho fa li liu o
   Allan would that thou were near me.

5. Allan of the curling ringlets,
   Sweet to me thy honey kisses.
   Allan would that thou were near me.
   Ho Ho fa li liu o
   Allan would that thou were near me.

3. *Ailein Ailein mo ghaol Ailein*
   Marcraich nan each seanga sunndach.
   Ailein dninn nach till thu'n taobhsa.
   Ho Ho fa li liu o
   Ailein dninn nach till thu'n taobhsa.

4. *Ailein dninn an leadain shoilleir*
   Shiubhlainn coille's doire dluth leat.
   Ailein dninn nach till thu'n taobhsa.
   Ho Ho fa li liu o
   Ailein dninn nach till thu'n taobhsa.

5. *Ailein dninn a'bhroillich bhoidhich*
   'S miles leam do phog na siucar.
   Ailein dninn nach till thu'n taobhsa.
   Ho Ho fa li liu o
   Ailein dninn nach till thu'n taobhsa.

FLOW GENTLY, SWEET AFTON

Scottish folksong
Words by Robert Burns
Melody by Alexander Hume

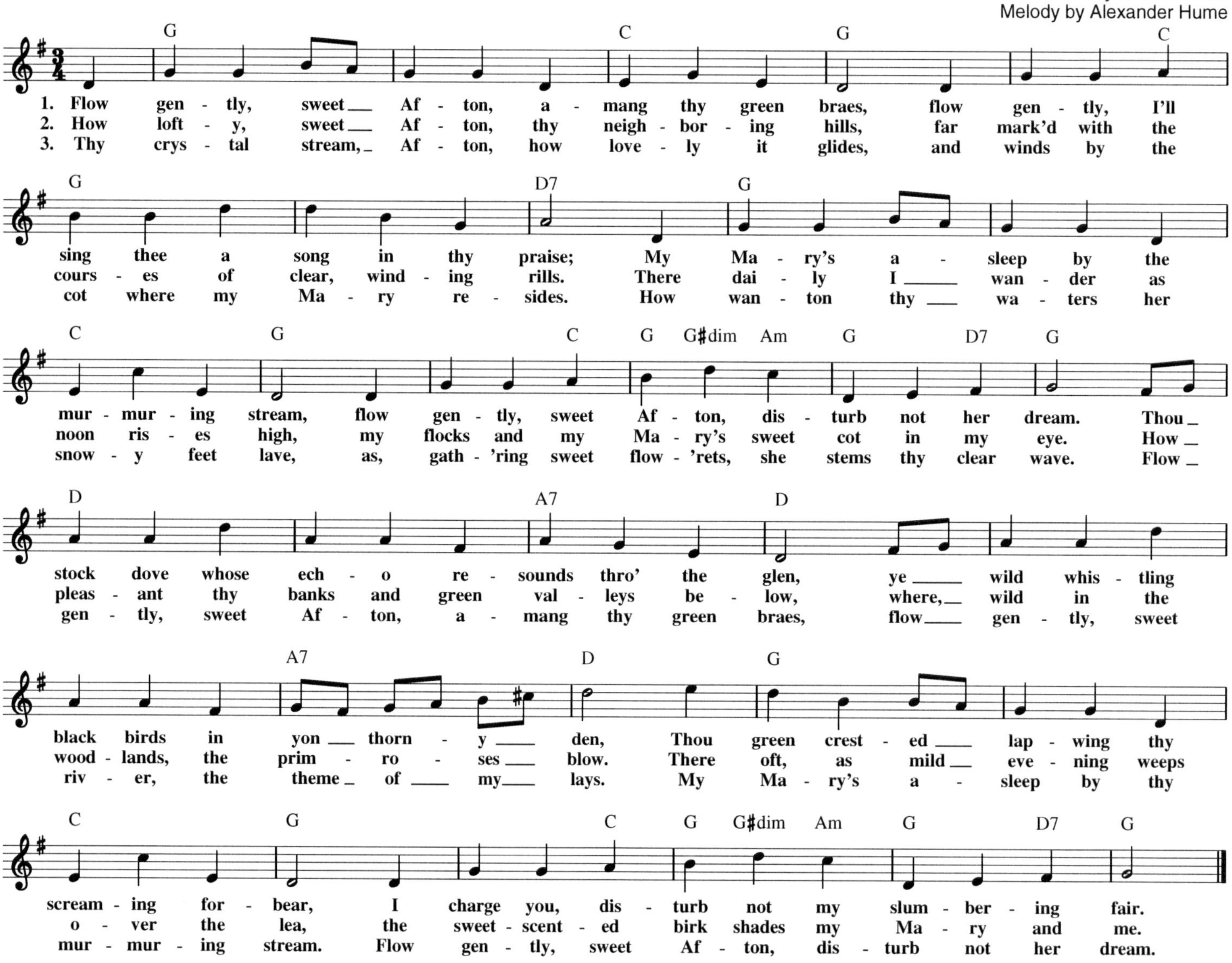

THE FLOWER OF SWEET STRABANE

Irish folksong

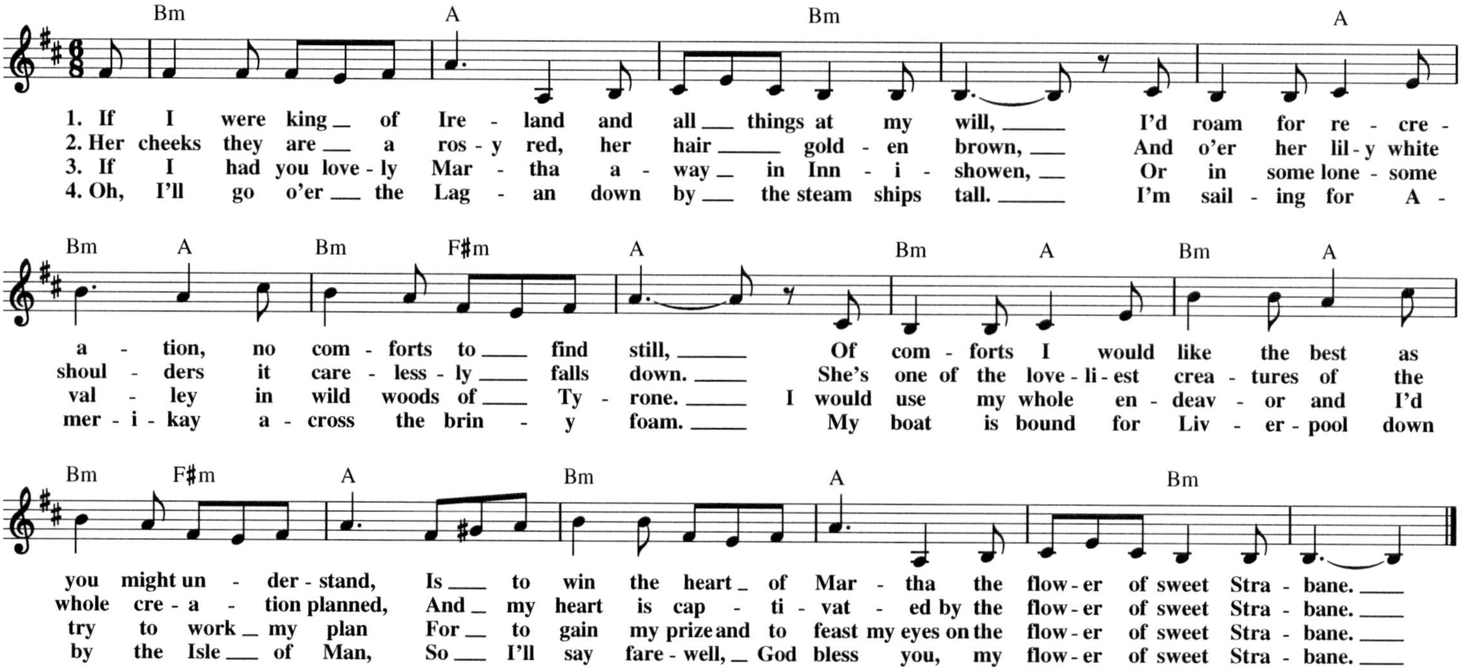

THE FLYING CLOUD

Irish folksong

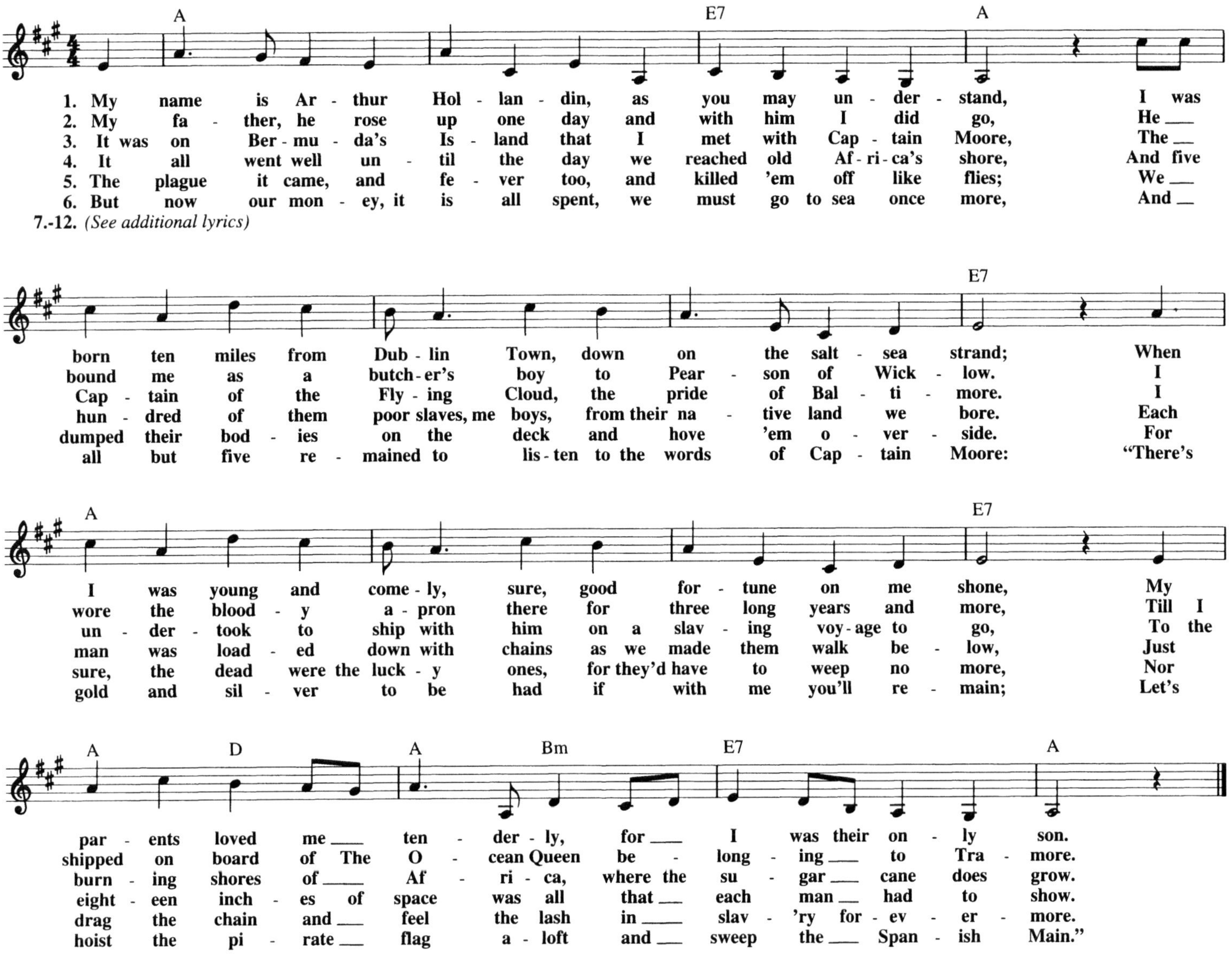

1. My name is Arthur Hollandin, as you may understand, I was born ten miles from Dublin Town, down on the salt-sea strand; When I was young and comely, sure, good fortune on me shone, My parents loved me tenderly, for I was their only son.

2. My father, he rose up one day and with him I did go, He bound me as a butcher's boy to Pearson of Wicklow. I wore the bloody apron there for three long years and more, Till I shipped on board of The Ocean Queen belonging to Tramore.

3. It was on Bermuda's Island that I met with Captain Moore, The Captain of the Flying Cloud, the pride of Baltimore. I undertook to ship with him on a slaving voyage to go, To the burning shores of Africa, where the sugar cane does grow.

4. It all went well until the day we reached old Africa's shore, And five hundred of them poor slaves, me boys, from their native land we bore. Each man was loaded down with chains as we made them walk below, Just eighteen inches of space was all that each man had to show.

5. The plague it came, and fever too, and killed 'em off like flies; We dumped their bodies on the deck and hove 'em over side. Sure, the dead were the lucky ones, for they'd have to weep no more, Nor drag the chain and feel the lash in slav'ry for evermore.

6. But now our money, it is all spent, we must go to sea once more, And all but five remained to listen to the words of Captain Moore: "There's gold and silver to be had if with me you'll remain; Let's hoist the pirate flag aloft and sweep the Spanish Main."

Additional Lyrics

7. The Flying Cloud was a Yankee ship, five hundred tons or more,
She could outsail any clipper ship hailing out of Baltimore,
With her canvas white as the driven snow and on it there's no specks,
And forty men and fourteen guns she carried below her decks.

8. We plundered many a gallant ship down on the Spanish Main,
Killed many a man and left his wife and children to remain,
To none we showed no kindness but gave them watery graves,
For the saying of our captain was: "Dead men tell no tales."

9. We ran and fought with many a ship both frigates and liners too,
Till, at last a British Man-O'-War, the Dunmow, hove in view,
She fired a shot across our bows as we ran before the wind,
And a chainshot cut our mainmast down and we fell far behind.

10. They beat our crew to quarters as they drew up alongside,
And soon across our quarterdeck there ran a crimson tide,
We fought until they killed our captain and twenty of our men,
Then a bombshell set our ship on fire, we had to surrender then.

11. It's now to Newgate we have come, bound down with iron chains,
For the sinking and the plundering of ships on the Spanish Main,
The judge he has condemned us and we are condemned to die.
Young men a warning by me take and shun all piracy.

12. Farewell to Dublin City and the girl that I adore,
I'll never kiss your cheek again nor hold your hand no more,
Whisky and bad company have made a wretch of me,
Young men, a warning by me take and shun all piracy.

THE FOGGY DEW

Irish folksong

1. O - ver the hills I ___ went one day; A ___ love - ly ___ maid I spied. ___
2. O - ver the hills I ___ went one morn, A - sing - ing ___ I did go. ___

___ With her coal - black ___ hair and her man - tle so green, An ___ im - age ___
Met this love - ly ___ maid with her coal - black hair, And she an - swered ___

to per - ceive. ___ Says I, "Dear girl, will you be my ___ bride?" And she
soft and low. ___ Said she, "Young man, I'll ___ be your ___ bride, If I

lift - ed her eyes of ___ blue. ___ She smiled and ___ said, "Young man,
know ___ that you'll be ___ true." ___ Oh, in my ___ arms, all ___

I'm to wed; I'm to meet him in the fog - gy dew. ___
of her charms Were ___ cast - ed in the fog - gy dew. ___

FOLLOW ME UP TO CARLOW

Irish folksong

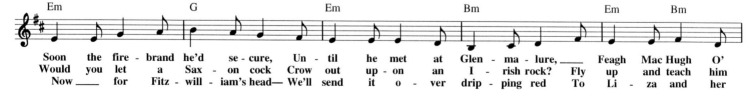

1. Lift, Mac Ca - hir Oge, your face, Brood - ing o'er the old dis - grace, That old Fitz - will - iam
2. See the swords of Glen Im - aal, Flash - ing o'er the En - glish Pale! See all the chil - dren
3. From Tas - sa - gart to Clon - more Flows a stream of Sax - on gore! O, great is Ror - y

stormed your place, And drove you to the fern, O! Grey said vic - to - ry was sure
of the Gael Be - neath O' Byrne's ___ ban - ners! Roos - ter of a fight - ing stock,
Oge O More At send - ing loons to Ha - des! White is sick and Lane is fled!

Soon the fire - brand he'd se - cure, Un - til he met at Glen - ma - lure, ___ Feagh Mac Hugh O'
Would you let a Sax - on cock Crow out up - on an I - rish rock? Fly up and teach him
Now ___ for Fitz - will - iam's head— We'll send it o - ver drip - ping red To Li - za and her

Byrne, O!
man - ners! } Curse and swear, Lord Kil - dare! Feagh will do what Feagh will dare; ___ And now, Fitz - will - iam,
la - dies!

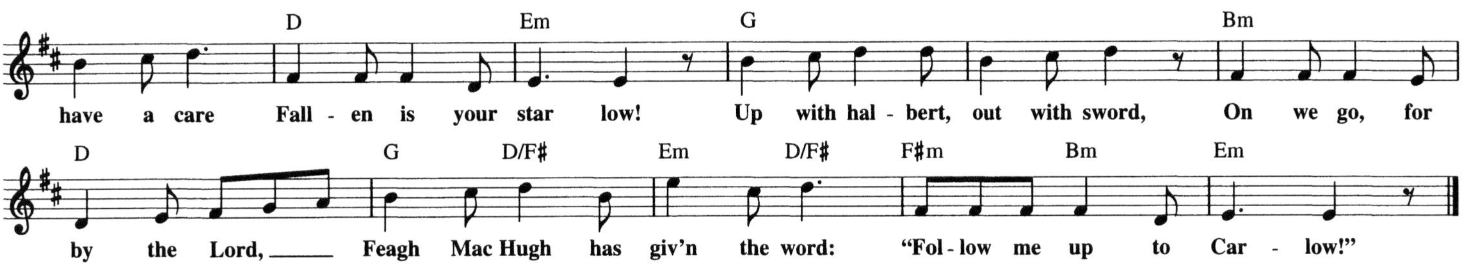

have a care Fall - en is your star low! Up with hal - bert, out with sword, On we go, for
by the Lord, _____ Feagh Mac Hugh has giv'n the word: "Fol - low me up to Car - low!"

FOR I HAD A SPIRIT ABOVE MY DEGREE

Irish folksong

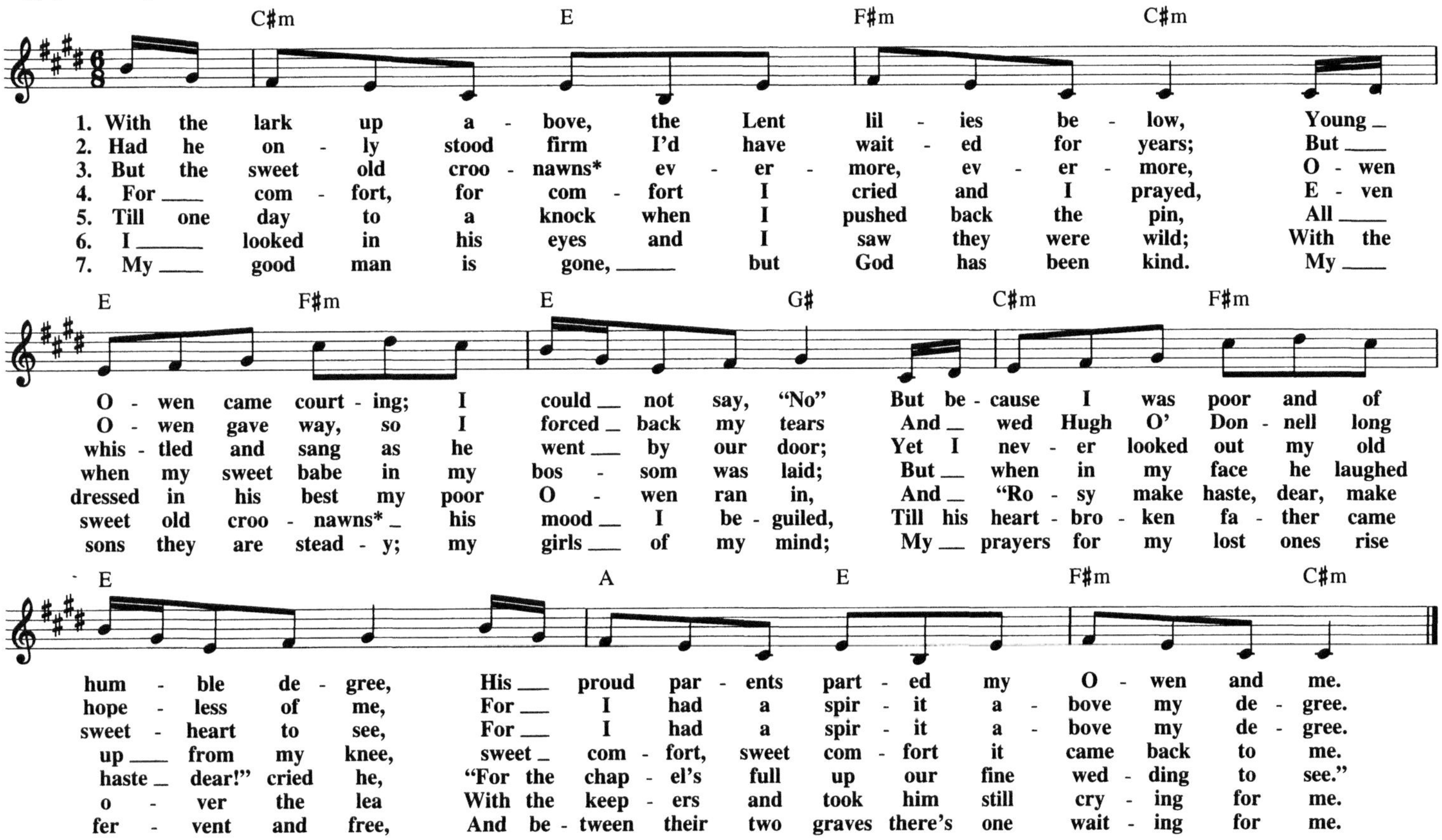

1. With the lark up a - bove, the Lent lil - ies be - low, Young _
2. Had he on - ly stood firm I'd have wait - ed for years; But _
3. But the sweet old croo - nawns* ev - er - more, ev - er - more, O - wen
4. For _ com - fort, for com - fort I cried and I prayed, E - ven
5. Till one day to a knock when I pushed back the pin, All _
6. I _____ looked in his eyes and I saw they were wild; With the
7. My _ good man is gone, _____ but God has been kind. My _

O - wen came court - ing; I could _ not say, "No" But be - cause I was poor and of
O - wen gave way, so I forced _ back my tears And _ wed Hugh O' Don - nell long
whis - tled and sang as he went _ by our door; Yet I nev - er looked out my old
when my sweet babe in my bos - om was laid; But _ when in my face he laughed
dressed in his best my poor O - wen ran in, And _ "Ro - sy make haste, dear, make
sweet old croo - nawns* _ his mood _ I be - guiled, Till his heart - bro - ken fa - ther came
sons they are stead - y; my girls _ of my mind; My _ prayers for my lost ones rise

hum - ble de - gree, His _ proud par - ents part - ed my O - wen and me.
hope - less of me, For _ I had a spir - it a - bove my de - gree.
sweet - heart to see, For _ I had a spir - it a - bove my de - gree.
up _ from my knee, sweet _ com - fort, sweet com - fort it came back to me.
haste _ dear!" cried he, "For the chap - el's full up our fine wed - ding to see."
o - ver the lea With the keep - ers and took him still cry - ing for me.
fer - vent and free, And be - tween their two graves there's one wait - ing for me.

country songs

THE FOUR MARYS

Scottish folksong

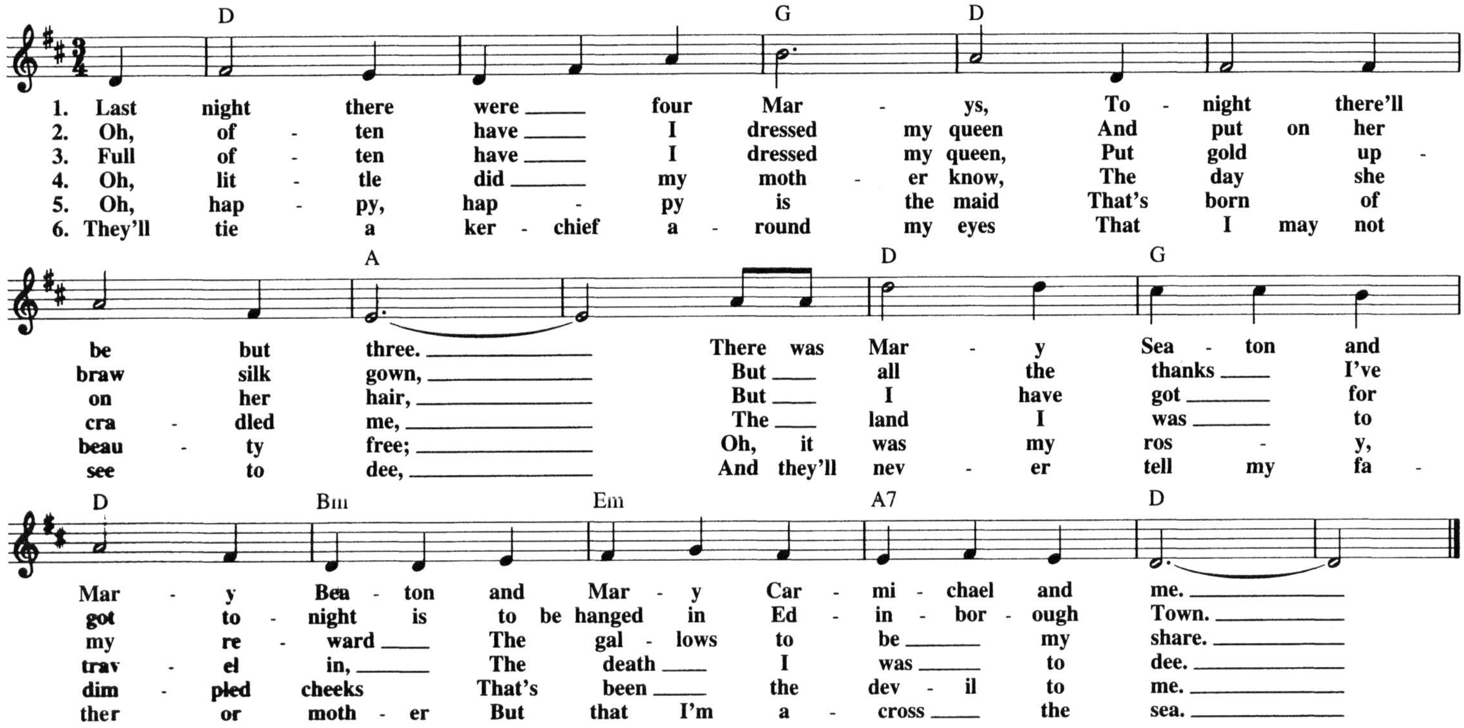

1. Last night there were _____ four Mar - ys, To - night there'll
2. Oh, of - ten have _____ I dressed my queen, And put on her
3. Full of - ten have _____ I dressed my queen, Put gold up -
4. Oh, lit - tle did _____ my moth - er know, The day she
5. Oh, hap - py, hap - py is the maid That's born of
6. They'll tie a ker - chief a - round my eyes That I may not

be but three. _____ There was Mar - y Sea - ton and
braw silk gown, _____ But _____ all the thanks _____ I've
on her hair, _____ But _____ I have got _____ for
cra - dled me, _____ The _____ land I was to
beau - ty free; _____ Oh, it was my ros - y,
see to dee, _____ And they'll nev - er tell my fa -

Mar - y Bea - ton and Mar - y Car - mi - chael and me. _____
got to - night is to be hanged in Ed - in - bor - ough Town. _____
my re - ward _____ The gal - lows to be _____ my share. _____
trav - el in, _____ The death I was to dee. _____
dim - pled cheeks That's been _____ the dev - il to me. _____
ther or moth - er But that I'm a - cross _____ the sea. _____

FROM THE COLD SOD THAT'S O'ER YOU

Irish folksong

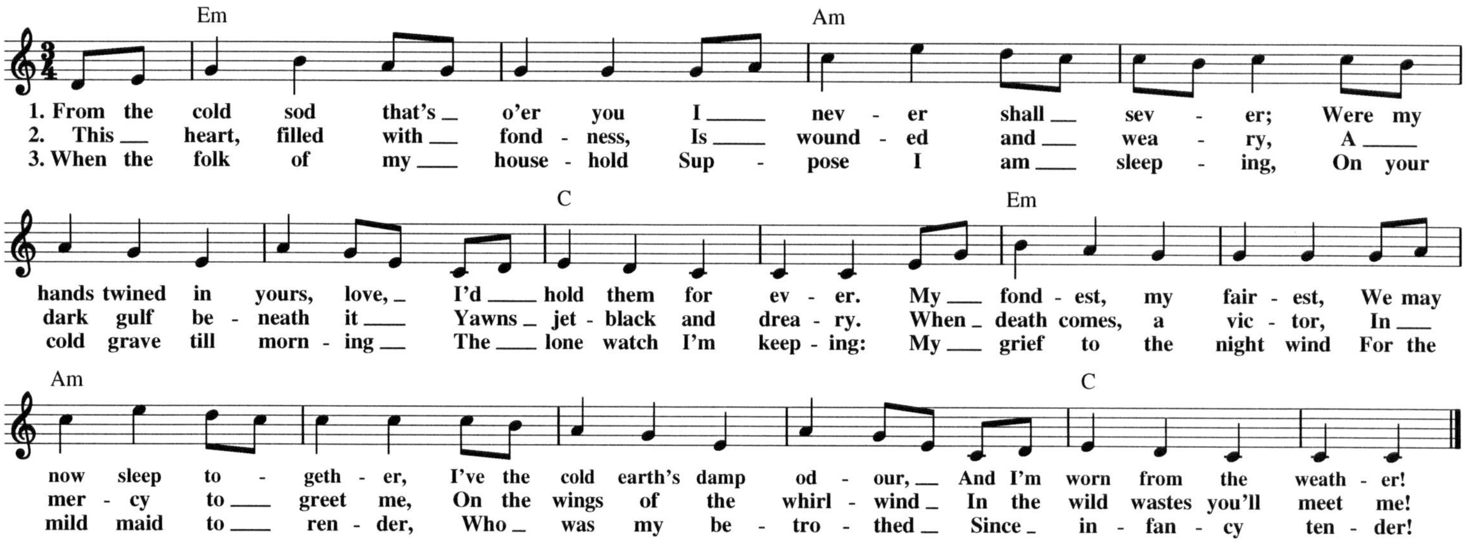

1. From the cold sod that's __ o'er you I ____ nev - er shall __ sev - er; Were my
2. This __ heart, filled with __ fond - ness, Is __ wound - ed and __ wea - ry, A __
3. When the folk of my __ house - hold Sup - pose I am __ sleep - ing, On your

hands twined in yours, love, __ I'd __ hold them for ev - er. My __ fond - est, my fair - est, We may
dark gulf be - neath it __ Yawns __ jet - black and drea - ry. When __ death comes, a vic - tor, In __
cold grave till morn - ing __ The __ lone watch I'm keep - ing: My __ grief to the night wind For the

now sleep to - geth - er, I've the cold earth's damp od - our, __ And I'm worn from the weath - er!
mer - cy to __ greet me, On the wings of the whirl - wind __ In the wild wastes you'll meet me!
mild maid to __ ren - der, Who __ was my be - tro - thed __ Since __ in - fan - cy ten - der!

Gaelic Lyrics

1. *Táim sínte ar do thuama, Is do gheóir ann do shíor me;*
   Dá mbeadh barr do dhá lámh agam Ní sgarfainn leat choíche
   A úilín is a annsacht, Is am domh-sa luí leat,
   Tá bola fuar na cré orm, Dath na gréine 's na gaoithe!

2. *Tá cló ar mo chroí-se 'Tá líonta le grá dhuit*
   Lionndubh ar thaobh thíos de Chomh cíordhubh le h-áirne.
   Is má bhaineann aon ní dhom 'S go gclaoifeadh an bás me,
   Bead-sa im shí gaoithe Romhat thíos ar na bánta!

3. *Nuair is dó le mo mhuinntir Go mbím-se ar mo leaba,*
   Ar do thuama 'sea bhím sínte Ó oíche go maidin:
   A' cur síos mo chruatan 'S a' crua-ghol go daingean.
   Tré mo chailín ciúin stuama Do luadh liom 'n-a leanbh!

FROM ERIN'S SHORES

Irish folksong
Words by Florence Hoare

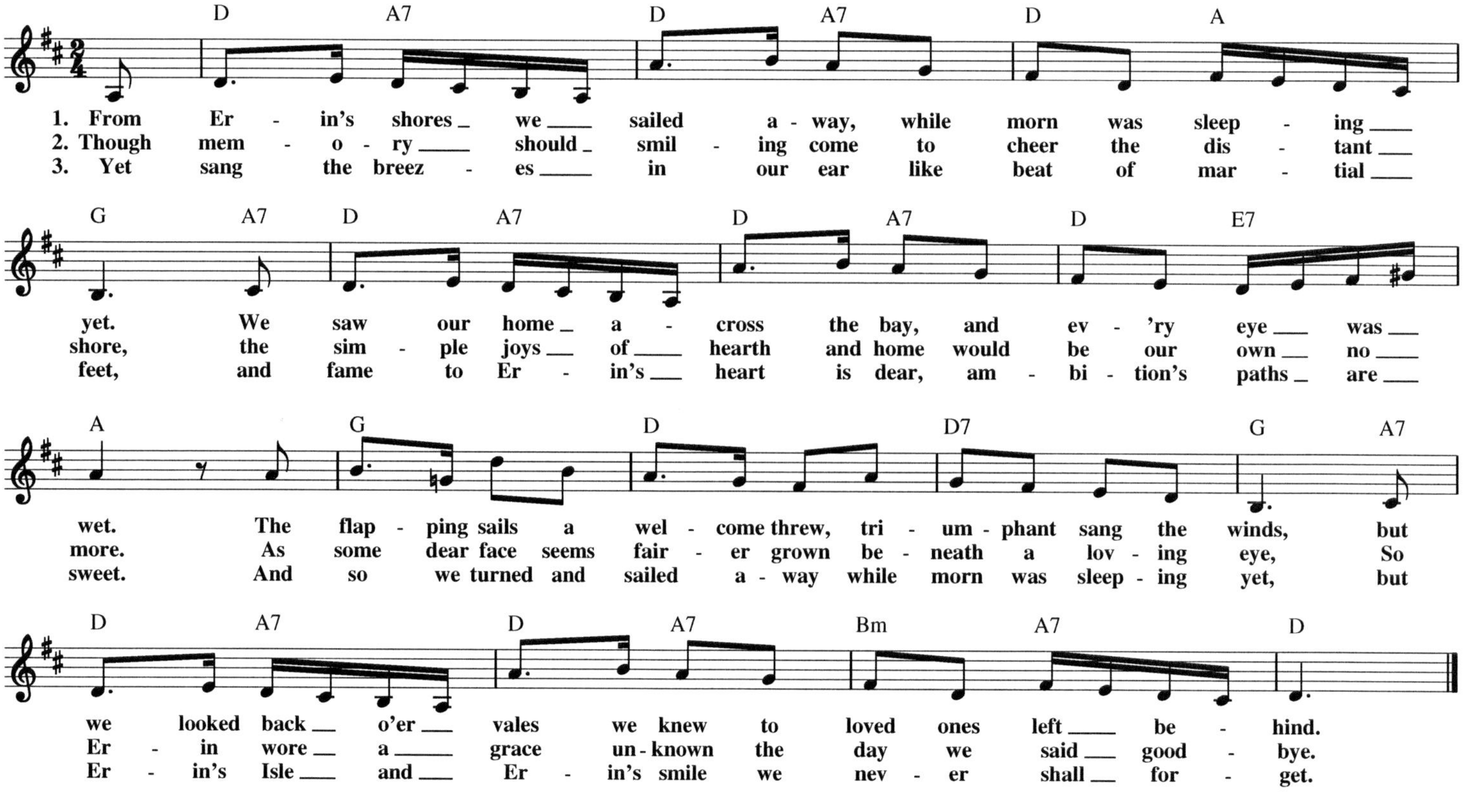

1. From Er - in's shores __ we __ sailed a - way, while morn was sleep - ing __
2. Though mem - o - ry __ should __ smil - ing come to cheer the dis - tant __
3. Yet sang the breez - es __ in our ear like beat of mar - tial __

yet. We saw our home __ a - cross the bay, and ev - 'ry eye __ was
shore, the sim - ple joys __ of __ hearth and home would be our own __ no
feet, and fame to Er - in's __ heart is dear, am - bi - tion's paths __ are

wet. The flap - ping sails a wel - come threw, tri - um - phant sang the winds, but
more. As some dear face seems fair - er grown be - neath a lov - ing eye, So
sweet. And so we turned and sailed a - way while morn was sleep - ing yet, but

we looked back __ o'er __ vales we knew to loved ones left __ be - hind.
Er - in wore __ a __ grace un - known the day we said __ good - bye.
Er - in's Isle __ and __ Er - in's smile we nev - er shall __ for - get.

THE GALBALLY FARMER

Irish folksong

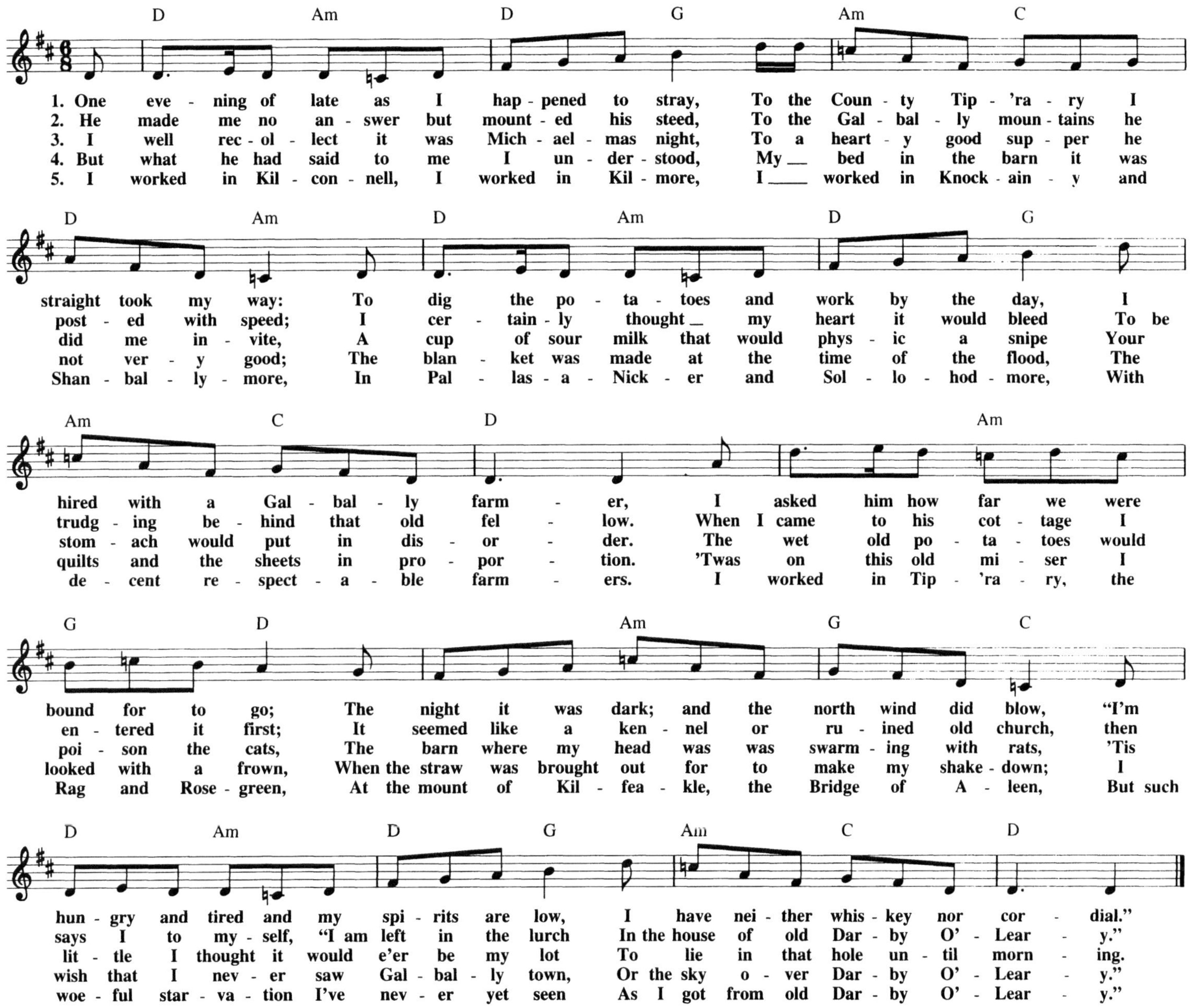

GIN I WERE

Scottish folksong

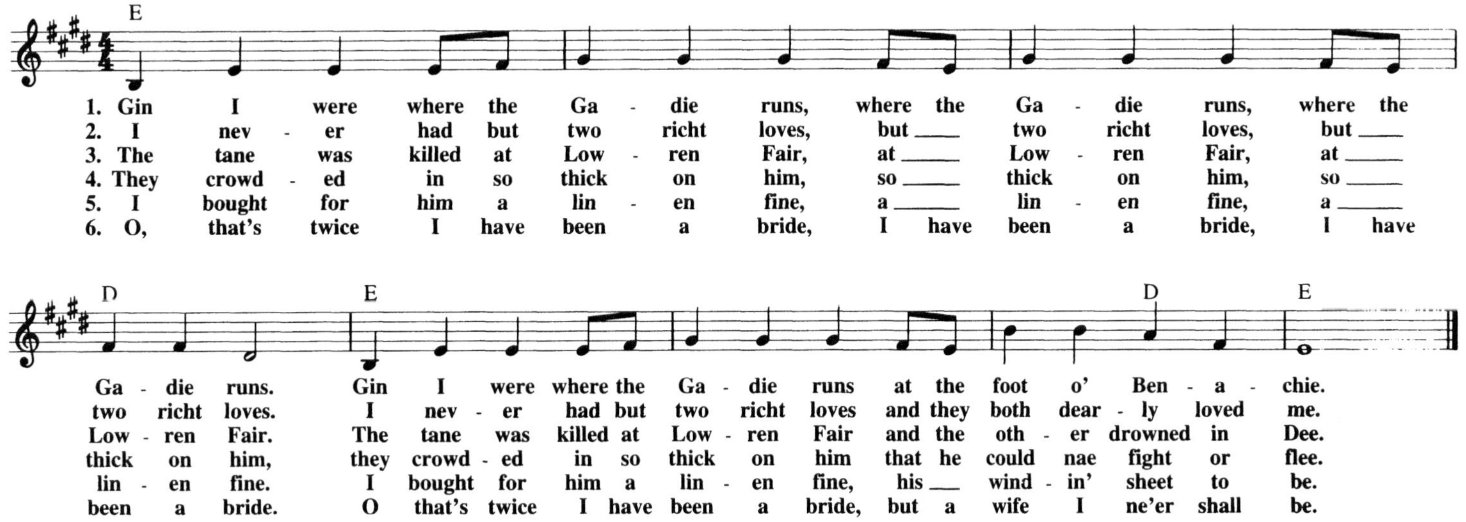

GALWAY CITY

Irish folksong

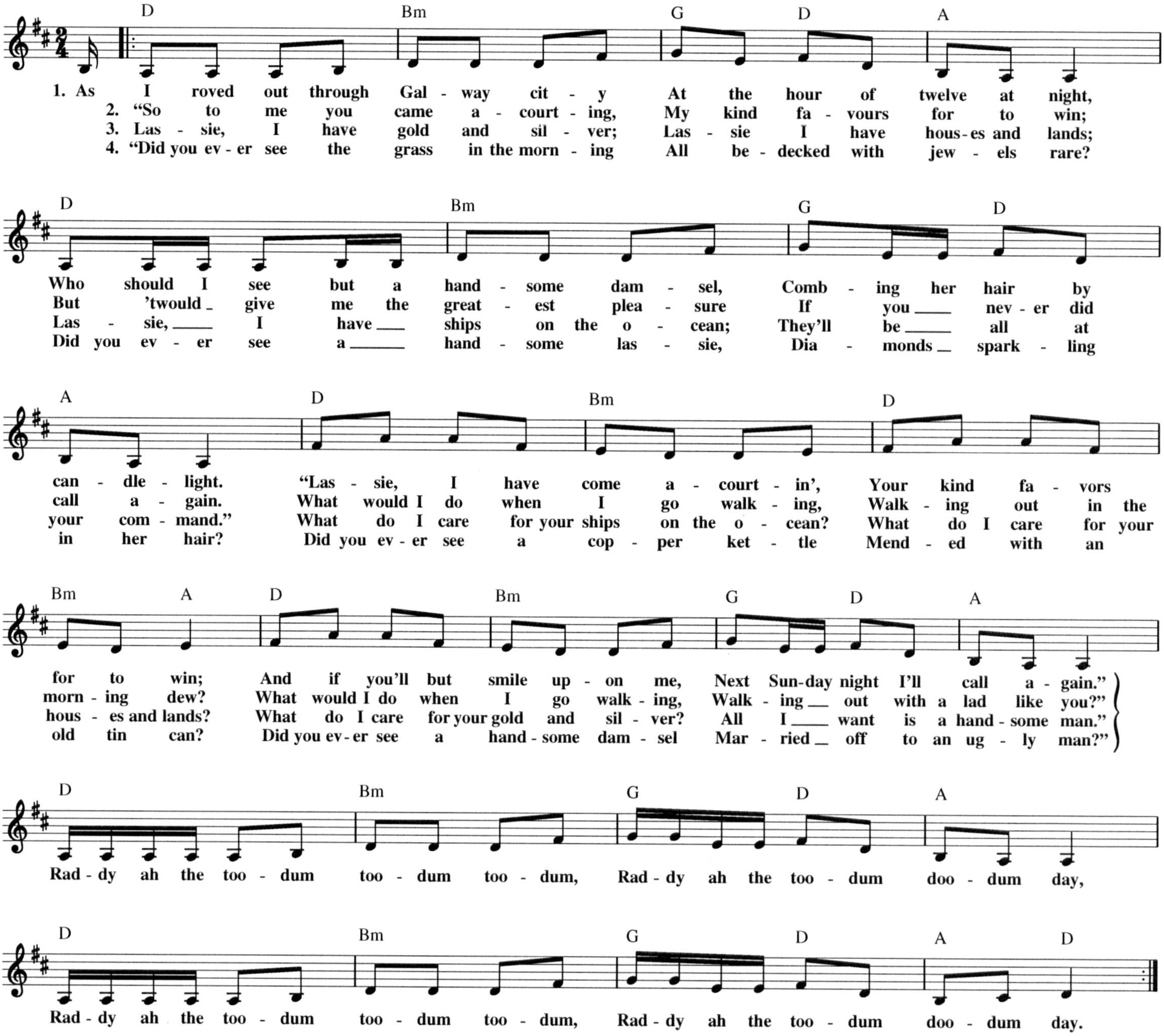

1. As I roved out through Gal - way cit - y At the hour of twelve at night,
2. "So to me you came a - court - ing, My kind fa - vours for to win;
3. Las - sie, I have gold and sil - ver; Las - sie I have hous - es and lands;
4. "Did you ev - er see the grass in the morn - ing All be - decked with jew - els rare?

Who should I see but a hand - some dam - sel, Comb - ing her hair by
But 'twould give me the great - est plea - sure If you nev - er did
Las - sie, I have ships on the o - cean; They'll be all at
Did you ev - er see a hand - some las - sie, Dia - monds spark - ling

can - dle - light. "Las - sie, I have come a - court - in', Your kind fa - vors
call a - gain. What would I do when I go walk - ing, Walk - ing out in the
your com - mand." What do I care for your ships on the o - cean? What do I care for your
your hair? Did you ev - er see a cop - per ket - tle Mend - ed with an

for to win; And if you'll but smile up - on me, Next Sun-day night I'll call a - gain."
morn - ing dew? What would I do when I go walk - ing, Walk - ing out with a lad like you?"
hous - es and lands? What do I care for your gold and sil - ver? All I want is a hand - some man."
old tin can? Did you ev - er see a hand - some dam - sel Mar - ried off to an ug - ly man?"

Rad - dy ah the too - dum too - dum too - dum, Rad - dy ah the too - dum doo - dum day,

Rad - dy ah the too - dum too - dum too - dum, Rad - dy ah the too - dum doo - dum day.

THE GALWAY PIPER

Irish folksong

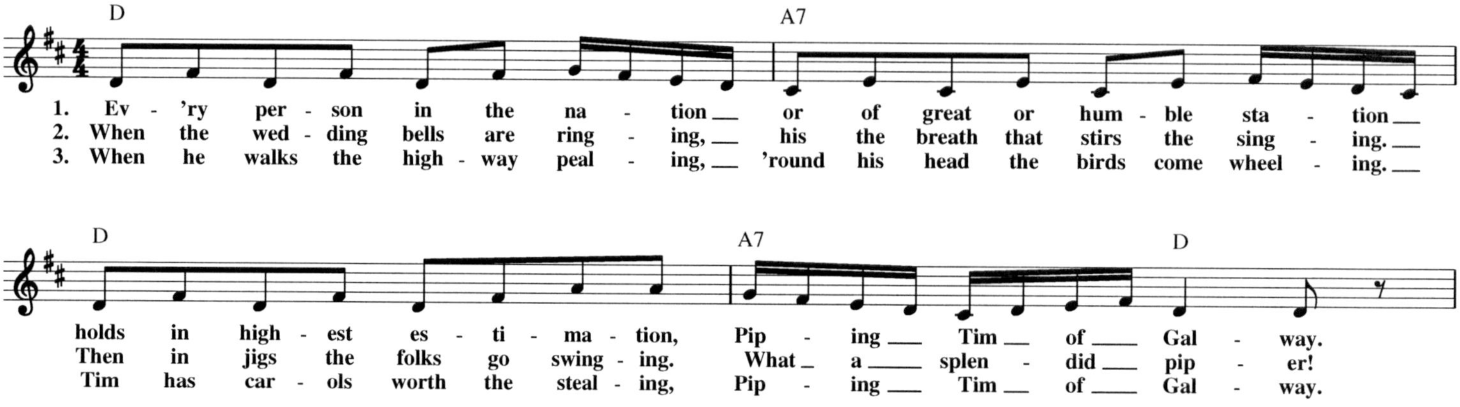

1. Ev - 'ry per - son in the na - tion or of great or hum - ble sta - tion
2. When the wed - ding bells are ring - ing, his the breath that stirs the sing - ing.
3. When he walks the high - way peal - ing, 'round his head the birds come wheel - ing.

holds in high - est es - ti - ma - tion, Pip - ing Tim of Gal - way.
Then in jigs the folks go swing - ing. What a splen - did pip - er!
Tim has car - ols worth the steal - ing, Pip - ing Tim of Gal - way.

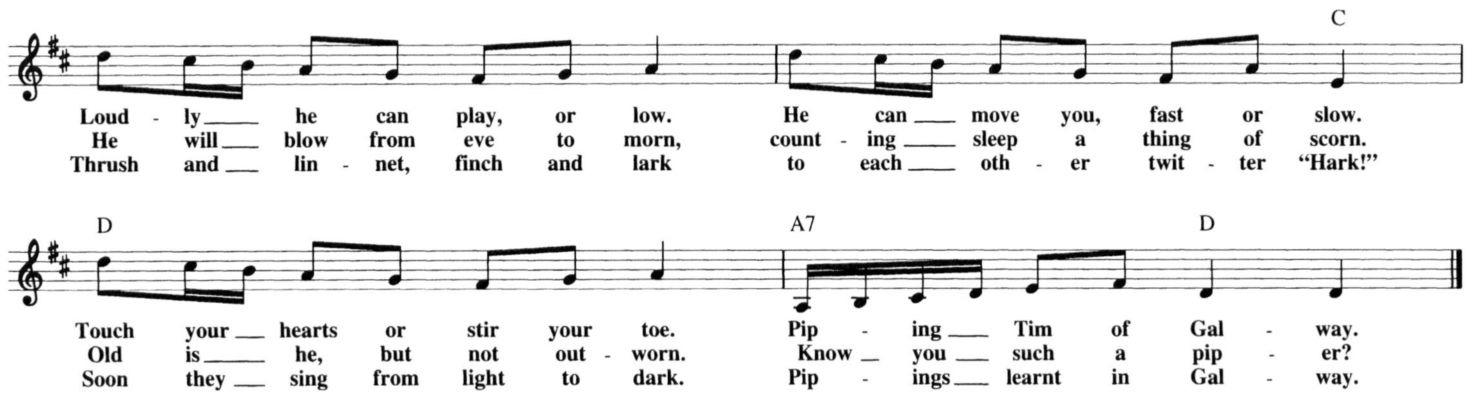

Loudly ___ he can play, or low. He can ___ move you, fast or slow.
He will ___ blow from eve to morn, count - ing ___ sleep a thing of scorn.
Thrush and ___ lin - net, finch and lark to each ___ oth - er twit - ter "Hark!"

Touch your ___ hearts or stir your toe. Pip - ing ___ Tim of Gal - way.
Old is ___ he, but not out - worn. Know ___ you ___ such a pip - er?
Soon they ___ sing from light to dark. Pip - ings ___ learnt in Gal - way.

THE GALWAY RACES

Irish folksong

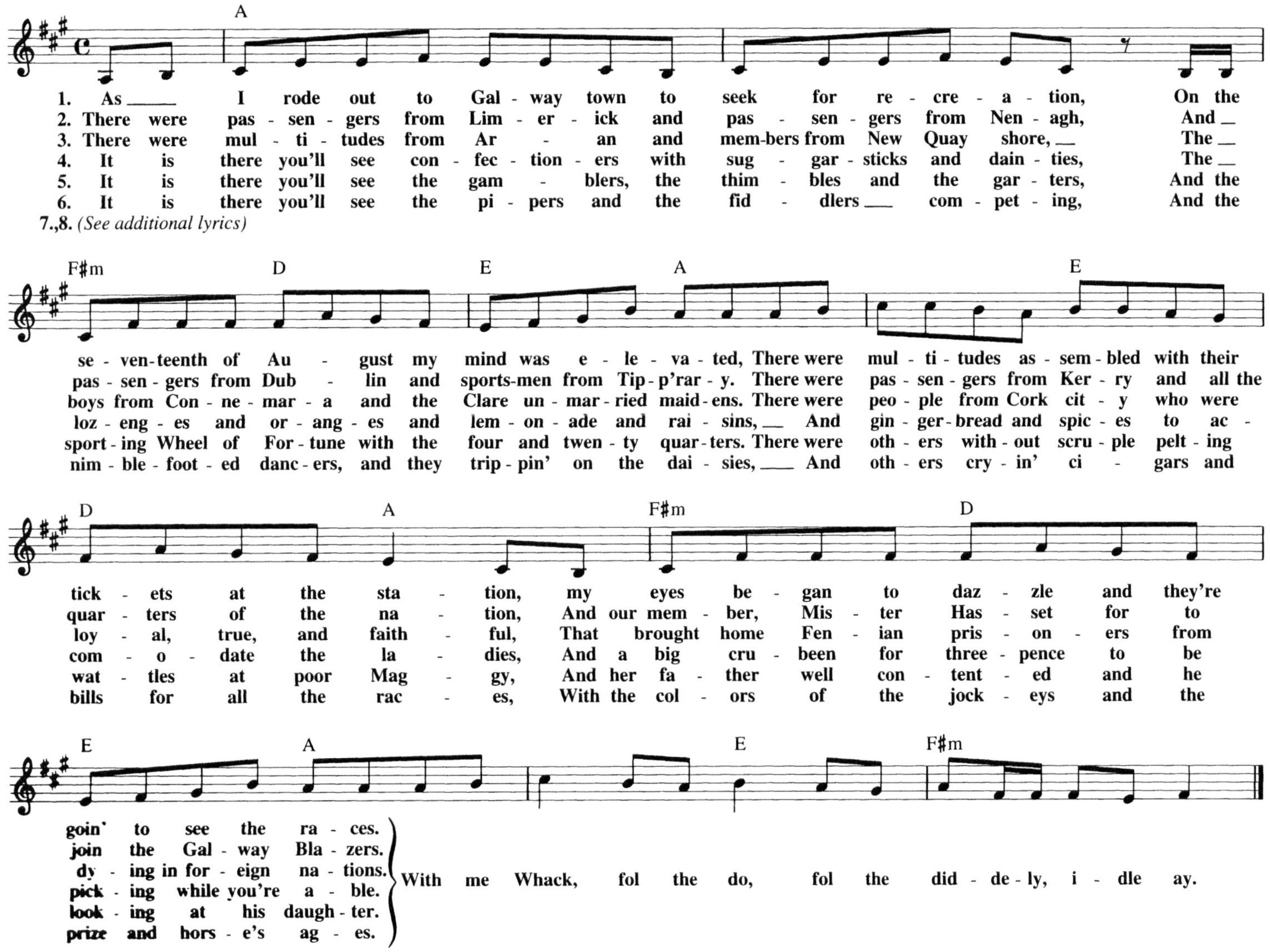

1. As ___ I rode out to Gal - way town to seek for re - cre - a - tion, On the
2. There were pas - sen - gers from Lim - er - ick and pas - sen - gers from Nen - agh, And ___
3. There were mul - ti - tudes from Ar - an and mem - bers from New Quay shore, ___ The ___
4. It is there you'll see con - fec - tion - ers with sug - ar - sticks and dain - ties, The ___
5. It is there you'll see the gam - blers, the thim - bles and the gar - ters, And the
6. It is there you'll see the pi - pers and the fid - dlers ___ com - pet - ing, And the

7.,8. *(See additional lyrics)*

se - ven - teenth of Au - gust my mind was e - le - va - ted, There were mul - ti - tudes as - sem - bled with their
pas - sen - gers from Dub - lin and sports - men from Tip - p'rar - y. There were pas - sen - gers from Ker - ry and all the
boys from Con - ne - mar - a and the Clare un - mar - ried maid - ens. There were peo - ple from Cork cit - y who were
loz - eng - es and or - ang - es and lem - on - ade and rai - sins, ___ And gin - ger - bread and spic - es to ac -
sport - ing Wheel of For - tune with the four and twen - ty quar - ters. There were oth - ers with - out scru - ple pelt - ing
nim - ble - foot - ed danc - ers, and they trip - pin' on the dai - sies, ___ And oth - ers cry - in' ci - gars and

tick - ets at the sta - tion, my eyes be - gan to daz - zle and they're
quar - ters of the na - tion, And our mem - ber, Mis - ter Has - set for to
loy - al, true, and faith - ful, That brought home Fen - ian pris - on - ers from
com - o - date the la - dies, And a big cru - been for three - pence to be
wat - tles at poor Mag - gy, And her fa - ther well con - tent - ed and he
bills for all the rac - es, With the col - ors of the jock - eys and the

goin' to see the ra - ces.
join the Gal - way Bla - zers.
dy - ing in for - eign na - tions. } With me Whack, fol the do, fol the did - de - ly, i - dle ay.
pick - ing while you're a - ble.
look - ing at his daugh - ter.
prize and hors - e's ag - es.

Additional Lyrics

7. It's there you'd see the jockeys and they mounted on most stately,
The pink and blue, the red and green, the emblem of our nation.
When the bell was rung for starting all the horses seemed impatient,
I thought they never stood on ground, their speed was so amazing.
Chorus

8. There was half a million people there of all denominations,
The Catholic, the Protestant, the Jew and Presbyterian.
There was yet no animosity, no matter what persuasion,
But fortune and hospitality inducing fresh acquaintance.
Chorus

THE GALWAY SHAWL

Irish folksong

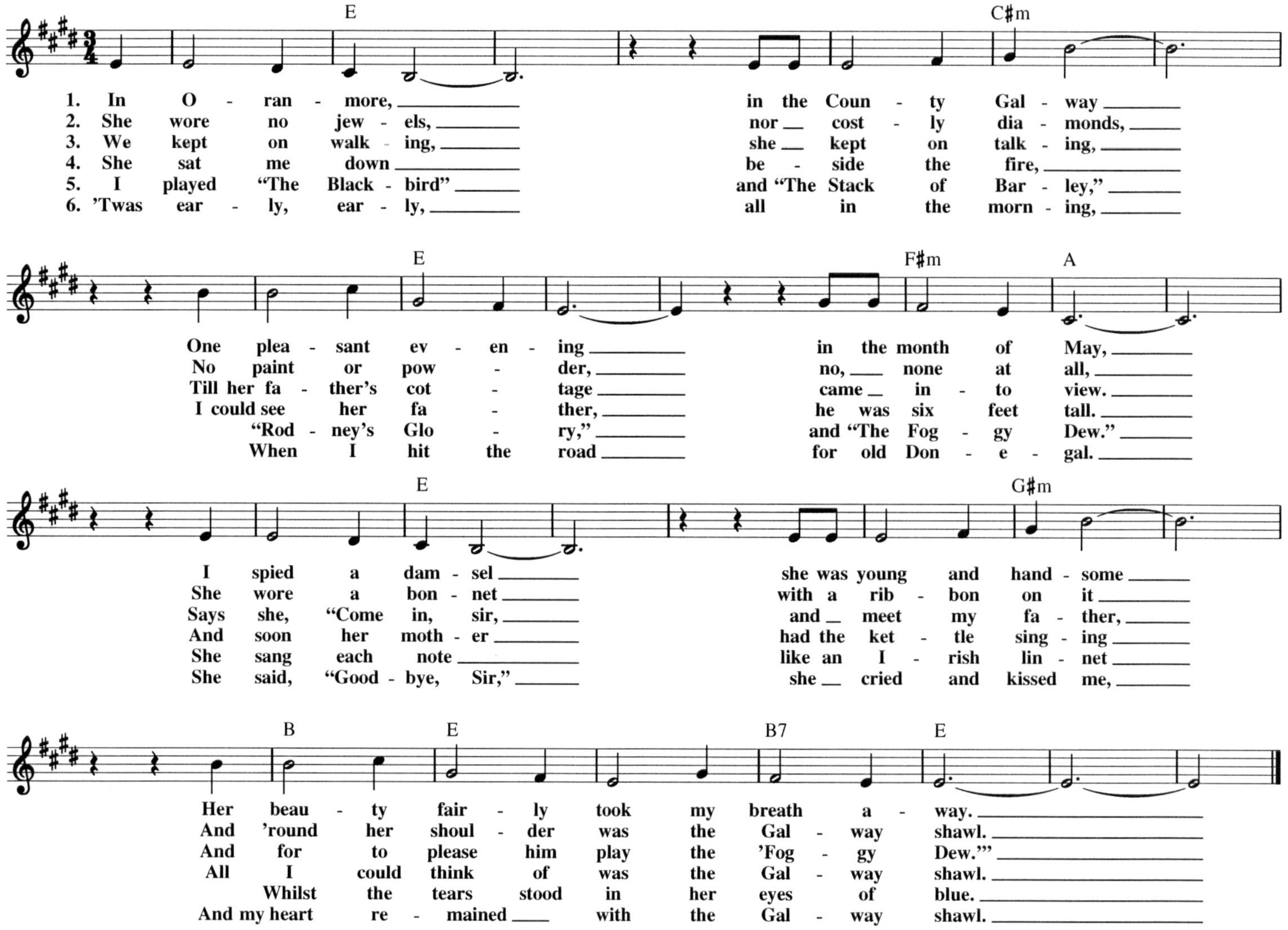

1. In O - ran - more, _____ in the Coun - ty Gal - way _____
2. She wore no jew - els, _____ nor __ cost - ly dia - monds, _____
3. We kept on walk - ing, _____ she __ kept on talk - ing, _____
4. She sat me down _____ be - side the fire, _____
5. I played "The Black - bird" _____ and "The Stack of Bar - ley," _____
6. 'Twas ear - ly, ear - ly, _____ all in the morn - ing, _____

One plea - sant ev - en - ing _____ in the month of May, _____
No paint or pow - der, _____ no, __ none at all, _____
Till her fa - ther's cot - tage _____ came __ in - to view. _____
I could see her fa - ther, _____ he was six feet tall. _____
"Rod - ney's Glo - ry," _____ and "The Fog - gy Dew." _____
When I hit the road _____ for old Don - e - gal. _____

I spied a dam - sel _____ she was young and hand - some _____
She wore a bon - net _____ with a rib - bon on it _____
Says she, "Come in, sir, _____ and __ meet my fa - ther, _____
And soon her moth - er _____ had the ket - tle sing - ing _____
She sang each note _____ like an I - rish lin - net _____
She said, "Good - bye, Sir," _____ she __ cried and kissed me, _____

Her beau - ty fair - ly took my breath a - way. _____
And 'round her shoul - der was the Gal - way shawl. _____
And for to please him play the 'Fog - gy Dew.'" _____
All I could think of was the Gal - way shawl. _____
Whilst the tears stood in her eyes of blue. _____
And my heart re - mained __ with the Gal - way shawl. _____

THE GAOL OF CLONMEL
(Príosún Chluain Meala)

Irish folksong

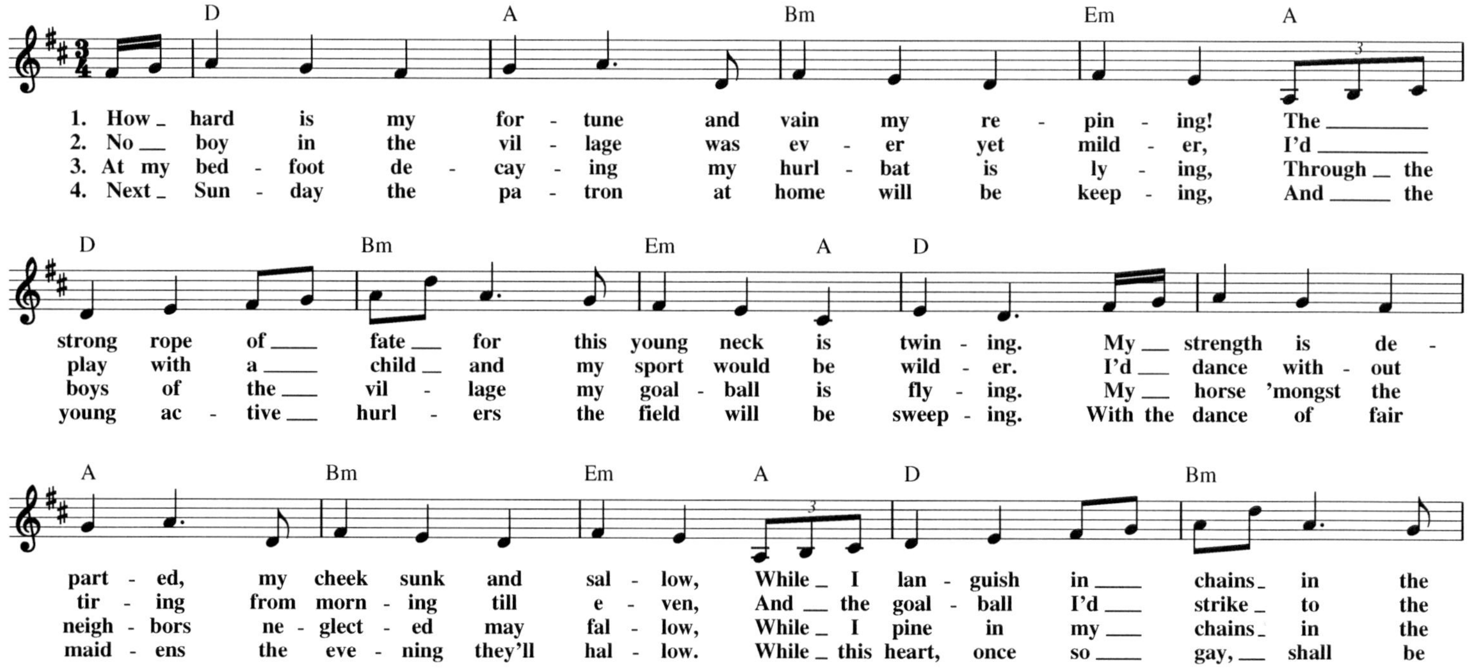

1. How _ hard is my for - tune and vain my re - pin - ing! The _____
2. No _ boy in the vil - lage was ev - er yet mild - er, I'd _____
3. At my bed - foot de - cay - ing my hurl - bat is ly - ing, Through __ the
4. Next _ Sun - day the pa - tron at home will be keep - ing, And _____ the

strong rope of ____ fate __ for this young neck is twin - ing. My __ strength is de -
play with a ____ child __ and my sport would be wild - er. I'd __ dance with - out
boys of the ___ vil - lage my goal - ball is fly - ing. My __ horse 'mongst the
young ac - tive __ hurl - ers the field will be sweep - ing. With the dance of fair

part - ed, my cheek sunk and sal - low, While _ I lan - guish in ____ chains _ in the
tir - ing, from morn - ing till e - ven, And _ the goal - ball I'd __ strike _ to the
neigh - bors ne - glect - ed may fal - low, While _ I pine in my ____ chains _ in the
maid - ens the eve - ning they'll hal - low. While _ this heart, once so ____ gay, _ shall be

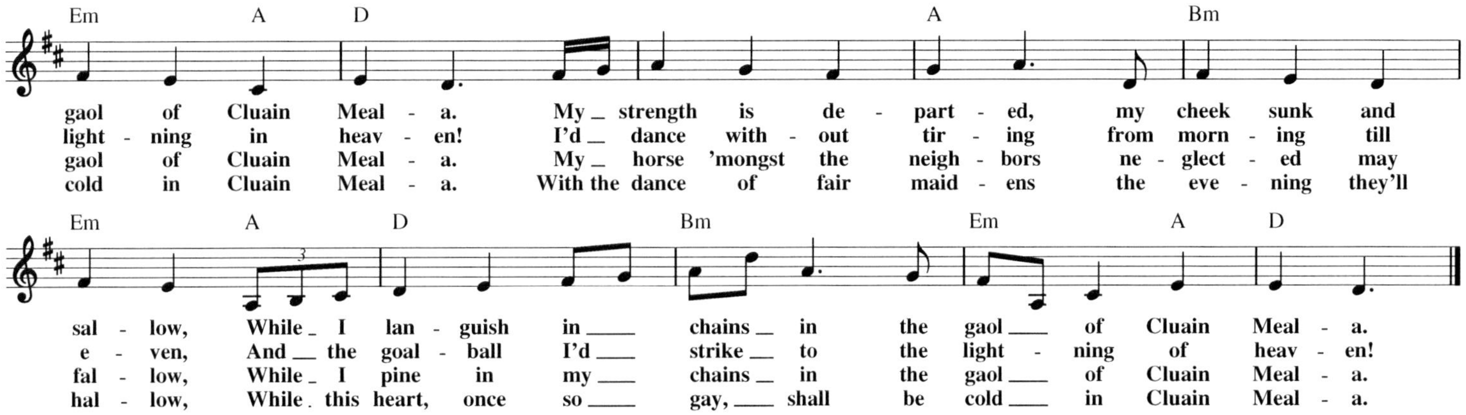

gaol of Cluain Meal - a. My _ strength is de - part - ed, my cheek sunk and
light - ning in heav - en! I'd _ dance with - out tir - ing from morn - ing till
gaol of Cluain Meal - a. My _ horse 'mongst the neigh - bors ne - glect - ed may
cold in Cluain Meal - a. With the dance of fair maid - ens the eve - ning they'll

sal - low, While _ I lan - guish in _____ chains _ in the gaol _____ of Cluain Meal - a.
e - ven, And _ the goal - ball I'd _____ strike _ to the light - ning of heav - en!
fal - low, While _ I pine in my _____ chains _ in the gaol _____ of Cluain Meal - a.
hal - low, While this heart, once so _____ gay, shall be cold _____ in Cluain Meal - a.

Gaelic Lyrics

1. *Ó! bliain is lá amáireach 'sea d'fhágas an baile*
   A' dul go h-Árd Pádraig, 'cur lásaí lem hata.
   Bhí Buachaillí Bána ann, is rás aca ar Eallaibh,
   Is mé go dúch uaigneach i bpríosún Chluain Meala.

2. *Tá mo shrian agus m'iallait ar iasacht le fada,*
   Mo chamán ar fiara fé iarthar mo leapa,
   Mo liathróid dá buala ag buachaillí an ghleanna—
   Is go mbuailfinn poc báire chomh h-árd leis na fearaibh!

3. *A Chiarraígh, bidh a' guí liom, is bog binn liom bhur nglórtha,*
   Is beag a shaoileas-sa choíche ná fillfinn-se beó orraibh:
   Go mbeidh ár dtrí cinn-ne ar trí spící mar sheó aca,
   Fé shneachta na h-oíche, is gach síon eile 'á ngeóidh chúinn!

4. *Go h-Uíbh Ráthach má théann tú, beir sgéal go dtí mo mhuinntir,*
   Go bhfuilim daor ar an bhfód so, is ná fuil beó agam ach go h-Aoine,
   Bailídh gléas tórraimh agus comhra bhreá im thímpal,
   Sin crích ar Ó Domhnaill, is go deó bídh a' guí leis!

GARRYOWEN

Irish folksong

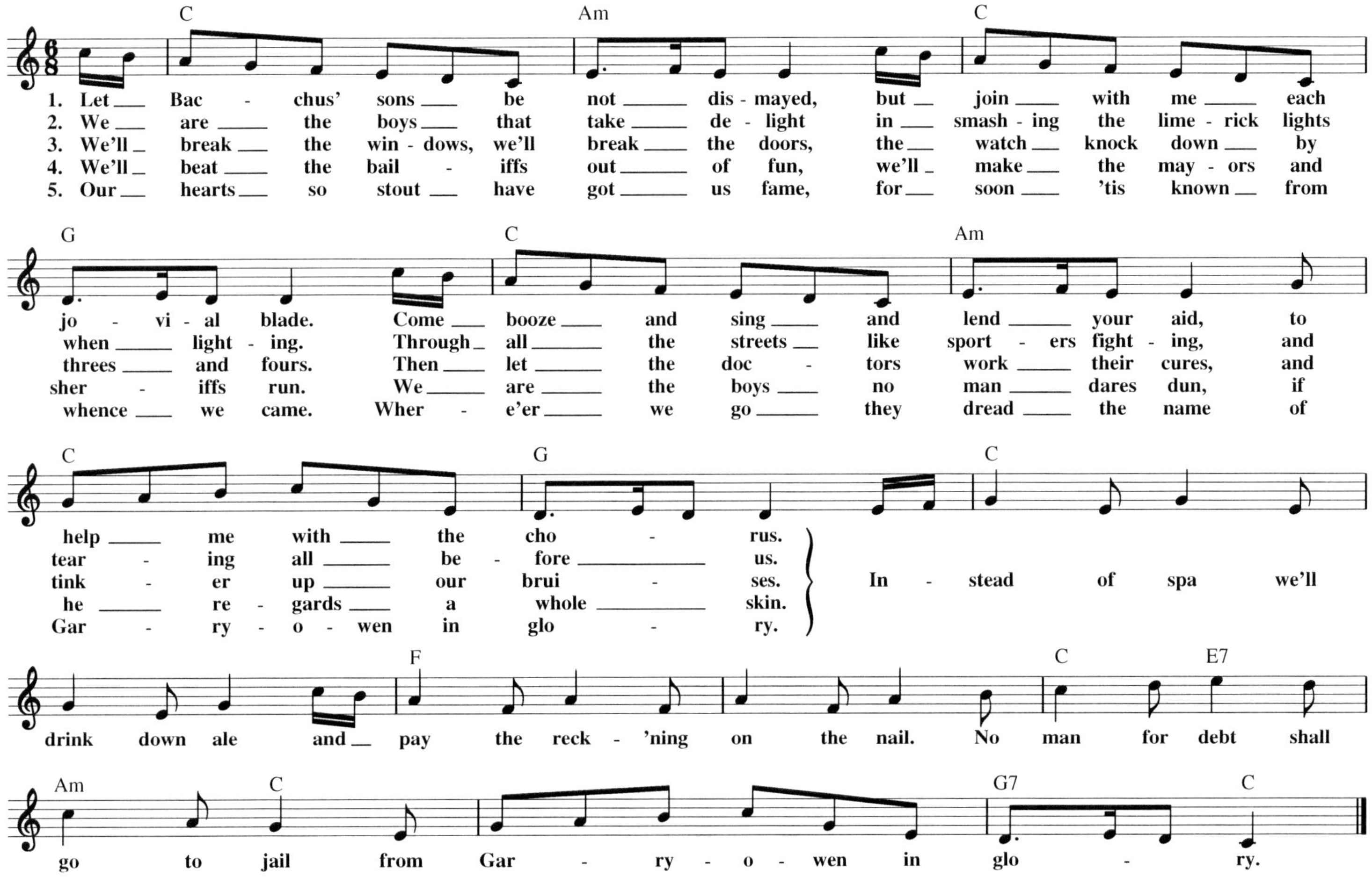

1. Let _ Bac - chus' sons _ be not _____ dis - mayed, but _ join _____ with me _____ each
2. We _ are _____ the boys _ that take _____ de - light in _ smash - ing the lime - rick lights
3. We'll _ break _ the win - dows, we'll break _____ the doors, the _ watch _ knock down _ by
4. We'll _ beat _ the bail - iffs out _____ of fun, we'll _ make _ the may - ors and
5. Our _ hearts _ so stout _ have got _____ us fame, for _ soon _ 'tis known _ from

jo - vi - al blade. Come _ booze _____ and sing _ and lend _____ your aid, to
when _____ light - ing. Through _ all the streets _ like sport - ers fight - ing, and
threes _____ and fours. Then _ let _____ the doc - tors work _____ their cures, and
sher - iffs run. We _____ are _____ the boys _ no man _____ dares dun, if
whence _____ we came. Wher - e'er _____ we go _____ they dread _____ the name of

help _____ me with _____ the cho - rus. }
tear - ing all _____ be - fore _____ us. }
tink - er up _____ our brui - ses. } In - stead of spa we'll
he _ re - gards _ a whole _____ skin. }
Gar - ry - o - wen in glo - ry. }

drink down ale and _ pay the reck - 'ning on the nail. No man for debt shall

go to jail from Gar - ry - o - wen in glo - ry.

THE GARDEN WHERE THE PRATIES GROW

Irish folksong

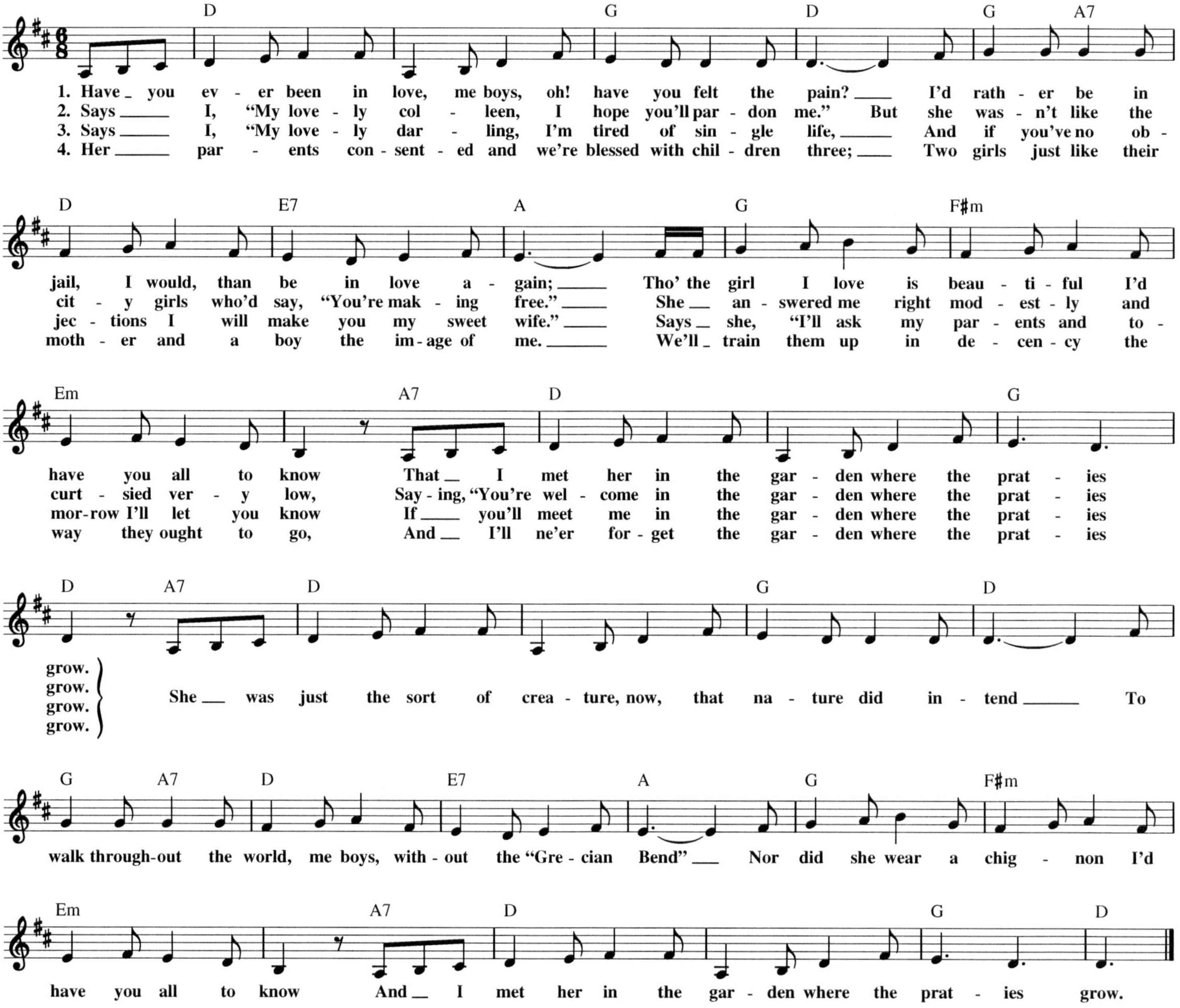

1. Have you ev-er been in love, me boys, oh! have you felt the pain? __ I'd rath-er be in
2. Says __ I, "My love-ly col-leen, I hope you'll par-don me." But she was-n't like the
3. Says __ I, "My love-ly dar-ling, I'm tired of sin-gle life, __ And if you've no ob-
4. Her __ par-ents con-sent-ed and we're blessed with chil-dren three; __ Two girls just like their

jail, I would, than be in love a-gain; __ Tho' the girl I love is beau-ti-ful I'd
cit-y girls who'd say, "You're mak-ing free." __ She an-swered me right mod-est-ly and
jec-tions I will make you my sweet wife." __ Says she, "I'll ask my par-ents and to-
moth-er and a boy the im-age of me. __ We'll train them up in de-cen-cy the

have you all to know That __ I met her in the gar-den where the prat-ies
curt-sied ver-y low, Say-ing, "You're wel-come in the gar-den where the prat-ies
mor-row I'll let you know If __ you'll meet me in the gar-den where the prat-ies
way they ought to go, And __ I'll ne'er for-get the gar-den where the prat-ies

grow.
grow.
grow.
grow.   She __ was just the sort of crea-ture, now, that na-ture did in-tend __ To

walk through-out the world, me boys, with-out the "Gre-cian Bend" __ Nor did she wear a chig-non I'd

have you all to know And __ I met her in the gar-den where the prat-ies grow.

THE GIRL I LEFT BEHIND ME

Irish folksong

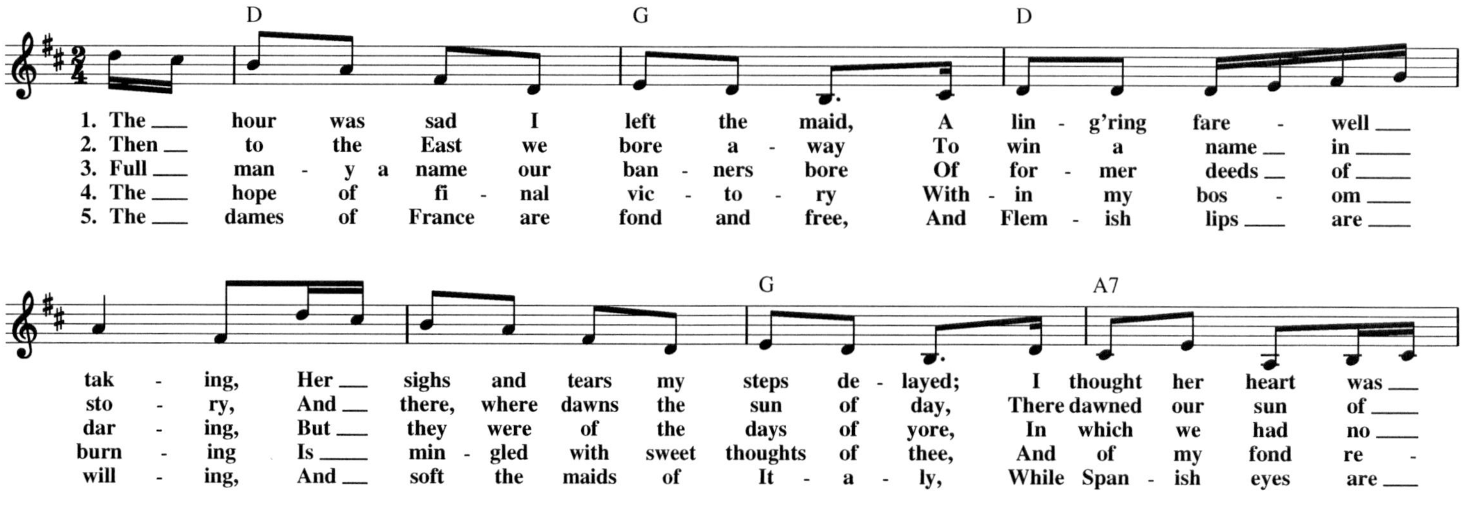

1. The __ hour was sad I left the maid, A lin-g'ring fare-well __
2. Then __ to the East we bore a-way To win a name __ in __
3. Full __ man-y a name our ban-ners bore Of for-mer deeds __ of __
4. The __ hope of fi-nal vic-to-ry With-in my bos-om __
5. The __ dames of France are fond and free, And Flem-ish lips __ are __

tak-ing, Her __ sighs and tears my steps de-layed; I thought her heart was __
sto-ry, And __ there, where dawns the sun of day, There dawned our sun of __
dar-ing, But __ they were of the days of yore, In which we had no __
burn-ing Is __ min-gled with sweet thoughts of thee, And of my fond re-
will-ing, And __ soft the maids of It-a-ly, While Span-ish eyes are __

D E7 D E7 A7
break - ing. In ___ hur - ried words her name I blessed, I breathed the vows that
glo - ry. Both ___ blazed in noon on Al - ma's heights When, in the past as -
shar - ing. But ___ now our lau - rels fresh - ly won With the old ones shall en -
turn - ing. But ___ should I ne'er re - turn a - gain, Still worth thy love thou'lt
thrill - ing. Still ___ though I bask be - neath their smile, Their charms quite fail to
Bm A7 D G A7 D
bind me, And ___ to my heart in an - guish pressed The girl I left be - hind me.
signed me, I ___ shared the glo - ry of that fight, Sweet girl I left be - hind me.
twined be, Still ___ wor - thy of his sire each son, Sweet girl I left be - hind me.
find me; Dis - hon - or's breath shall nev - er stain The name I leave be - hind me.
bind me, And my heart falls back to Er - in's Isle To the girl I left be - hind me.

THE GOLDEN JUBILEE

Irish folksong

G C G
1. Way down in the Coun - ty Ker - ry. In the place they call Tra - lee, A fine old coup - le
2. Ah, well do ___ I re - mem - ber when we danced on the vil - lage green, You held me in your
3. Ah, well do ___ I re - mem - ber when ___ first I was your bride, In the lit - tle chap - el
Em A7 D7 G
they lived there, called Kate and Pat Mc - Gee. They were goin' to hold a par - ty on their
arms, dear Pat and called me your col - leen. Your ___ hair was like the ra - ven's wing, but ___
yon - der there, where we sat side by side. Of ___ good things we've had man - y, of ___
C G Em A7 D7 G
gold - en ju - bi - lee, And Kate said she to Pat Mc - Gee, "Come lis - ten here to me."
now 'tis turn - ing grey, Come o - ver here, ol' sweet - heart dear, and hear what I've to say.
trou - bles we've had few: Come o - ver here, ol' sweet - heart dear, and here's what you must do.
C G
"Put on your ol' knee breech - es, And your coat of em - 'rald green Take off that hat, me
Em A7 D7 G
dar - lin' Pat, put on your ol' Cau - been. For to - day's our gold - en wed - ding, And we
C G Em A7 D7 G
want them all to know The way we looked when we were wed, just fif - ty years a - go."

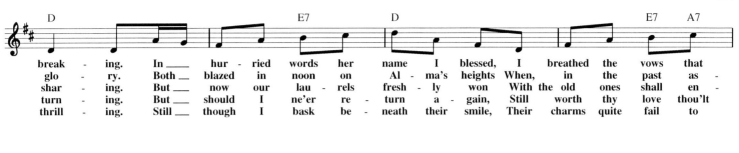

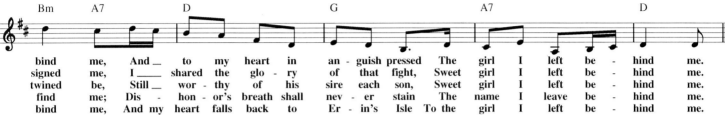

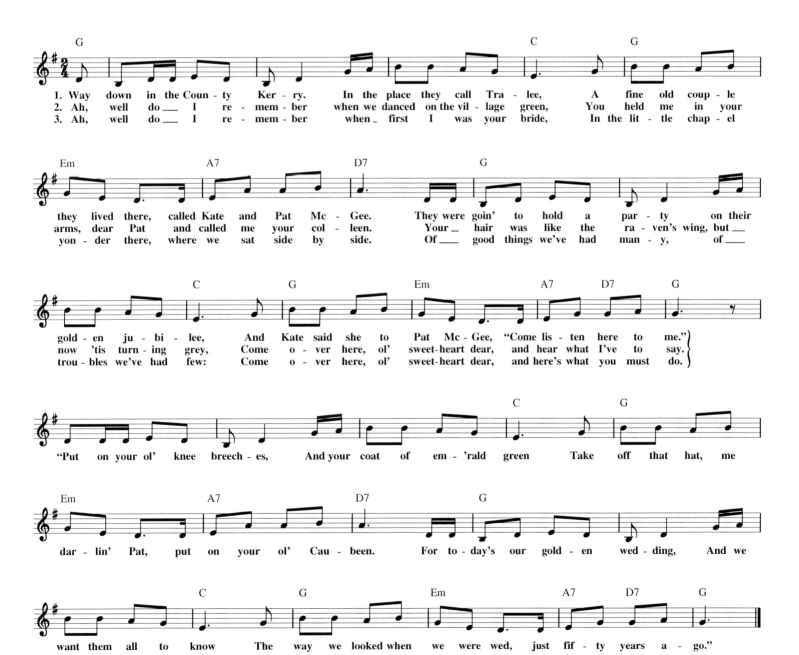

THE GIRLS OF COLERAINE

Irish folksong

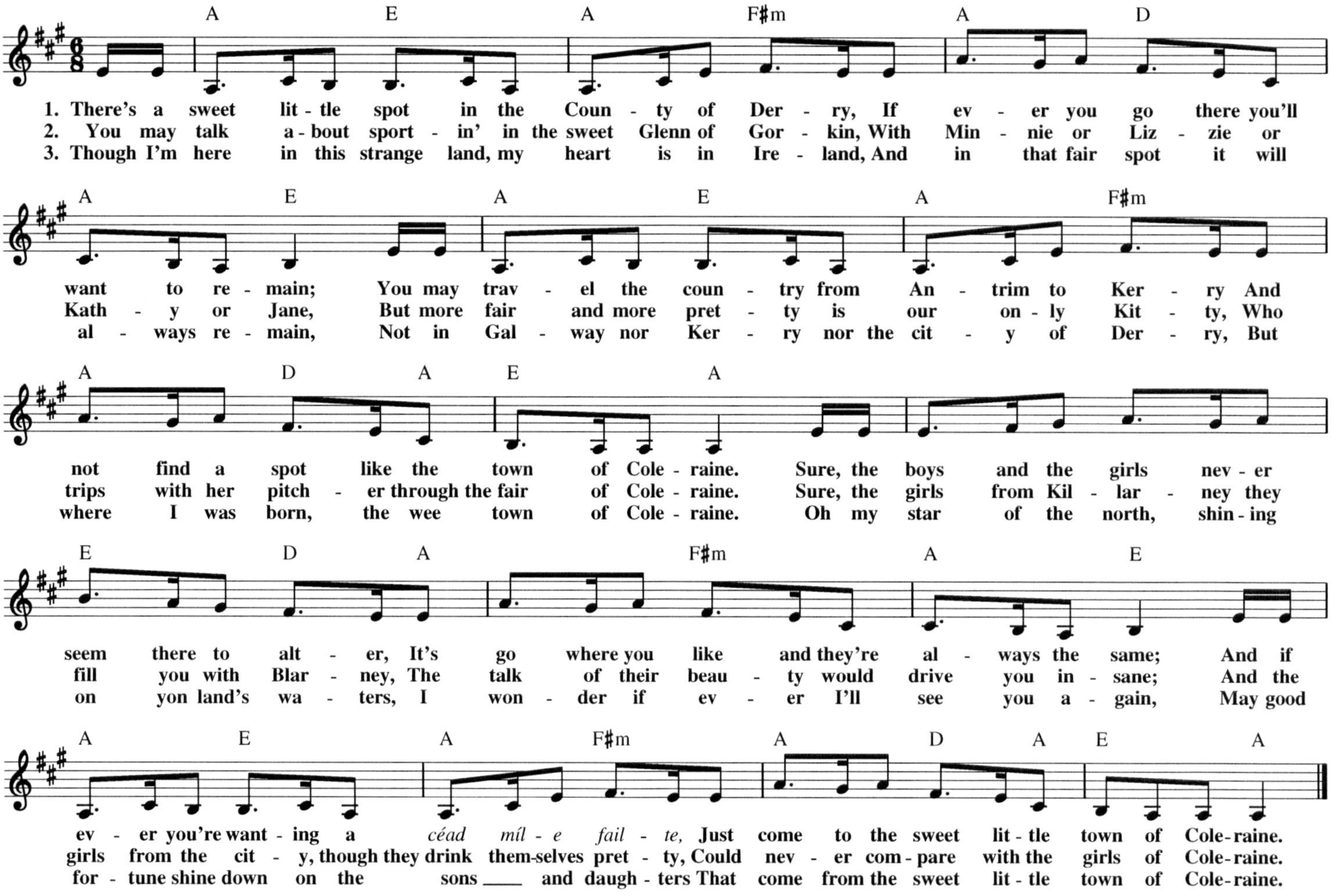

1. There's a sweet lit - tle spot in the Coun - ty of Der - ry, If ev - er you go there you'll
2. You may talk a - bout sport - in' in the sweet Glenn of Gor - kin, With Min - nie or Liz - zie or
3. Though I'm here in this strange land, my heart is in Ire - land, And in that fair spot it will

want to re - main; You may trav - el the coun - try from An - trim to Ker - ry And
Kath - y or Jane, But more fair and more pret - ty is our on - ly Kit - ty, Who
al - ways re - main, Not in Gal - way nor Ker - ry nor the cit - y of Der - ry, But

not find a spot like the town of Cole - raine. Sure, the boys and the girls nev - er
trips with her pitch - er through the fair of Cole - raine. Sure, the girls from Kil - lar - ney they
where I was born, the wee town of Cole - raine. Oh my star of the north, shin - ing

seem there to al - ter, It's go where you like and they're al - ways the same; And if
fill you with Blar - ney, The talk of their beau - ty would drive you in - sane; And the
on yon land's wa - ters, I won - der if ev - er I'll see you a - gain, May good

ev - er you're want - ing a *céad míl - e fail - te,* Just come to the sweet lit - tle town of Cole - raine.
girls from the cit - y, though they drink them-selves pret - ty, Could nev - er com - pare with the girls of Cole - raine.
for - tune shine down on the sons ___ and daugh - ters That come from the sweet lit - tle town of Cole - raine.

THE GREAT SILKIE

Scottish folksong

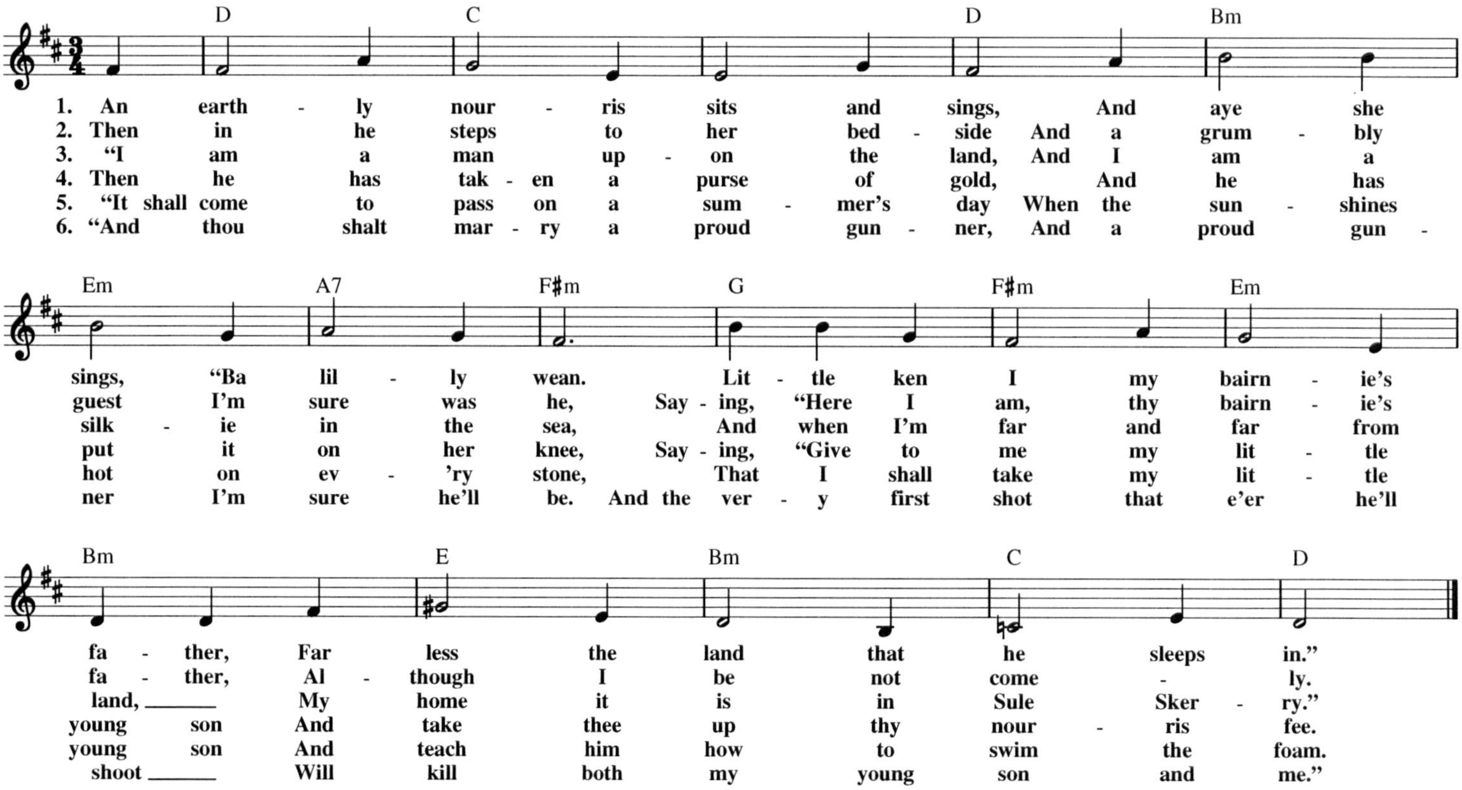

1. An earth - ly nour - ris sits and sings, And aye she
2. Then in he steps to her bed - side And a grum - bly
3. "I am a man up - on the land, And I am a
4. Then he has tak - en a purse of gold, And he has
5. "It shall come to pass on a sum - mer's day When the sun shines
6. "And thou shalt mar - ry a proud gun - ner, And a proud gun -

sings, "Ba lil - ly wean. Lit - tle ken I my bairn - ie's
guest I'm sure was he, Say - ing, "Here I am, thy bairn - ie's
silk - ie in the sea, And when I'm far and far from
put it on her knee, Say - ing, "Give to me my lit - tle
hot on ev - 'ry stone, That I shall take my lit - tle
ner I'm sure he'll be. And the ver - y first shot that e'er he'll

fa - ther, Far less the land that he sleeps in."
fa - ther, Al - though I be not come - ly.
land, ___ My home it is in Sule Sker - ry."
young son And take thee up thy nour - ris fee.
young son And teach him how to swim the foam.
shoot ___ Will kill both my young son and me."

THE GREEN FIELDS OF AMERICA

Irish folksong

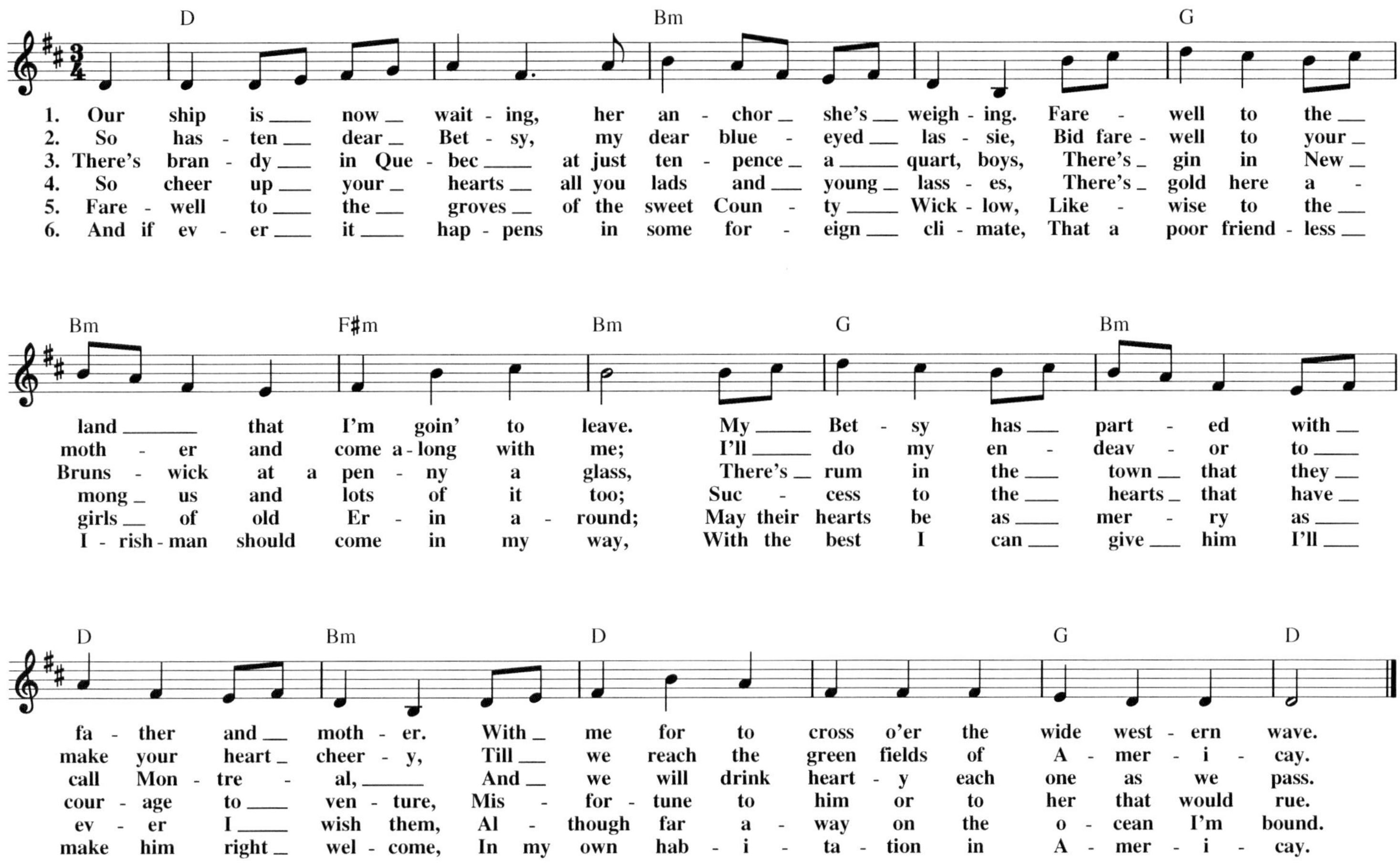

GREEN GROW THE RASHES, O

Scottish folksong
By Robert Burns

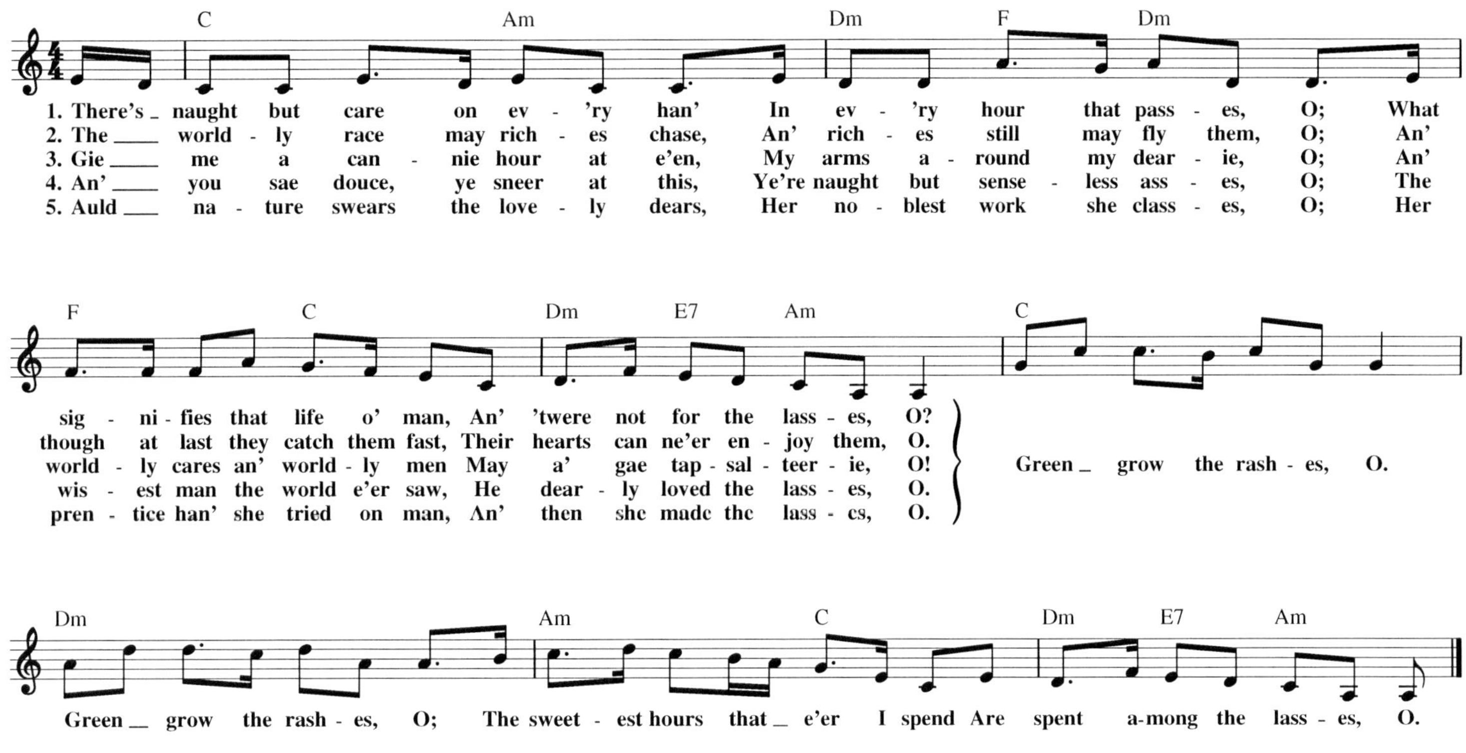

GREEN GROWS THE LAUREL

Irish folksong

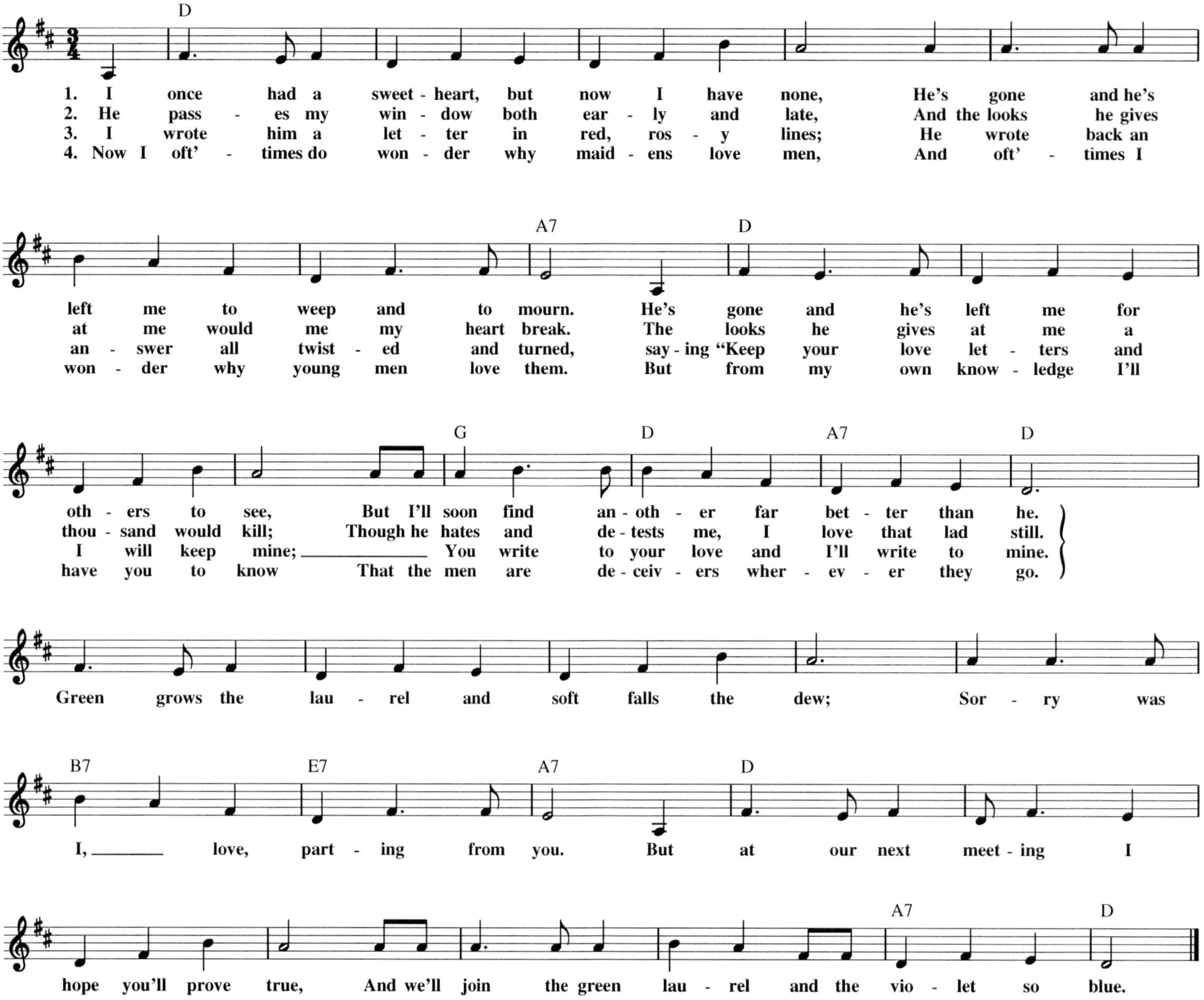

1. I once had a sweet-heart, but now I have none, He's gone and he's
2. He pass-es my win-dow both ear-ly and late, And the looks he gives
3. I wrote him a let-ter in red, ros-y lines; He wrote back an
4. Now I oft'-times do won-der why maid-ens love men, And oft'-times I

left me to weep and to mourn. He's gone and he's left me for
at me would me my heart break. The looks he gives at me a
an-swer all twist-ed and turned, say-ing "Keep your love let-ters and
won-der why young men love them. But from my own know-ledge I'll

oth-ers to see, But I'll soon find an-oth-er far bet-ter than he.
thou-sand would kill; Though he hates and de-tests me, I love that lad still.
I will keep mine; You write to your love and I'll write to mine.
have you to know That the men are de-ceiv-ers wher-ev-er they go.

Green grows the lau-rel and soft falls the dew; Sor-ry was

I, love, part-ing from you. But at our next meet-ing I

hope you'll prove true, And we'll join the green lau-rel and the vio-let so blue.

THE HARP OF DUNVEGAN
(Clarsach Shil-Leoid)

Folksong from the Hebrides

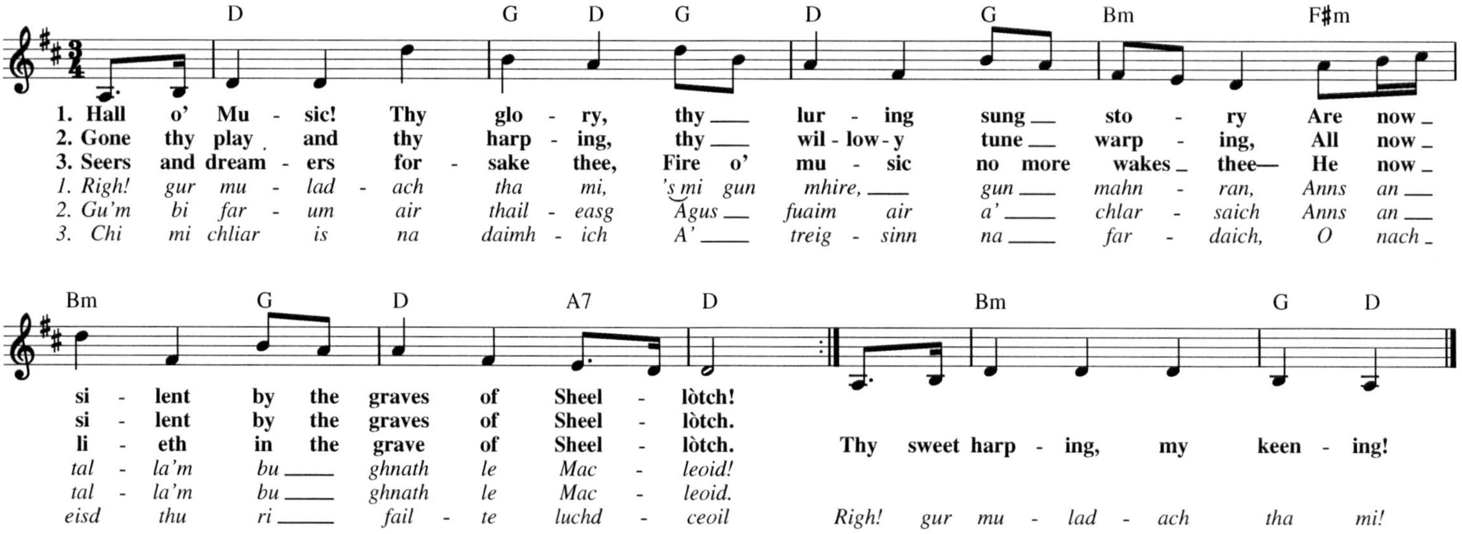

1. Hall o' Mu-sic! Thy glo-ry, thy lur-ing sung sto-ry Are now
2. Gone thy play and thy harp-ing, thy wil-low-y tune warp-ing, All now
3. Seers and dream-ers for-sake thee, Fire o' mu-sic no more wakes thee— He now

si-lent by the graves of Sheel-lòtch!
si-lent by the graves of Sheel-lòtch.
li-eth in the grave of Sheel-lòtch. Thy sweet harp-ing, my keen-ing!

THE HARP THAT ONCE

Irish popular song
Words by Thomas Moore

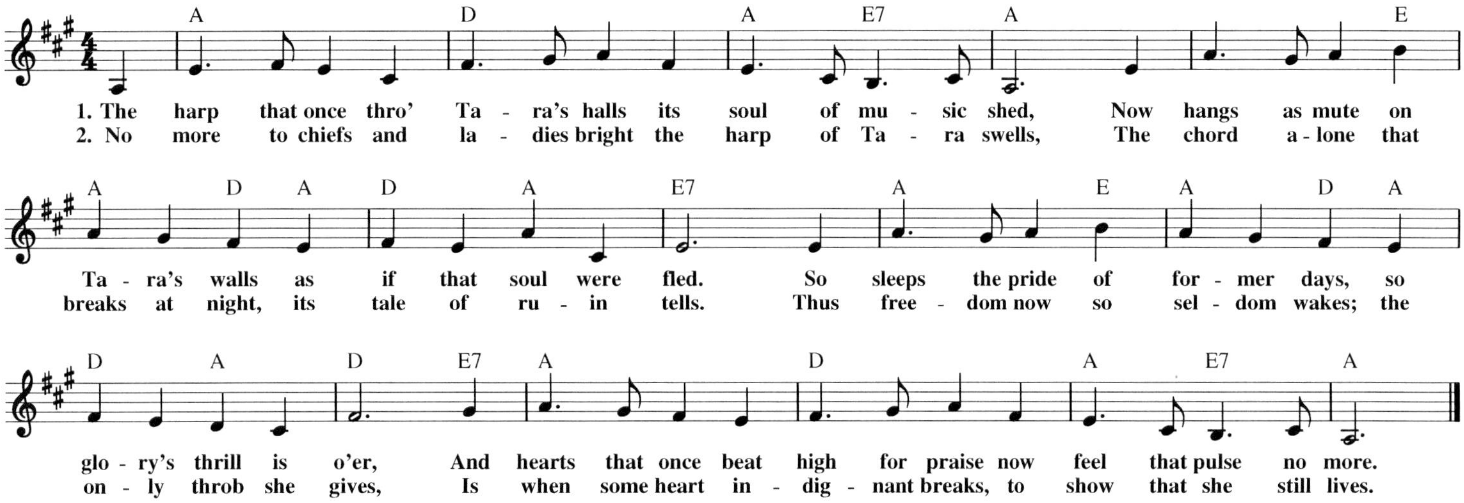

THE HARPER
(An Clarsair)

Folksong from the Hebrides

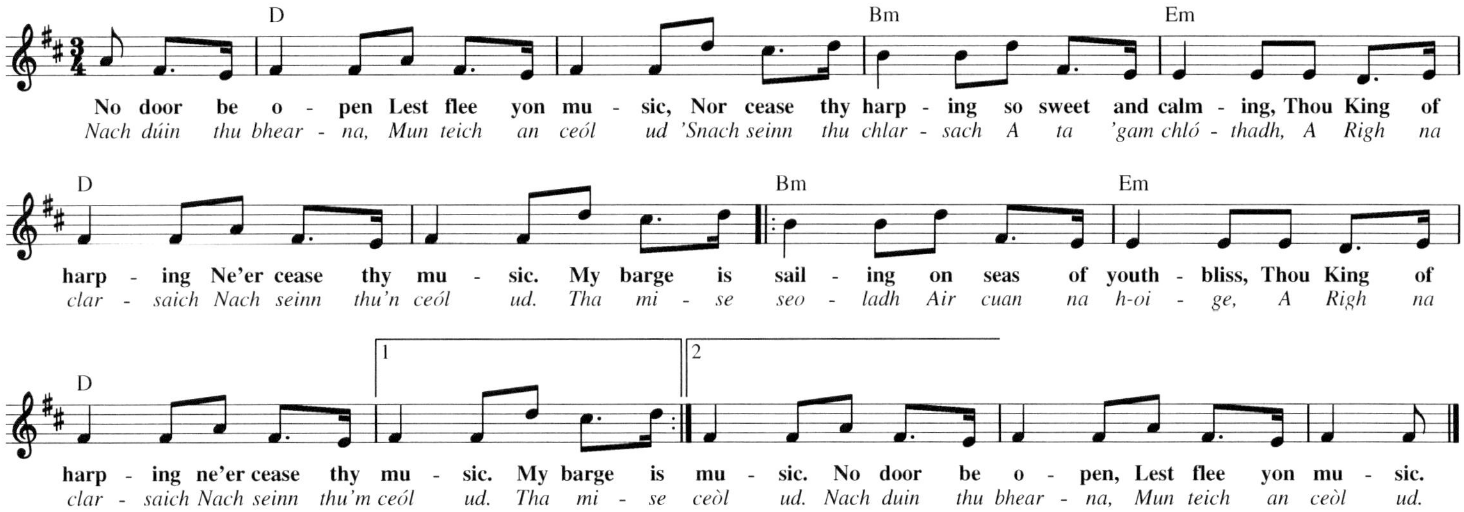

HARRIGAN

Words and Music by
George M. Cohan

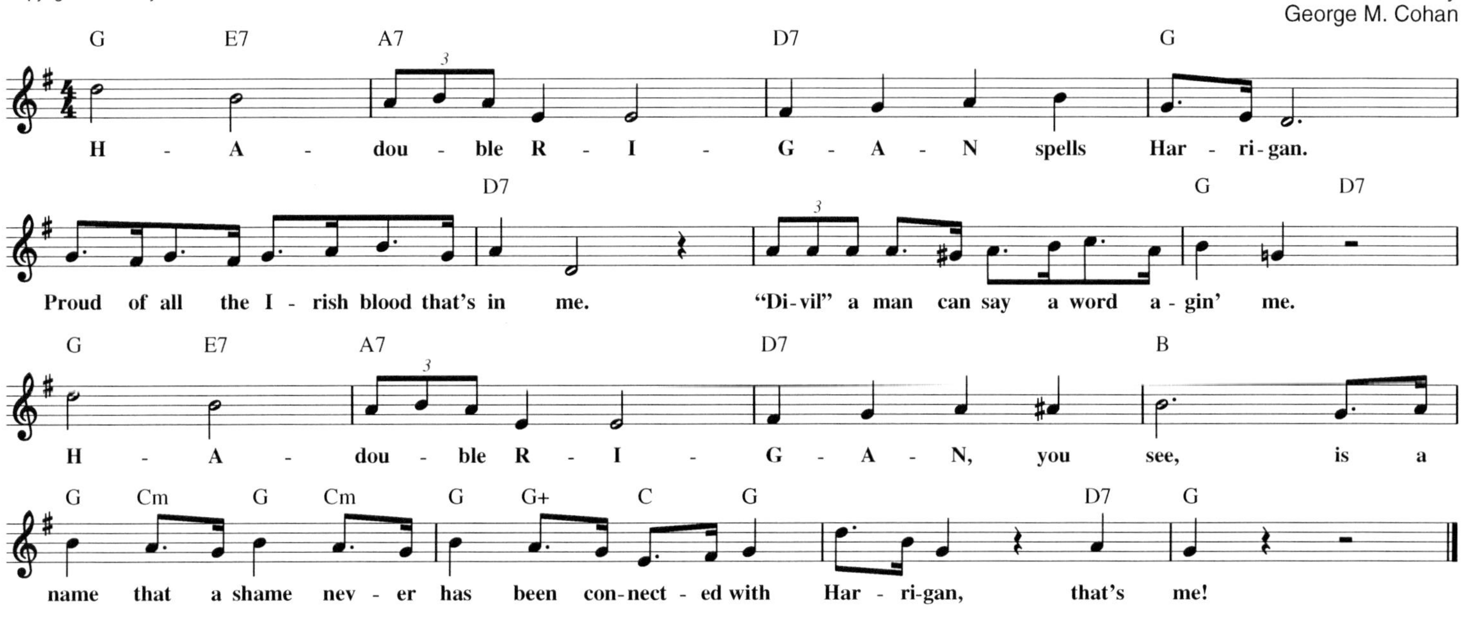

＃106

HAS ANYBODY HERE SEEN KELLY?

Words and Music by C.W. Murphy
and Will Letters

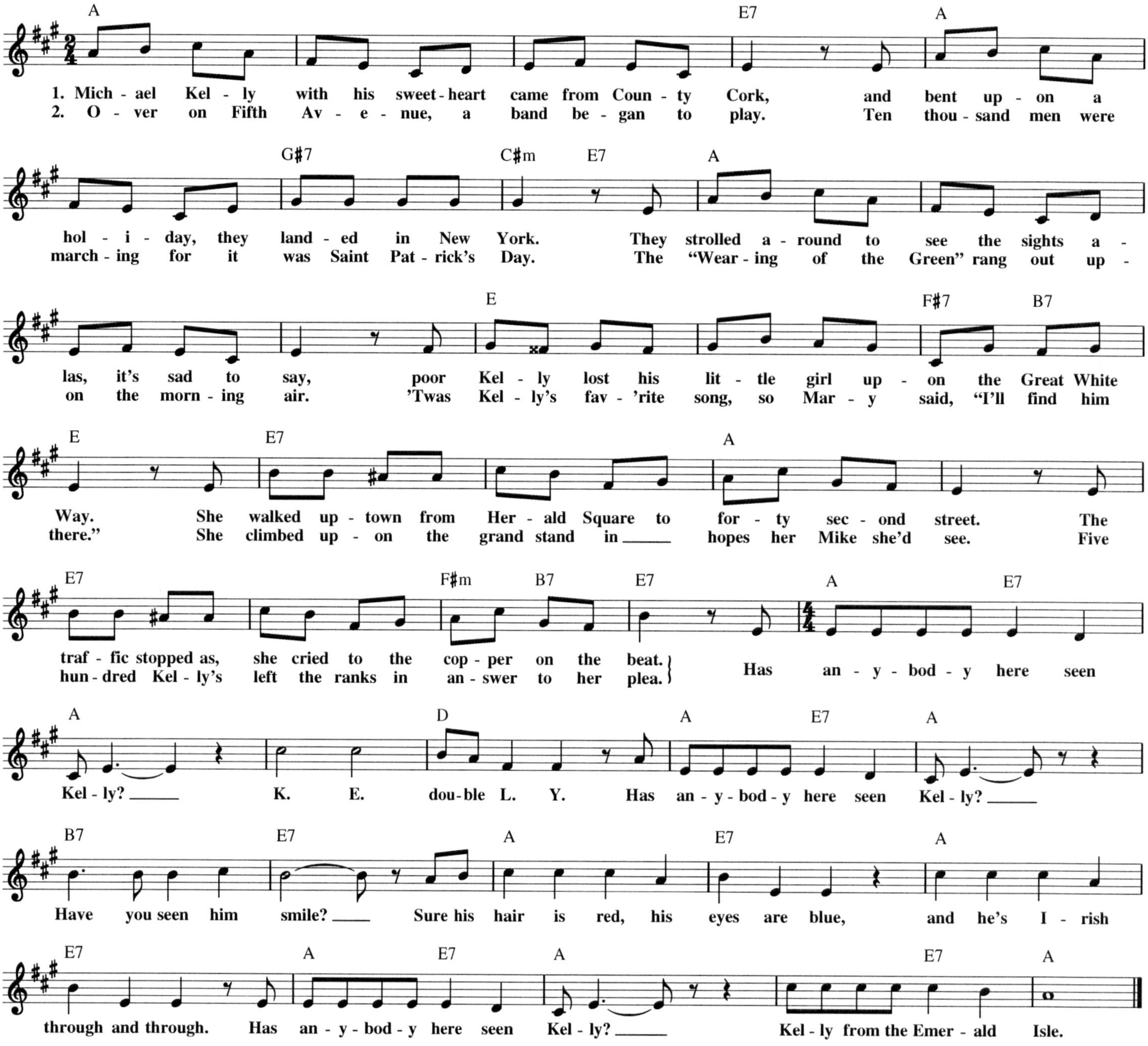

HAS SORROW THY YOUNG DAYS SHADED?

Irish folksong
Words by Thomas Moore

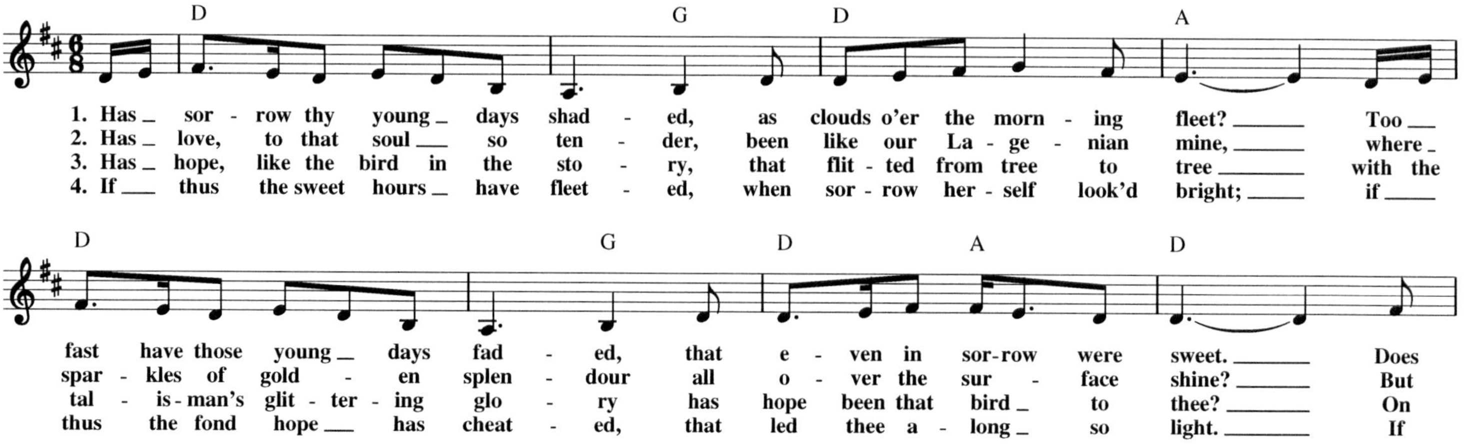

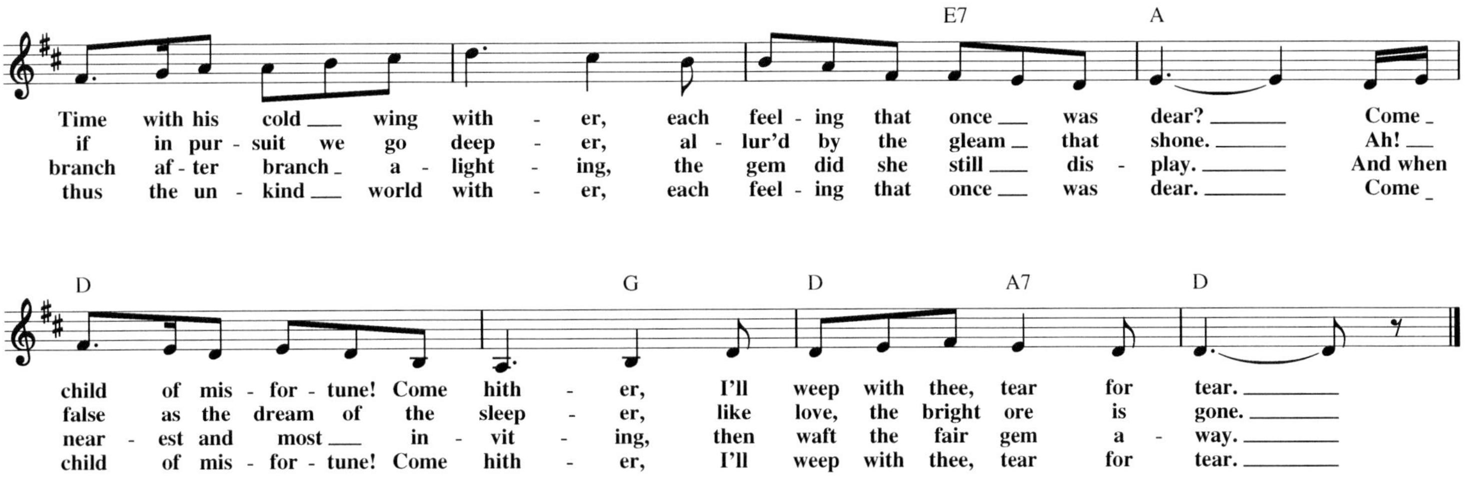

Time with his cold ___ wing with - er, each feel - ing that once ___ was dear? _____ Come _
if in pur - suit we go deep - er, al - lur'd by the gleam _ that shone. _____ Ah! ___
branch af - ter branch _ a - light - ing, the gem did she still ___ dis - play. _____ And when
thus the un - kind ___ world with - er, each feel - ing that once ___ was dear. _____ Come _

child of mis - for - tune! Come hith - er, I'll weep with thee, tear for tear. _____
false as the dream of the sleep - er, like love, the bright ore is gone. _____
near - est and most ___ in - vit - ing, then waft the fair gem a - way. _____
child of mis - for - tune! Come hith - er, I'll weep with thee, tear for tear. _____

THE HAT MY FATHER WORE

Words and Music by
Edwin Ferguson

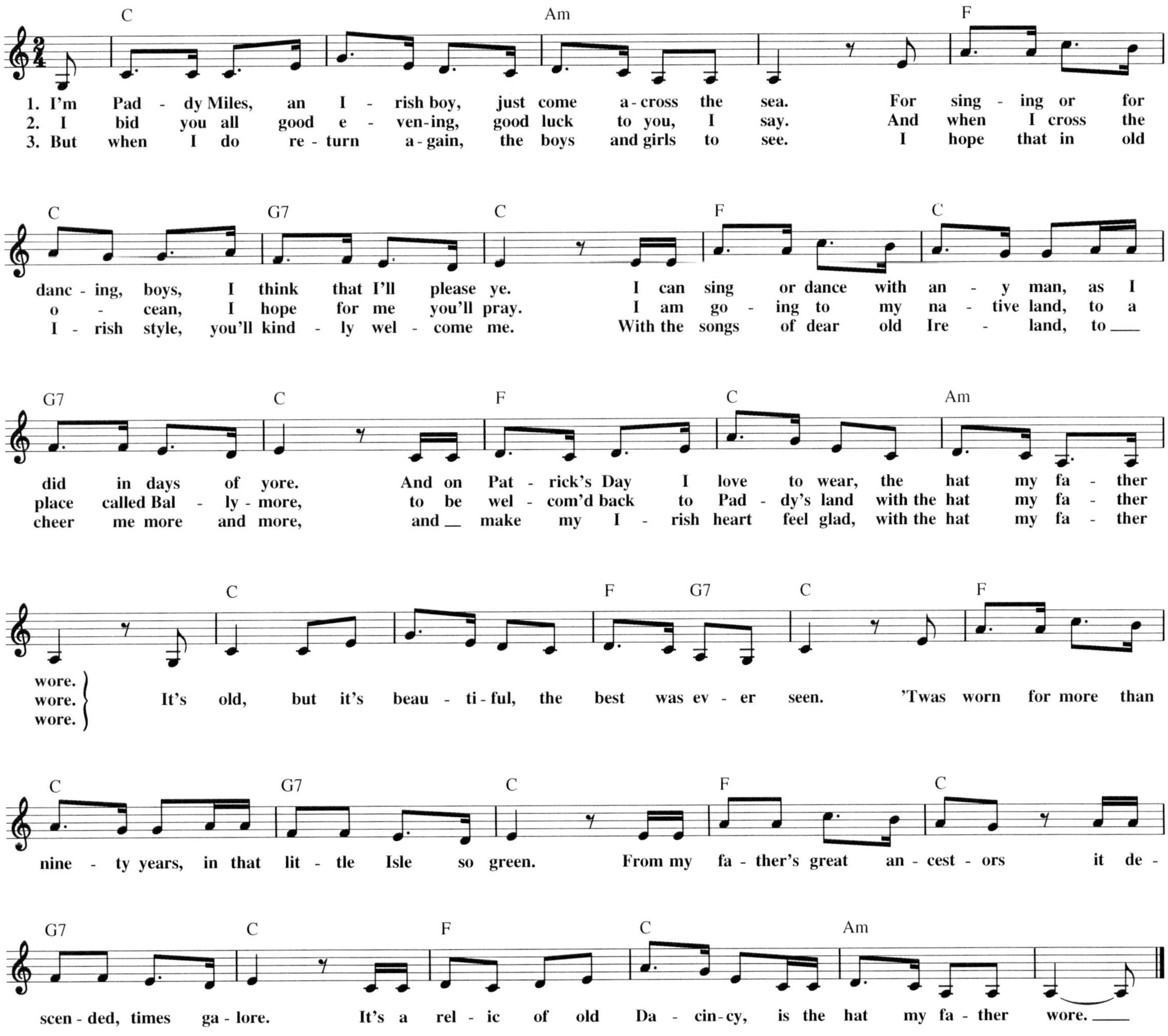

1. I'm Pad - dy Miles, an I - rish boy, just come a - cross the sea. For sing - ing or for
2. I bid you all good e - ven - ing, good luck to you, I say. And when I cross the
3. But when I do re - turn a - gain, the boys and girls to see. I hope that in old

danc - ing, boys, I think that I'll please ye. I can sing or dance with an - y man, as I
o - cean, I hope for me you'll pray. I am go - ing to my na - tive land, to a
I - rish style, you'll kind - ly wel - come me. With the songs of dear old Ire - land, to ___

did in days of yore. And on Pat - rick's Day I love to wear, the hat my fa - ther
place called Bal - ly - more, to be wel - com'd back to Pad - dy's land with the hat my fa - ther
cheer me more and more, and ___ make my I - rish heart feel glad, with the hat my fa - ther

wore. }
wore. }   It's old, but it's beau - ti - ful, the best was ev - er seen. 'Twas worn for more than
wore. }

nine - ty years, in that lit - tle Isle so green. From my fa - ther's great an - cest - ors it de -

scen - ded, times ga - lore. It's a rel - ic of old Da - cin - cy, is the hat my fa - ther wore. ___

HIELAND LADDIE

Scottish folksong

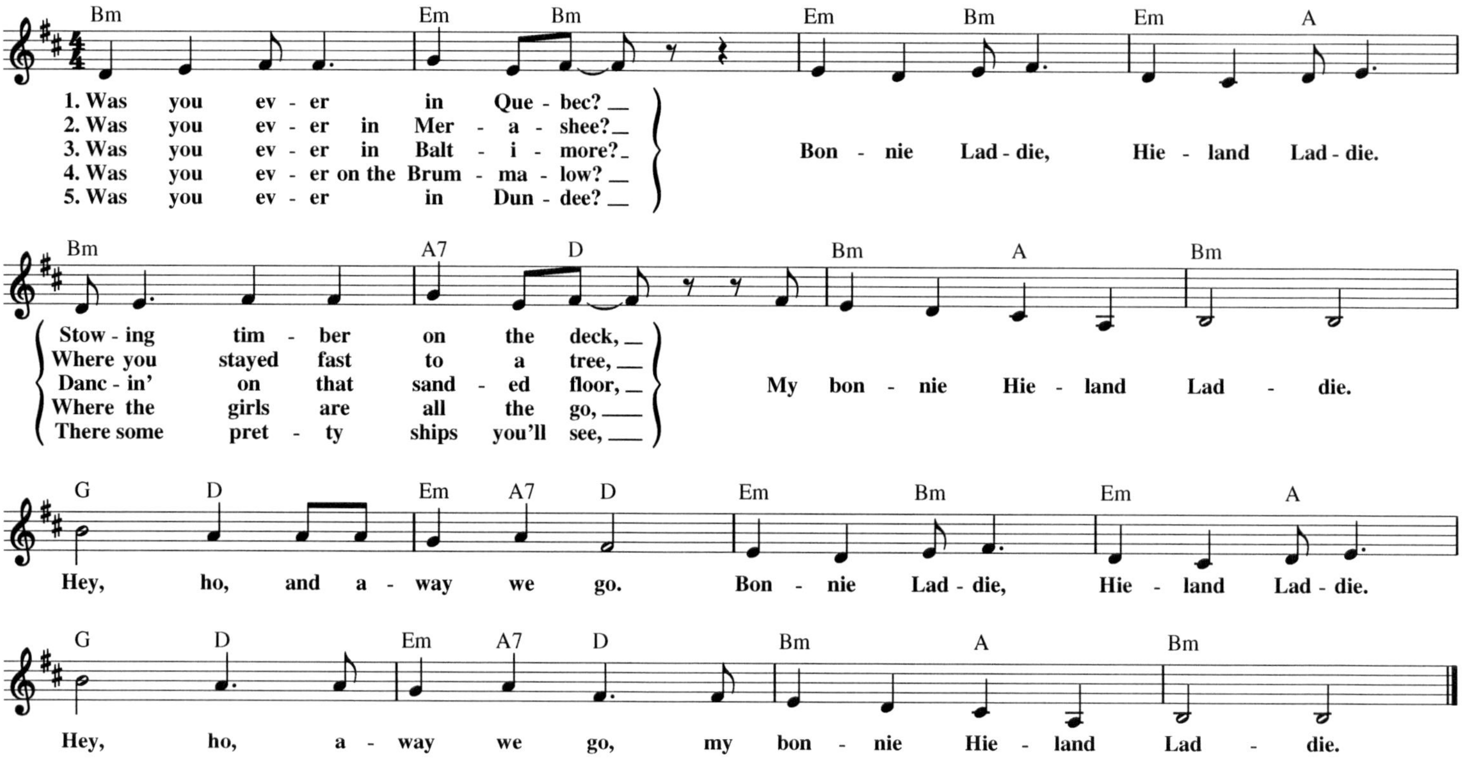

1. Was you ev - er in Que - bec? ___
2. Was you ev - er in Mer - a - shee? ___
3. Was you ev - er in Balt - i - more? ___
4. Was you ev - er on the Brum - ma - low? ___
5. Was you ev - er in Dun - dee? ___

Bon - nie Lad - die, Hie - land Lad - die.

Stow - ing tim - ber on the deck, ___
Where you stayed fast to a tree, ___
Danc - in' on that sand - ed floor, ___
Where the girls are all the go, ___
There some pret - ty ships you'll see, ___

My bon - nie Hie - land Lad - die.

Hey, ho, and a - way we go. Bon - nie Lad - die, Hie - land Lad - die.

Hey, ho, a - way we go, my bon - nie Hie - land Lad - die.

A HIGHLAND LAD MY LOVE WAS BORN

Scottish folksong
Words by Robert Burns

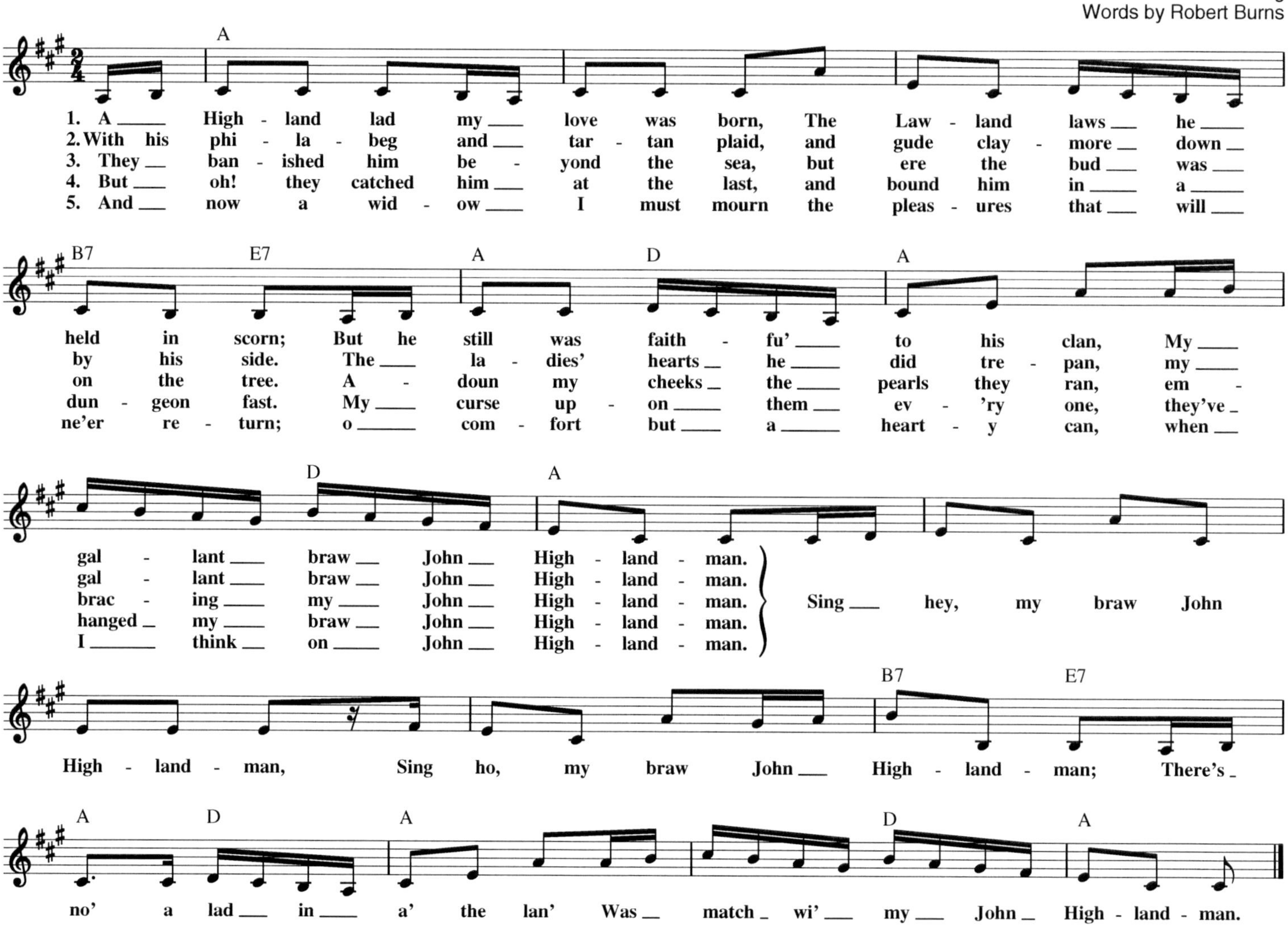

1. A ___ High - land lad my ___ love was born, The Law - land laws ___ he ___
2. With his phi - la - beg and ___ tar - tan plaid, and gude clay - more ___ down
3. They ___ ban - ished him be - yond the sea, but ere the bud ___ was ___
4. But ___ oh! they catched him ___ at the last, and bound him in ___ a ___
5. And ___ now a wid - ow ___ I must mourn the pleas - ures that ___ will ___

held in scorn; But he still was faith - fu' ___ to his clan, My ___
by his side. The ___ la - dies' hearts ___ he ___ did tre - pan, my ___
on the tree. A - doun my cheeks ___ the ___ pearls they ran, em -
dun - geon fast. My ___ curse up - on ___ them ___ ev - 'ry one, they've ___
ne'er re - turn; o ___ com - fort but ___ a ___ heart - y can, when ___

gal - lant ___ braw ___ John ___ High - land - man.
gal - lant ___ braw ___ John ___ High - land - man.
brac - ing ___ my ___ John ___ High - land - man.
hanged ___ my ___ braw ___ John ___ High - land - man.
I ___ think ___ on ___ John ___ High - land - man.

Sing ___ hey, my braw John

High - land - man, Sing ho, my braw John ___ High - land - man; There's ___

no' a lad ___ in ___ a' the lan' Was ___ match ___ wi' ___ my ___ John ___ High - land - man.

THE HOUNDS OF FILEMORE

Irish folksong

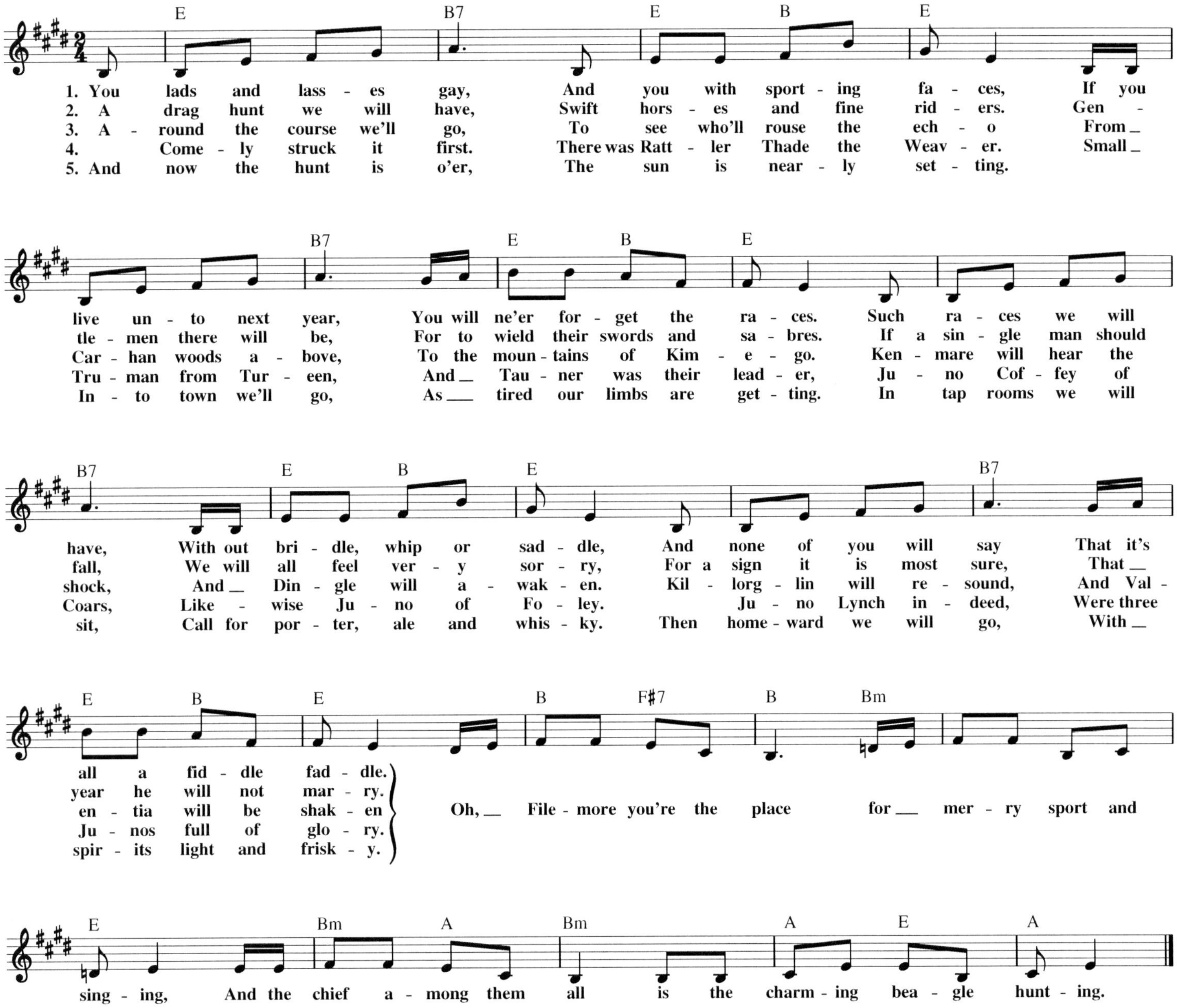

1. You lads and lass - es gay, And you with sport - ing fa - ces, If you
2. A drag hunt we will have, Swift hors - es and fine rid - ers. Gen -
3. A - round the course we'll go, To see who'll rouse the ech - o From _
4. Come - ly struck it first. There was Ratt - ler Thade the Weav - er. Small _
5. And now the hunt is o'er, The sun is near - ly set - ting.

live un - to next year, You will ne'er for - get the ra - ces. Such ra - ces we will
tle - men there will be, For to wield their swords and sa - bres. If a sin - gle man should
Car - han woods a - bove, To the moun - tains of Kim - e - go. Ken - mare will hear the
Tru - man from Tur - een, And _ Tau - ner was their lead - er, Ju - no Cof - fey of
In - to town we'll go, As _ tired our limbs are get - ting. In tap rooms we will

have, With out bri - dle, whip or sad - dle, And none of you will say That it's
fall, We will all feel ver - y sor - ry, For a sign it is most sure, That _
shock, And _ Din - gle will a - wak - en. Kil - lorg - lin will re - sound, And Val -
Coars, Like - wise Ju - no of Fo - ley. Ju - no Lynch in - deed, Were three
sit, Call for por - ter, ale and whis - ky. Then home - ward we will go, With _

all a fid - dle fad - dle.)
year he will not mar - ry.
en - tia will be shak - en   Oh, _ File - more you're the place for _ mer - ry sport and
Ju - nos full of glo - ry.
spir - its light and frisk - y.

sing - ing, And the chief a - mong them all is the charm - ing bea - gle hunt - ing.

HURREE HURROO

Scottish folksong

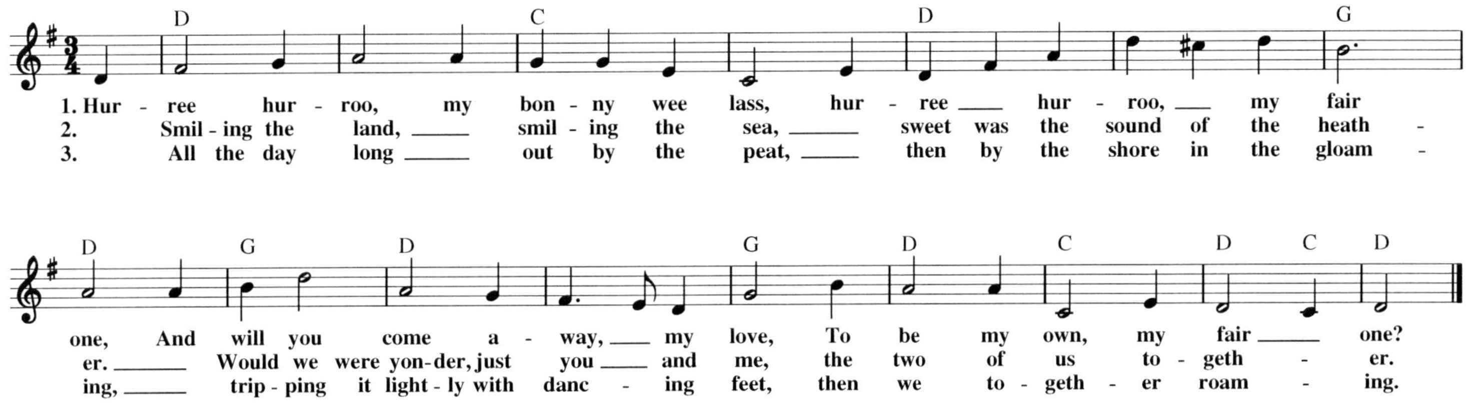

1. Hur - ree hur - roo, my bon - ny wee lass, hur - ree _ hur - roo, _ my fair
2. Smil - ing the land, _ smil - ing the sea, _ sweet was the sound of the heath -
3. All the day long _ out by the peat, _ then by the shore in the gloam -

one, And will you come a - way, _ my love, To be my own, my fair _ one?
er. _ Would we were yon - der, just you _ and me, the two of us to - geth - er.
ing, _ trip - ping it light - ly with danc - ing feet, then we to - geth - er roam - ing.

THE HILLS OF KERRY

Irish folksong

HUNTING THE HARE
(Hela'r 'Sgyvarnog)

Welsh folksong

I HAD FIFTEEN DOLLARS IN MY INSIDE POCKET

Words and Music by
Harry Kennedy

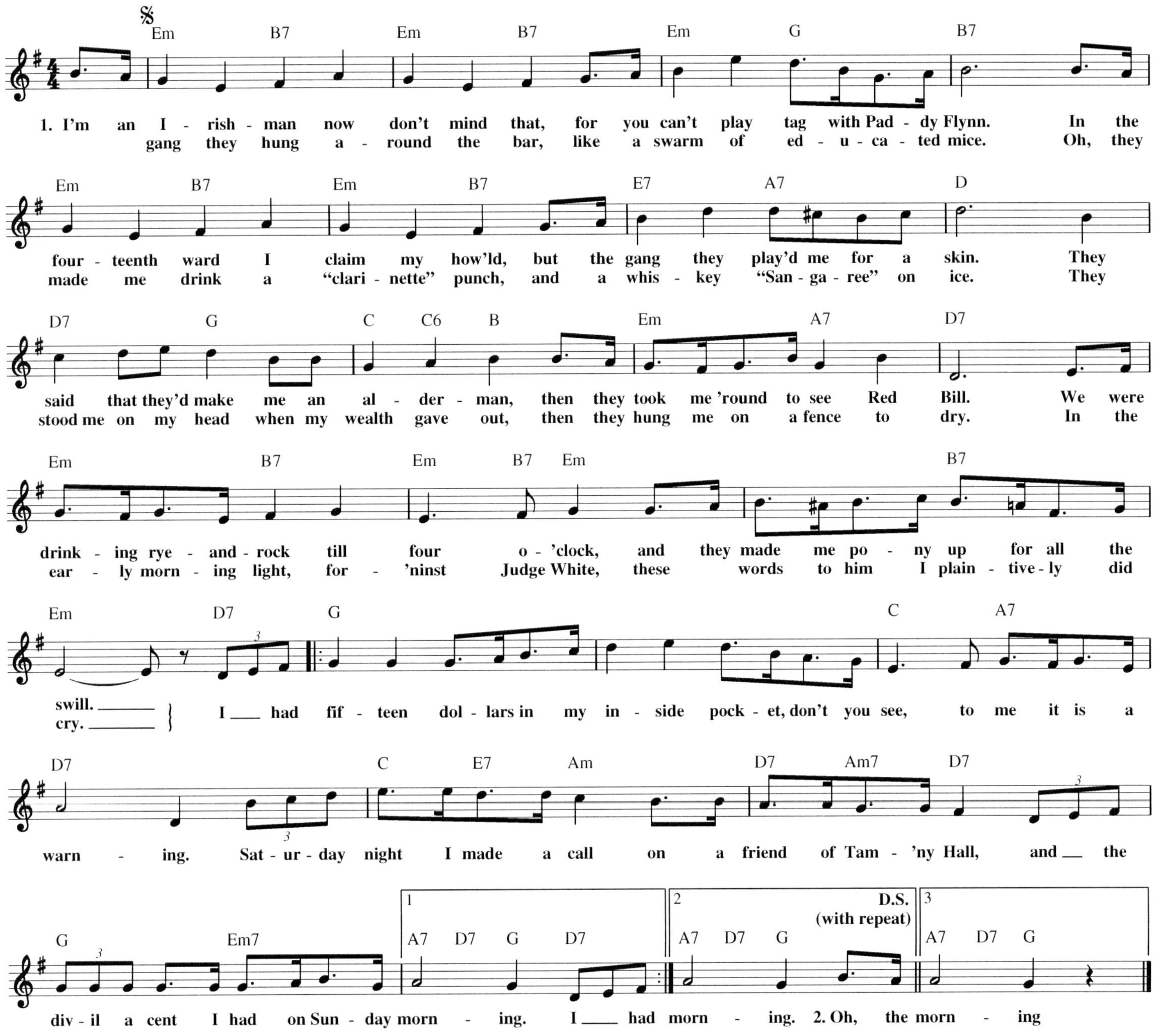

I KNOW WHERE I'M GOING

Scottish folksong

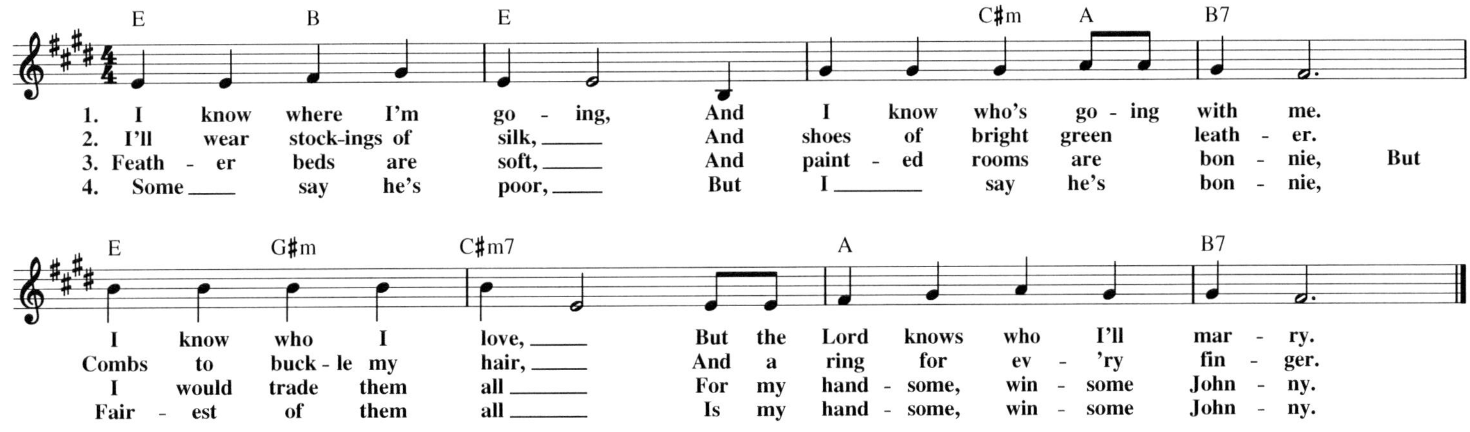

I KNOW MY LOVE

Irish folksong

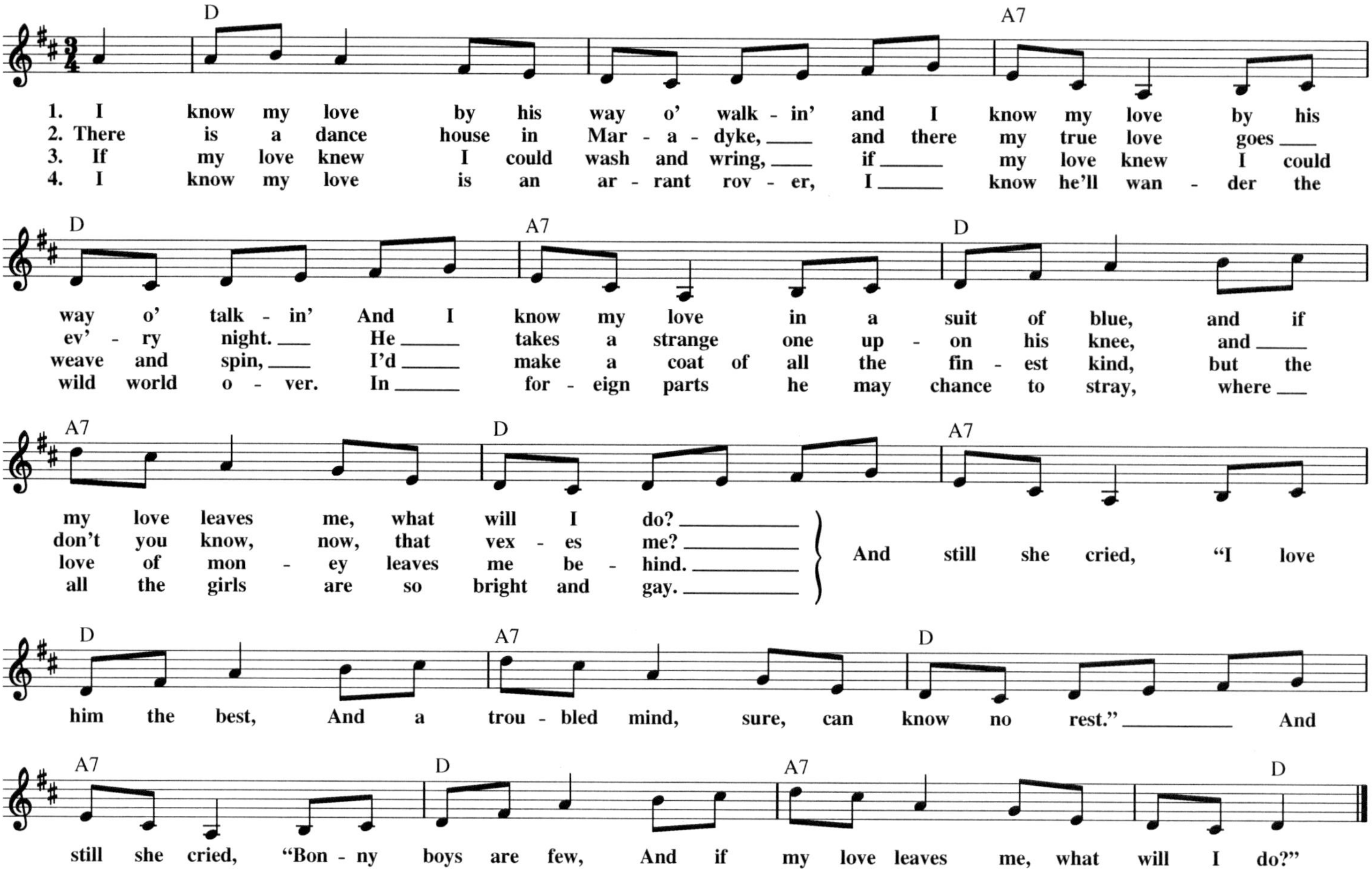

1. I know my love by his way o' walk-in' and I know my love by his
2. There is a dance house in Mar - a - dyke, ___ and there my true love goes ___
3. If my love knew I could wash and wring, ___ if ___ my love knew I could
4. I know my love is an ar - rant rov - er, I ___ know he'll wan - der the

way o' talk - in' And I know my love in a suit of blue, and if
ev' - ry night. ___ He ___ takes a strange one up - on his knee, and ___
weave and spin, ___ I'd ___ make a coat of all the fin - est kind, but the
wild world o - ver. In ___ for - eign parts he may chance to stray, where ___

my love leaves me, what will I do? ___
don't you know, now, that vex - es me? ___ } And still she cried, "I love
love of mon - ey leaves me be - hind. ___
all the girls are so bright and gay. ___

him the best, And a trou - bled mind, sure, can know no rest." ___ And

still she cried, "Bon - ny boys are few, And if my love leaves me, what will I do?"

"I THANK YOU, MA'AM," SAYS DAN

Irish folksong

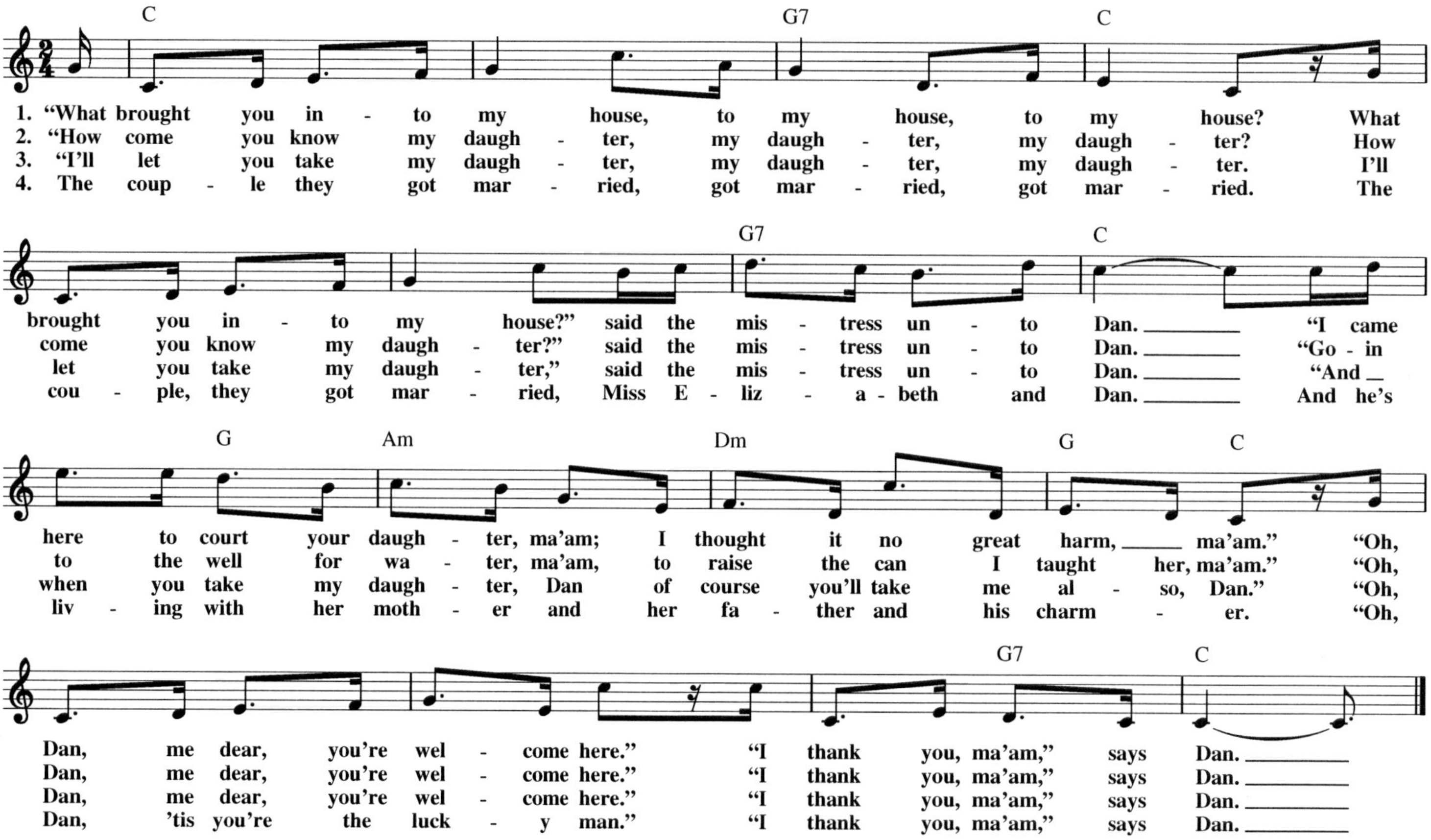

1. "What brought you in - to my house, to my house, to my house? What
2. "How come you know my daugh - ter, my daugh - ter, my daugh - ter? How
3. "I'll let you take my daugh - ter, my daugh - ter, my daugh - ter. I'll
4. The coup - le they got mar - ried, got mar - ried, got mar - ried. The

brought you in - to my house?" said the mis - tress un - to Dan. ___ "I came
come you know my daugh - ter?" said the mis - tress un - to Dan. ___ "Go - in
let you take my daugh - ter," said the mis - tress un - to Dan. ___ "And ___
cou - ple, they got mar - ried, Miss E - liz - a - beth and Dan. ___ And he's

here to court your daugh - ter, ma'am; I thought it no great harm, ___ ma'am." "Oh,
to the well for wa - ter, ma'am, to raise the can I taught her, ma'am." "Oh,
when you take my daugh - ter, Dan of course you'll take me al - so, Dan." "Oh,
liv - ing with her moth - er and her fa - ther and his charm - er. "Oh,

Dan, me dear, you're wel - come here." "I thank you, ma'am," says Dan. ___
Dan, me dear, you're wel - come here." "I thank you, ma'am," says Dan. ___
Dan, me dear, you're wel - come here." "I thank you, ma'am," says Dan. ___
Dan, 'tis you're the luck - y man." "I thank you, ma'am," says Dan. ___

I NEVER WILL MARRY

Irish folksong

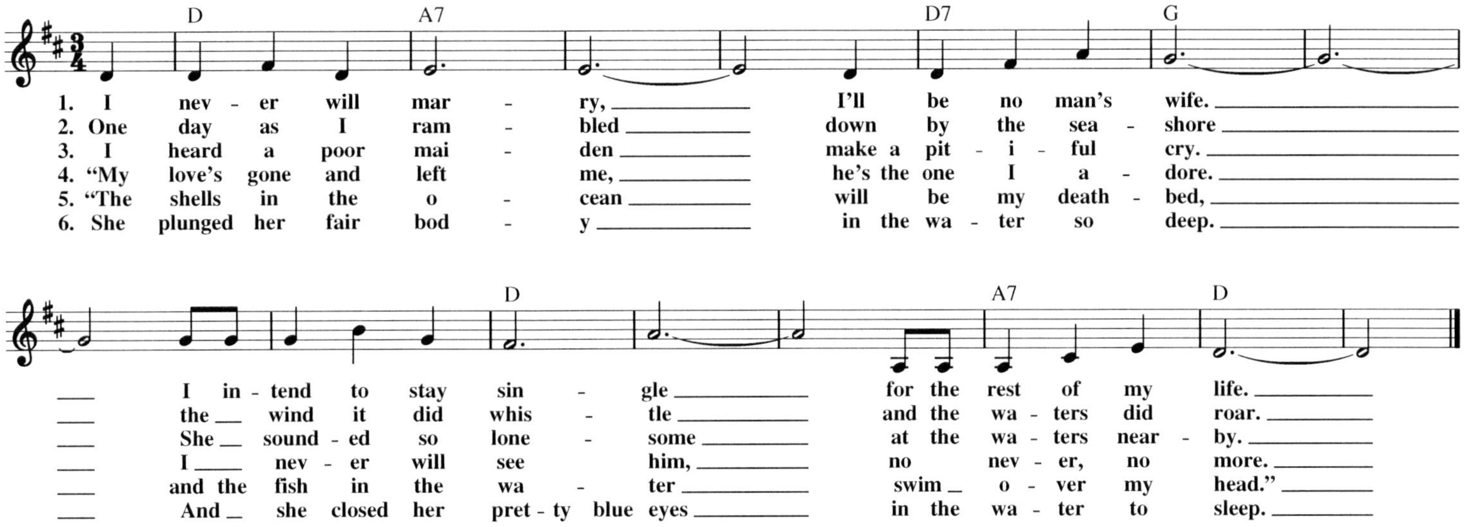

1. I nev - er will mar - ry, I'll be no man's wife.
2. One day as I ram - bled down by the sea - shore
3. I heard a poor mai - den make a pit - i - ful cry.
4. "My love's gone and left me, he's the one I a - dore.
5. "The shells in the o - cean will be my death - bed,
6. She plunged her fair bod - y in the wa - ter so deep.

__ I in - tend to stay sin - gle for the rest of my life.
__ the __ wind it did whis - tle and the wa - ters did roar.
__ She __ sound - ed so lone - some at the wa - ters near - by.
__ I __ nev - er will see him, no nev - er, no more.
__ and the fish in the wa - ter swim __ o - ver my head."
__ And __ she closed her pret - ty blue eyes in the wa - ter to sleep.

I'LL TAKE YOU HOME AGAIN, KATHLEEN

By Thomas P. Westendoff

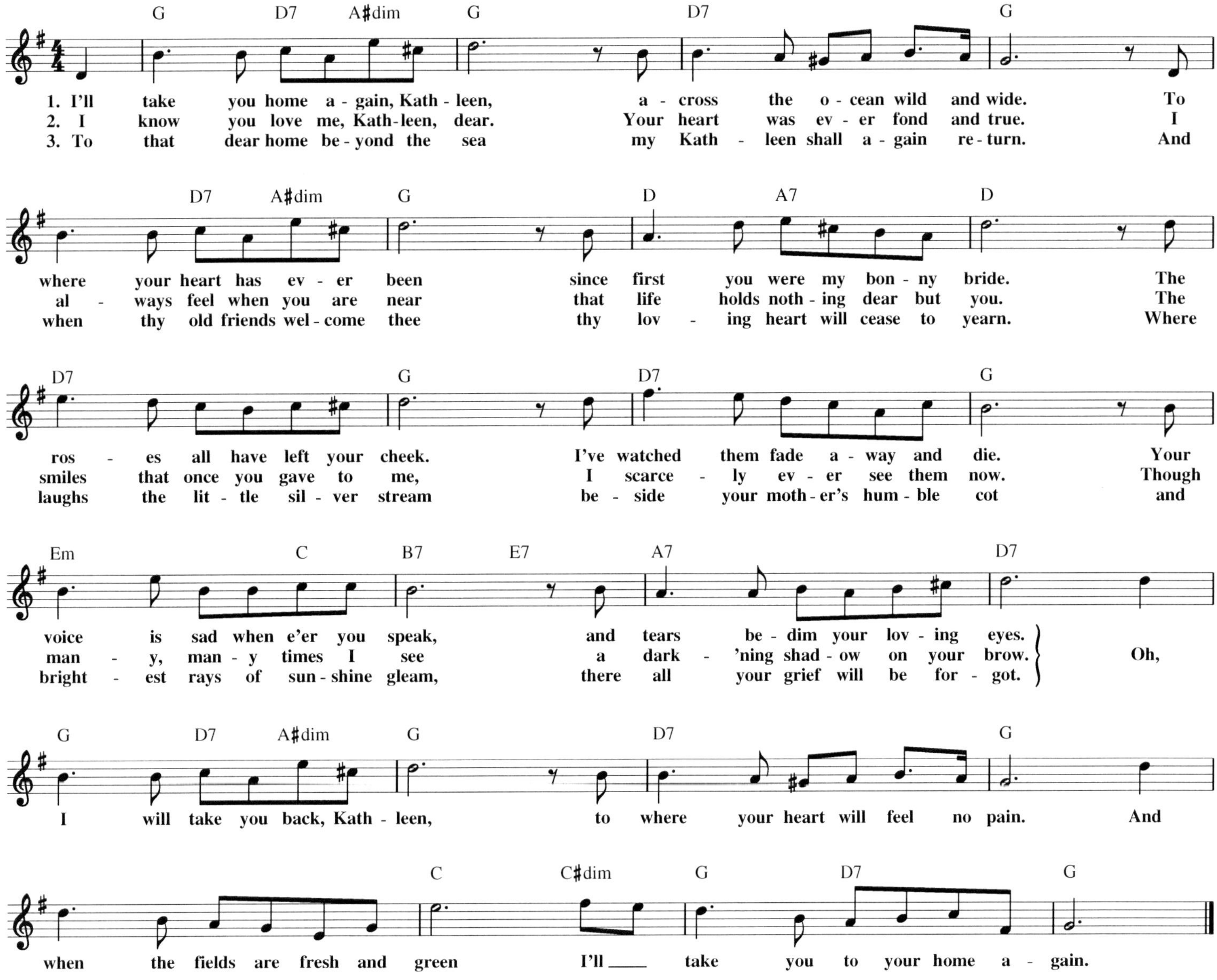

1. I'll take you home a - gain, Kath - leen, a - cross the o - cean wild and wide. To
2. I know you love me, Kath-leen, dear. Your heart was ev - er fond and true. I
3. To that dear home be - yond the sea my Kath - leen shall a - gain re - turn. And

where your heart has ev - er been since first you were my bon - ny bride. The
al - ways feel when you are near that life holds noth - ing dear but you. The
when thy old friends wel - come thee thy lov - ing heart will cease to yearn. Where

ros - es all have left your cheek. I've watched them fade a - way and die. Your
smiles that once you gave to me, I scarce - ly ev - er see them now. Though
laughs the lit - tle sil - ver stream be - side your moth - er's hum - ble cot and

voice is sad when e'er you speak, and tears be - dim your lov - ing eyes.
man - y, man - y times I see a dark - 'ning shad - ow on your brow. Oh,
bright - est rays of sun - shine gleam, there all your grief will be - got.

I will take you back, Kath - leen, to where your heart will feel no pain. And

when the fields are fresh and green I'll __ take you to your home a - gain.

I'LL TELL MY MA

Irish folksong

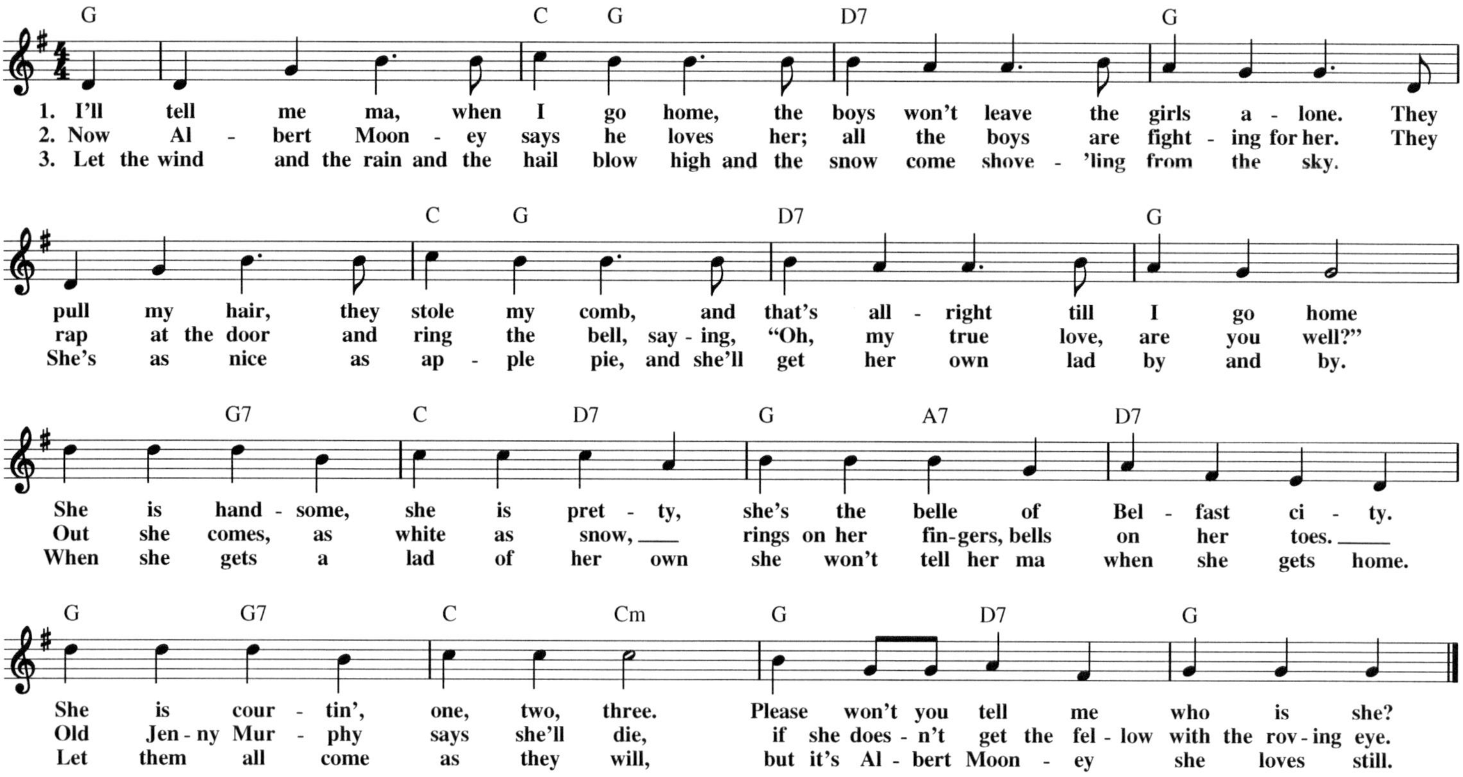

1. I'll tell me ma, when I go home, the boys won't leave the girls a-lone. They pull my hair, they stole my comb, and that's all-right till I go home. She is hand-some, she is pret-ty, she's the belle of Bel-fast ci-ty. She is cour-tin', one, two, three. Please won't you tell me who is she?

2. Now Al-bert Moon-ey says he loves her; all the boys are fight-ing for her. They rap at the door and ring the bell, say-ing, "Oh, my true love, are you well?" Out she comes, as white as snow, rings on her fin-gers, bells on her toes. Old Jen-ny Mur-phy says she'll die, if she does-n't get the fel-low with the rov-ing eye.

3. Let the wind and the rain and the hail blow high and the snow come shove-'ling from the sky. She's as nice as ap-ple pie, and she'll get her own lad by and by. When she gets a lad of her own she won't tell her ma when she gets home. Let them all come as they will, but it's Al-bert Moon-ey she loves still.

I'VE GOT RINGS ON MY FINGERS

Words by Weston and Barnes
Music by Maurice Scott

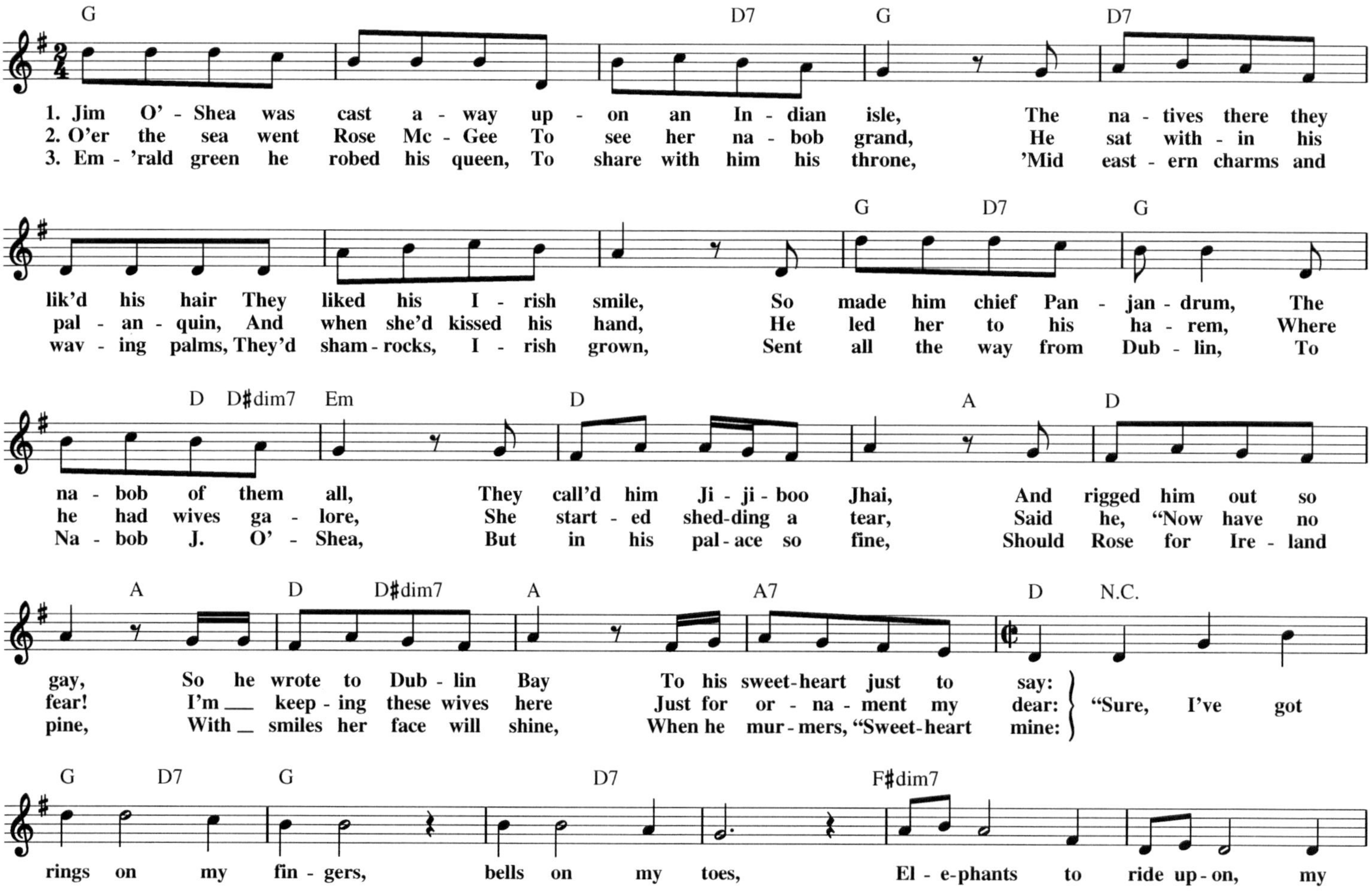

1. Jim O'-Shea was cast a-way up-on an In-dian isle, The na-tives there they lik'd his hair They liked his I-rish smile, So made him chief Pan-jan-drum, The na-bob of them all, They call'd him Ji-ji-boo Jhai, And rigged him out so gay, So he wrote to Dub-lin Bay To his sweet-heart just to say: "Sure, I've got rings on my fin-gers, bells on my toes, El-e-phants to ride up-on, my

2. O'er the sea went Rose Mc-Gee To see her na-bob grand, He sat with-in his pal-an-quin, And when she'd kissed his hand, She start-ed shed-ding a tear, Said he, "Now have no fear! I'm keep-ing these wives here Just for or-na-ment my dear:

3. Em-'rald green he robed his queen, To share with him his throne, 'Mid east-ern charms and wav-ing palms, They'd sham-rocks, I-rish grown, Sent all the way from Dub-lin, To Na-bob J. O'-Shea, But in his pal-ace so fine, Should Rose for Ire-land pine, With smiles her face will shine, When he mur-mers, "Sweet-heart mine:

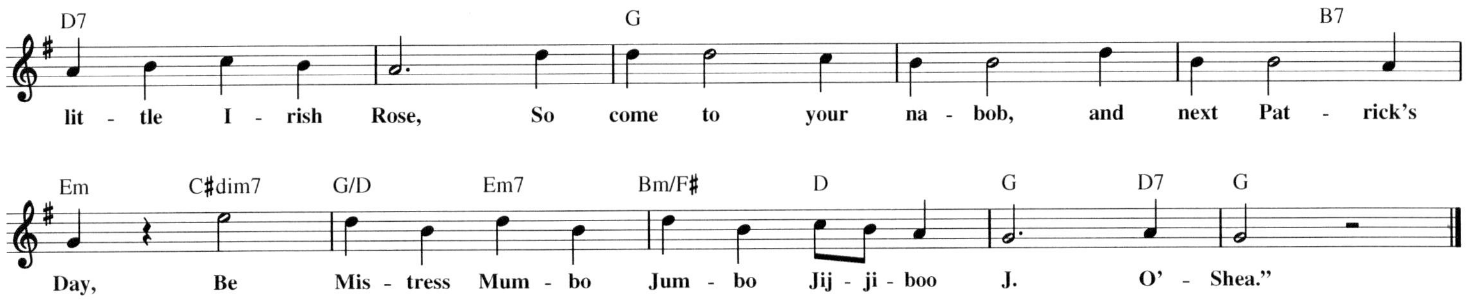

lit - tle I - rish Rose, So come to your na - bob, and next Pat - rick's

Day, Be Mis - tress Mum - bo Jum - bo Jij - ji - boo J. O' - Shea."

I'M A POOR STRANGER

Irish folksong

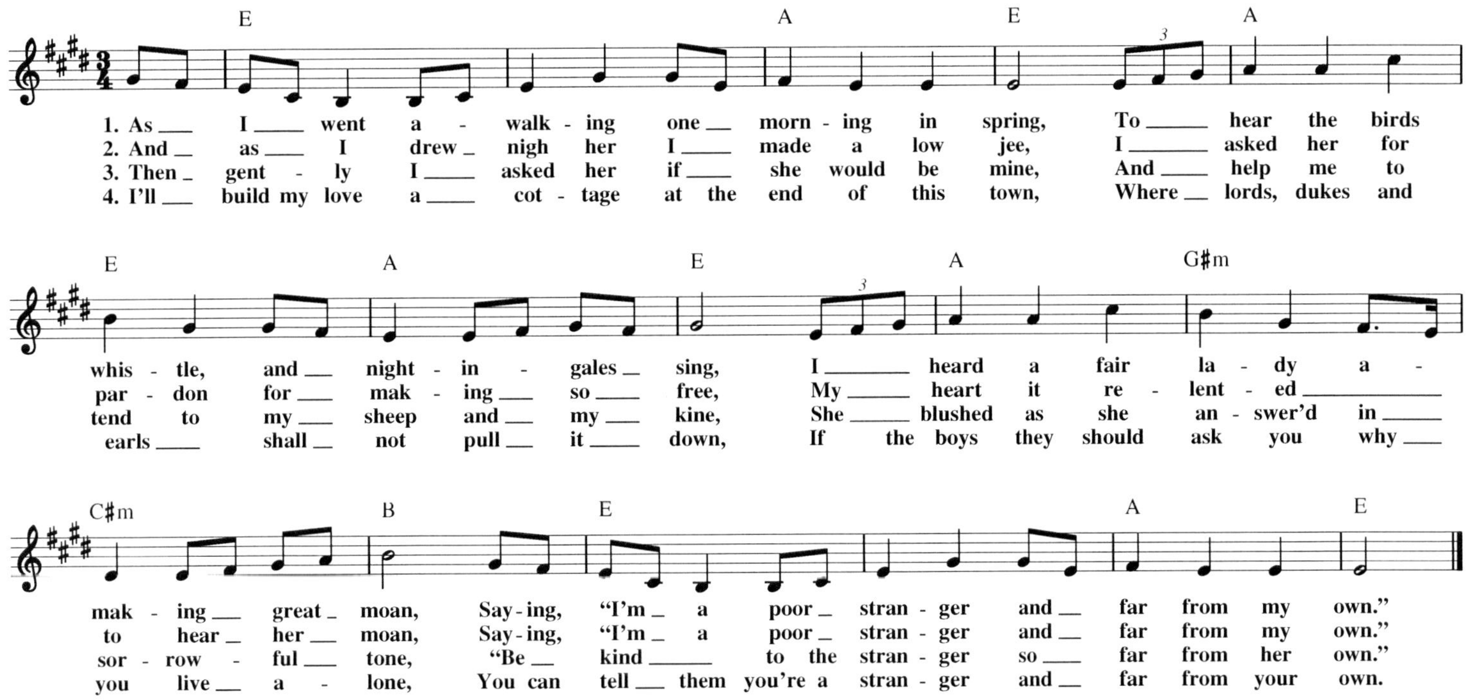

1. As ___ I ___ went a - walk - ing one ___ morn - ing in spring, To ___ hear the birds
2. And ___ as ___ I drew ___ nigh her I ___ made a low jee, I ___ asked her for
3. Then ___ gent - ly I ___ asked her if ___ she would be mine, And ___ help me to
4. I'll ___ build my love a ___ cot - tage at the end of this town, Where ___ lords, dukes and

whis - tle, and ___ night - in - gales ___ sing, I ___ heard a fair la - dy a -
par - don for ___ mak - ing ___ so ___ free, My ___ heart it re - lent - ed ___
tend to my ___ sheep and ___ my ___ kine, She ___ blushed as she an - swer'd in ___
earls ___ shall ___ not pull ___ it ___ down, If the boys they should ask you why ___

mak - ing ___ great ___ moan, Say - ing, "I'm ___ a poor ___ stran - ger and ___ far from my own."
to hear ___ her ___ moan, Say - ing, "I'm ___ a poor ___ stran - ger and ___ far from my own."
sor - row - ful ___ tone, "Be ___ kind ___ to the stran - ger so ___ far from her own."
you live ___ a - lone, You can tell ___ them you're a stran - ger and ___ far from your own.

IN SCARTAGLEN THERE LIVED A LASS

Irish folksong

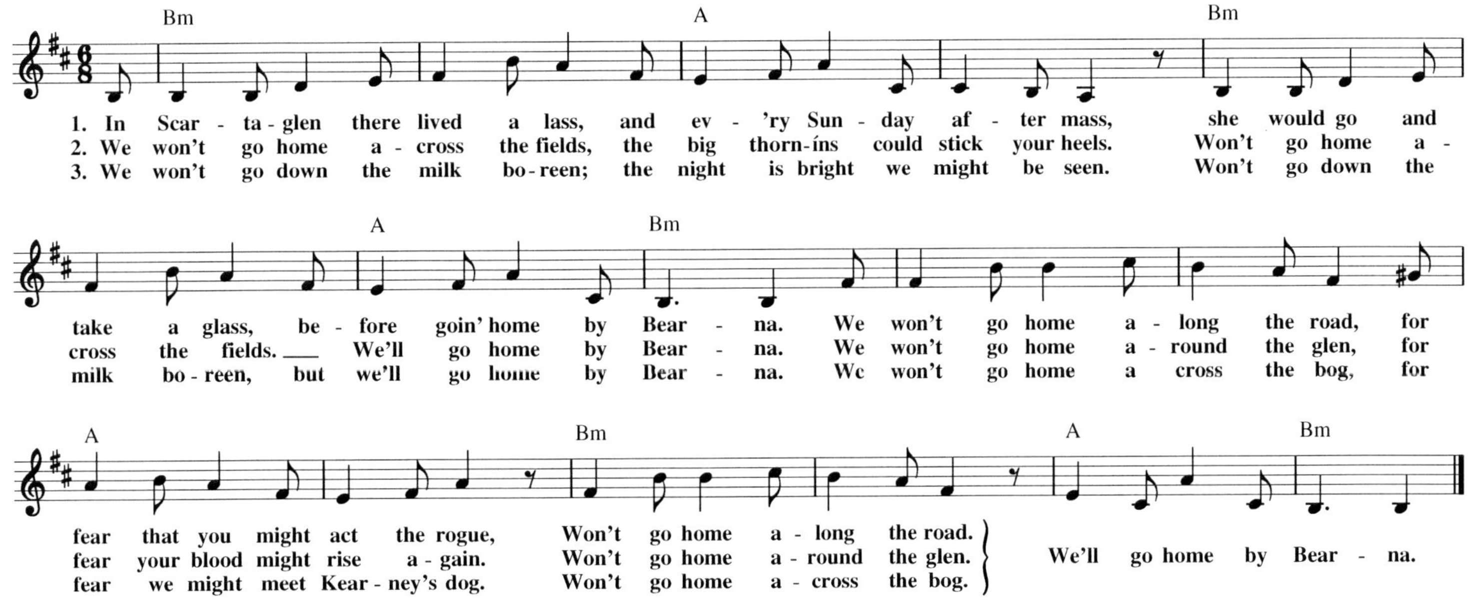

1. In Scar - ta - glen there lived a lass, and ev - 'ry Sun - day af - ter mass, she would go and
2. We won't go home a - cross the fields, the big thorn - íns could stick your heels. Won't go home a -
3. We won't go down the milk bo - reen; the night is bright we might be seen. Won't go down the

take a glass, be - fore goin' home by Bear - na. We won't go home a - long the road, for
cross the fields. ___ We'll go home by Bear - na. We won't go home a - round the glen, for
milk bo - reen, but we'll go home by Bear - na. We won't go home a cross the bog, for

fear that you might act the rogue, Won't go home a - long the road. }
fear your blood might rise a - gain. Won't go home a - round the glen. } We'll go home by Bear - na.
fear we might meet Kear - ney's dog. Won't go home a - cross the bog.

IN GLENDALOUGH LIVED A YOUNG SAINT

Irish folksong

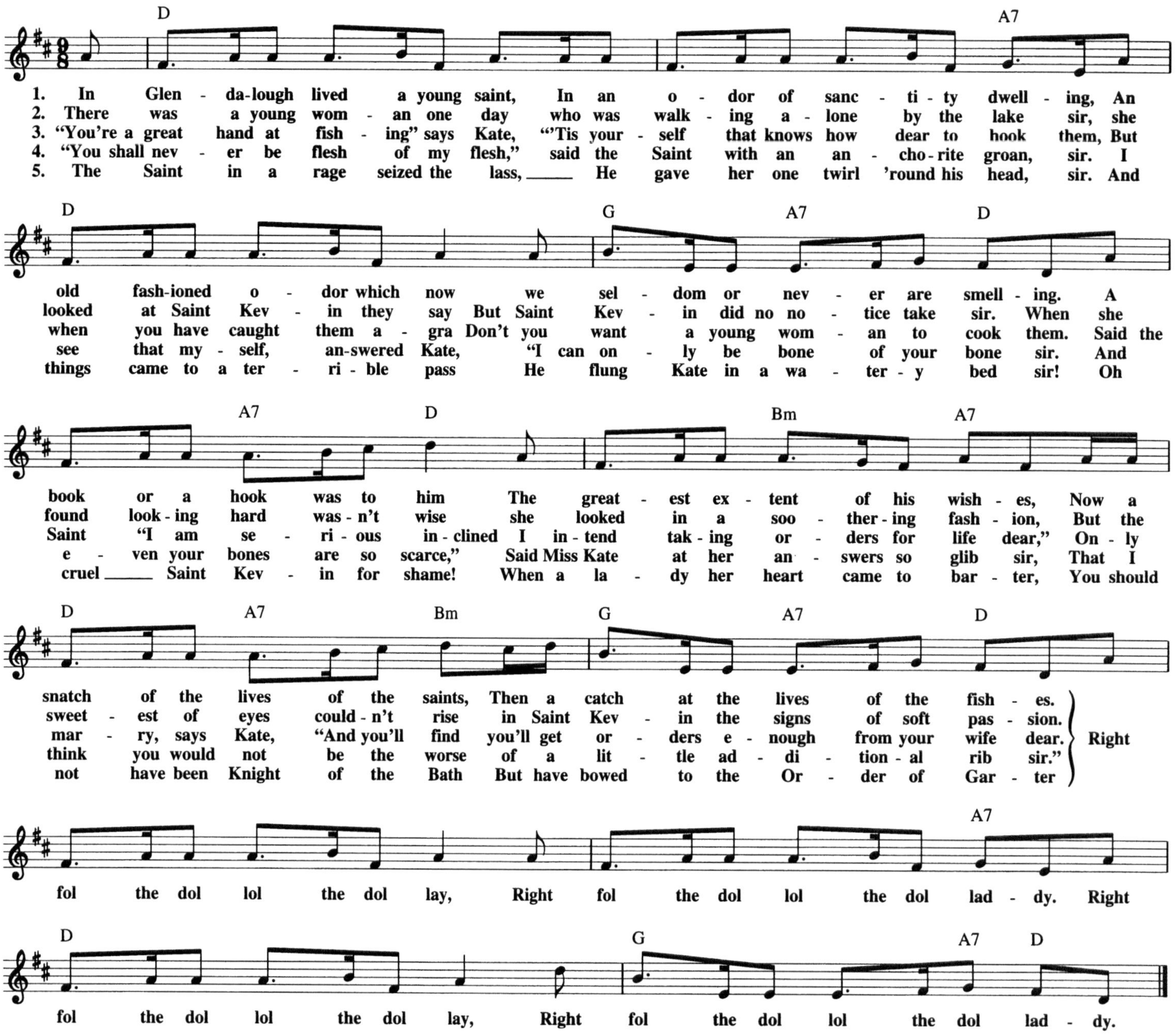

1. In Glen-da-lough lived a young saint, In an o-dor of sanc-ti-ty dwell-ing, An
2. There was a young wom-an one day who was walk-ing a-lone by the lake sir, she
3. "You're a great hand at fish-ing" says Kate, "'Tis your-self that knows how dear to hook them, But
4. "You shall nev-er be flesh of my flesh," said the Saint with an an-cho-rite groan, sir. I
5. The Saint in a rage seized the lass,_____ He gave her one twirl 'round his head, sir. And

old fash-ioned o-dor which now we sel-dom or nev-er are smell-ing. A
looked at Saint Kev-in they say But Saint Kev-in did no no-tice take sir. When she
when you have caught them a-gra Don't you want a young wom-an to cook them. Said the
see that my-self, an-swered Kate, "I can on-ly be bone of your bone sir. And
things came to a ter-ri-ble pass He flung Kate in a wa-ter-y bed sir! Oh

book or a hook was to him The great-est ex-tent of his wish-es, Now a
found look-ing hard was-n't wise she looked in a soo-ther-ing fash-ion, But the
Saint "I am se-ri-ous in-clined I in-tend tak-ing or-ders for life dear," On-ly
e-ven your bones are so scarce," Said Miss Kate at her an-swers so glib sir, That I
cruel_____ Saint Kev-in for shame! When a la-dy her heart came to bar-ter, You should

snatch of the lives of the saints, Then a catch at the lives of the fish-es.
sweet-est of eyes could-n't rise in Saint Kev-in the signs of soft pas-sion.
mar-ry, says Kate, "And you'll find you'll get or-ders e-nough from your wife dear." Right
think you would not be the worse of a lit-tle ad-di-tion-al rib sir."
not have been Knight of the Bath But have bowed to the Or-der of Gar-ter

fol the dol lol the dol lay, Right fol the dol lol the dol lad-dy. Right

fol the dol lol the dol lay, Right fol the dol lol the dol lad-dy.

IRISH ASTRONOMY

Irish popular song
By C.G. Hapline

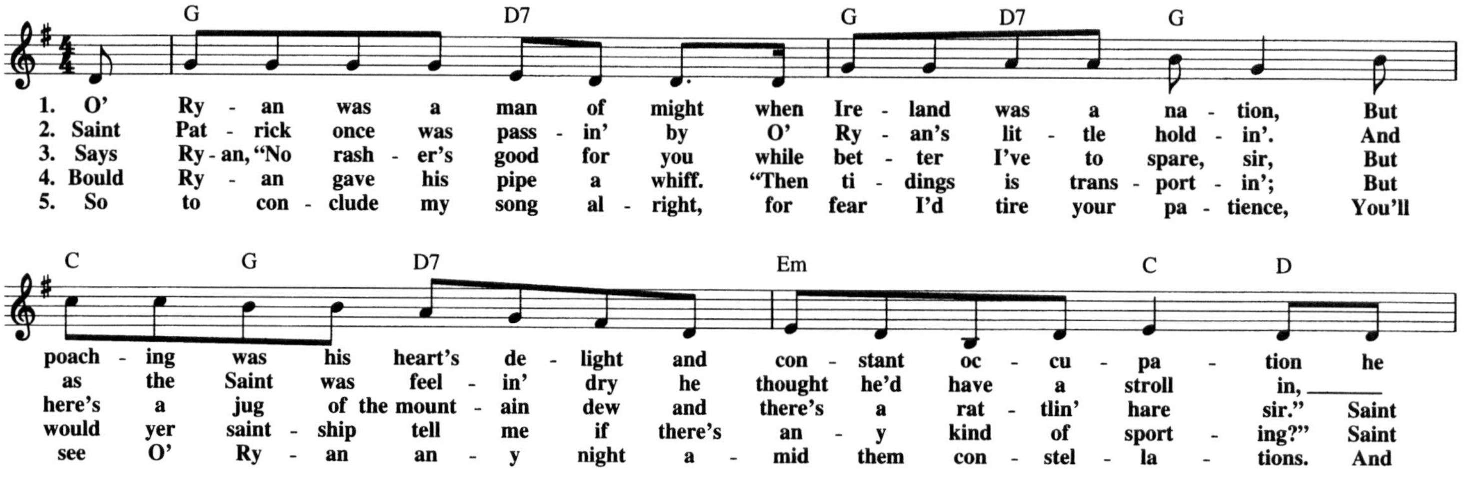

1. O' Ry-an was a man of might when Ire-land was a na-tion, But
2. Saint Pat-rick once was pass-in' by O' Ry-an's lit-tle hold-in'. And
3. Says Ry-an, "No rash-er's good for you while bet-ter I've to spare, sir, But
4. Bould Ry-an gave his pipe a whiff. "Then ti-dings is trans-port-in'; But
5. So to con-clude my song al-right, for fear I'd tire your pa-tience, You'll

poach-ing was his heart's de-light and con-stant oc-cu-pa-tion he
as the Saint was feel-in' dry he thought he'd have a stroll in,_____
here's a jug of the mount-ain dew and there's a rat-tlin' hare sir." Saint
would yer saint-ship tell me if there's an-y kind of sport-ing?" Saint
see O' Ry-an an-y night a-mid them con-stel-la-tions. And

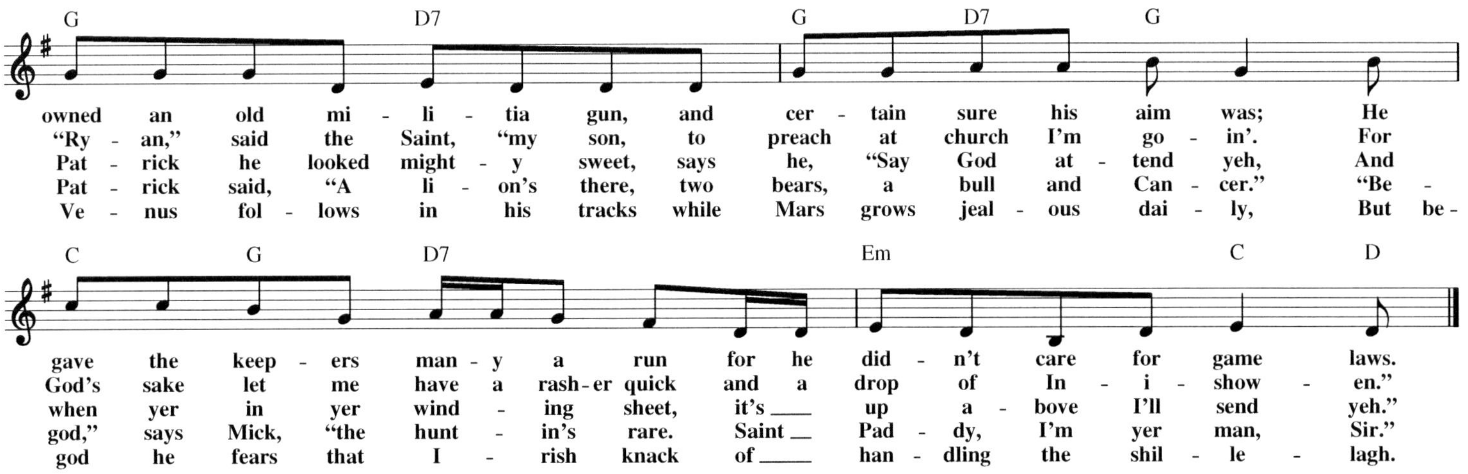

owned an old mi - li - tia gun, and cer - tain sure his aim was; He
"Ry - an," said the Saint, "my son, to preach at church I'm go - in'. For
Pat - rick he looked might - y sweet, says he, "Say God at - tend yeh, And
Pat - rick said, "A li - on's there, two bears, a bull and Can - cer." "Be -
Ve - nus fol - lows in his tracks while Mars grows jeal - ous dai - ly,

gave the keep - ers man - y a run for he did - n't care for game laws.
God's sake let me have a rash - er quick and a drop of In - i - show - en."
when yer in yer wind - ing sheet, it's _____ up a - bove I'll send yeh."
god," says Mick, "the hunt - in's rare. Saint _____ Pad - dy, I'm yer man, Sir."
god he fears that I - rish knack of _____ han - dling the shil - le - lagh.

THE IRISH WASHERWOMAN

Irish folksong

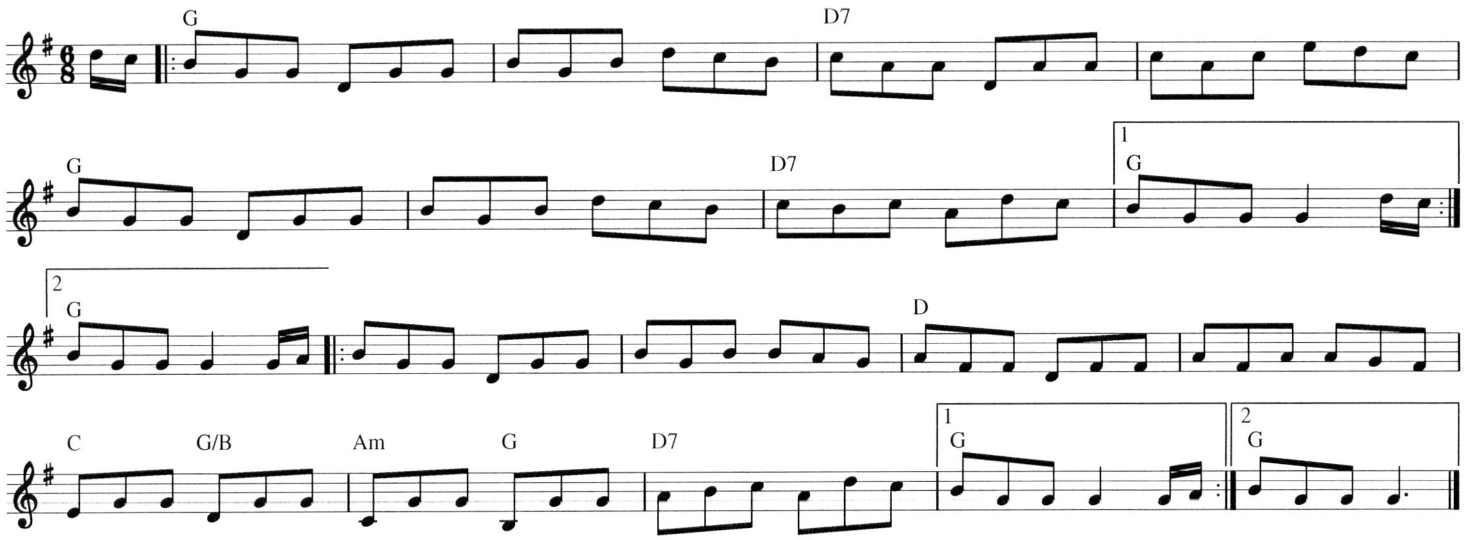

THE IRISH WEDDING

Words and Music by
Charles Dibdin

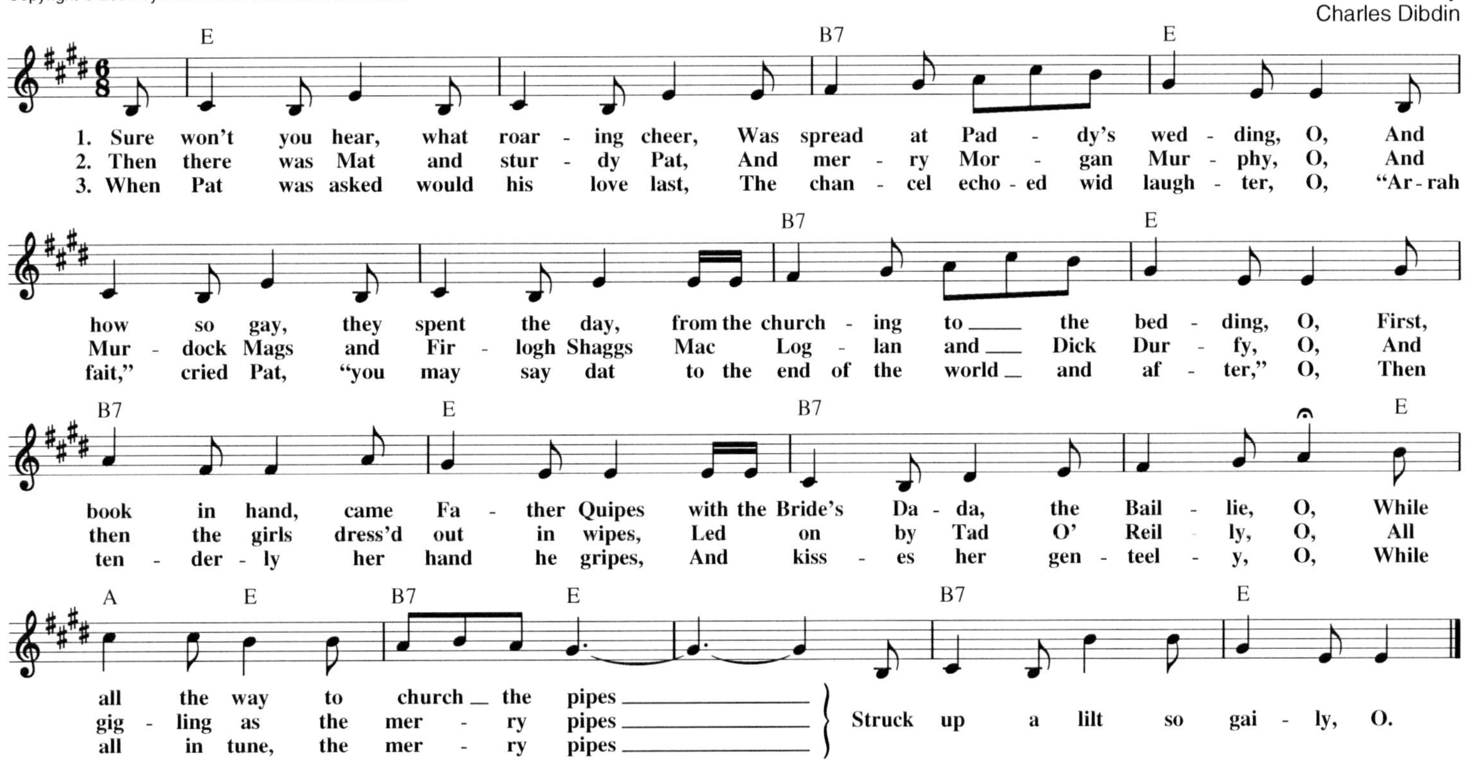

1. Sure won't you hear, what roar - ing cheer, Was spread at Pad - dy's wed - ding, O, And
2. Then there was Mat and stur - dy Pat, And mer - ry Mor - gan Mur - phy, O, And
3. When Pat was asked would his love last, The chan - cel echo - ed wid laugh - ter, O, "Ar - rah

how so gay, they spent the day, from the church - ing to _____ the bed - ding, O, First,
Mur - dock Mags and Fir - logh Shaggs Mac Log - lan and _____ Dick Dur - fy, O, And
fait," cried Pat, "you may say dat to the end of the world _____ and af - ter," O, Then

book in hand, came Fa - ther Quipes with the Bride's Da - da, the Bail - lie, O, While
then the girls dress'd out in wipes, Led on by Tad O' Reil - ly, O, All
ten - der - ly her hand he gripes, And kiss - es her gen - teel - y, O, While

all the way to church _____ the pipes _____
gig - ling as the mer - ry pipes _____ } Struck up a lilt so gai - ly, O.
all in tune, the mer - ry pipes _____

118

THE IRISH GIRL

Copyright © 2000 by HAL LEONARD CORPORATION

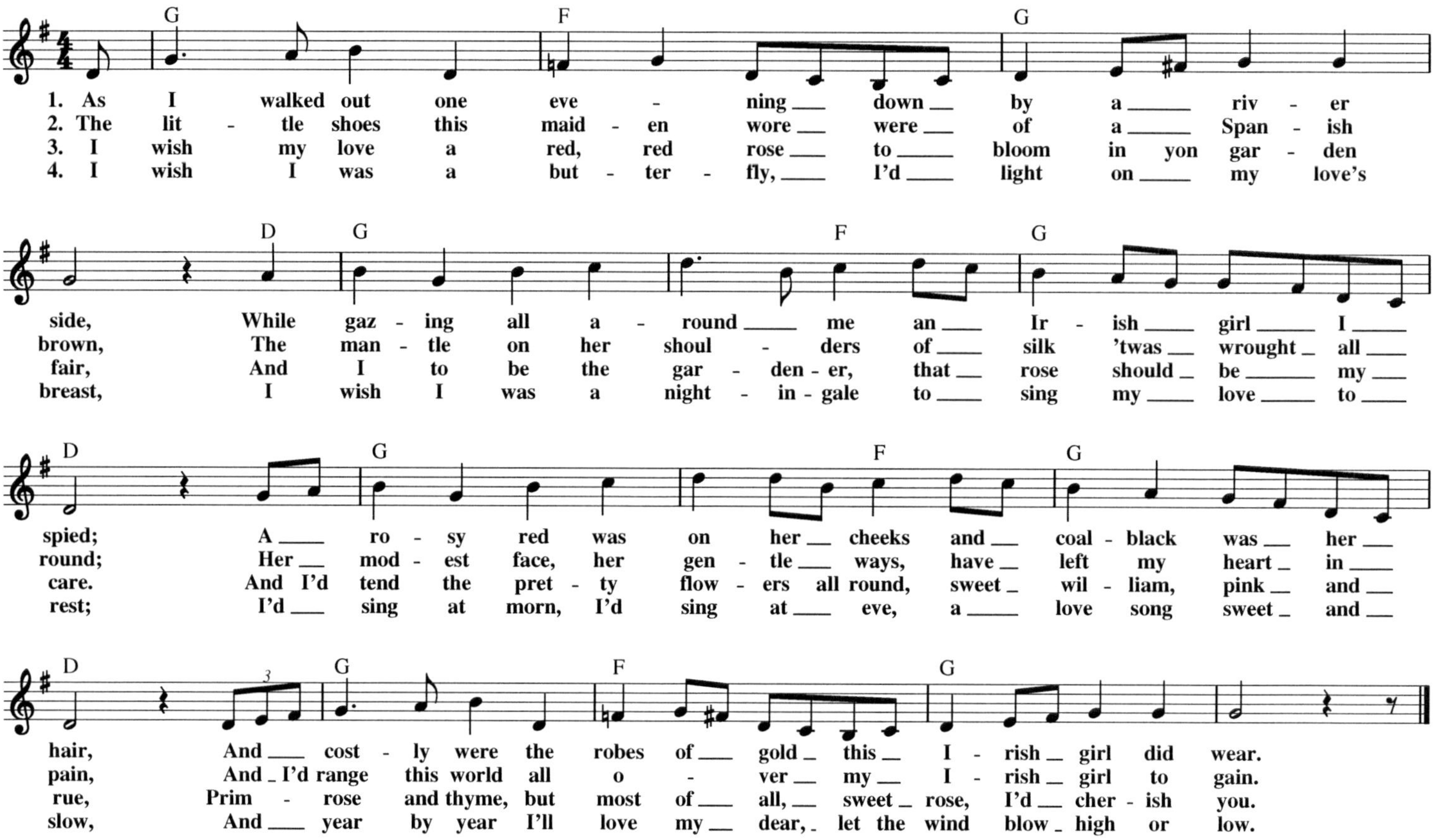

THE IRISH ROVER

Irish folksong

Copyright © 2001 by HAL LEONARD CORPORATION

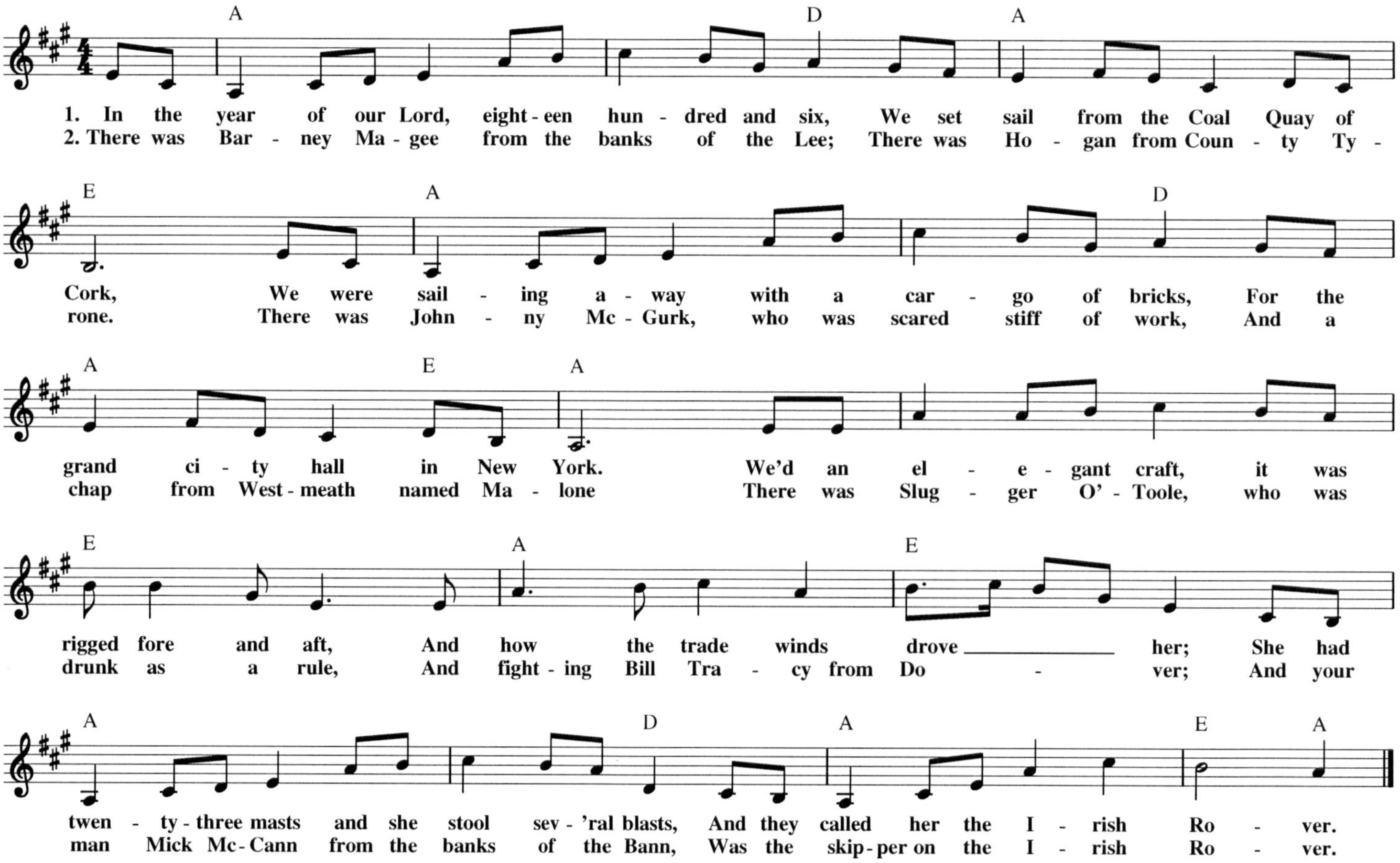

THE IRISHMAN'S EPISTLE

Irish folksong

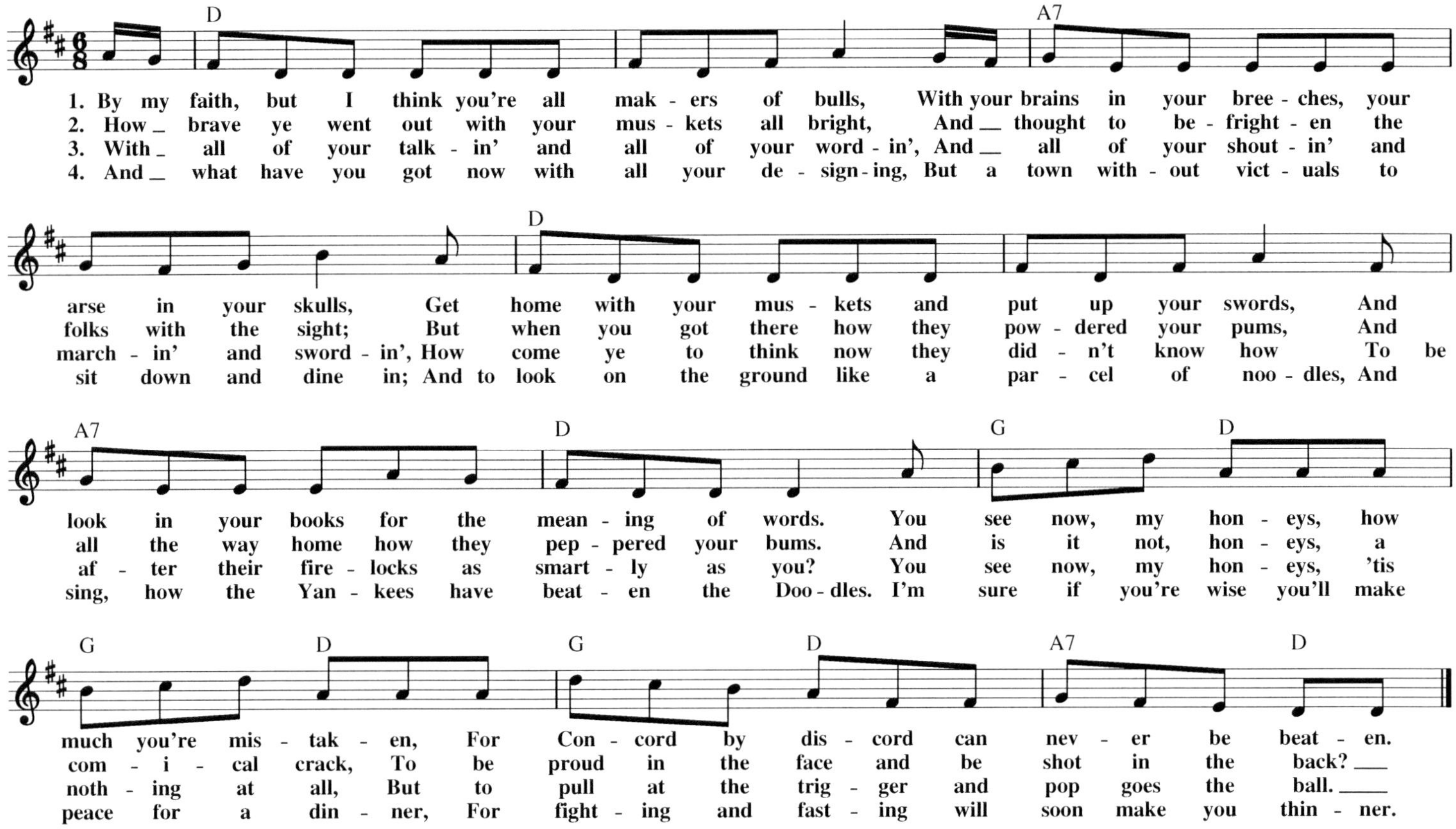

1. By my faith, but I think you're all mak - ers of bulls, With your brains in your bree - ches, your
2. How _ brave ye went out with your mus - kets all bright, And _ thought to be fright - en the
3. With _ all of your talk - in' and all of your word - in', And _ all of your shout - in' and
4. And _ what have you got now with all your de - sign - ing, But a town with - out vict - uals to

arse in your skulls, Get home with your mus - kets and put up your swords, And
folks with the sight; But when you got there how they pow - dered your pums, And
march - in' and sword - in', How come ye to think now they did - n't know how To be
sit down and dine in; And to look on the ground like a par - cel of noo - dles, And

look in your books for the mean - ing of words. You see now, my hon - eys, how
all the way home how they pep - pered your bums. And is it not, hon - eys, a
af - ter their fire - locks as smart - ly as you? You see now, my hon - eys, 'tis
sing, how the Yan - kees have beat - en the Doo - dles. I'm sure if you're wise you'll make

much you're mis - tak - en, For Con - cord by dis - cord can nev - er be beat - en.
com - i - cal crack, To be proud in the face and be shot in the back? ___
noth - ing at all, But to pull at the trig - ger and pop goes the ball. ____
peace for a din - ner, For fight - ing and fast - ing will soon make you thin - ner.

THE IRISHMAN'S SHANTY

Words and Music by
Emmet Driscoll

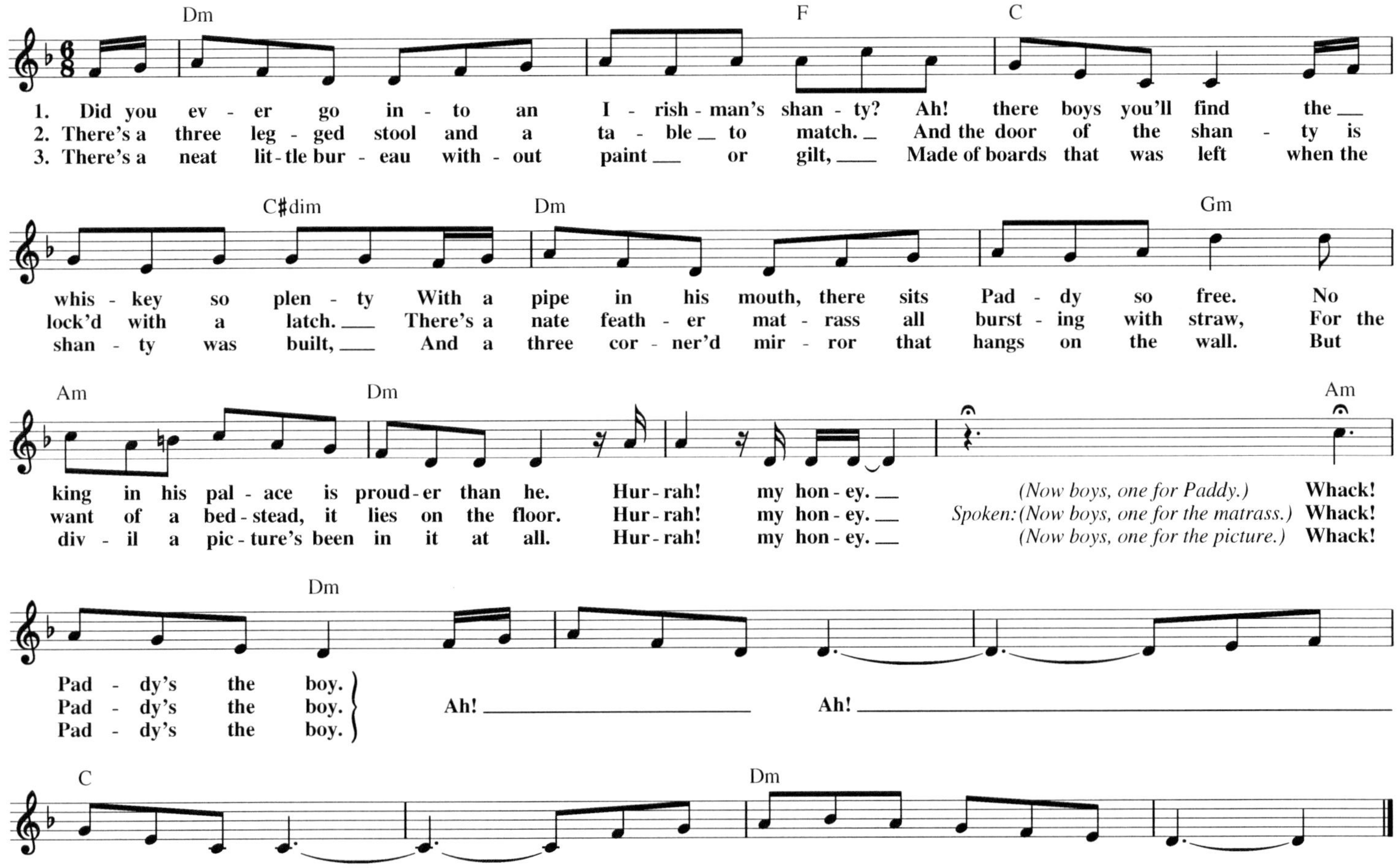

1. Did you ev - er go in - to an I - rish - man's shan - ty? Ah! there boys you'll find the ___
2. There's a three leg - ged stool and a ta - ble _ to match. _ And the door of the shan - ty is
3. There's a neat lit - tle bur - eau with - out paint ___ or gilt, ___ Made of boards that was left when the

whis - key so plen - ty With a pipe in his mouth, there sits Pad - dy so free. No
lock'd with a latch. ___ There's a nate feath - er mat - rass all burst - ing with straw, For the
shan - ty was built, ___ And a three cor - ner'd mir - ror that hangs on the wall. But

king in his pal - ace is proud - er than he. Hur - rah! my hon - ey. ___ *(Now boys, one for Paddy.)* **Whack!**
want of a bed - stead, it lies on the floor. Hur - rah! my hon - ey. ___ *Spoken:(Now boys, one for the matrass.)* **Whack!**
div - il a pic - ture's been in it at all. Hur - rah! my hon - ey. ___ *(Now boys, one for the picture.)* **Whack!**

Pad - dy's the boy. ⎫
Pad - dy's the boy. ⎬   Ah! _____   Ah! _____
Pad - dy's the boy. ⎭

_____ Ah! _____   Ah! _____

JOHN RILEY

Irish folksong

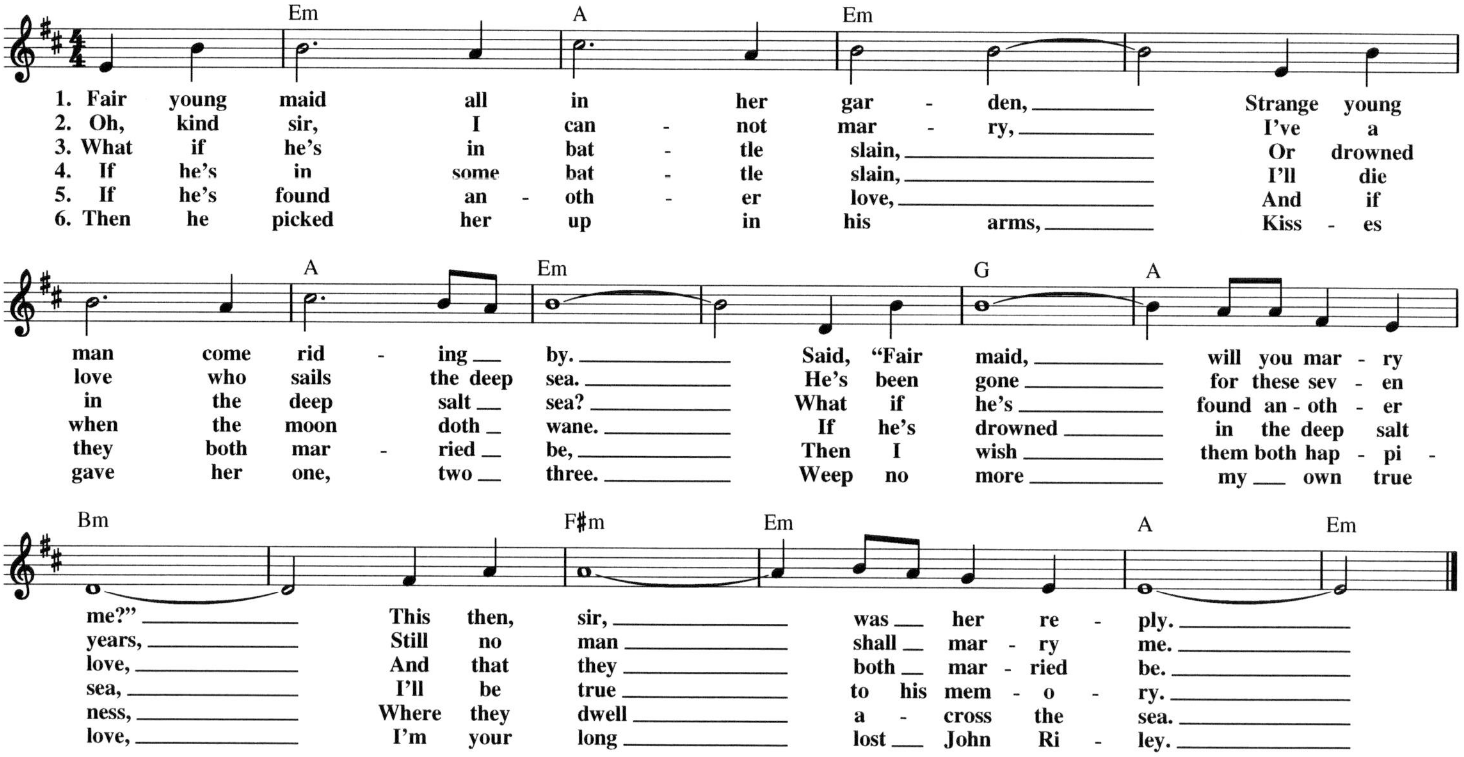

1. Fair young maid all in her gar - den, Strange young
2. Oh, kind sir, I can - not mar - ry, I've a
3. What if he's in bat - tle slain, Or drowned
4. If he's in some bat - tle slain, I'll die
5. If he's found an - oth - er love, And if
6. Then he picked her up in his arms, Kiss - es

man come rid - ing by. Said, "Fair maid, will you mar - ry
love who sails the deep sea. He's been gone for these sev - en
in the deep salt sea? What if he's found an - oth - er
when the moon doth wane. If he's drowned in the deep salt
they both mar - ried be, Then I wish them both hap - pi
gave her one, two three. Weep no more my own true

me?" This then, sir, was her re - ply.
years, Still no man shall mar - ry me.
love, And that they both mar - ried be.
sea, I'll be true to his mem - o - ry.
ness, Where they dwell a - cross the sea.
love, I'm your long lost John Ri - ley.

JOHNNY I HARDLY KNEW YE

Irish folksong

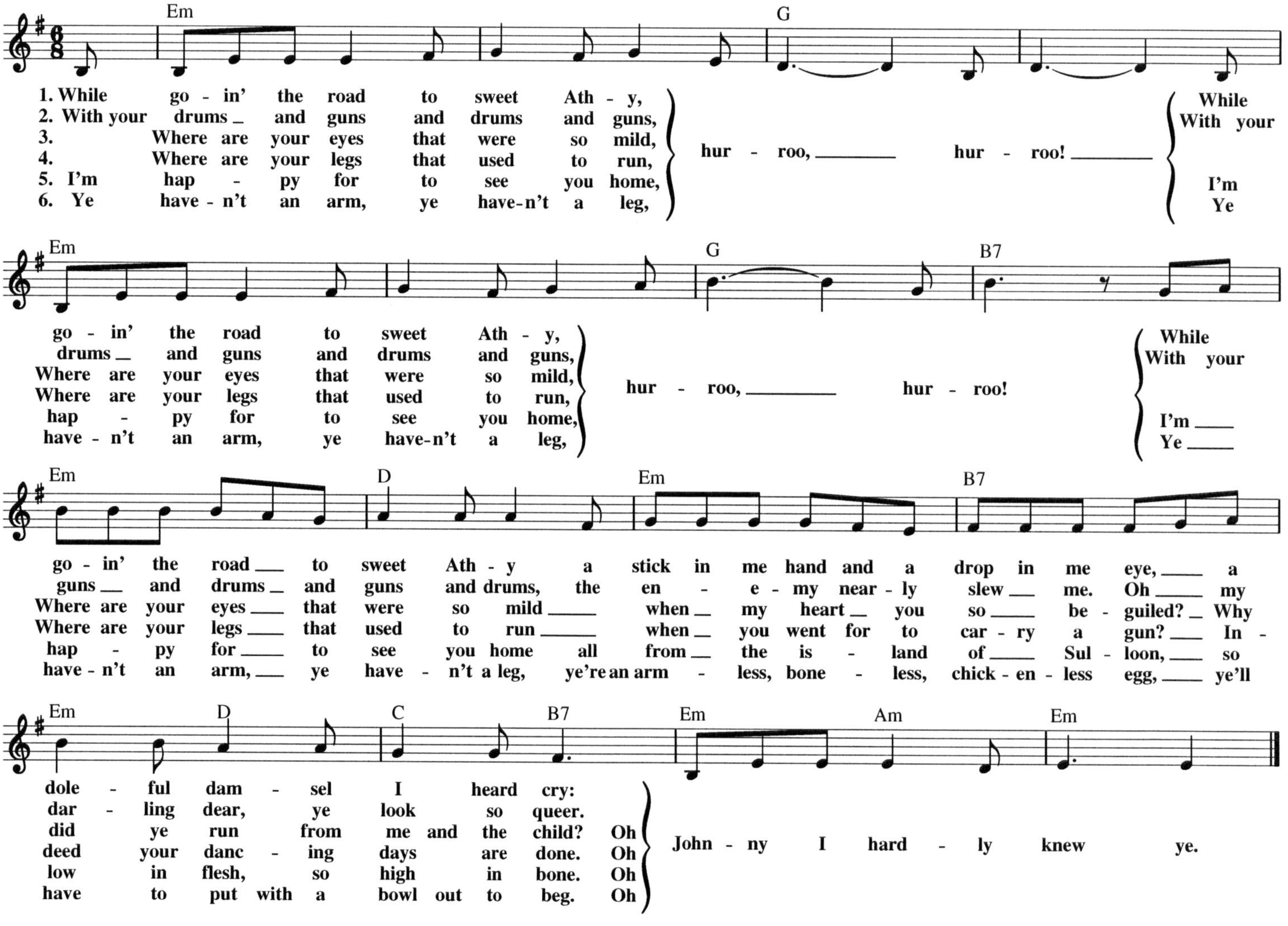

1. While go - in' the road to sweet Ath - y, hur - roo, hur - roo! While
2. With your drums and guns and drums and guns, With your
3. Where are your eyes that were so mild, hur - roo, hur - roo!
4. Where are your legs that used to run,
5. I'm hap - py for to see you home, I'm
6. Ye have - n't an arm, ye have-n't a leg, Ye

go - in' the road to sweet Ath - y, hur - roo, hur - roo! While
drums and guns and drums and guns, With your
Where are your eyes that were so mild, I'm
Where are your legs that used to run, Ye
hap - py for to see you home,
have - n't an arm, ye have - n't a leg,

go - in' the road to sweet Ath - y a stick in me hand and a drop in me eye, a
guns and drums and guns and drums, the en - e - my near - ly slew me. Oh my
Where are your eyes that were so mild when my heart you so be - guiled? Why
Where are your legs that used to run when you went for to car - ry a gun? In
hap - py for to see you home all from the is - land of Sul - loon, so
have - n't an arm, ye have - n't a leg, ye're an arm - less, bone - less, chick - en - less egg, ye'll

dole - ful dam - sel I heard cry:
dar - ling dear, ye look so queer. Oh John - ny I hard - ly knew ye.
did ye run from me and the child? Oh
deed your danc - ing days are done. Oh
low in flesh, so high in bone. Oh
have to put with a bowl out to beg. Oh

JUG OF PUNCH

Irish folksong

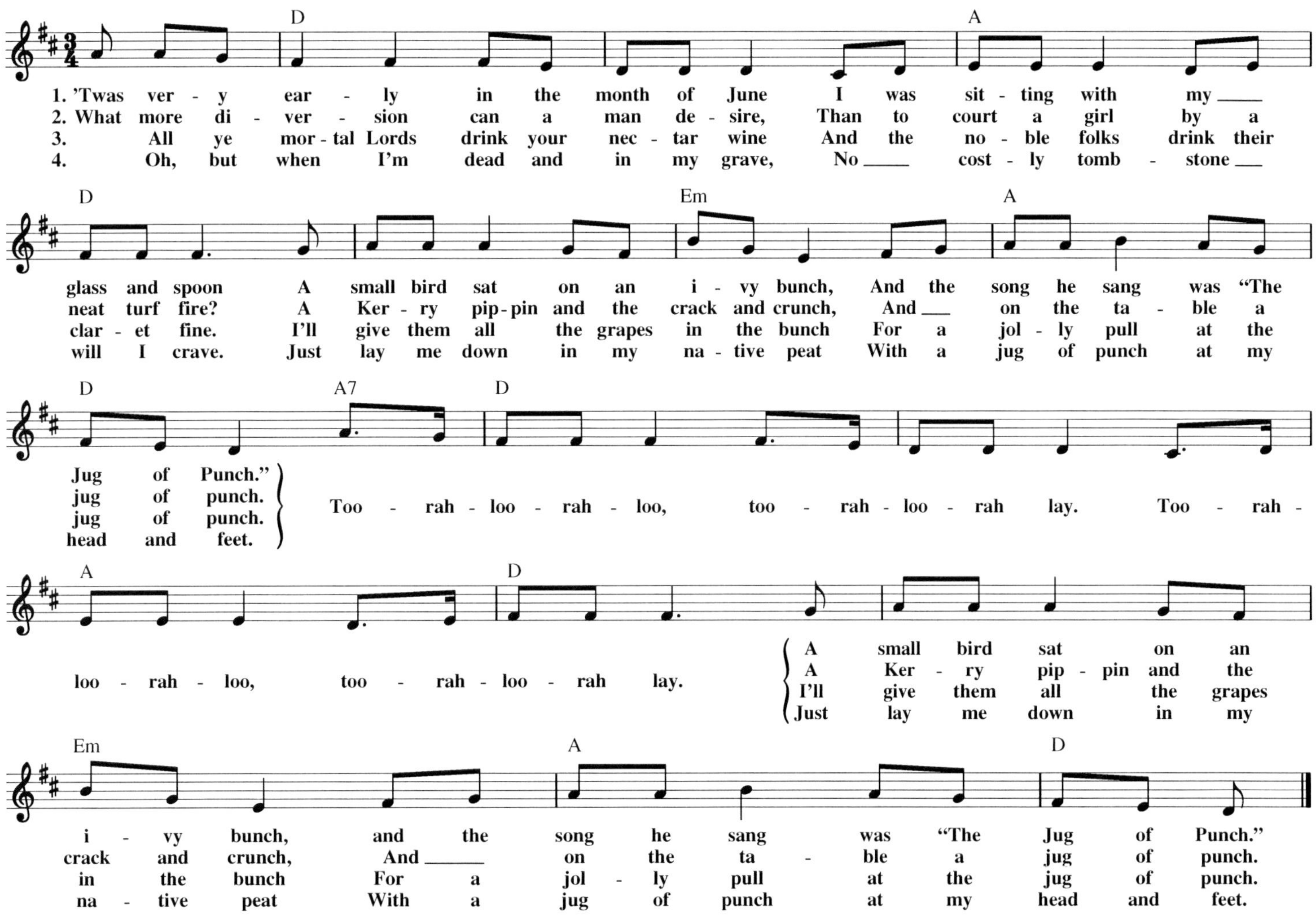

KELLY, THE BOY FROM KILLANN

Words and Music by
P.J. McCall

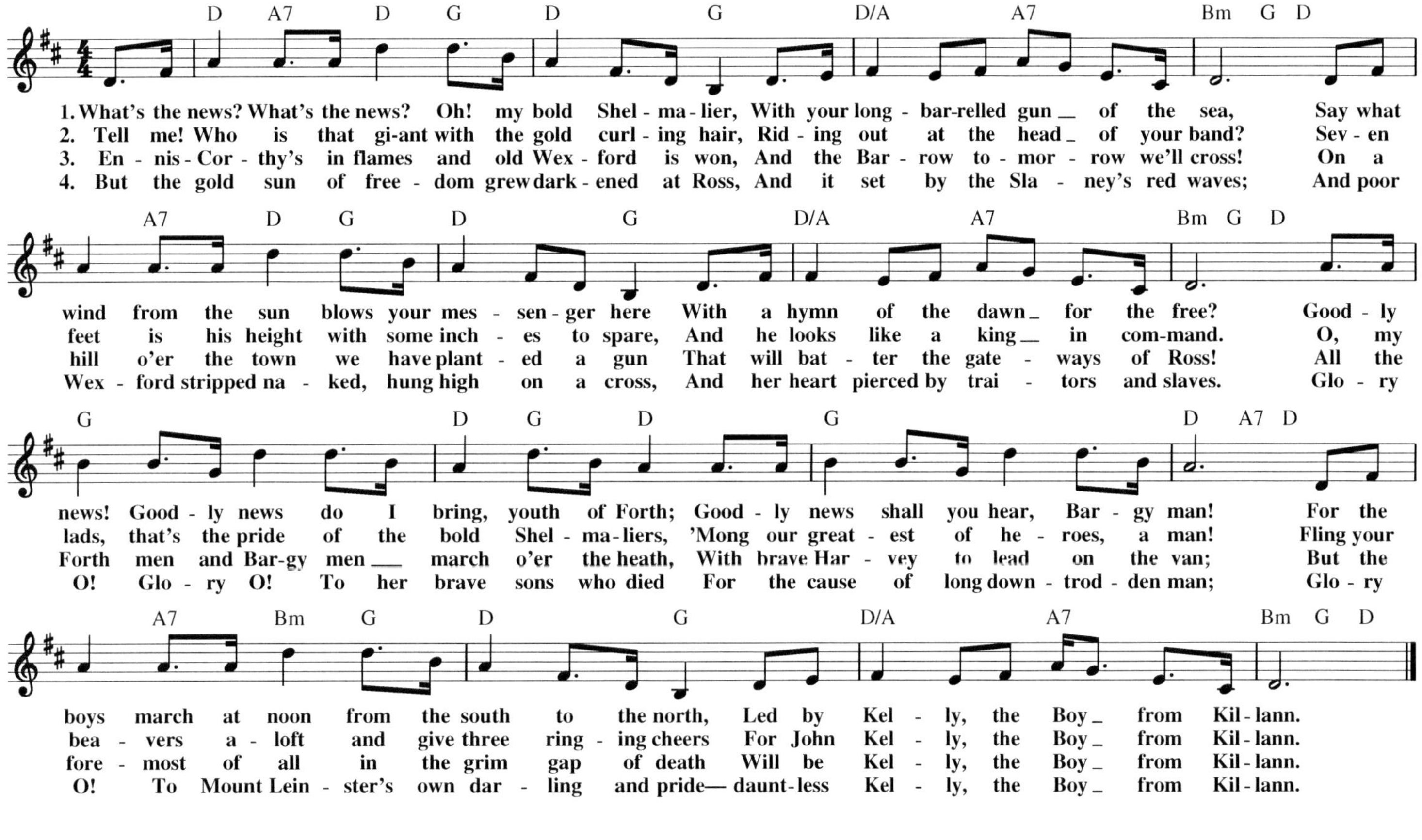

KATHLEEN MAVOURNEEN

Words by Annie Barry Crawford
Music by F.W.N. Crouch

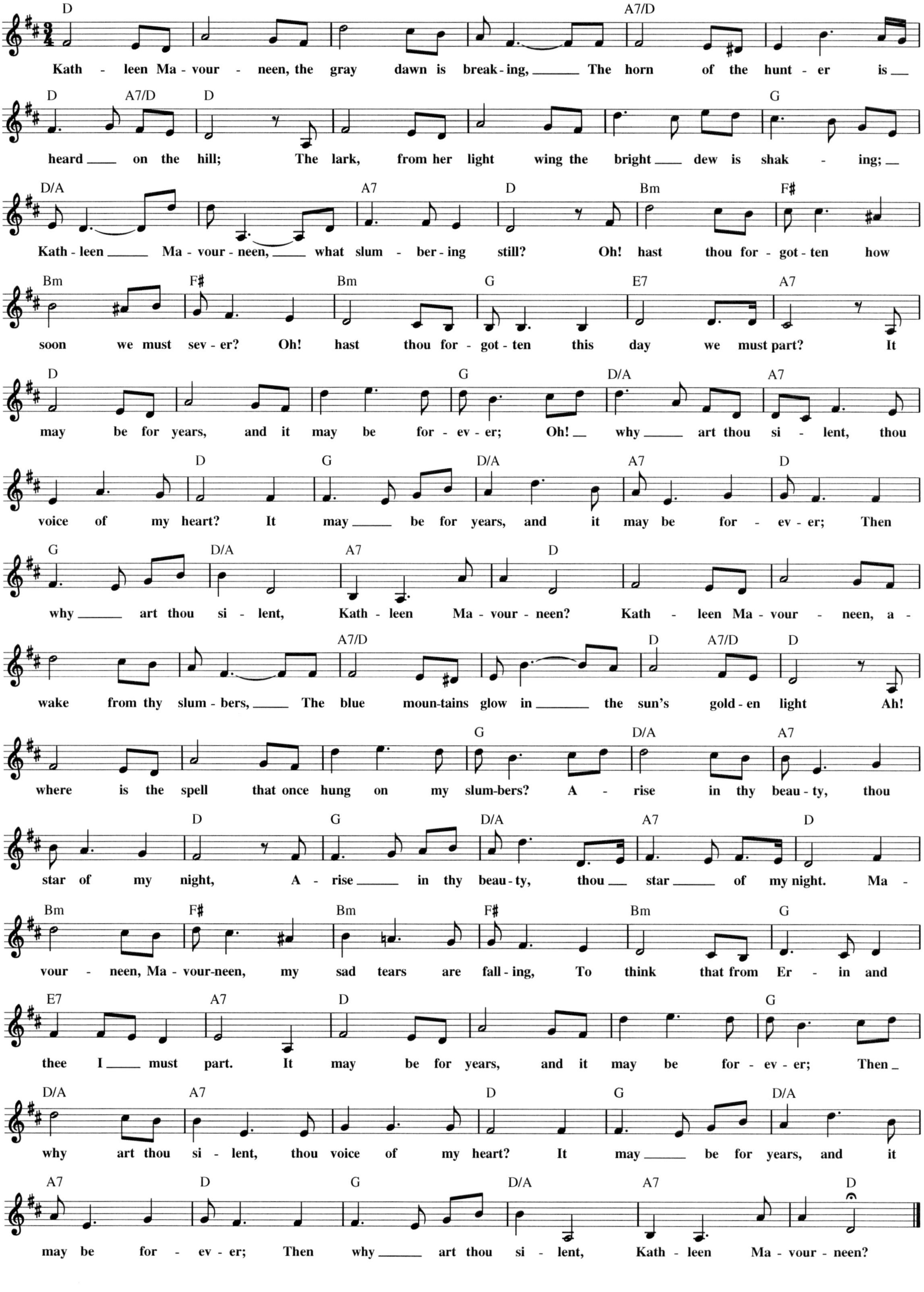

THE KERRY COW

Irish folksong

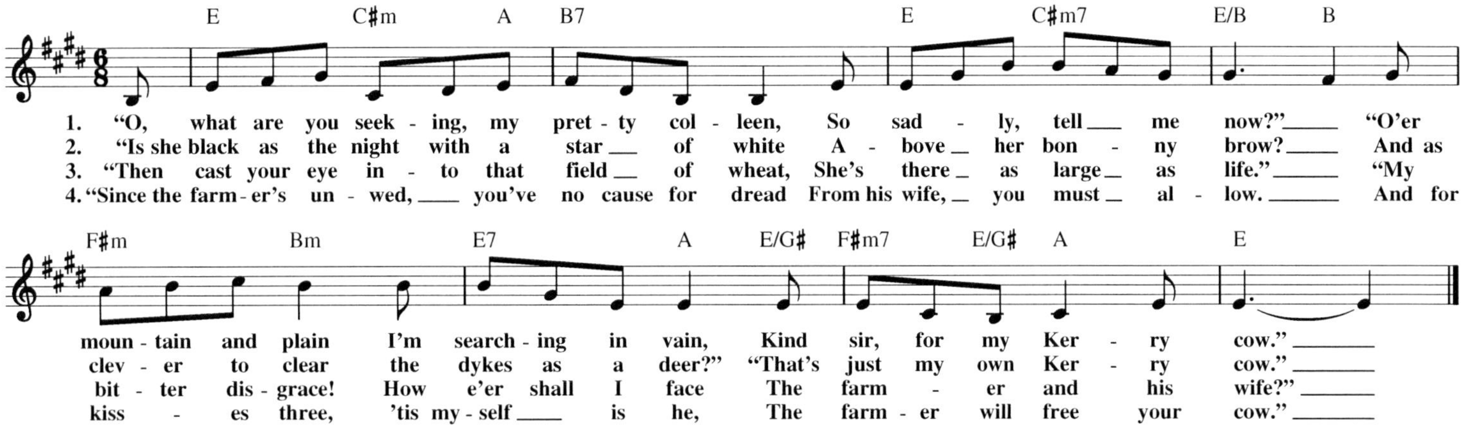

THE KERRY REEL

Irish folksong

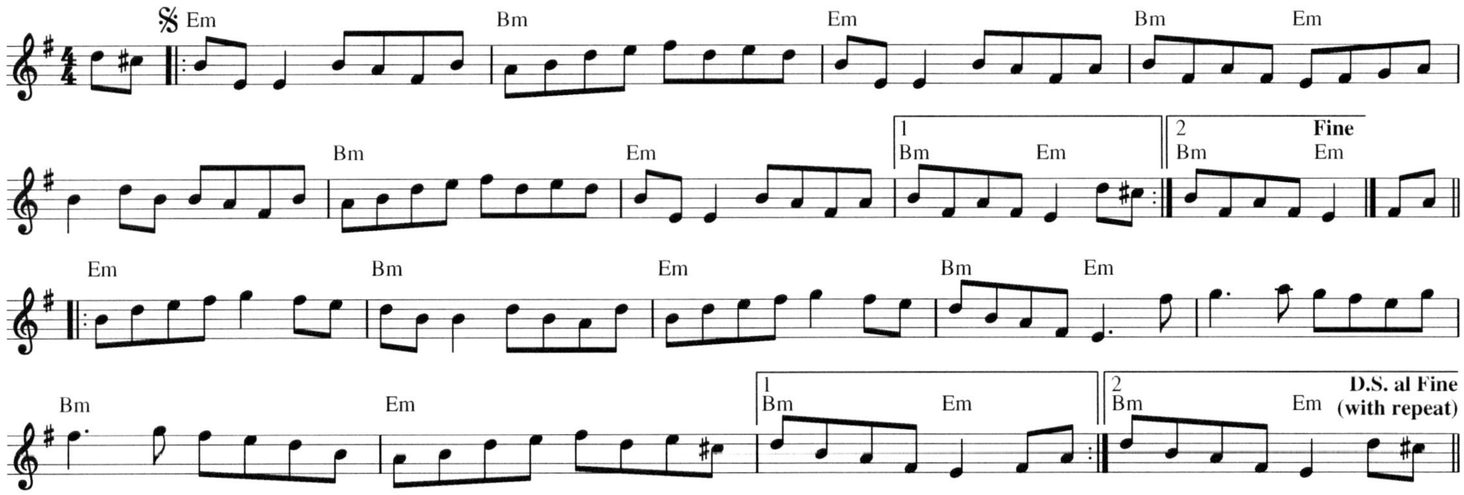

KEVIN BARRY

Irish folksong

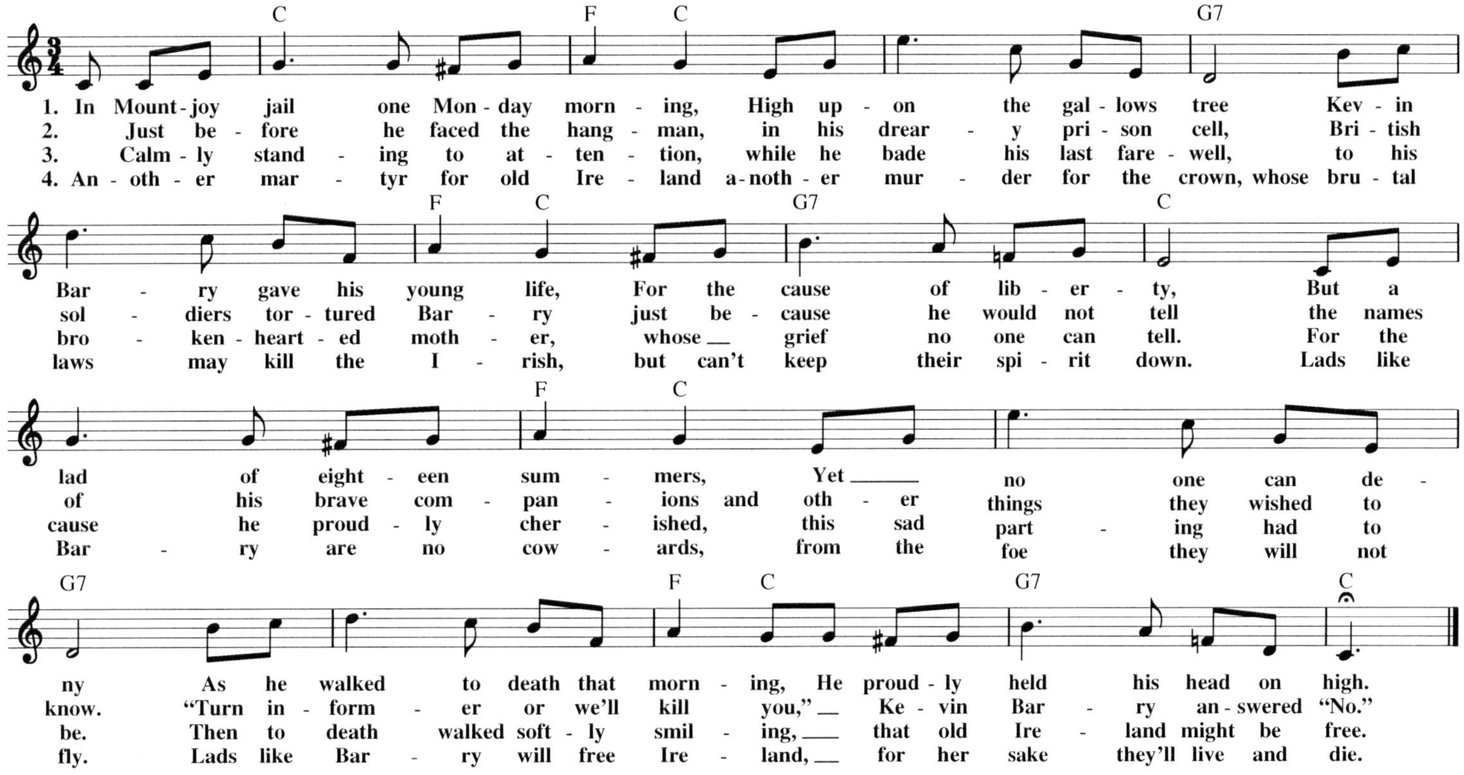

124

THE KERRY DANCE

Words and Music by
James L. Molloy

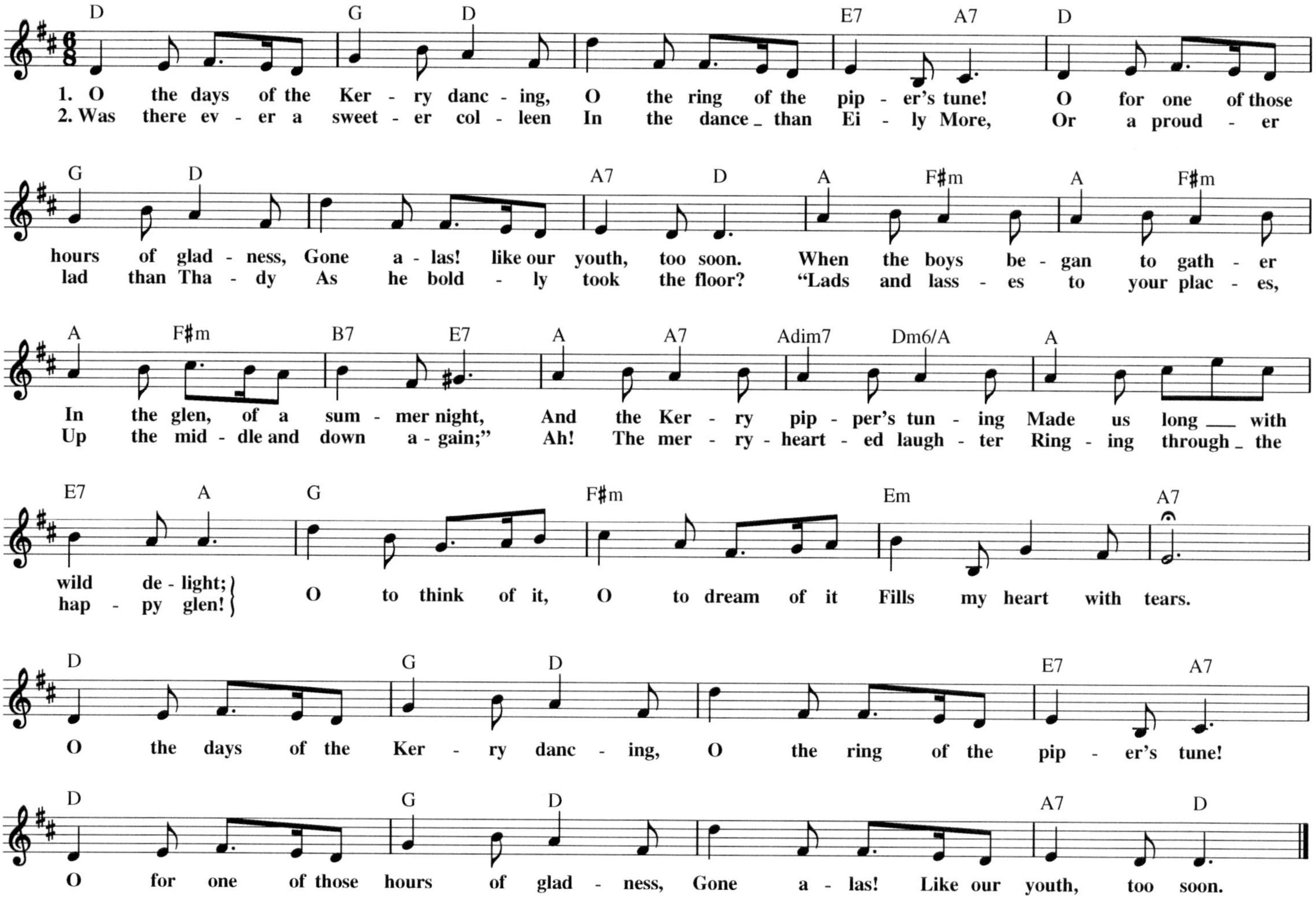

KILGARY MOUNTAIN

Irish folksong

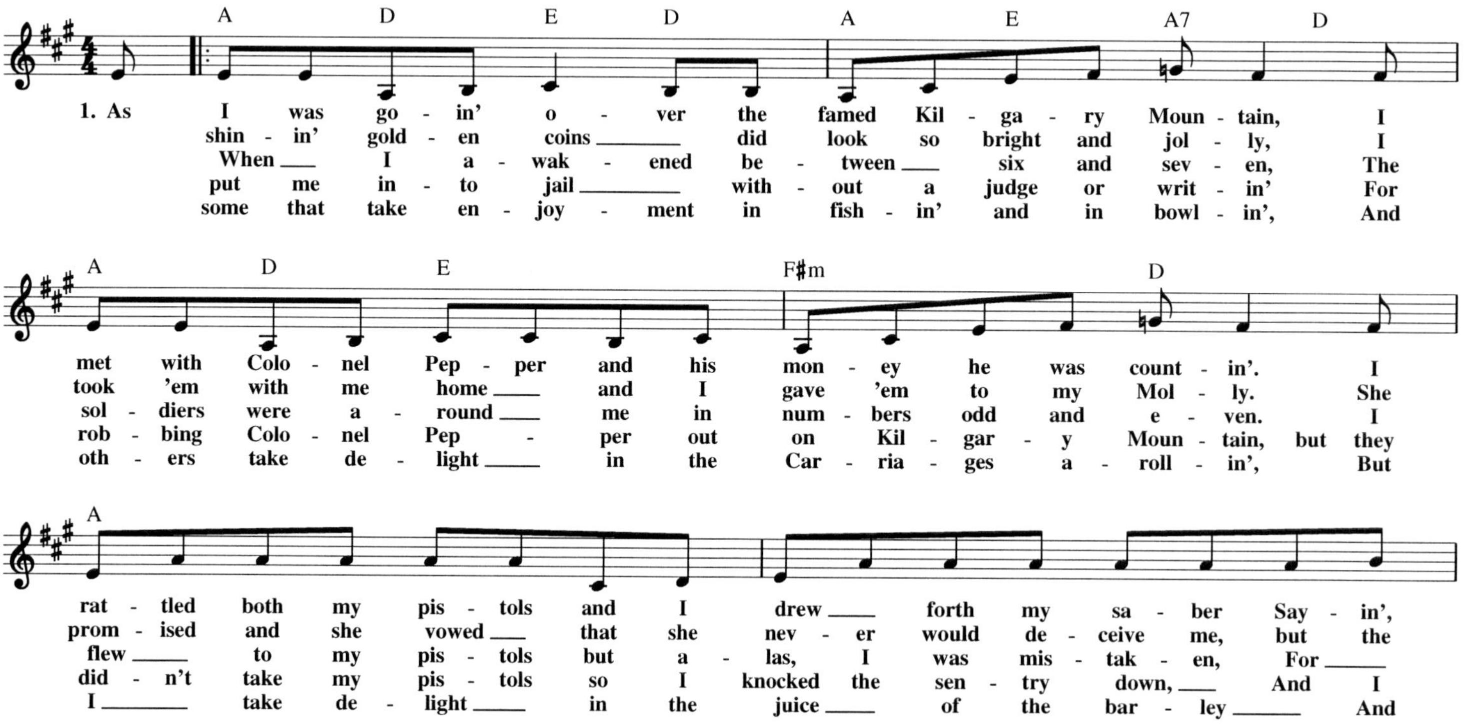

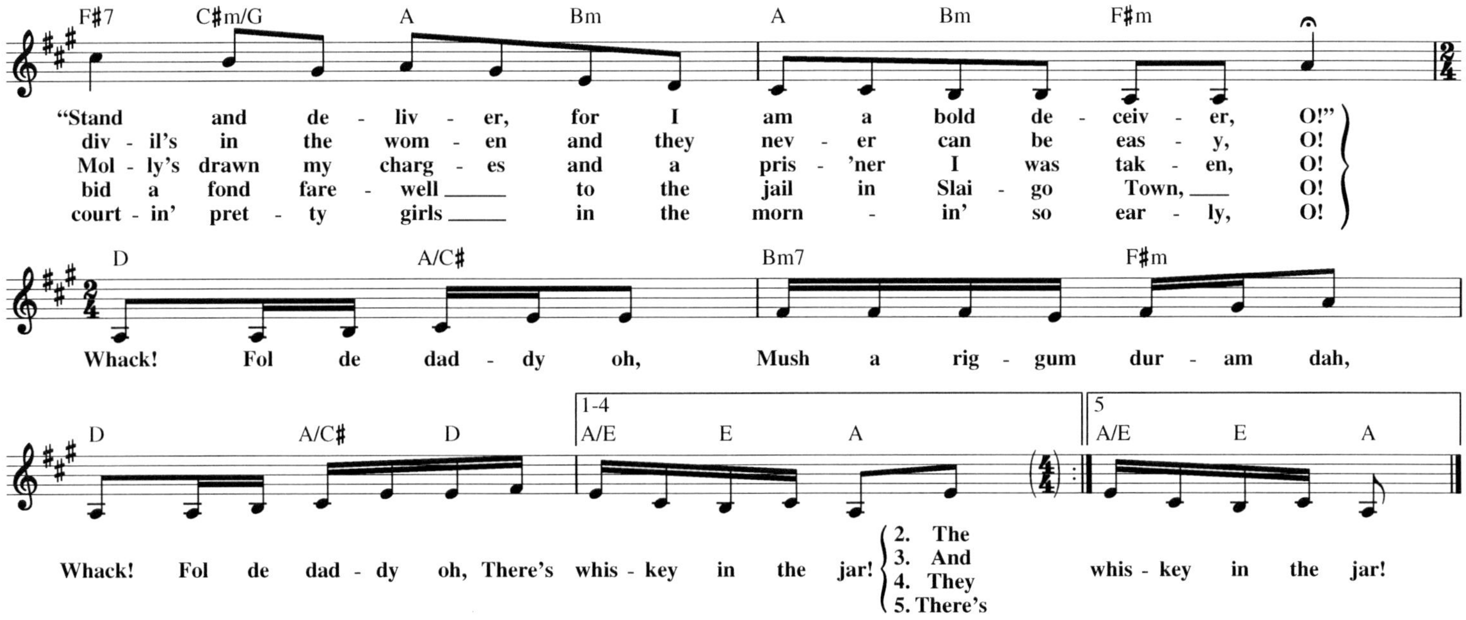
F#7 C#m/G A Bm A Bm F#m
"Stand and de - liv - er, for I am a bold de - ceiv - er, O!"
div - il's in the wom - en and they nev - er can be eas - y, O!
Mol - ly's drawn my charg - es and a pris - 'ner I was tak - en, O!
bid a fond fare - well to the jail in Slai - go Town, O!
court - in' pret - ty girls in the morn - in' so ear - ly, O!
D A/C# Bm7 F#m
Whack! Fol de dad - dy oh, Mush a rig - gum dur - am dah,
D A/C# D
1-4
A/E E A
5
A/E E A
Whack! Fol de dad - dy oh, There's whis - key in the jar!
2. The
3. And
4. They
5. There's
whis - key in the jar!

KILLARNEY

Words and Music by
M.W. Balfe

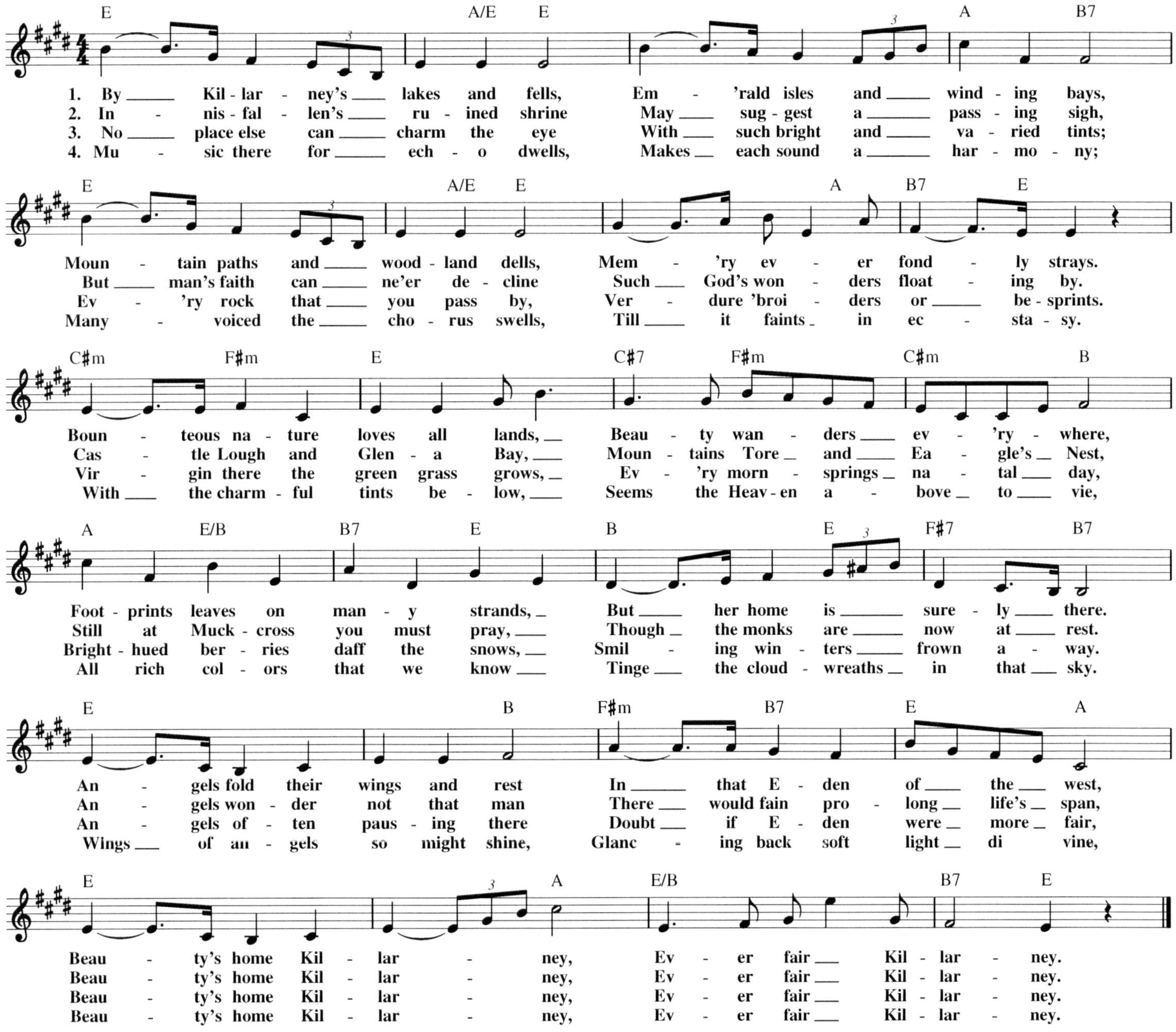
1. By Kil - lar - ney's lakes and fells, Em - 'rald isles and wind - ing bays,
2. In - nis - fal - len's ru - ined shrine May sug - gest a pass - ing sigh,
3. No place else can charm the eye With such bright and va - ried tints;
4. Mu - sic there for ech - o dwells, Makes each sound a har - mo - ny;
Moun - tain paths and wood - land dells, Mem - 'ry ev - er fond - ly strays.
But man's faith can ne'er de - cline Such God's won - ders float - ing by.
Ev - 'ry rock that you pass by, Ver - dure 'broi - ders or be - sprints.
Many - voiced the cho - rus swells, Till it faints in ec - sta - sy.
Boun - teous na - ture loves all lands, Beau - ty wan - ders ev - 'ry - where,
Cas - tle Lough and Glen - a Bay, Moun - tains Tore and Ea - gle's Nest,
Vir - gin there the green grass grows, Ev - 'ry morn - springs na - tal day,
With the charm - ful tints be - low, Seems the Heav - en a - bove to vie,
Foot - prints leaves on man - y strands, But her home is sure - ly there.
Still at Muck - cross you must pray, Though the monks are now at rest.
Bright - hued ber - ries daff the snows, Smil - ing win - ters frown a - way.
All rich col - ors that we know Tinge the cloud - wreaths in that sky.
An - gels fold their wings and rest In that E - den of the west,
An - gels won - der not that man There would fain pro - long life's span,
An - gels of - ten paus - ing there Doubt if E - den were more fair,
Wings of an - gels so might shine, Glanc - ing back soft light di - vine,
Beau - ty's home Kil - lar - ney, Ev - er fair Kil - lar - ney.
Beau - ty's home Kil - lar - ney, Ev - er fair Kil - lar - ney.
Beau - ty's home Kil - lar - ney, Ev - er fair Kil - lar - ney.
Beau - ty's home Kil - lar - ney, Ev - er fair Kil - lar - ney.

126

KIRSTEEN
(Co bhios agad, Chairistiona)

Folksong from the Hebrides

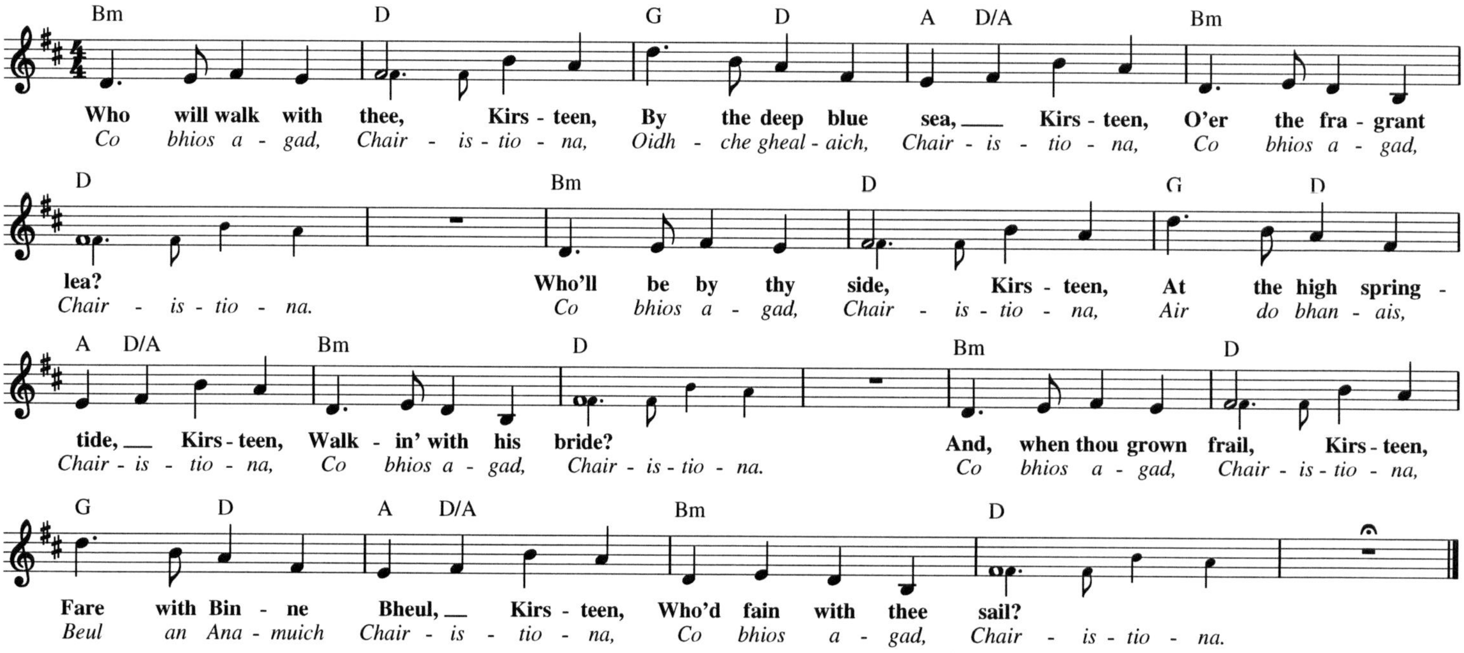

KITTY OF COLERAINE

Irish folksong

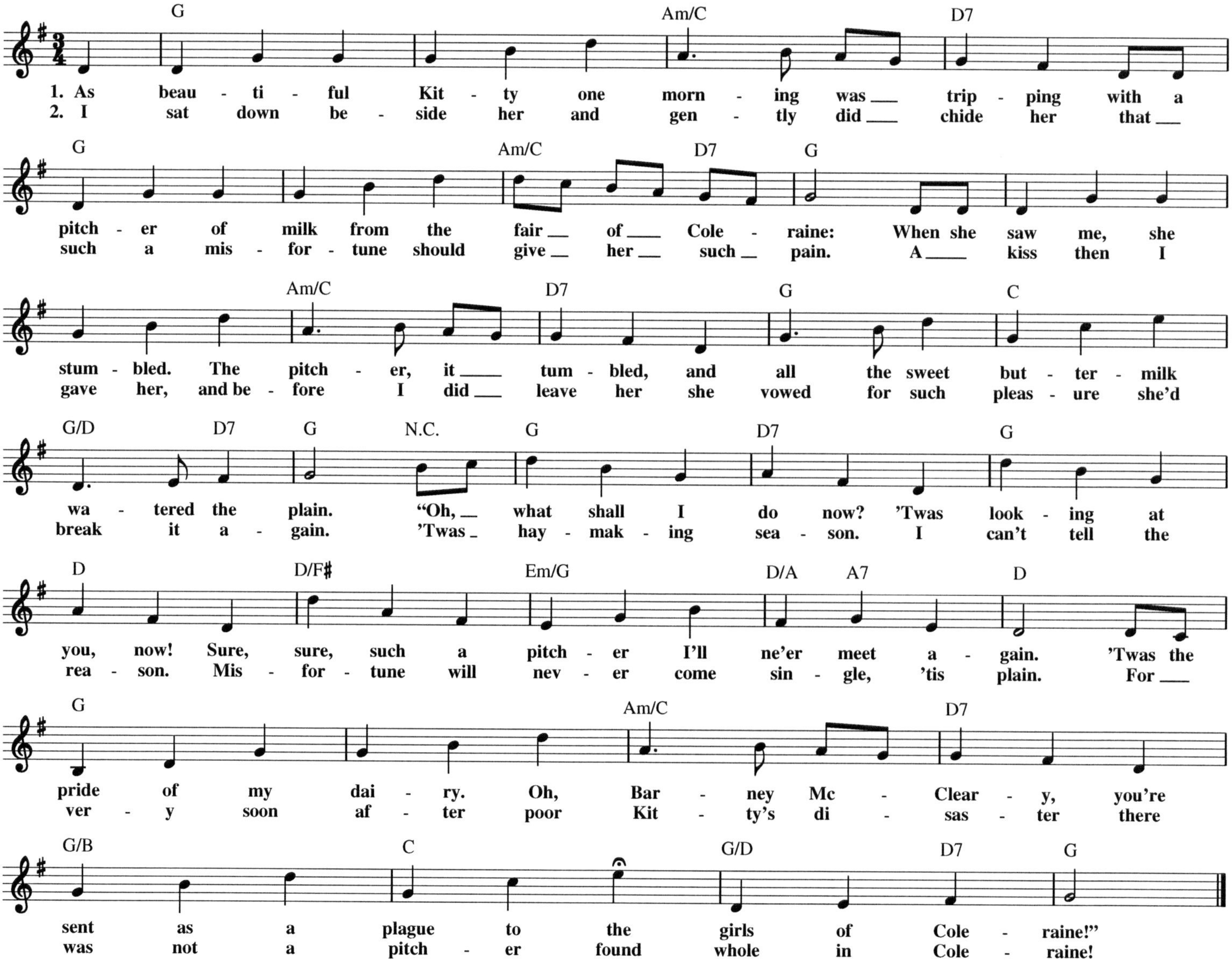

KISHMUL'S GALLEY
(Á Bhirlinn Bharrach)

Folksong from the Hebrides

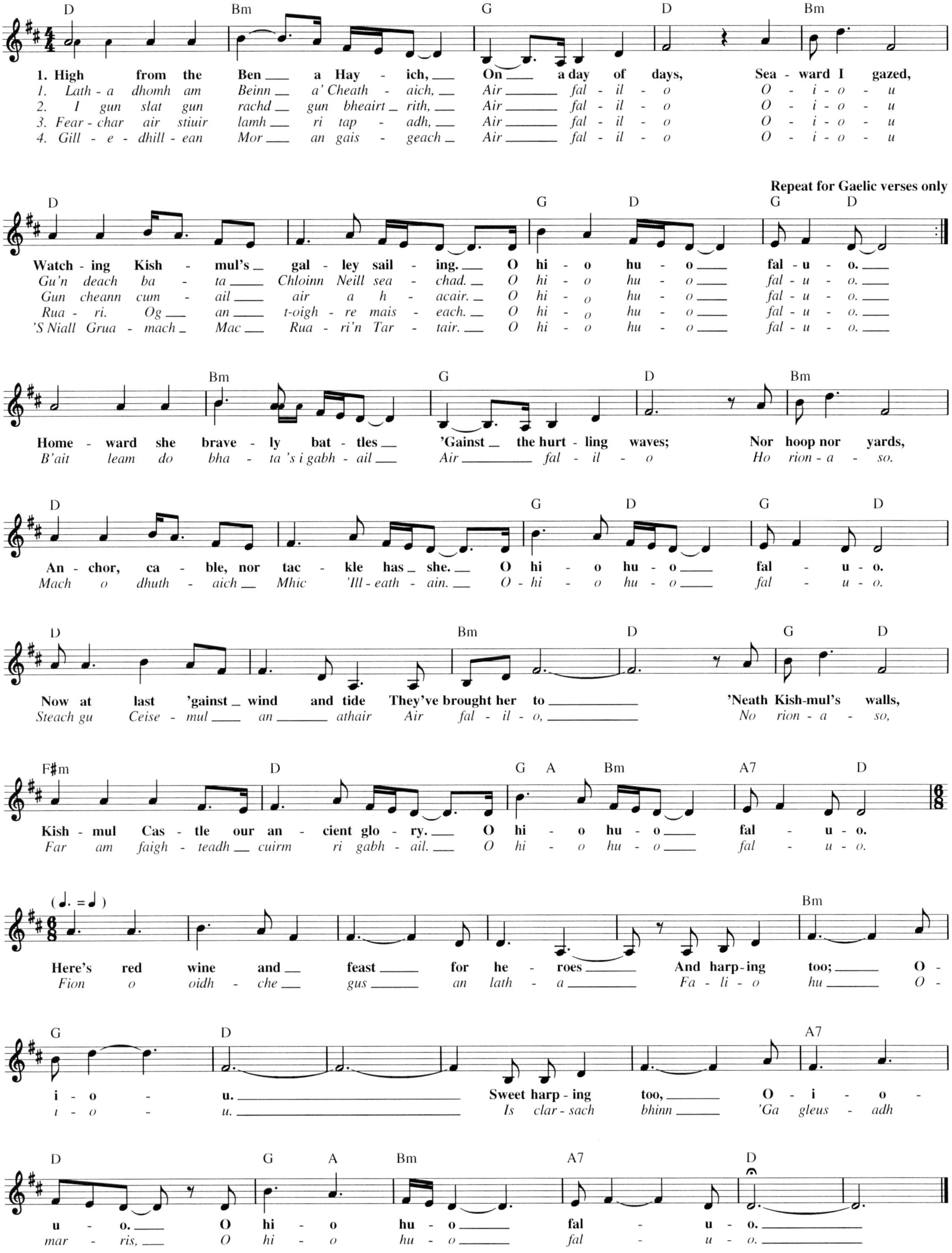

THE LAMBS ON THE GREEN HILLS

Irish folksong

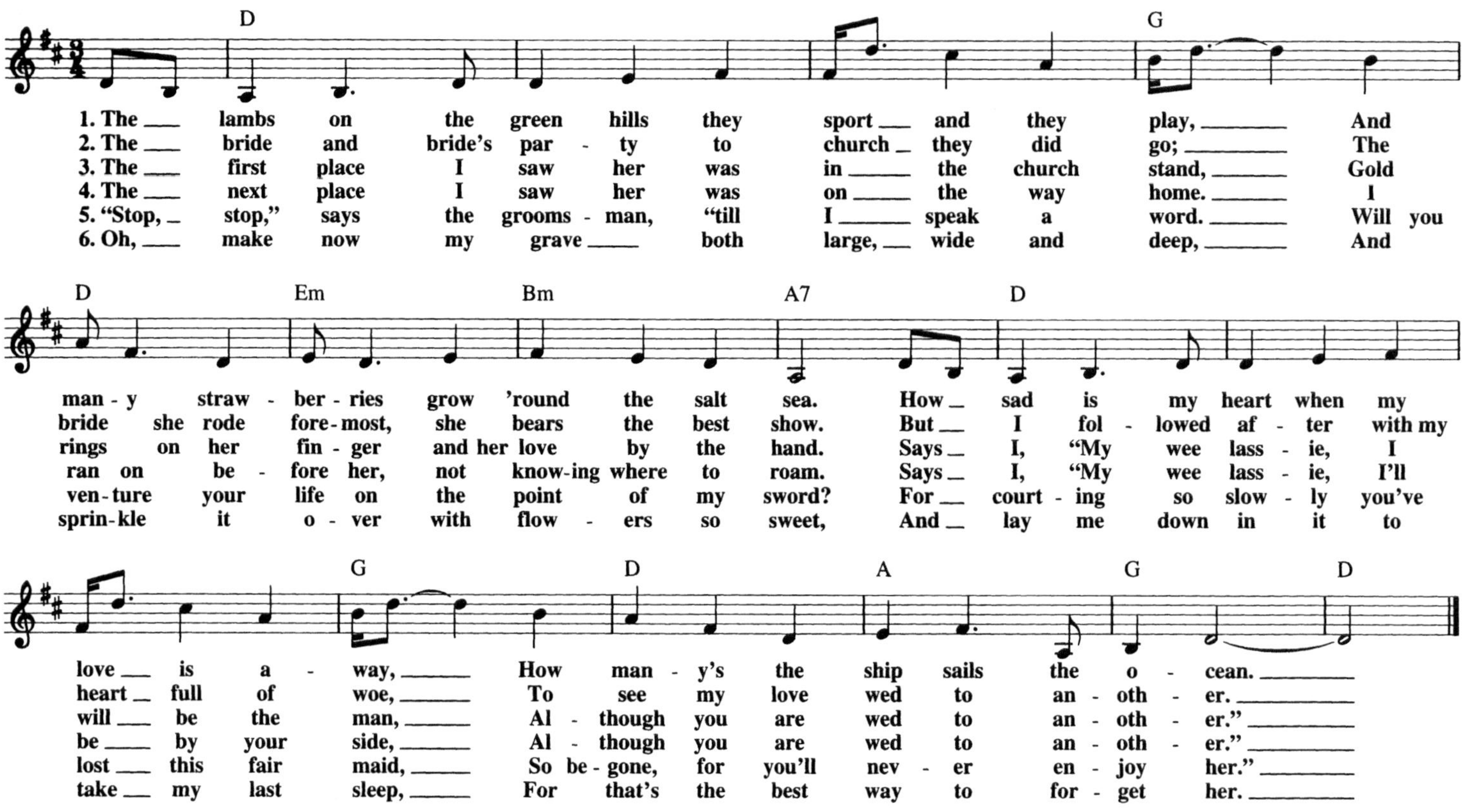

1. The ___ lambs on the green hills they sport ___ and they play, _____ And
2. The ___ bride and bride's par - ty to church ___ they did go; _____ The
3. The ___ first place I saw her was in _____ the church stand, _____ Gold
4. The ___ next place I saw her was on _____ the way home. _____ I
5. "Stop, _ stop," says the grooms - man, "till I _____ speak a word. _____ Will you
6. Oh, ___ make now my grave _____ both large, ___ wide and deep, _____ And

man - y straw - ber - ries grow 'round the salt sea. How ___ sad is my heart when my
bride she rode fore - most, she bears the best show. But ___ I fol - lowed af - ter with my
rings on her fin - ger and her love by the hand. Says ___ I, "My wee lass - ie, I
ran on be - fore her, not know - ing where to roam. Says ___ I, "My wee lass - ie, I'll
ven - ture your life on the point of my sword? For ___ court - ing so slow - ly you've
sprin - kle it o - ver with flow - ers so sweet, And ___ lay me down in it to

love ___ is a - way, _____ How man - y's the ship sails the o - cean. _____
heart _ full of woe, _____ To see my love wed to an - oth - er. _____
will ___ be the man, _____ Al - though you are wed to an - oth - er." _____
be ___ by your side, _____ Al - though you are wed to an - oth - er." _____
lost ___ this fair maid, _____ So be - gone, for you'll nev - er en - joy her." _____
take ___ my last sleep, _____ For that's the best way to for - get her. _____

LANIGAN'S BALL

Words by Tony Pastor
Music by Neil Bryant

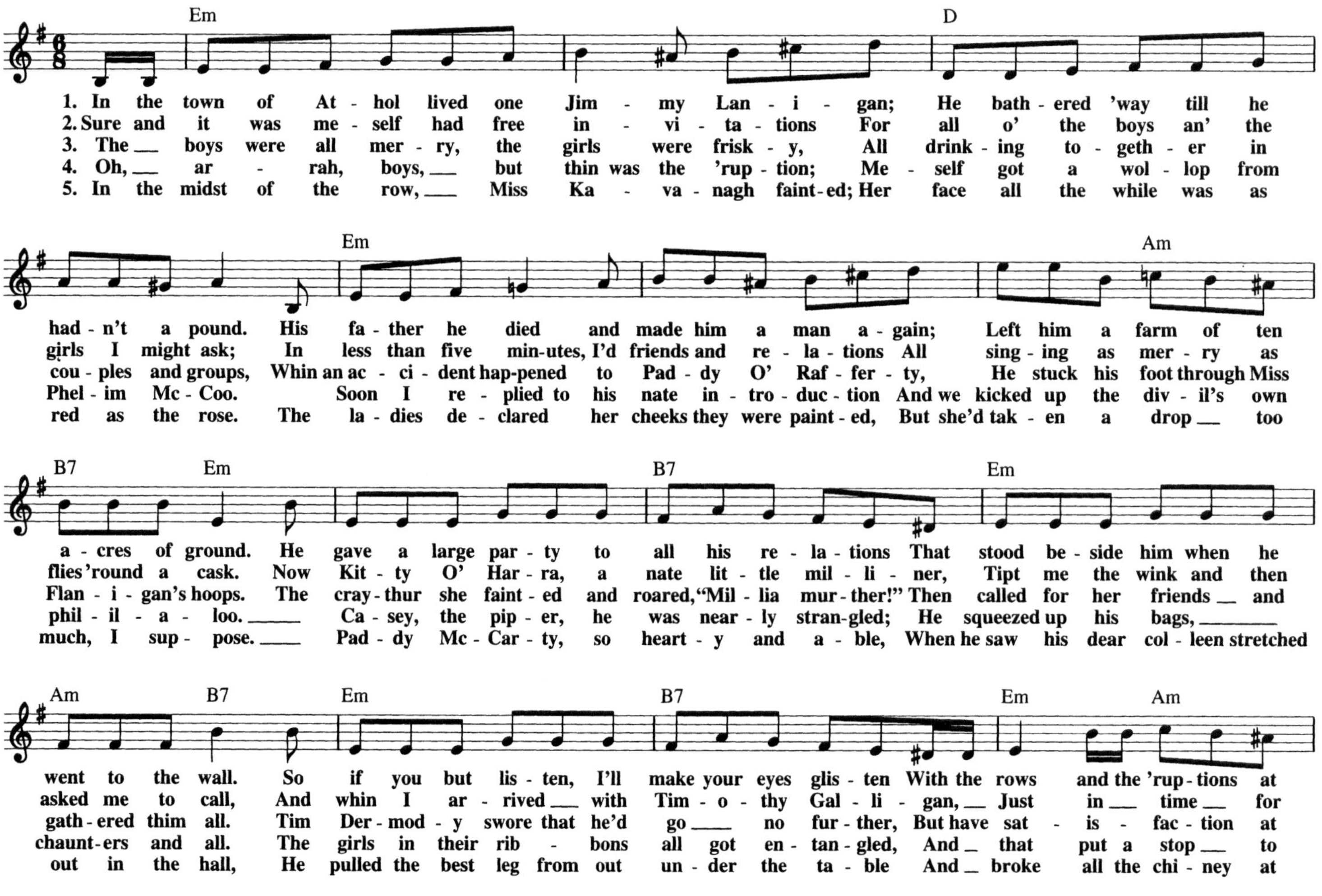

1. In the town of At - hol lived one Jim - my Lan - i - gan; He bath - ered 'way till he
2. Sure and it was me - self had free in - vi - ta - tions For all o' the boys an' the
3. The ___ boys were all mer - ry, the girls were frisk - y, All drink - ing to - geth - er in
4. Oh, ___ ar - rah, boys, ___ but thin was the 'rup - tion; Me - self got a wol - lop from
5. In the midst of the row, ___ Miss Ka - va - nagh faint - ed; Her face all the while was as

had - n't a pound. His fa - ther he died and made him a man a - gain; Left him a farm of ten
girls I might ask; In less than five min - utes, I'd friends and re - la - tions All sing - ing as mer - ry as
cou - ples and groups, Whin an ac - ci - dent hap - pened to Pad - dy O' Raf - fer - ty, He stuck his foot through Miss
Phel - im Mc - Coo. Soon I re - plied to his nate in - tro - duc - tion And we kicked up the div - il's own
red as the rose. The la - dies de - clared her cheeks they were paint - ed, But she'd tak - en a drop ___ too

a - cres of ground. He gave a large par - ty to all his re - la - tions That stood be - side him when he
flies 'round a cask. Now Kit - ty O' Har - ra, a nate lit - tle mil - li - ner, Tipt me the wink and then
Flan - i - gan's hoops. The cray - thur she faint - ed and roared, "Mil - lia mur - ther!" Then called for her friends ___ and
phil - il - a - loo. ___ Ca - sey, the pip - er, he was near - ly stran - gled; He squeezed up his bags, _____
much, I sup - pose. ___ Pad - dy Mc - Car - ty, so heart - y and a - ble, When he saw his dear col - leen stretched

went to the wall. So if you but lis - ten, I'll make your eyes glis - ten With the rows and the 'rup - tions at
asked me to call, And whin I ar - rived ___ with Tim - o - thy Gal - li - gan, ___ Just in ___ time for
gath - ered them all. Tim Der - mod - y swore that he'd go ___ no fur - ther, But have sat - is - fac - tion at
chaunt - ers and all. The girls in their rib - bons all got en - tan - gled, And ___ that put a stop ___ to
out in the hall, He pulled the best leg from out un - der the ta - ble And ___ broke all the chi - ney at

Lan - i - gan's Ball.
Lan - i - gan's Ball.
Lan - i - gan's Ball.
Lan - i - gan's Ball.
Lan - i - gan's Ball.

Whack! fal, lal, fal, lal, tal, lad - ed - dy. Whack! fal, lal, fal,

lal, tal, lad - ed - dy. Whack! fal, lal, fal, lal, tal, lad - ed - dy. Whack! hur - roo! __ for Lan - i - gan's Ball.

Whack! fal, lal, fal, lal, tal, lad - ed - dy. Whack! fal, lal, fal, lal, tal, lad - ed - dy.

Whack! fal, lal, fal, lal, tal, lad - ed - dy. Whack! hur - roo! __ for Lan - i - gan's Ball.

THE LARK IN THE CLEAR AIR

Irish folksong
Words and Music by
Sir Samuel Ferguson

1. Dear __ thoughts are __ in my mind, and __ my soul __ soars en -
2. I shall tell her __ all my love, all __ my soul's __ ad - o -

chant - ed As I hear the __ sweet lark sing in __ the clear __ air of the day. For a
ra - tion, And I think she __ will hear me, and __ will __ not say me nay. It is

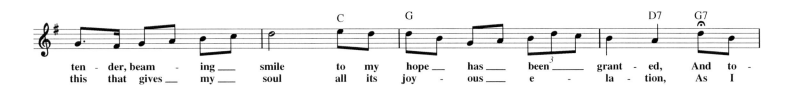

ten - der, beam - ing __ smile to my hope __ has __ been __ grant - ed, And to -
this that gives __ my __ soul all its joy - ous e - la - tion, As I

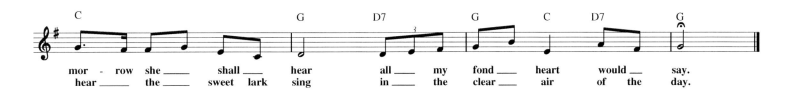

mor - row she __ shall __ hear all __ my fond __ heart would __ say.
hear __ the __ sweet lark sing in __ the clear __ air of the day.

THE LARK IN THE MORNING

Irish folksong

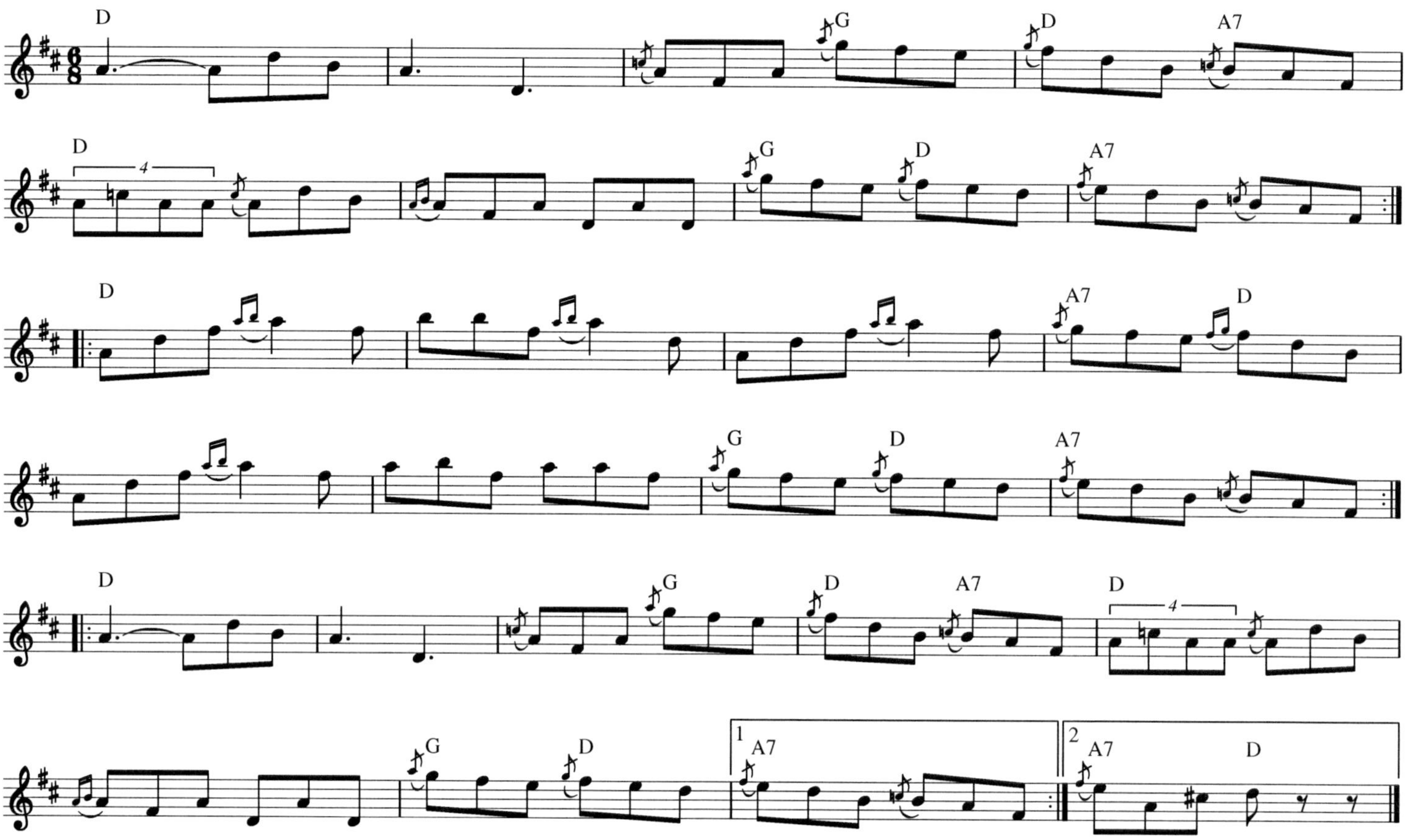

THE LAY OF DIARMAD

Folksong from the Hebrides

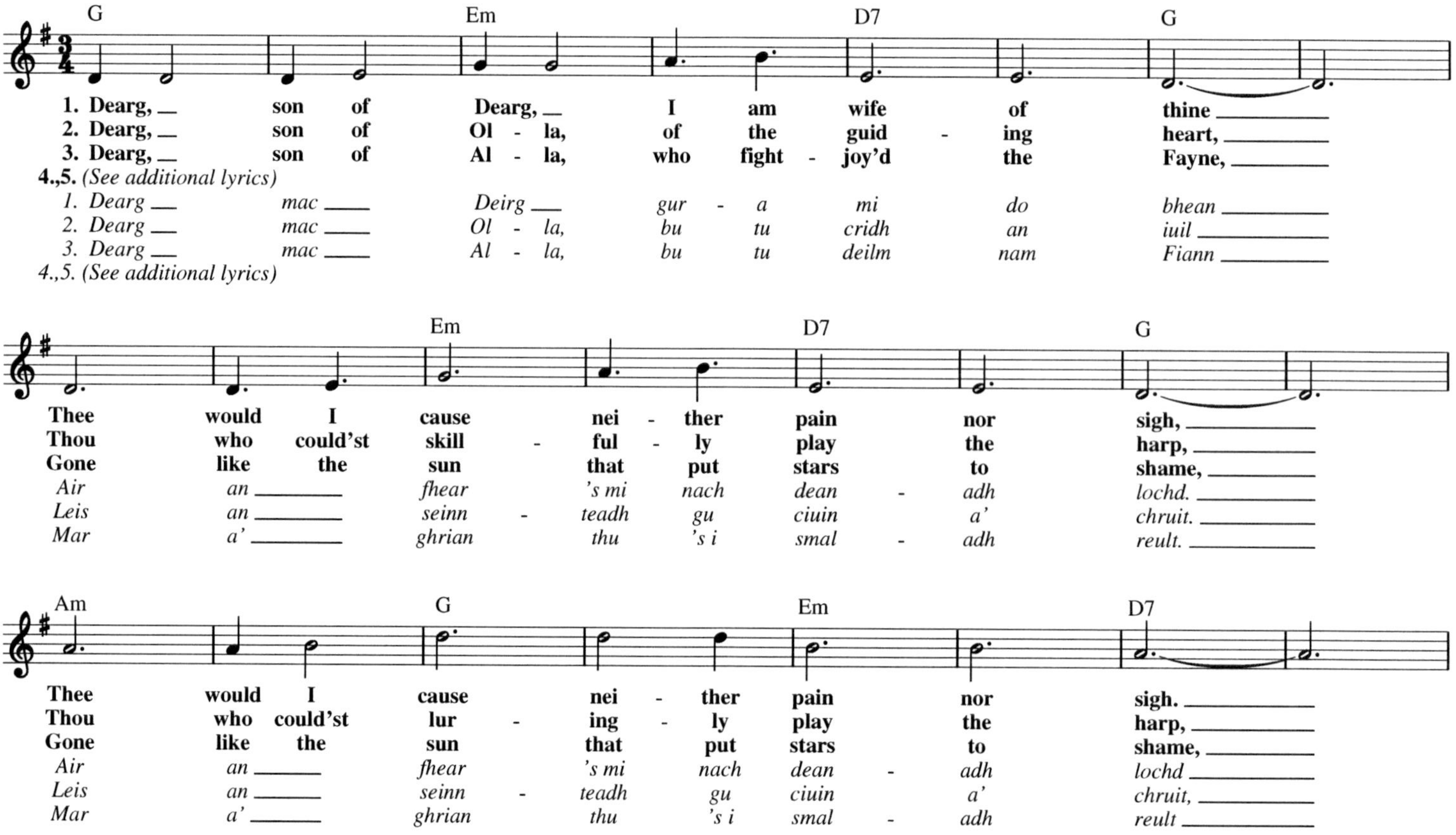

1. Dearg, __ son of Dearg, __ I am wife of thine _____
2. Dearg, __ son of Ol - la, of the guid - ing heart, _____
3. Dearg, __ son of Al - la, who fight - joy'd the Fayne, _____
4.,5. *(See additional lyrics)*
1. *Dearg* __ *mac* __ *Deirg* __ *gur - a mi do bhean* _____
2. *Dearg* __ *mac* __ *Ol - la, bu tu cridh an iuil* _____
3. *Dearg* __ *mac* __ *Al - la, bu tu deilm nam Fiann* _____
4.,5. *(See additional lyrics)*

Thee would I cause nei - ther pain nor sigh, _____
Thou who could'st skill - ful - ly play the harp, _____
Gone like the sun that put stars to shame, _____
Air an _____ *fhear 's mi nach dean - adh lochd.* _____
Leis an _____ *seinn - teadh gu ciuin a' chruit.* _____
Mar a' _____ *ghrian thu 's i smal - adh reult.* _____

Thee would I cause nei - ther pain nor sigh. _____
Thou who could'st lur - ing - ly play the harp, _____
Gone like the sun that put stars to shame, _____
Air an _____ *fhear 's mi nach dean - adh lochd* _____
Leis an _____ *seinn - teadh gu ciuin a' chruit,* _____
Mar a' _____ *ghrian thu 's i smal - adh reult* _____

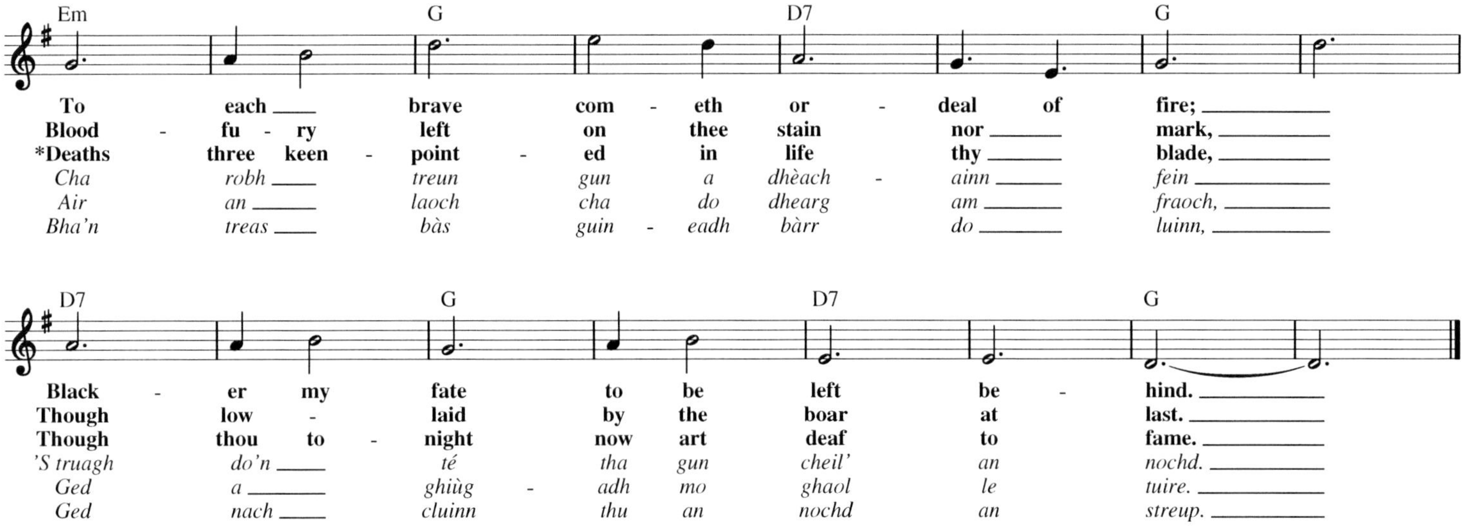

Em			G			D7			G	
To	each	brave	com	eth	or	deal	of	fire;		
Blood	fu - ry	left	on	thee	stain	nor		mark,		
*Deaths	three keen	point - ed	in	life	thy		blade,			
Cha	*robh*	*treun*	*gun*	*a*	*dhèach*	*ainn*		*fein*		
Air	*an*	*laoch*	*cha*	*do*	*dhearg*	*am*		*fraoch,*		
Bha'n	*treas*	*bàs*	*guin - eadh*	*bàrr*	*do*		*luinn,*			

D7			G			D7			G	
Black - er	my	fate	to	be	left	be -	hind.			
Though	low -	laid	by	the	boar	at	last.			
Though	thou to -	night	now	art	deaf	to	fame.			
'S truagh	*do'n*	*té*	*tha*	*gun*	*cheil'*	*an*	*nochd.*			
Ged	*a*	*ghiùg - adh*	*mo*	*ghaol*	*le*	*tuire.*				
Ged	*nach*	*cluinn*	*thu*	*an*	*nochd*	*an*	*streup.*			

Additional Lyrics

4. I see thy hawk and I see thy hound;
Keen in thy love their hunt-trail they found,
Keen in thy love their hunt-trail they found.
Dear to thee were we all three I trow;
Now let all three be to thee for shroud.

5. Shed we no tear on our brave, but sing
That we tonight deathwatch a king,
That we tonight deathwatch a king.
Stately calm, openhanded our mien,
For we tonight deathwatch a king.

4. Chi mi'n t-seabhag agus chi mi 'n cù
Leanadh dlùth fo do shuil 'san t-seilg.
Leanadh dlùth fo do shuil 'san t-seilg
'S o'n a b'ait le mo Dhearg an triuir
Theid an triuir anns an uir le Dearg.

5. 'S dùth dhuinn arral is cha dhèoir an nochd,
Sinn ri faire mu ghealchorp bu righ.
Sinn ri faire mu ghealchorp bu righ
'S duth d'ar caithris bhi gu flathail fial
B'e sid riamh maise Dheirg 'na chlìth.

*Deaths three: "The foe who has come, the foe who will come, the foe who is there now."

LET ERIN REMEMBER THE DAYS OF OLD

Irish popular song
Words by Thomas Moore

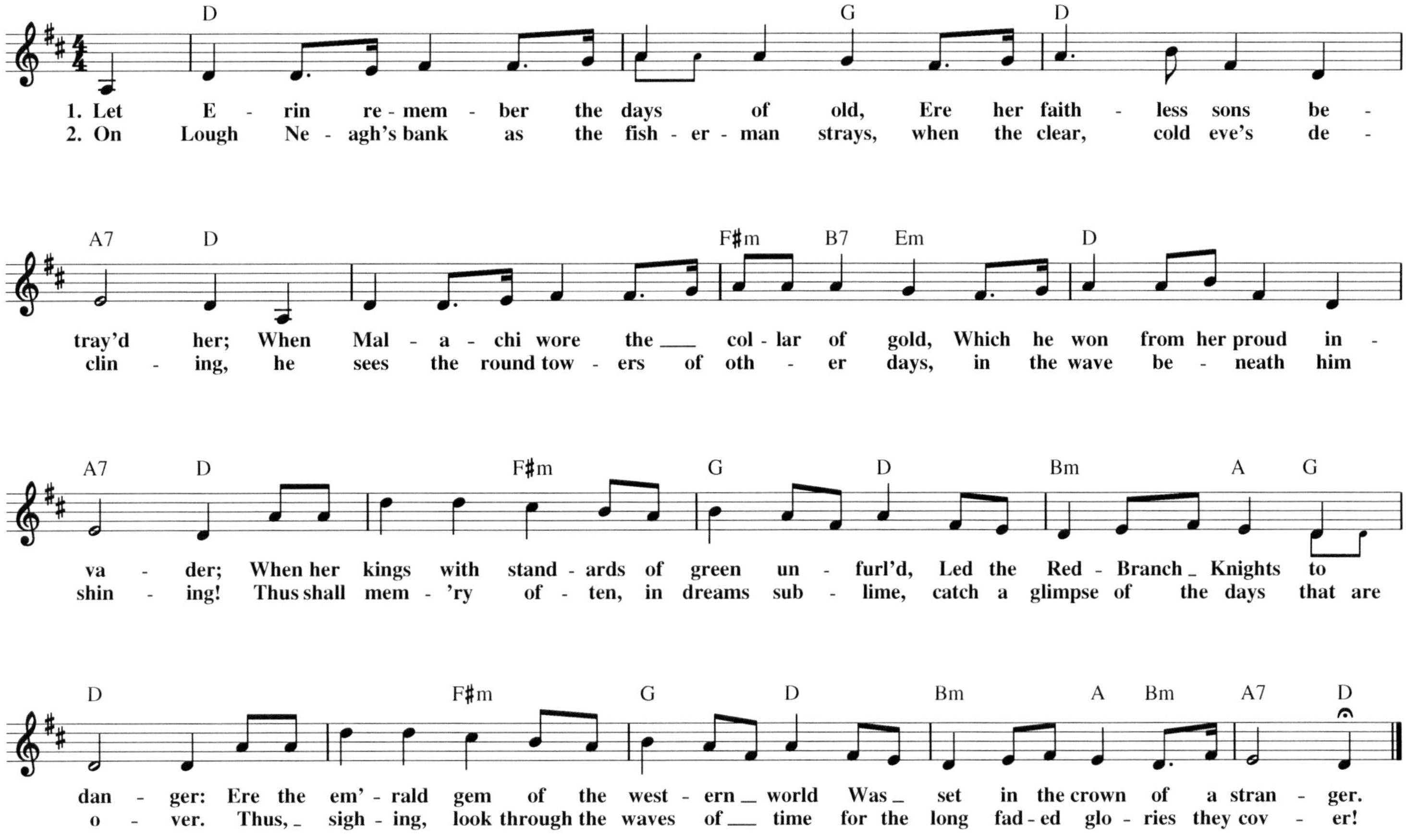

1. Let E - rin re - mem - ber the days of old, Ere her faith - less sons be -
2. On Lough Ne - agh's bank as the fish - er - man strays, when the clear, cold eve's de -

tray'd her; When Mal - a - chi wore the col - lar of gold, Which he won from her proud in -
clin - ing, he sees the round tow - ers of oth - er days, in the wave be - neath him

va - der; When her kings with stand - ards of green un - furl'd, Led the Red - Branch Knights to
shin - ing! Thus shall mem - 'ry of - ten, in dreams sub - lime, catch a glimpse of the days that are

dan - ger: Ere the em' - rald gem of the west - ern world Was set in the crown of a stran - ger.
o - ver. Thus, sigh - ing, look through the waves of time for the long fad - ed glo - ries they cov - er!

LET HIM GO—LET HIM TARRY

Words and Music by Cliff Gordon,
Max Maurice and Carl Yale

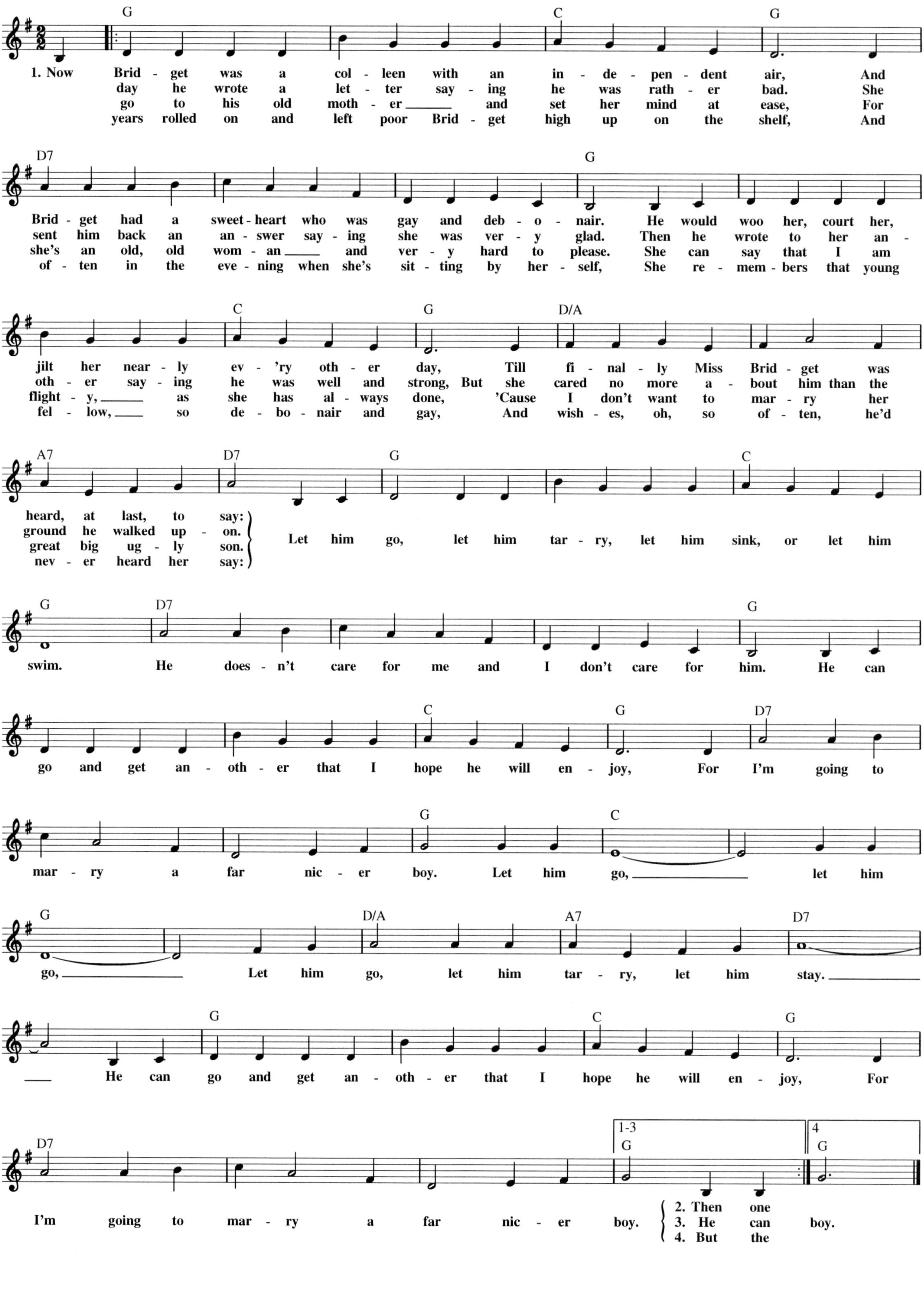

A LITTLE BIT OF HEAVEN

Words by J. Keirn Brennan
Music by Ernest R. Ball

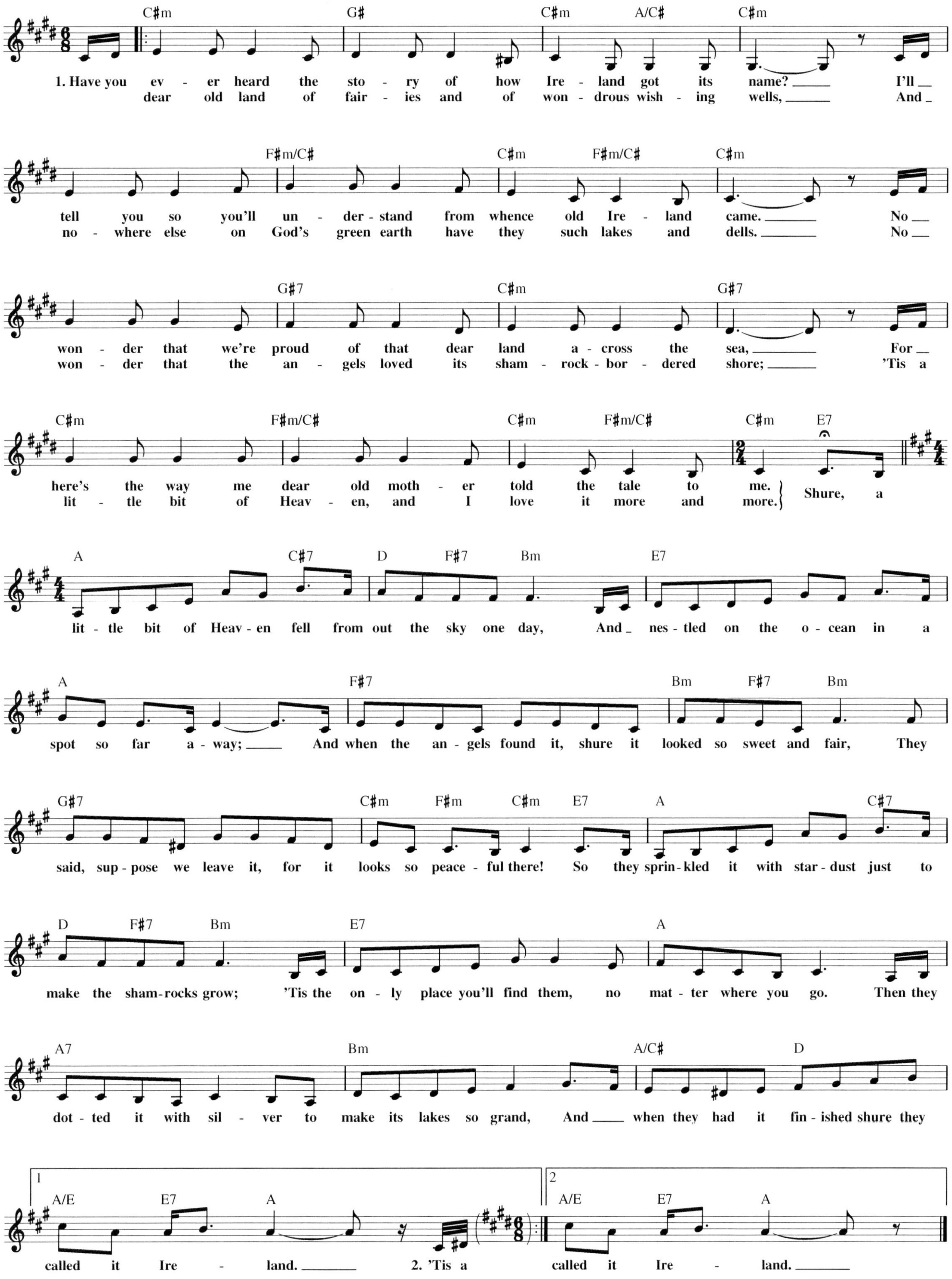

LIMERICK IS BEAUTIFUL

Irish popular song
Words by Michael Scanlon

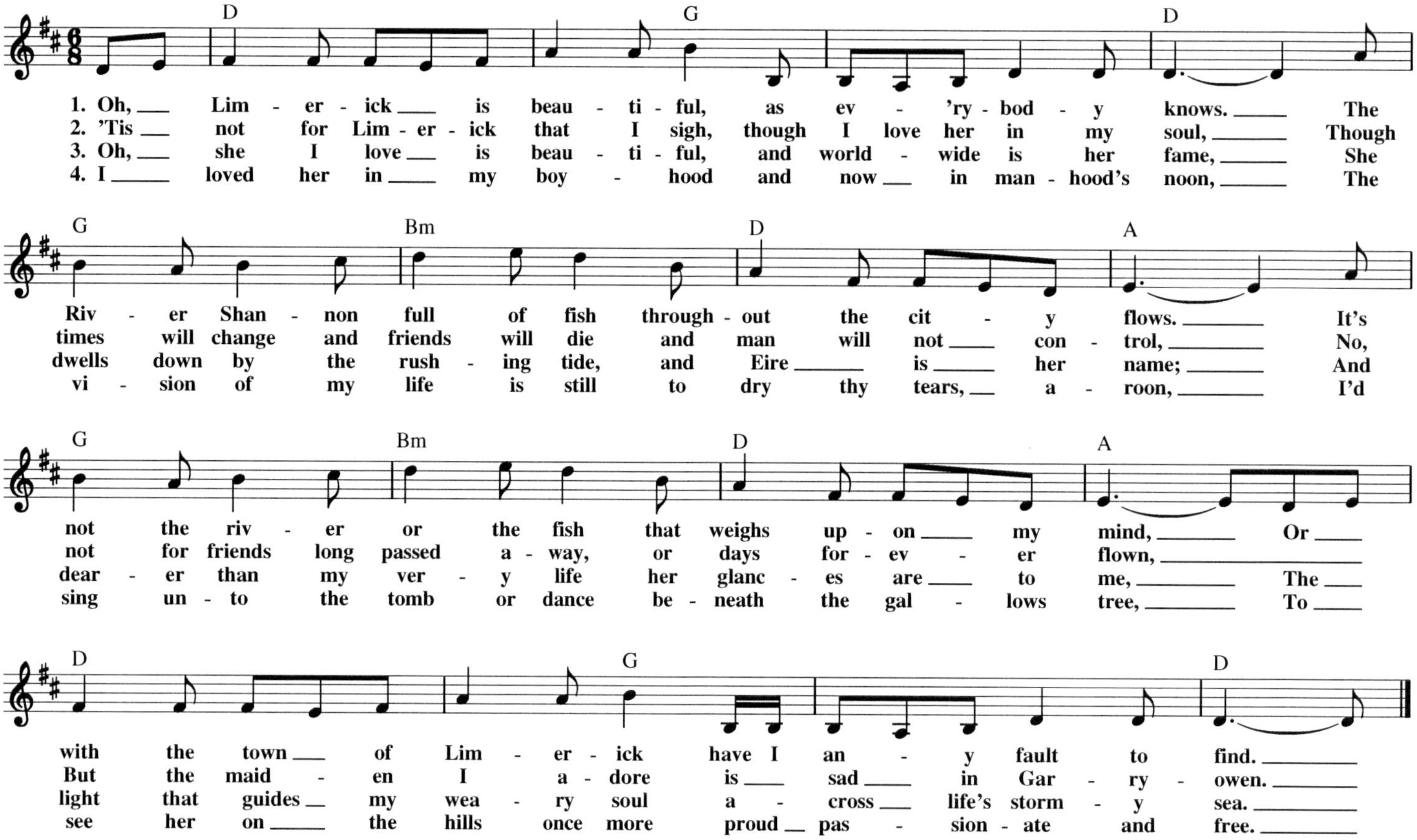

1. Oh, Limerick is beautiful, as ev'rybody knows. The
2. 'Tis not for Limerick that I sigh, though I love her in my soul, Though
3. Oh, she I love is beautiful, and world-wide is her fame, She
4. I loved her in my boyhood and now in manhood's noon, The

River Shannon full of fish throughout the city flows. It's
times will change and friends will die and man will not control. No,
dwells down by the rushing tide, and Eire is her name; And
vision of my life is still to dry thy tears, aroon, I'd

not the river or the fish that weighs upon my mind, Or
not for friends long passed away, or days forever flown, But
dearer than my very life her glances are to me, The
sing unto the tomb or dance beneath the gallows tree, To

with the town of Limerick have I any fault to find.
But the maiden I adore is sad in Garryowen.
light that guides my weary soul across life's stormy sea.
see her on the hills once more proud passionate and free.

THE LITTLE BUNCH OF RUSHES
(An Beinnsín Luachra)

Irish folksong

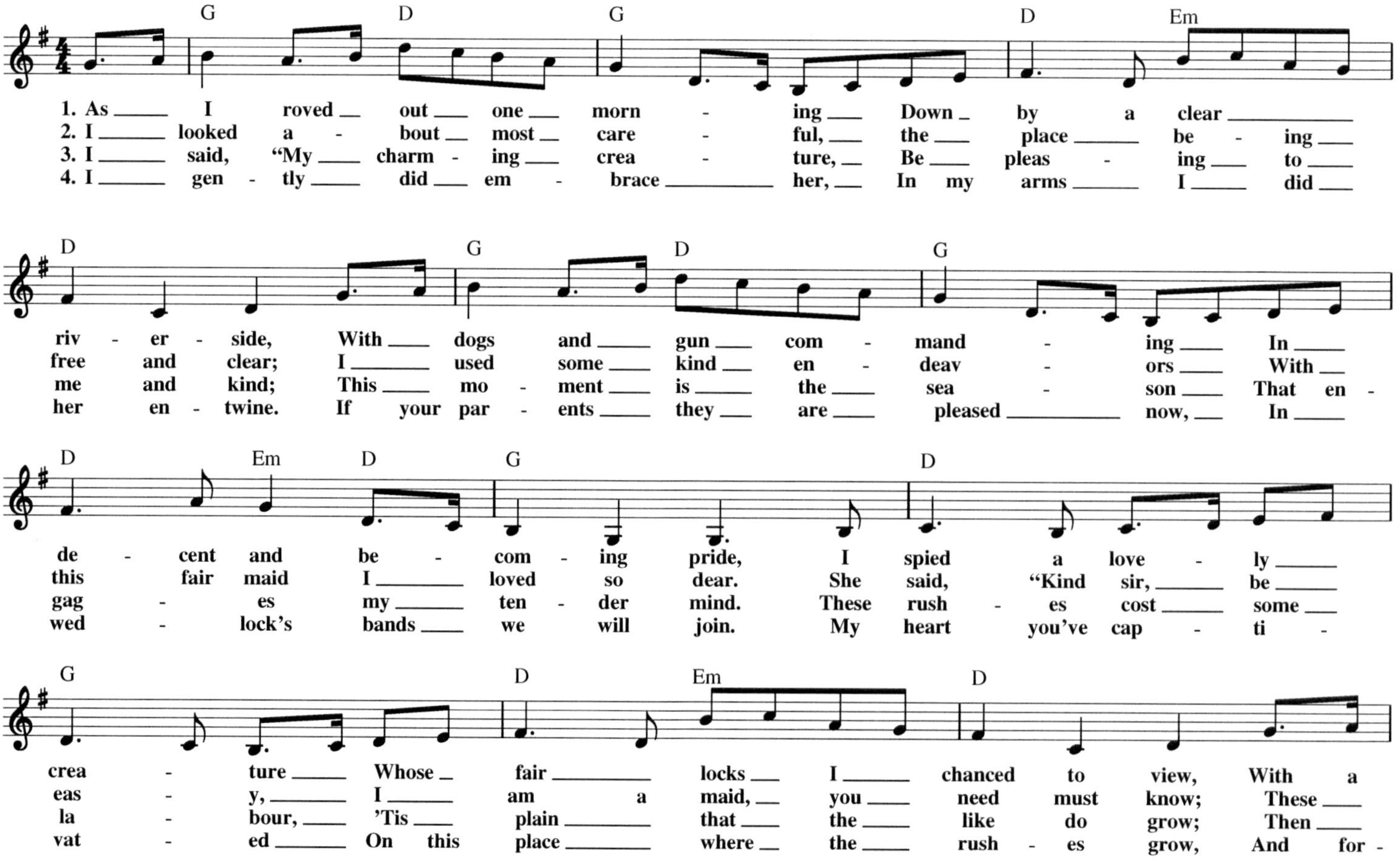

1. As I roved out one morning Down by a clear
2. I looked about most careful, the place being
3. I said, "My charming creature, Be pleasing to
4. I gently did embrace her, In my arms I did

riverside, With dogs and gun commanding In
free and clear; I used some kind endeavors, With
me and kind; This moment is the season That en-
her entwine. If your parents they are pleased now, In

decent and becoming pride, I spied a lovely
this fair maid I loved so dear. She said, "Kind sir, be
gages my tender mind. These rushes cost some
wedlock's bands we will join. My heart you've capti-

creature Whose fair locks I chanced to view, With a
easy, I am a maid, you need must know; These
labour, 'Tis plain that the like do grow; Then
vated On this place where the rushes grow, And for-

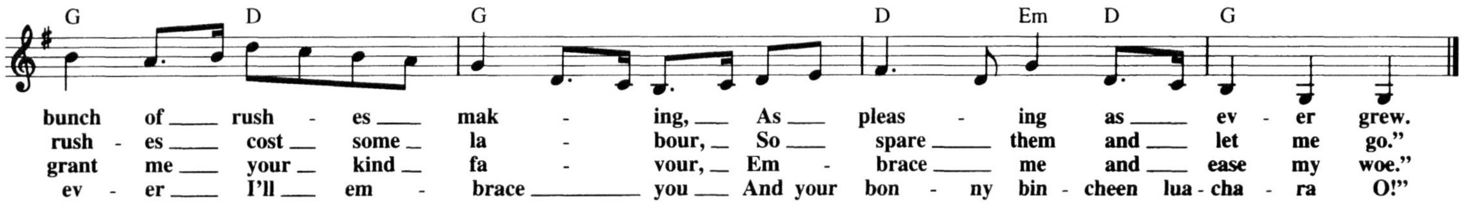

bunch of ___ rush - es ___ mak - ing, ___ As ___ pleas - ing as ___ ev - er grew.
rush - es ___ cost ___ some ___ la - bour, ___ So ___ spare ___ them and ___ let me go."
grant me ___ your ___ kind ___ fa - vour, ___ Em - brace ___ me and ___ ease my woe."
ev - er ___ I'll ___ em - brace ___ you ___ And your bon - ny bin - cheen lua - cha - ra O!"

Gaelic Lyrics

1. Ó! maidin aoibhinn uaibhreach
   Ar bhruach na coille is glaise bláth,
   Bhí mo ghadhairín liom a' gluaiseacht
   Go h-uasal is mo ghunna im láimh.
   Casadh orm stua-bhean
   Ba ruaidhe ghile dheise bhreá,
   Agus birtín léithi buailte
   Dhen luachair ba dheise bláth.

2. Is d'fhéachas ar na cuantaibh,
   'S do bhí an t-uaigneas againn um neóin,
   Do dhruideas leis an stuaire
   Is d'fhuaduíos uaithi cúpla póg.
   'Sé dúirt sí liom go h-uaibhreach,
   "Fan uaim is ná cuir orm stró,
   'S ná sgaip mo bheinnsín luachra
   Is a bhfuaireas dá thrioblóid."

3. "A chailín bhig na luachra,
   A' leigfeá-sa do bheart ar lár?
   Nó a' dtiocfá liom i n-uaigneas
   Faoi bhruach na coille is glaise bláth?
   Sagairt ní bhfuíodh sgéal air,
   Nó éinneach dá bhfuil le fáil,
   Go dtiocfaidh cainn! don chéirseach
   Nó béarla don londubh bhreá."

4. "A chailín bhig na luachra,
   Glac suaineas is fan go réidh;
   Ní cáll duit a bheith uaibhreach
   I n-uaigneas is tú leat féin.
   Má sgaip mé do chuid luachra,
   Is dual go bhfuil cuid tar h'éis;
   Bainfead beinnse muar dhuit,
   Is ualach mar thuille léi."

THE LITTLE SAUCEPAN
(Sospan Vach)

Welsh folksong

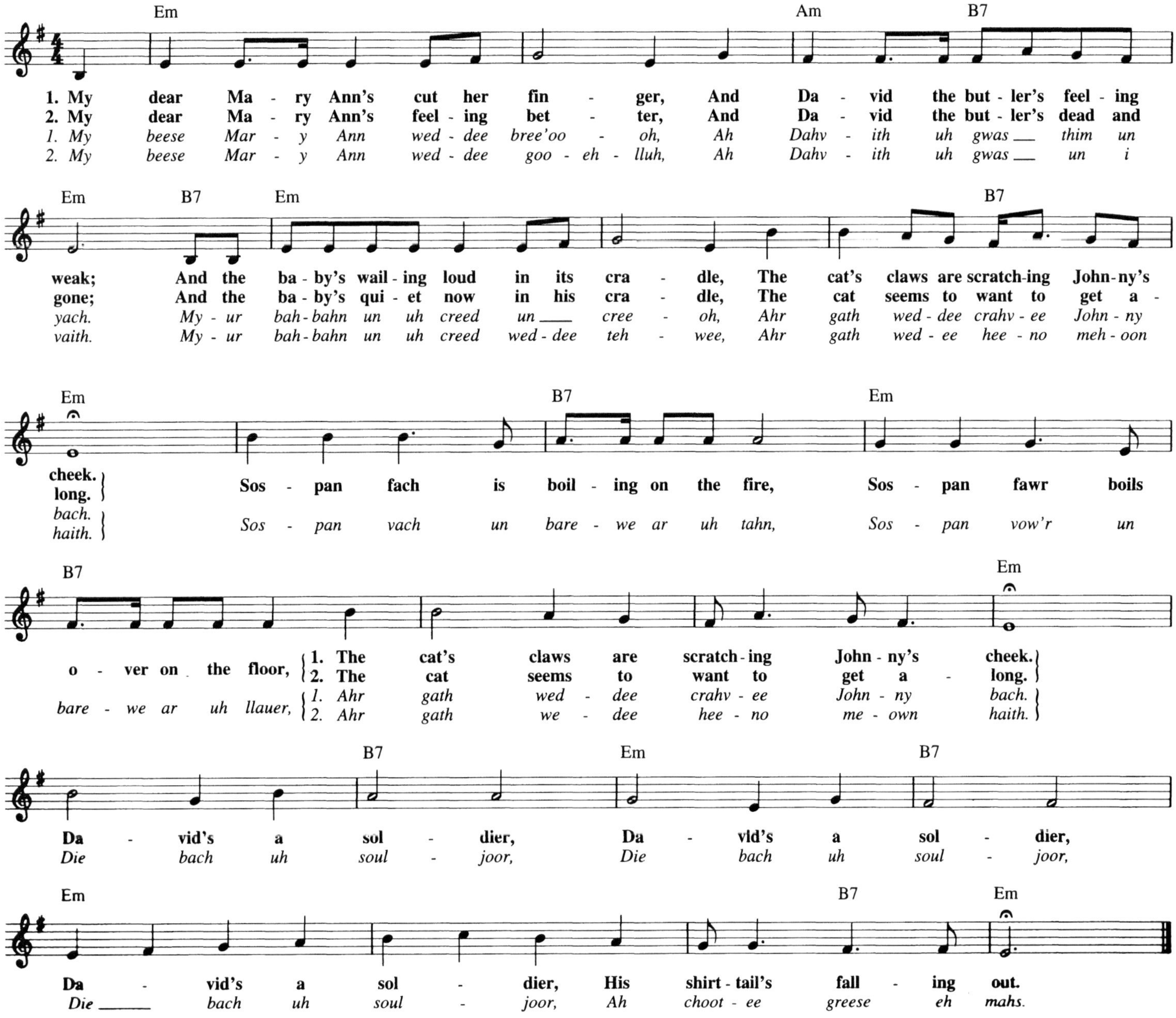

1. My dear Ma - ry Ann's cut her fin - ger, And Da - vid the but - ler's feel - ing
2. My dear Ma - ry Ann's feel - ing bet - ter, And Da - vid the but - ler's dead and
1. My beese Mar - y Ann wed - dee bree'oo - oh, Ah Dahv - ith uh gwas ___ thim un
2. My beese Mar - y Ann wed - dee goo - eh - lluh, Ah Dahv - ith uh gwas ___ un i

weak; And the ba - by's wail - ing loud in its cra - dle, The cat's claws are scratch-ing John-ny's
gone; And the ba - by's qui - et now in his cra - dle, The cat seems to want to get a -
yach. My - ur bah-bahn un uh creed un ___ cree - oh, Ahr gath wed - dee crahv - ee John - ny
vaith. My - ur bah-bahn un uh creed wed - dee teh - wee, Ahr gath wed - ee hee - no meh - oon

cheek. }
long. }
bach. }
haith. }
Sos - pan fach is boil - ing on the fire, Sos - pan fawr boils
Sos - pan vach un bare - we ar uh tahn, Sos - pan vow'r un

o - ver on the floor, { 1. The cat's claws are scratch-ing John - ny's cheek. }
{ 2. The cat seems to want to get a - long. }
bare - we ar uh llauer, { 1. Ahr gath wed - dee crahv - ee John - ny bach. }
{ 2. Ahr gath we - dee hee - no me - own haith. }

Da - vid's a sol - dier, Da - vid's a sol - dier,
Die bach uh soul - joor, Die bach uh soul - joor,

Da - vid's a sol - dier, His shirt - tail's fall - ing out.
Die ___ bach uh soul - joor, Ah choot - ee greese eh mahs.

LOCH LOMOND

Scottish folksong

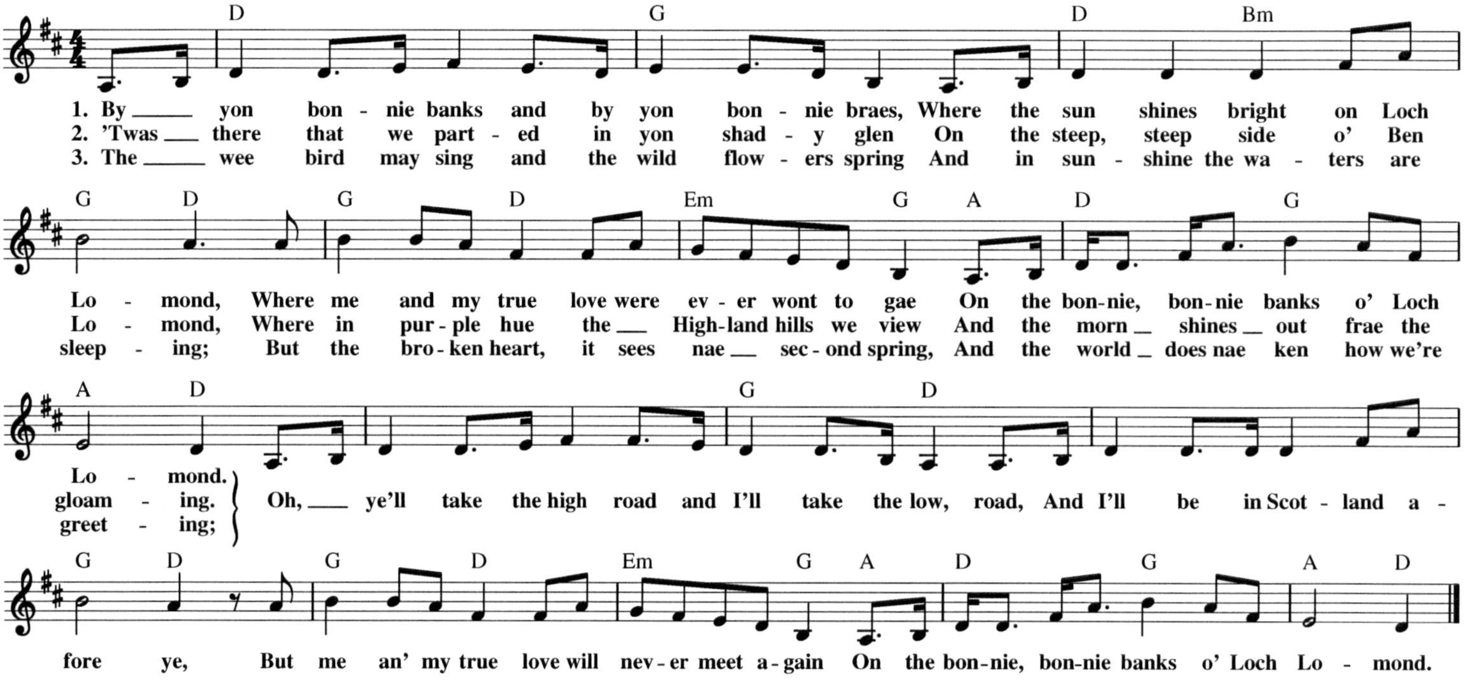

LOCHBROOM LOVE SONG
(Mhàiri Laghach)

Words by J. MacDonald
Folksong from the Hebrides

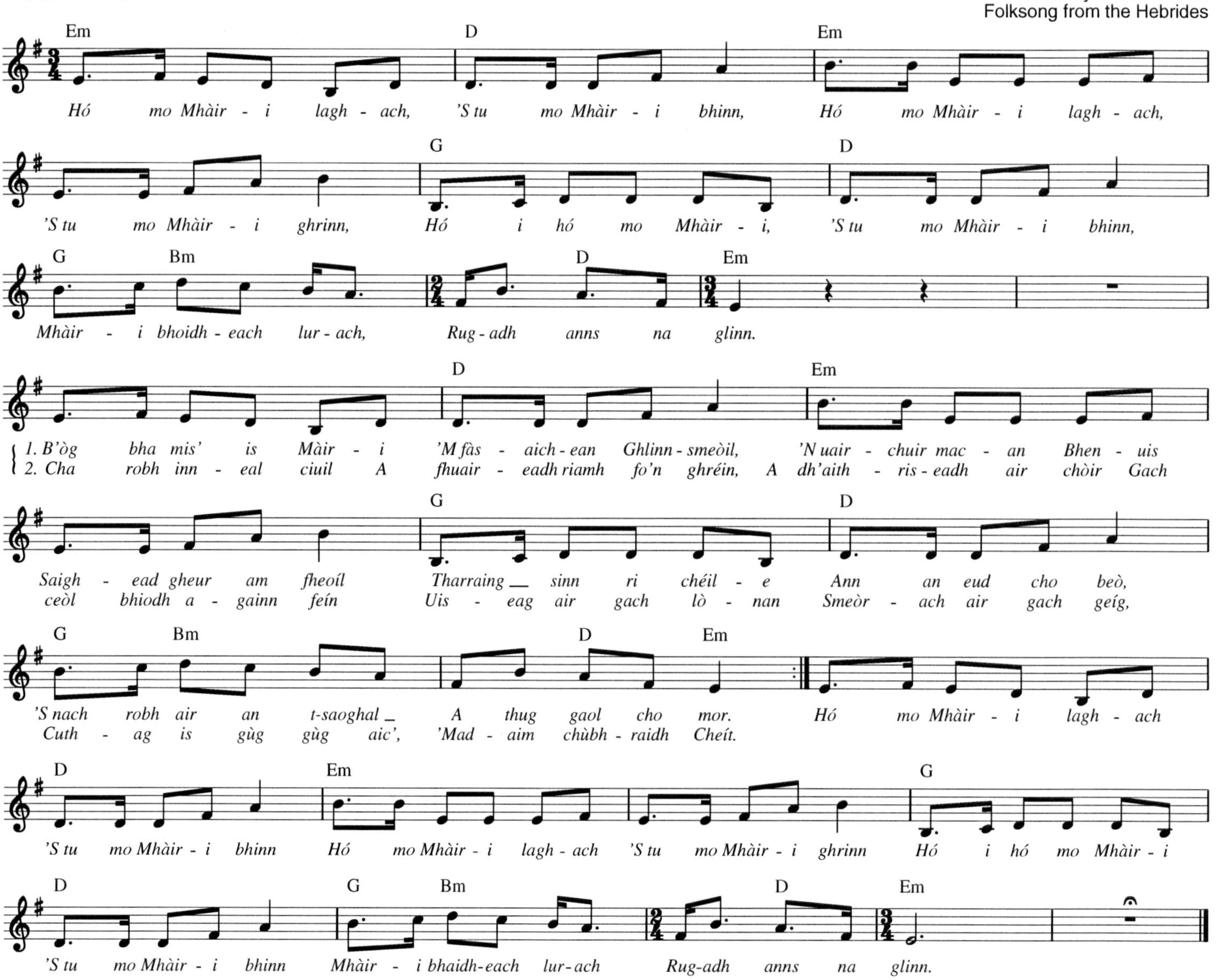

LOCH LEVEN LOVE LAMENT
(Chuir mo leannan cul rium fhein)

Folksong from the Hebrides

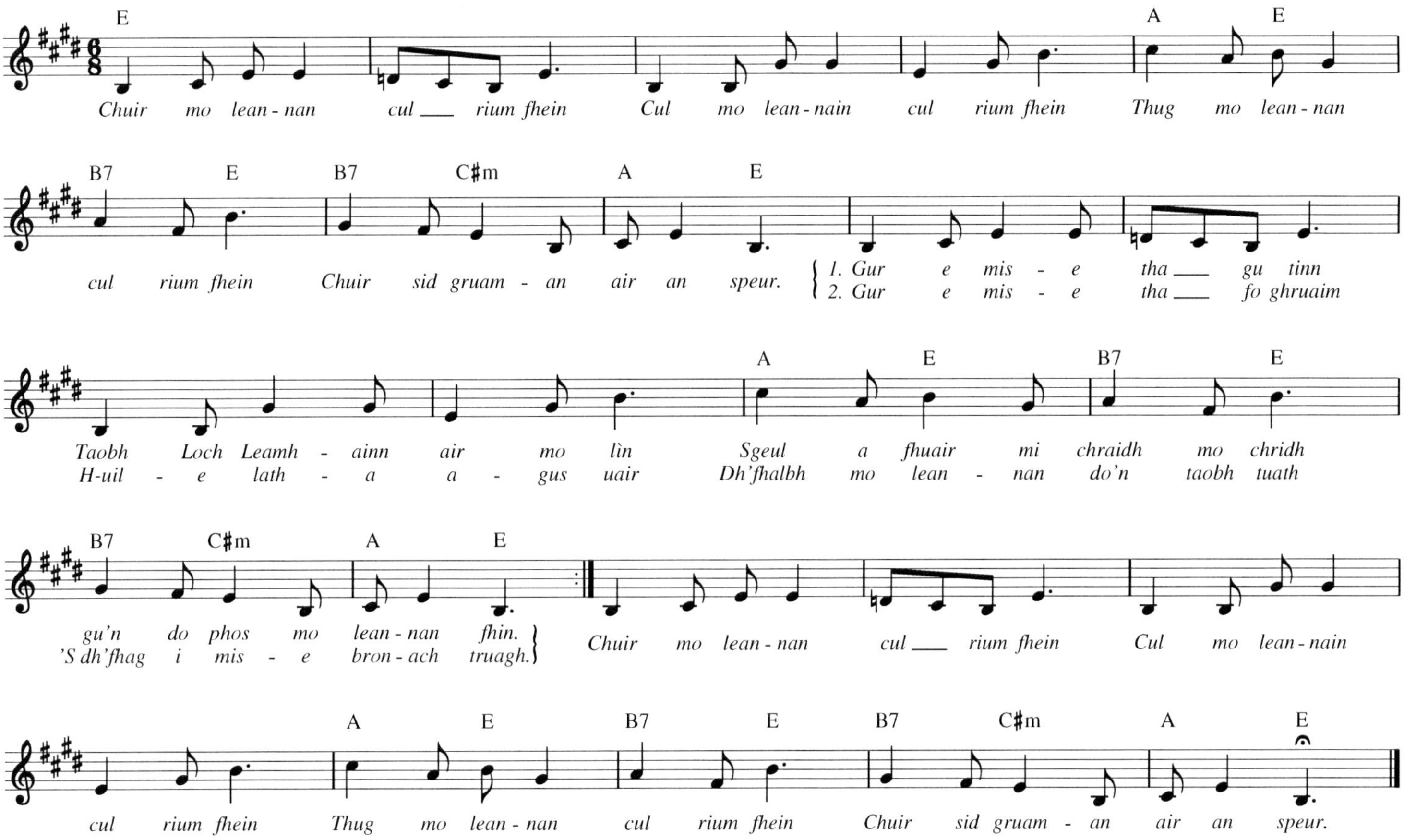

THE LOST CHILD

Irish folksong

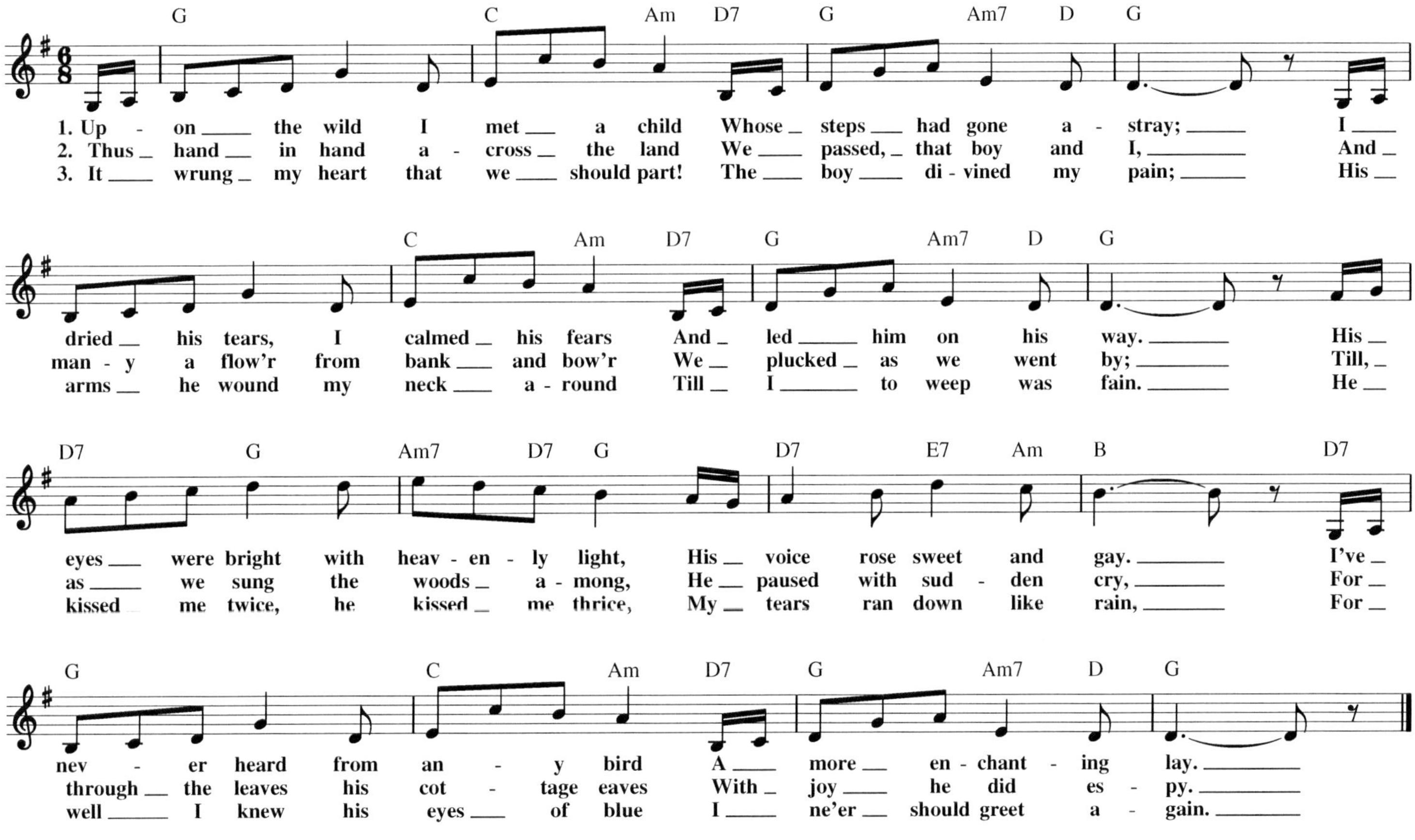

LOUGH SHEELIN'S SIDE

Irish folksong

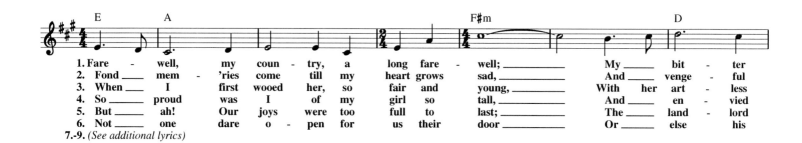

1. Fare - well, my coun - try, a long fare - well; My bit - ter
2. Fond mem - 'ries come till my heart grows sad, And venge - ful
3. When I first wooed her, so fair and young, With her art - less
4. So proud was I of my girl so tall, And en - vied
5. But ah! Our joys were too full to last; The land - lord
6. Not one dare o - pen for us their door Or else his

7.-9. *(See additional lyrics)*

an - guish no tongue can tell, For I must fly o'er the o - cean
thoughts till my brain goes mad, When I think of Ei - leen my fair young
airs and her guile - less tongue, All oth - er maid - ens she far out -
most by the young men all, When I brought her blush - ing with bash - ful
ven - geance would reach them sure; My Ei - leen faint in my arms

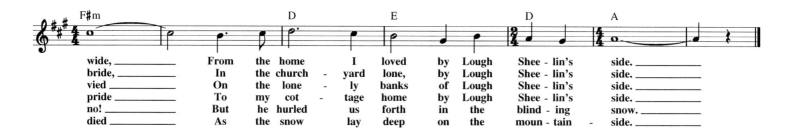

wide, From the home I loved by Lough Shee - lin's side.
bride, In the church - yard lone, by Lough Shee - lin's side.
vied On the lone - ly banks of Lough Shee - lin's side.
pride To my cot - tage home by Lough Shee - lin's side.
no! But he hurled us forth in the blind - ing snow.
died As the snow lay deep on the moun - tain - side.

Additional Lyrics

7. I raised my hand to the heavens above,
And I said one prayer for my lifeless love;
May the God of justice, I wildly cried,
Avenge the death of my murdered bride.

8. We laid her down in the churchyard low,
Where in the springtime sweet daisies grow;
I shed no tears, for the fount has dried,
On that woeful night by Lough Sheelin's side.

9. Farewell, my country, farewell for e'er;
The big ship's waiting, I must prepare.
But my fond heart it shall still abide
In my Eileen's grave by Lough Sheelin's side.

LOVE AT MY HEART

Irish folksong

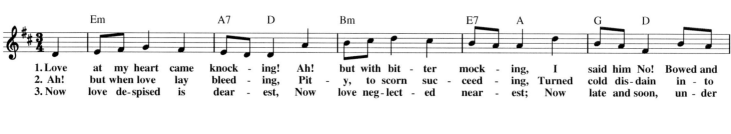

1. Love at my heart came knock - ing! Ah! but with bit - ter mock - ing, I said him No! Bowed and
2. Ah! but when love lay bleed - ing, Pit - y, to scorn suc - ceed - ing, Turned cold dis - dain in - to
3. Now love de - spised is dear - est, Now love neg - lect - ed near - est; Now late and soon, un - der

bade him go Far, far a - way, heigh - ho! Far, far a - way, heigh - ho!
poign - ant pain, Till I too loved a - gain, Till I too loved a - gain.
sun and moon, O heart o' mine, keep love's tune! O heart o' mine, keep love's tune!

THE LOVE-WANDERING

Folksong from the Hebrides

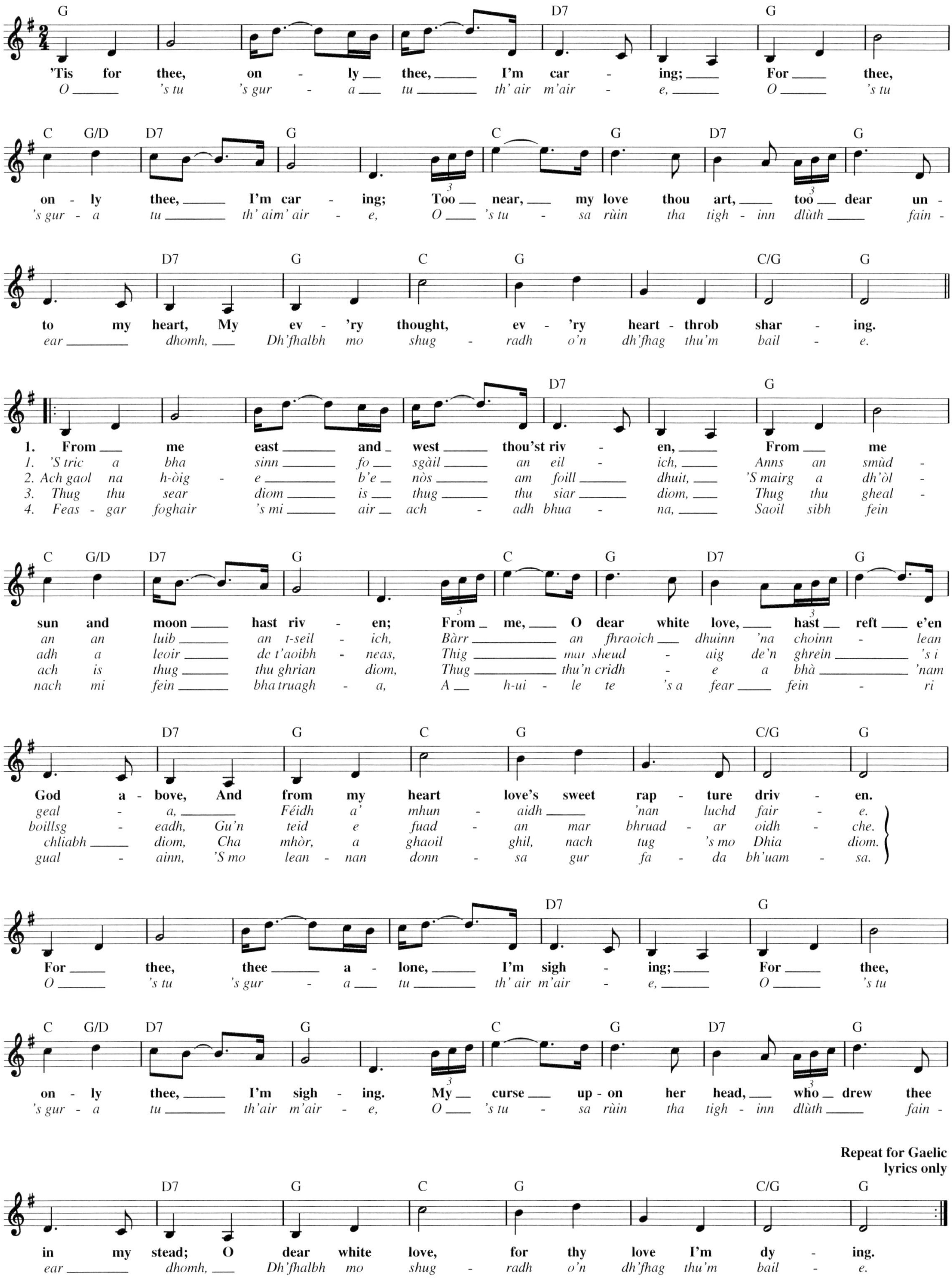
'Tis for thee, on - ly thee, I'm car - ing; For thee,
O 's tu 's gur - a tu th' air m'air - e, O 's tu
on - ly thee, I'm car - ing; Too near, my love thou art, too dear un -
's gur - a tu th' aim' air - e, O 's tu - sa rùin tha tigh - inn dlùth fain -
to my heart, My ev - 'ry thought, ev - 'ry heart - throb shar - ing.
ear dhomh, Dh'fhalbh mo shug - radh o'n dh'fhag thu'm bail - e.
1. From me east and west thou'st riv - en, From me
1. 'S tric a bha sinn fo sgàil an eil - ich, Anns an smùd -
2. Ach gaol na h-òig - e b'e nòs am foill dhuit, 'S mairg a dh'òl -
3. Thug thu sear diom is thug thu siar diom, Thug thu gheal -
4. Feas - gar foghair 's mi air ach - adh bhua - na, Saoil sibh fein
sun and moon hast riv - en; From me, O dear white love, hast reft e'en
an an luib an t-seil - ich, Bàrr an fhraoich dhuinn 'na choinn - lean
adh a leoir de t'aoibh - neas, Thig mar sheud - aig de'n ghrein 's i
ach is thug thu ghrian diom, Thug thu'n cridh - e a bhà 'nam
nach mi fein bha truagh - a, A h-ui - le te 's a fear fein - ri
God a - bove, And from my heart love's sweet rap - ture driv - en.
geal - a, Féidh a' mhun - aidh 'nan luchd fair - e.
boillsg - eadh, Gu'n teid e fuad - an mar bhruad - ar oidh - che.
chliabh diom, Cha mhòr, a ghaoil ghil, nach tug 's mo Dhia diom.
gual - ainn, 'S mo lean - nan donn - sa gur fa - da bh'uam - sa.
For thee, thee a - lone, I'm sigh - ing; For thee,
O 's tu 's gur - a tu th' air m'air - e, O 's tu
on - ly thee, I'm sigh - ing. My curse up - on her head, who drew thee
's gur - a tu th'air m'air - e, O 's tu - sa rùin tha tigh - inn dlùth fain -
Repeat for Gaelic lyrics only
in my stead; O dear white love, for thy love I'm dy - ing.
ear dhomh, Dh'fhalbh mo shug - radh o'n dh'fhag thu'm bail - e.

LOVELY LEITRIM

Words and Music by
P. Fitzpatrick

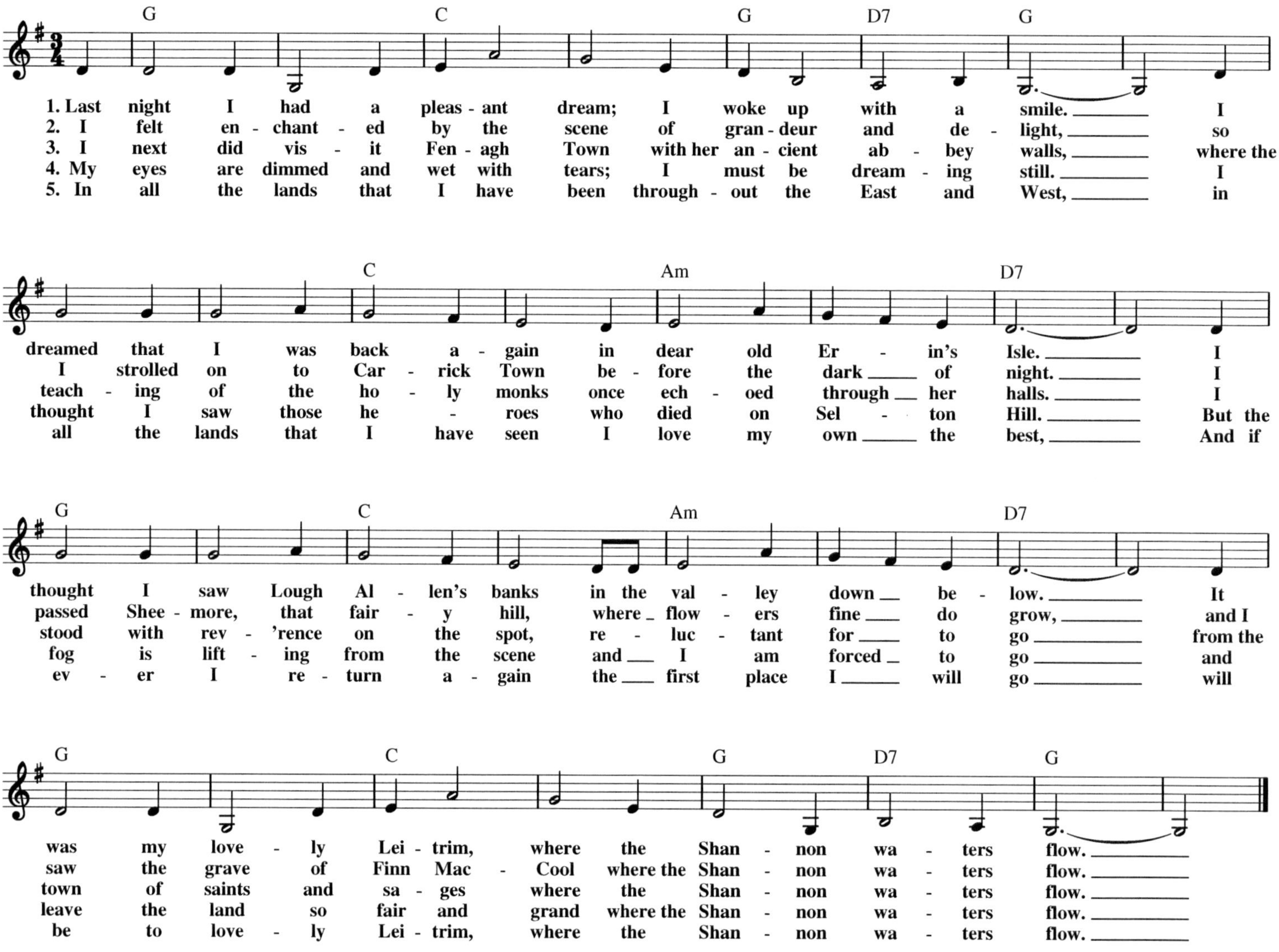

1. Last night I had a pleas-ant dream; I woke up with a smile. _____ I
2. I felt en-chant-ed by the scene of gran-deur and de-light, _____ so
3. I next did vis-it Fen-agh Town with her an-cient ab-bey walls, _____ where the
4. My eyes are dimmed and wet with tears; I must be dream-ing still. _____ I
5. In all the lands that I have been through-out the East and West, _____ in

dreamed that I was back a-gain in dear old Er-in's Isle. _____ I
I strolled on to Car-rick Town be-fore the dark _____ of night. _____ I
teach-ing of the ho-ly monks once ech-oed through _____ her halls. _____ I
thought I saw those he-roes who died on Sel-ton Hill. _____ But the
all the lands that I have seen I love my own _____ the best, _____ And if

thought I saw Lough Al-len's banks in the val-ley down _____ be-low. _____ It
passed Shee-more, that fair-y hill, where _ flow-ers fine _____ do grow, _____ and I
stood with rev-'rence on the spot, re-luc-tant for _____ to go _____ from the
fog is lift-ing from the scene and _____ I am forced _____ to go _____ and
ev-er I re-turn a-gain the _____ first place I _____ will go _____ will

was my love-ly Lei-trim, where the Shan-non wa-ters flow.
saw the grave of Finn Mac-Cool where the Shan-non wa-ters flow. _____
town of saints and sa-ges where the Shan-non wa-ters flow. _____
leave the land so fair and grand where the Shan-non wa-ters flow. _____
be to love-ly Lei-trim, where the Shan-non wa-ters flow. _____

THE LURE OF THE FAIRY HILL
(Ghillebhinn)

Folksong from the Hebrides

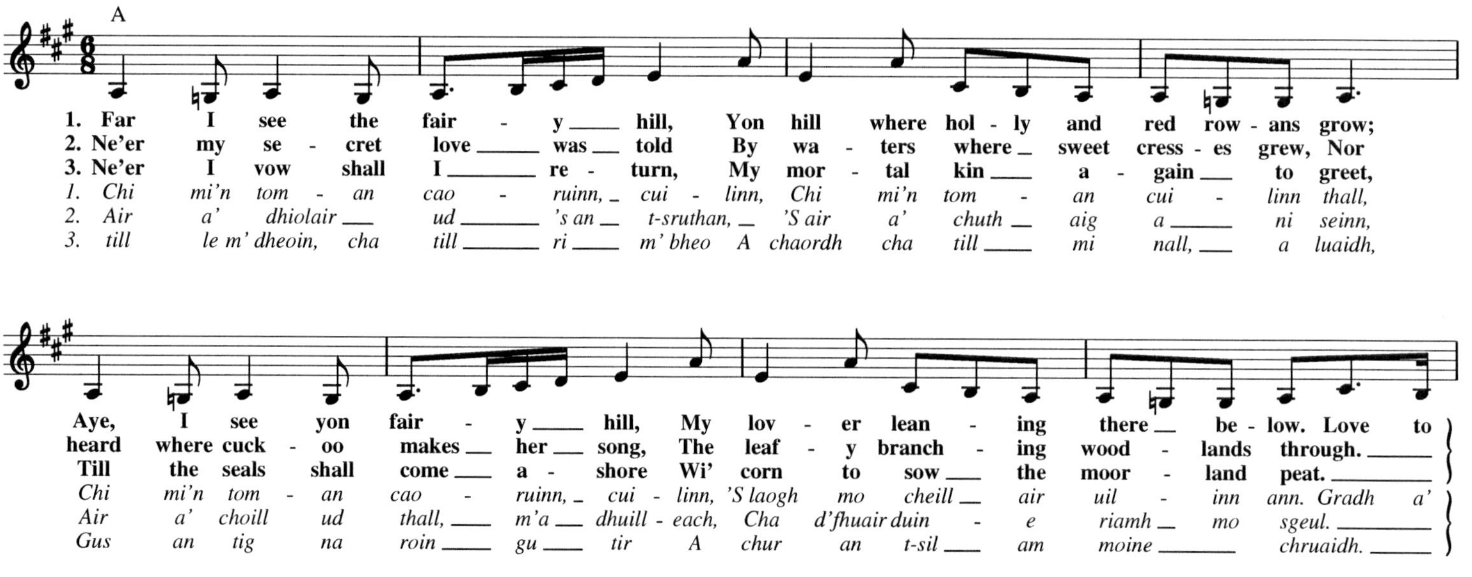

1. Far I see the fair-y _____ hill, Yon hill where hol-ly and red row-ans grow;
2. Ne'er my se-cret love _____ was _____ told By wa-ters where _ sweet cress-es grew, Nor
3. Ne'er I vow shall I _____ re-turn, My mor-tal kin _____ a-gain _____ to greet,

1. Chi mi'n tom-an cao-ruinn, _ cui-linn, Chi mi'n tom-an cui-linn thall,
2. Air a' dhiolair _____ ud _____ 's an _ t-sruthan, _ 'S air a' chuth _ aig a _____ ni seinn,
3. till le m' dheoin, cha till _____ ri m' bheo A chaordh cha till _____ mi nall, _ a luaidh,

Aye, I see yon fair-y _____ hill, My lov-er lean-ing there _ be-low. Love to
heard where cuck-oo makes _ her song, The leaf-y branch-ing wood-lands through. _____
Till the seals shall come a-shore Wi' corn to sow _ the moor-land peat. _____

Chi mi'n tom-an cao-ruinn, _ cui-linn, 'S laogh mo cheill _ air uil-inn ann. Gradh a'
Air a' choill ud thall, _ m'a _ dhuill-each, Cha d'fhuair duin-e riamh _ mo sgeul. _____
Gus an tig na roin _ gu _ tir A chur an t-sil _ am moine _____ chruaidh.

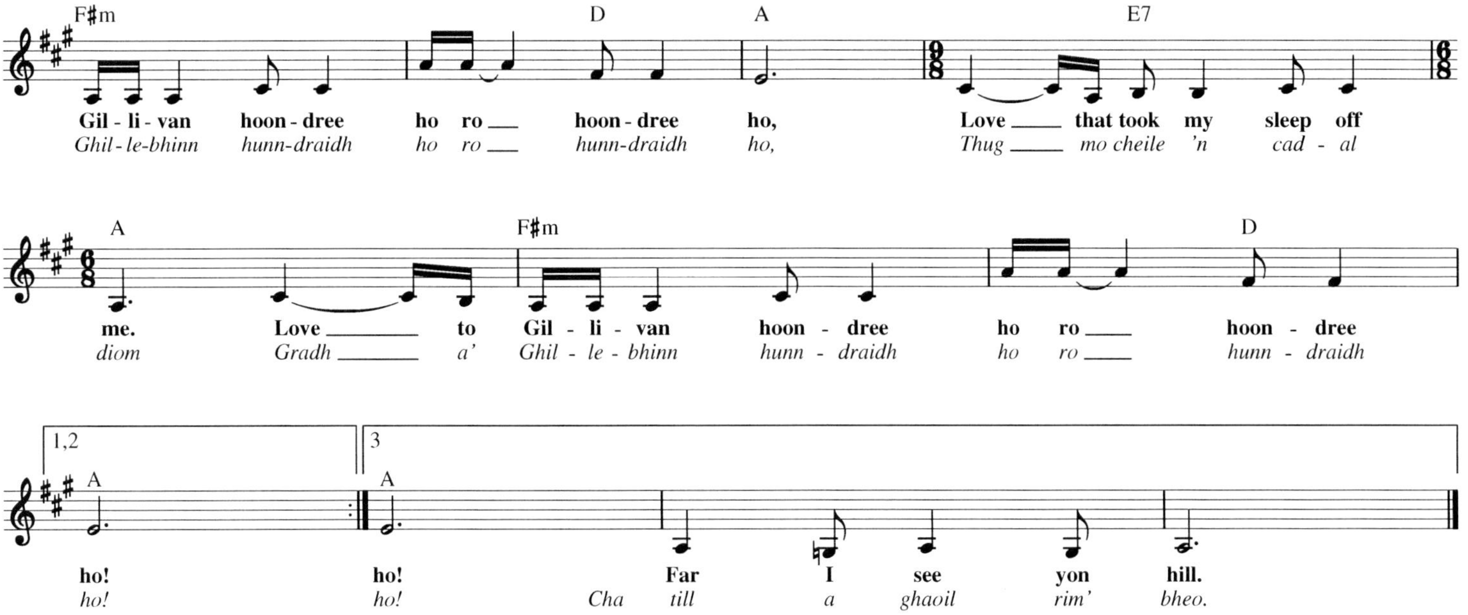

THE LOW-BACKED CAR

Irish folksong
Words by Samuel Lover

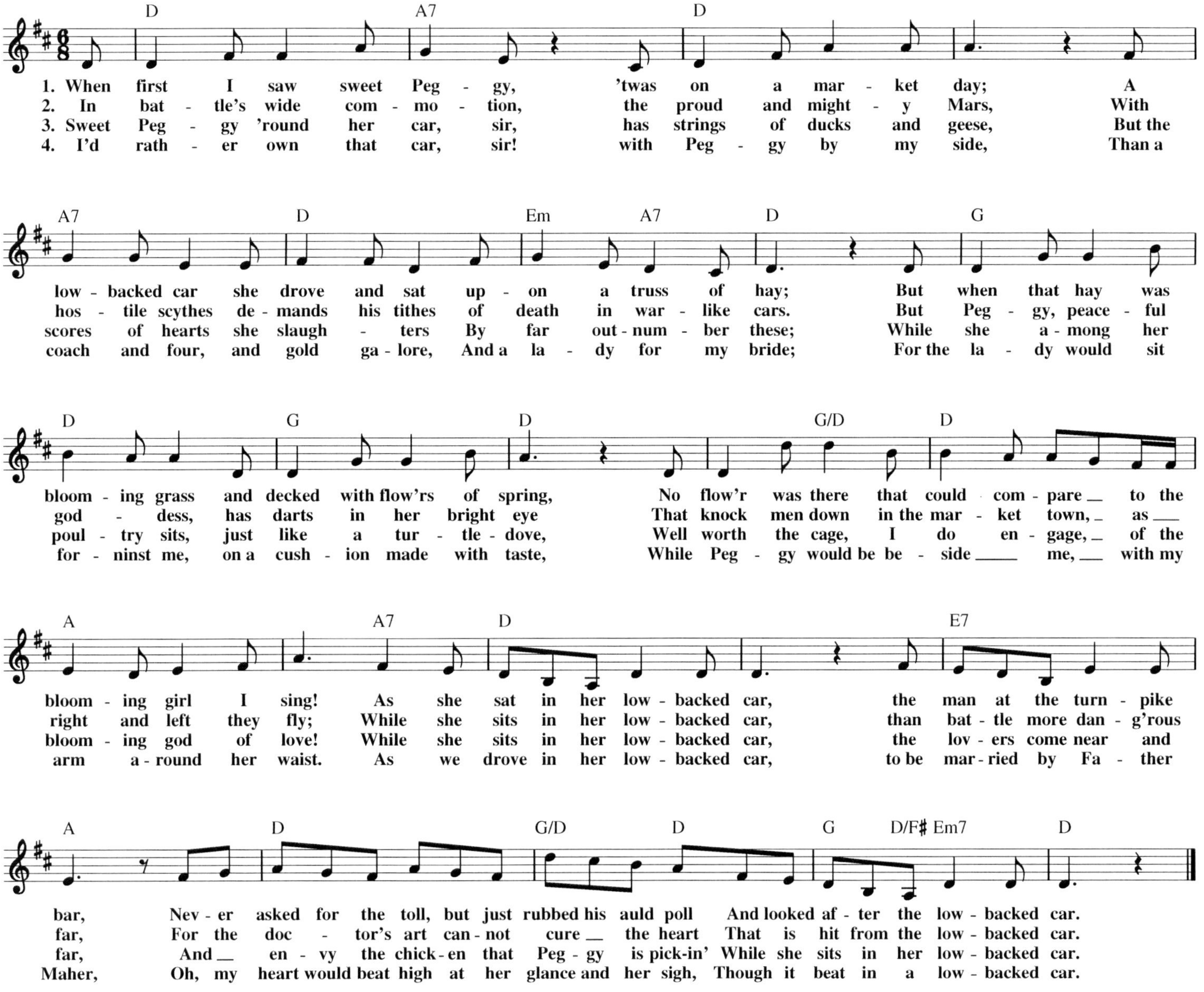

MacPHERSON'S FAREWELL

Scottish folksong

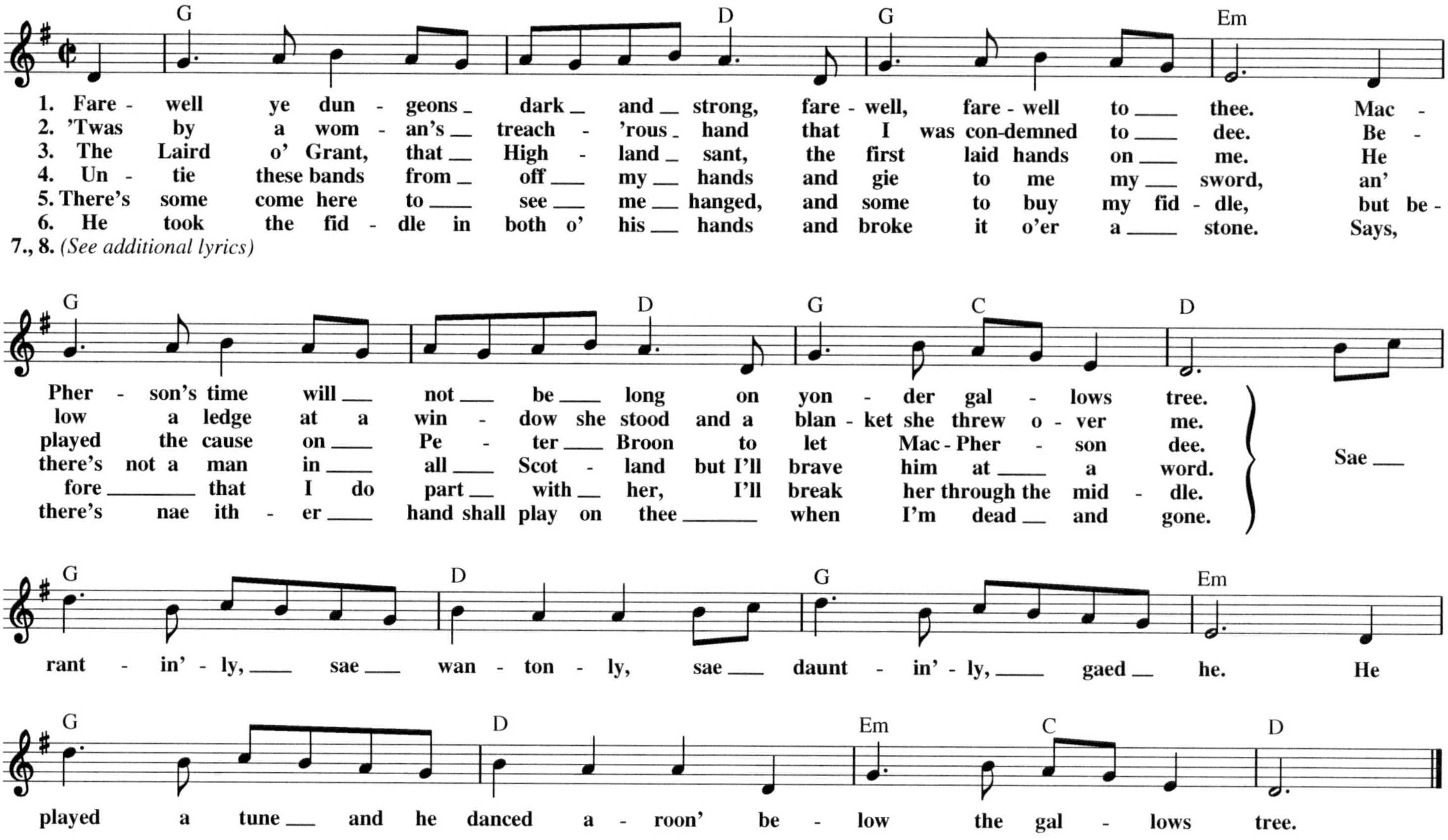

1. Fare - well ye dun - geons dark and strong, fare - well, fare - well to thee. Mac -
2. 'Twas by a wom - an's treach - 'rous hand that I was con-demned to dee. Be -
3. The Laird o' Grant, that High - land sant, the first laid hands on me. He
4. Un - tie these bands from off my hands and gie to me my sword, an'
5. There's some come here to see me hanged, and some to buy my fid - dle, but be -
6. He took the fid - dle in both o' his hands and broke it o'er a stone. Says,

7., 8. *(See additional lyrics)*

Pher - son's time will not be long on yon - der gal - lows tree.
low a ledge at a win - dow she stood and a blan - ket she threw o - ver me.
played the cause on Pe - ter Broon to let Mac - Pher - son dee.
there's not a man in all Scot - land but I'll brave him at a word.
fore that I do part with her, I'll break her through the mid - dle.
there's nae ith - er hand shall play on thee when I'm dead and gone.

Sae

rant - in' - ly, sae wan - ton - ly, sae daunt - in' - ly, gaed he. He

played a tune and he danced a - roon' be - low the gal - lows tree.

Additional Lyrics

7. O little did my mother think
When first she cradled me,
That I would turn a rovin' boy
And die on the gallows tree.

8. The reprieve was comin' o'er the brig o' Banff
To let MacPherson free,
But they pit the clock a quarter afore
And hanged him to the tree.

MACUSHLA

Words by Josephine V. Rowe
Music by Dermot MacMurrough

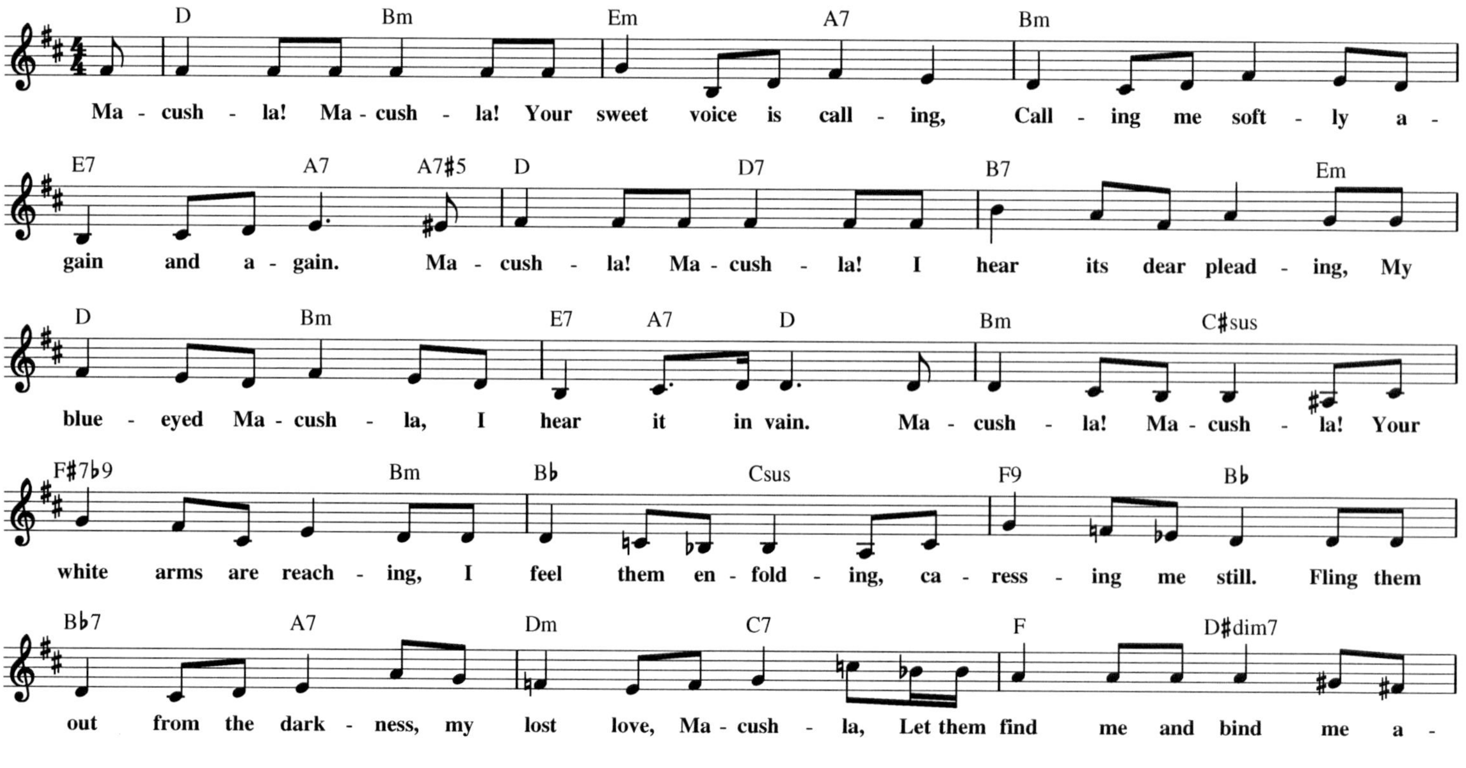

Ma - cush - la! Ma - cush - la! Your sweet voice is call - ing, Call - ing me soft - ly a -

gain and a - gain. Ma - cush - la! Ma - cush - la! I hear its dear plead - ing, My

blue - eyed Ma - cush - la, I hear it in vain. Ma - cush - la! Ma - cush - la! Your

white arms are reach - ing, I feel them en - fold - ing, ca - ress - ing me still. Fling them

out from the dark - ness, my lost love, Ma - cush - la, Let them find me and bind me a -

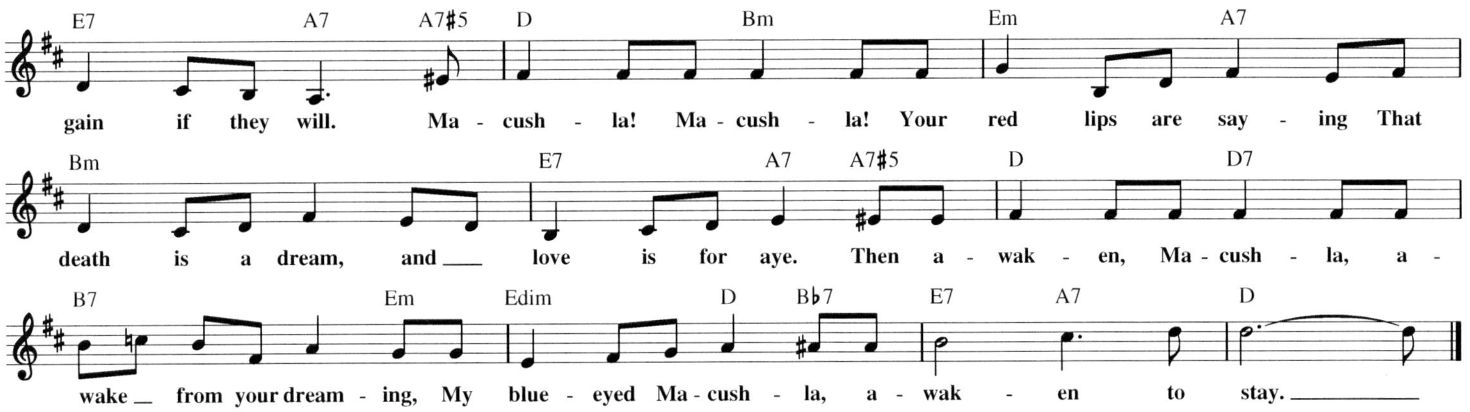

gain if they will. Ma - cush - la! Ma - cush - la! Your red lips are say - ing That

death is a dream, and ____ love is for aye. Then a - wak - en, Ma - cush - la, a -

wake __ from your dream - ing, My blue - eyed Ma - cush - la, a - wak - en to stay. _____

THE MAGIC MIST

Irish folksong

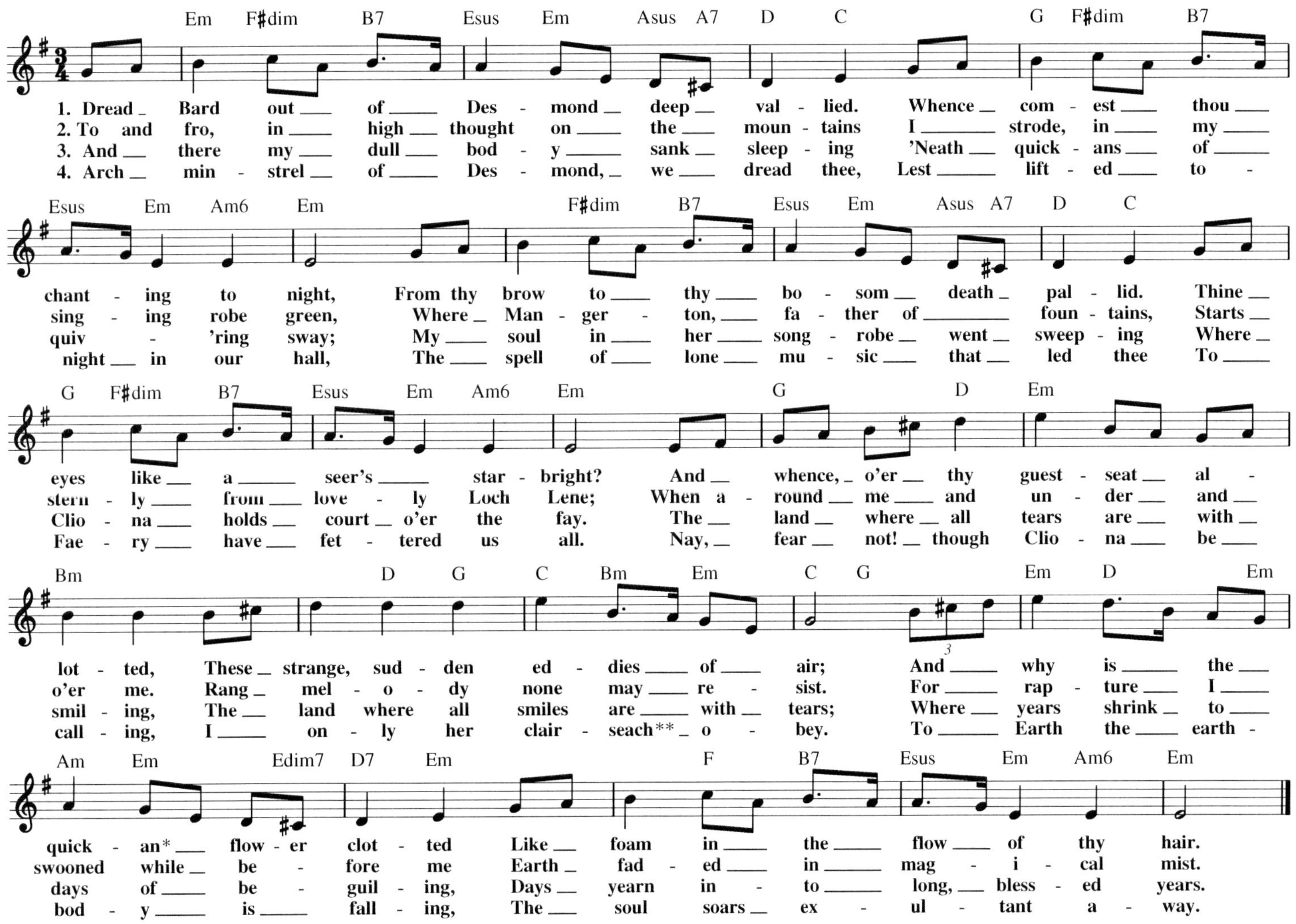

1. Dread _ Bard out __ of ____ Des - mond deep _ val - lied. Whence _ com - est ___ thou ___
2. To and fro, in ___ high __ thought on ___ the __ moun - tains I _____ strode, in ____ my ____
3. And __ there my ___ dull __ bod - y _____ sank _ sleep - ing 'Neath __ quick - ans ___ of ___
4. Arch _ min - strel of ____ Des - mond, we __ dread thee, Lest ____ lift - ed to -

chant - ing to night, From thy brow to ____ thy ___ bo - som __ death pal - lid. Thine __
sing - ing robe green, Where _ Man - ger - ton, ___ fa - ther of _____ foun - tains, Starts __
quiv - 'ring sway; My ___ soul in ___ her _ song - robe went _ sweep - ing Where __
night __ in our hall, The __ spell of ___ lone mu - sic ___ that __ led thee To ____

eyes like __ a _____ seer's _____ star - bright? And __ whence, _ o'er __ thy guest - seat __ al -
stern - ly ____ from ___ love - ly Loch Lene; When a - round _ me ___ and un - der __ and __
Clio - na ___ holds ___ court _ o'er the fay. The __ land __ where __ all tears are __ with __
Fae - ry have ___ fet - tered us all. Nay, __ fear _ not! _ though Clio - na be __

lot - ted, These _ strange, sud - den ed - dies of ___ air; And ____ why is ___ the __
o'er me. Rang _ mel - o - dy none may ___ re - sist. For ____ rap - ture __ I __
smil - ing, The _ land where all smiles are ___ with _ tears; Where ___ years shrink _ to __
call - ing, I __ on - ly her clair - seach** _ o - bey. To ____ Earth the ___ earth -

quick - an* __ flow - er clot - ted Like __ foam in ___ the ____ flow of thy hair.
swooned while _ be - fore me Earth _ fad - ed in ___ mag - i - cal mist.
days of ___ be - guil - ing, Days _ yearn in - to long, _ bless - ed years.
bod - y ___ is ___ fall - ing, The __ soul soars _ ex - ul - tant a - way.

*Elder flower
**harp

A MAN OF DOUBLE DEED

Irish folksong

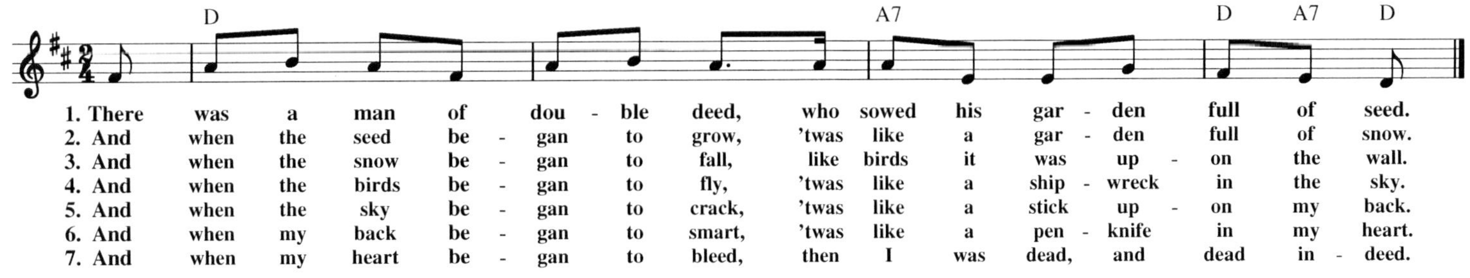

1. There was a man of dou - ble deed, who sowed his gar - den full of seed.
2. And when the seed be - gan to grow, 'twas like a gar - den full of snow.
3. And when the snow be - gan to fall, like birds it was up - on the wall.
4. And when the birds be - gan to fly, 'twas like a ship - wreck in the sky.
5. And when the sky be - gan to crack, 'twas like a stick up - on my back.
6. And when my back be - gan to smart, 'twas like a pen - knife in my heart.
7. And when my heart be - gan to bleed, then I was dead, and dead in - deed.

MAID OF FIFE-E-O

Irish folksong

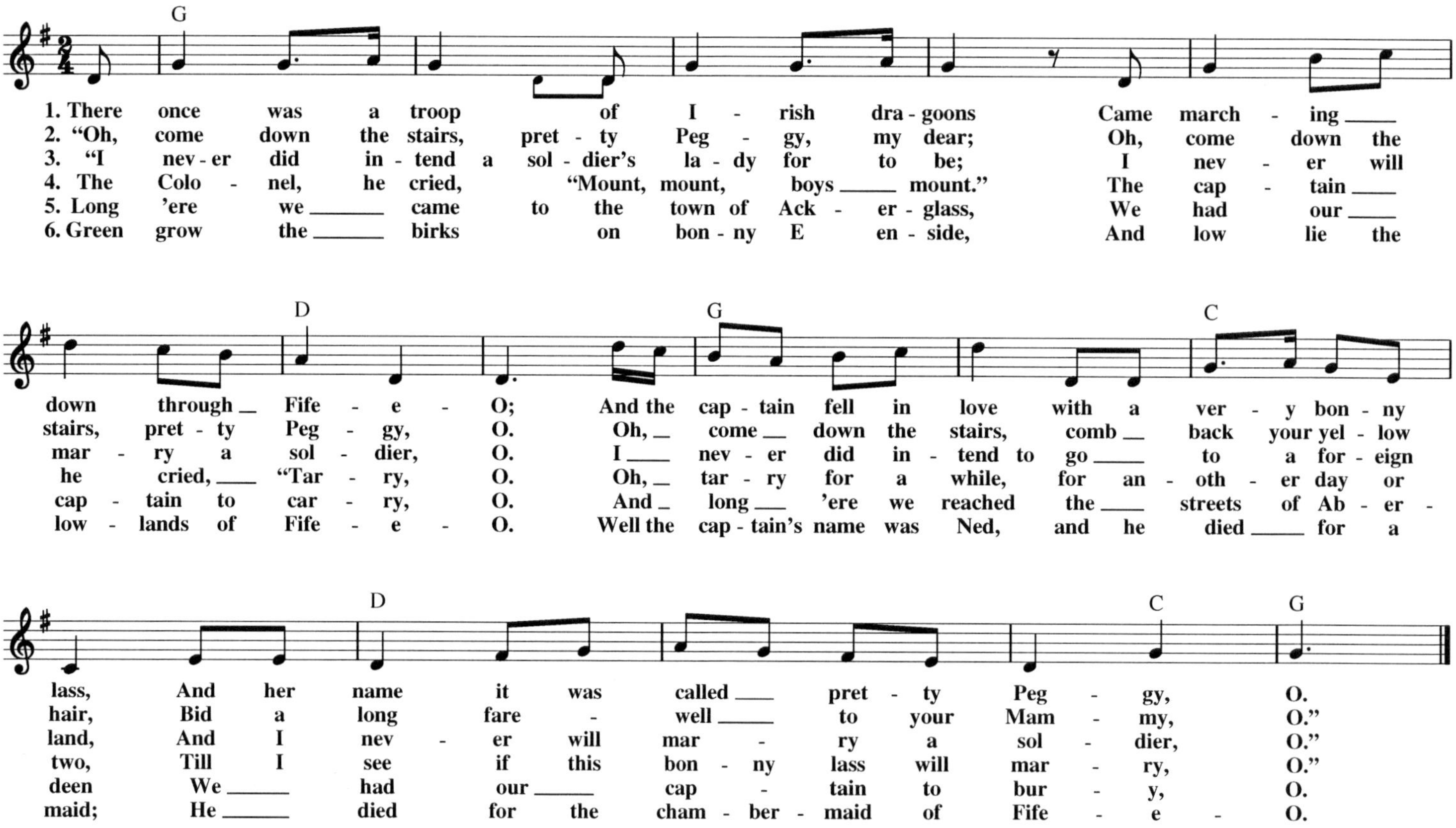

1. There once was a troop of I - rish dra - goons Came march - ing ____
2. "Oh, come down the stairs, pret - ty Peg - gy, my dear; Oh, come down the
3. "I nev - er did in - tend a sol - dier's la - dy for to be; I nev - er will
4. The Colo - nel, he cried, "Mount, mount, boys ____ mount." The cap - tain ____
5. Long 'ere we ____ came to the town of Ack - er - glass, We had our ____
6. Green grow the ____ birks on bon - ny E en - side, And low lie the

down through __ Fife - e - O; And the cap - tain fell in love with a ver - y bon - ny
stairs, pret - ty Peg - gy, O. Oh, __ come down the stairs, comb __ back your yel - low
mar - ry a sol - dier, O. I __ nev - er did in - tend to go __ to a for - eign
he cried, ____ "Tar - ry, O. Oh, __ tar - ry for a while, for an - oth - er day or
cap - tain to car - ry, O. And __ long ____ 'ere we reached the ____ streets of Ab - er -
low - lands of Fife - e - O. Well the cap - tain's name was Ned, and he died ____ for a

lass, And her name it was called ____ pret - ty Peg - gy, O.
hair, Bid a long fare - well ____ to your Mam - my, O."
mar - ry a sol - dier, O."
land, And I nev - er will mar - ry a sol - dier, O."
two, Till I see if this bon - ny lass will mar - ry, O."
deen We ____ had our ____ cap - tain to bur - y, O.
maid; He ____ died for the cham - ber - maid of Fife - e - O.

THE MAID OF SLIEVENAMON

Irish folksong
Words by Charles Kickham

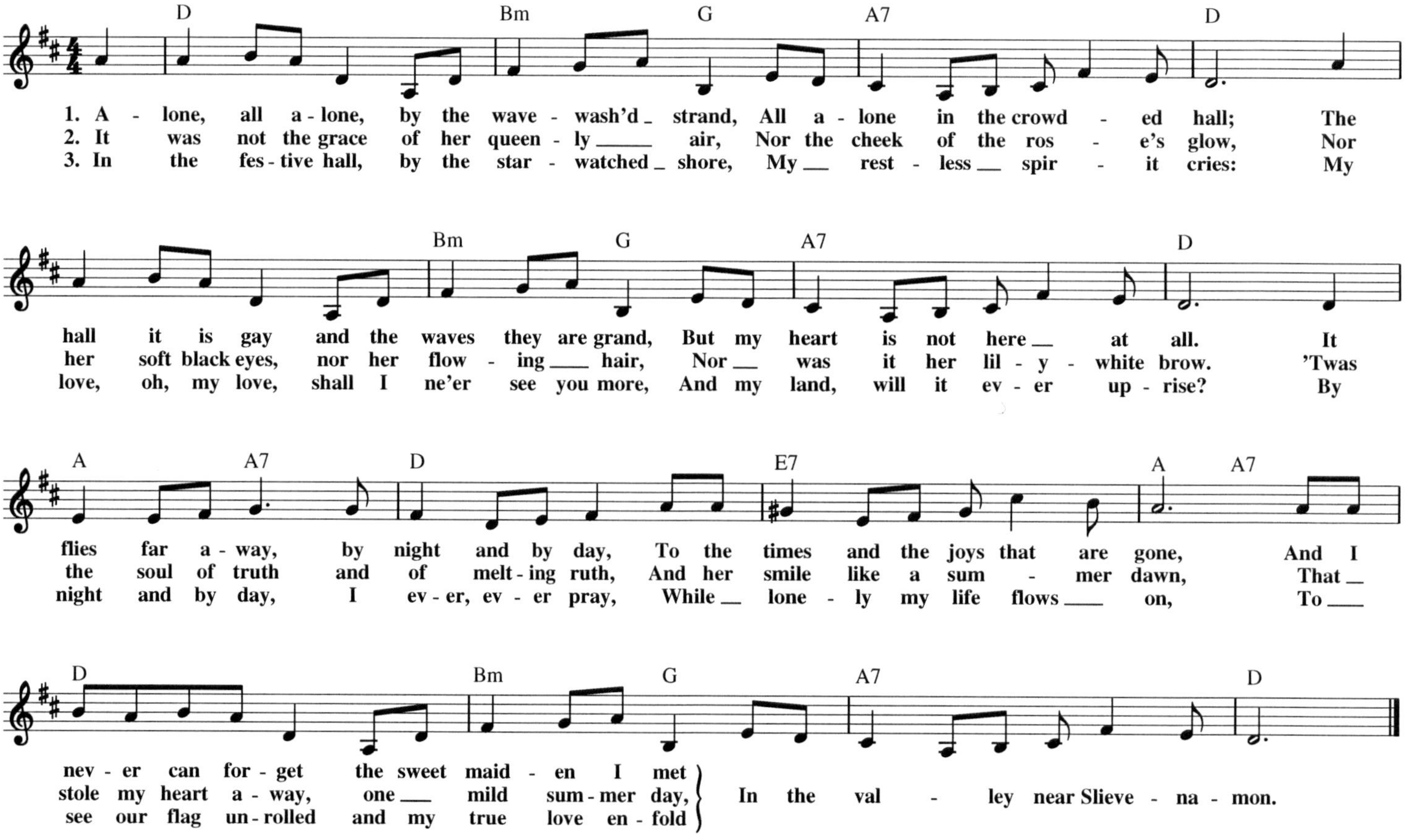

1. A - lone, all a - lone, by the wave - wash'd _ strand, All a - lone in the crowd - ed hall; The
2. It was not the grace of her queen - ly ____ air, Nor the cheek of the ros - e's glow, Nor
3. In the fes - tive hall, by the star - watched _ shore, My ____ rest - less ____ spir - it cries: My

hall it is gay and the waves they are grand, But my heart is not here __ at all. It
her soft black eyes, nor her flow - ing ___ hair, Nor __ was it her lil - y - white brow. 'Twas
love, oh, my love, shall I ne'er see you more, And my land, will it ev - er up - rise? By

flies far a - way, by night and by day, To the times and the joys that are gone, And I
the soul of truth and of melt - ing ruth, And her smile like a sum - mer dawn, That __
night and by day, I ev - er, ev - er pray, While lone - ly my life flows ____ on, To ____

nev - er can for - get the sweet maid - en I met
stole my heart a - way, one ____ mild sum - mer day, } In the val - ley near Slieve - na - mon.
see our flag un - rolled and my true love en - fold

THE MAID OF THE SWEET BROWN KNOWE*

Irish folksong

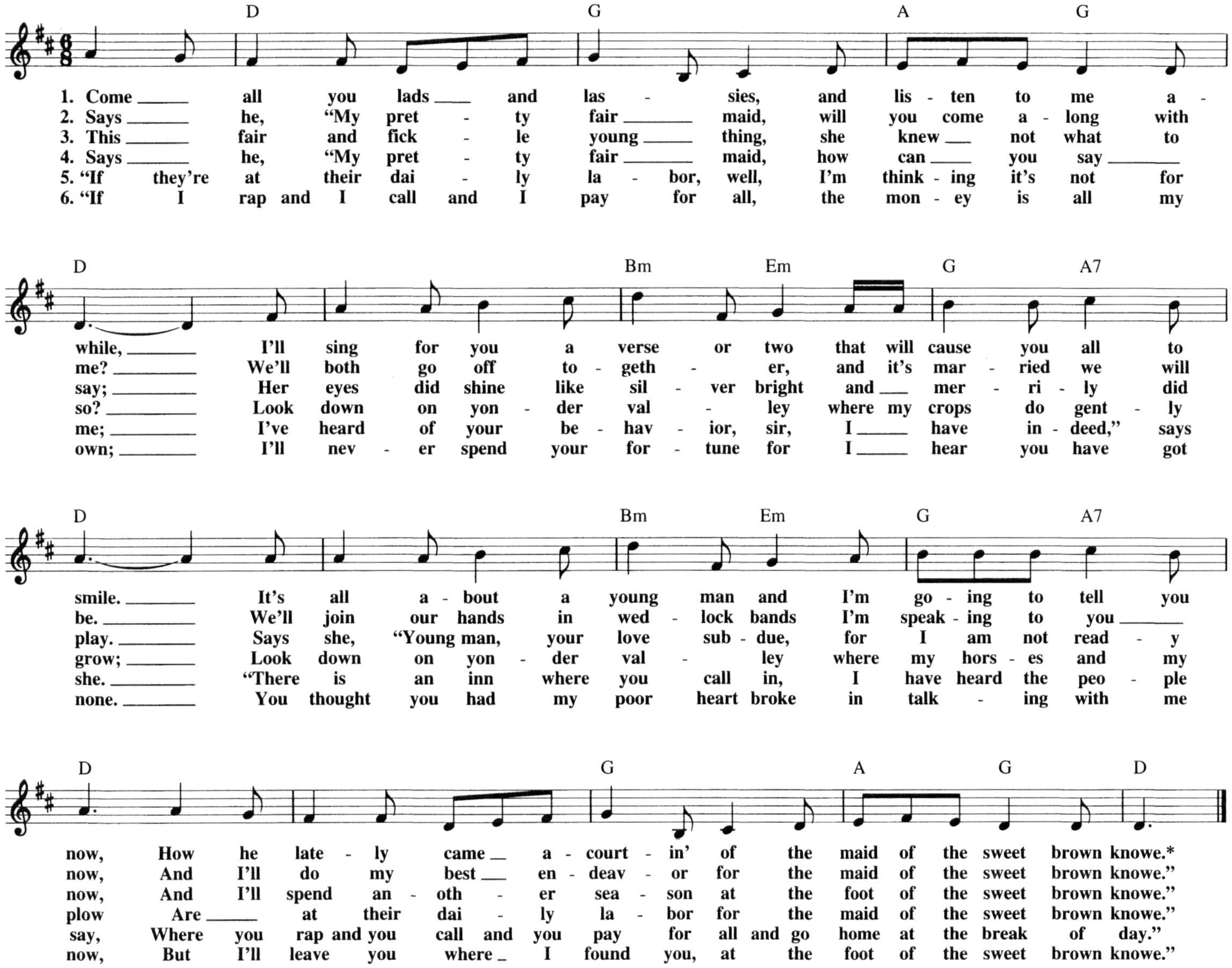

1. Come _____ all you lads _____ and las - sies, and lis - ten to me a -
2. Says _____ he, "My pret - ty fair _____ maid, will you come a - long with
3. This _____ fair and fick - le young _____ thing, she knew _____ not what to
4. Says _____ he, "My pret - ty fair _____ maid, how can _____ you say _____
5. "If they're at their dai - ly la - bor, well, I'm think - ing it's not for
6. "If I rap and I call and I pay for all, the mon - ey is all my

while, _____ I'll sing for you a verse or two that will cause you all to
me? _____ We'll both go off to - geth - er, and it's mar - ried we will
say; _____ Her eyes did shine like sil - ver bright and mer - ri - ly did
so? _____ Look down on yon - der val - ley where my crops do gent - ly
me; _____ I've heard of your be - hav - ior, sir, I _____ have in - deed," says
own; _____ I'll nev - er spend your for - tune for I _____ hear you have got

smile. _____ It's all a - bout a young man and I'm go - ing to tell you
be. _____ We'll join our hands in wed - lock bands I'm speak - ing to you _____
play. _____ Says she, "Young man, your love sub - due, for I am not read - y
grow; _____ Look down on yon - der val - ley where my hors - es and my
she. _____ "There is an inn where you call in, I have heard the peo - ple
none. _____ You thought you had my poor heart broke in talk - ing with me

now, How he late - ly came _____ a - court - in' of the maid of the sweet brown knowe.*
now, And I'll do my best _____ en - deav - or for the maid of the sweet brown knowe."
now, And I'll spend an - oth - er sea - son at the foot of the sweet brown knowe."
plow Are _____ at their dai - ly la - bor for the maid of the sweet brown knowe."
say, Where you rap and you call and you pay for all and go home at the break of day."
now, But I'll leave you where _ I found you, at the foot of the sweet brown knowe."

*small hill or knoll

MARY FAIR
(A Mhairi Bhan)

Folksong from the Hebrides

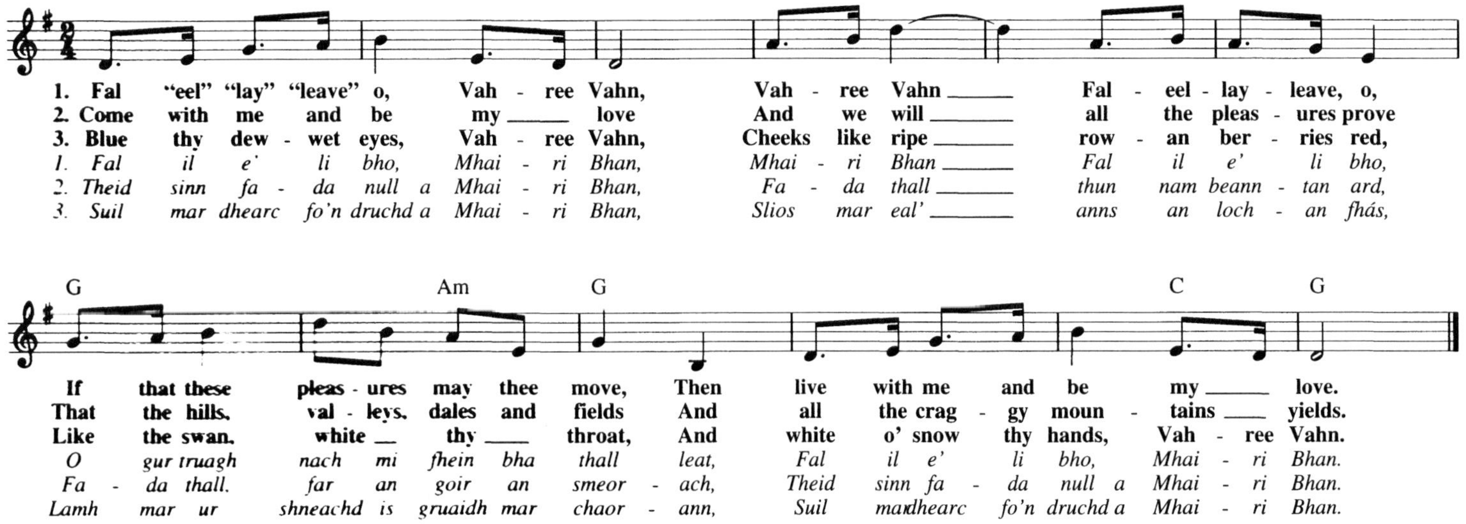

1. Fal "eel" "lay" "leave" o, Vah - ree Vahn, Vah - ree Vahn _____ Fal - eel - lay - leave, o,
2. Come with me and be my _____ love And we will _____ all the pleas - ures prove
3. Blue thy dew - wet eyes, Vah - ree Vahn, Cheeks like ripe _____ row - an ber - ries red,
1. Fal il e' li bho, Mhai - ri Bhan, Mhai - ri Bhan _____ Fal il e' li bho,
2. Theid sinn fa - da null a Mhai - ri Bhan, Fa - da thall _____ thun nam beann - tan ard,
3. Suil mar dhearc fo'n druchd a Mhai - ri Bhan, Slios mar eal' _____ anns an loch - an fhás,

If that these pleas - ures may thee move, Then live with me and be my _____ love.
That the hills, val - leys, dales and fields And all the crag - gy moun - tains _____ yields.
Like the swan, white _ thy _ throat, And white o' snow thy hands, Vah - ree Vahn.
O gur truagh nach mi fhein bha thall leat, Fal il e' li bho, Mhai - ri Bhan.
Fa - da thall. far an goir an smeor - ach, Theid sinn fa - da null a Mhai - ri Bhan.
Lamh mar ur shneachd is gruaidh mar chaor - ann, Suil mardhearc fo'n druchd a Mhai - ri Bhan.

MASTER McGRATH

Irish folksong

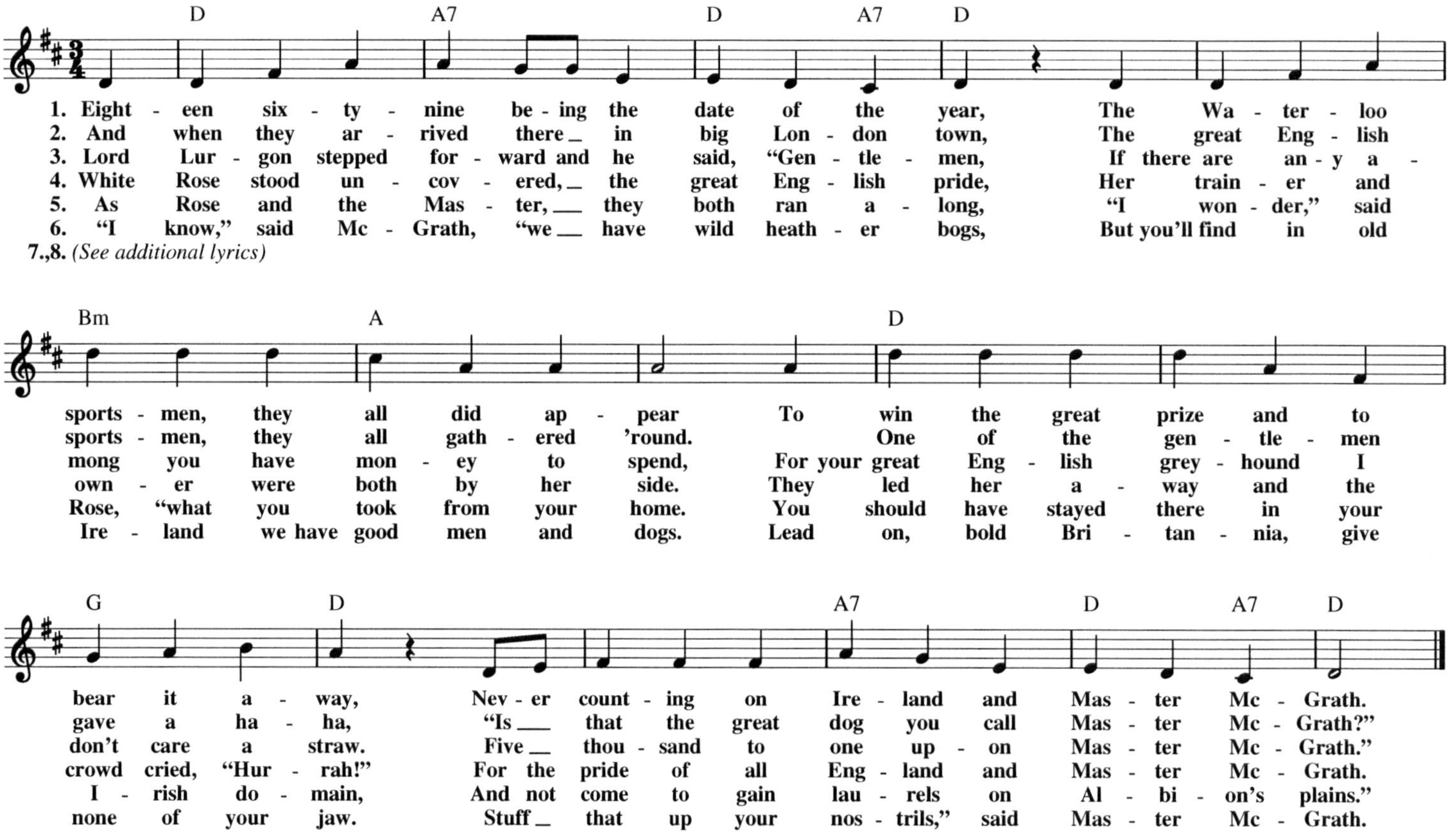

1. Eight - een six - ty - nine be - ing the date of the year, The Wa - ter - loo
2. And when they ar - rived there in big Lon - don town, The great Eng - lish
3. Lord Lur - gon stepped for - ward and he said, "Gen - tle - men, If there are an - y a -
4. White Rose stood un - cov - ered, the great Eng - lish pride, Her train - er and
5. As Rose and the Mas - ter, they both ran a - long, "I won - der," said
6. "I know," said Mc - Grath, "we have wild heath - er bogs, But you'll find in old

7., 8. *(See additional lyrics)*

sports - men, they all did ap - pear. To win the great prize and to
sports - men, they all gath - ered 'round. One of the gen - tle - men
own - er were both by her side. They led her a - way and the
Rose, "what you took from your home. You should have stayed there in your
Ire - land we have good men and dogs. Lead on, bold Bri - tan - nia, give

bear it a - way, Nev - er count - ing on Ire - land and Mas - ter Mc - Grath.
gave a ha - ha, "Is that the great dog you call Mas - ter Mc - Grath?"
don't care a straw. Five thou - sand to one up - on Mas - ter Mc - Grath."
crowd cried, "Hur - rah!" For the pride of all Eng - land and Mas - ter Mc - Grath.
I - rish do - main, And not come to gain lau - rels on Al - bi - on's plains."
none of your jaw. Stuff that up your nos - trils," said Mas - ter Mc - Grath.

Additional Lyrics

7. The hare she led on, what a beautiful view,
As swift as the wind o'er the green fields she flew.
He jumped on her back and he held up his paw;
"Three cheers for old Ireland," said Master McGrath.

8. I've known many greyhounds that filled me with pride
In the days that are gone and it can't be denied,
But the greatest and the bravest the world ever saw
Was our champion of champions, brave Master McGrath.

McPHERSON'S LAMENT

Irish folksong

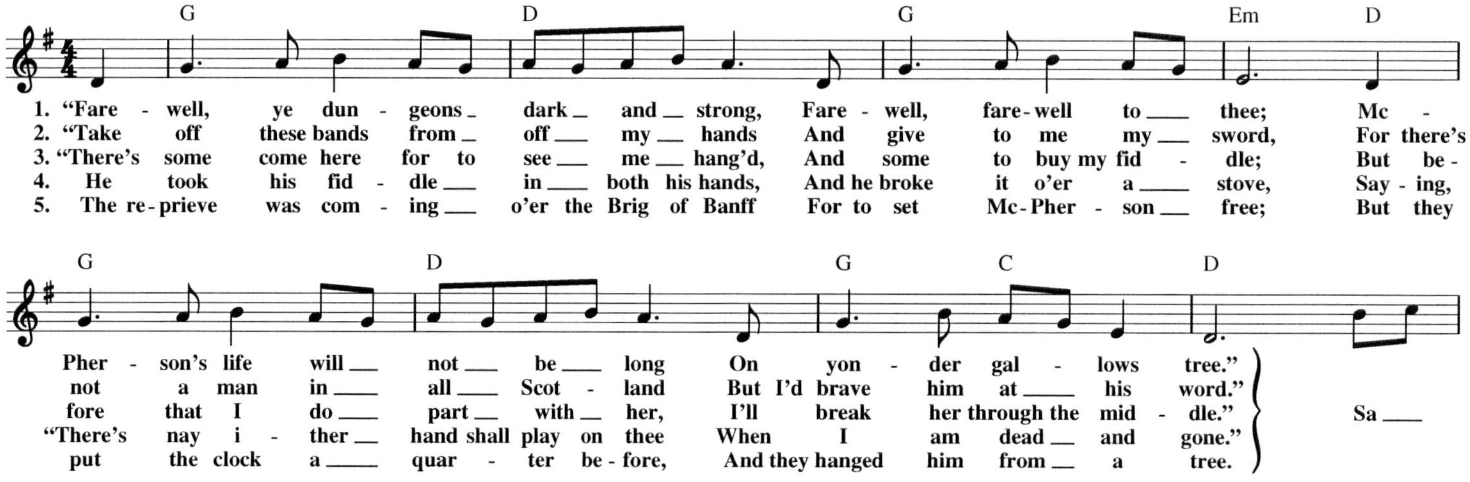

1. "Fare - well, ye dun - geons dark and strong, Fare - well, fare - well to thee; Mc -
2. "Take off these bands from off my hands And give to me my sword, For there's
3. "There's some come here for to see me hang'd, And some to buy my fid - dle; But be -
4. He took his fid - dle in both his hands, And he broke it o'er a stove, Say - ing,
5. The re - prieve was com - ing o'er the Brig of Banff For to set Mc - Pher - son free; But they

Pher - son's life will not be long On yon - der gal - lows tree."
not a man in all Scot - land But I'd brave him at his word."
fore that I do part with her, I'll break her through the mid - dle." Sa -
"There's nay i - ther hand shall play on thee When I am dead and gone."
put the clock a quar - ter be - fore, And they hanged him from a tree.

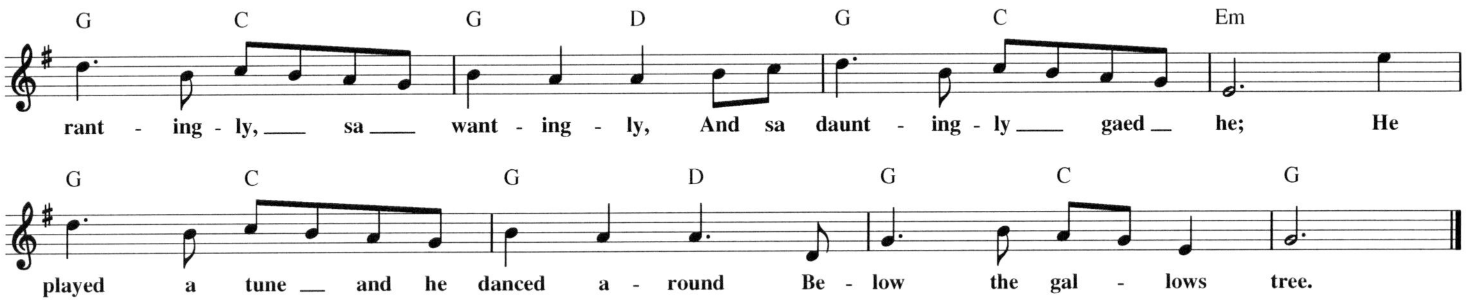

McSORLEY'S TWINS

Words and Music by
Gustave Phillips

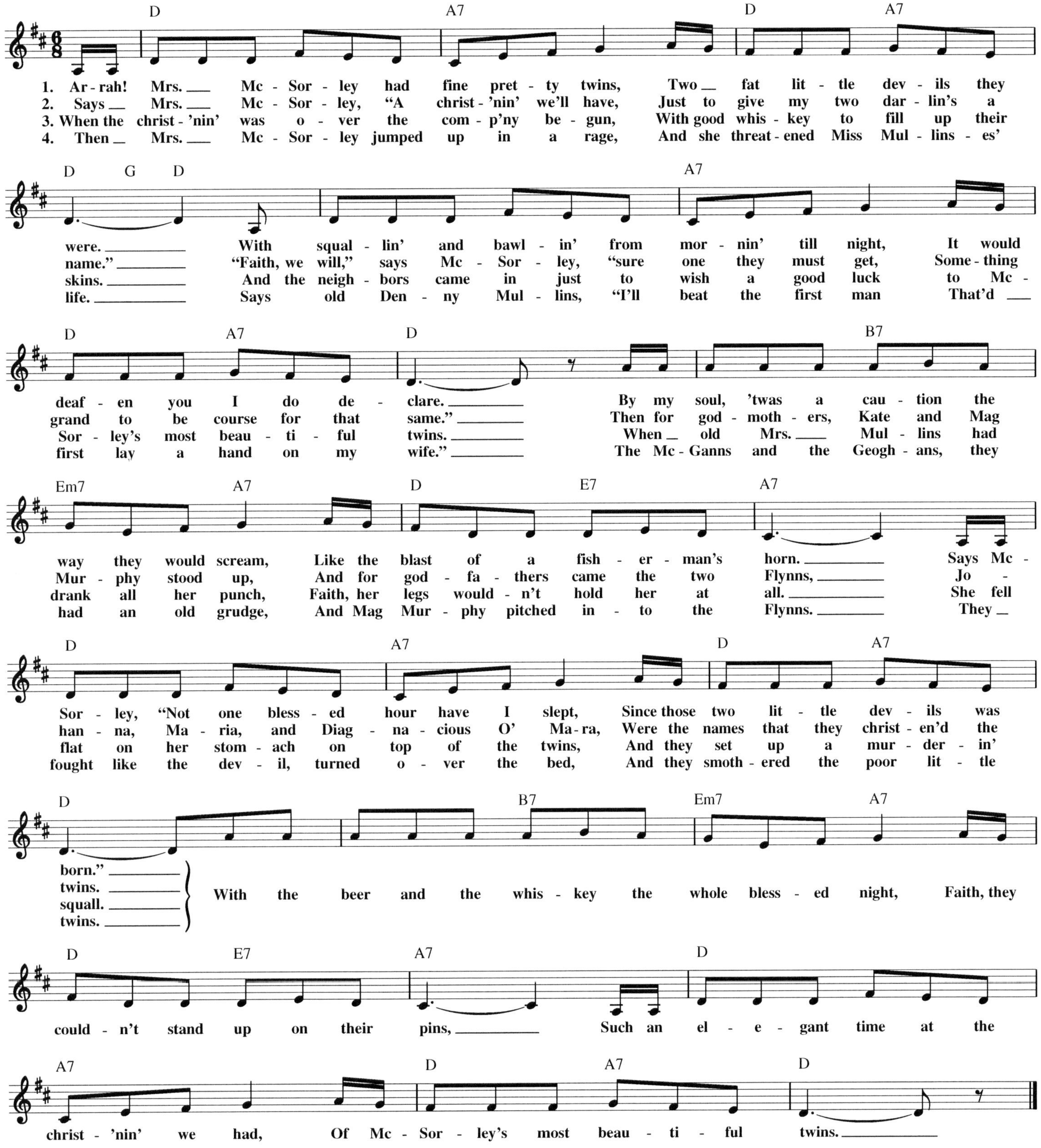

McCAFFERY

Irish folksong

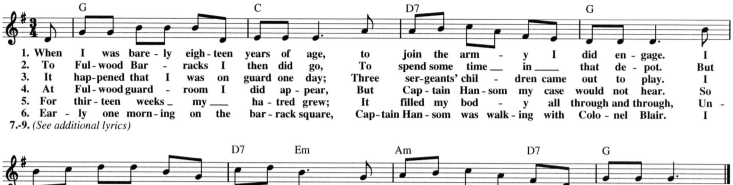

1. When I was bare-ly eigh-teen years of age, to join the arm - y I did en - gage. I
2. To Ful-wood Bar - racks I then did go, To spend some time __ in __ that de - pot. But
3. It hap-pened that I was on guard one day; Three ser-geants' chil - dren came out to play. I
4. At Ful-wood guard - room I did ap-pear, But Cap-tain Han-som my case would not hear. So
5. For thir-teen weeks __ my __ ha - tred grew; It filled my bod - y all through and through, Un-
6. Ear - ly one morn-ing on the bar - rack square, Cap-tain Han-som was walk - ing with Colo - nel Blair. I

7.-9. *(See additional lyrics)*

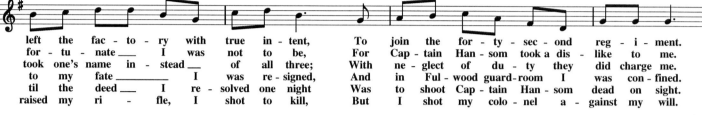

left the fac - to - ry with true in - tent, To join the for - ty - sec - ond reg - i - ment.
for - tu - nate __ I was not to be, For Cap - tain Han - som took a dis - like to me.
took one's name in - stead __ of all three; With ne - glect of du - ty they did charge me.
to my fate __ I was re - signed, And in Ful - wood guard-room I was con - fined.
til the deed __ I re - solved one night Was to shoot Cap - tain Han - som dead on sight.
raised my ri - fle, I shot to kill, But I shot my colo - nel a - gainst my will.

Additional Lyrics

7. I done the deed, I shed the blood.
   At Liverpool Assizes my trial I stood.
   Judge says to me, "McCaffery,
   Prepare yourself for the gallows tree."

8. I had no father to take my part,
   Likewise no mother to break her heart.
   Only one pal and a girl was she—
   She'd have laid down her life for McCaffery.

9. Come all you young Irishmen, come listen to me,
   Have nothing to do with the British Army.
   For only lies and tyranny
   Made a murderer out of McCaffery.

MEN OF HARLECH
(Rhyfelgyrch Gwyr Harlech)

Welsh folksong
Words by Ceriog

See the flames of fires like hell there, Fie - ry tongues that ache and swell there.
Well - uh goil - kairth wen un flam - yo, Ah thav - ode - i tahn un bloyth - yo,

Hear the brave man's bat - tle yell there: On - ward as we go.
Ahr eer dew - rion thod ee dah - ro, Een - wythe et on een.

Hear the war cries, ar - mor clash - ing, Chief - tains urge the right - eous thrash - ing,
Gahn - von - llev i tuh - ois - og - yon, Llice gel - on - yon, troost ar - vog - yon

Sol - diers ride on hors - es dash - ing, On - ward as we go.
Ah char - lom - yod uh march - og - yon, Creig - ar grieg ah green!

Ar - fon sings on al - ways, Of her might and glo - ry.
Ahr - von beeth nee or - veeth, Ken - eer un dra - guh weeth,

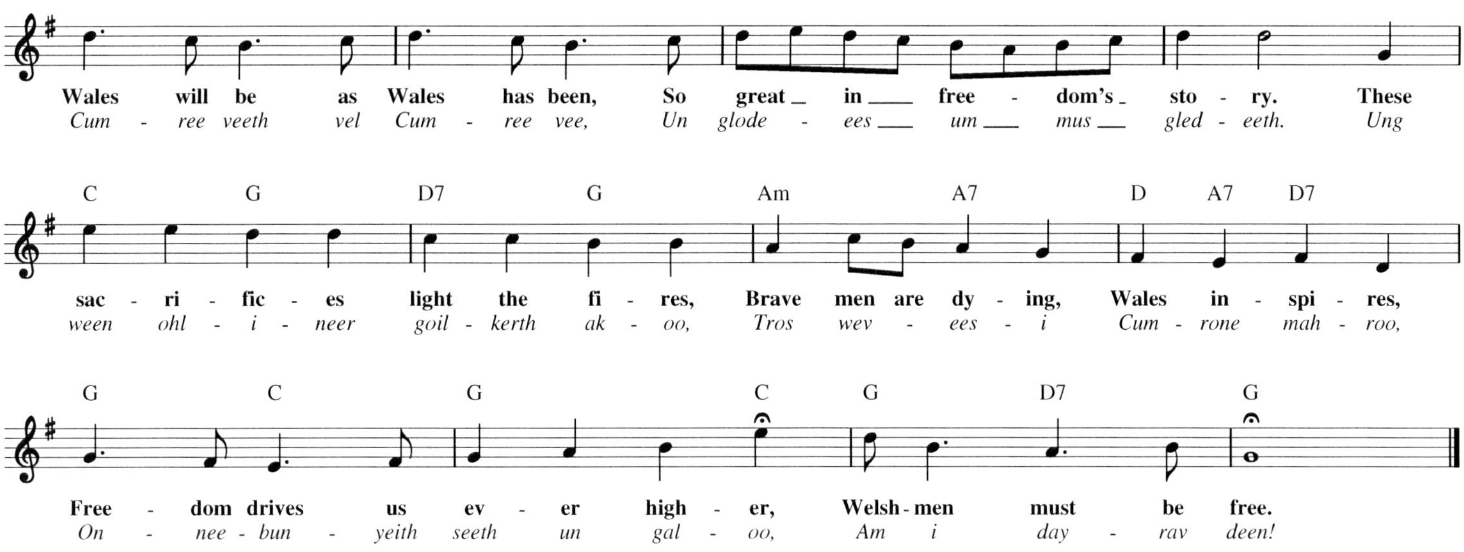

Wales will be as Wales has been, So great _ in ____ free - dom's _ sto - ry. These
Cum - ree veeth vel Cum - ree vee, Un glode - ees ____ um ____ mus ____ gled - eeth. Ung

sac - ri - fic - es light the fi - res, Brave men are dy - ing, Wales in - spi - res,
ween ohl - i - neer goil - kerth ak - oo, Tros wev - ees - i Cum - rone mah - roo,

Free - dom drives us ev - er high - er, Welsh - men must be free.
On - nee - bun - yeith seeth un gal - oo, Am i day - rav deen!

THE MEN OF THE WEST

Irish folksong
By William Rooney

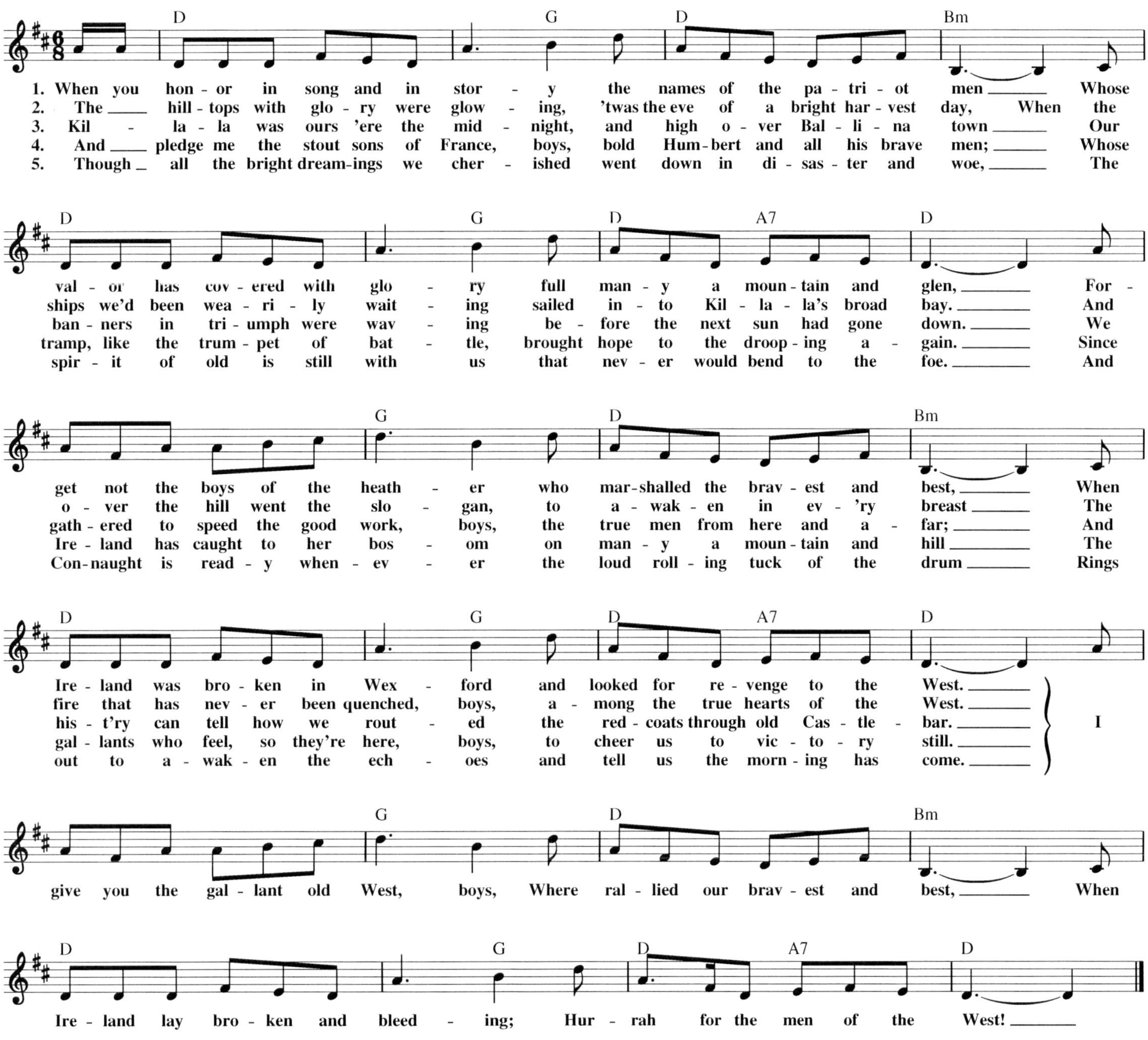

1. When you hon - or in song and in stor - y the names of the pa - tri - ot men ____ Whose
2. The ____ hill - tops with glo - ry were glow - ing, 'twas the eve of a bright har - vest day, When the
3. Kil - la - la was ours 'ere the mid - night, and high o - ver Bal - li - na town ____ Our
4. And ____ pledge me the stout sons of France, boys, bold Hum - bert and all his brave men; ____ Whose
5. Though ____ all the bright dream - ings we cher - ished went down in di - sas - ter and woe, ____ The

val - or has cov - ered with glo - ry full man - y a moun - tain and glen, ____ For -
ships we'd been wea - ri - ly wait - ing sailed in - to Kil - la - la's broad bay. ____ And
ban - ners in tri - umph were wav - ing be - fore the next sun had gone down. ____ We
tramp, like the trum - pet of bat - tle, brought hope to the droop - ing a - gain. ____ Since
spir - it of old is still with us that nev - er would bend to the foe. ____ And

get not the boys of the heath - er who mar - shalled the brav - est and best, ____ When
o - ver the hill went the slo - gan, to a - wak - en in ev - 'ry breast ____ The
gath - ered to speed the good work, boys, the true men from here and a - far; ____ And
Ire - land has caught to her bos - om on man - y a moun - tain and hill ____ The
Con - naught is read - y when - ev - er the loud roll - ing tuck of the drum ____ Rings

Ire - land was bro - ken in Wex - ford and looked for re - venge to the West. ____
fire that has nev - er been quenched, boys, a - mong the true hearts of the West. ____
his - t'ry can tell how we rout - ed the red - coats through old Cas - tle - bar. ____
gal - lants who feel, so they're here, boys, to cheer us to vic - to - ry still. ____
out to a - wak - en the ech - oes and tell us the morn - ing has come. ____

I

give you the gal - lant old West, boys, Where ral - lied our brav - est and best, ____ When

Ire - land lay bro - ken and bleed - ing; Hur - rah for the men of the West! ____

THE MERCHANT'S DAUGHTER

Irish folksong

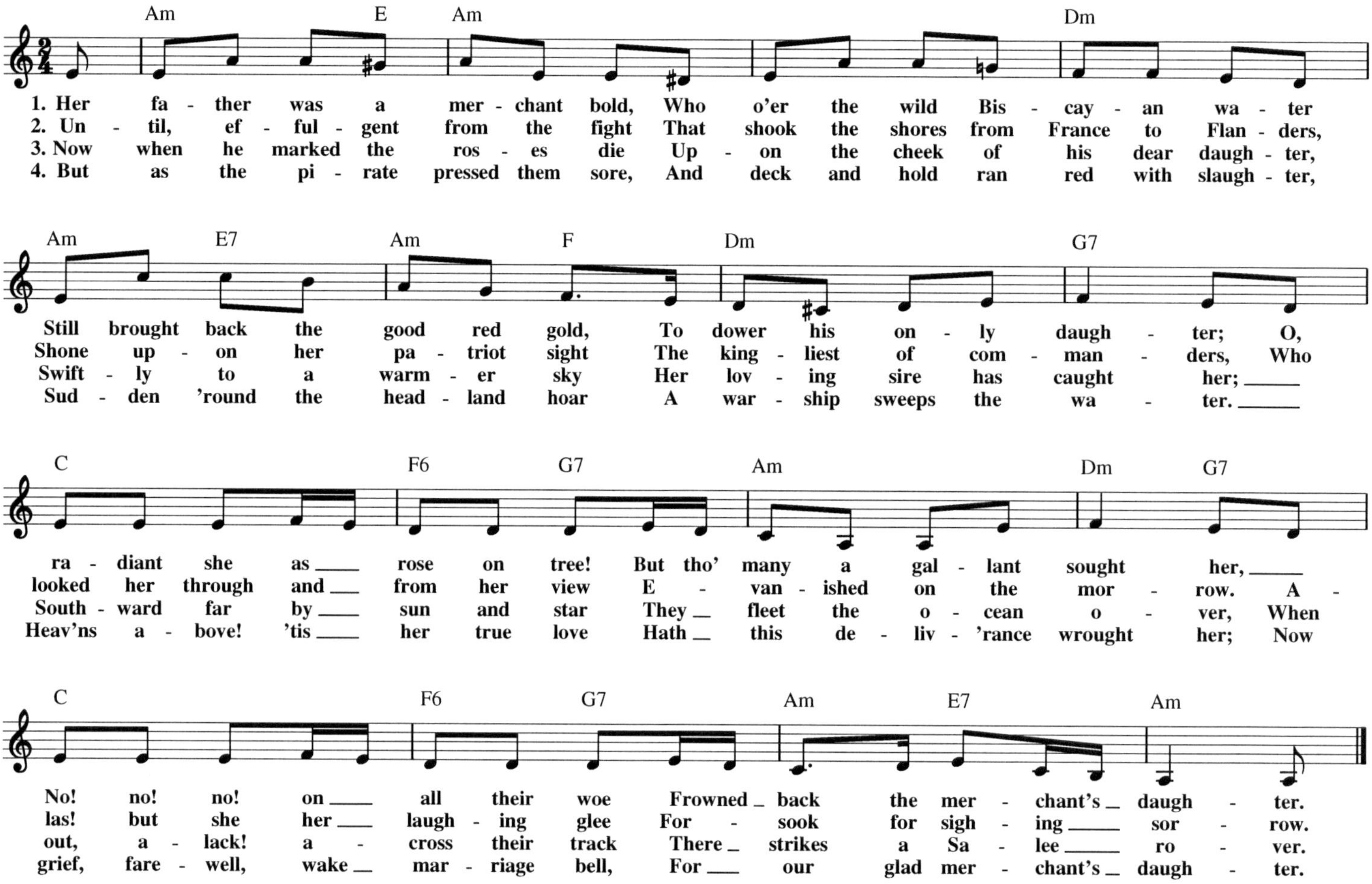

1. Her father was a merchant bold, Who o'er the wild Biscayan water
2. Until, effulgent from the fight That shook the shores from France to Flanders,
3. Now when he marked the roses die Upon the cheek of his dear daughter,
4. But as the pirate pressed them sore, And deck and hold ran red with slaughter,

Still brought back the good red gold, To dower his only daughter; O,
Shone upon her patriot sight The kingliest of commanders, Who
Swiftly to a warmer sky Her loving sire has caught her;
Sudden 'round the headland hoar A warship sweeps the water.

radiant she as rose on tree! But tho' many a gallant sought her,
looked her through and from her view E vanished on the morrow. A-
Southward far by sun and star They fleet the ocean over, When
Heav'ns above! 'tis her true love Hath this deliv'rance wrought her; Now

No! no! no! on all their woe Frowned back the merchant's daughter.
las! but she her laughing glee Forsook for sighing sorrow.
out, a lack! across their track There strikes a Salee rover.
grief, farewell, wake marriage bell, For our glad merchant's daughter.

MERMAID SONG

Irish folksong

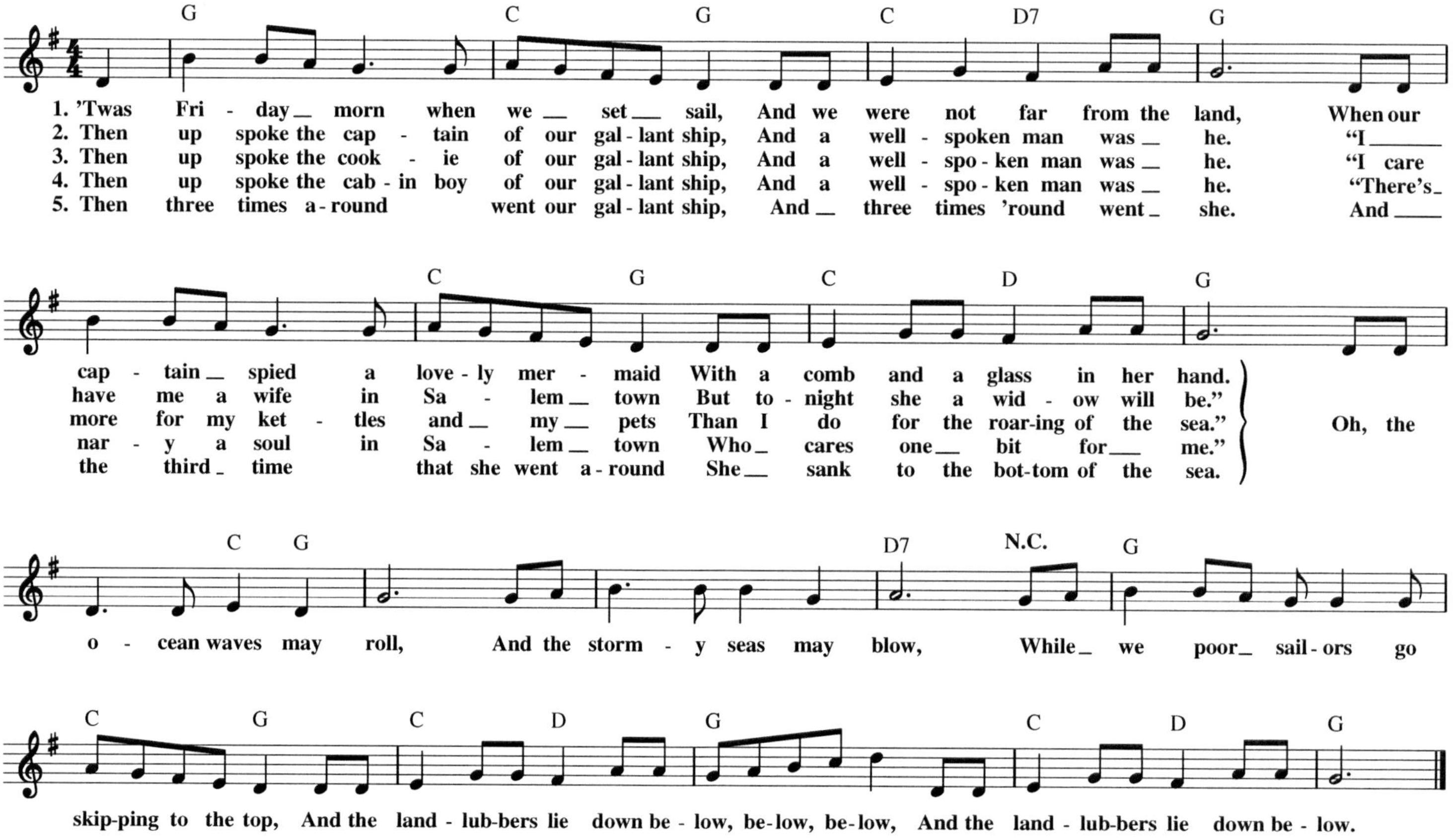

1. 'Twas Friday morn when we set sail, And we were not far from the land, When our
2. Then up spoke the captain of our gallant ship, And a well-spoken man was he. "I
3. Then up spoke the cookie of our gallant ship, And a well-spoken man was he. "I care
4. Then up spoke the cabin boy of our gallant ship, And a well-spoken man was he. "There's
5. Then three times a-round went our gallant ship, And three times 'round went she. And

captain spied a lovely mermaid With a comb and a glass in her hand.
have me a wife in Salem town But to-night she a widow will be."
more for my kettles and my pets Than I do for the roaring of the sea."
nary a soul in Salem town Who cares one bit for me."
the third time that she went a-round She sank to the bottom of the sea.

Oh, the

ocean waves may roll, And the storm-y seas may blow, While we poor sailors go

skipping to the top, And the landlubbers lie down below, be-low, be-low, And the landlubbers lie down below.

MICK McGUIRE

Irish folksong

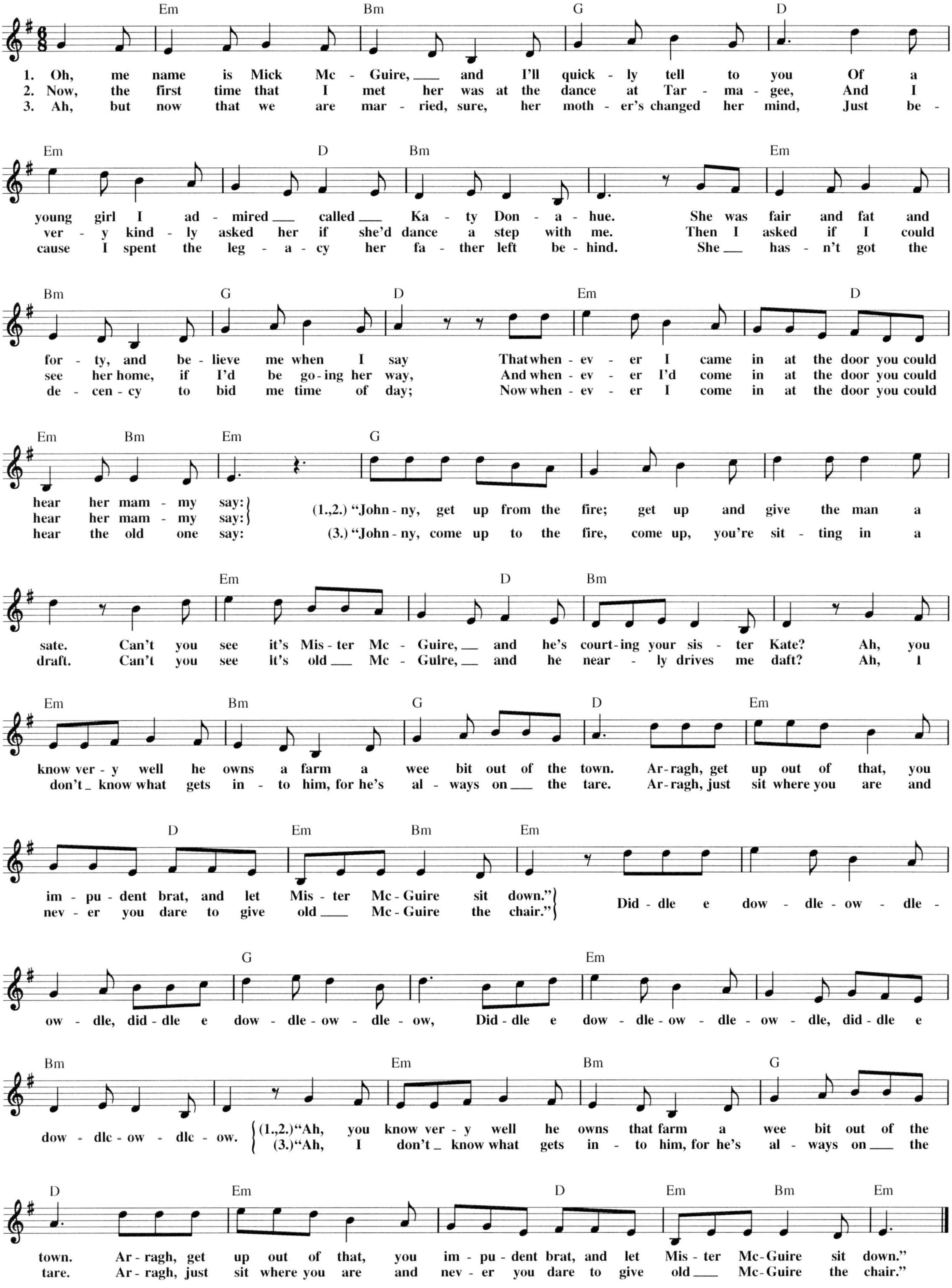
Em Bm G D
1. Oh, me name is Mick Mc - Guire, and I'll quick - ly tell to you Of a
2. Now, the first time that I met her was at the dance at Tar - ma - gee, And I
3. Ah, but now that we are mar - ried, sure, her moth - er's changed her mind, Just be -
Em D Bm Em
young girl I ad - mired called Ka - ty Don - a - hue. She was fair and fat and
ver - y kind - ly asked her if she'd dance a step with me. Then I asked if I could
cause I spent the leg - a - cy her fa - ther left be - hind. She has - n't got the
Bm G D Em D
for - ty, and be - lieve me when I say That when - ev - er I came in at the door you could
see her home, if I'd be go - ing her way, And when - ev - er I'd come in at the door you could
de - cen - cy to bid me time of day; Now when - ev - er I come in at the door you could
Em Bm Em G
hear her mam - my say: (1.,2.) "John - ny, get up from the fire; get up and give the man a
hear her mam - my say:
hear the old one say: (3.) "John - ny, come up to the fire, come up, you're sit - ting in a
Em D Bm
sate. Can't you see it's Mis - ter Mc - Guire, and he's court - ing your sis - ter Kate? Ah, you
draft. Can't you see it's old Mc - Guire, and he near - ly drives me daft? Ah, I
Em Bm G D Em
know ver - y well he owns a farm a wee bit out of the town. Ar - ragh, get up out of that, you
don't know what gets in - to him, for he's al - ways on the tare. Ar - ragh, just sit where you are and
D Em Bm Em
im - pu - dent brat, and let Mis - ter Mc - Guire sit down."
nev - er you dare to give old Mc - Guire the chair."
Did - dle e dow - dle - ow - dle -
G Em
ow - dle, did - dle e dow - dle - ow - dle - ow, Did - dle e dow - dle - ow - dle - ow - dle, did - dle e
Bm Em Bm G
dow - dle - ow - dle - ow. (1.,2.) "Ah, you know ver - y well he owns that farm a wee bit out of the
(3.) "Ah, I don't know what gets in - to him, for he's al - ways on the
D Em D Em Bm Em
town. Ar - ragh, get up out of that, you im - pu - dent brat, and let Mis - ter Mc - Guire sit down."
tare. Ar - ragh, just sit where you are and nev - er you dare to give old Mc - Guire the chair."

THE MERMAID'S CROON
(Crònan na Maighdinn-Mhara)

Folksong from the Hebrides

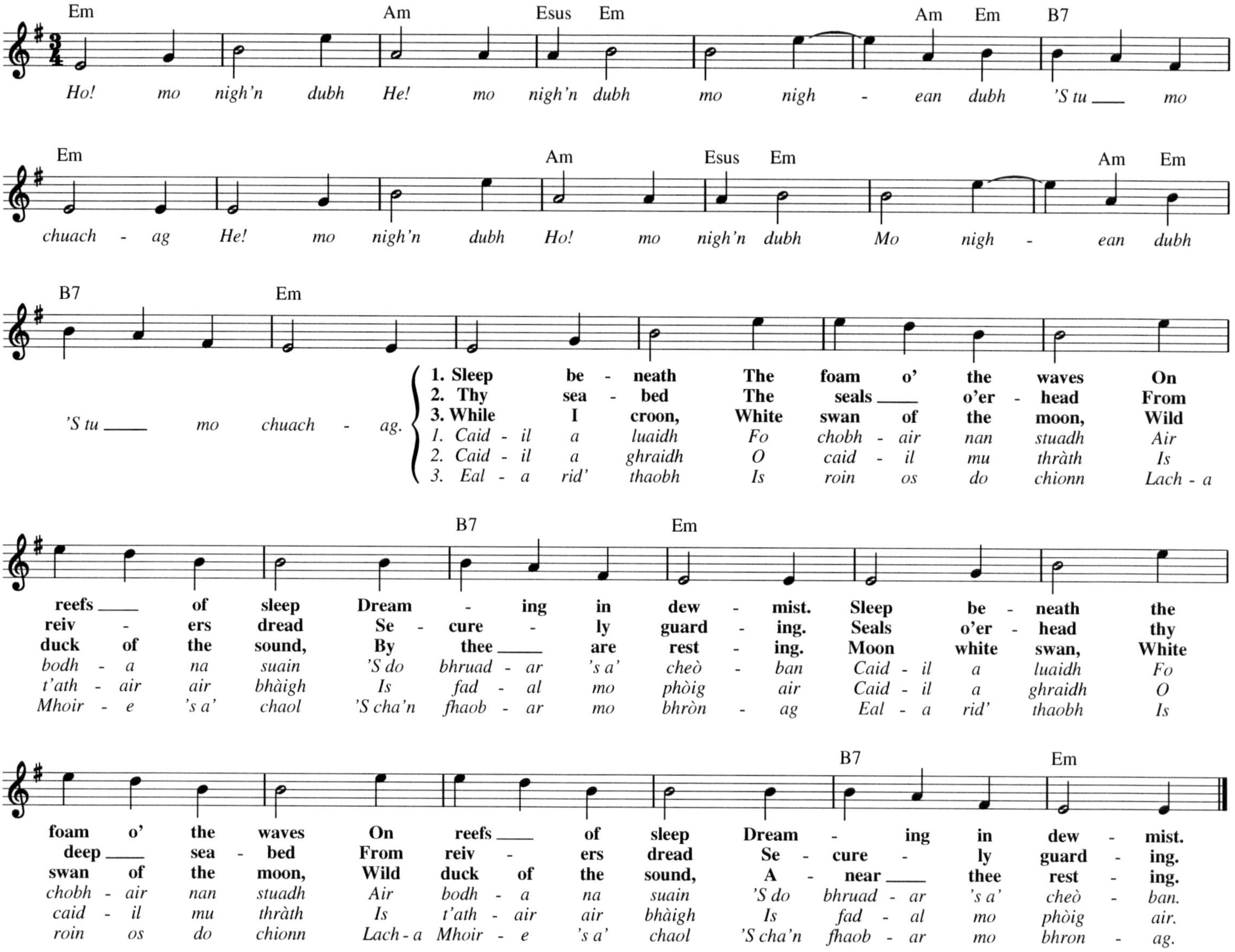

MICHAEL ROY OF BROOKLYN CITY

Irish popular song

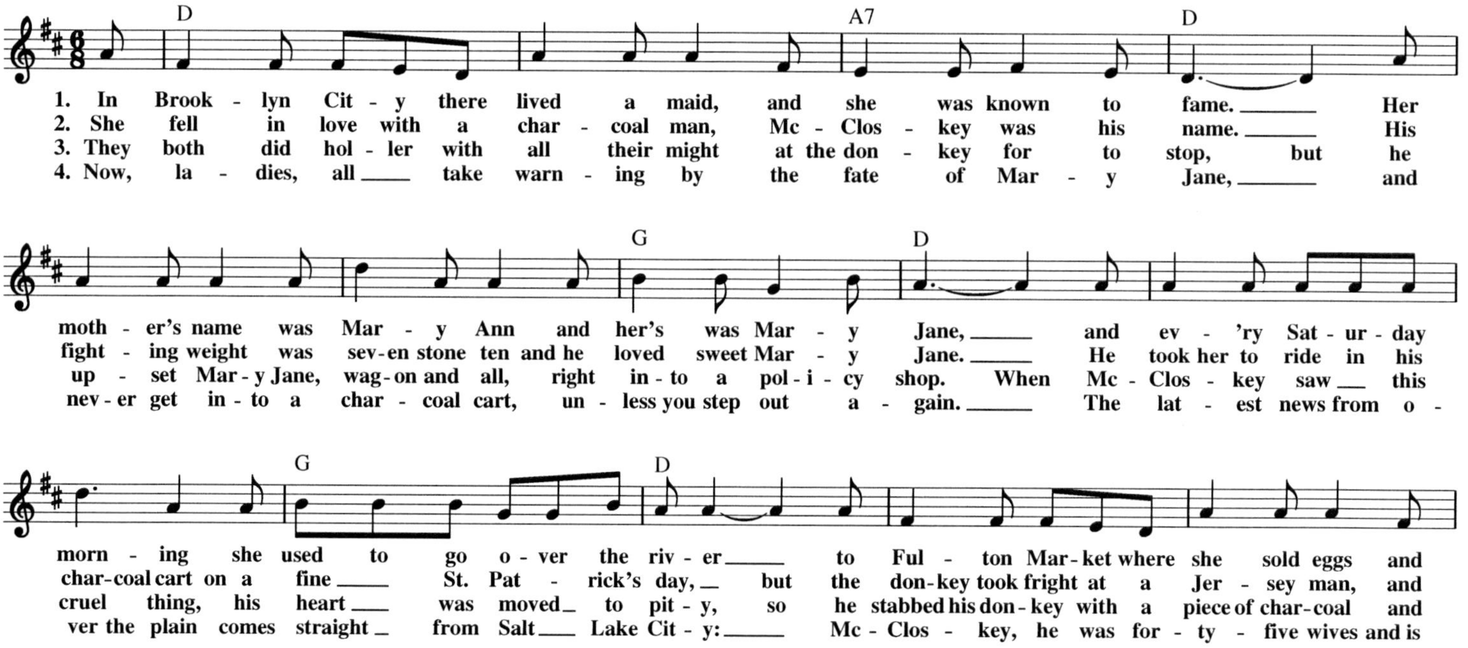

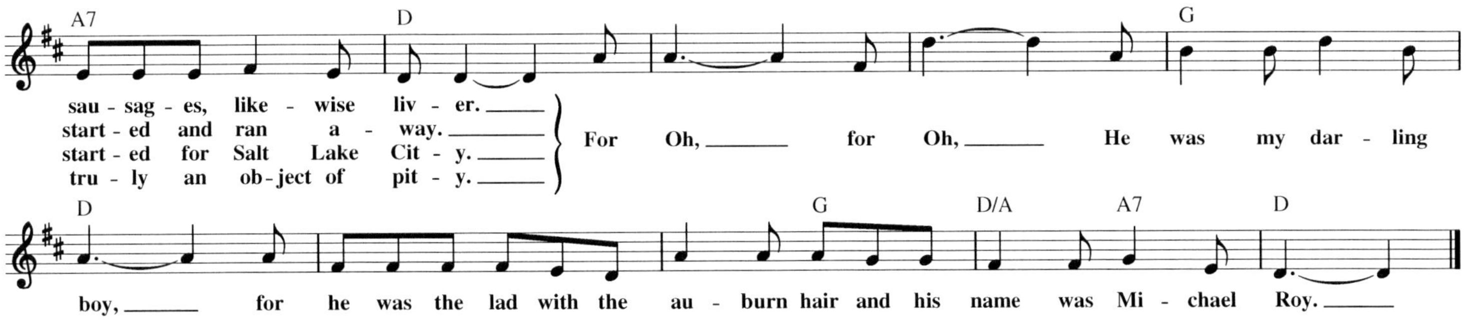

sau - sag - es, like - wise liv - er. _____ }
start - ed and ran a - way. _____ }
start - ed for Salt Lake Cit - y. _____ }
tru - ly an ob - ject of pit - y. _____ }
For Oh, _____ for Oh, _____ He was my dar - ling

boy, _____ for he was the lad with the au - burn hair and his name was Mi - chael Roy. _____

MILKING CROON
(Cronan Bleoghain)

Folksong from the Hebrides

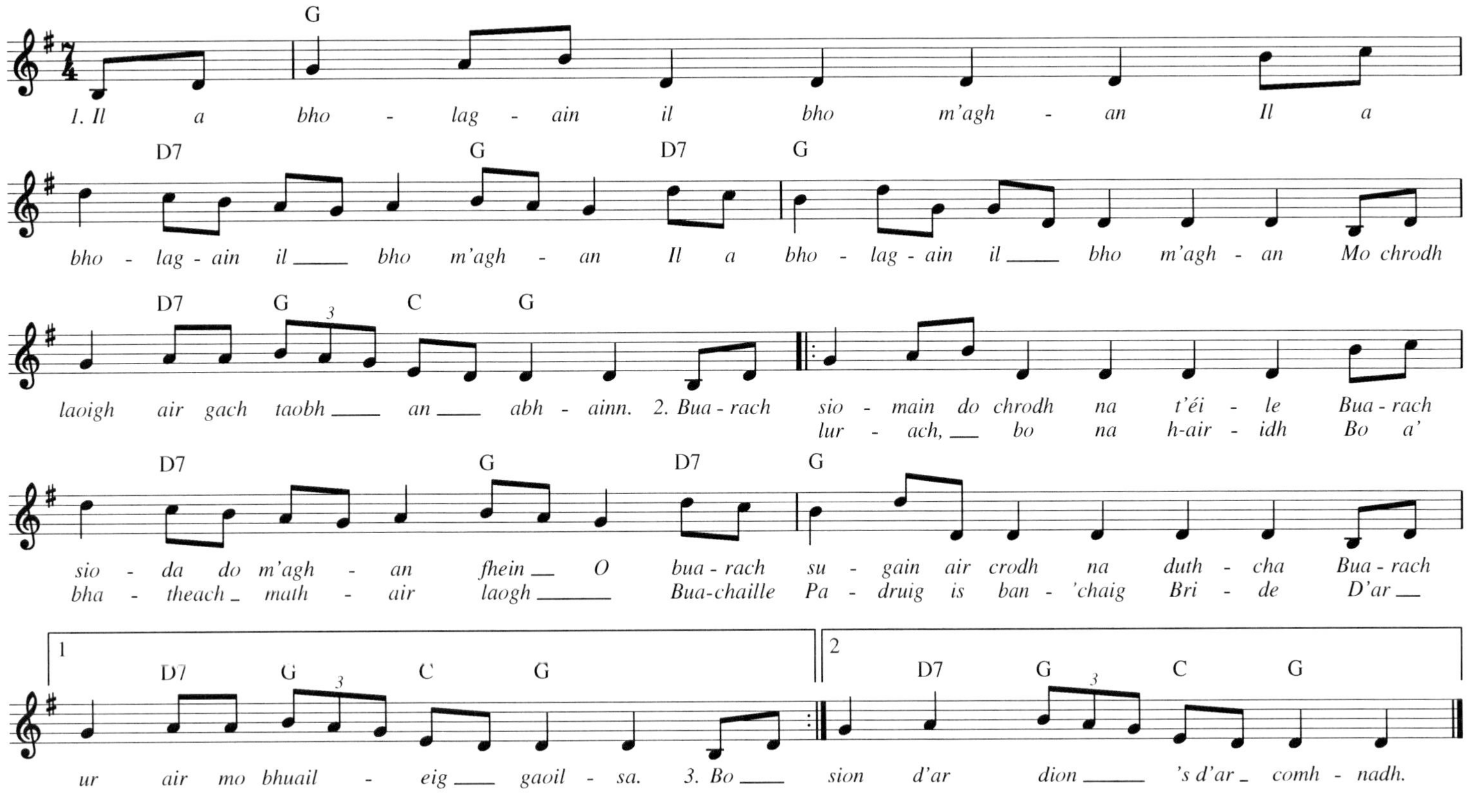

1. Il a bho - lag - ain il bho m'agh - an Il a

bho - lag - ain il _____ bho m'agh - an Il a bho - lag - ain il _____ bho m'agh - an Mo chrodh

laoigh air gach taobh _____ an _____ abh - ainn. 2. Bua - rach sio - main do chrodh na t'éi - le Bua - rach
lur - ach, _____ bo na h-air - idh Bo a'

sio - da do m'agh - an fhein _____ O bua - rach su - gain air crodh na duth - cha Bua - rach
bha - theach _ math - air laogh _____ Bua-chaille Pa - druig is ban - 'chaig Bri - de D'ar _____

1
ur air mo bhuail - eig _____ gaoil - sa. 3. Bo _____

2
sion d'ar dion _____ 's d'ar _ comh - nadh.

MILKING SONG
(Oran Buaile)

Folksong from the Hebrides

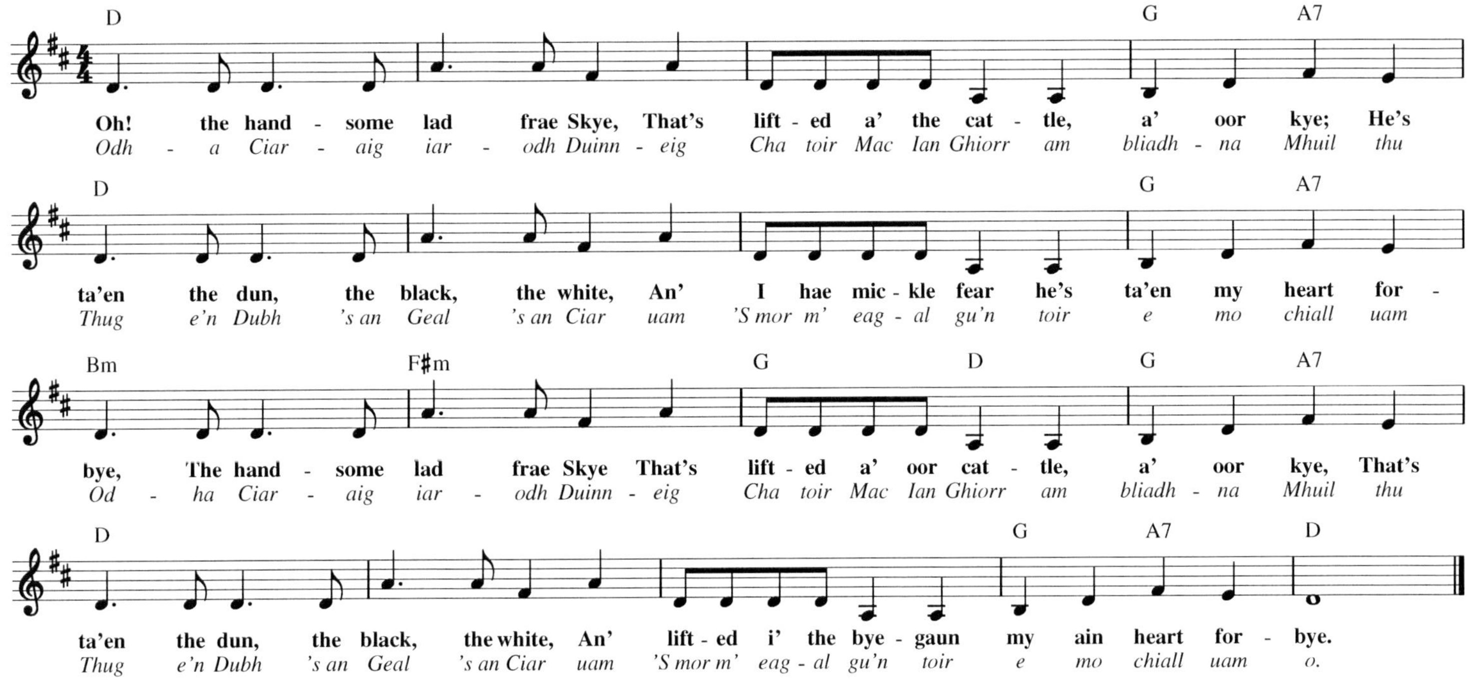

Oh! the hand - some lad frae Skye, That's lift - ed a' the cat - tle, a' oor kye; He's
Odh - a Ciar - aig iar - odh Duinn - eig Cha toir Mac Ian Ghiorr am bliadh - na Mhuil thu

ta'en the dun, the black, the white, An' I hae mic - kle fear he's ta'en my heart for -
Thug e'n Dubh 's an Geal 's an Ciar uam 'S mor m' eag - al gu'n toir e mo chiall uam

bye, The hand - some lad frae Skye That's lift - ed a' oor cat - tle, a' oor kye, That's
Od - ha Ciar - aig iar - odh Duinn - eig Cha toir Mac Ian Ghiorr am bliadh - na Mhuil thu

ta'en the dun, the black, the white, An' lift - ed i' the bye - gaun my ain heart for - bye.
Thug e'n Dubh 's an Geal 's an Ciar uam 'S mor m' eag - al gu'n toir e mo chiall uam o.

THE MINSTREL BOY

Irish popular song
Words by Thomas Moore

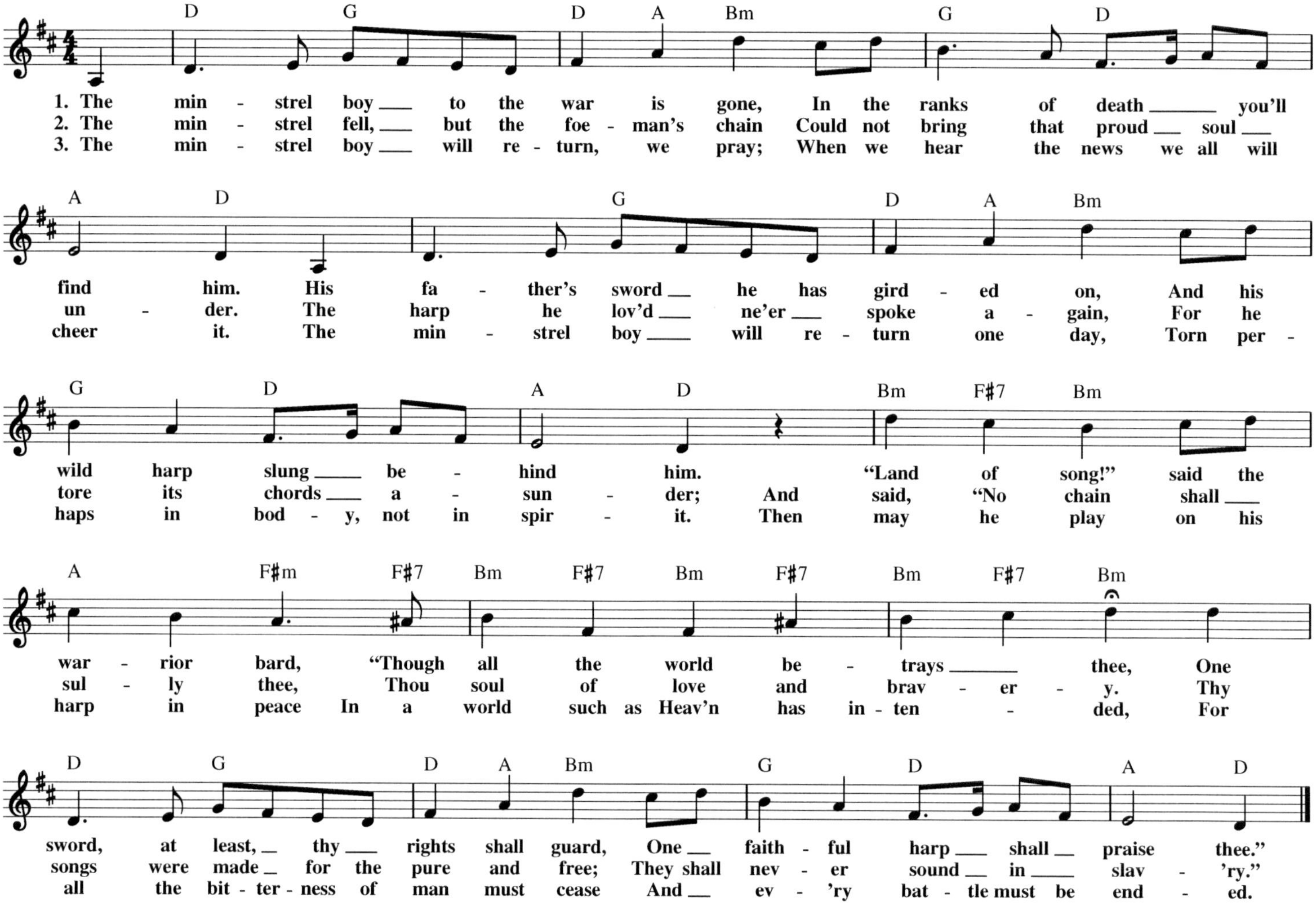

1. The min - strel boy ___ to the war is gone, In the ranks of death _____ you'll
2. The min - strel fell, ___ but the foe - man's chain Could not bring that proud ___ soul ___
3. The min - strel boy ___ will re - turn, we pray; When we hear the news we all will

find him. His fa - ther's sword ___ he has gird - ed on, And his
un - der. The harp he lov'd ___ ne'er ___ spoke a - gain, For he
cheer it. The min - strel boy ___ will re - turn one day, Torn per -

wild harp slung ____ be - hind him. "Land of song!" said the
tore its chords ___ a - sun - der; And said, "No chain shall ___
haps in bod - y, not in spir - it. Then may he play on his

war - rior bard, "Though all the world be - trays ____ thee, One
sul - ly thee, Thou soul of love and brav - er - y. Thy
harp in peace In a world such as Heav'n has in - ten - ded, For

sword, at least, ___ thy ___ rights shall guard, One ___ faith - ful harp ___ shall ___ praise thee."
songs were made ___ for the pure and free; They shall nev - er sound ___ in ____ slav - 'ry."
all the bit - ter - ness of man must cease And ___ ev - 'ry bat - tle must be end - ed.

MR. MOSES RI-TOORAL-I-AY

Irish folksong

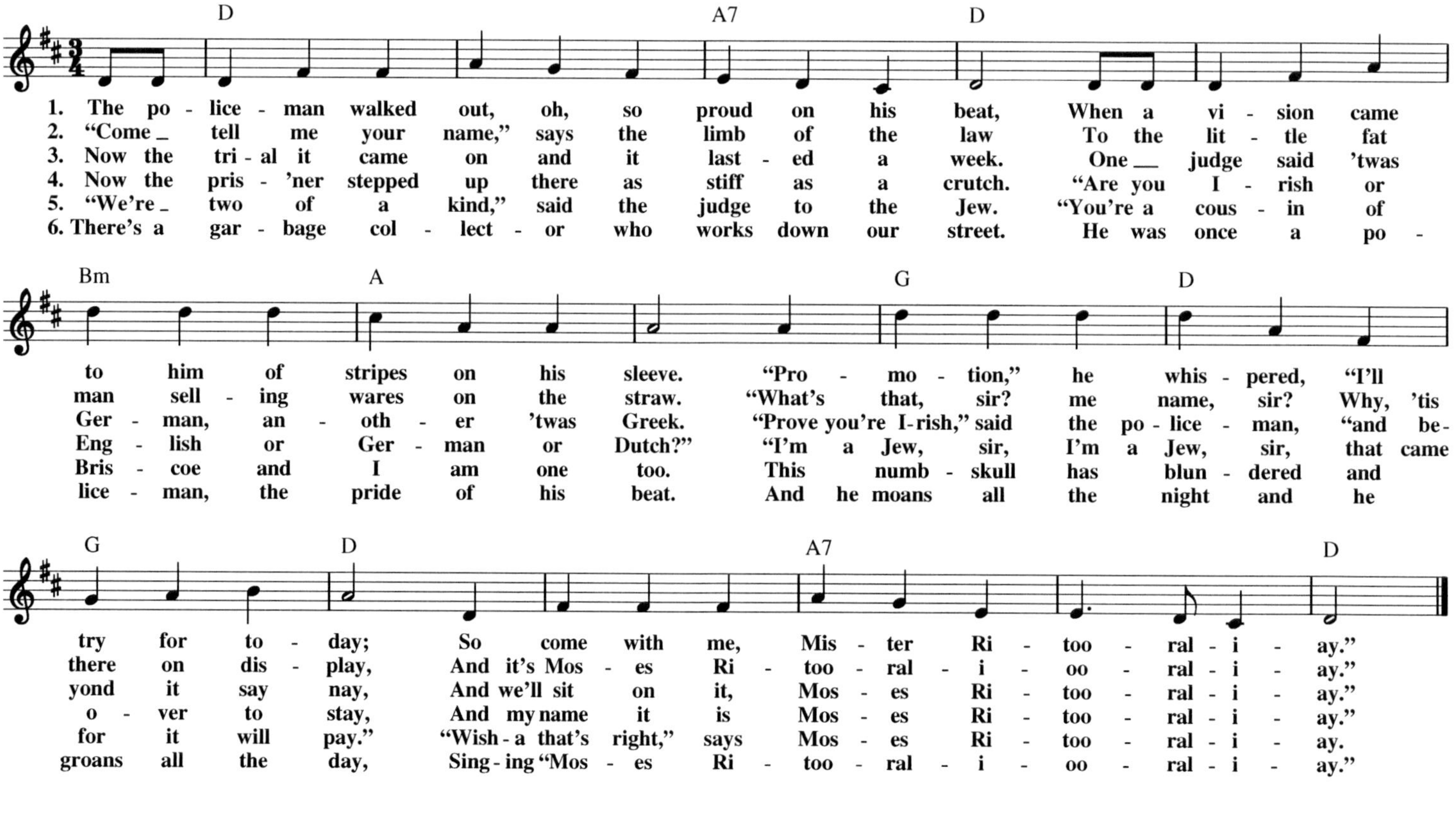

1. The po - lice - man walked out, oh, so proud on his beat, When a vi - sion came
2. "Come ___ tell me your name," says the limb of the law To the lit - tle fat
3. Now the tri - al it came on and it last - ed a week. One ___ judge said 'twas
4. Now the pris - 'ner stepped up there as stiff as a crutch. "Are you I - rish or
5. "We're ___ two of a kind," said the judge to the Jew. "You're a cous - in of
6. There's a gar - bage col - lect - or who works down our street. He was once a po -

to him of stripes on his sleeve. "Pro - mo - tion," he whis - pered, "I'll
man sell - ing wares on the straw. "What's that, sir? me name, sir? Why, 'tis
Ger - man, an - oth - er 'twas Greek. "Prove you're I - rish," said the po - lice - man, "and be -
Eng - lish or Ger - man or Dutch?" "I'm a Jew, sir, I'm a Jew, sir, that came
Bris - coe and I am one too. This numb - skull has blun - dered and
lice - man, the pride of his beat. And he moans all the night and he

try for to - day; So come with me, Mis - ter Ri - too - ral - i - ay."
there on dis - play, And it's Mos - es Ri - too - ral - i - oo - ral - i - ay."
yond it say nay, And we'll sit on it, Mos - es Ri - too - ral - i - ay."
o - ver to stay, And my name it is Mos - es Ri - too - ral - i - ay."
for it will pay." "Wish - a that's right," says Mos - es Ri - too - ral - i - ay.
groans all the day, Sing - ing "Mos - es Ri - too - ral - i - oo - ral - i - ay."

MRS. MURPHY'S CHOWDER

Irish popular song

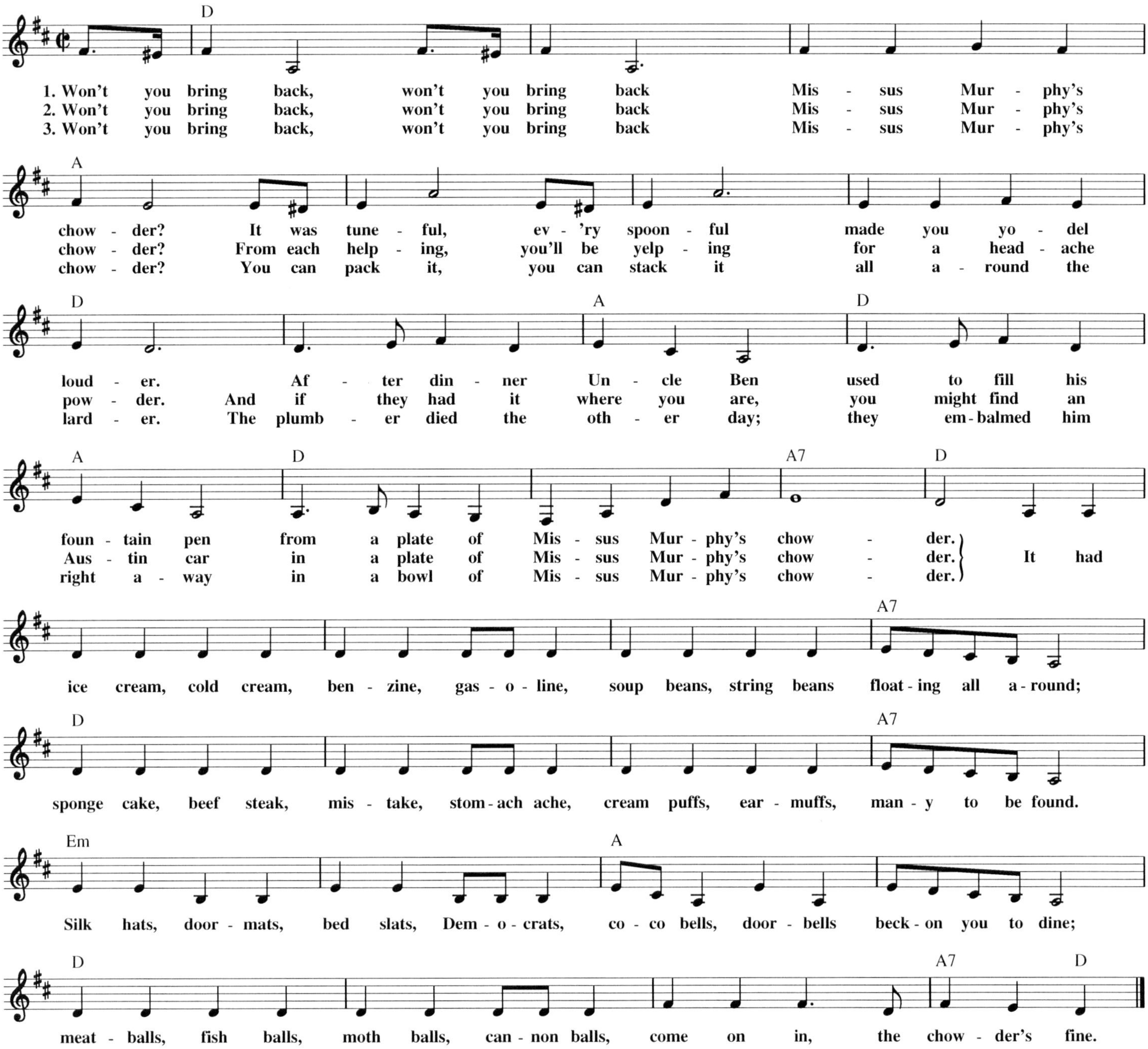

1. Won't you bring back, won't you bring back Mis - sus Mur - phy's
2. Won't you bring back, won't you bring back Mis - sus Mur - phy's
3. Won't you bring back, won't you bring back Mis - sus Mur - phy's

chow - der? It was tune - ful, ev - 'ry spoon - ful made you yo - del
chow - der? From each help - ing, you'll be yelp - ing for a head - ache
chow - der? You can pack it, you can stack it all a - round the

loud - er. Af - ter din - ner Un - cle Ben used to fill his
pow - der. And if they had it where you are, you might find an
lard - er. The plumb - er died the oth - er day; they em - balmed him

foun - tain pen from a plate of Mis - sus Mur - phy's chow - der.
Aus - tin car in a plate of Mis - sus Mur - phy's chow - der. It had
right a - way in a bowl of Mis - sus Mur - phy's chow - der.

ice cream, cold cream, ben - zine, gas - o - line, soup beans, string beans float - ing all a - round;

sponge cake, beef steak, mis - take, stom - ach ache, cream puffs, ear - muffs, man - y to be found.

Silk hats, door - mats, bed slats, Dem - o - crats, co - co bells, door - bells beck - on you to dine;

meat - balls, fish balls, moth balls, can - non balls, come on in, the chow - der's fine.

MO GHRÁ-SA MO DHIA

Irish folksong

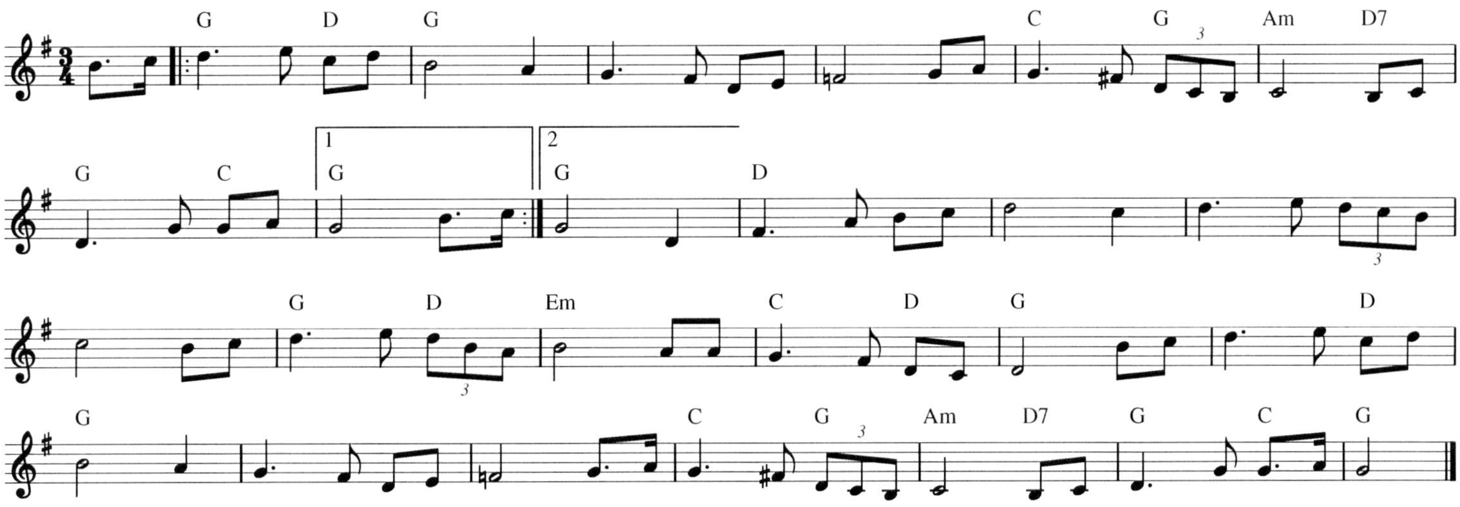

MRS. McGRATH

Irish folksong

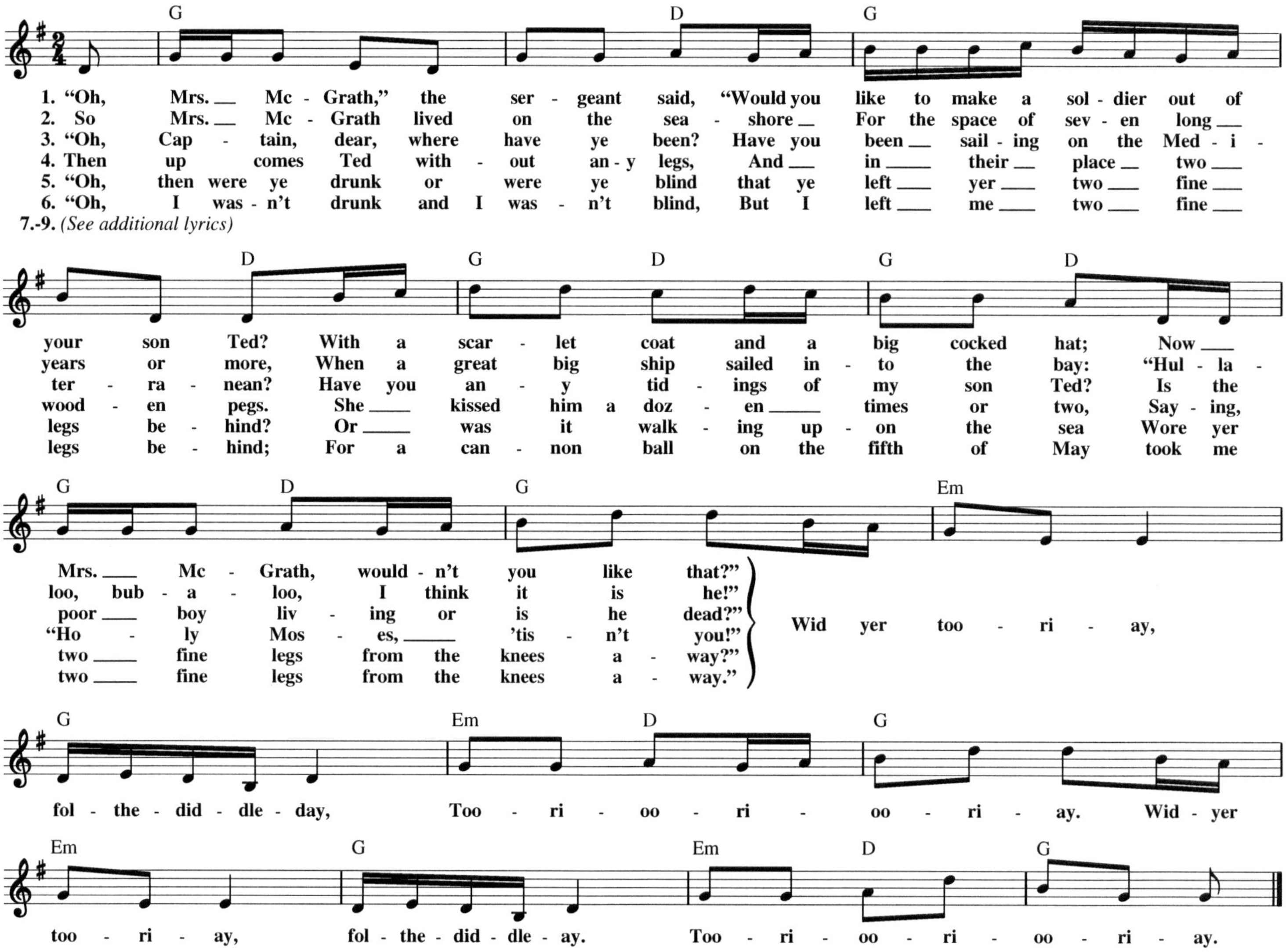

1. "Oh, Mrs. McGrath," the sergeant said, "Would you like to make a soldier out of
2. So Mrs. McGrath lived on the seashore For the space of seven long
3. "Oh, Captain, dear, where have ye been? Have you been sailing on the Medi-
4. Then up comes Ted without any legs, And in their place two
5. "Oh, then were ye drunk or were ye blind that ye left yer two fine
6. "Oh, I wasn't drunk and I wasn't blind, But I left me two fine

7.-9. *(See additional lyrics)*

your son Ted? With a scarlet coat and a big cocked hat; Now
years or more, When a great big ship sailed into the bay: "Hul-la-
terra-nean? Have you any tidings of my son Ted? Is the
wood-en pegs. She kissed him a dozen times or two, Say-ing,
legs be-hind? Or was it walk-ing up-on the sea Wore yer
legs be-hind; For a can-non ball on the fifth of May took me

Mrs. McGrath, would-n't you like that?" }
loo, bub-a-loo, I think it is he!" }
poor boy liv-ing or is he dead?" } Wid yer too-ri-ay,
"Ho-ly Mos-es, 'tis-n't you!" }
two fine legs from the knees a-way?" }
two fine legs from the knees a-way." }

fol-the-did-dle-day, Too-ri-oo-ri-oo-ri-ay. Wid yer

too-ri-ay, fol-the-did-dle-ay. Too-ri-oo-ri-oo-ri-ay.

Additional Lyrics

7. "Oh, then, Teddy me boy," the widow cried,
"Yer two fine legs were yer mama's pride.
Them stumps of a tree wouldn't do at all,
Why didn't ye run from the big cannon ball?"

8. "All foreign wars I do proclaim
Between Don John and the King of Spain.
But by Heavens I'll make them rue the time
That they swept the legs from a child of mine."

9. "Oh then, if I had ye back again,
I'd never let ye go to fight the King of Spain.
For I'd rather my Ted as he used to be
Than the King of France and his whole Navy."

MOLLY BAWN

Words and Music by
Samuel Lover

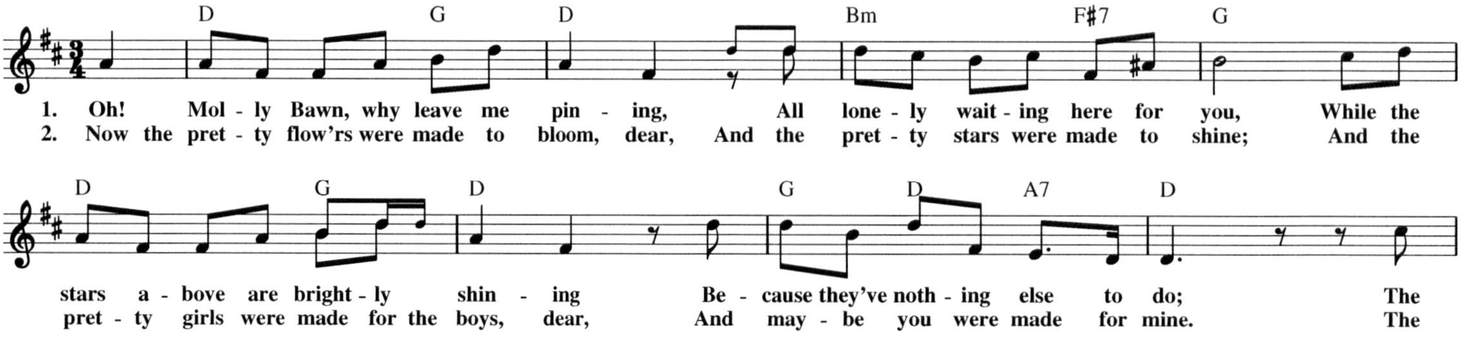

1. Oh! Mol-ly Bawn, why leave me pin-ing, All lone-ly wait-ing here for you, While the
2. Now the pret-ty flow'rs were made to bloom, dear, And the pret-ty stars were made to shine; And the

stars a-bove are bright-ly shin-ing Be-cause they've noth-ing else to do; The
pret-ty girls were made for the boys, dear, And may-be you were made for mine. The

157

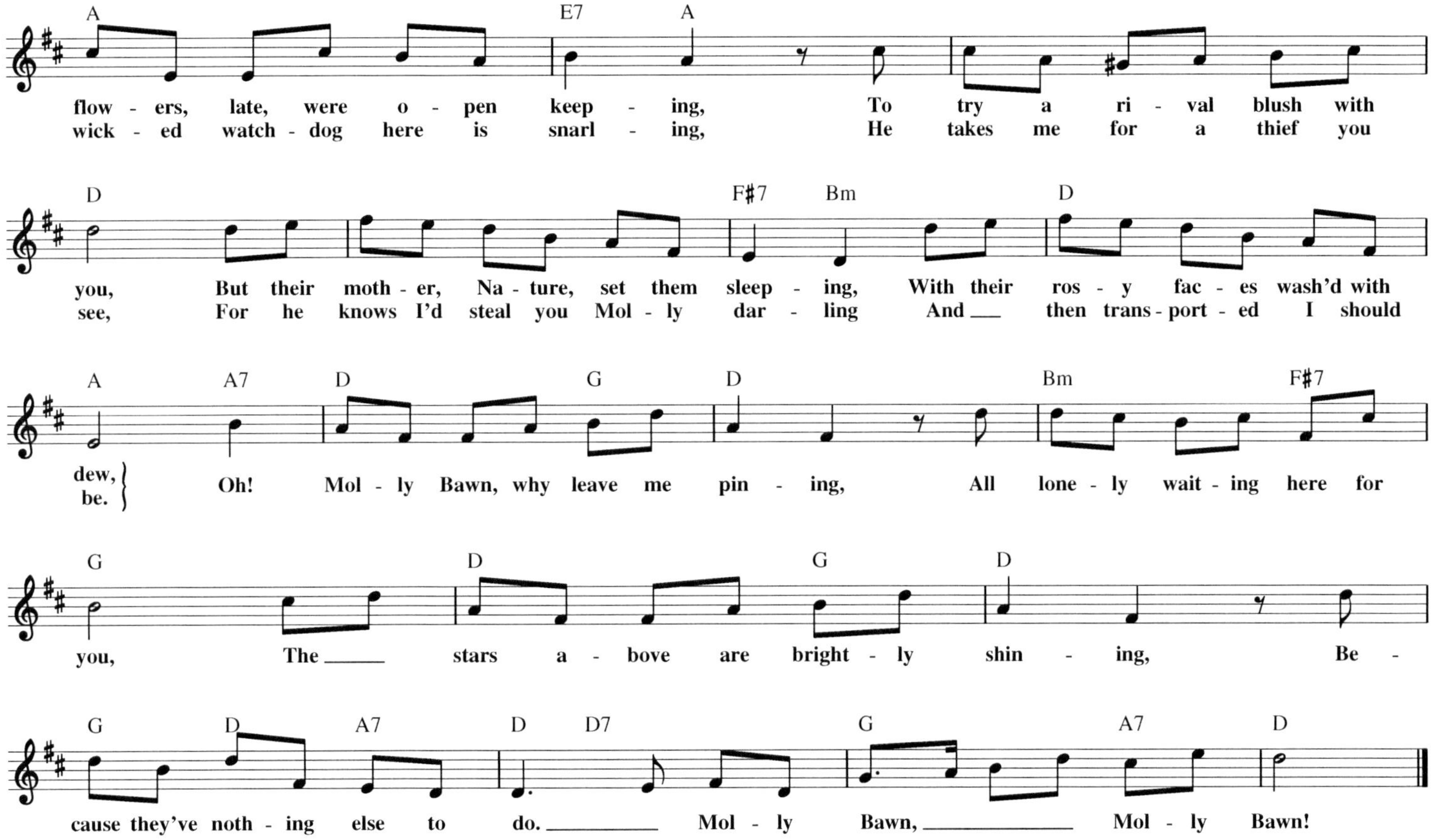

MOLLY BRANNIGAN

Irish folksong

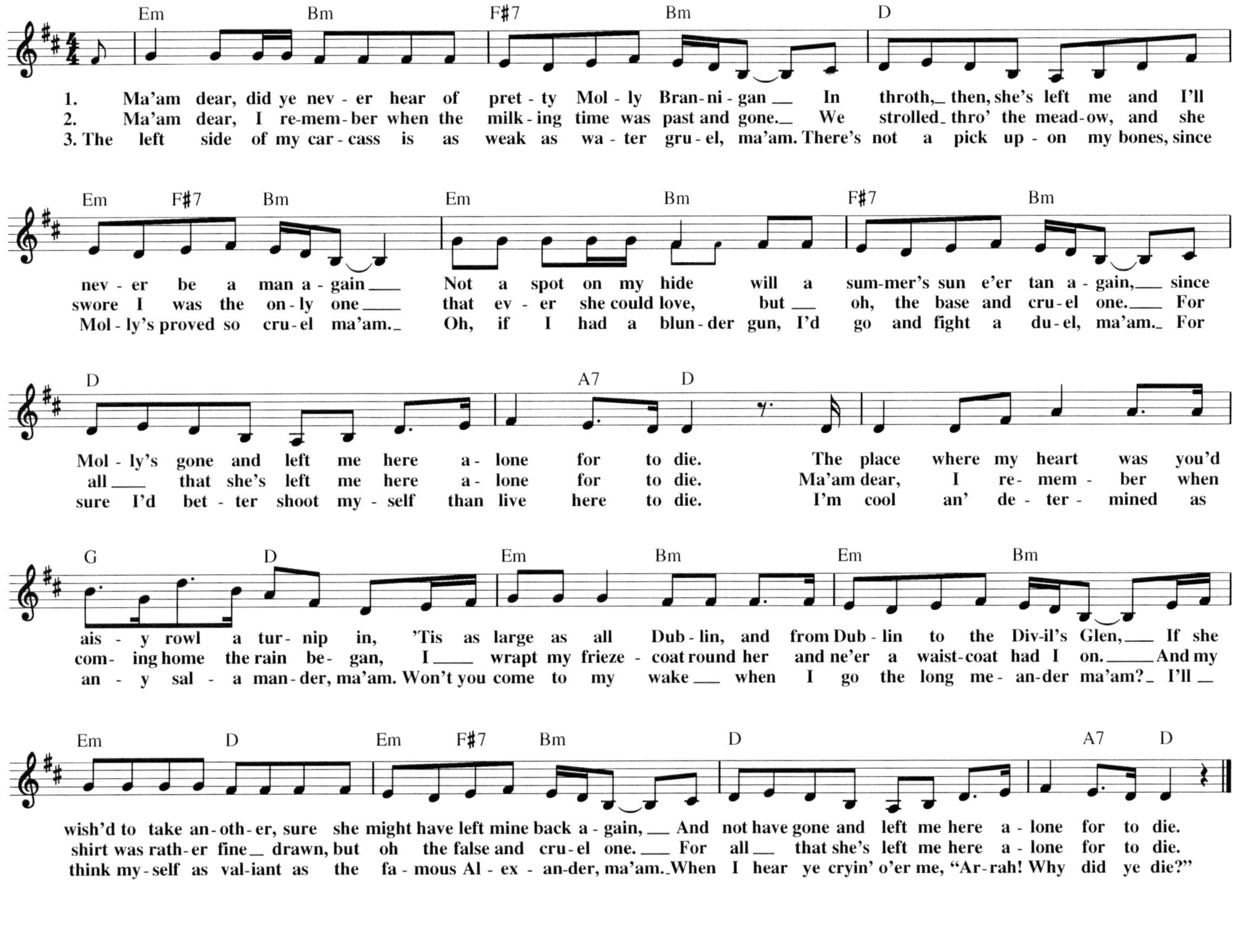

MOLLY MALONE
(Cockles and Mussels)

Irish folksong

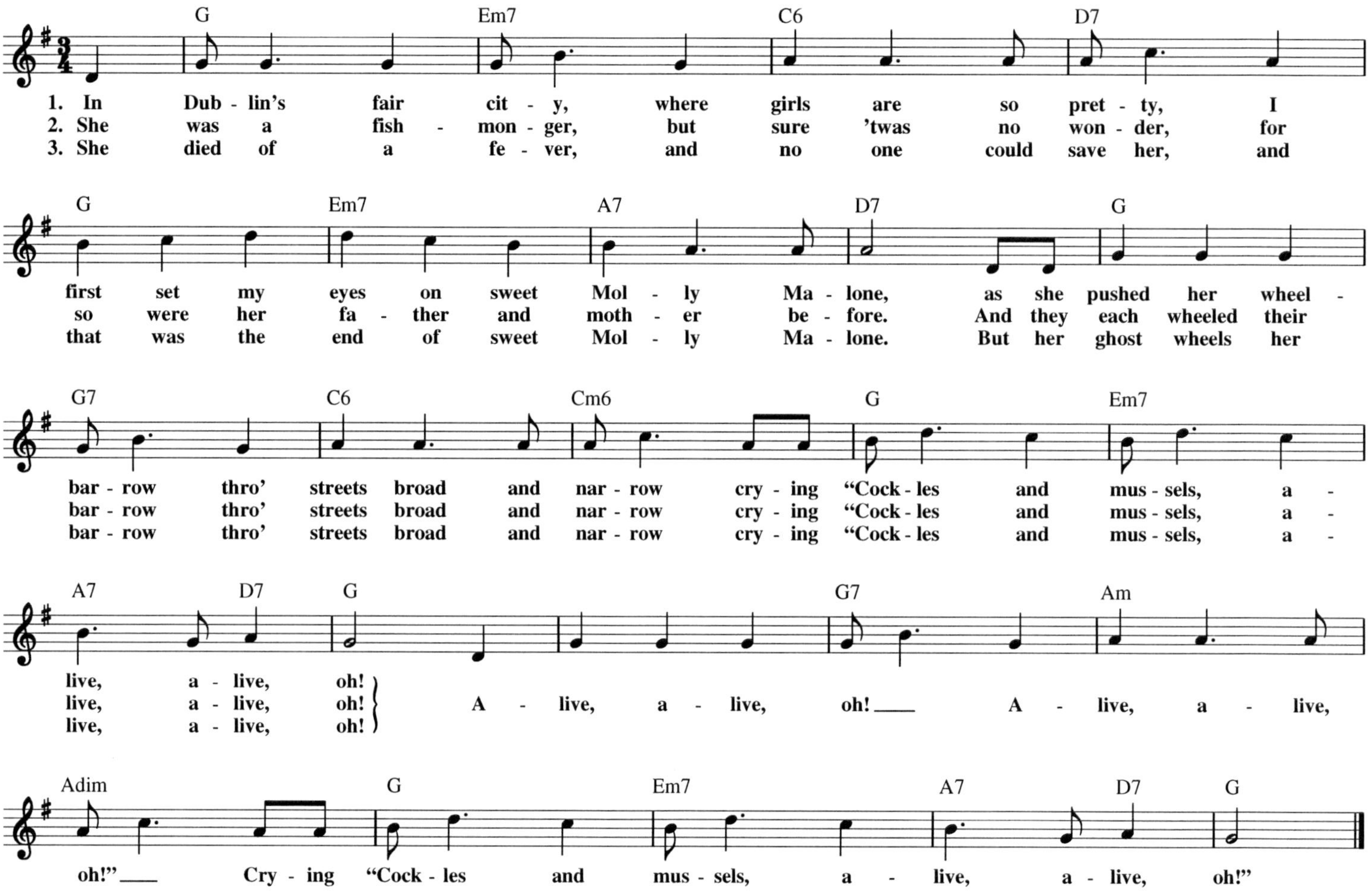

1. In Dub - lin's fair cit - y, where girls are so pret - ty, I
2. She was a fish - mon - ger, but sure 'twas no won - der, for
3. She died of a fe - ver, and no one could save her, and

first set my eyes on sweet Mol - ly Ma - lone, as she pushed her wheel -
so were her fa - ther and moth - er be - fore. And they each wheeled their
that was the end of sweet Mol - ly Ma - lone. But her ghost wheels her

bar - row thro' streets broad and nar - row cry - ing "Cock - les and mus - sels, a -
bar - row thro' streets broad and nar - row cry - ing "Cock - les and mus - sels, a -
bar - row thro' streets broad and nar - row cry - ing "Cock - les and mus - sels, a -

live, a - live, oh!
live, a - live, oh! A - live, a - live, oh! ___ A - live, a - live,
live, a - live, oh!

oh!" ___ Cry - ing "Cock - les and mus - sels, a - live, a - live, oh!"

MORGAN MAGAN

Irish folksong

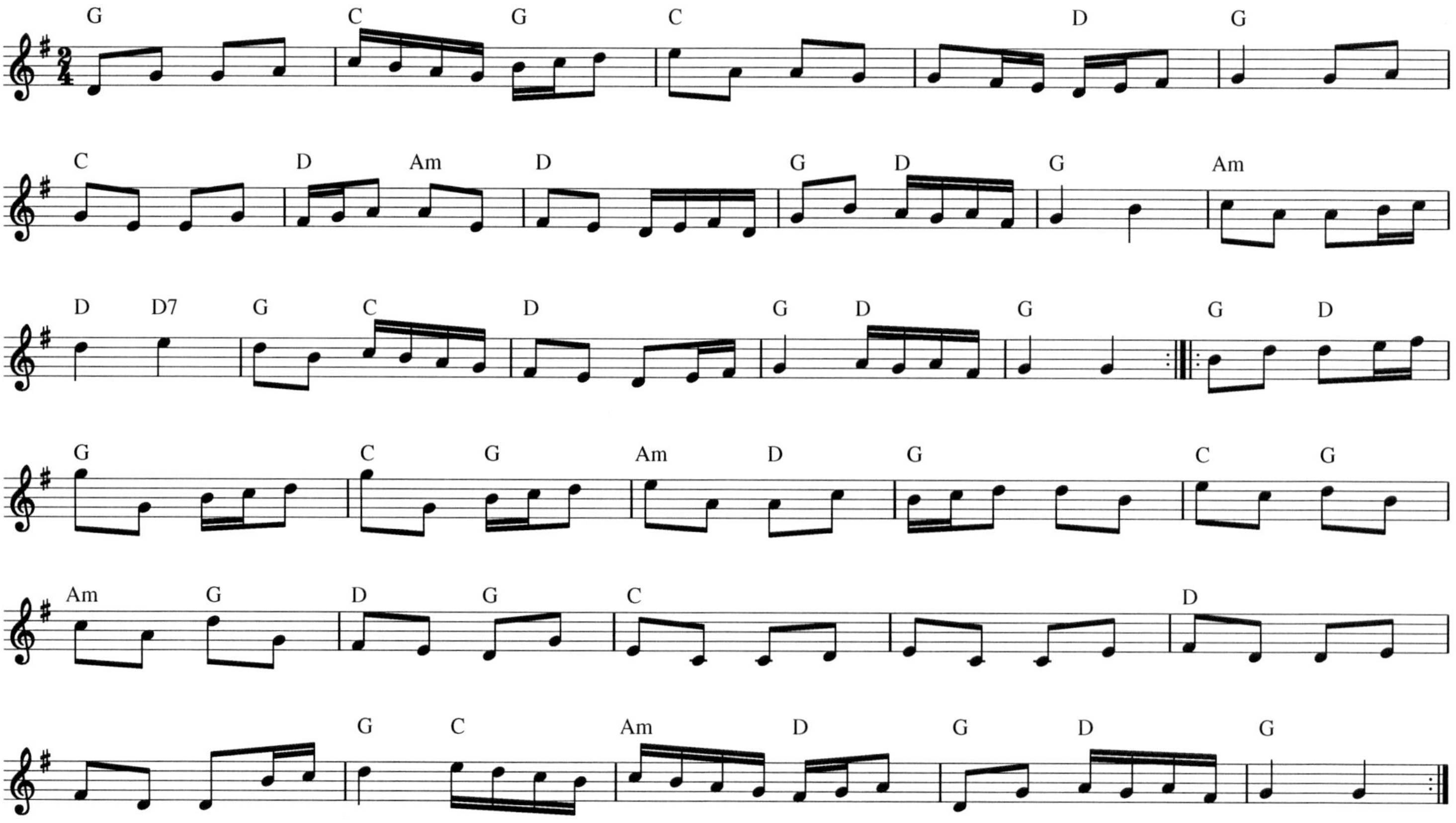

MORRISSEY AND THE RUSSIAN SAILOR

Irish folksong

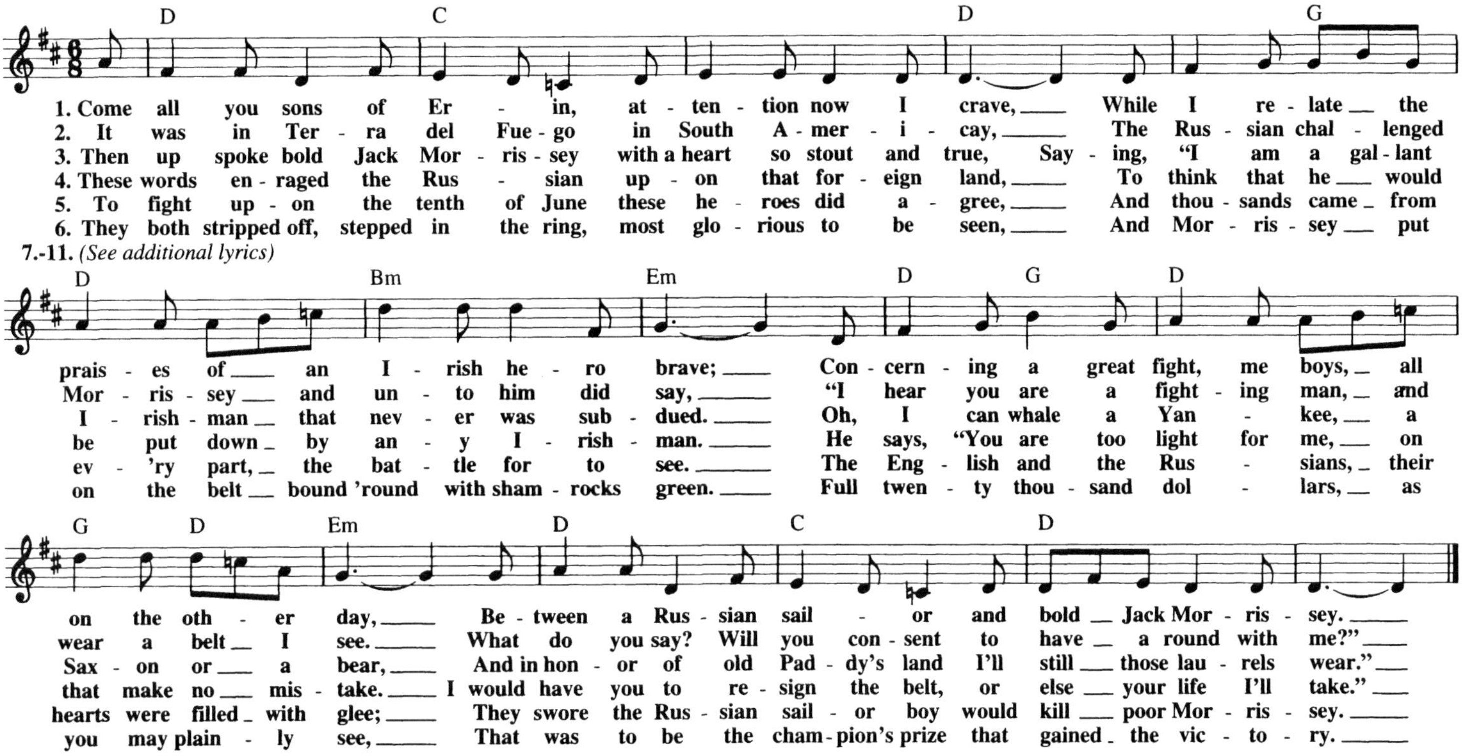

1. Come all you sons of Er - in, at - ten - tion now I crave, ___ While I re - late ___ the
2. It was in Ter - ra del Fue - go in South A - mer - i - cay, ___ The Rus - sian chal - lenged
3. Then up spoke bold Jack Mor - ris - sey with a heart so stout and true, Say - ing, "I am a gal - lant
4. These words en - raged the Rus - sian up - on that for - eign land, To think that he ___ would
5. To fight up - on the tenth of June these he - roes did a - gree, And thou - sands came ___ from
6. They both stripped off, stepped in the ring, most glo - rious to be seen, ___ And Mor - ris - sey ___ put

7.-11. *(See additional lyrics)*

prais - es of ___ an I - rish he - ro brave; ___ Con - cern - ing a great fight, me boys, ___ all
Mor - ris - sey ___ and un - to him did say, ___ "I hear you are a fight - ing man, ___ and
I - rish - man ___ that nev - er was sub - dued. ___ Oh, I can whale a Yan - kee, ___ a
be put down ___ by an - y I - rish - man. ___ He says, "You are too light for me, ___ on
ev - 'ry part, ___ the bat - tle for to see. ___ The Eng - lish and the Rus - sians, ___ their
on the belt ___ bound 'round with sham - rocks green. ___ Full twen - ty thou - sand dol - lars, ___ as

on the oth - er day, ___ Be - tween a Rus - sian sail - or and bold ___ Jack Mor - ris - sey. ___
wear a belt ___ I see. ___ What do you say? Will you con - sent to have ___ a round with me?" ___
Sax - on or ___ a bear, ___ And in hon - or of old Pad - dy's land I'll still ___ those lau - rels wear." ___
that make no ___ mis - take. ___ I would have you to re - sign the belt, or else ___ your life I'll take." ___
hearts were filled ___ with glee; ___ They swore the Rus - sian sail - or boy would kill ___ poor Mor - ris - sey. ___
you may plain - ly see, ___ That was to be the cham - pion's prize that gained ___ the vic - to - ry. ___

Additional Lyrics

7. They both shook hands, walked round the ring, commencing then to fight.
It filled each Irish heart with joy for to behold the sight.
The Russian, he floored Morrissey up to the eleventh round,
With English, Russian and Saxon cheers the valley did resound.

8. A minute and a half our hero lay before he could rise.
The word went all around the field: "He's dead," were all their cries.
But Morrissey raised manfully, and raising from the ground,
From that until the twentieth the Russian he put down.

9. Up to the thirty-seventh round 'twas fall and fall about,
Which made the burly sailor to keep a sharp lookout.
The Russian called his second and asked for a glass of wine.
Our Irish hero smiled and said, "The battle will be mine."

10. The thirty-eighth decided all. The Russian felt the smart
When Morrissey, with a fearful blow, he struck him o'er the heart.
A doctor he was called on to open up a vein.
He said it was quite useless, he would never fight again.

11. Our hero conquered Thompson, the Yankee Clipper too;
The Benicia boy and Shepherd he nobly did subdue.
So let us fill a flowing bowl and drink a health galore
To brave Jack Morrissey and Paddies evermore.

MY MARY OF THE CURLING HAIR

Words and Music by
Gerald Griffin

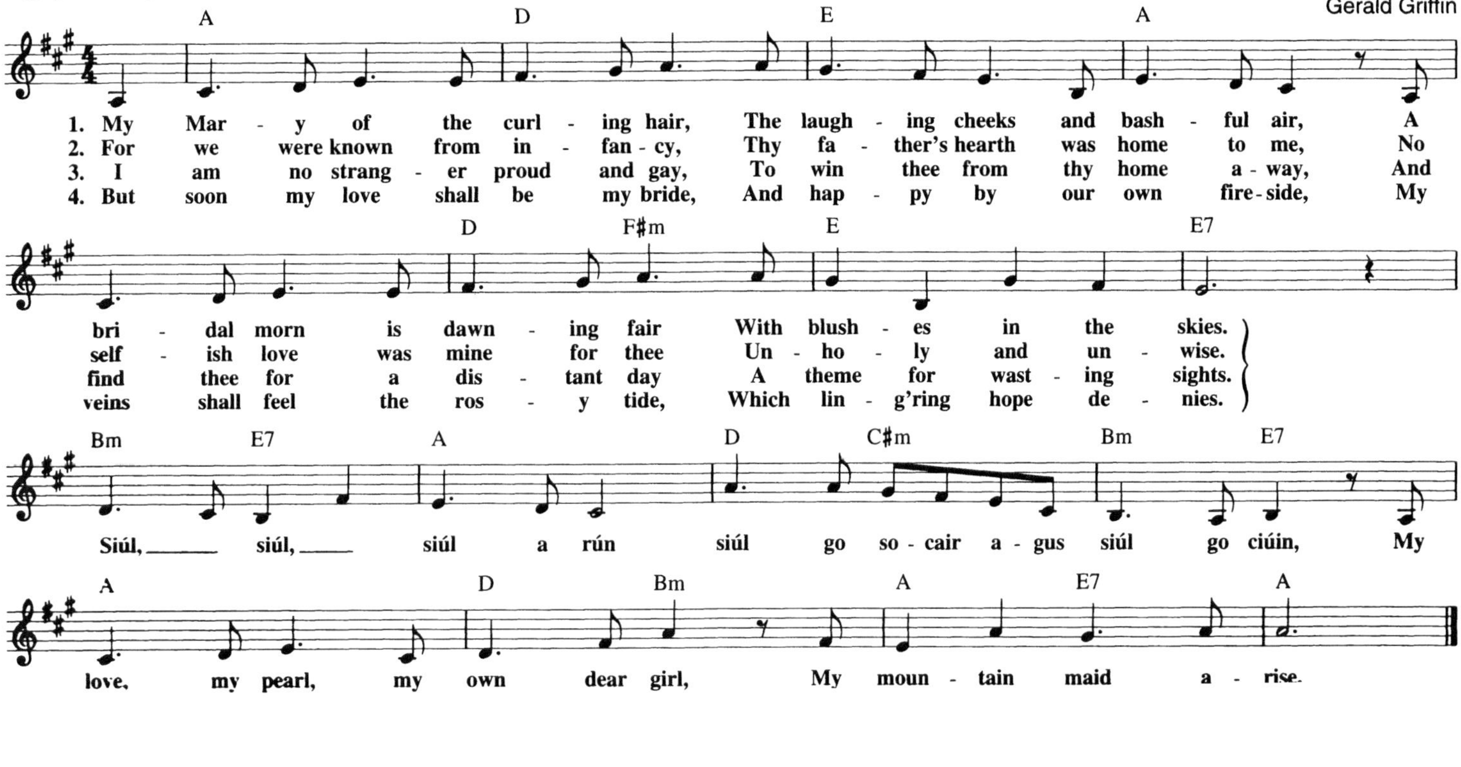

1. My Mar - y of the curl - ing hair, The laugh - ing cheeks and bash - ful air, A
2. For we were known from in - fan - cy, Thy fa - ther's hearth was home to me, No
3. I am no strang - er proud and gay, To win thee from thy home a - way, And
4. But soon my love shall be my bride, And hap - py by our own fire - side, My

bri - dal morn is dawn - ing fair With blush - es in the skies.
self - ish love was mine for thee Un - ho - ly and un - wise.
find thee for a dis - tant day A theme for wast - ing sights.
veins shall feel the ros - y tide, Which lin - g'ring hope de - nies.

Siúl, ___ siúl, ___ siúl a rún siúl go so - cair a - gus siúl go ciúin, My

love, my pearl, my own dear girl, My moun - tain maid a - rise.

MOTHER MACHREE

Words by Rida Johnson Young
Music by Chauncey Olcott and Ernest R. Ball

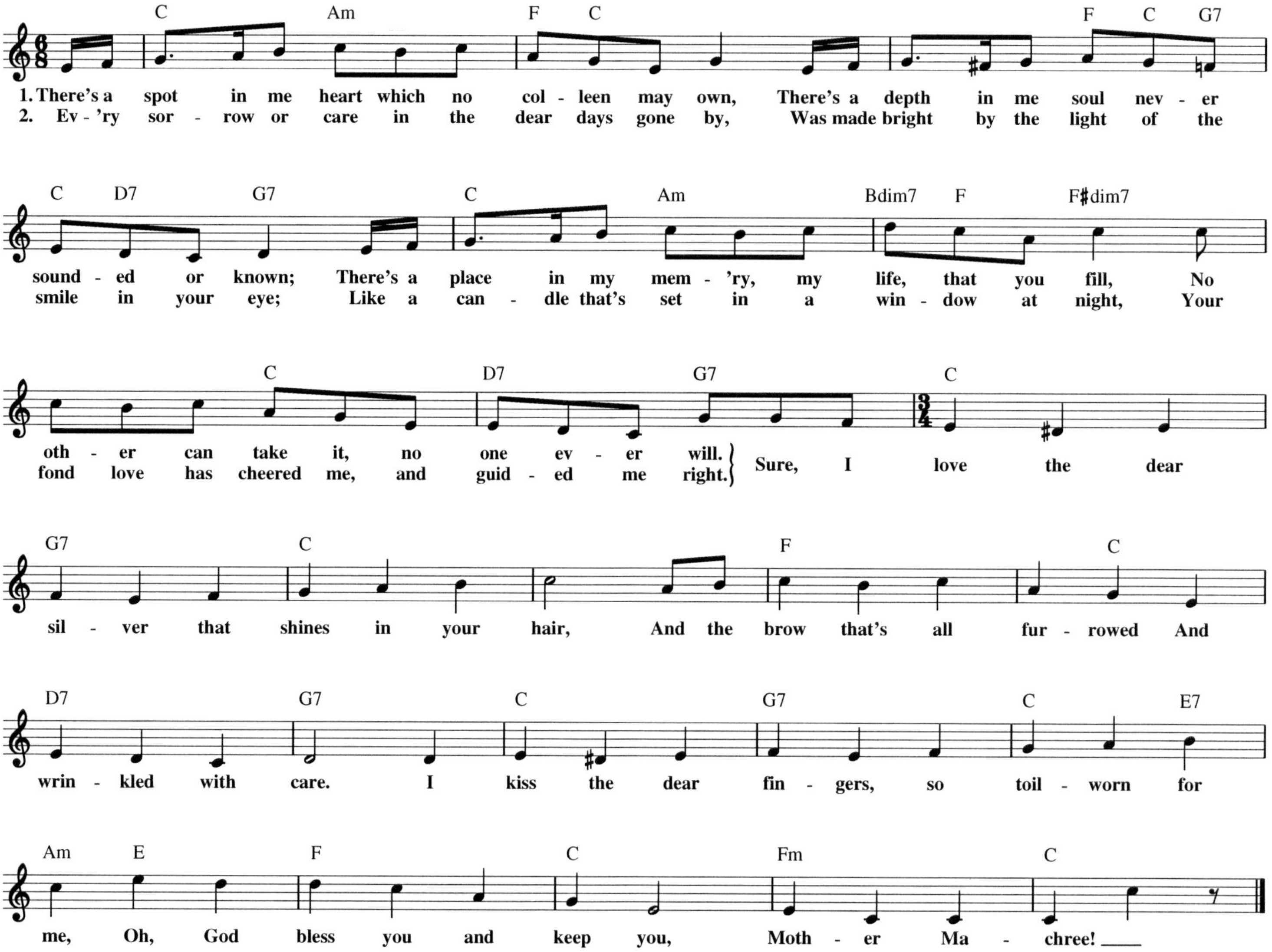

1. There's a spot in me heart which no col-leen may own, There's a depth in me soul nev-er
2. Ev-'ry sor-row or care in the dear days gone by, Was made bright by the light of the

sound-ed or known; There's a place in my mem-'ry, my life, that you fill, No
smile in your eye; Like a can-dle that's set in a win-dow at night, Your

oth-er can take it, no one ev-er will.} Sure, I love the dear
fond love has cheered me, and guid-ed me right.}

sil-ver that shines in your hair, And the brow that's all fur-rowed And

wrin-kled with care. I kiss the dear fin-gers, so toil-worn for

me, Oh, God bless you and keep you, Moth-er Ma-chree! ___

MOUNTAINS OF MOURNE

Irish folksong
Words by Percy French

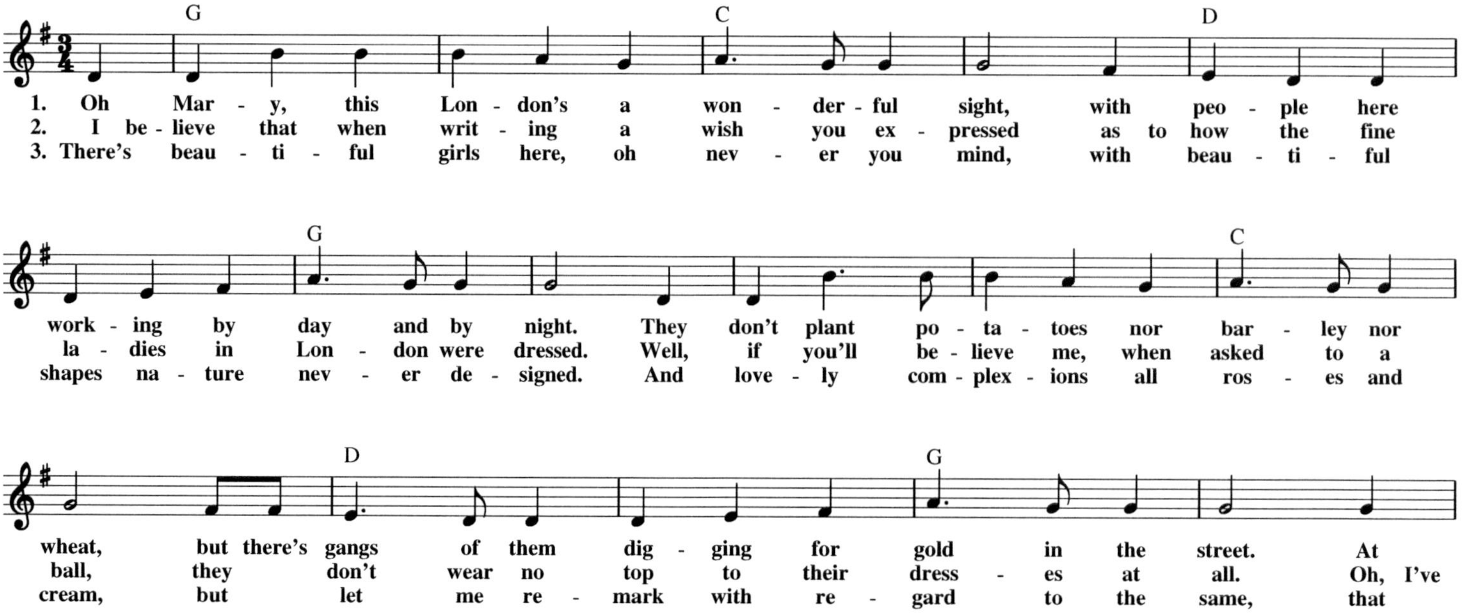

1. Oh Mar-y, this Lon-don's a won-der-ful sight, with peo-ple here
2. I be-lieve that when writ-ing a wish you ex-pressed as to how the fine
3. There's beau-ti-ful girls here, oh nev-er you mind, with beau-ti-ful

work-ing by day and by night. They don't plant po-ta-toes nor bar-ley nor
la-dies in Lon-don were dressed. Well, if you'll be-lieve me, when asked to a
shapes na-ture nev-er de-signed. And love-ly com-plex-ions all ros-es and

wheat, but there's gangs of them dig-ging for gold in the street. At
ball, they don't wear no top to their dress-es at all. Oh, I've
cream, but let me re-mark with re-gard to the same, that

THE MULLIGAN GUARD

Words by Edward Harrigan
Music by David Braham

MULL FISHER'S LOVE SONG
(O Mhairead Og!)

Folksong from the Hebrides

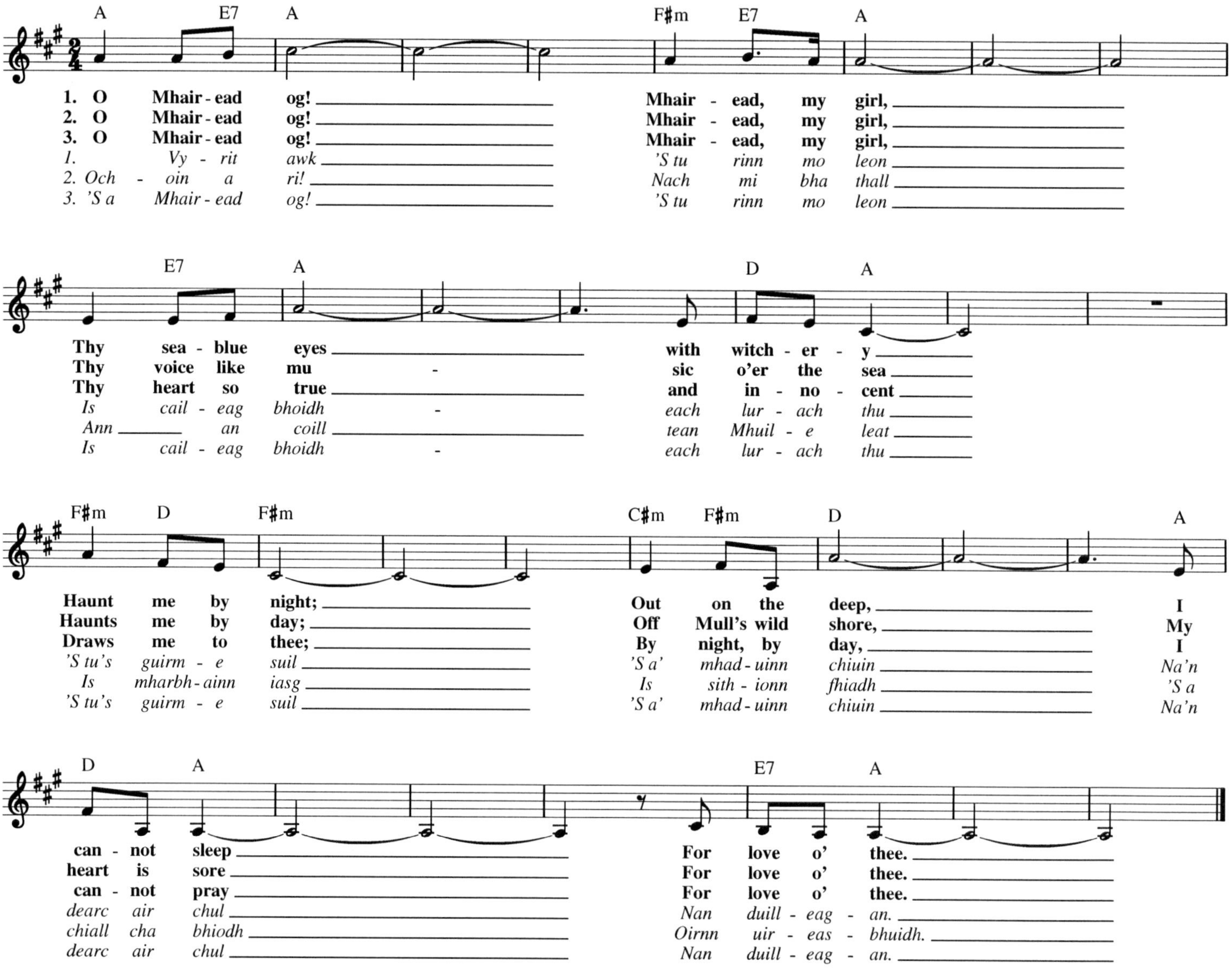

MY BONNIE LIES OVER THE OCEAN

Scottish folksong

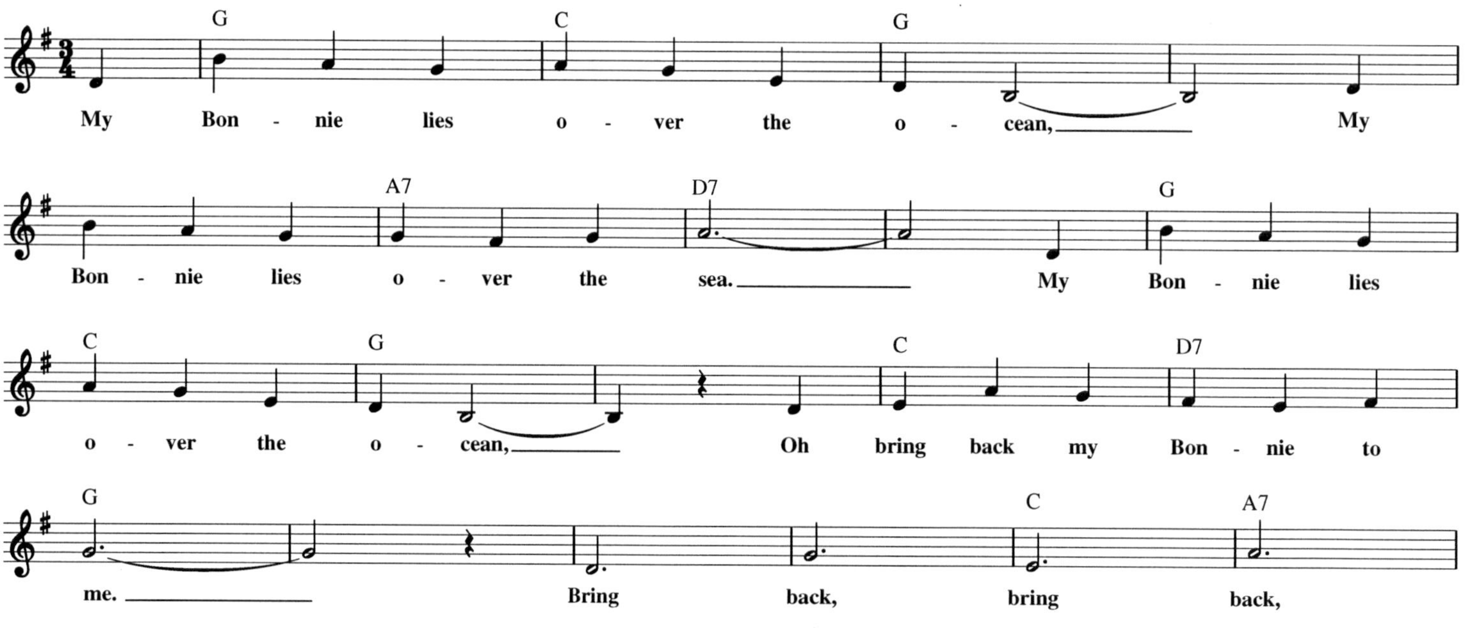

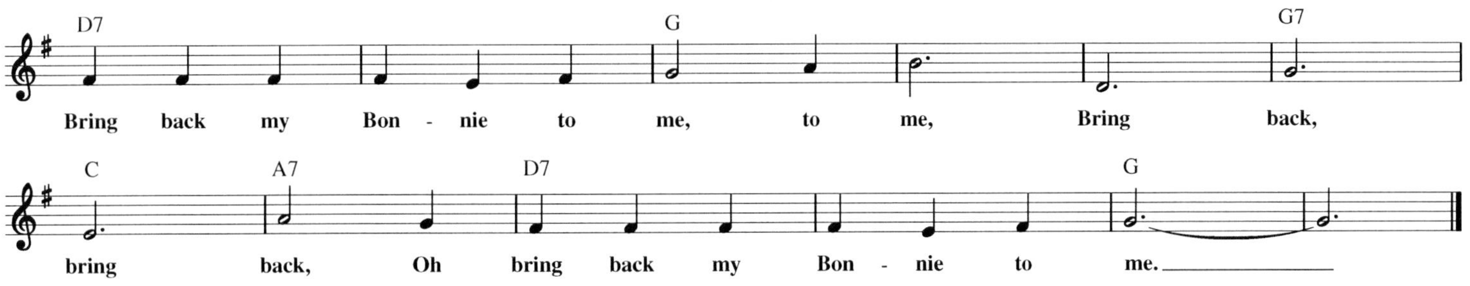

MY WILD IRISH ROSE

Words and Music by
Chauncey Olcott

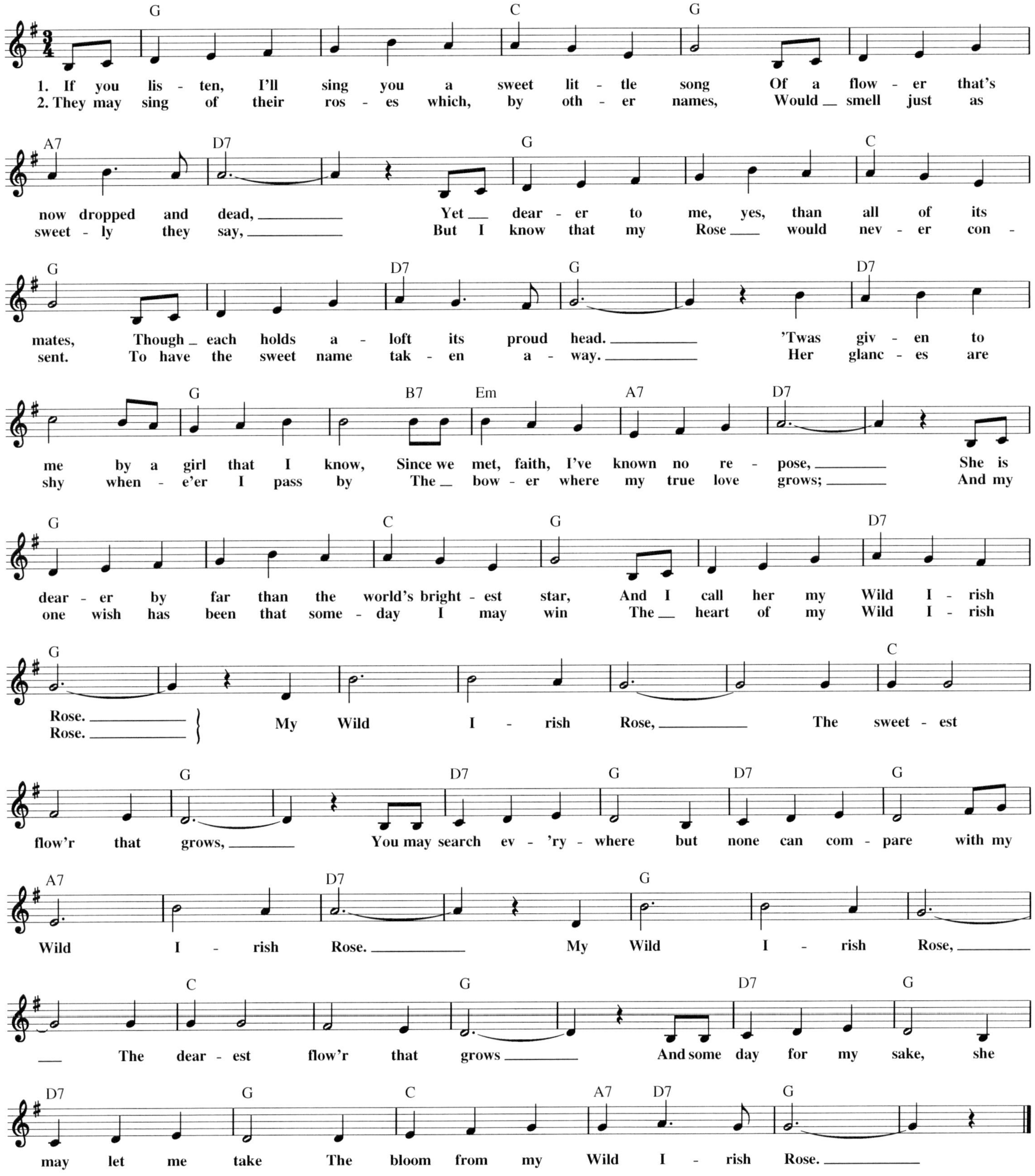

MY LUVE IS LIKE A RED, RED ROSE

Scottish folksong
Words by Robert Burns

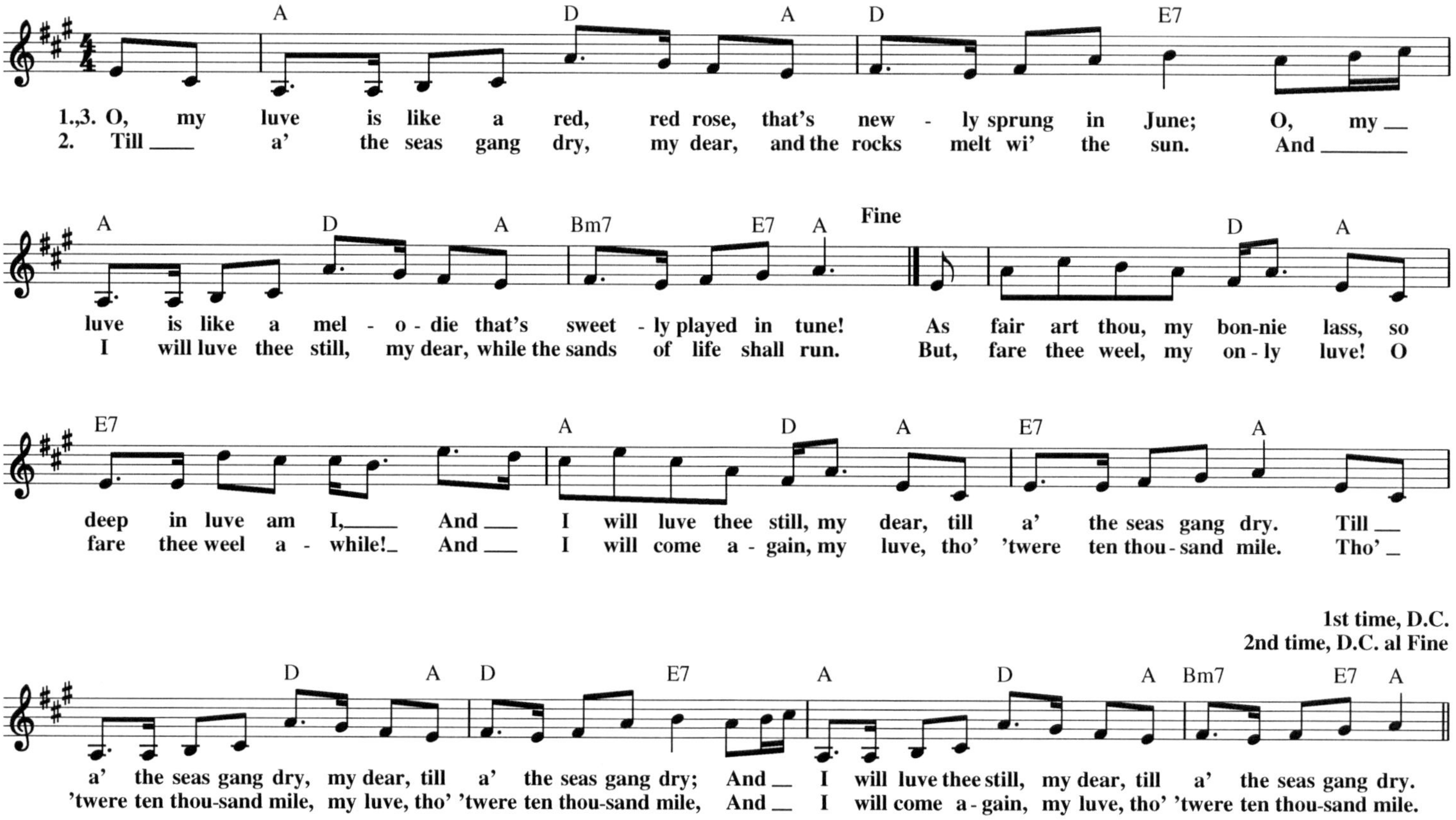

MY NAME IS KELLY
(But I'm Livin' the Life of Reilly)

Words and Music by Harry Pease,
Edward G. Nelson and Neuman Fier

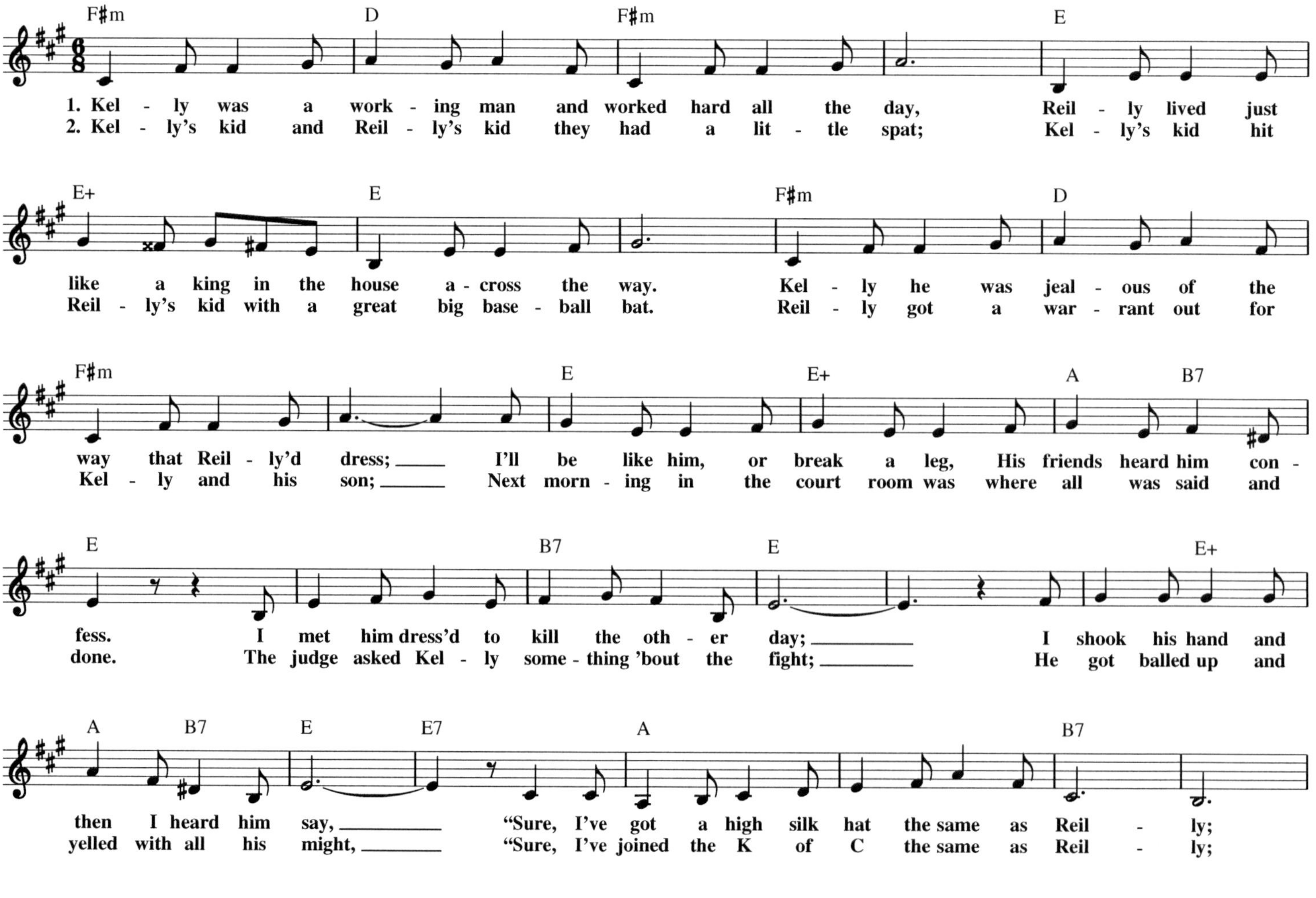

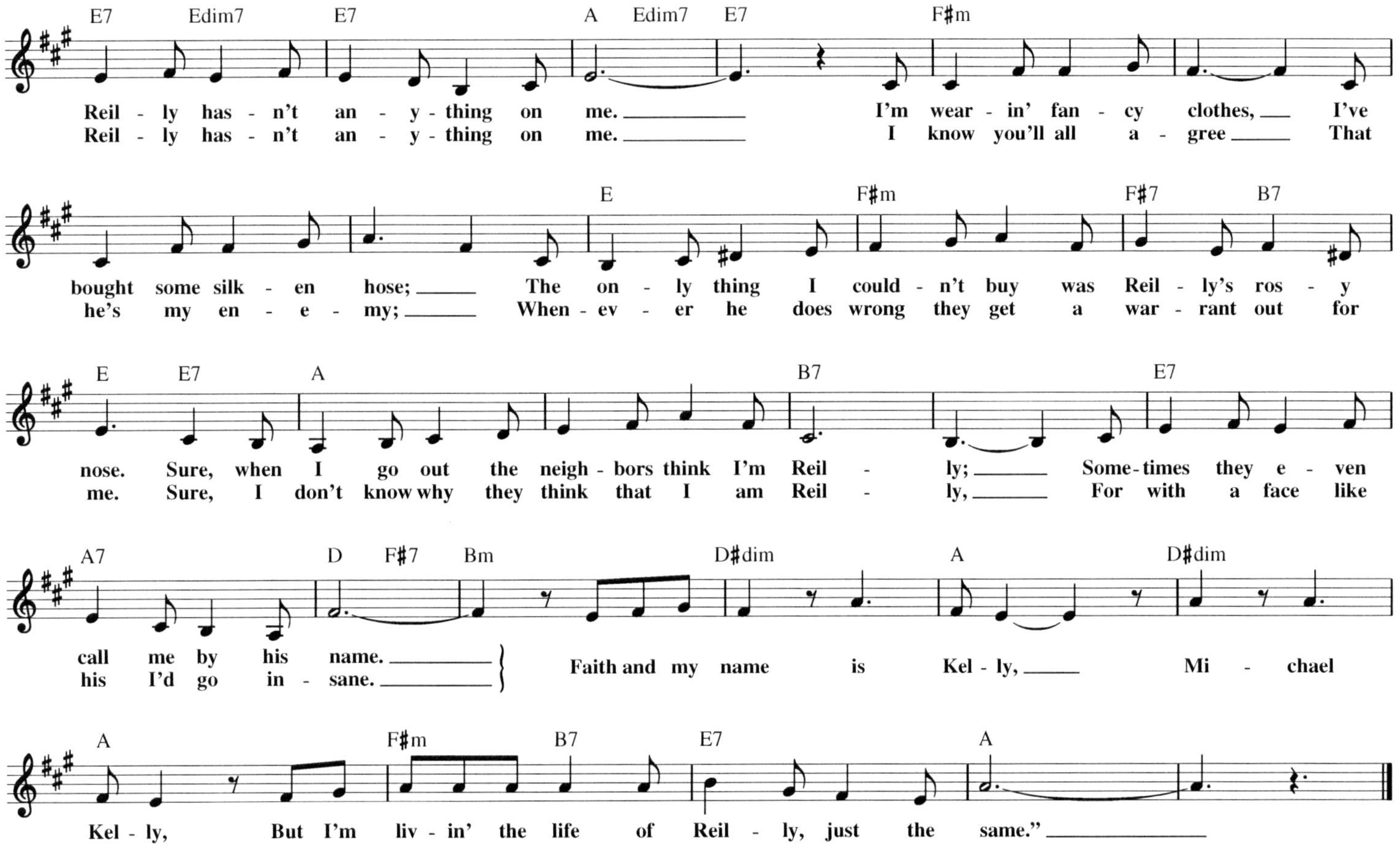
E7 Edim7 E7 A Edim7 E7 F#m
Reil - ly has - n't an - y - thing on me. I'm wear - in' fan - cy clothes, I've
Reil - ly has - n't an - y - thing on me. I know you'll all a - gree That
E F#m F#7 B7
bought some silk - en hose; The on - ly thing I could - n't buy was Reil - ly's ros - y
he's my en - e - my; When - ev - er he does wrong they get a war - rant out for
E E7 A B7 E7
nose. Sure, when I go out the neigh - bors think I'm Reil - ly; Some - times they e - ven
me. Sure, I don't know why they think that I am Reil - ly, For with a face like
A7 D F#7 Bm D#dim A D#dim
call me by his name.
his I'd go in - sane.
Faith and my name is Kel - ly, Mi - chael
A F#m B7 E7 A
Kel - ly, But I'm liv - in' the life of Reil - ly, just the same."

THE NEXT MARKET DAY

Irish folksong

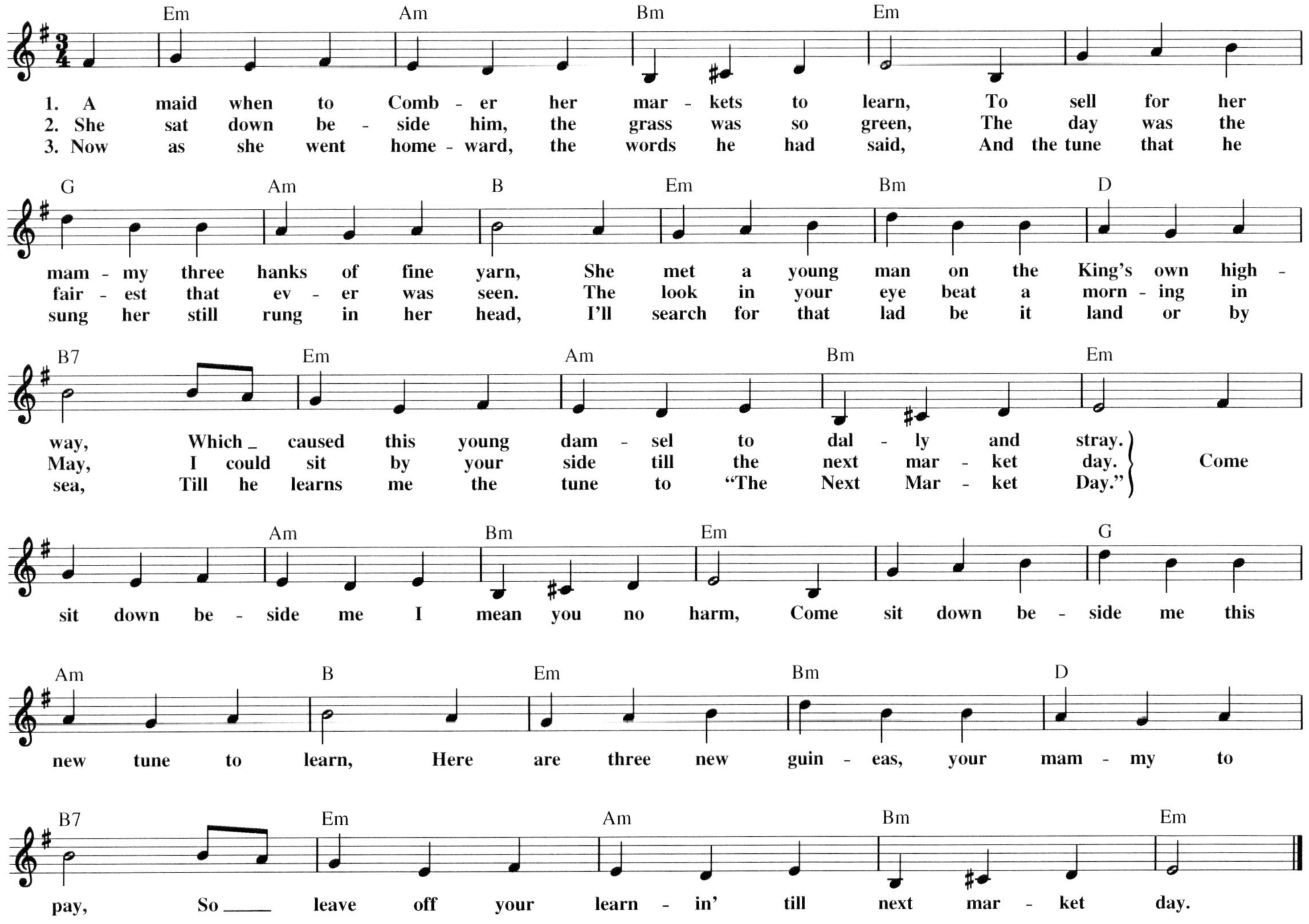
Em Am Bm Em
1. A maid when to Comb - er her mar - kets to learn, To sell for her
2. She sat down be - side him, the grass was so green, The day was the
3. Now as she went home - ward, the words he had said, And the tune that he
G Am B Em Bm D
mam - my three hanks of fine yarn, She met a young man on the King's own high -
fair - est that ev - er was seen. The look in your eye beat a morn - ing in
sung her still rung in her head, I'll search for that lad be it land or by
B7 Em Am Bm Em
way, Which caused this young dam - sel to dal - ly and stray.
May, I could sit by your side till the next mar - ket day.
sea, Till he learns me the tune to "The Next Mar - ket Day."
Come
Am Bm Em G
sit down be - side me I mean you no harm, Come sit down be - side me this
Am B Em Bm D
new tune to learn, Here are three new guin - eas, your mam - my to
B7 Em Am Bm Em
pay, So leave off your learn - in' till next mar - ket day.

NELL FLAHERTY'S DRAKE

Irish folksong

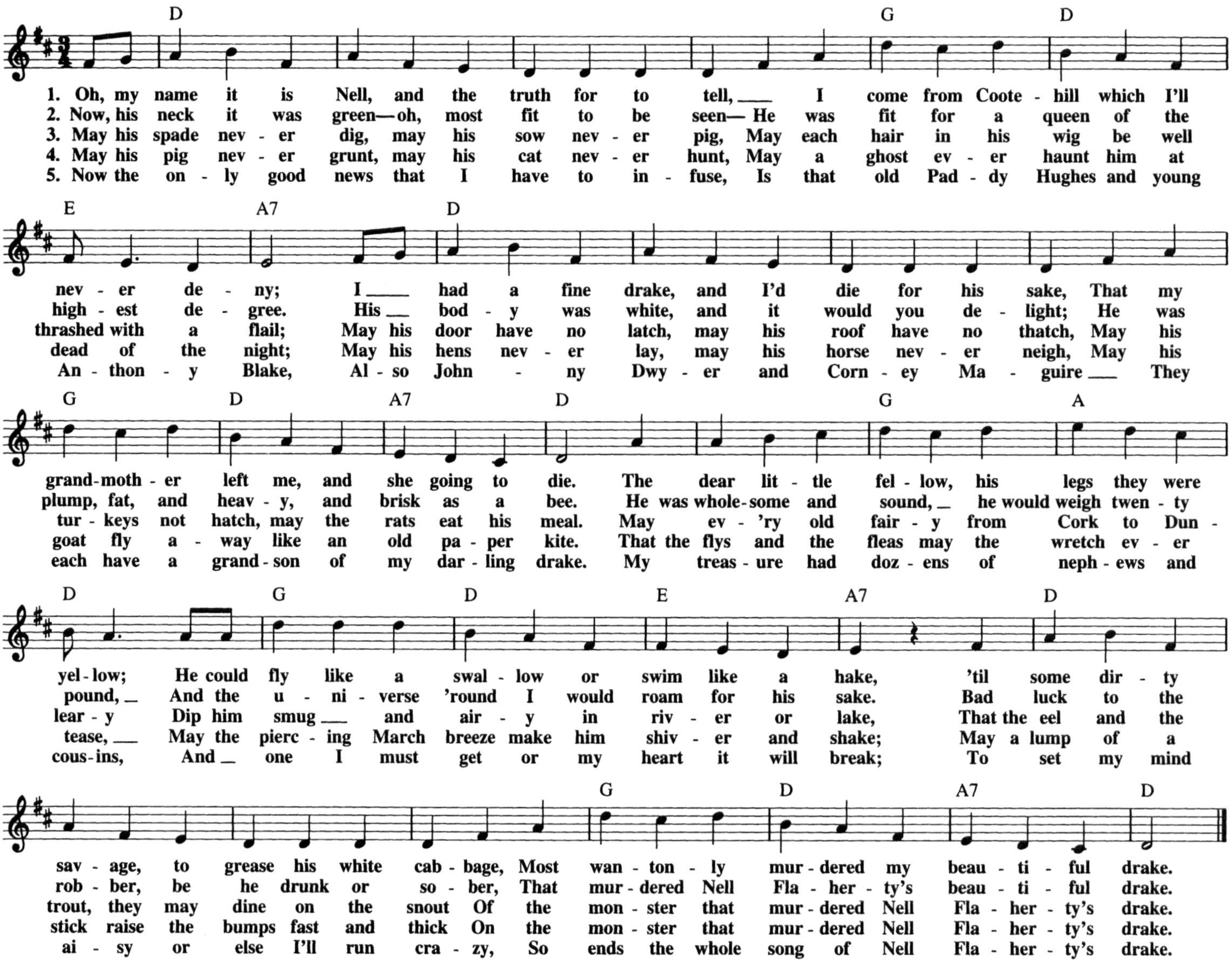

1. Oh, my name it is Nell, and the truth for to tell, ___ I come from Coote - hill which I'll
2. Now, his neck it was green—oh, most fit to be seen— He was fit for a queen of the
3. May his spade nev - er dig, may his sow nev - er pig, May each hair in his wig be well
4. May his pig nev - er grunt, may his cat nev - er hunt, May a ghost ev - er haunt him at
5. Now the on - ly good news that I have to in - fuse, Is that old Pad - dy Hughes and young

nev - er de - ny; I ___ had a fine drake, and I'd die for his sake, That my
high - est de - gree. His ___ bod - y was white, and it would you de - light; He was
thrashed with a flail; May his door have no latch, may his roof have no thatch, May his
dead of the night; May his hens nev - er lay, may his horse nev - er neigh, May his
An - thon - y Blake, Al - so John - ny Dwy - er and Corn - ey Ma - guire ___ They

grand-moth - er left me, and she going to die. The dear lit - tle fel - low, his legs they were
plump, fat, and heav - y, and brisk as a bee. He was whole-some and sound, ___ he would weigh twen - ty
tur - keys not hatch, may the rats eat his meal. May ev - 'ry old fair - y from Cork to Dun -
goat fly a - way like an old pa - per kite. That the flys and the fleas may the wretch ev - er
each have a grand-son of my dar - ling drake. My treas - ure had doz - ens of neph - ews and

yel - low; He could fly like a swal - low or swim like a hake, 'til some dir - ty
pound, ___ And the u - ni - verse 'round I would roam for his sake. Bad luck to the
lear - y Dip him smug ___ and air - y in riv - er or lake, That the eel and the
tease, ___ May the pierc - ing March breeze make him shiv - er and shake; May a lump of a
cous - ins, And ___ one I must get or my heart it will break; To set my mind

sav - age, to grease his white cab - bage, Most wan - ton - ly mur - dered my beau - ti - ful drake.
rob - ber, be he drunk or so - ber, That mur - dered Nell Fla - her - ty's beau - ti - ful drake.
trout, they may dine on the snout Of the mon - ster that mur - dered Nell Fla - her - ty's drake.
stick raise the bumps fast and thick On the mon - ster that mur - dered Nell Fla - her - ty's drake.
ai - sy or else I'll run cra - zy, So ends the whole song of Nell Fla - her - ty's drake.

NO IRISH NEED APPLY

Irish folksong

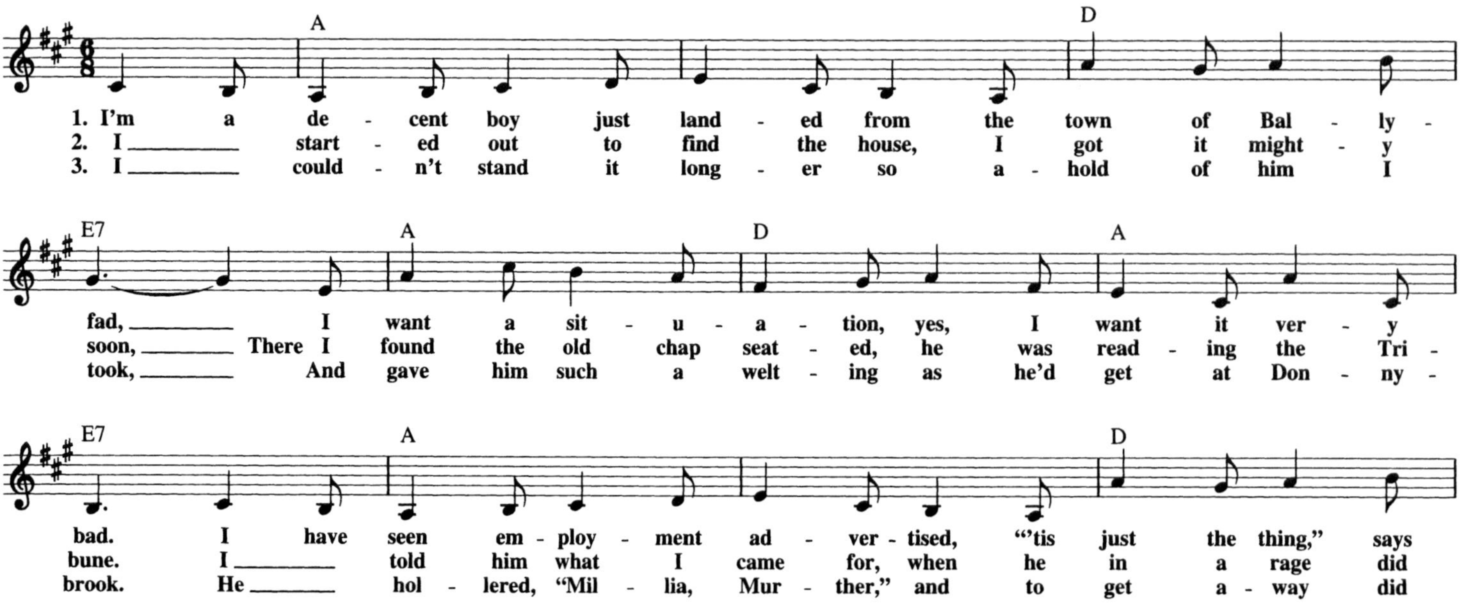

1. I'm a de - cent boy just land - ed from the town of Bal - ly -
2. I ___ start - ed out to find the house, I got it might - y
3. I ___ could - n't stand it long - er so a - hold of him I

fad, _____ I want a sit - u - a - tion, yes, I want it ver - y
soon, _____ There I found the old chap seat - ed, he was read - ing the Tri -
took, _____ And gave him such a welt - ing as he'd get at Don - ny -

bad. I have seen em - ploy - ment ad - ver - tised, "tis just the thing," says
bune. I ___ told him what I came for, when he in a rage did
brook. He ___ hol - lered, "Mil - lia, Mur - ther," and to get a - way did

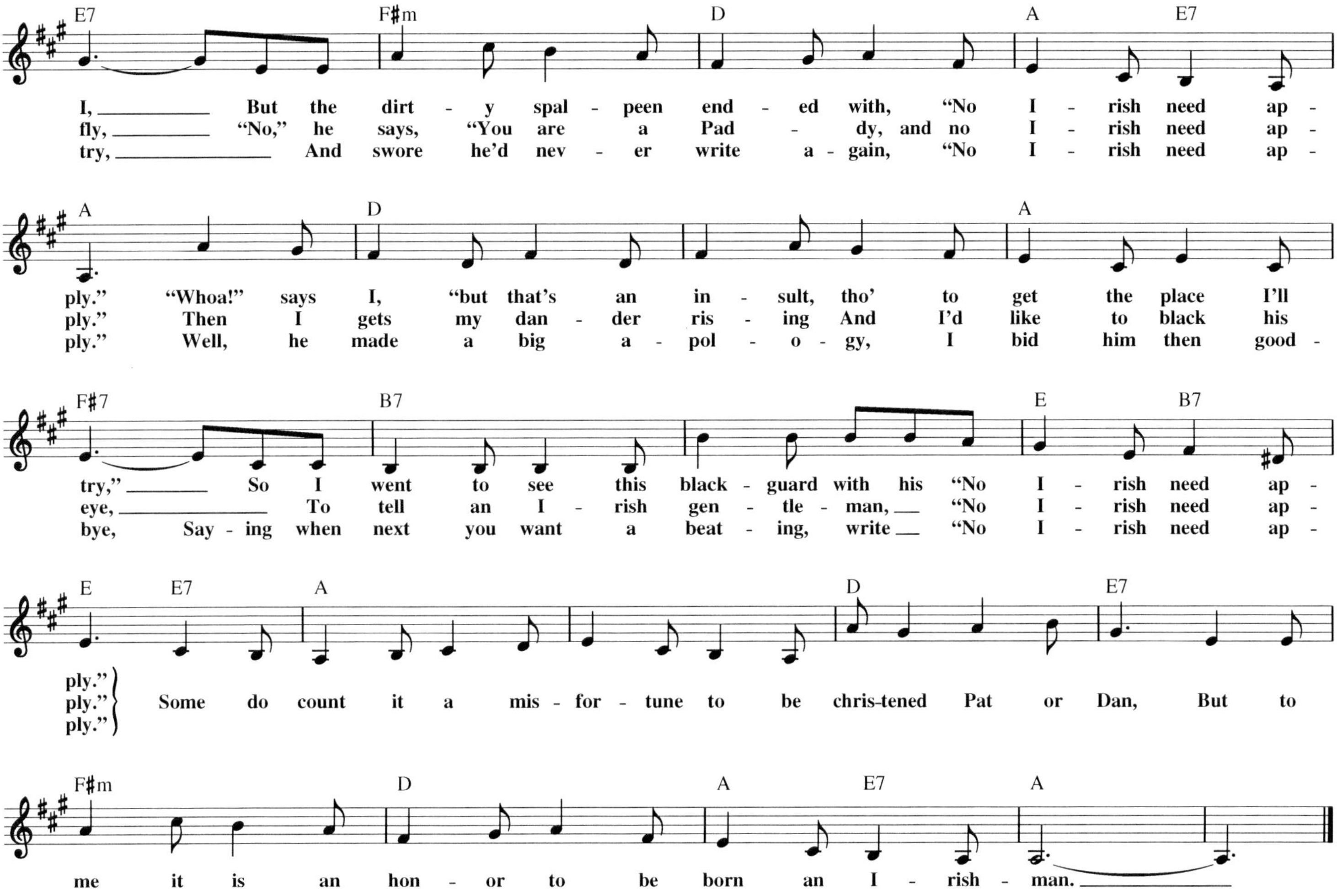

I, _____ But the dirt - y spal - peen end - ed with, "No I - rish need ap -
fly, _____ "No," he says, "You are a Pad - dy, and no I - rish need ap -
try, _____ And swore he'd nev - er write a - gain, "No I - rish need ap -

ply." "Whoa!" says I, "but that's an in - sult, tho' to get the place I'll
ply." Then I gets my dan - der ris - ing And I'd like to black his
ply." Well, he made a big a - pol - o - gy, I bid him then good -

try," _____ So I went to see this black - guard with his "No I - rish need ap -
eye, _____ To tell an I - rish gen - tle - man, __ "No I - rish need ap -
bye, Say - ing when next you want a beat - ing, write __ "No I - rish need ap -

ply."
ply." } Some do count it a mis - for - tune to be chris-tened Pat or Dan, But to
ply."

me it is an hon - or to be born an I - rish - man. _____

NONE CAN LOVE LIKE AN IRISHMAN

Irish folksong

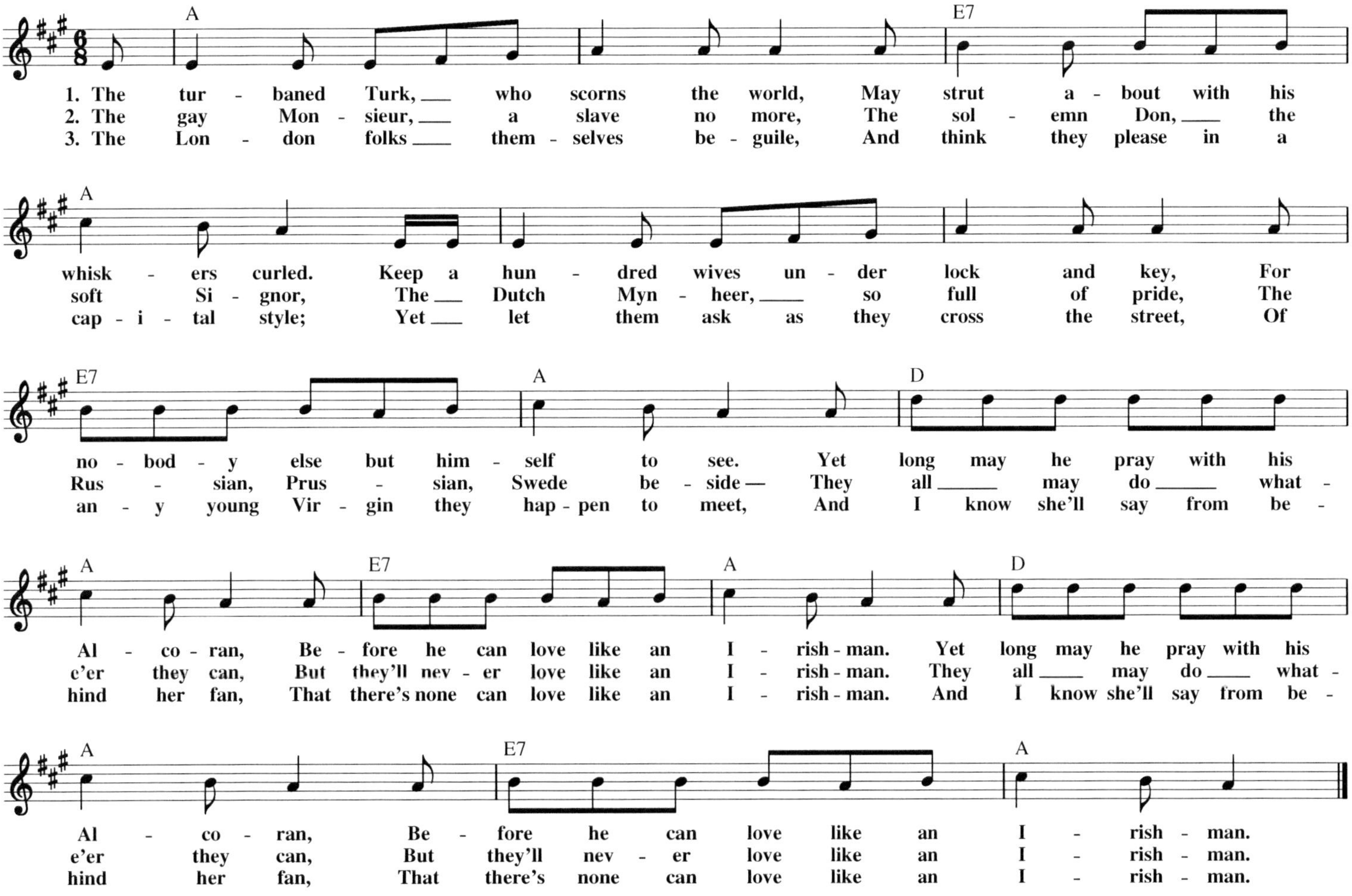

1. The tur - baned Turk, __ who scorns the world, May strut a - bout with his
2. The gay Mon - sieur, __ a slave no more, The sol - emn Don, __ the
3. The Lon - don folks __ them - selves be - guile, And think they please in a

whisk - ers curled. Keep a hun - dred wives un - der lock and key, For
soft Si - gnor, The __ Dutch Myn - heer, __ so full of pride, The
cap - i - tal style; Yet __ let them ask as they cross the street, Of

no - bod - y else but him - self to see. Yet long may he pray with his
Rus - sian, Prus - sian, Swede be - side— They all _____ may do _____ what -
an - y young Vir - gin they hap - pen to meet, And I know she'll say from be -

Al - co - ran, Be - fore he can love like an I - rish - man. Yet long may he pray with his
e'er they can, But they'll nev - er love like an I - rish - man. They all _____ may do _____ what -
hind her fan, That there's none can love like an I - rish - man. And I know she'll say from be -

Al - co - ran, Be - fore he can love like an I - rish - man.
e'er they can, But they'll nev - er love like an I - rish - man.
hind her fan, That there's none can love like an I - rish - man.

NORA

Words and Music by
Sean O' Casey

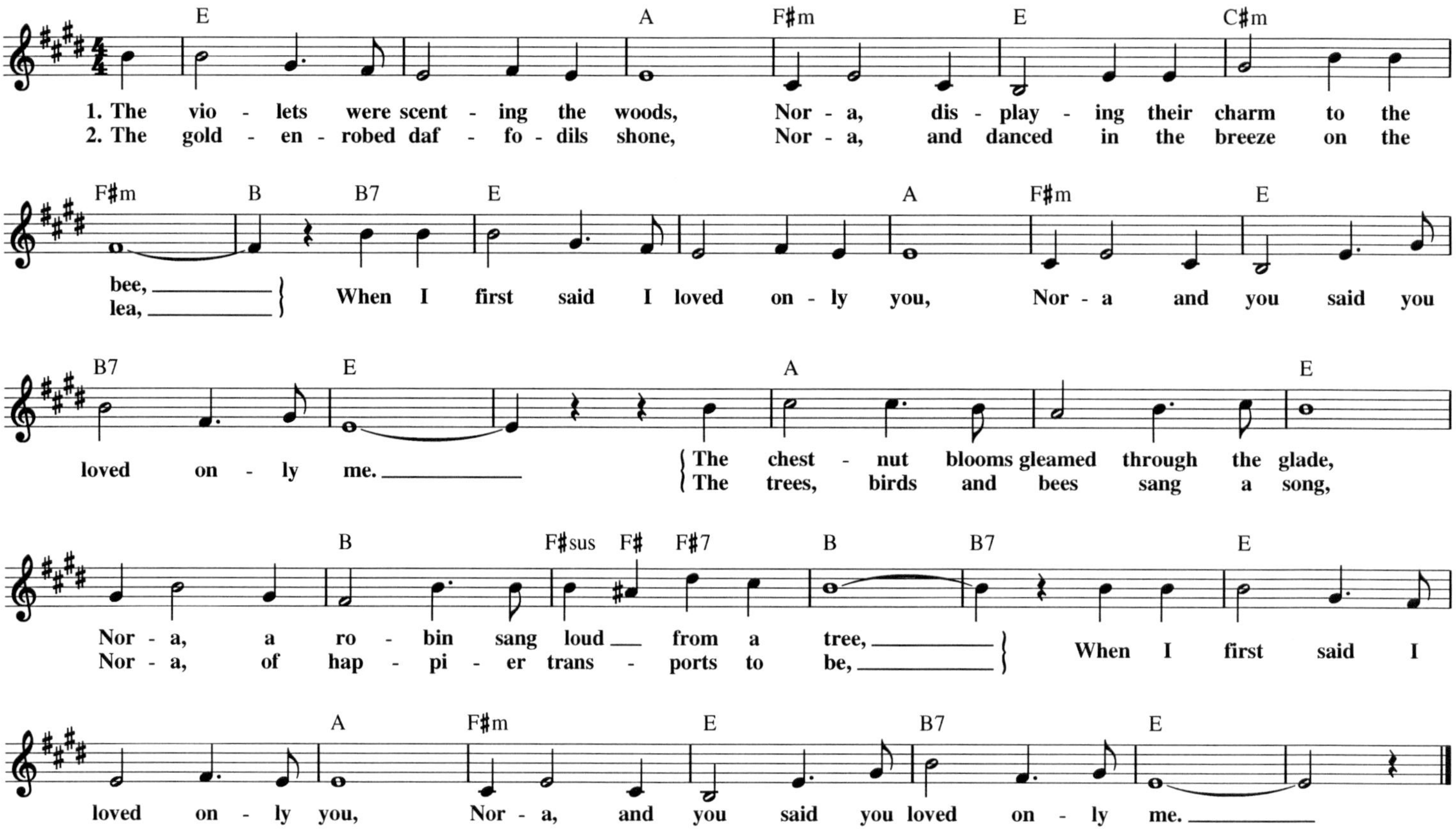

1. The vio - lets were scent - ing the woods, Nor - a, dis - play - ing their charm to the
2. The gold - en - robed daf - fo - dils shone, Nor - a, and danced in the breeze on the

bee, _____ When I first said I loved on - ly you, Nor - a and you said you
lea, _____

B7 E A F#m E
loved on - ly me. _____ The chest - nut blooms gleamed through the glade,
The trees, birds and bees sang a song,

Nor - a, a ro - bin sang loud ___ from a tree, _____ When I first said I
Nor - a, of hap - pi - er trans - ports to be, _____

loved on - ly you, Nor - a, and you said you loved on - ly me. _____

NORAH O'NEALE

Irish folksong

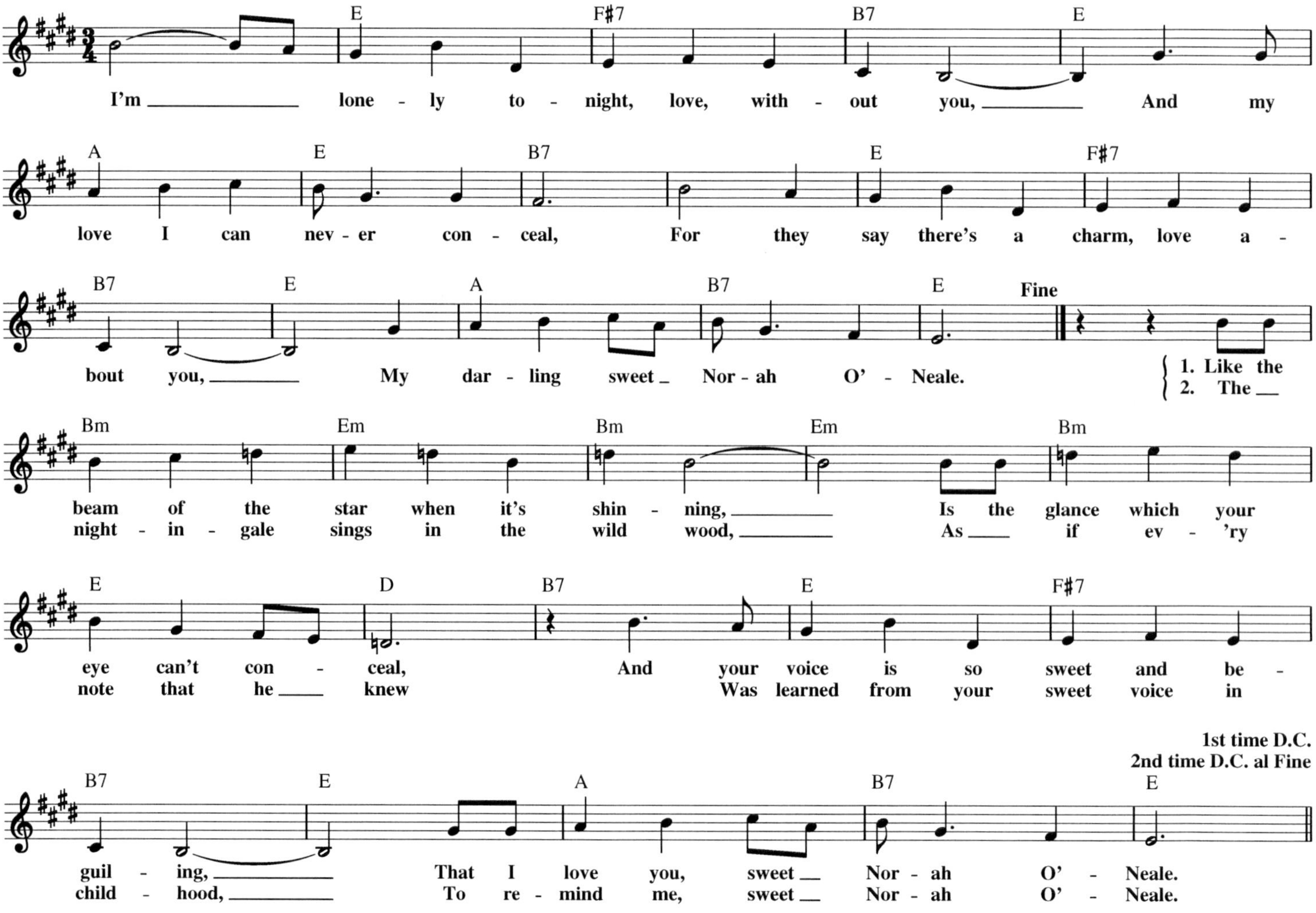

I'm _____ lone - ly to - night, love, with - out you, _____ And my

love I can nev - er con - ceal, For they say there's a charm, love a -

bout you, _____ My dar - ling sweet _ Nor - ah O' - Neale.

1. Like the
2. The ___

beam of the star when it's shin - ing, _____ Is the glance which your
night - in - gale sings in the wild wood, _____ As ___ if ev - 'ry

eye can't con - ceal, And your voice is so sweet and be -
note that he ___ knew Was learned from your sweet voice in

1st time D.C.
2nd time D.C. al Fine

guil - ing, _____ That I love you, sweet _ Nor - ah O' - Neale.
child - hood, _____ To re - mind me, sweet _ Nor - ah O' - Neale.

O LOVE, 'TIS A CALM STARRY NIGHT

Irish folksong

O WOMAN WASHING BY THE RIVER

Irish folksong

Additional Lyrics

2. *Seo è annso mo theach mór maiseach,*
    Is iomdha leann úr is leann sean ann,
    Is isomdha mil bhui 'gus céir bheach ann,
    Is iomdha seanduine ar a nasg ann.
    Is iomdha buachaill cúl-donn cas ann,
    Is iomdha cailin cúi-bhui deas ann.
    Tá dhá bhean déag ag iomchar mac ann,
    Tá an oiread eile re n-a n-ais ann.

170

O'DONNELL ABOO

Irish folksong
by Michael Joseph McCann

O'HARA'S CUP

Irish folksong

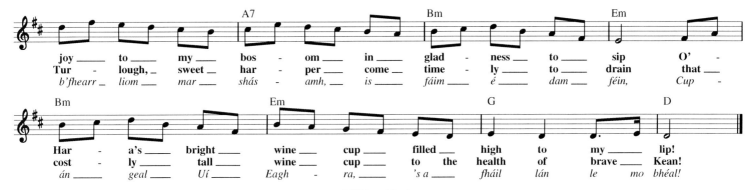

joy to my bos-om in glad-ness to sip O'-
Tur - lough, sweet har - per come time - ly to drain that
b'fhearr liom mar shás - amh, is fáim é dam féin, Cup-

Har - a's bright wine cup filled high to my lip!
cost - ly tall wine cup to the health of brave Kean!
án geal Uí Eagh - ra, 's a fháil lán le mo bhéal!

Additional Lyrics
2. *God é siúd dob áil dam,
's a liacht ádh maith 'n-a dhéidh?
'Sé deir ollamh na h-áite,
dar mo láimh-se ní bréag:
A Thrialaigh Bhriain ádhmhail,
tar tráth fá mo dhéin,
Go n-ólam as an tsár-chupán
sláinte bhreá Chéin!*

THE OLD CRONE'S LILT

Folksong from the Hebrides

When I was young, a mai-den So shy I was, So shy I was, Al-
Nuair bha mi fhein 'nam mhaigh - dean Bu bhan - ail mi, Bu bhan - ail mi Gu'm

though the lads were keen then To greet me lass, To greet me lass, When
biodh na fir 'gam fhaigh - neachd Gu coth - to - mach Gu coth - ro - mach Nuair

I was young, a mai-den So shy I was, So shy I was, Al-
bha mi fhein 'nam mhaigh - dean Bu bhan - ail mi, Bu bhan - ail mi, Gu'm

though the lads were keen then, To greet me lass, To greet me lass, But
biodh na fir 'gam fhaigh - neachd Gu coth - ro - mach Gu coth - ro - mach Ach

now when old and gray, I come hir-plin' down, Come hir-plin' down, There's
mi - se bho'n a liath mi, Gur cail - leach mi Gur cail - leach mi 'S cha'n

scarce a lad will say me "Good e'e-nin' crone Good e'e-nin' crone," But
fhaigh mi fiu na poi - ge Bho fhear a - ca Bho fhear a - ca Ach

now when old and gray, I come hir-plin' down, Come hir-plin' down. There's
mi - se bho'n a liath mi, Gur cail - leach mi Gur cail - leach mi 'Scha'n

scarce a lad will say me, "Good e'e-nin' crone, Good e'e-nin' crone," When
fhaigh mi fiu na poi - ge Bho fhear a - ca, Bho fhear a - ca. Nuair

I was young, a mai-den So shy I was, So shy I was.
bha mi fhein 'nam mhaigh - dean, Bu bhan - ail mi, Bu bhan - ail mi.

OFT IN THE STILLY NIGHT

Irish folksong

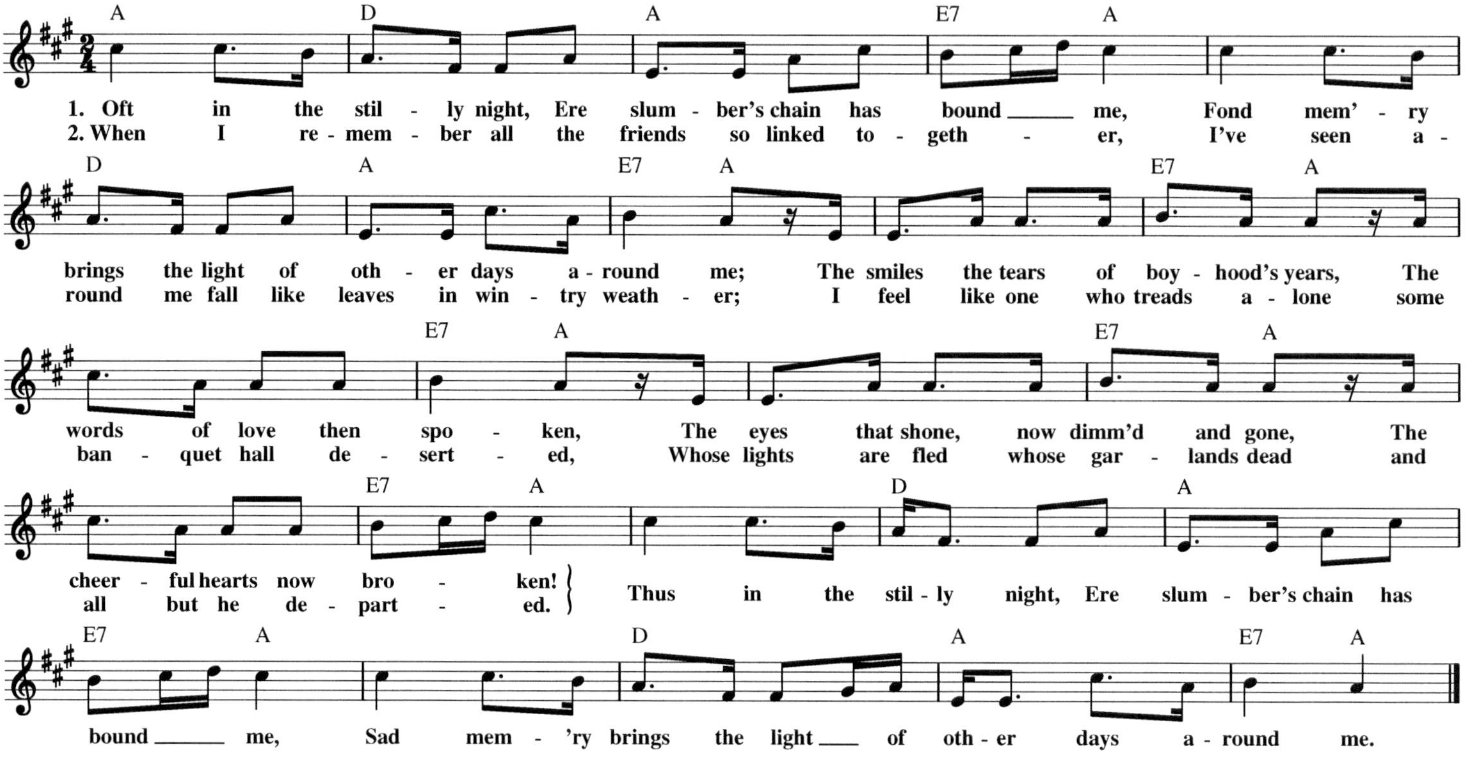

1. Oft in the stil - ly night, Ere slum - ber's chain has bound _____ me, Fond mem' - ry
2. When I re - mem - ber all the friends so linked to - geth - er, I've seen a -

brings the light of oth - er days a - round me; The smiles the tears of boy - hood's years, The
round me fall like leaves in win - try weath - er; I feel like one who treads a - lone some

words of love then spo - ken, The eyes that shone, now dimm'd and gone, The
ban - quet hall de - sert - ed, Whose lights are fled whose gar - lands dead and

cheer - ful hearts now bro - ken! } Thus in the stil - ly night, Ere slum - ber's chain has
all but he de - part - ed. }

bound _____ me, Sad mem - 'ry brings the light _____ of oth - er days a - round me.

OH ROWAN TREE

Scottish folksong
Words by Lady Carolina Nairne

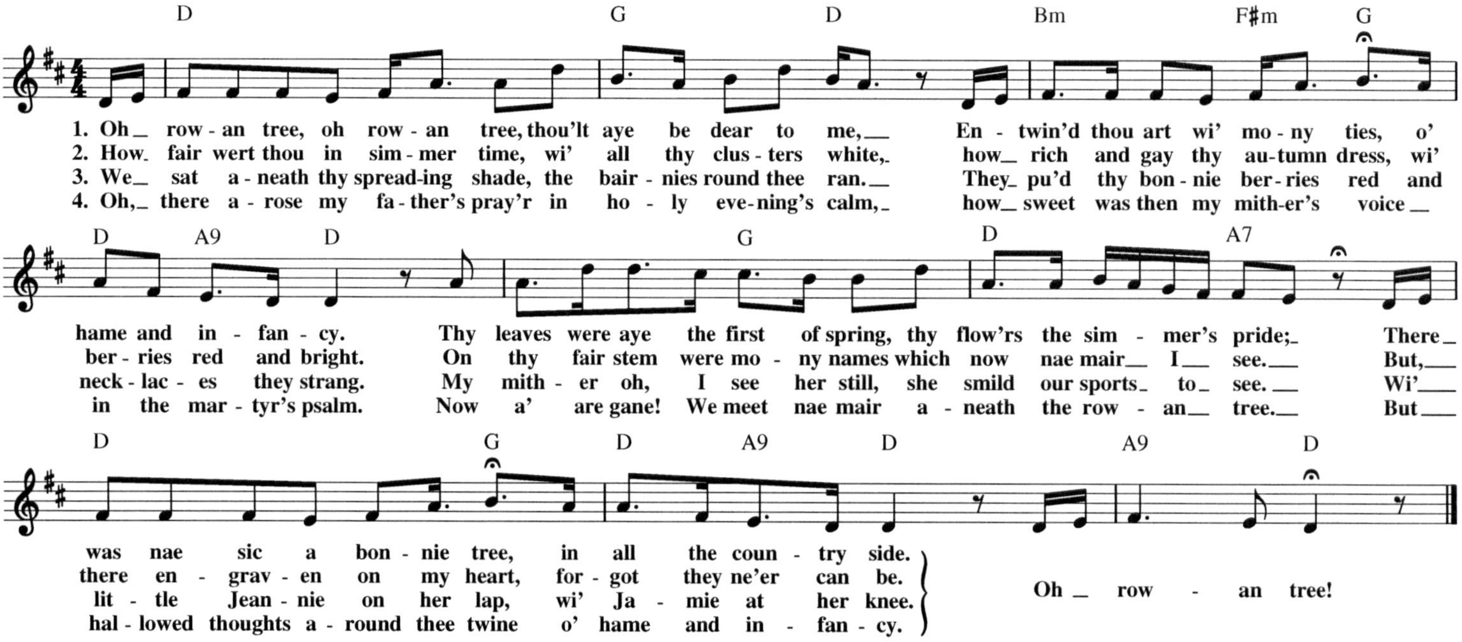

1. Oh __ row - an tree, oh row - an tree, thou'lt aye be dear to me, __ En - twin'd thou art wi' mo - ny ties, o'
2. How __ fair wert thou in sim - mer time, wi' all thy clus - ters white, __ how __ rich and gay thy au - tumn dress, wi'
3. We __ sat a - neath thy spread-ing shade, the bair - nies round thee ran. __ They __ pu'd thy bon - nie ber - ries red and
4. Oh, __ there a - rose my fa - ther's pray'r in ho - ly eve - ning's calm, __ how __ sweet was then my mith - er's voice __

hame and in - fan - cy. Thy leaves were aye the first of spring, thy flow'rs the sim - mer's pride; __ There __
ber - ries red and bright. On thy fair stem were mo - ny names which now nae mair __ I __ see. __ But, __
neck - lac - es they strang. My mith - er oh, I see her still, she smild our sports __ to __ see. __ Wi' __
in the mar - tyr's psalm. Now a' are gane! We meet nae mair a - neath the row - an __ tree. __ But __

was nae sic a bon - nie tree, in all the coun - try side. }
there en - grav - en on my heart, for - got they ne'er can be. }
neck - lac - es they strang. My mith - er oh, I see her still, } Oh __ row - an tree!
lit - tle Jean - ie on her lap, wi' Ja - mie at her knee. }
hal - lowed thoughts a - round thee twine o' hame and in - fan - cy. }

OICHE NOLLAG

Irish folksong

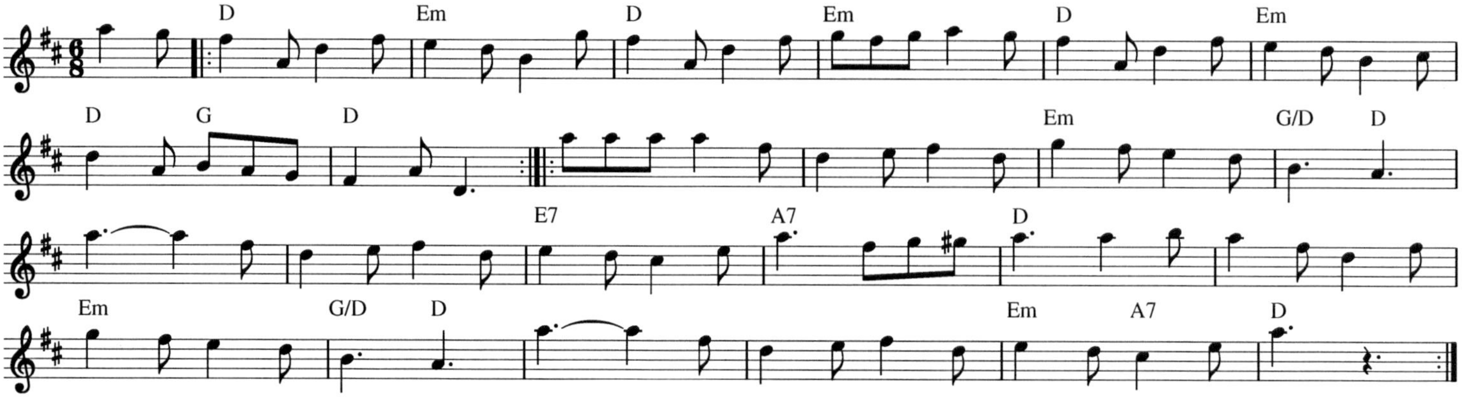

THE OLD ORANGE FLUTE

Irish folksong

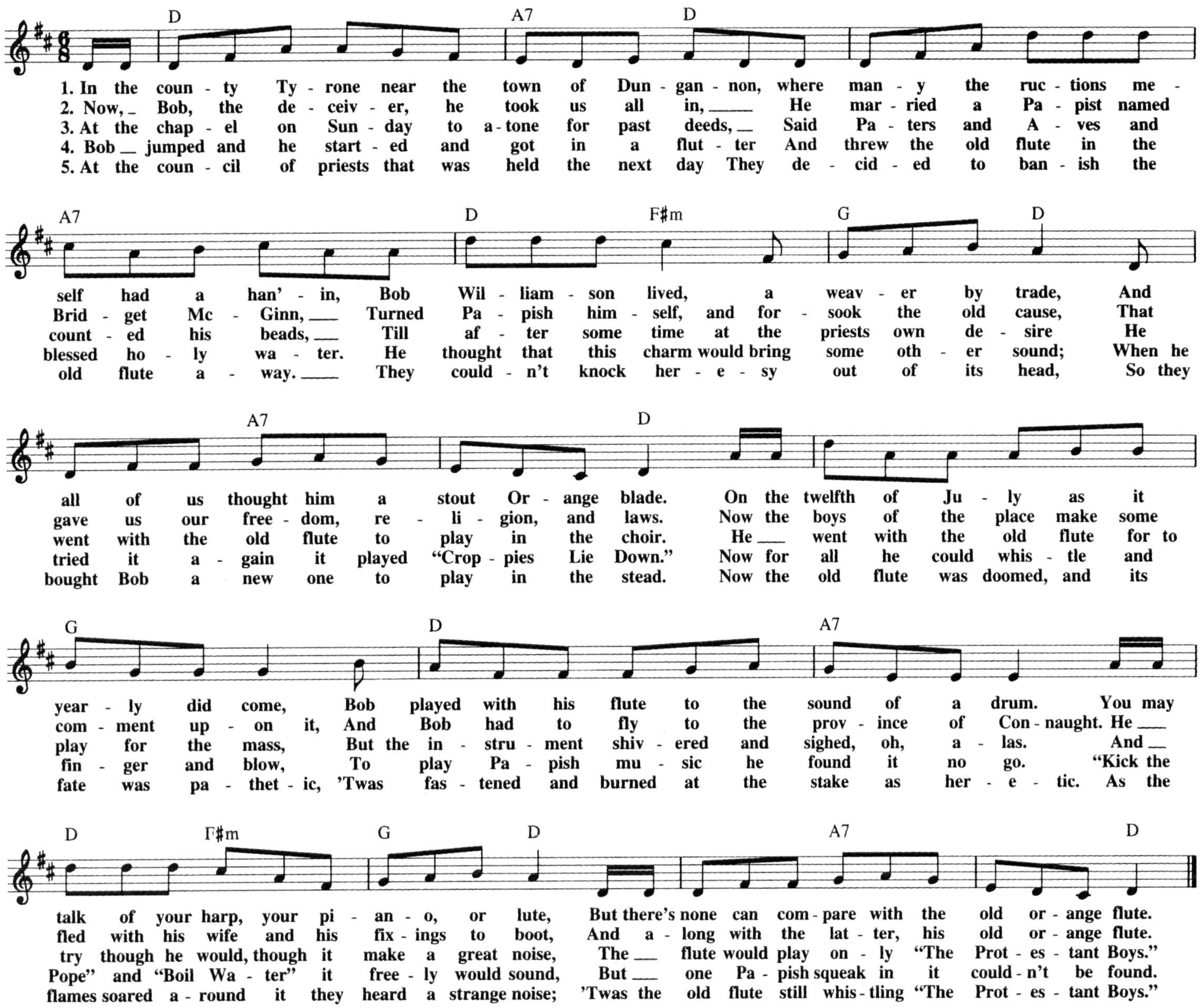

1. In the coun - ty Ty - rone near the town of Dun - gan - non, where man - y the ruc - tions me -
2. Now, _ Bob, the de - ceiv - er, he took us all in, _ He mar - ried a Pa - pist named
3. At the chap - el on Sun - day to a - tone for past deeds, _ Said Pa - ters and A - ves and
4. Bob _ jumped and he start - ed and got in a flut - ter And threw the old flute in the
5. At the coun - cil of priests that was held the next day They de - cid - ed to ban - ish the

self had a han' - in, Bob Wil - liam - son lived, a weav - er by trade, And
Brid - get Mc - Ginn, _ Turned Pa - pish him - self, and for - sook the old cause, That
count - ed his beads, Till af - ter some time at the priests own de - sire He
blessed ho - ly wa - ter. He thought that this charm would bring some oth - er sound; When he
old flute a - way. _ They could - n't knock her - e - sy out of its head, So they

all of us thought him a stout Or - ange blade. On the twelfth of Ju - ly as it
gave us our free - dom, re - li - gion, and laws. Now the boys of the place make some
went with the old flute to play in the choir. He _ went with the old flute for to
tried it a - gain it played "Crop - pies Lie Down." Now for all he could whis - tle and
bought Bob a new one to play in the stead. Now the old flute was doomed, and its

year - ly did come, Bob played with his flute to the sound of a drum. You may
com - ment up - on it, And Bob had to fly to the prov - ince of Con - naught. He _
play for the mass, But the in - stru - ment shiv - ered and sighed, oh, a - las. And _
fin - ger and blow, To play Pa - pish mu - sic he found it no go. "Kick the
fate was pa - thet - ic, 'Twas fas - tened and burned at the stake as her - e - tic. As the

talk of your harp, your pi - an - o, or lute, But there's none can com - pare with the old or - ange flute.
fled with his wife and his fix - ings to boot, And a - long with the lat - ter, his old or - ange flute.
try though he would, though it make a great noise, The _ flute would play on - ly "The Prot - es - tant Boys."
Pope" and "Boil Wa - ter" it free - ly would sound, But _ one Pa - pish squeak in it could - n't be found.
flames soared a - round it they heard a strange noise; 'Twas the old flute still whis - tling "The Prot - es - tant Boys."

THE OLD TURF FIRE

Irish folksong

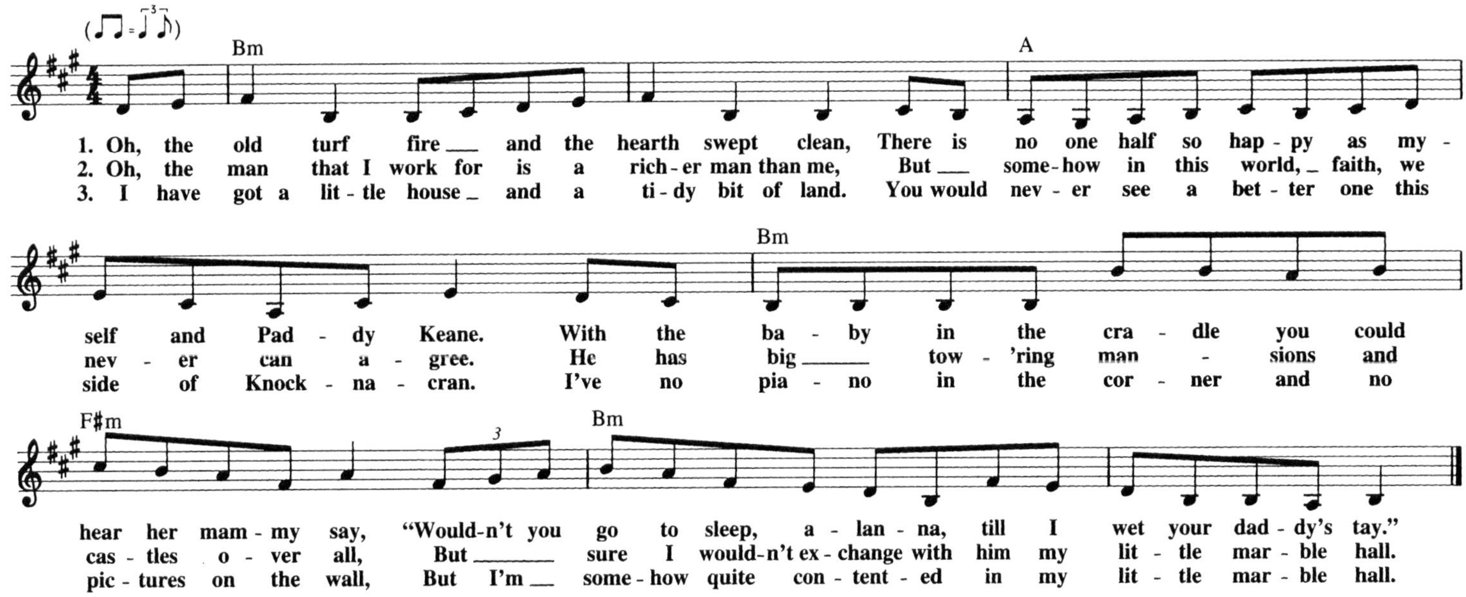

1. Oh, the old turf fire _ and the hearth swept clean, There is no one half so hap - py as my -
2. Oh, the man that I work for is a rich - er man than me, But _ some - how in this world, _ faith, we
3. I have got a lit - tle house _ and a ti - dy bit of land. You would nev - er see a bet - ter one this

self and Pad - dy Keane. With the ba - by in the cra - dle you could
nev - er can a - gree. He has big _ tow - 'ring man - sions and
side of Knock - na - cran. I've no pi - a - no in the cor - ner and no

hear her mam - my say, "Would - n't you go to sleep, a - lan - na, till I wet your dad - dy's tay."
cas - tles o - ver all, But _ sure I would - n't ex - change with him my lit - tle mar - ble hall.
pic - tures on the wall, But I'm _ some - how quite con - tent - ed in my lit - tle mar - ble hall.

THE OLD TRIANGLE

Irish folksong

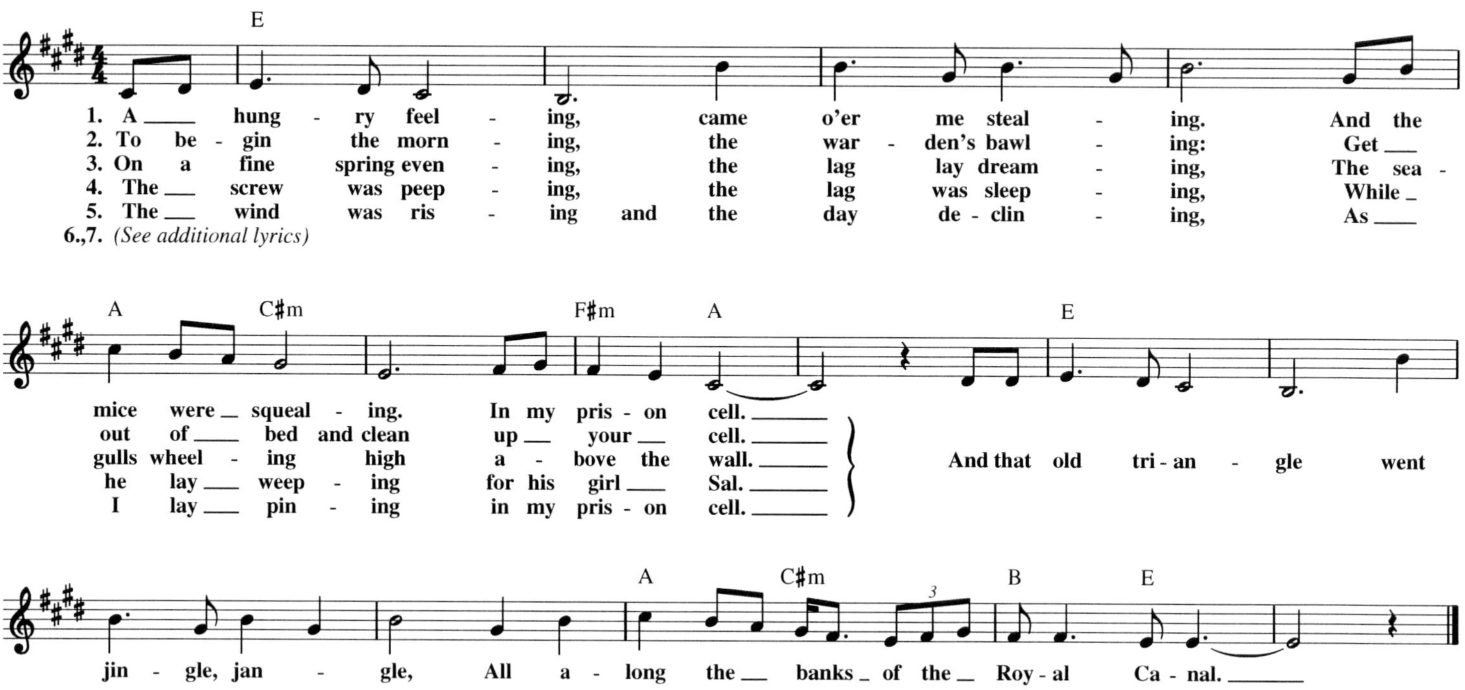

1. A _____ hung - ry feel - ing, came o'er me steal - ing. And the
2. To be - gin the morn - ing, the war - den's bawl - ing: Get _____
3. On a fine spring even - ing, the lag lay dream - ing, The sea -
4. The _____ screw was peep - ing, the lag was sleep - ing, While _____
5. The _____ wind was ris - ing and the day de - clin - ing, As _____
6.,7. *(See additional lyrics)*

mice were _ squeal - ing. In my pris - on cell. _____
out of _____ bed and clean up _____ your _____ cell. _____
gulls wheel - ing high a - bove the wall. _____
he lay _____ weep - ing for his girl _____ Sal. _____
I lay _____ pin - ing in my pris - on cell. _____

And that old tri - an - gle went

jin - gle, jan - gle, All a - long the _ banks _ of the _ Roy - al Ca - nal. _____

Additional Lyrics

6. In the female prison there are seventy women,
I wish it was with them that I did dwell,
Then that old triangle could jingle jangle
Along the banks of the Royal Canal.

7. The day was dying and the wind was sighing,
As I lay crying in my prison cell,
And the old triangle went jingle, jangle
Along the banks of the Royal Canal.

ON THE BANKS OF ALLAN WATER

Scottish folksong

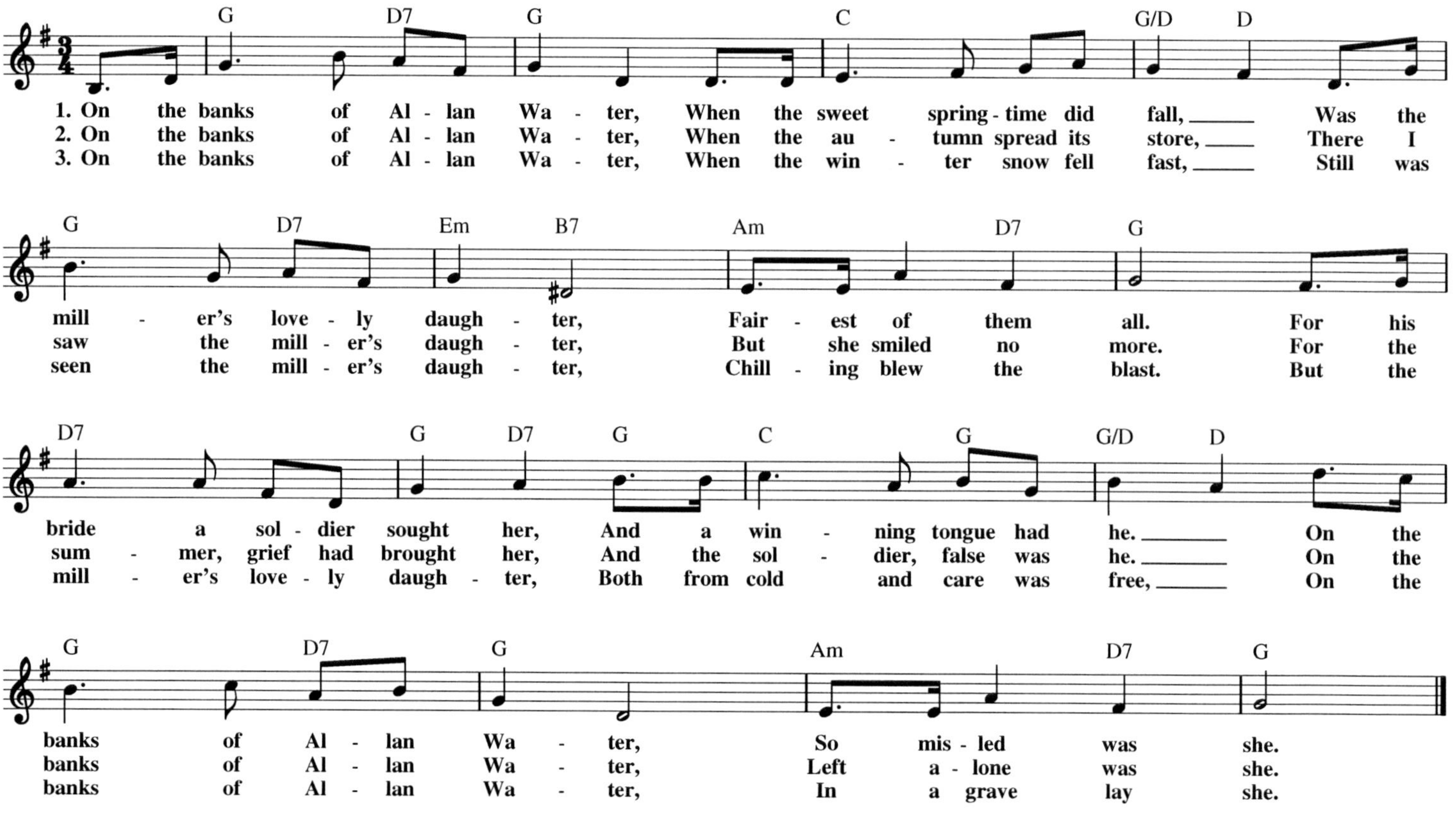

1. On the banks of Al - lan Wa - ter, When the sweet spring - time did fall, _____ Was the
2. On the banks of Al - lan Wa - ter, When the au - tumn spread its store, _____ There I
3. On the banks of Al - lan Wa - ter, When the win - ter snow fell fast, _____ Still was

mill - er's love - ly daugh - ter, Fair - est of them all. For his
saw the mill - er's daugh - ter, But she smiled no more. For the
seen the mill - er's daugh - ter, Chill - ing blew the blast. But the

bride a sol - dier sought her, And a win - ning tongue had he. _____ On the
sum - mer, grief had brought her, And the sol - dier, false was he. _____ On the
mill - er's love - ly daugh - ter, Both from cold and care was free, _____ On the

banks of Al - lan Wa - ter, So mis - led was she.
banks of Al - lan Wa - ter, Left a - lone was she.
banks of Al - lan Wa - ter, In a grave lay she.

ON THE BANKS OF THE ROSES

Irish folksong

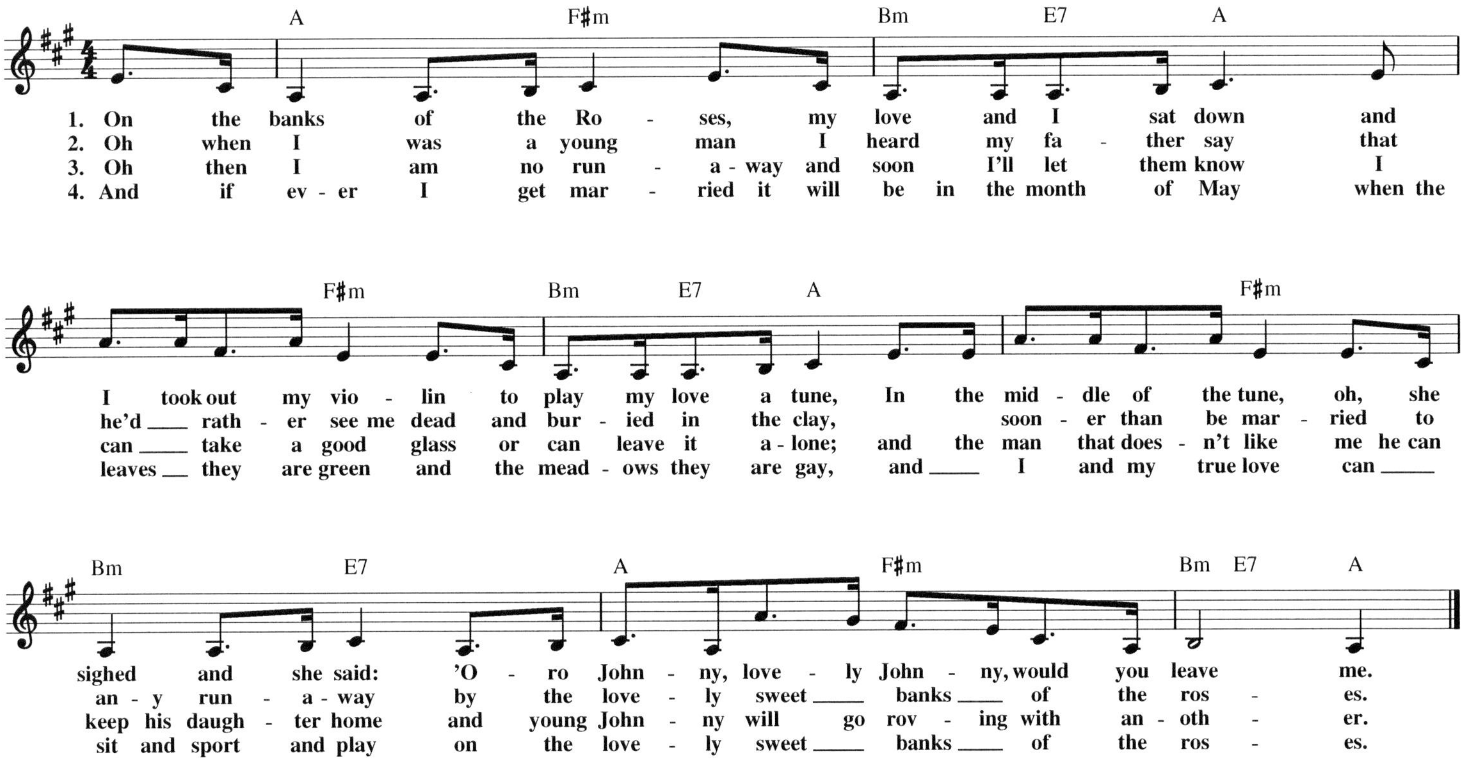

1. On the banks of the Ro - ses, my love and I sat down and
2. Oh when I was a young man I heard my fa - ther say and that
3. Oh then I am no run - a - way and soon I'll let them know I
4. And if ev - er I get mar - ried it will be in the month of May when the

I took out my vio - lin to play my love a tune, In the mid - dle of the tune, oh, she
he'd ___ rath - er see me dead and bur - ied in the clay, soon - er than be mar - ried to
can ___ take a good glass or can leave it a - lone; and the man that does - n't like me he can
leaves ___ they are green and the mead - ows they are gay, and ___ I and my true love can ___

sighed and she said: 'O - ro John - ny, love - ly John - ny, would you leave me.
an - y run - a - way by the love - ly sweet ___ banks ___ of the ros - es.
keep his daugh - ter home and young John - ny will go rov - ing with an - oth - er.
sit and sport and play on the love - ly sweet ___ banks ___ of the ros - es.

OVER THE MOOR TO MAGGIE

Irish folksong

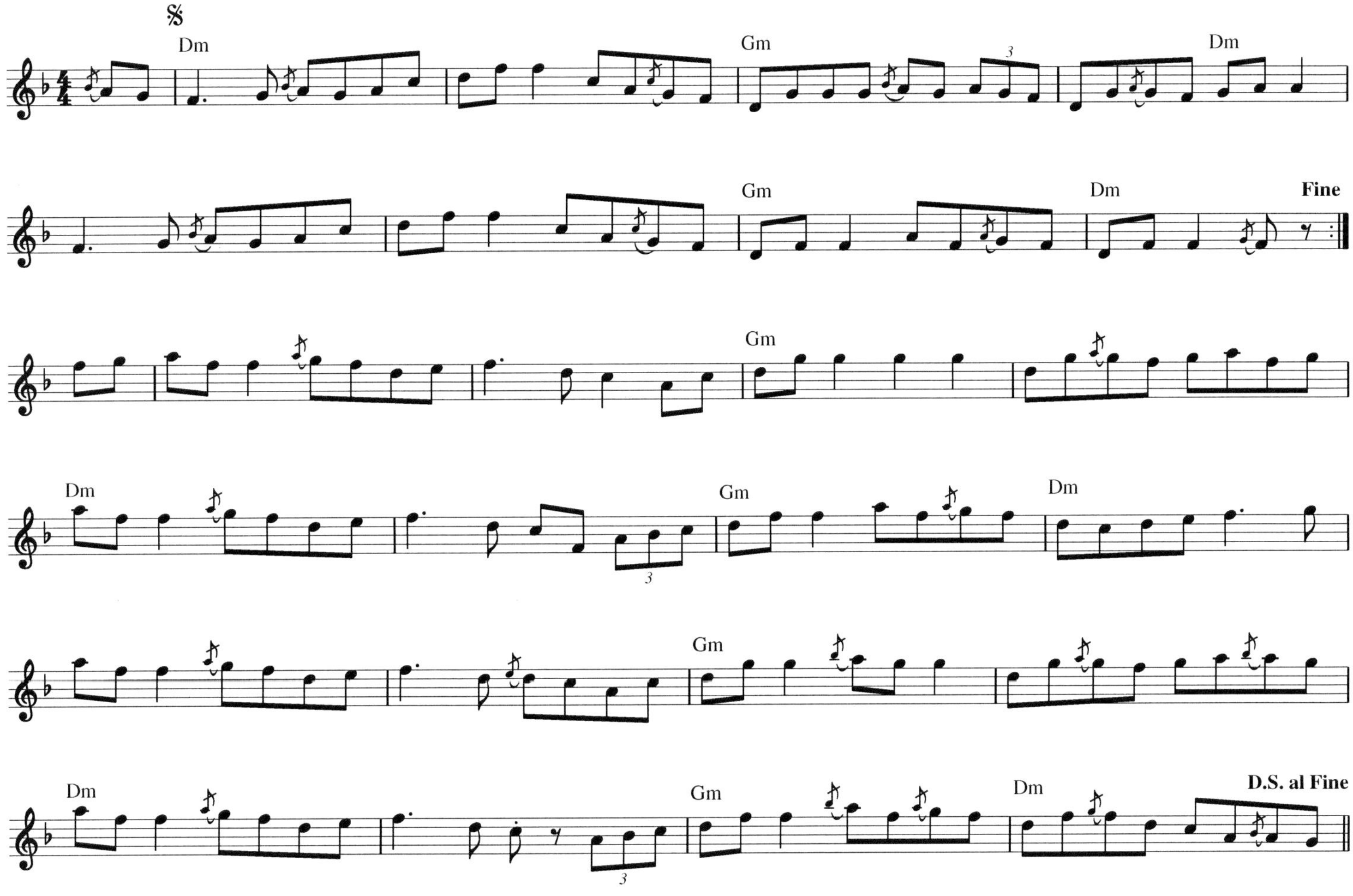

OWEN CÓIR

Irish folksong

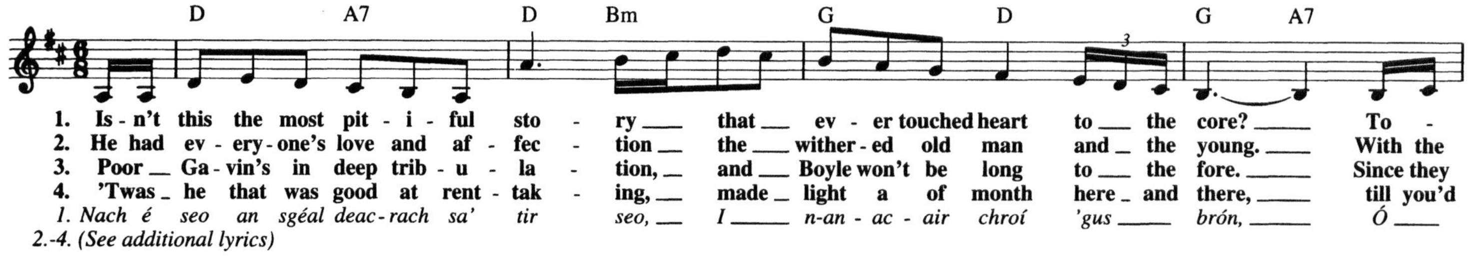

1. Is - n't this the most pit - i - ful sto - ry ___ that ___ ev - er touched heart to ___ the core? ___ To -
2. He had ev - ery - one's love and af - fec - tion ___ the ___ with - er - ed old man and ___ the young. ___ With the
3. Poor ___ Ga - vin's in deep trib - u - la - tion, ___ and ___ Boyle won't be long to ___ the fore. ___ Since they
4. 'Twas ___ he that was good at rent - tak - ing, ___ made ___ light a of month here ___ and there, ___ till you'd

1. Nach é seo an sgéal deac - rach sa' tir seo, ___ I ___ n-an - ac - air chroí 'gus ___ brón, Ó

2.-4. (See additional lyrics)

day we saw O - wen to glo - ry ___ From ___ Creag - an - a - line to Fall - more. ___ Such
high - est and low - est con - nec - tion ___ the ___ praise of his big heart was sung. ___ With the
lost their best friend in cre - a - tion ___ their ___ hearts are with grief brim - ming o'er. ___ There
sell the frieze cloth you'd be mak - ing ___ or your young hei - fer calf at the fair. ___ 'Twas

fhág - as tú Creag - án a' Lín - e ___ Go ___ dté tú go dtí'n Fál Mór? ___ A

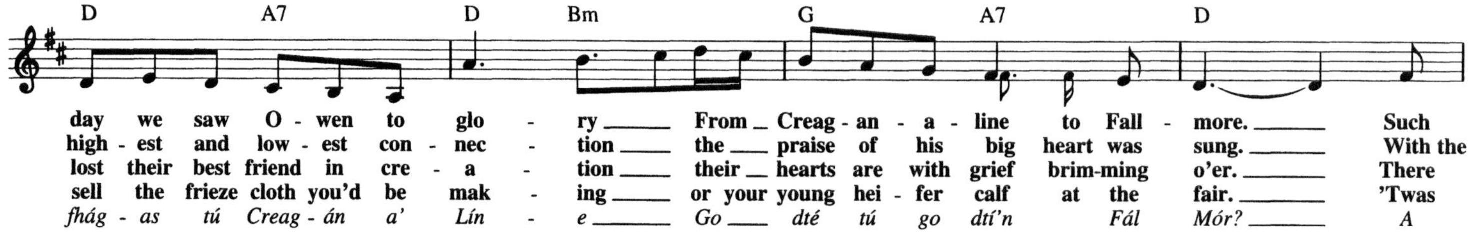

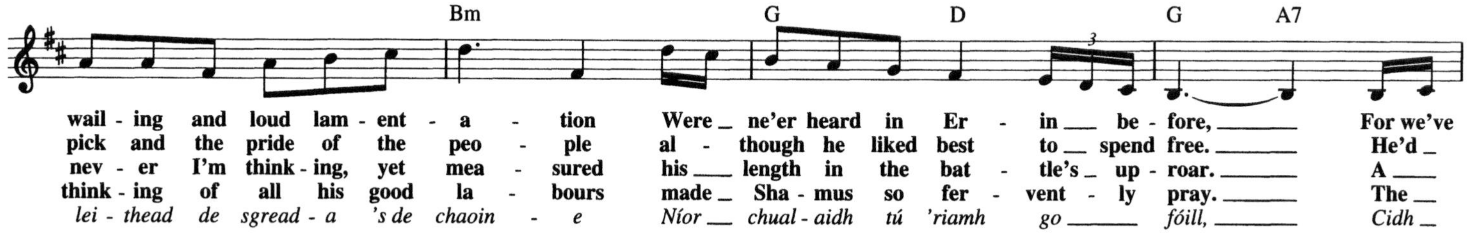

wail - ing and loud lam - ent - a - tion Were ___ ne'er heard in Er - in be - fore, ___ For we've
pick and the pride of the peo - ple al - though he liked best to ___ spend free. ___ He'd
nev - er I'm think - ing, yet mea - sured his ___ length in the bat - tle's up - roar. ___ A
think - ing of all his good la - bours made ___ Sha - mus so fer - vent - ly pray. ___ The ___

lei - thead de sgread - a 's de chaoin - e Níor ___ chual - aidh tú 'riamh go ___ fóill, ___ Cidh ___

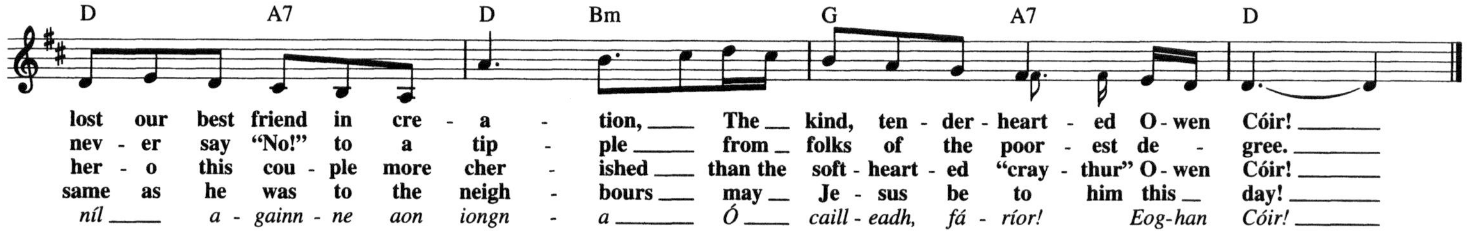

lost our best friend in cre - a - tion, ___ The ___ kind, ten - der - heart - ed O - wen Cóir! ___
nev - er say "No!" to a tip - ple ___ from ___ folks of the poor - est de - gree. ___
her - o this cou - ple more cher - ished ___ than the soft - heart - ed "cray - thur" O - wen Cóir! ___
same as he was to the neigh - bours ___ may ___ Je - sus be to him this ___ day! ___

níl ___ a - gainn - ne aon iongn - a ___ Ó ___ caill - eadh, fá - ríor! Eog - han Cóir!

Additional Lyrics

2. *Bhí grá agus gean ag gach n-aon air,*
   An seanduine críon 's an t-óg,
   Bhí an saidhbhir 's an daidhbhir i ngnaoi leis
   Mar gheall ar a chroí maith mór
   Le togha 'gus le rogha na tire
   Do chaitheadh sé piosai óir.
   'S e daoine bocht' eile nior spid leis
   Buidéal den tsibin d'ól.

3. *Tá Antoine Ó Gabháin a' caoine,*
   'S ni bheidh Seán Ó Baoghail i bhfad beó,
   Ó cailleadh a gcaraid san tir seo,
   'Sé d'fhágaibh a gcroi faoi bhrón.
   I n-anacair chathair nior sineadh,
   'Sé mheasaim, fá liag ná fód
   Aoinneach ba mheasa don dis-se
   Ná an duine bocht maol, Eoghan Cóir!

4. *Ba ró-mhaith a' tógbháil an chiosa é,*
   Ba bheag aige mi nó dhó,
   Go ndioltaí an bhó ar an aonach,
   Nó an giota do bhiodh san tseól.
   'Sé dúirt Séamus Pheadair Mhic Riabhaigh,
   Is é ag agairt ar Ri na ndeór,
   "Do réir mar bhi seisean do dhaoinibh,
   Gurab amhlaidh bheas Criosta dhó!"

O'ROURKE'S REVEL ROUT

Irish folksong

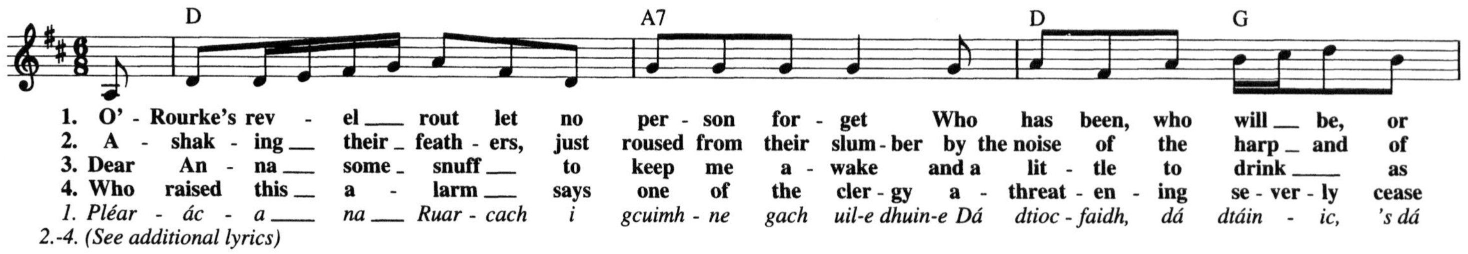

1. O' - Rourke's rev - el ___ rout let no per - son for - get Who has been, who will ___ be, or
2. A - shak - ing their ___ feath - ers, just roused from their slum - ber by the noise of the harp ___ and of
3. Dear An - na ___ some ___ snuff to keep me a - wake and a lit - tle to drink ___ as
4. Who raised this ___ a - larm ___ says one of the cler - gy a - threat - en - ing se - ver - ly cease

1. Pléar - ác - a ___ na ___ Ruar - cach i gcuimh - ne gach uil - e dhuin - e Dá dtioc - faidh, dá dtáin - ic, 's dá

2.-4. (See additional lyrics)

nev - er was yet. See sev - en score hogs in the morn - ing we slay, ___ With
feet ___ with - out num - ber. The sons of O' - Rourke ___ bounced up in a throng ___ each
long as I speak. Good heav - en how strange ___ what must peo - ple think ___ af - ter
fight - ing I charge ye. A good knot - ted staff the full of his hand in -

mair - eann go fóill: Seacht bhfi - chid muc, ___ mart ag - us caor - a Dhá

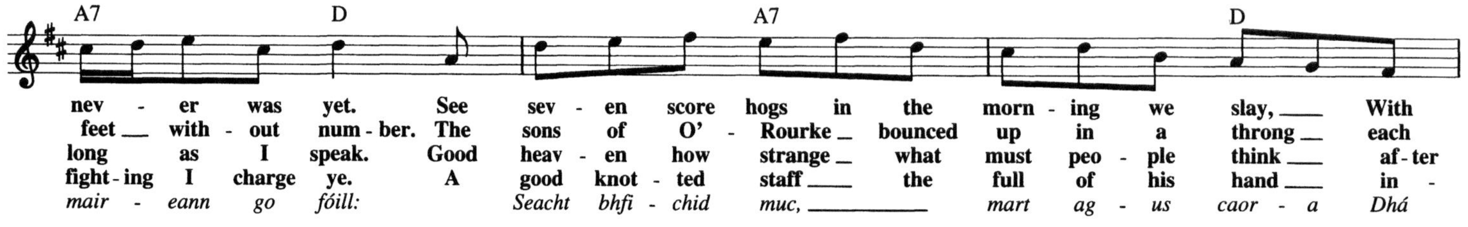

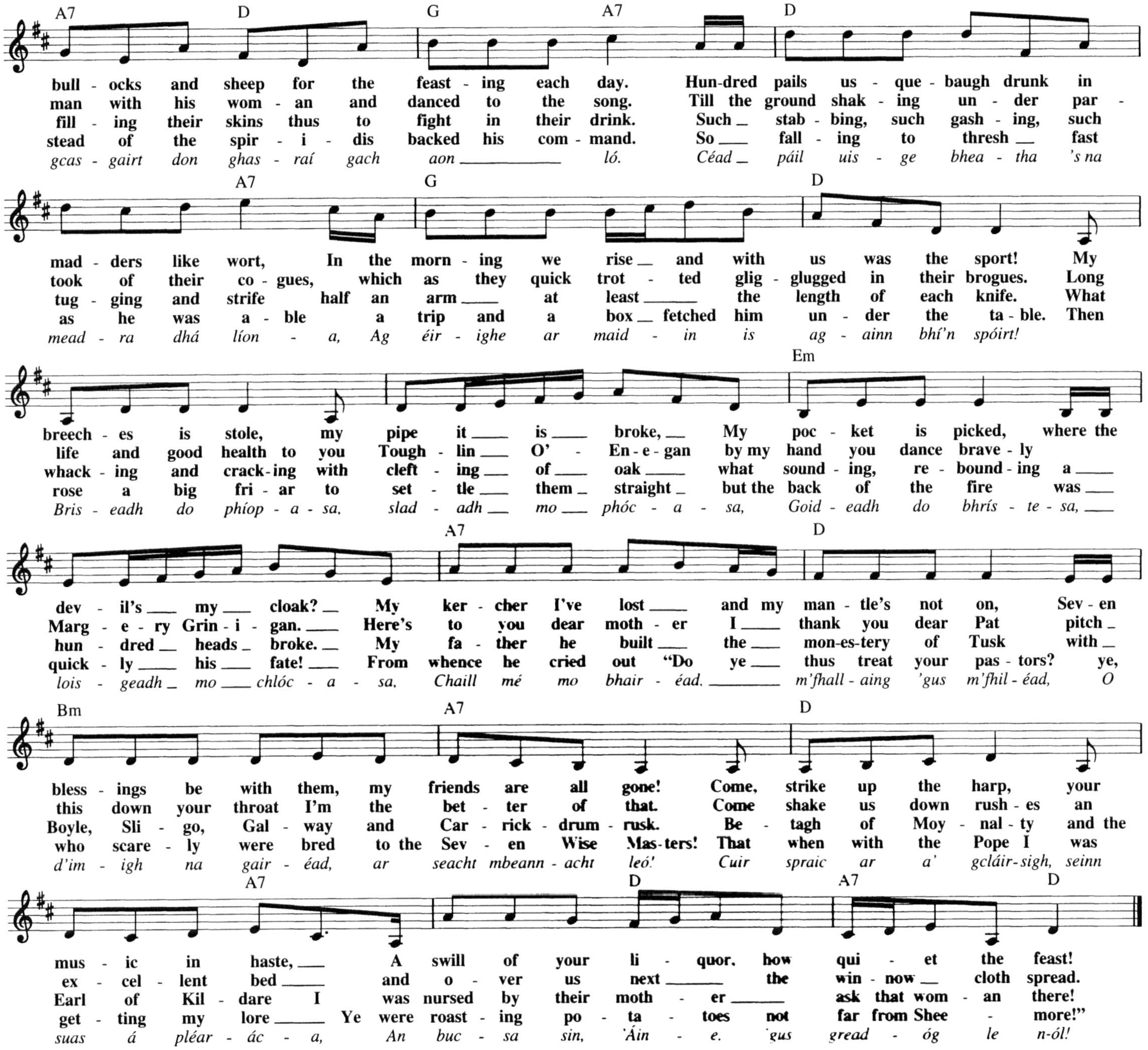

Additional Lyrics

2. *Lucht leanamhna na Ruarcach a' cratha a gcleiti.*
Tráth chuala siad tormán nó troimpléasg an cheóil:
D'éirigh gach aon aca gan coisreaca 'n-a leabaidh.
Is a bhean leis ar strachailt in gach aon chórn.
Nár láidir an seasamh don talamh bhí fútha,
Gan réaba le sodar agus glug ins gach bróig!
Saol agus sláinte dhuit, 'Mh'leachlainn Ui
Fhionnagáin!
Dar mo láimh is maith a dhamhsuíos tú,
'Mhársail Ní Ghriodagáin!
Here's to you, 'mháthair, I pledge you, God save you!
Beir ar a' sgála so, sgag é in do sgóig.
Craith fúinn an tsráideóg, sin tharuinn an bhán-phluid.
Tugthar ar sáith dhúinn de lionn-choirm chóir!

3. *A Árd-Ri na gcarad, cébi 'tchifeadh an ghasraí*
Ar líona a gcraicní nó ar lasa san ól!
Cnáimh righe bacaird ar fad in gach sgin aca,
A' gearra 's a' cosgairt go mór, mór, mór;
A slisneachu daruch ar lasu a' gubháil fríd a chéile,
A' buala, a' greada, a' losga 's a' dódh.
A bhodaigh, 'sé m'athair-se chuir Mainistir na
Búille suas,
Sligeach is Gaillimh is Caraidh Dhroma Rúisgthe fós.
Iarla Chill' Dara agus Biadhtach Mhuí n-Ealta,
Siad d'oil agus d'altrium mé, fiosraigh so de Mhór.
Tóig suas a' t'ádhmad agus buail an t-alárm air,
Preab ionsa táirr agus cic ionsa tóin!

4. *"Cé thóig a' t-alárm so?" ar aon den Eaglais.*
Ag éirghe 'n-a sheasamh 's a' bagairt go mór;
Ni h-é spairgeas uisge coisreactha ghlac sé sa gcíora
Ach bata maith darach, bog-lán dóirn!
Tráth shíl sé na caithmhílidh a chasgairt 's a chíora,
Do fágadh an sagart 'n-a mheall chasta fán mbórd.
D'éirigh na bráithre a' tárrtháil na bruíne.
Is fágadh an t-Athair Gáirdian ar a thárr
'n-áirde sa ngríosai.
"Tráth bhínn-se ag an bPápa ar stuidéar na ngrásta,
'S a' glaca na ngrádhamh thall ins a' Róimh,
'Sé an Seven Wise Masters bhi agad ar do tháirr,
Is tú a' rósta na bprátaí láimh leis a' tSidh Mhór!"

PADDY DOYLE'S BOOTS

Irish folksong

THE PALATINE'S DAUGHTER

Irish folksong

PADDY UPON THE CANAL

Irish folksong

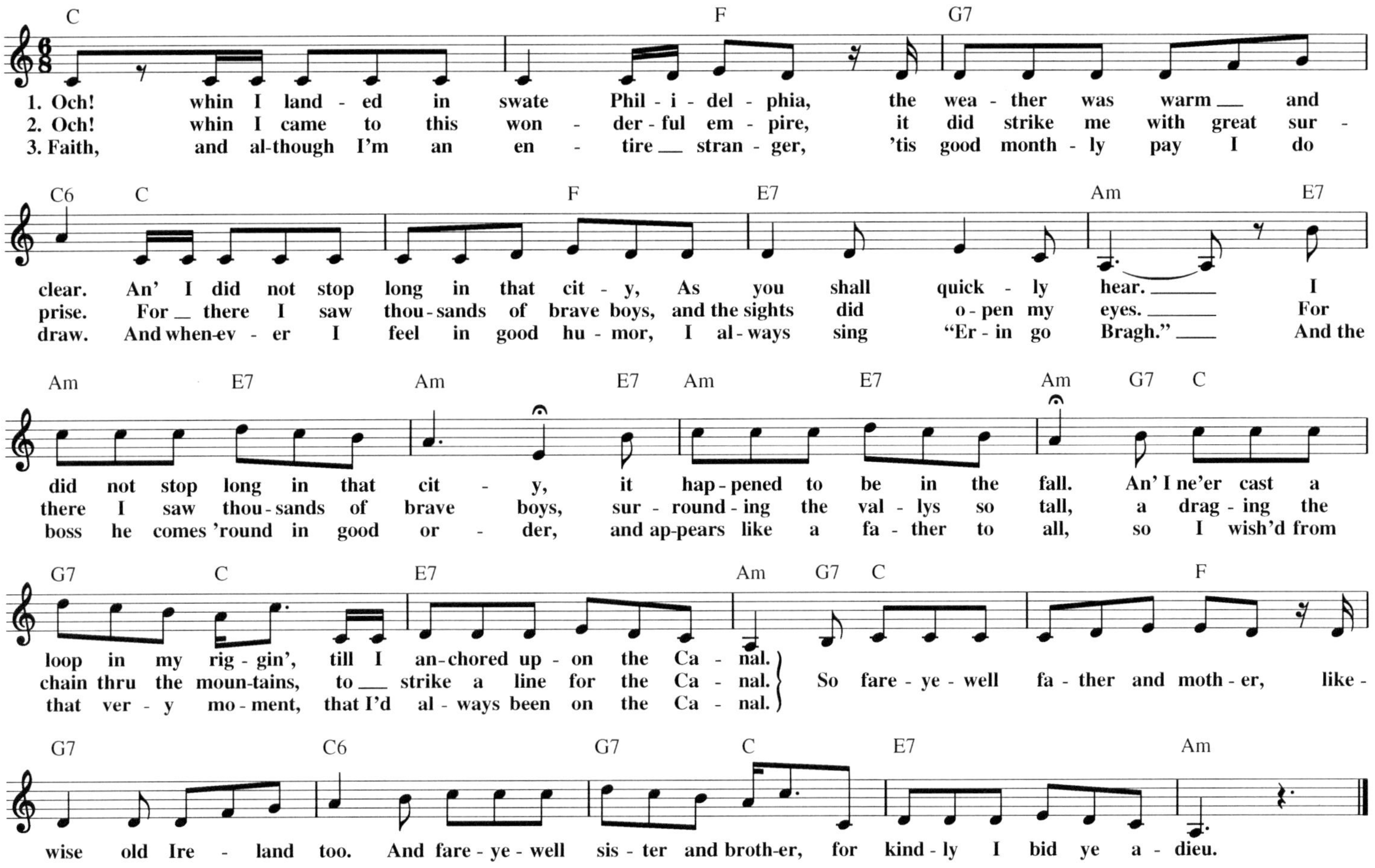

1. Och! whin I land-ed in swate Phil-i-del-phia, the wea-ther was warm and clear. An' I did not stop long in that cit-y, As you shall quick-ly hear. I did not stop long in that cit-y, it hap-pened to be in the fall. An' I ne'er cast a loop in my rig-gin', till I an-chored up-on the Ca-nal.

2. Och! whin I came to this won-der-ful em-pire, it did strike me with great sur-prise. For there I saw thou-sands of brave boys, and the sights did o-pen my eyes. For there I saw thou-sands of brave boys, sur-round-ing the val-lys so tall, a drag-ing the chain thru the moun-tains, to strike a line for the Ca-nal.

3. Faith, and al-though I'm an en-tire stran-ger, 'tis good month-ly pay I do draw. And when-ev-er I feel in good hu-mor, I al-ways sing "Er-in go Bragh." And the boss he comes 'round in good or-der, and ap-pears like a fa-ther to all, so I wish'd from that ver-y mo-ment, that I'd al-ways been on the Ca-nal.

So fare-ye-well fa-ther and moth-er, like-wise old Ire-land too. And fare-ye-well sis-ter and broth-er, for kind-ly I bid ye a-dieu.

THE PARTING GLASS

Irish folksong

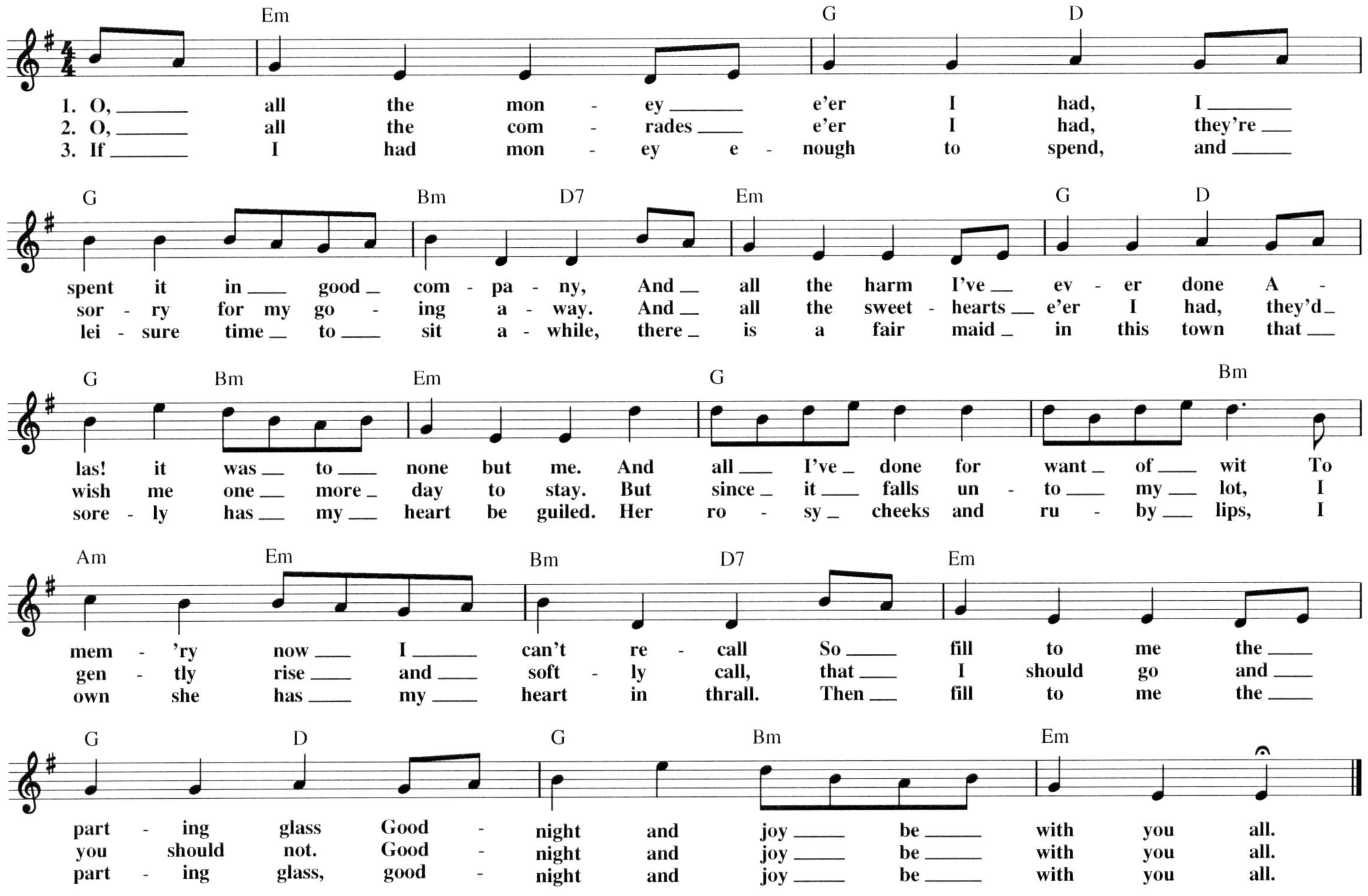

1. O, all the mon-ey e'er I had, I spent it in good com-pa-ny, And all the harm I've ev-er done A-las! it was to none but me. And all I've done for want of wit To mem-'ry now I can't re-call So fill to me the part-ing glass Good-night and joy be with you all.

2. O, all the com-rades e'er I had, they're sor-ry for my go-ing a-way. And all the sweet-hearts e'er I had, they'd wish me one more day to stay. But since it falls un-to my lot, I gen-tly rise and soft-ly call, that I should go and you should not. Good-night and joy be with you all.

3. If I had mon-ey e-nough to spend, and lei-sure time to sit a-while, there is a fair maid in this town that sore-ly has my heart be-guiled. Her ro-sy cheeks and ru-by lips, I own she has my heart in thrall. Then fill to me the part-ing glass, good-night and joy be with you all.

180

PAT MALLOY

Copyright © 2001 by HAL LEONARD CORPORATION

Irish folksong

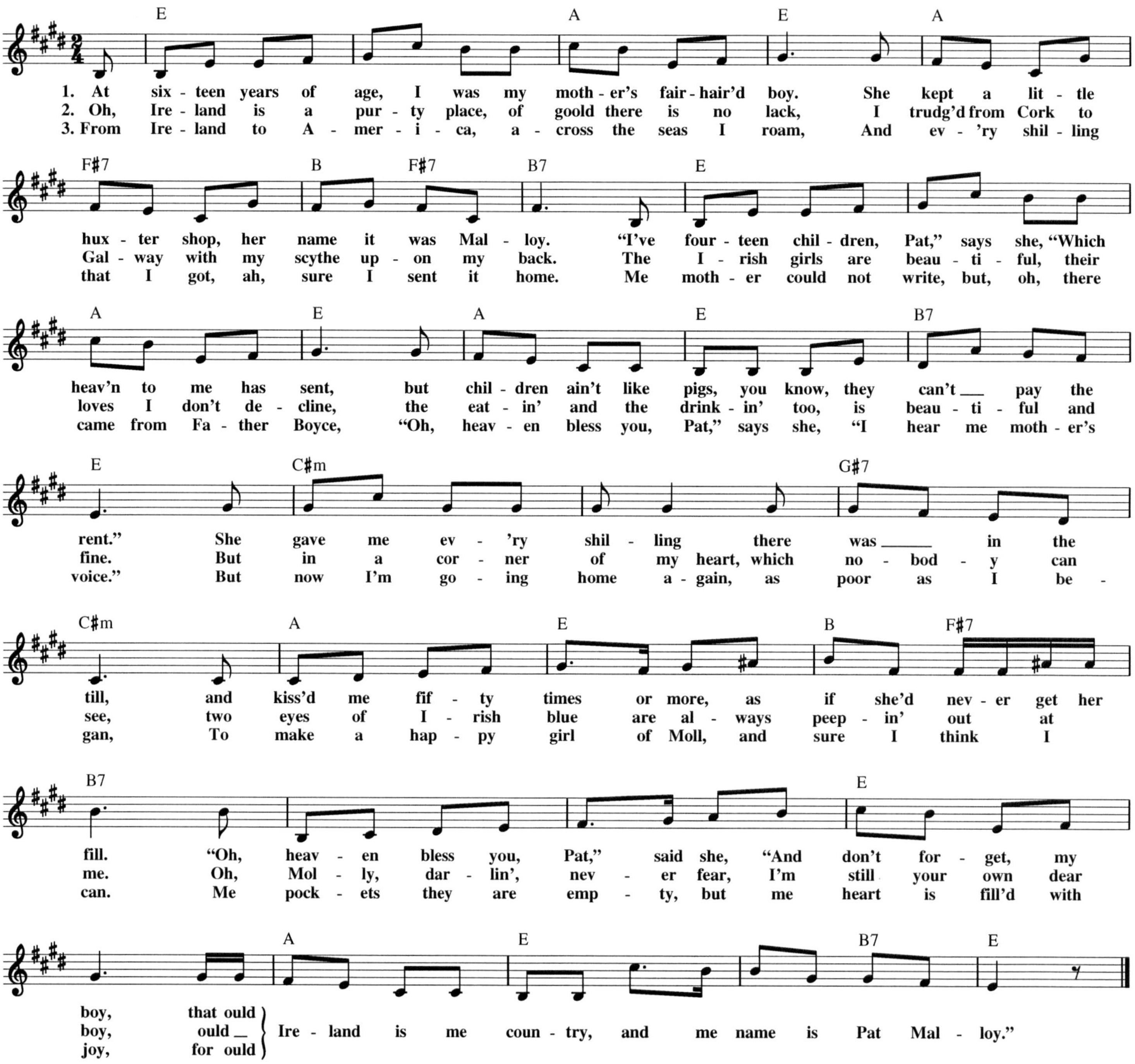

1. At six - teen years of age, I was my moth - er's fair - hair'd boy. She kept a lit - tle
2. Oh, Ire - land is a pur - ty place, of goold there is no lack, I trudg'd from Cork to
3. From Ire - land to A - mer - i - ca, a - cross the seas I roam, And ev - 'ry shil - ling

hux - ter shop, her name it was Mal - loy. "I've four - teen chil - dren, Pat," says she, "Which
Gal - way with my scythe up - on my back. The I - rish girls are beau - ti - ful, their
that I got, ah, sure I sent it home. Me moth - er could not write, but, oh, there

heav'n to me has sent, but chil - dren ain't like pigs, you know, they can't ___ pay the
loves I don't de - cline, the eat - in' and the drink - in' too, is beau - ti - ful and
came from Fa - ther Boyce, "Oh, heav - en bless you, Pat," says she, "I hear me moth - er's

rent." She gave me ev - 'ry shil - ling there was ___ in the
fine. But in a cor - ner of my heart, which no - bod - y can
voice." But now I'm go - ing home a - gain, as poor as I be -

till, and kiss'd me fif - ty times or more, as if she'd nev - er get her
see, two eyes of I - rish blue are al - ways peep - in' out at
gan, To make a hap - py girl of Moll, and sure I think I

fill. "Oh, heav - en bless you, Pat," said she, "And don't for - get, my
me. Oh, Mol - ly, dar - lin', nev - er fear, I'm still your own dear
can. Me pock - ets they are emp - ty, but me heart is fill'd with

boy, that ould
boy, ould ___   } Ire - land is me coun - try, and me name is Pat Mal - loy."
joy, for ould

THE PEACOCK MARCH

Copyright © 2001 by HAL LEONARD CORPORATION

Irish folksong

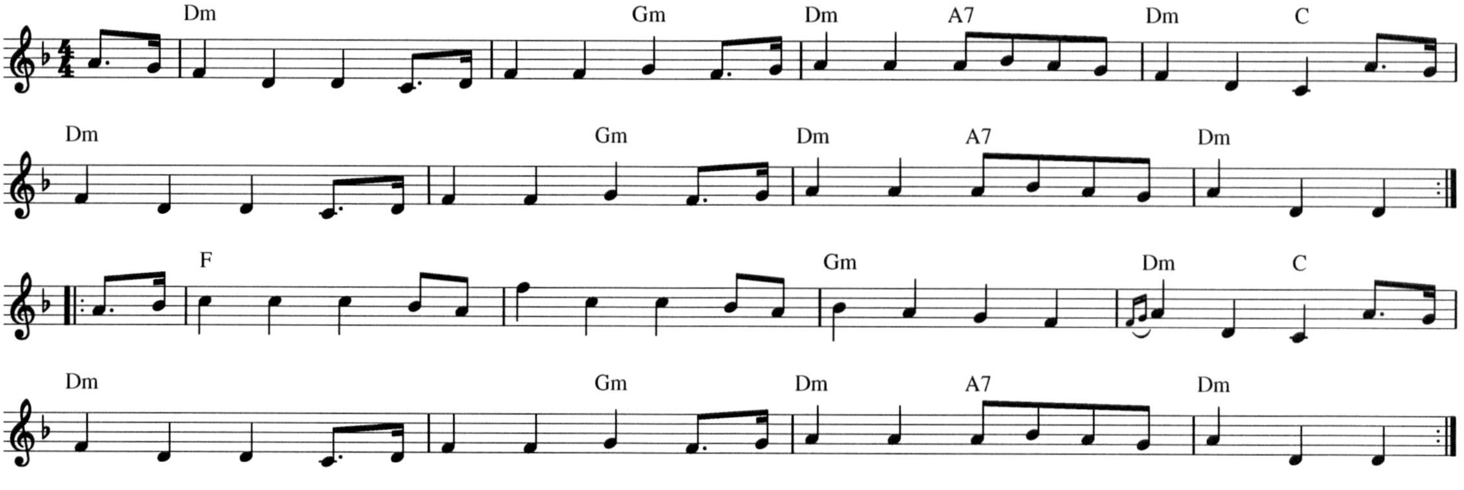

PHIL THE FLUTER

Irish folksong

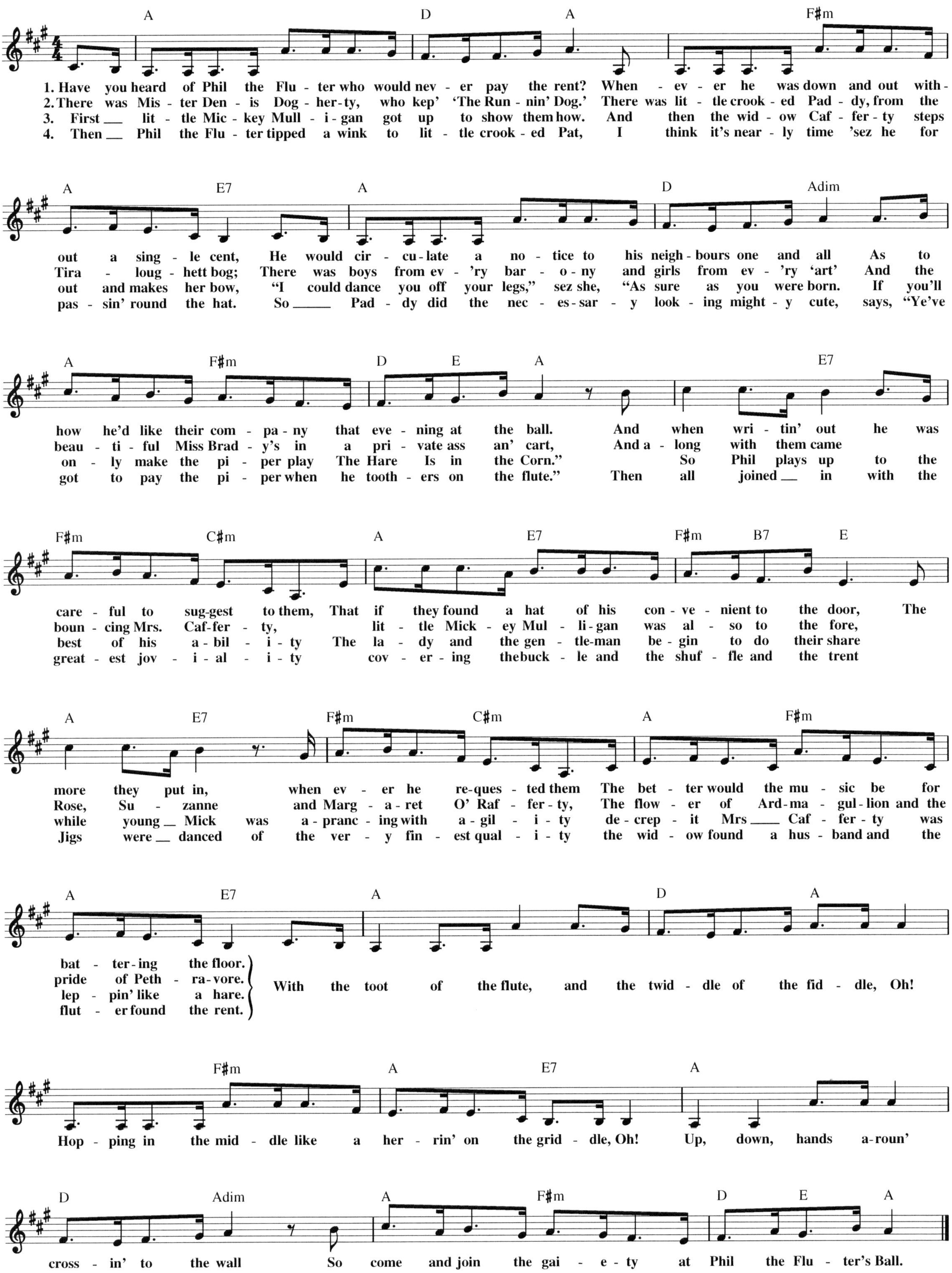

1. Have you heard of Phil the Flu - ter who would nev - er pay the rent? When - ev - er he was down and out with -
2. There was Mis - ter Den - is Dog - her - ty, who kep' 'The Run - nin' Dog.' There was lit - tle crook - ed Pad - dy, from the
3. First __ lit - tle Mic - key Mull - i - gan got up to show them how. And then the wid - ow Caf - fer - ty steps
4. Then __ Phil the Flu - ter tipped a wink to lit - tle crook - ed Pat, I think it's near - ly time 'sez he for

out a sing - le cent, He would cir - cu - late a no - tice to his neigh - bours one and all As to
Tira - loug - hett bog; There was boys from ev - 'ry bar - o - ny and girls from ev - 'ry 'art' And the
out and makes her bow, "I could dance you off your legs," sez she, "As sure as you were born. If you'll
pas - sin' round the hat. So ____ Pad - dy did the nec - es - sar - y look - ing might - y cute, says, "Ye've

how he'd like their com - pa - ny that eve - ning at the ball. And when wri - tin' out he was
beau - ti - ful Miss Brad - y's in a pri - vate ass an' cart, And a - long with them came
on - ly make the pi - per play The Hare Is in the Corn." So Phil plays up to the
got to pay the pi - per when he tooth - ers on the flute." Then all joined __ in with the

care - ful to sug - gest to them, That if they found a hat of his con - ve - nient to the door, The
boun - cing Mrs. Caf - fer - ty, lit - tle Mick - ey Mul - li - gan was al - so to the fore,
best of his a - bil - i - ty The la - dy and the gen - tle - man be - gin to do their share
great - est jov - i - al - i - ty cov - er - ing the buck - le and the shuf - fle and the trent

more they put in, when ev - er he re - ques - ted them The bet - ter would the mu - sic be for
Rose, Su - zanne and Marg - a - ret O' Raf - fer - ty, The flow - er of Ard - ma - gul - lion and the
while young __ Mick was a - pranc - ing with a - gil - i - ty de - crep - it Mrs ___ Caf - fer - ty was
Jigs were __ danced of the ver - y fin - est qual - i - ty the wid - ow found a hus - band and the

bat - ter - ing the floor. ⎫
pride of Peth - ra - vore. ⎪ With the toot of the flute, and the twid - dle of the fid - dle, Oh!
lep - pin' like a hare. ⎬
flut - er found the rent. ⎭

Hop - ping in the mid - dle like a her - rin' on the grid - dle, Oh! Up, down, hands a-roun'

cross - in' to the wall So come and join the gai - e - ty at Phil the Flu - ter's Ball.

PEGGY GORDON

Irish folksong

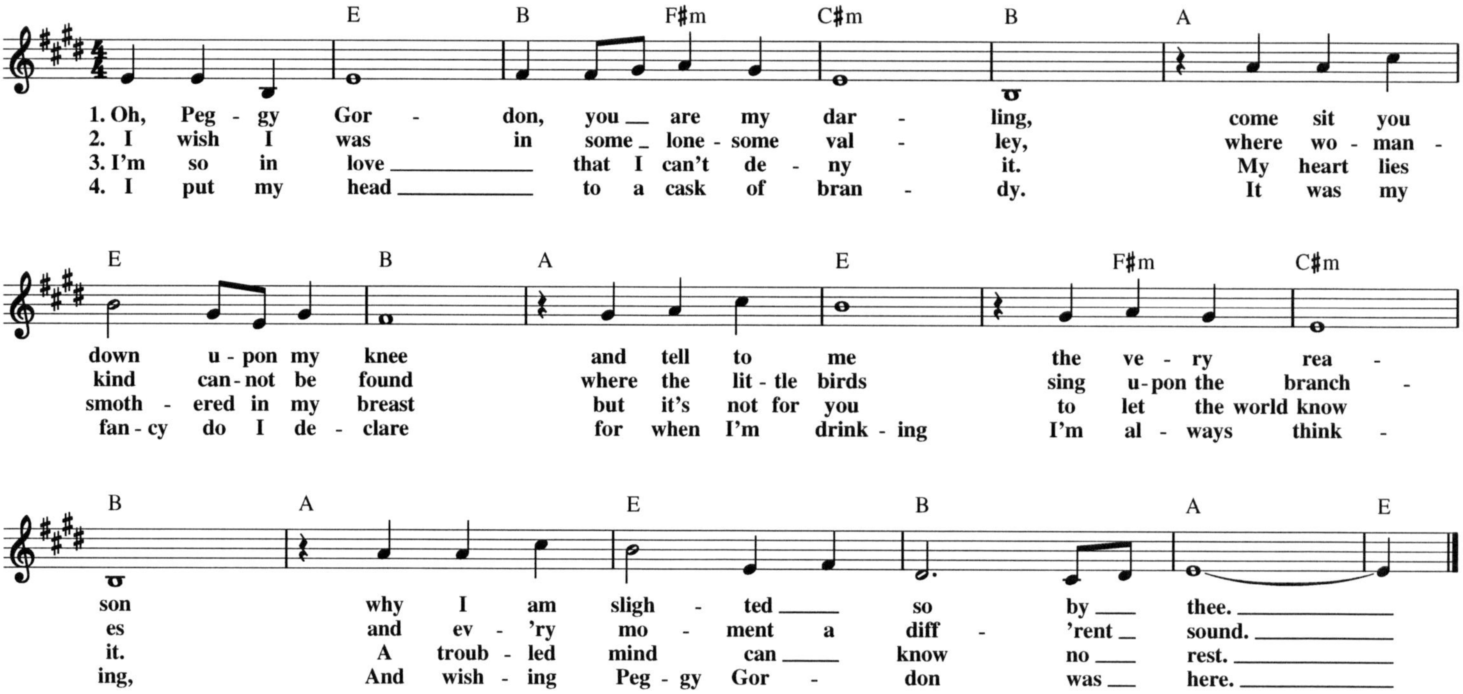

1. Oh, Peg-gy Gor - don, you __ are my dar - ling, come sit you
2. I wish I was in some _ lone - some val - ley, where wo - man -
3. I'm so in love __ that I can't de - ny it. My heart lies
4. I put my head __ to a cask of bran - dy. It was my

down u - pon my knee and tell to me the ve - ry rea -
kind can - not be found where the lit - tle birds sing u - pon the branch -
smoth - ered in my breast but it's not for you to let the world know
fan - cy do I de - clare for when I'm drink - ing I'm al - ways think -

son why I am sligh - ted __ so by __ thee. __
es and ev - 'ry mo - ment a diff - 'rent _ sound. __
it. A troub - led mind can __ know no __ rest. __
ing, And wish - ing Peg - gy Gor - don was __ here. __

PEG O' MY HEART

Words by Alfred Bryan
Music by Fred Fischer

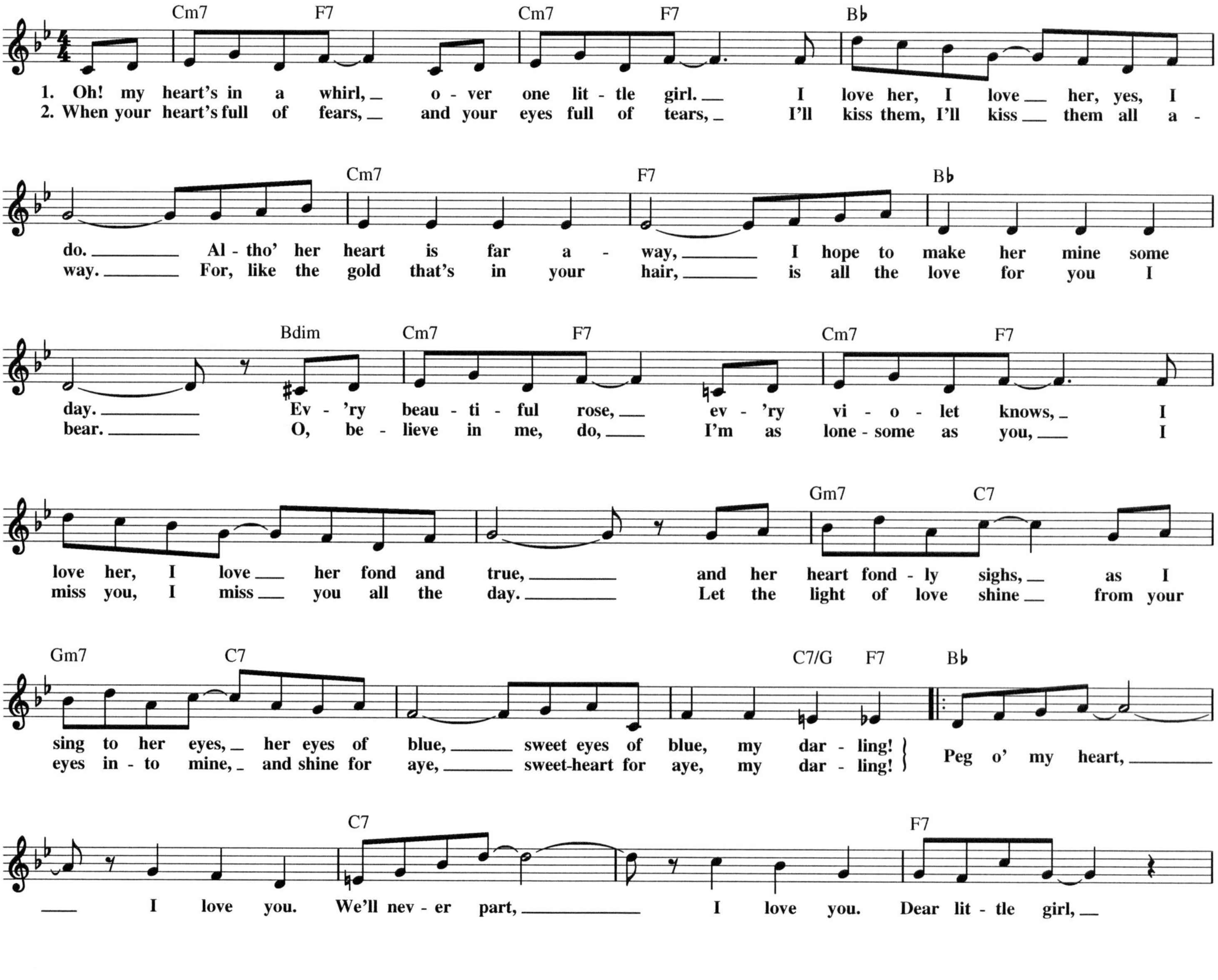

1. Oh! my heart's in a whirl, _ o - ver one lit - tle girl. __ I love her, I love __ her, yes, I
2. When your heart's full of fears, _ and your eyes full of tears, _ I'll kiss them, I'll kiss __ them all a -

do. __ Al - tho' her heart is far a - way, __ I hope to make her mine some
way. __ For, like the gold that's in your hair, __ is all the love for you I

day. __ Ev - 'ry beau - ti - ful rose, __ ev - 'ry vi - o - let knows, _ I
bear. __ O, be - lieve in me, do, __ I'm as lone - some as you, __ I

love her, I love __ her fond and true, __ and her heart fond - ly sighs, _ as I
miss you, I miss __ you all the day. __ Let the light of love shine __ from your

sing to her eyes, _ her eyes of blue, __ sweet eyes of blue, my dar - ling! } Peg o' my heart, __
eyes in - to mine, _ and shine for aye, __ sweet-heart for aye, my dar - ling! }

__ I love you. We'll nev - er part, __ I love you. Dear lit - tle girl, __

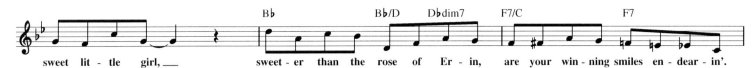

sweet lit - tle girl, ___ sweet - er than the rose of Er - in, are your win - ning smiles en - dear - in'.

Peg o' my heart, _____ your glanc - es with I - rish art _____ en - trance us. Come, be my own, _

come, make your home _ in my heart.   heart. _____

PORTLÁIRGE

Irish folksong

Brightly

1. Ó do bhios - sa lá i Port - láir - ge,   Fol dow fol dee fol the dad eye um,   Bhi _ fion is punch ar
Oh dhu vee - sah law Burth - law - rig-eh,   Vee _ feen iss punch err
2.,3. (See additional lyrics)

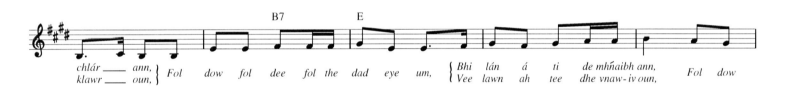

chlár ___ ann,   Fol dow fol dee fol the dad eye um,   Bhi lán á ti de mhńaibh ann,   Fol dow
klawr ___ oun,   Vee lawn ah tee dhe vnaw-iv oun,

fol dee fol the dad eye um,   Ag - us mise ag ól a sláin - te,   Fol dow fol dee fol the dad eye um.
Og-gus mish egg ohl ah slawn - teh,

Additional Lyrics

2. Agus d' éaluigh bean ó Rath liom,
   Og-gus thale-ig ban oh Raw lum,

   Fol dow fol dee fol the dad eye um,

   Agus triúr ó Thiobraid Árann,
   Og-gus throor oh Hibb-ar-idh Awr-on,

   Fol dow fol dee fol the dad eye um,

   Ni raibh a muintir sásta,
   Nee rev ah mween-thar saws-tha,

   Fol dow fol dee fol the dad eye um,

   Ni rabhadar ach leath-shásta,
   Nee row-dhar ock lah-haws-tha,

   Fol dow fol dee fol the dad eye um.

3. Ó raghadsa ón Charraig amárach,
   Oh ride-sah oan Korr-igg am-awr-ock,

   Fol dow fol dee fol the dad eye um,

   Agus tabharfad cailin bréa liom,
   Og-gus thaur-hadh koll-een brah lum,

   Fol dow fol dee fol the dad eye um,

   Gabhfaimid trid an Bhearnan,
   Go-meedh treedh on Vaar-nan,

   Fol dow fol dee fol the dad eye um,

   Ó thuaidh go Thiobraid Árann,
   Oh how-ig guh Hibb-ar-idh Awr-on

   Fol dow fol dee fol the dad eye um.

THE PORTUGUESE SAILOR

Irish folksong

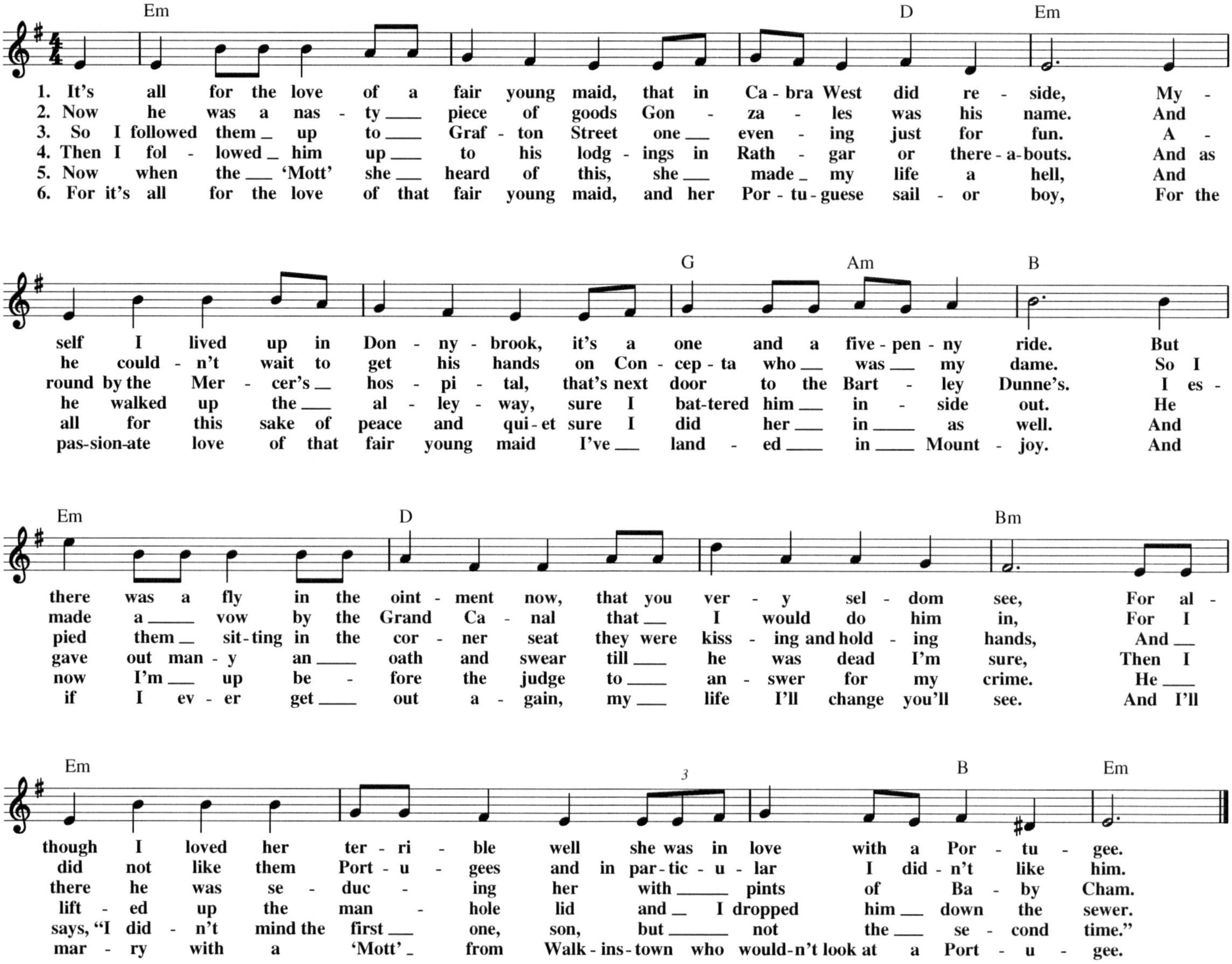

1. It's all for the love of a fair young maid, that in Ca-bra West did re-side, My-
2. Now he was a nas-ty piece of goods Gon-za-les was his name. And
3. So I followed them up to Graf-ton Street one even-ing just for fun. A-
4. Then I fol-lowed him up to his lodg-ings in Rath-gar or there-a-bouts. And as
5. Now when the 'Mott' she heard of this, she made my life a hell, And
6. For it's all for the love of that fair young maid, and her Por-tu-guese sail-or boy, For the

self I lived up in Don-ny-brook, it's a one and a five-pen-ny ride. But
he could-n't wait to get his hands on Con-cep-ta who was my dame. So I
round by the Mer-cer's hos-pi-tal, that's next door to the Bart-ley Dunne's. I es-
he walked up the al-ley-way, sure I bat-tered him in-side out. He
all for this sake of peace and qui-et sure I did her in as well. And
pas-sion-ate love of that fair young maid I've land-ed in Mount-joy. And

there was a fly in the oint-ment now, that you ver-y sel-dom see, For al-
made a vow by the Grand Ca-nal that I would do him in, For I
pied them sit-ting in the cor-ner seat they were kiss-ing and hold-ing hands, And
gave out man-y an oath and swear till he was dead I'm sure, Then I
now I'm up be-fore the judge to an-swer for my crime. He
if I ev-er get out a-gain, my life I'll change you'll see. And I'll

though I loved her ter-ri-ble well she was in love with a Por-tu-gee.
did not like them Port-u-gees and in par-tic-u-lar I did-n't like him.
caped them he was se-duc-ing her with pints of Ba-by Cham.
lift-ed up the man-hole lid and I dropped him down the sewer.
says, "I did-n't mind the first one, son, but not the se-cond time."
mar-ry with a 'Mott' from Walk-ins-town who would-n't look at a Port-u-gee.

THE PRATIES, THEY GROW SMALL

Irish folksong

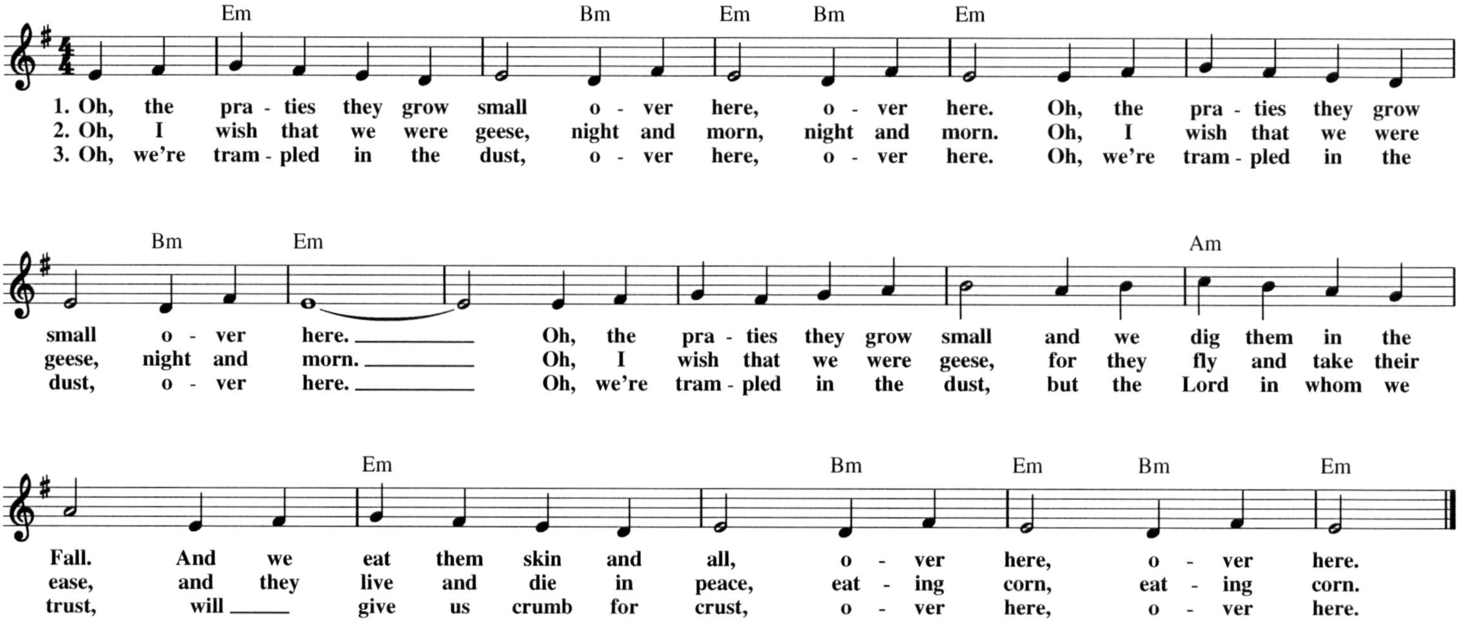

1. Oh, the pra-ties they grow small o-ver here, o-ver here. Oh, the pra-ties they grow
2. Oh, I wish that we were geese, night and morn, night and morn. Oh, I wish that we were
3. Oh, we're tram-pled in the dust, o-ver here, o-ver here. Oh, we're tram-pled in the

small o-ver here. Oh, the pra-ties they grow small and we dig them in the
geese, night and morn. Oh, I wish that we were geese, for they fly and take their
dust, o-ver here. Oh, we're tram-pled in the dust, but the Lord in whom we

Fall. And we eat them skin and all, o-ver here, o-ver here.
ease, and they live and die in peace, eat-ing corn, eat-ing corn.
trust, will give us crumb for crust, o-ver here, o-ver here.

THE PRETTY GIRL MILKING HER COW

Irish popular song
Words by Thomas Moore

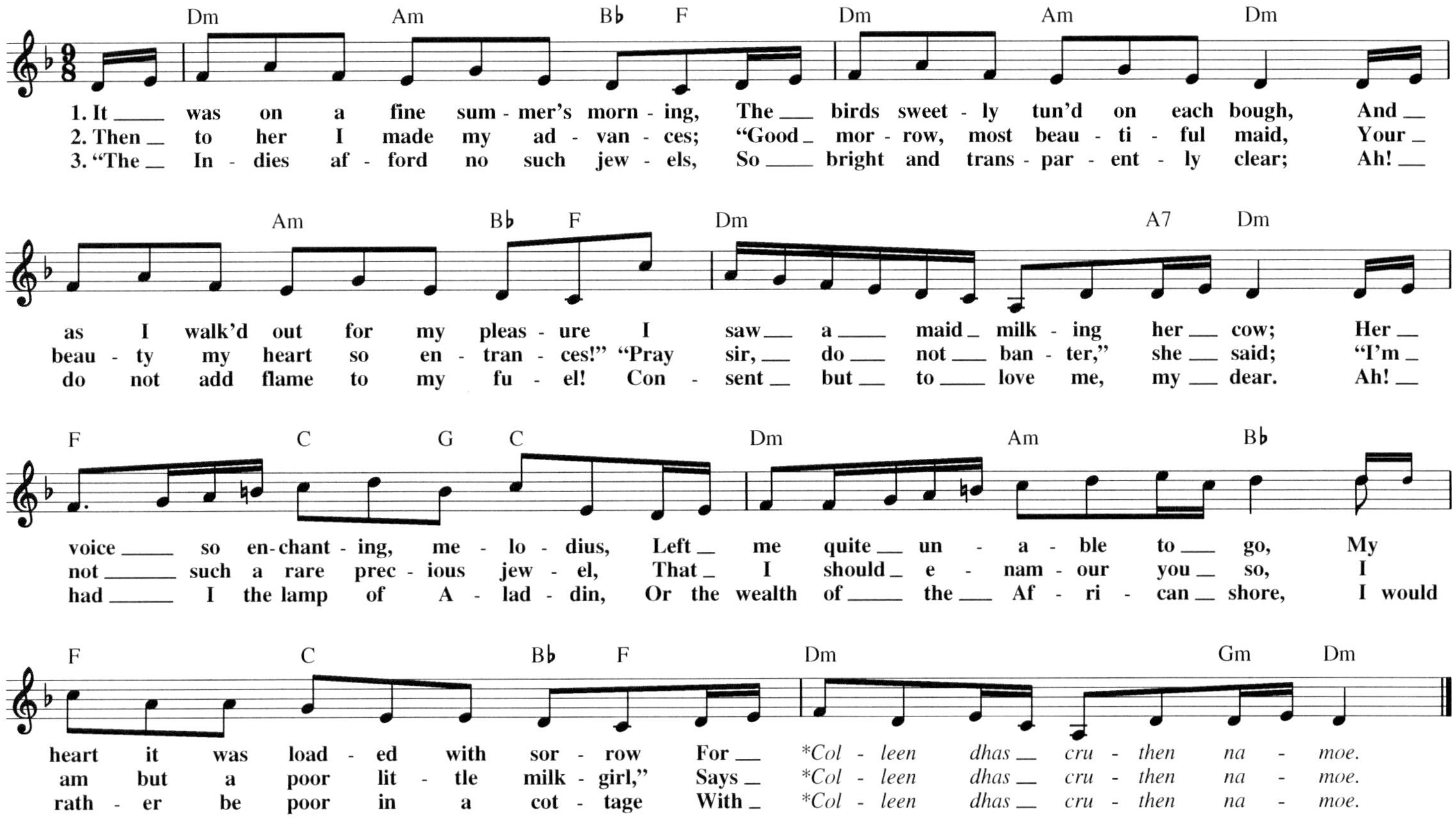

1. It ____ was on a fine sum-mer's morn-ing, The ____ birds sweet-ly tun'd on each bough, And ____
2. Then ____ to her I made my ad-van-ces; "Good ____ mor-row, most beau-ti-ful maid, Your ____
3. "The ____ In-dies af-ford no such jew-els, So ____ bright and trans-par-ent-ly clear; Ah! ____

as I walk'd out for my pleas-ure I saw ____ a ____ maid ____ milk-ing her ____ cow; Her ____
beau-ty my heart so en-tran-ces!" "Pray sir, ____ do ____ not ____ ban-ter," she ____ said; "I'm ____
do not add flame to my fu-el! Con-sent ____ but ____ to ____ love me, my ____ dear. Ah! ____

voice _____ so en-chant-ing, me-lo-dius, Left ____ me quite ____ un-a-ble to ____ go, My
not _____ such a rare prec-ious jew-el, That ____ I should ____ e-nam-our you ____ so, I
had _____ I the lamp of A-lad-din, Or the wealth of _____ the ____ Af-ri-can ____ shore, I would

heart it was load-ed with sor-row For ____ *Col-leen dhas ____ cru-then na-moe.
am but a poor lit-tle milk-girl," Says ____ *Col-leen dhas ____ cru-then na-moe.
rath-er be poor in a cot-tage With ____ *Col-leen dhas ____ cru-then na-moe.

*Pretty girl milking her cow.

PULLING THE SEA-DULSE

Folksong from the Hebrides

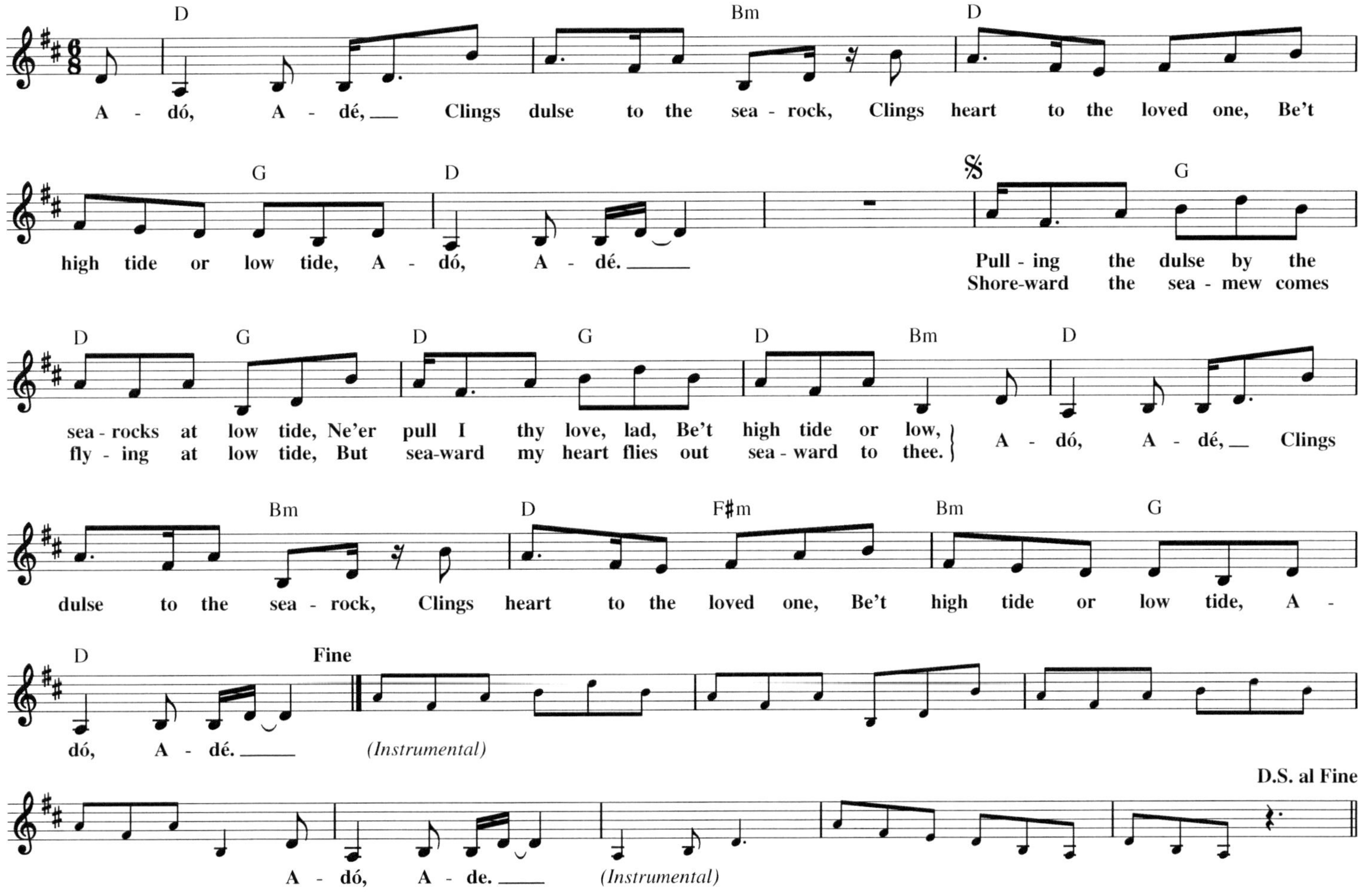

A - dó, A - dé, ____ Clings dulse to the sea-rock, Clings heart to the loved one, Be't

high tide or low tide, A - dó, A - dé. _____ Pull-ing the dulse by the
Shore-ward the sea-mew comes

sea-rocks at low tide, Ne'er pull I thy love, lad, Be't high tide or low, A - dó, A - dé, ____ Clings
fly-ing at low tide, But sea-ward my heart flies out sea-ward to thee.

dulse to the sea-rock, Clings heart to the loved one, Be't high tide or low tide, A -

Fine

dó, A - dé. _____ (Instrumental)

D.S. al Fine

A - dó, A - de. _____ (Instrumental)

PULSE OF MY HEART

Irish folksong

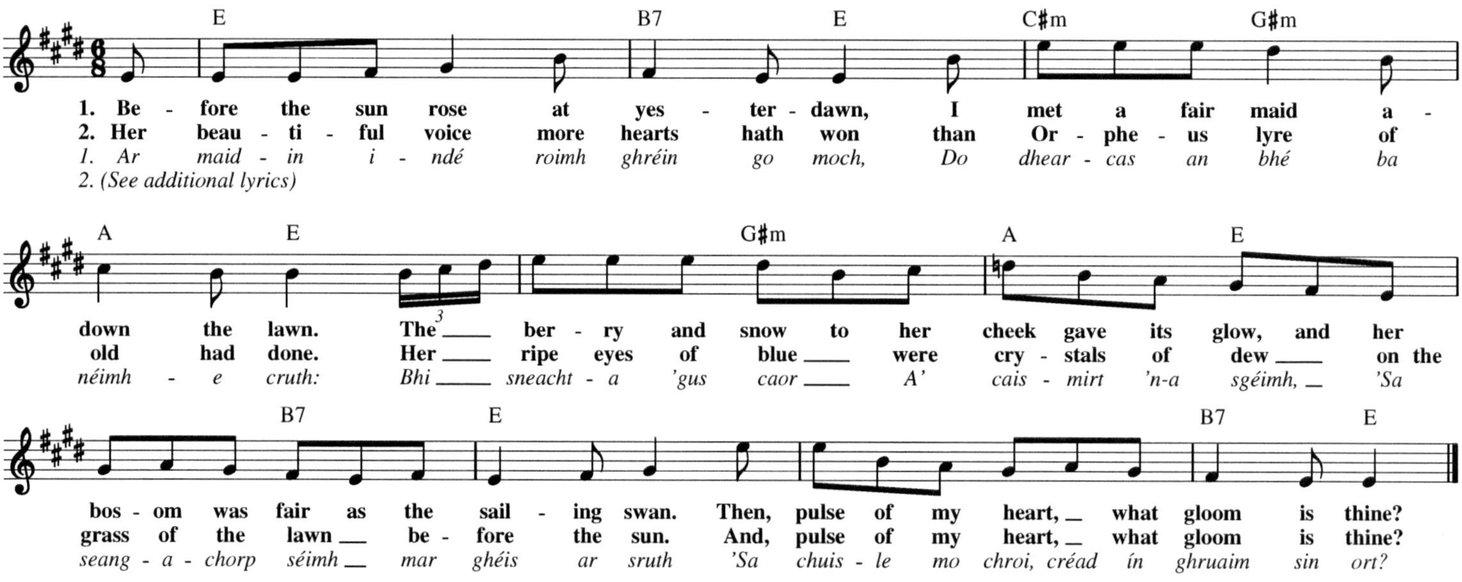

1. Be - fore the sun rose at yes - ter - dawn, I met a fair maid a-
2. Her beau - ti - ful voice more hearts hath won than Or - phe - us lyre of

1. Ar maid - in i - ndé roimh ghréin go moch, Do dhear - cas an bhé ba
2. (See additional lyrics)

down the lawn. The____ ber - ry and snow to her cheek gave its glow, and her
old had done. Her____ ripe eyes of blue____ were cry - stals of dew____ on the

néimh - e cruth: Bhi____ sneacht - a 'gus caor____ A' cais - mirt 'n-a sgéimh, ___ 'Sa

bos - om was fair as the sail - ing swan. Then, pulse of my heart, __ what gloom is thine?
grass of the lawn ___ be - fore the sun. And, pulse of my heart, __ what gloom is thine?

seang - a - chorp séimh ___ mar ghéis ar sruth 'Sa chuis - le mo chroi, créad ín ghruaim sin ort?

Additional Lyrics

2. *Ba bhinne guth caomh a béil le sult*
   Ná Orpheus do léig go faon na tuirc:
   Bhi a reamhar-rosg réidh
   Mar chriostal na mbraon
   Ar sheamair ghlais fhéir roimh ghréin go moch-
   'S a chuisle mo chroi, créad i'n ghruaim sin ort?

PUTTING THE TAUNT
(Cur Na Tamailte)

Folksong from the Hebrides

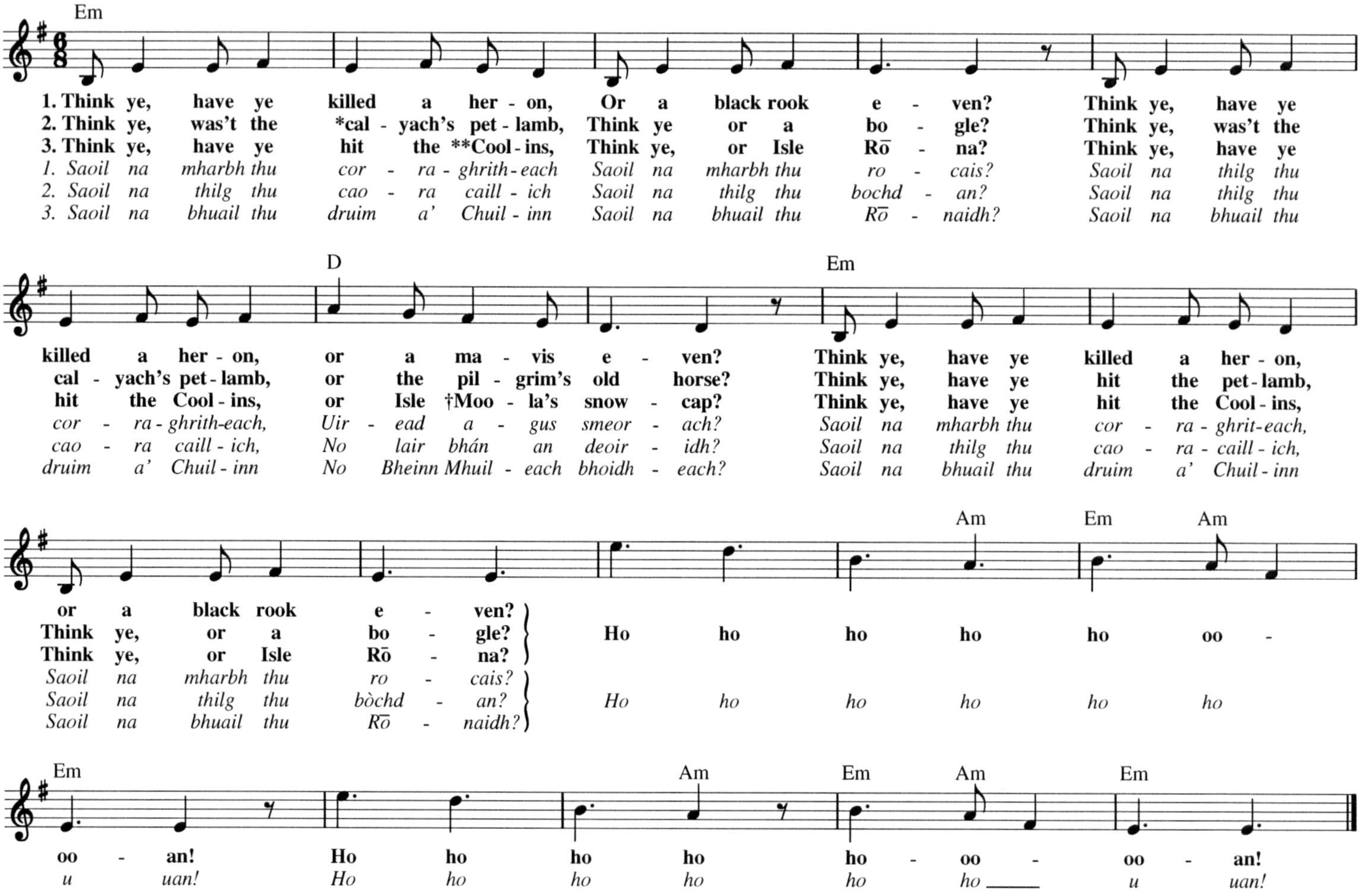

1. Think ye, have ye killed a her - on, Or a black rook e - ven? Think ye, have ye
2. Think ye, was't the *cal - yach's pet - lamb, Think ye or a bo - gle? Think ye, was't the
3. Think ye, have ye hit the **Cool - ins, Think ye, or Isle Rō - na? Think ye, have ye

1. Saoil na mharbh thu cor - ra - ghrith-each Saoil na mharbh thu ro - cais? Saoil na thilg thu
2. Saoil na thilg thu cao - ra caill - ich Saoil na thilg thu bochd - an? Saoil na thilg thu
3. Saoil na bhuail thu druim a' Chuil - inn Saoil na bhuail thu Rō - naidh? Saoil na bhuail thu

killed a her - on, or a ma - vis e - ven? Think ye, have ye killed a her - on,
cal - yach's pet - lamb, or the pil - grim's old horse? Think ye, have ye hit the pet - lamb,
hit the Cool - ins, or Isle †Moo - la's snow - cap? Think ye, have ye hit the Cool - ins,

cor - ra - ghrith-each, Uir - ead a - gus smeor - ach? Saoil na mharbh thu cor - ra - ghrit-each,
cao - ra caill - ich, No lair bhán an deor - idh? Saoil na thilg thu cao - ra - caill - ich,
druim a' Chuil - inn No Bheinn Mhuil - each bhoidh - each? Saoil na bhuail thu druim a' Chuil - inn

or a black rook e - ven?
Think ye, or a bo - gle? Ho ho ho ho ho oo -
Think ye, or Isle Rō - na?
Saoil na mharbh thu ro - cais?
Saoil na thilg thu bòchd - an? Ho ho ho ho ho ho
Saoil na bhuail thu Rō - naidh?

oo - an! Ho ho ho ho ho - oo - oo - an!
u uan! Ho ho ho ho ho ho ____ u uan!

*cailleach = old wife
**the hills of Skye and Rūm
†mull

PUTTING OUT TO SEA

Folksong from the Hebrides

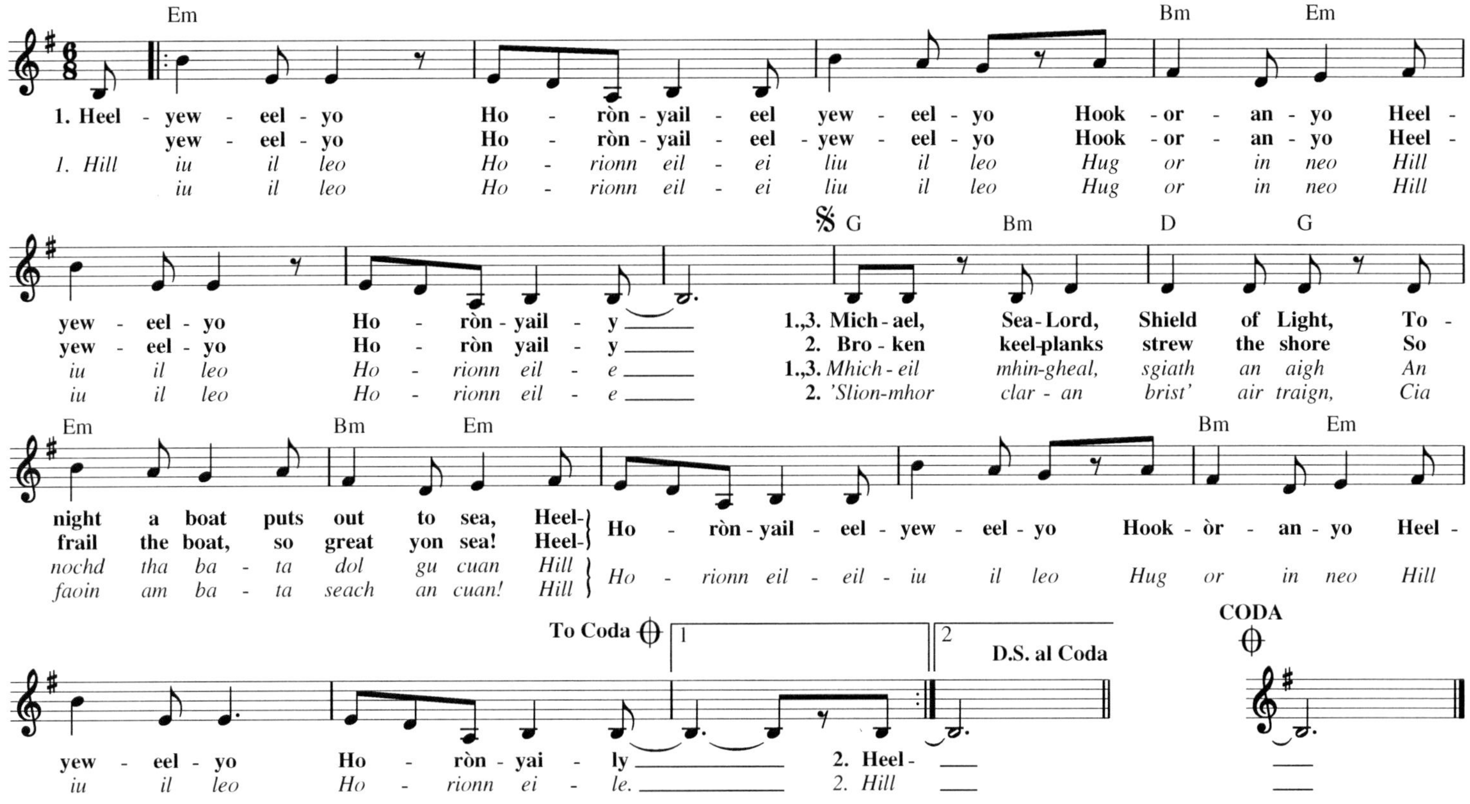

THE QUEEN OF CONNEMARA

Irish folksong

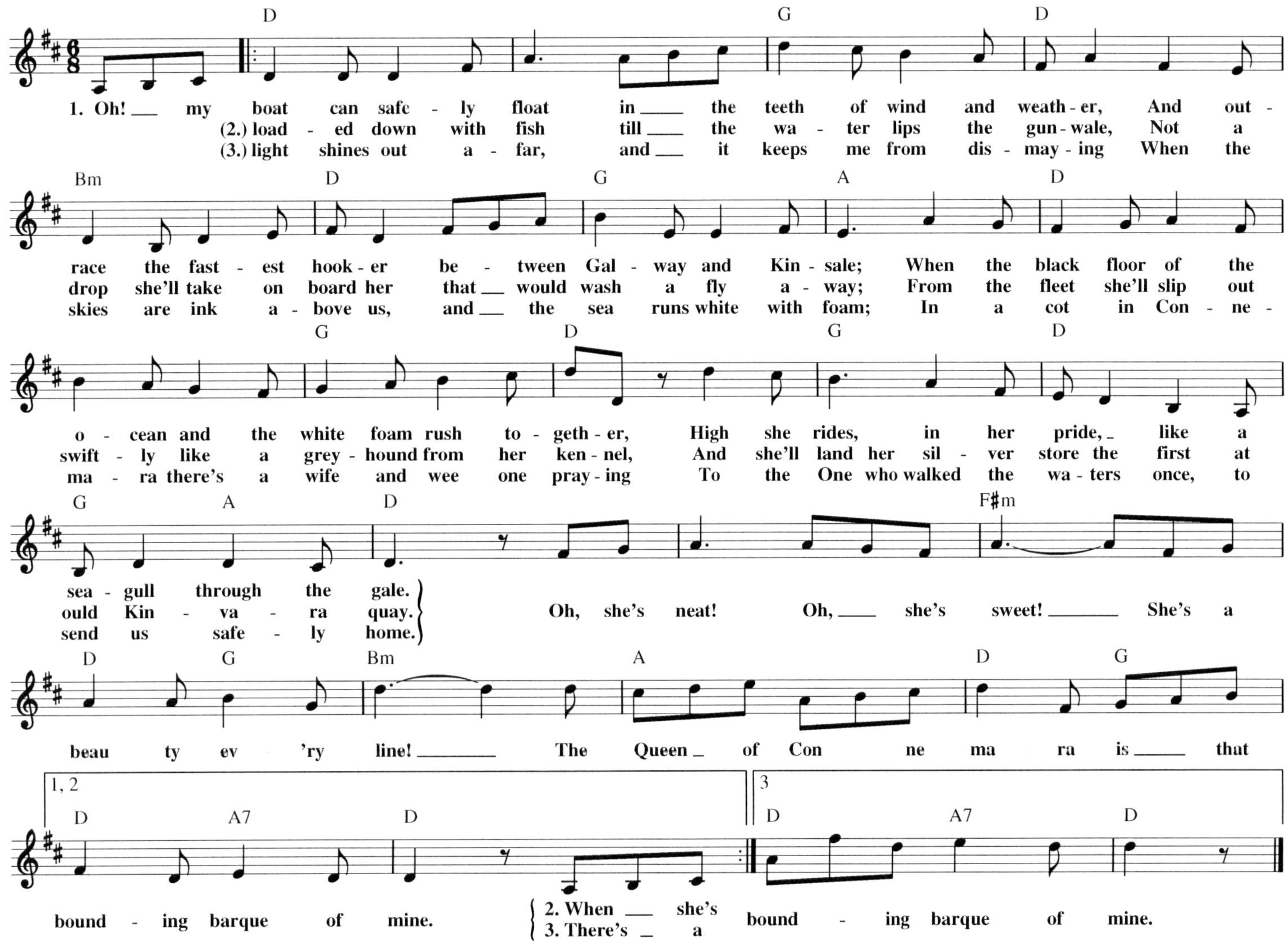

RAGLAN ROAD

Irish folksong

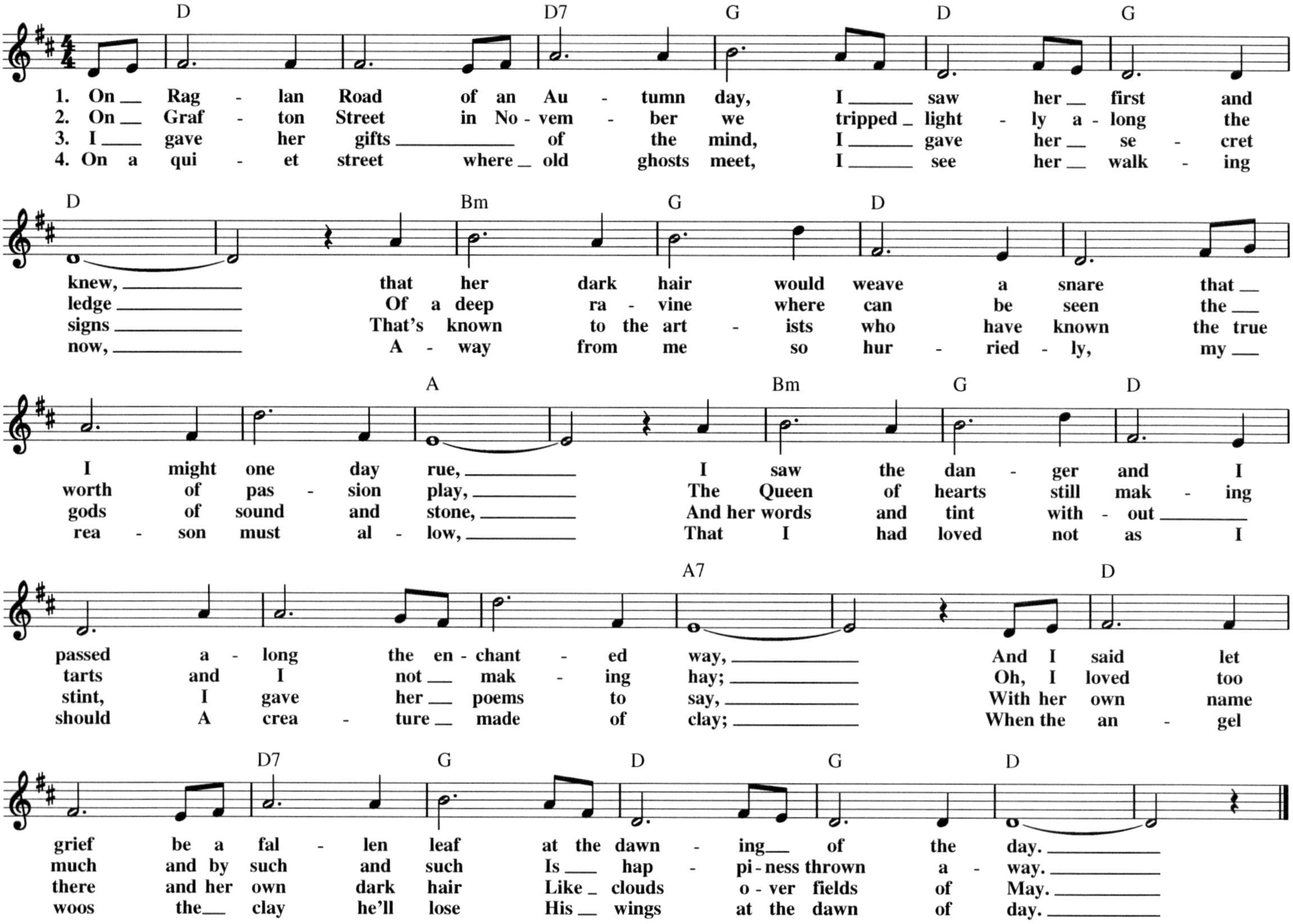

1. On __ Rag - lan Road of an Au - tumn day, I _____ saw her __ first and
2. On __ Graf - ton Street in No - vem - ber we tripped _ light - ly a - long the
3. I ____ gave her gifts _____ of the mind, I _____ gave her _ se - cret
4. On a qui - et street where _ old ghosts meet, I _____ see her _ walk - ing

knew, _____ that her dark hair would weave a snare that __
ledge _____ Of a deep dark ra - vine where can be seen the __
signs _____ That's known to the art - ists who have known the true
now, _____ A - way from me so hur - ried - ly, my __

I might one day rue, _____ I saw the dan - ger and I
worth of pas - sion play, _____ The Queen of hearts still mak - ing
gods of sound and stone, _____ And her words and tint with - out __
rea - son must al - low, _____ That I had loved not as I

passed a - long the en - chant - ed way, _____ And I said let
tarts and I not __ mak - ing hay; _____ Oh, I loved too
stint, I gave her _ poems to say, _____ With her own name
should A crea - ture _ made of clay; _____ When the an - gel

grief be a fal - len leaf at the dawn - ing __ of the day. _____
much and by such and such Is __ hap - pi - ness thrown a - way. _____
there and her own dark hair Like _ clouds o - ver fields of May. _____
woos the _ clay he'll lose His _ wings at the dawn of day. _____

RAKE AND RAMBLING BOY

Irish folksong

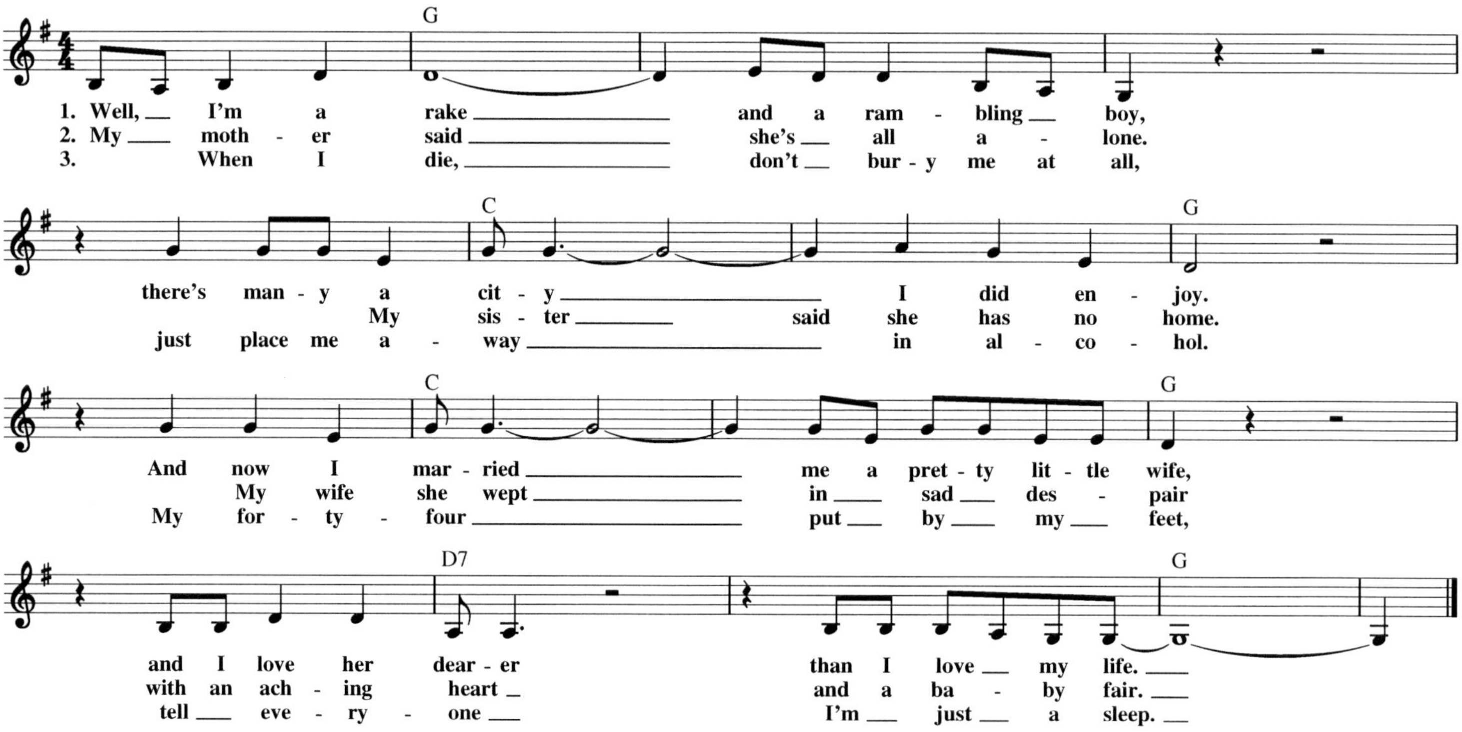

1. Well, __ I'm a rake _____ and a ram - bling __ boy,
2. My __ moth - er said _____ she's __ all a - lone.
3. When I die, _____ don't __ bur - y me at all,

there's man - y a cit - y _____ I did en - joy.
My sis - ter _____ said she has no home.
just place me a - way _____ in al - co - hol.

And now I mar - ried _____ me a pret - ty lit - tle wife,
My wife she wept _____ in sad des - pair
My for - ty - four _____ put __ by __ my __ feet,

and I love her dear - er than I love __ my life. __
with an ach - ing heart _ and a ba - by fair. __
tell __ eve - ry - one __ I'm __ just _ a sleep. __

REAL OLD MOUNTAIN DEW

Irish folksong

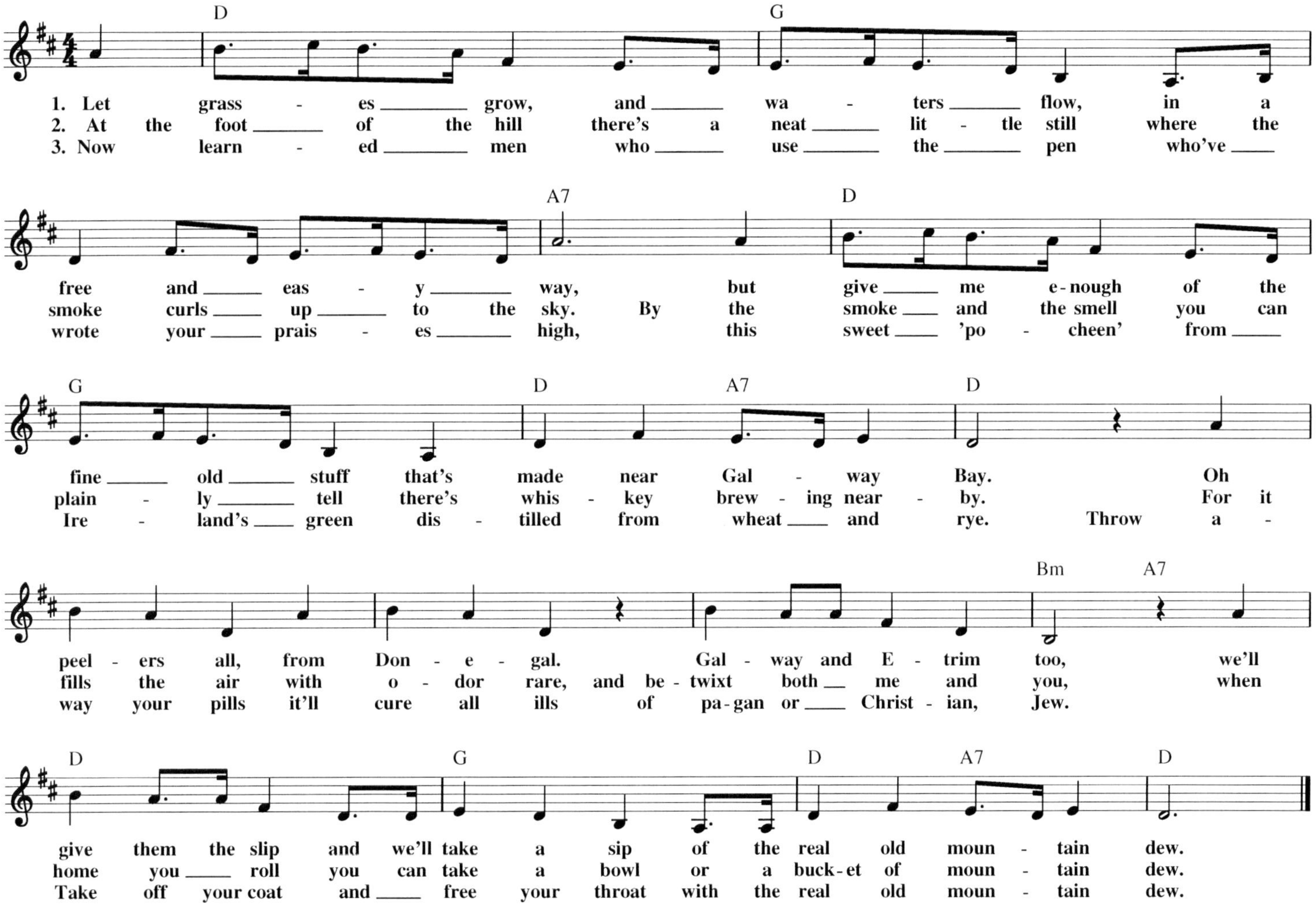

1. Let grass - es grow, and waters flow, in a free and eas - y way, but give me e-nough of the fine old stuff that's made near Gal - way Bay. Oh give them the slip and we'll take a sip of the real old moun - tain dew.
2. At the foot of the hill there's a neat lit - tle still where the smoke curls up to the sky. By the smoke and the smell you can plain - ly tell there's whis - key brew - ing near - by. For it fills the air with o - dor rare, and be - twixt both me and you, when home you roll you can take a bowl or a buck-et of moun - tain dew.
3. Now learn - ed men who use the pen who've wrote your prais - es high, this sweet 'po - cheen' from peel - ers all, from Don - e - gal. Gal - way and E - trim too, we'll way your pills it'll cure all ills of pa-gan or Christ - ian, Jew. Take off your coat and free your throat with the real old moun - tain dew.

REYNARD THE FOX

Irish folksong

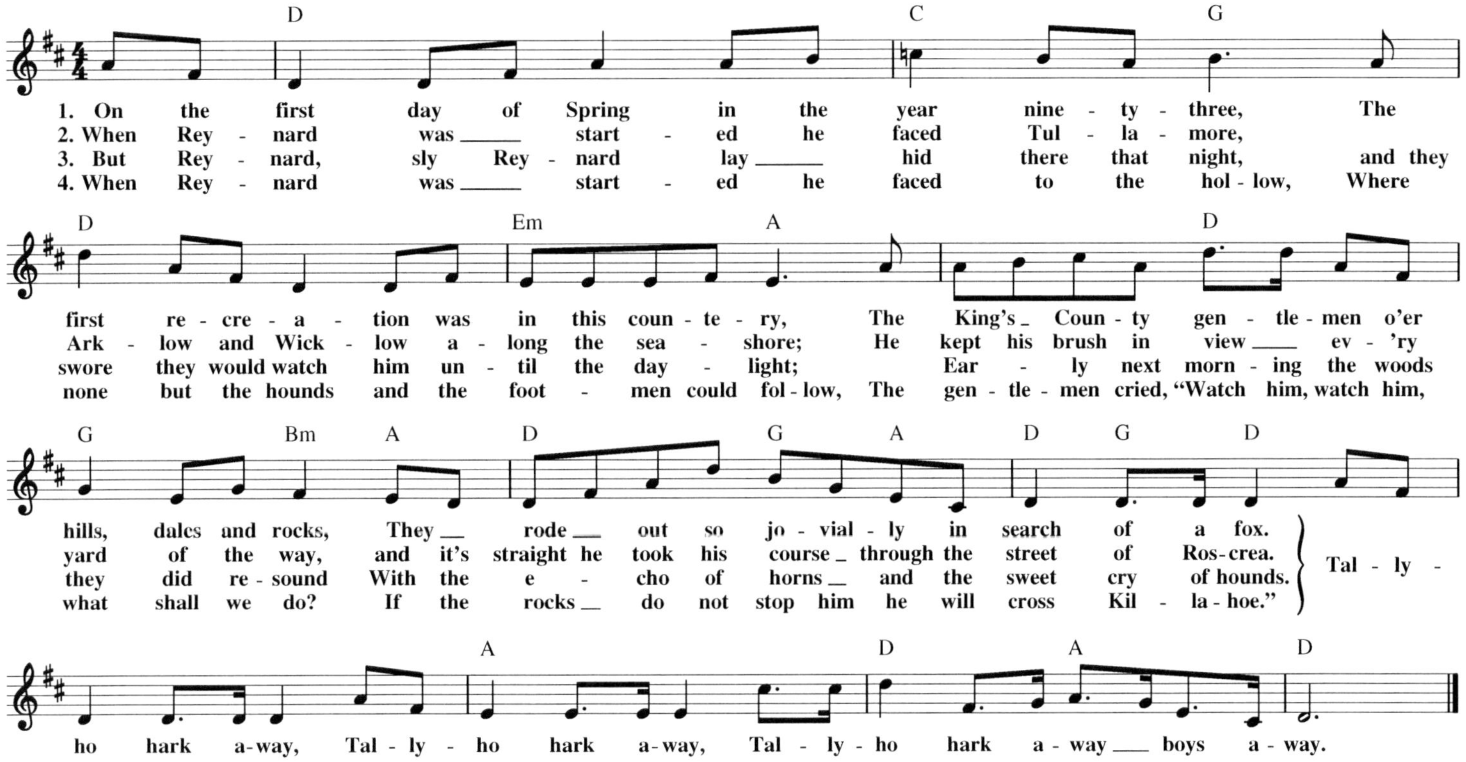

1. On the first day of Spring in the year nine - ty - three, The first re-cre-a - tion was in this coun - te-ry, The King's Coun - ty gen - tle-men o'er hills, dales and rocks, They rode out so jo - vial - ly in search of a fox. Tal - ly - ho hark a-way, Tal - ly-ho hark a-way, Tal - ly - ho hark a - way boys a - way.
2. When Rey - nard was start - ed he faced Tul - la - more, Ark - low and Wick - low a - long the sea - shore; He kept his brush in view ev - 'ry yard of the way, and it's straight he took his course through the street of Ros-crea.
3. But Rey - nard, sly Rey - nard lay hid there that night, and they swore they would watch him un - til the day - light; Ear - ly next morn - ing the woods they did re-sound With the e - cho of horns and the sweet cry of hounds.
4. When Rey - nard was start - ed he faced to the hol - low, Where none but the hounds and the foot - men could fol - low, The gen - tle - men cried, "Watch him, watch him, what shall we do? If the rocks do not stop him he will cross Kil - la - hoe."

THE RISING OF THE MOON

Irish folksong
By John Keegan Casey

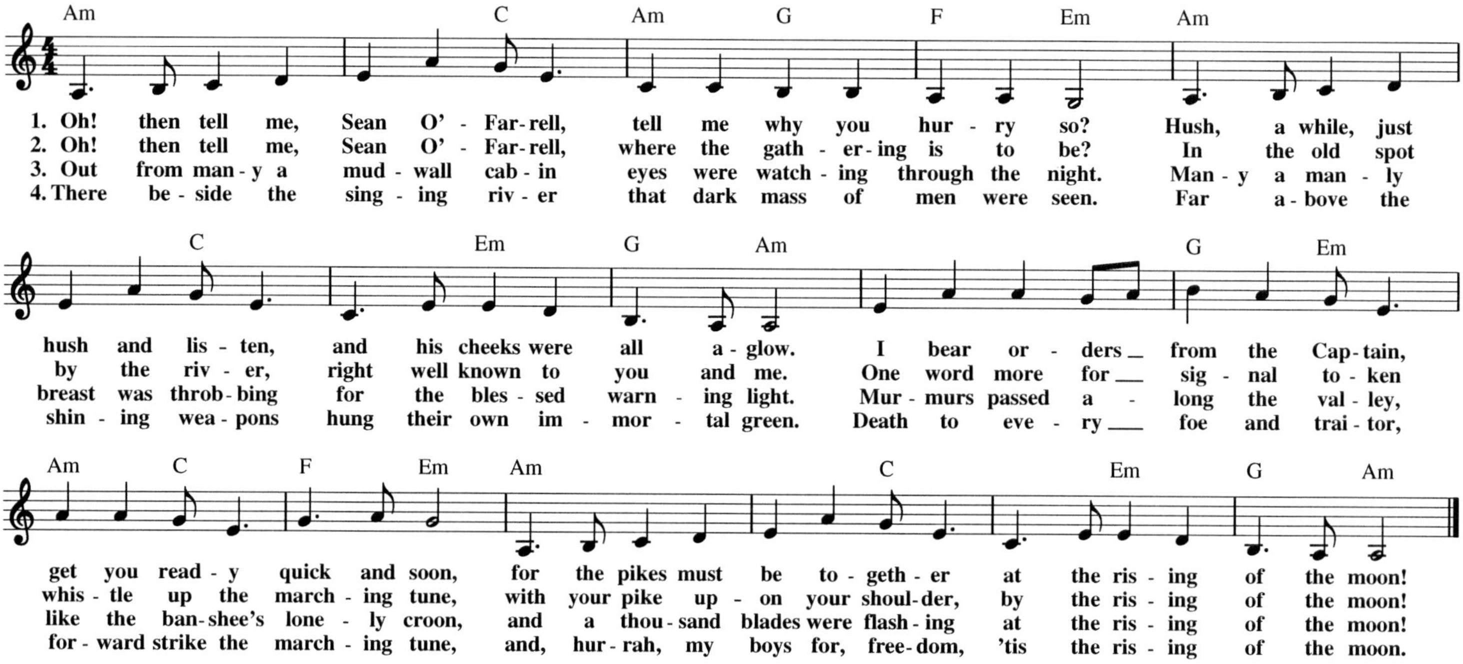

1. Oh! then tell me, Sean O'-Far-rell, tell me why you hur-ry so? Hush, a while, just
2. Oh! then tell me, Sean O'-Far-rell, where the gath-er-ing is to be? In the old spot
3. Out from man-y a mud-wall cab-in eyes were watch-ing through the night. Man-y a man-ly
4. There be-side the sing-ing riv-er that dark mass of men were seen. Far a-bove the

hush and lis-ten, and his cheeks were all a-glow. I bear or-ders _ from the Cap-tain,
by the riv-er, right well known to you and me. One word more for _ sig-nal to-ken
breast was throb-bing for the bles-sed warn-ing light. Mur-murs passed a - long the val-ley,
shin-ing wea-pons hung their own im-mor-tal green. Death to eve-ry _ foe and trai-tor,

get you read-y quick and soon, for the pikes must be to-geth-er at the ris-ing of the moon!
whis-tle up the march-ing tune, with your pike up-on your shoul-der, by the ris-ing of the moon!
like the ban-shee's lone-ly croon, and a thou-sand blades were flash-ing at the ris-ing of the moon!
for-ward strike the march-ing tune, and, hur-rah, my boys for, free-dom, 'tis the ris-ing of the moon.

THE ROAD TO THE ISLES

Scottish folksong

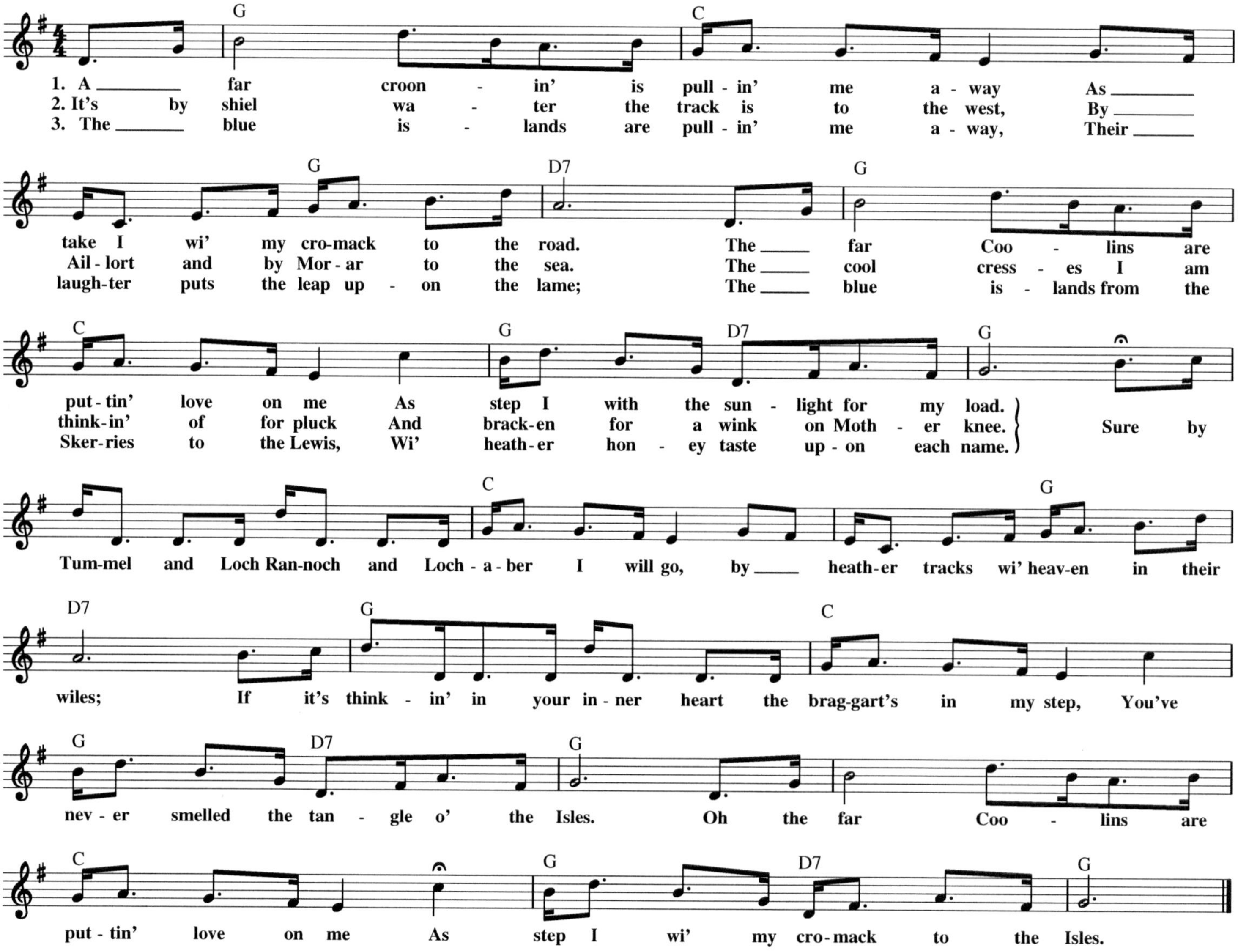

1. A _____ far croon - in' is pull - in' me a - way As _____
2. It's by shiel wa - ter the track is to the west, By _____
3. The _____ blue is - lands are pull - in' me a - way, Their _____

take I wi' my cro-mack to the road. The _____ far Coo - lins are
Ail - lort and by Mor - ar to the sea. The _____ cool cress - es I am
laugh-ter puts the leap up - on the lame; The _____ blue is - lands from the

put - tin' love on me As step I with the sun - light for my load. }
think - in' of for pluck And brack-en for a wink on Moth - er knee. } Sure by
Sker - ries to the Lewis, Wi' heath-er hon - ey taste up - on each name. }

Tum-mel and Loch Ran-noch and Loch - a - ber I will go, by _____ heath-er tracks wi' heav-en in their

wiles; If it's think - in' in your in - ner heart the brag-gart's in my step, You've

nev - er smelled the tan - gle o' the Isles. Oh the far Coo - lins are

put - tin' love on me As step I wi' my cro-mack to the Isles.

A RICH IRISH LADY

Irish folksong

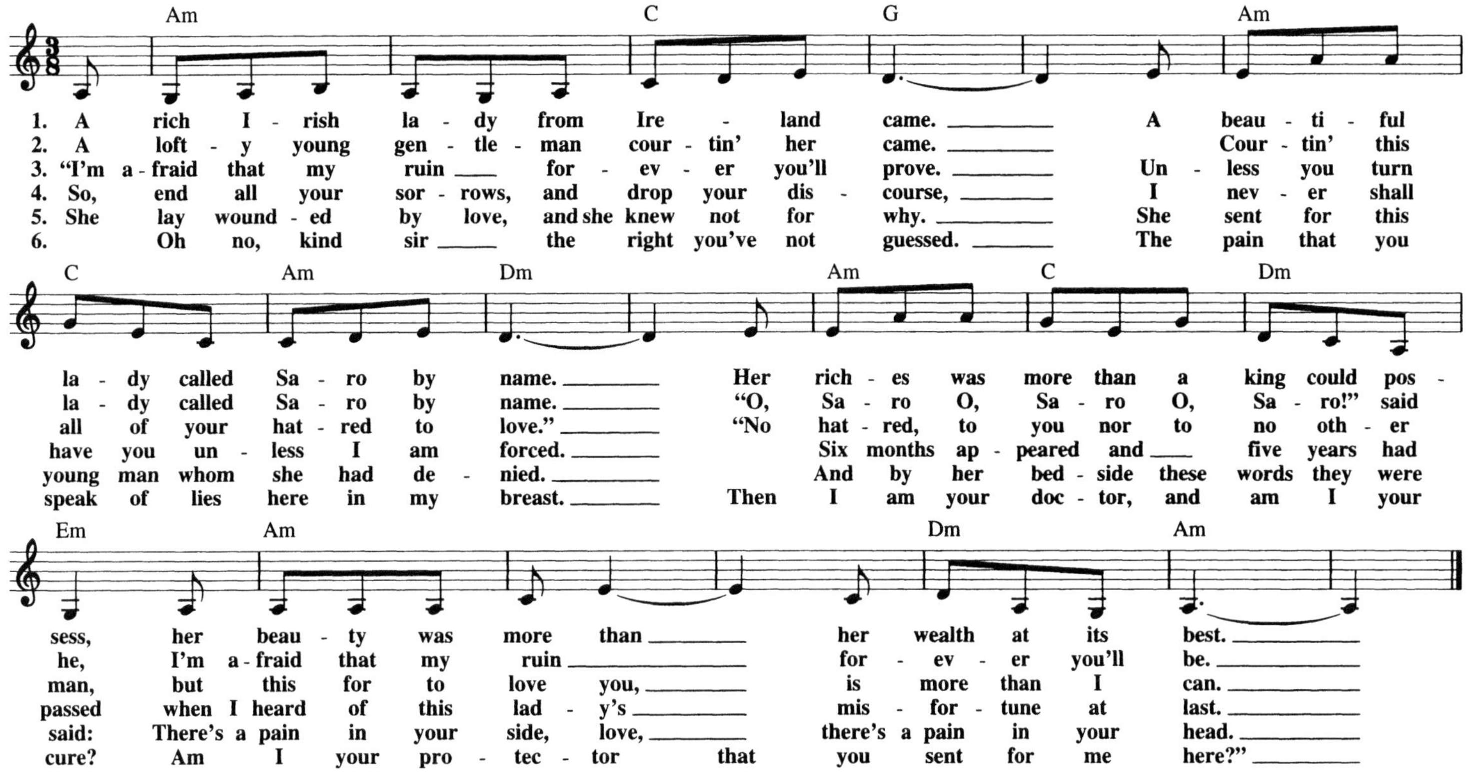

THE ROCKS OF BAWN

Irish folksong

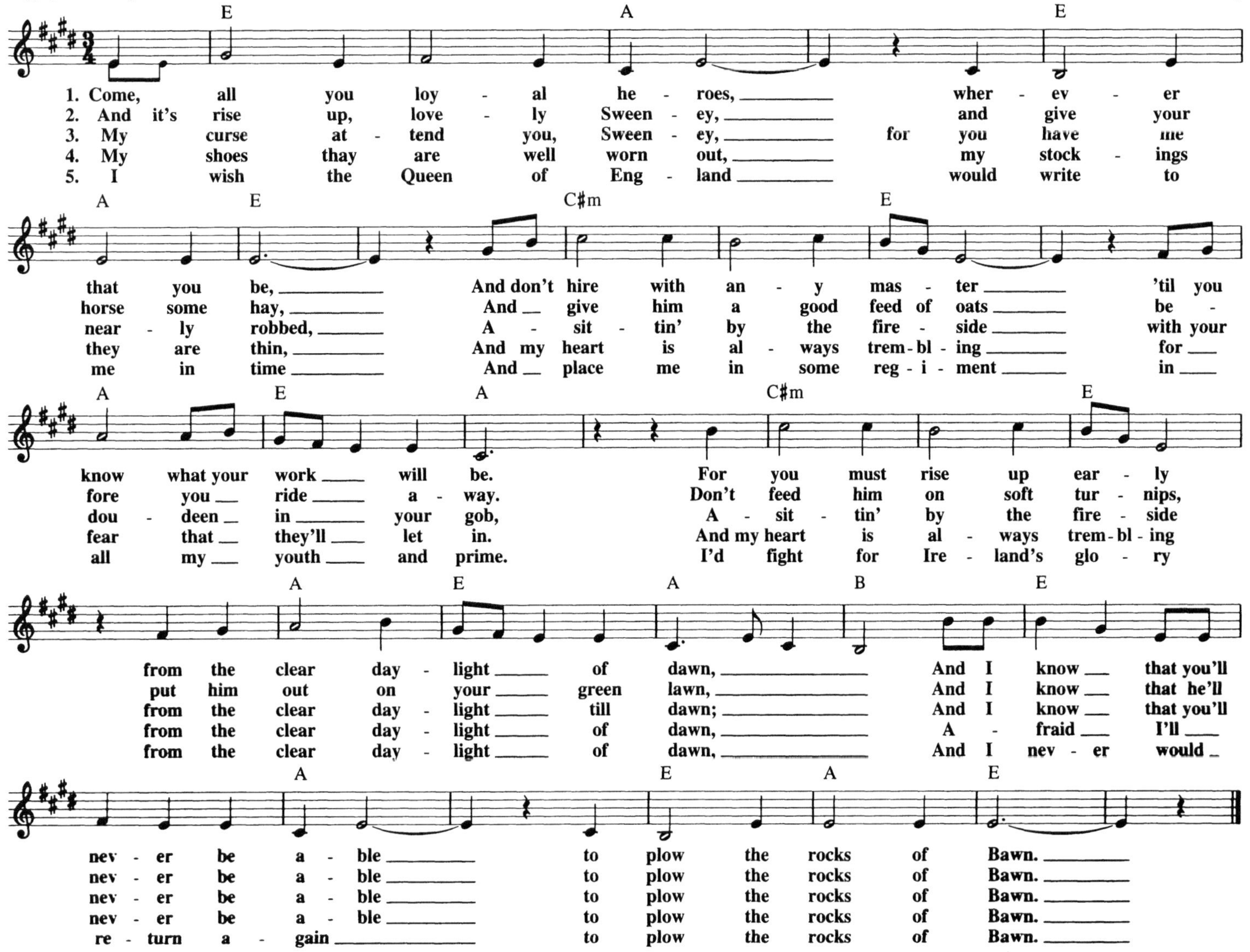

192

RODDY McCORLEY

Irish folksong

Copyright © 2000 by HAL LEONARD CORPORATION

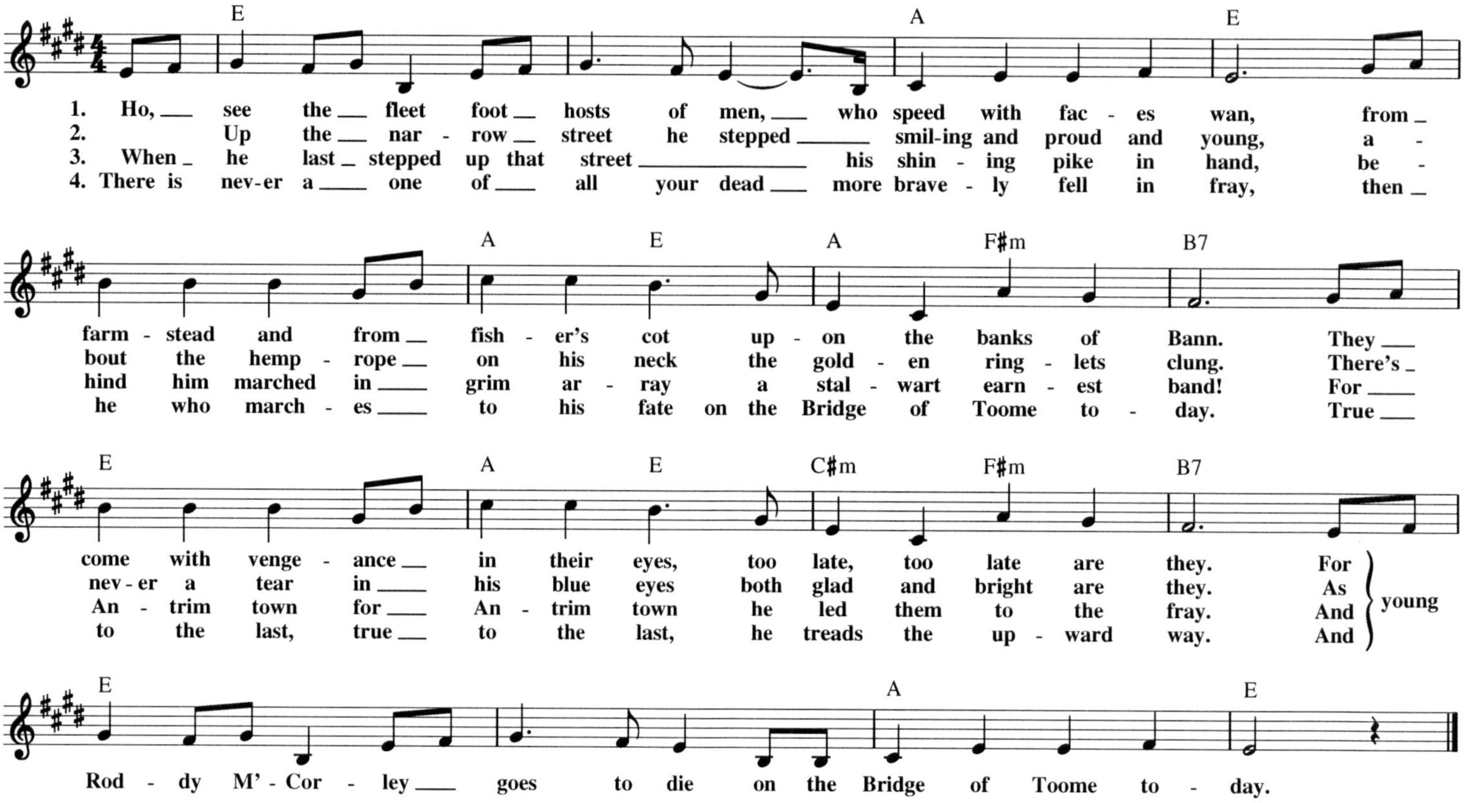

RORY O'MOORE

Words and Music by
Samuel Lover

Copyright © 2001 by HAL LEONARD CORPORATION

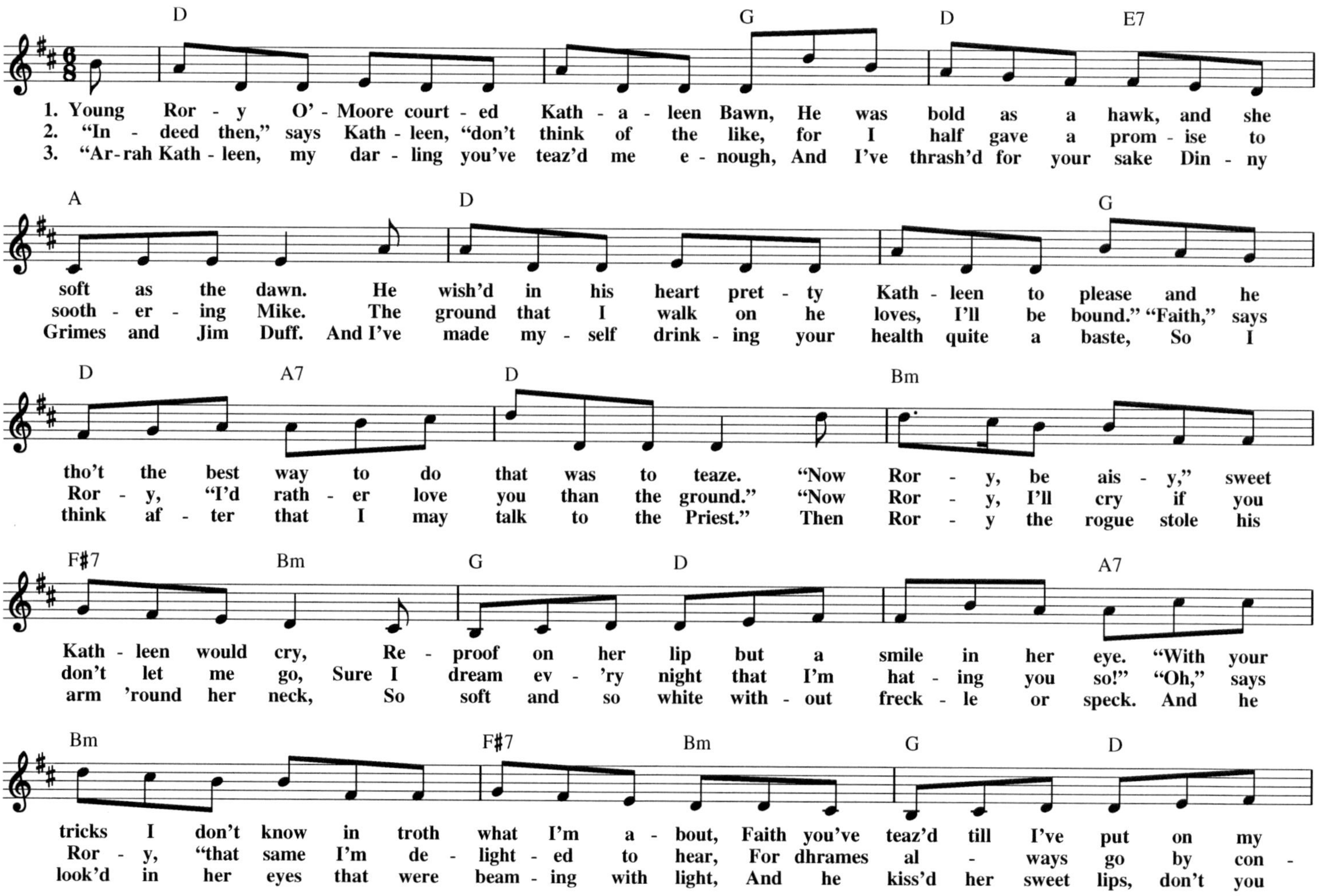

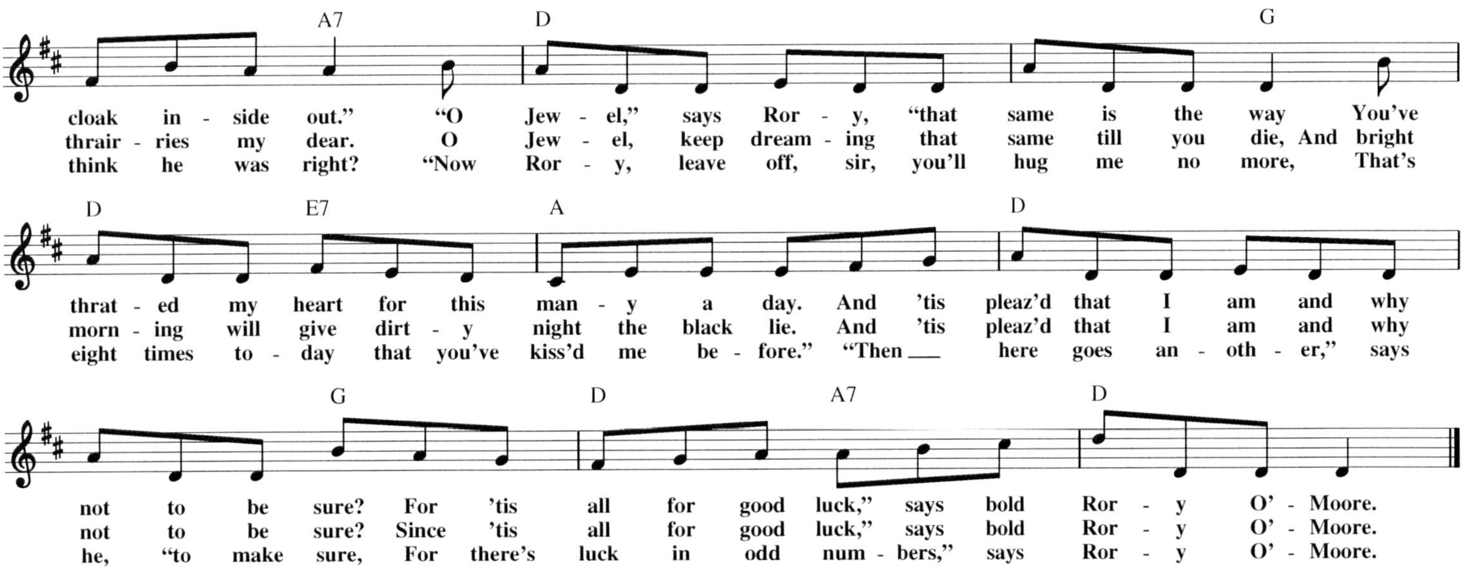

cloak in - side out." "O Jew - el," says Ror - y, "that same is the way You've
thrair - ries my dear. O Jew - el, keep dream - ing that same till you die, And bright
think he was right? "Now Ror - y, leave off, sir, you'll hug me no more, That's

thrat - ed my heart for this man - y a day. And 'tis pleaz'd that I am and why
morn - ing will give dirt - y night the black lie. And 'tis pleaz'd that I am and why
eight times to - day that you've kiss'd me be - fore." "Then ___ here goes an - oth - er," says

not to be sure? For 'tis all for good luck," says bold Ror - y O' - Moore.
not to be sure? Since 'tis all for good luck," says bold Ror - y O' - Moore.
he, "to make sure, For there's luck in odd num - bers," says Ror - y O' - Moore.

ROSIN THE BEAU

Irish folksong

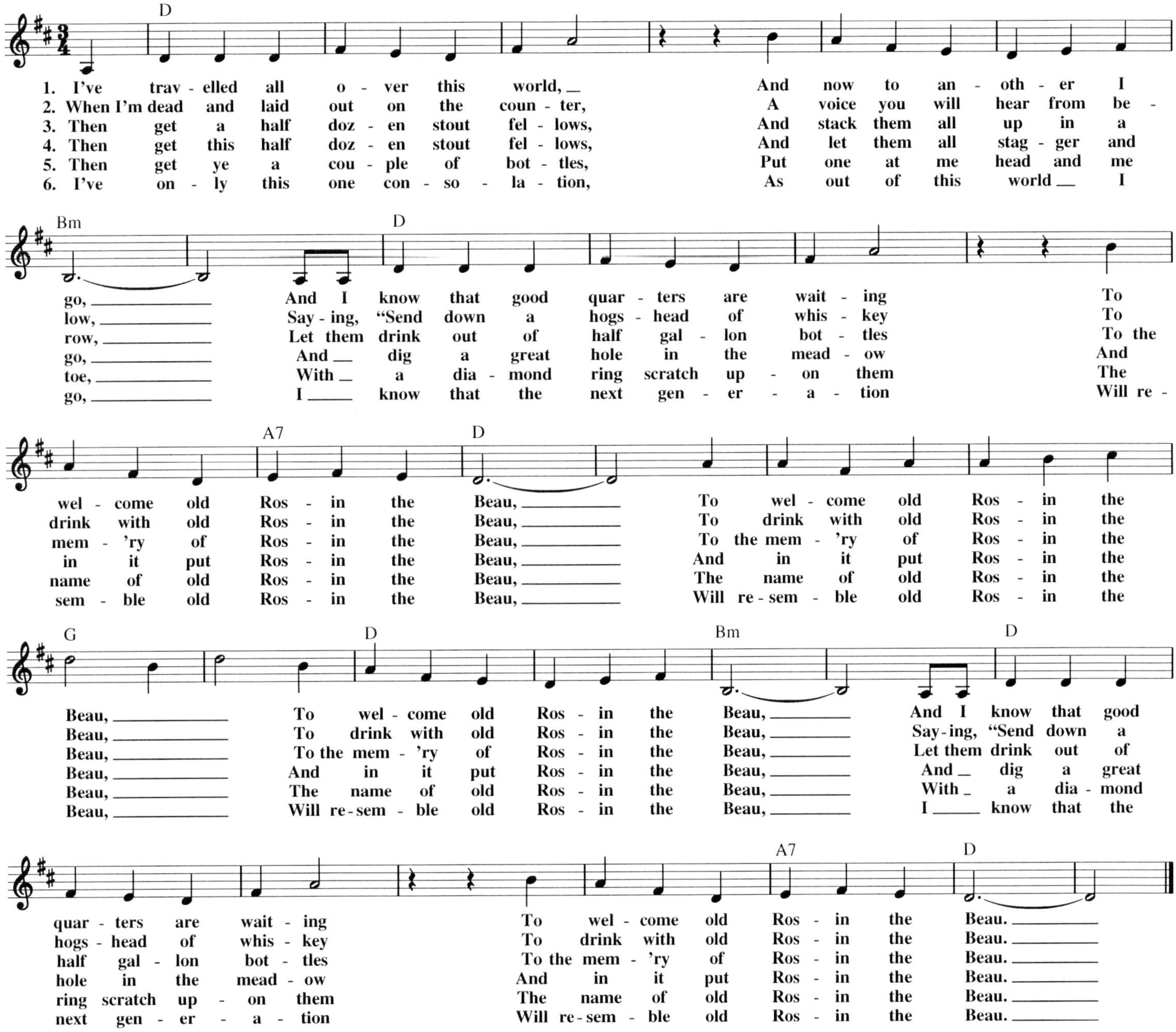

1. I've trav - elled all o - ver this world, ___ And now to an - oth - er I
2. When I'm dead and laid out on the coun - ter, A voice you will hear from be -
3. Then get a half doz - en stout fel - lows, And stack them all up in a
4. Then get this half doz - en stout fel - lows, And let them all stag - ger and
5. Then get ye a cou - ple of bot - tles, Put one at me head and me
6. I've on - ly this one con - so - la - tion, As out of this world ___ I

go, ___ And I know that good quar - ters are wait - ing To
low, ___ Say - ing, "Send down a hogs - head of whis - key To
row, ___ Let them drink out of half gal - lon bot - tles To the
go, ___ And ___ dig a great hole in the mead - ow And
toe, ___ With ___ a dia - mond ring scratch up - on them The
go, ___ I ___ know that the next gen - er - a - tion Will re -

wel - come old Ros - in the Beau, ___ To wel - come old Ros - in the
drink with old Ros - in the Beau, ___ To drink with old Ros - in the
mem - 'ry of Ros - in the Beau, ___ To the mem - 'ry of Ros - in the
in it put Ros - in the Beau, ___ And in it put Ros - in the
name of old Ros - in the Beau, ___ The name of old Ros - in the
sem - ble old Ros - in the Beau, ___ Will re - sem - ble old Ros - in the

Beau, ___ To wel - come old Ros - in the Beau, ___ And I know that good
Beau, ___ To drink with old Ros - in the Beau, ___ Say - ing, "Send down a
Beau, ___ To the mem - 'ry of Ros - in the Beau, ___ Let them drink out of
Beau, ___ And in it put Ros - in the Beau, ___ And ___ dig a great
Beau, ___ The name of old Ros - in the Beau, ___ With ___ a dia - mond
Beau, ___ Will re - sem - ble old Ros - in the Beau, ___ I know that the

quar - ters are wait - ing To wel - come old Ros - in the Beau. ___
hogs - head of whis - key To drink with old Ros - in the Beau. ___
half gal - lon bot - tles To the mem - 'ry of Ros - in the Beau. ___
hole in the mead - ow And in it put Ros - in the Beau. ___
ring scratch up - on them The name of old Ros - in the Beau. ___
next gen - er - a - tion Will re - sem - ble old Ros - in the Beau. ___

THE ROSE OF ALLENDALE

Irish folksong

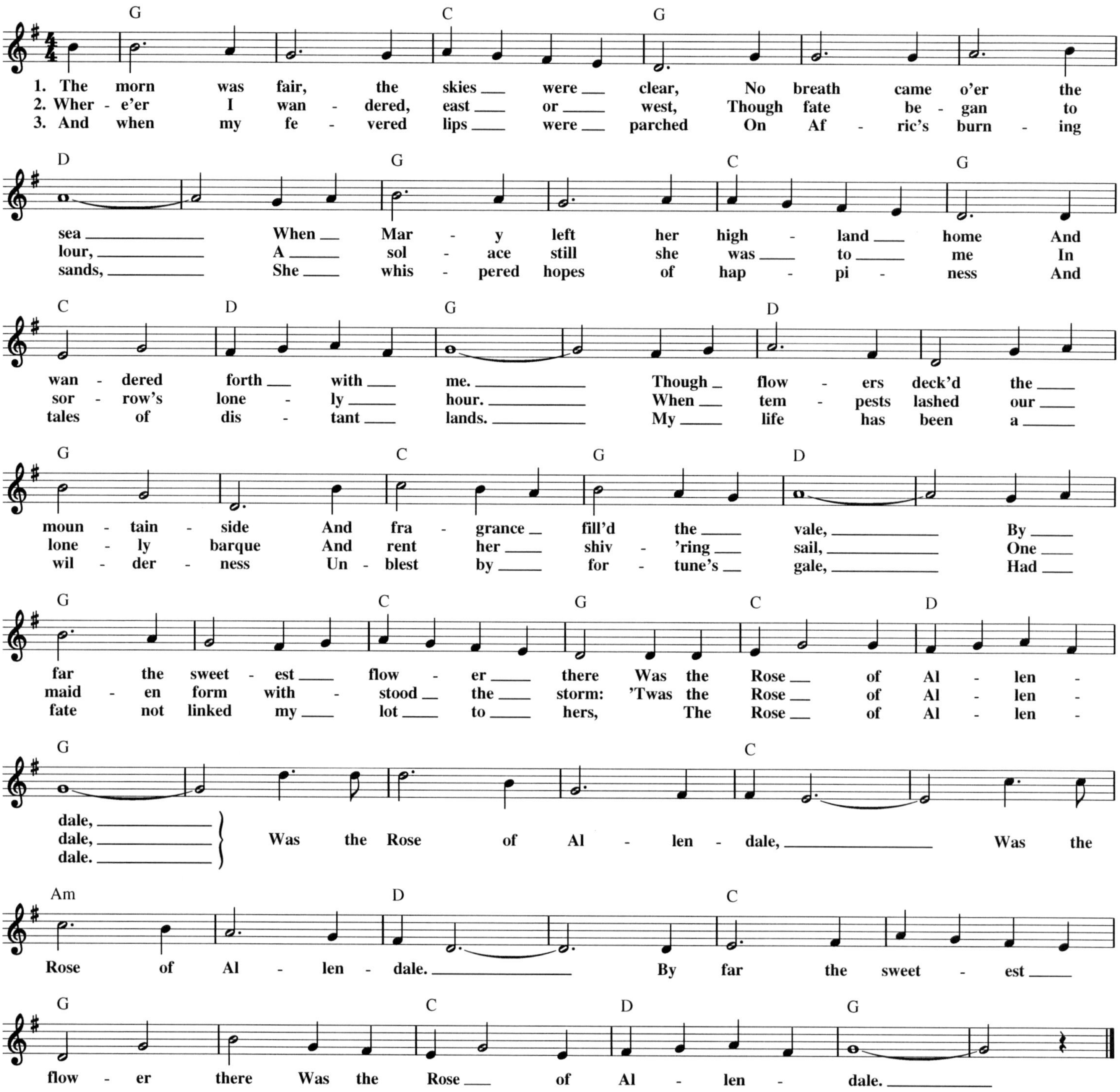

1. The morn was fair, the skies were clear, No breath came o'er the
2. Wher - e'er I wan - dered, east or west, Though fate be - gan to
3. And when my fe - vered lips were parched On Af - ric's burn - ing

sea When Mar - y left her high - land home And
lour, A sol - ace still she was to me In
sands, She whis - pered hopes of hap - pi - ness And

wan - dered forth with me. Though flow - ers deck'd the
sor - row's lone - ly hour. When tem - pests lashed our
tales of dis - tant lands. My life has been a

moun - tain - side And fra - grance fill'd the vale, By
lone - ly barque And rent her shiv - 'ring sail, One
wil - der - ness Un - blest by for - tune's gale, Had

far the sweet - est flow - er there Was the Rose of Al - len -
maid - en form with - stood the storm: 'Twas the Rose of Al - len -
fate not linked my lot to hers, The Rose of Al - len -

dale,
dale, Was the Rose of Al - len - dale, Was the
dale.

Rose of Al - len - dale. By far the sweet - est

flow - er there Was the Rose of Al - len - dale.

THE ROSE OF TRALEE

Words by C. Mordaunt Spencer
Music by Charles W. Glover

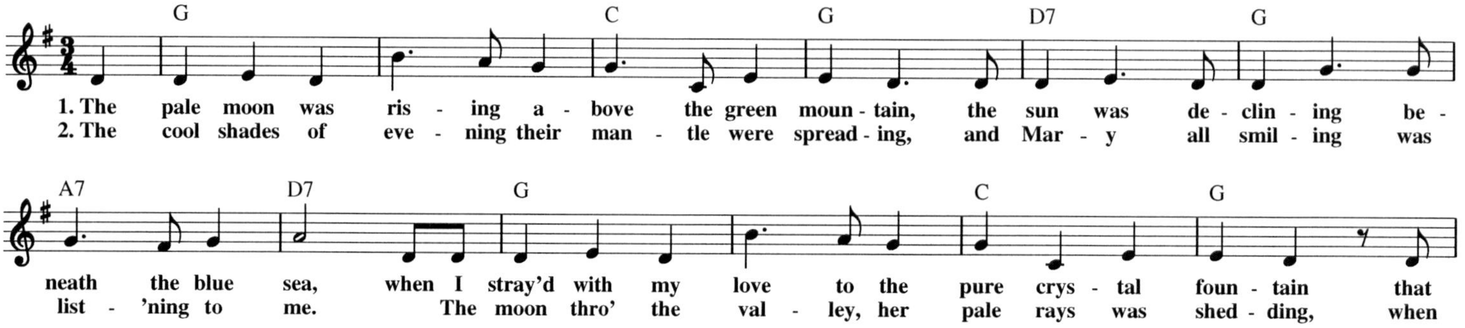

1. The pale moon was ris - ing a - bove the green moun - tain, the sun was de - clin - ing be -
2. The cool shades of eve - ning their man - tle were spread - ing, and Mar - y all smil - ing was

neath the blue sea, when I stray'd with my love to the pure crys - tal foun - tain that
list - 'ning to me. The moon thro' the val - ley, her pale rays was shed - ding, when

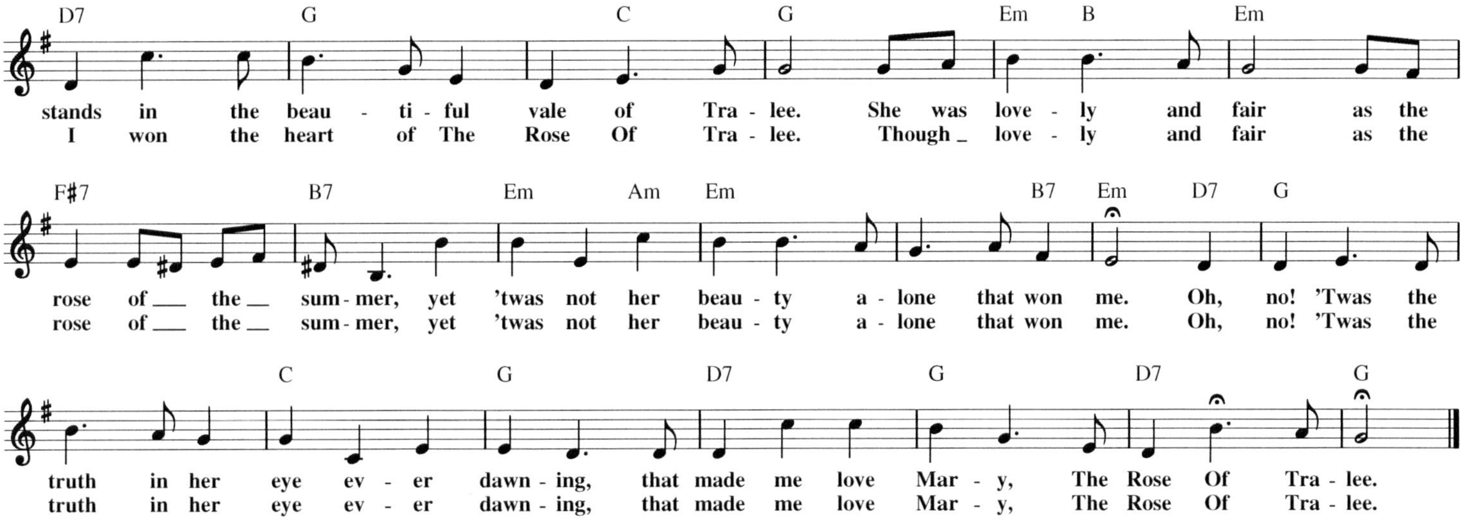

stands in the beau-ti-ful vale of Tra-lee. She was love-ly and fair as the
I won the heart of The Rose Of Tra-lee. Though love-ly and fair as the

rose of __ the __ sum-mer, yet 'twas not her beau-ty a-lone that won me. Oh, no! 'Twas the
rose of __ the __ sum-mer, yet 'twas not her beau-ty a-lone that won me. Oh, no! 'Twas the

truth in her eye ev-er dawn-ing, that made me love Mar-y, The Rose Of Tra-lee.
truth in her eye ev-er dawn-ing, that made me love Mar-y, The Rose Of Tra-lee.

THE SAILOR'S HORNPIPE

Irish folksong

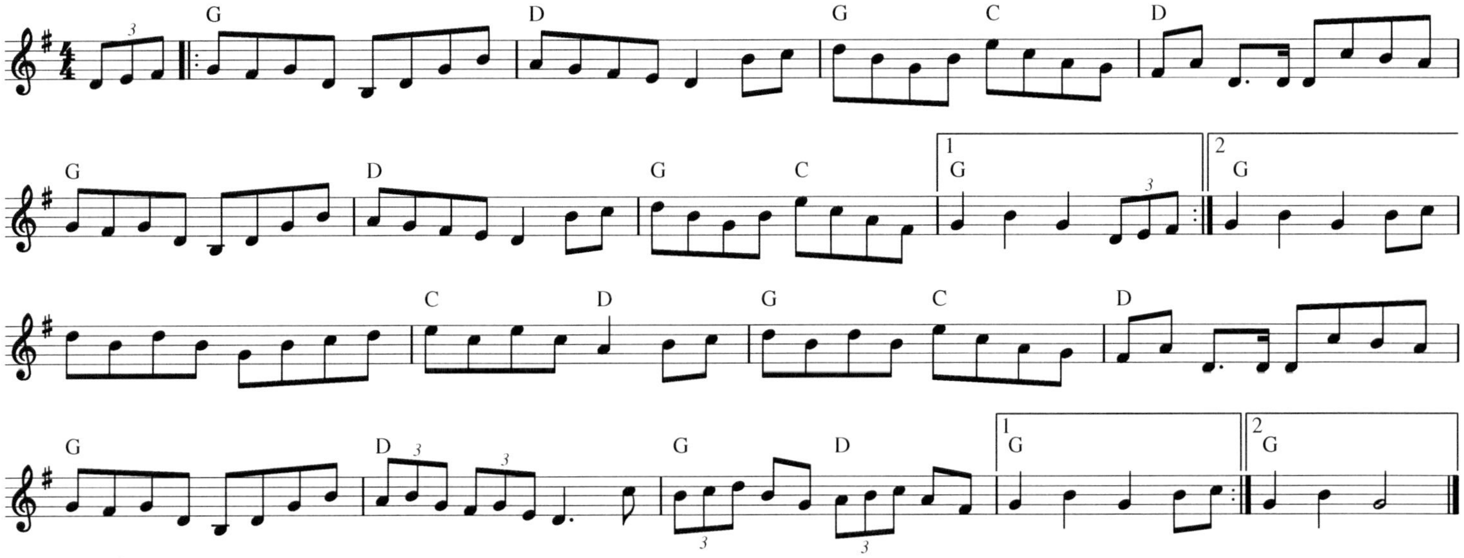

SCOTS WHA HAE

Scottish folksong
Words by Robert Burns

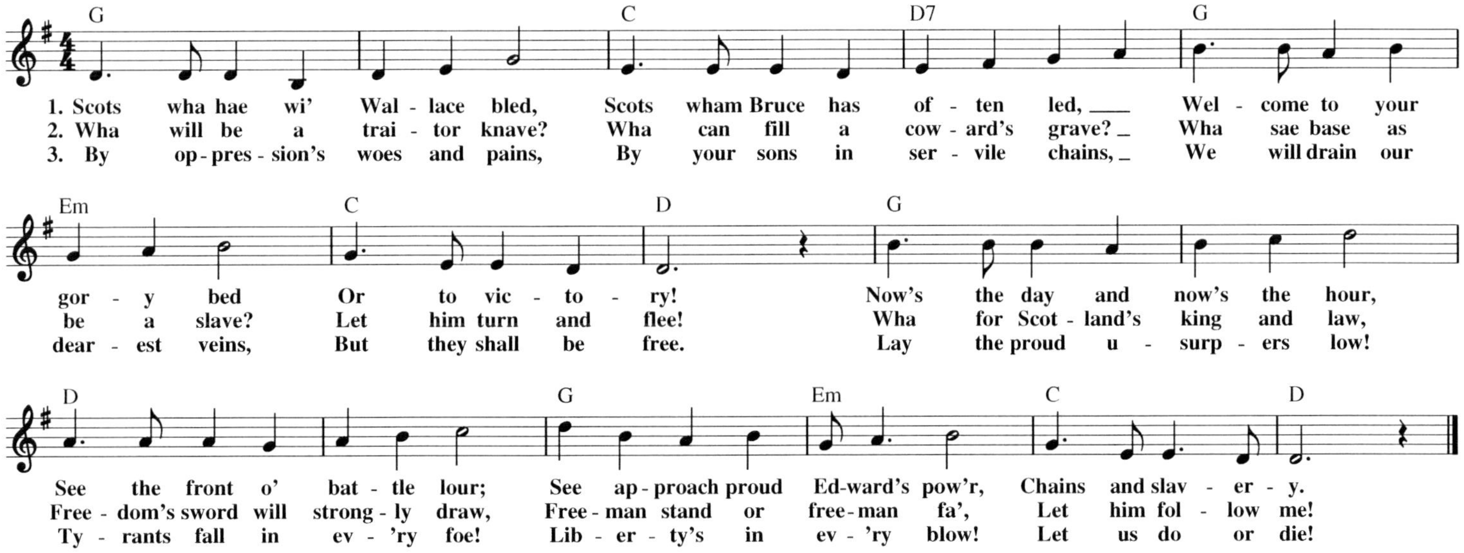

1. Scots wha hae wi' Wal-lace bled, Scots wham Bruce has of-ten led, __ Wel-come to your
2. Wha will be a trai-tor knave? Wha can fill a cow-ard's grave? _ Wha sae base as
3. By op-pres-sion's woes and pains, By your sons in ser-vile chains, _ We will drain our

gor-y bed Or to vic-to-ry! Now's the day and now's the hour,
be a slave? Let him turn and flee! Wha for Scot-land's king and law,
dear-est veins, But they shall be free. Lay the proud u-surp-ers low!

See the front o' bat-tle lour; See ap-proach proud Ed-ward's pow'r, Chains and slav-er-y.
Free-dom's sword will strong-ly draw, Free-man stand or free-man fa', Let him fol-low me!
Ty-rants fall in ev-'ry foe! Lib-er-ty's in ev-'ry blow! Let us do or die!

SEA-BIRD TO HER CHICKS
('S è mo nighean a ni ceol)

Folksong from the Hebrides

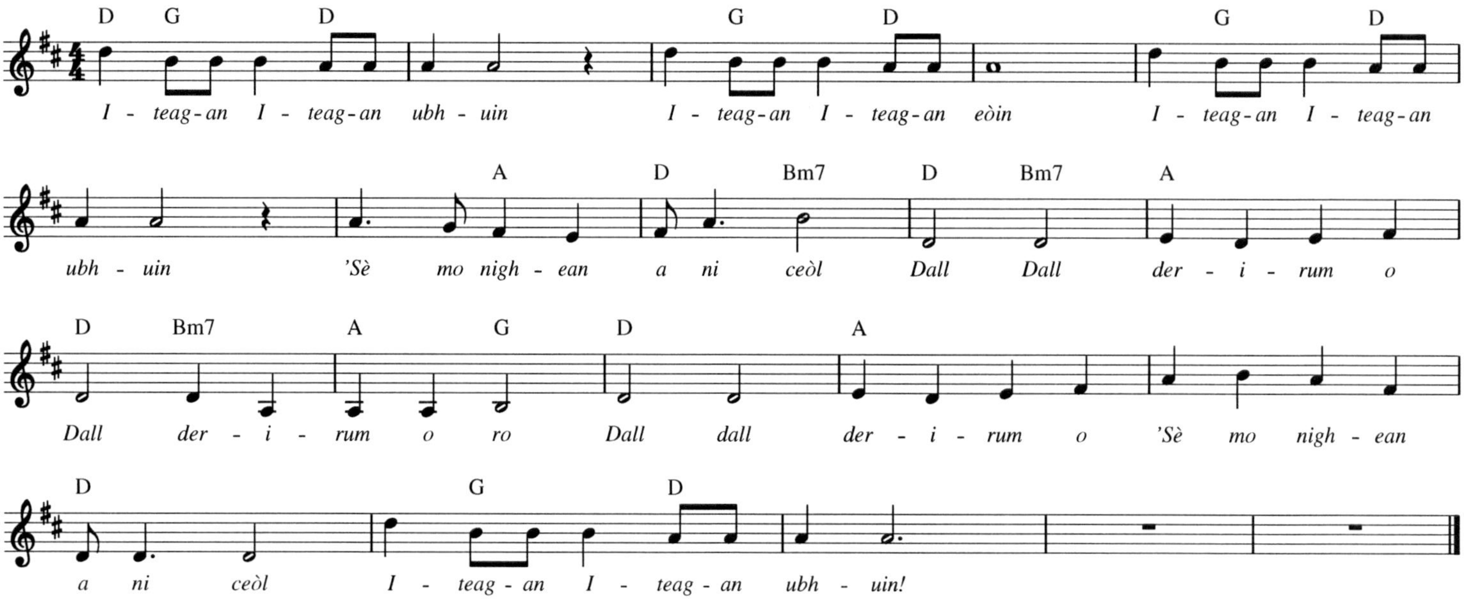

SEA-SOUNDS
(Gair na Mara)

Folksong from the Hebrides

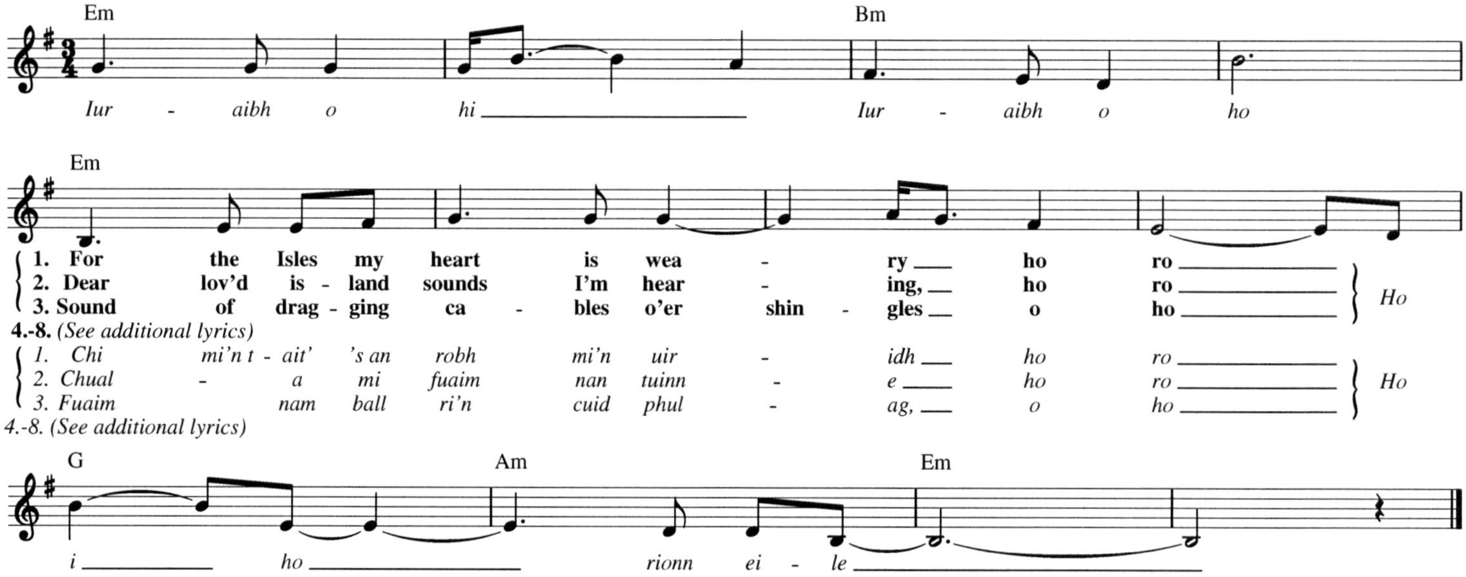

Additional Lyrics

4. Would I might see Iuraibh o ho
   Sound of seamen's voices ringing
   Ho ro ho rionn eile

5. Iuraibh o hi Iuraibh o ho
   Sound of oars that rend the waves, ho ro
   Ho i ho rionn eile

6. Iuraibh o hi Iuraibh o ho
   Sound of sand drift 'mong the muran, ho ro
   Ho i ho rionn eile

7. Iuraibh o hi Iuraibh o ho
   From the isles of muran a curach o ho
   Ho i ho rionn eile

8. Would I might hear Iuraibh o ho
   Boat of currach from the isles rowing
   Ho ro ho rionn eile

4. Iuraibh o hi Iuraibh o ho
   Fuáim nan Gall ri'n cuid luingis
   Ho ro ho rionn eile

5. Iuraibh o hi Iuraibh o ho
   Fuaim nan ramh a'reubadh tuinne o ro
   Ho i ho rionn eile

6. Iuraibh o hi Iuraibh o ho
   Fuáim an tsiabain ris a' mhuran, ho ro
   Ho i ho rionn eile

7. Iuraibh o hi Iuraibh o ho
   Cha'n fhaic mi bata no curach, o ho
   Ho i ho rionn eile

8. Iuraibh o hi Iuraibh o ho
   A' tilleadh o thir nan tuinne
   Ho ro ho rionn eile

SEA MOODS
(Bruadar Mara)

Folksong from the Hebrides

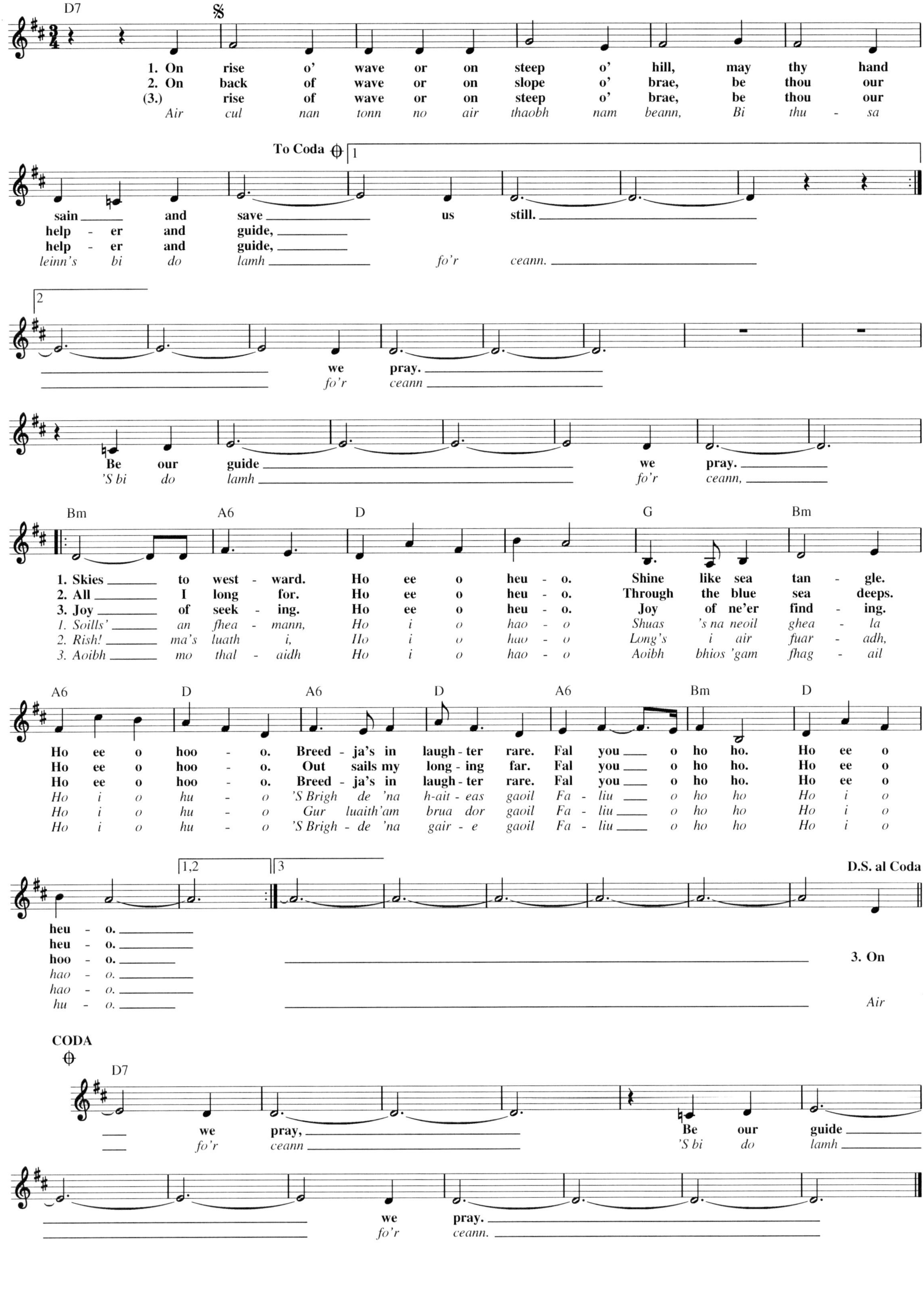

THE SEA-QUEST
(Am Bròn Binn)

Folksong from the Hebrides

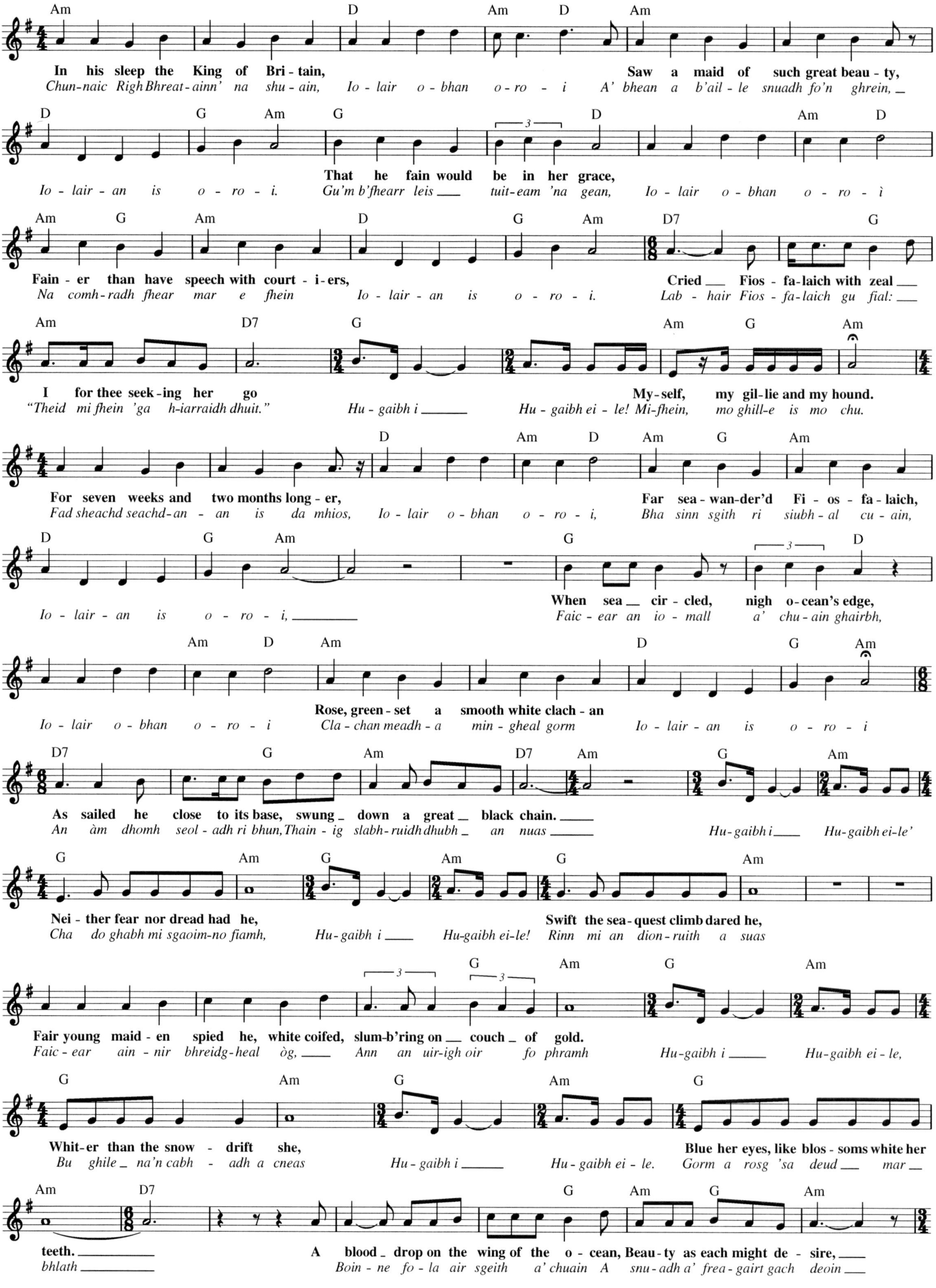

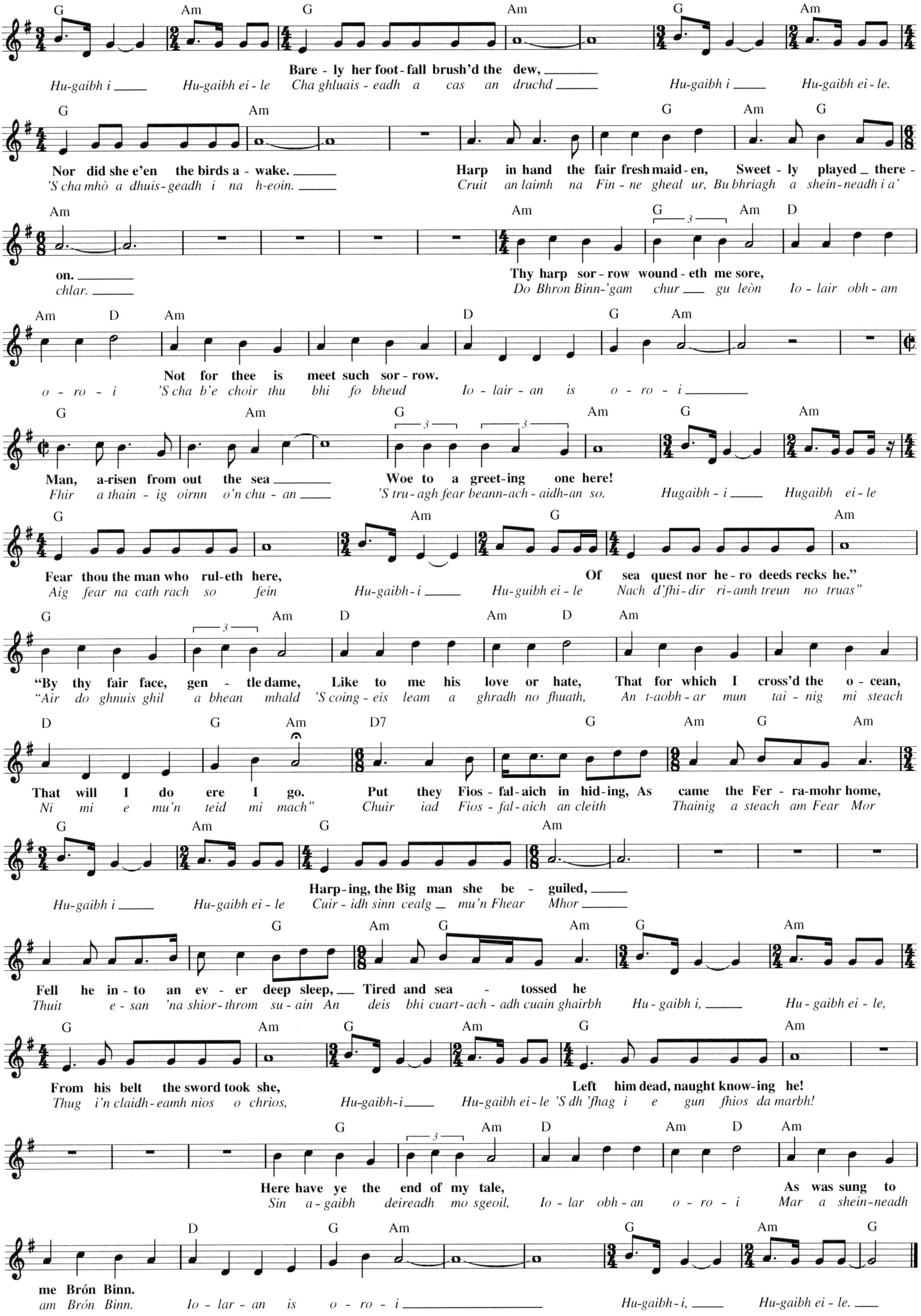
Bare - ly her foot - fall brush'd the dew,
Hu-gaibh i Hu-gaibh ei - le Cha ghluais - eadh a cas an druchd Hu-gaibh i Hu-gaibh ei - le.
Nor did she e'en the birds a - wake. Harp in hand the fair fresh maid - en, Sweet - ly played there -
'S cha mhò a dhuis-geadh i na h-eoin. Cruit an laimh na Fin - ne gheal ur, Bu bhriagh a shein-neadh i a'
on. Thy harp sor - row wound - eth me sore,
chlar. Do Bhron Binn-'gam chur gu leòn Io - lair obh - am
Not for thee is meet such sor - row.
o - ro - i 'S cha b'e choir thu bhi fo bheud Io - lair - an is o - ro - i
Man, a-risen from out the sea Woe to a greet-ing one here!
Fhir a thain - ig oirnn o'n chu - an 'S tru - agh fear beann-ach - aidh-an so. Hugaibh - i Hugaibh ei - le
Fear thou the man who rul-eth here, Of sea quest nor he - ro deeds recks he."
Aig fear na cath rach so fein Hu-gaibh - i Hu-guibh ei - le Nach d'fhi - dir ri-amh treun no truas"
"By thy fair face, gen - tle dame, Like to me his love or hate, That for which I cross'd the o - cean,
"Air do ghnuis ghil a bhean mhald 'S coing - eis leam a ghradh no fhuath, An t-aobh - ar mun tai - nig mi steach
That will I do ere I go. Put they Fios - fal-aich in hid-ing, As came the Fer - ra-mohr home,
Ni mi e mu'n teid mi mach" Chuir iad Fios - fal - aich an cleith Thainig a steach am Fear Mor
Harp - ing, the Big man she be - guiled,
Hu-gaibh i Hu-gaibh ei - le Cuir - idh sinn cealg mu'n Fhear Mhor
Fell he in - to an ev - er deep sleep, Tired and sea - tossed he
Thuit e - san 'na shior-throm su - ain An deis bhi cuart-ach - adh cuain ghairbh Hu - gaibh i, Hu - gaibh ei - le,
From his belt the sword took she, Left him dead, naught know-ing he!
Thug i'n claidh-eamh nios o chrios, Hu-gaibh-i Hu-gaibh ei - le 'S dh 'fhag i e gun fhios da marbh!
Here have ye the end of my tale, As was sung to
Sin a - gaibh deireadh mo sgeoil, Io - lar obh - an o - ro - i Mar a shein-neadh
me Brón Binn.
am Brón Binn. Io - lar - an is o - ro - i Hu-gaibh - i, Hu-gaibh ei - le.

SEA SORROW
(Am Bron Mara)

Folksong from the Hebrides

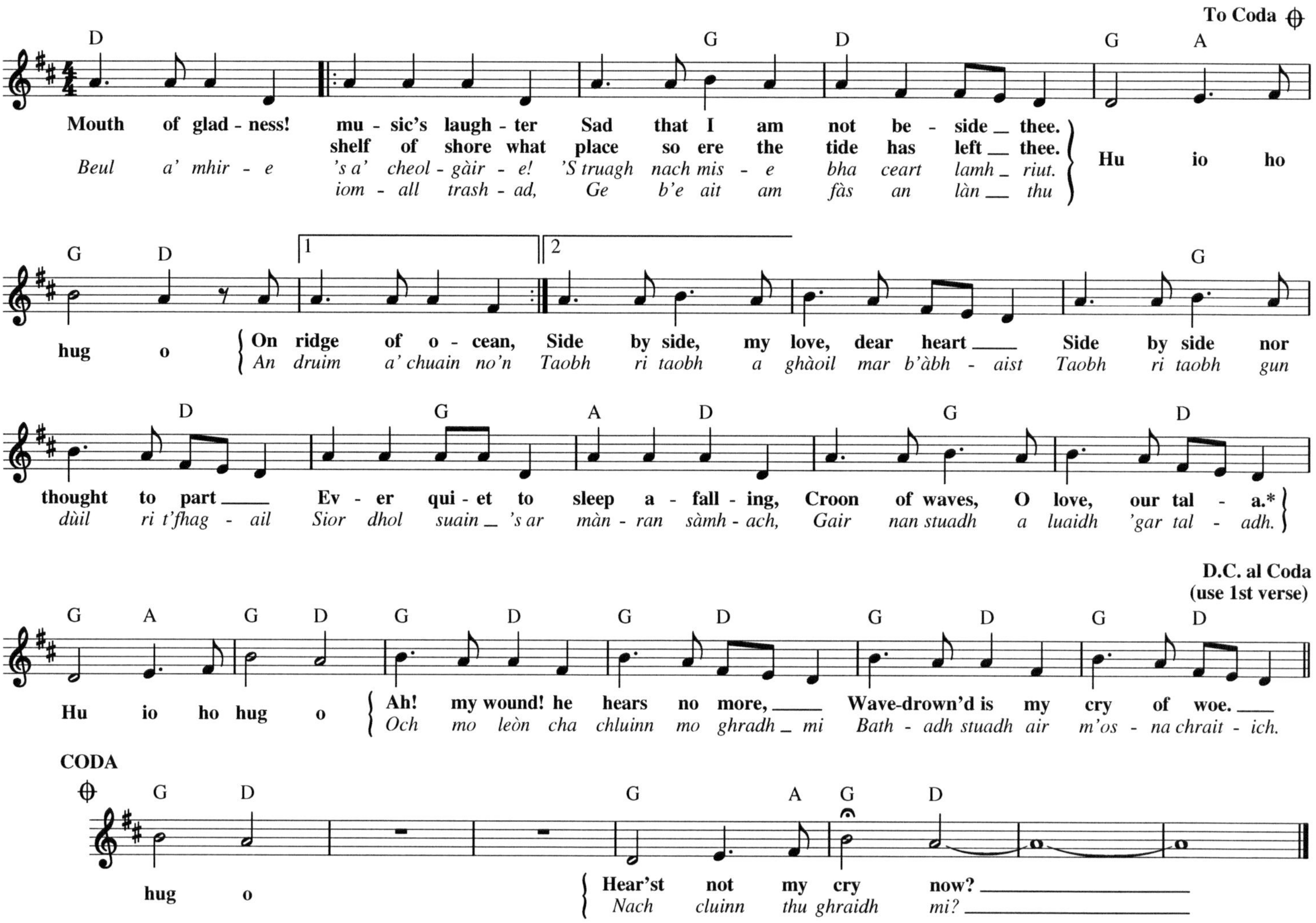

Mouth of glad-ness! mu-sic's laugh-ter Sad that I am not be-side _ thee.
shelf of shore what place so ere the tide has left _ thee.
Beul a' mhir-e 's a' cheol-gàir-e! 'S truagh nach mis-e bha ceart lamh _ riut.
iom-all trash-ad, Ge b'e ait am fàs an làn _ thu

Hu io ho hug o

On ridge of o-cean, Side by side, my love, dear heart ____ Side by side nor
An druim a' chuain no'n Taobh ri taobh a ghàoil mar b'àbh-aist Taobh ri taobh gun

thought to part ____ Ev-er qui-et to sleep a-fall-ing, Croon of waves, O love, our tal-a.*
dùil ri t'fhag-ail Sior dhol suain _ 's ar màn-ran sàmh-ach, Gair nan stuadh a luaidh 'gar tal-adh.

D.C. al Coda
(use 1st verse)

Hu io ho hug o

Ah! my wound! he hears no more, ____ Wave-drown'd is my cry of woe. ____
Och mo leòn cha chluinn mo ghradh _ mi Bath-adh stuadh air m'os-na chrait-ich.

CODA

hug o

Hear'st not my cry now? _____
Nach cluinn thu ghraidh mi? _____

Bantrachas-cuain

Gura mis' tha fo mhulad
'S mi air tulaich na h-àiridh;

Mi bhi faicinn nan rillean
Anns an linne 'gam bathadh;

Ged is oil leam gach aon diubh,
Fear mo ghaoil gur e chraidh mi,

'Se mo cheist do chul dualach
'Ga shior-luadh air bharr sàile;

'S tu 'nad shìneadh 'san tiùrra,
Far 'na bhrùchd a' mhuir-làn thu.

Righ! nach robh thu 'nad chadal
Ann an Clachan na Tràghad;

Ann an Eaglais na Trianaid,
Far an lionmhor do chàirdean;

Gu 'm biodh deoir mo dha shùla
Mar an drùchd glasadh t'fhàile.

Faic, a Dhia, mar tha mise—
Bean gun mhisneach gu bràth mi;

Bean gun mhac gun fhear-tighe,
Bean gun aighear gun slainte;

Ged bu shunndach an Nollaig
'S dubh dorranach Caisg dhomh.

* lulling song

THE SEAGULL OF THE LAND-UNDER-WAVES

Folksong from the Hebrides

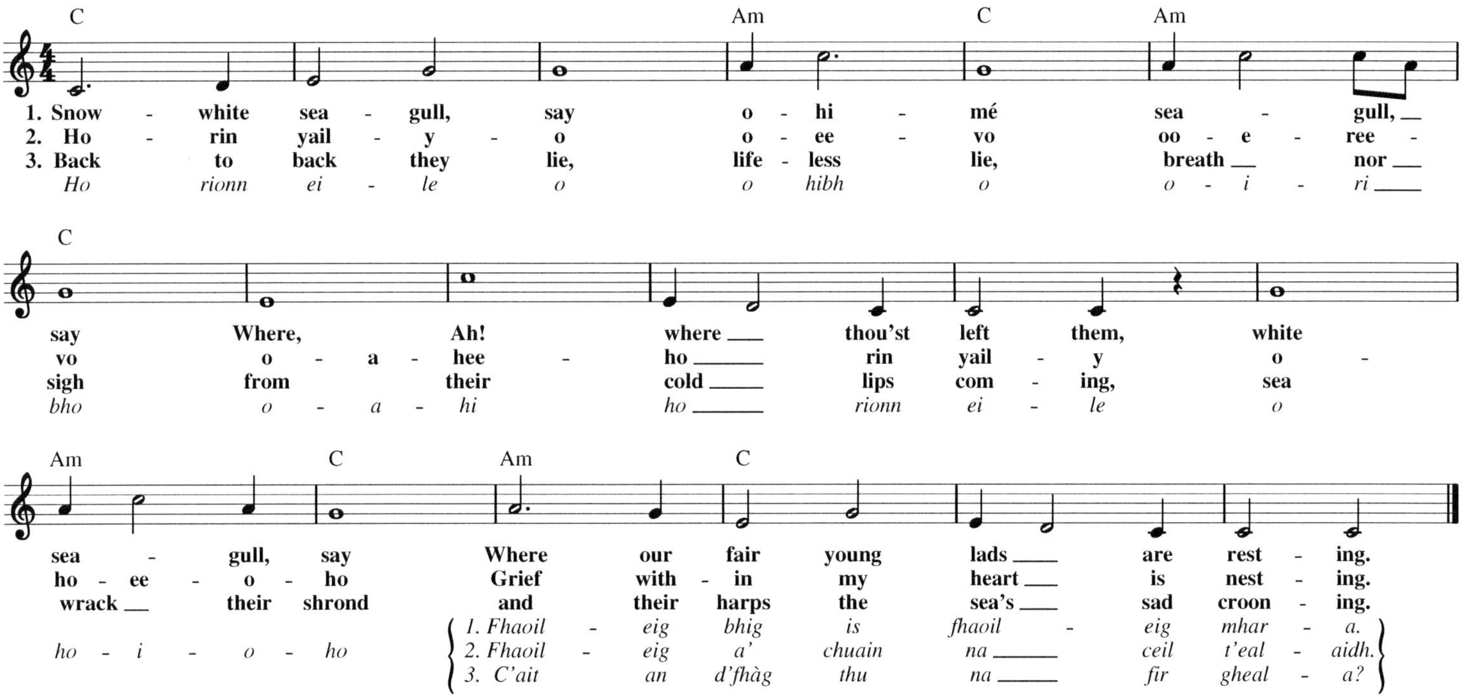

1. Snow-white sea-gull, say o - hi - mé sea - gull, say Where, Ah! where thou'st left them, white sea - gull, say Where our fair young lads are rest-ing.
2. Ho - rin yail - y - o o - ee - vo oo - e - ree - vo o - a - hee - ho rin yail - y - o ho - ee - o - ho Grief with-in my heart is nest-ing.
3. Back to back they lie, life-less lie, breath nor sigh from their cold lips com-ing, sea wrack their shrond and their harps the sea's sad croon-ing.

Ho rionn ei - le o o hibh o o - i - ri bho o - a - hi ho rionn ei - le o ho - i - o - ho
{ 1. Fhaoil - eig bhig is fhaoil - eig mhar - a.
2. Fhaoil - eig a' chuain na ceil t'eal - aidh.
3. C'ait an d'fhàg thu na fir gheal - a? }

THE SEAL-WOMAN'S CROON
(An Cadal trom)

Folksong from the Hebrides

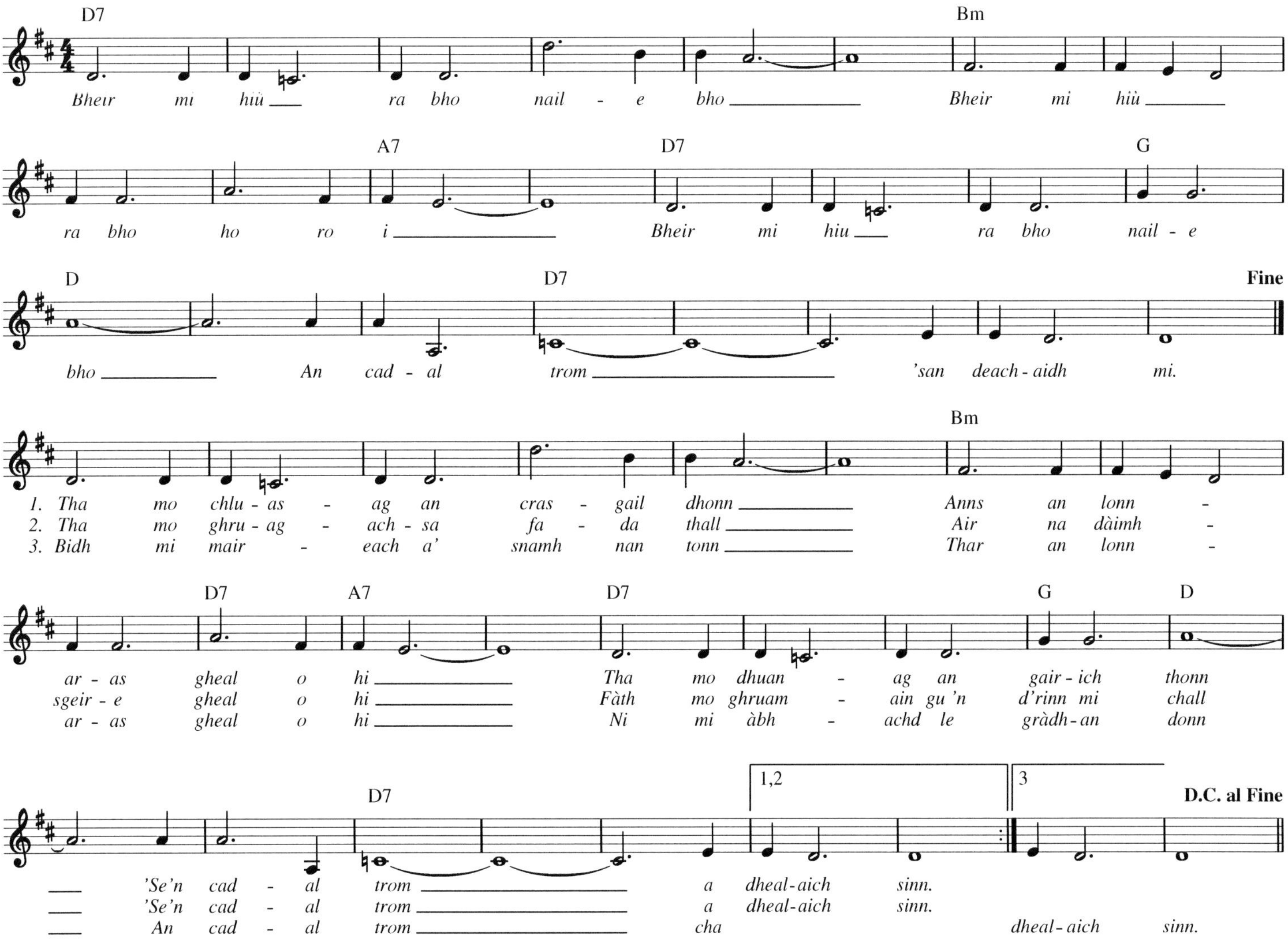

Bheir mi hiù ra bho nail - e bho Bheir mi hiù
ra bho ho ro i Bheir mi hiu ra bho nail - e
bho An cad - al trom 'san deach - aidh mi.

1. Tha mo chlu - as - ag an cras - gail dhonn Anns an lonn - ar - as gheal o hi Tha mo dhuan - ag an gair - ich thonn
2. Tha mo ghru - ag - ach - sa fa - da thall Air na dàimh sgeir - e gheal o hi Fàth mo ghruam - ain gu'n d'rinn mi chall
3. Bidh mi mair - each a' snamh nan tonn Thar an lonn - ar - as gheal o hi Ni mi àbh - achd le gràdh - an donn

[1,2]
'Se'n cad - al trom a dheal-aich sinn.
'Se'n cad - al trom a dheal-aich sinn.

[3]
An cad - al trom cha dheal-aich sinn.

D.C. al Fine

THE SENTRY BOX

Irish folksong

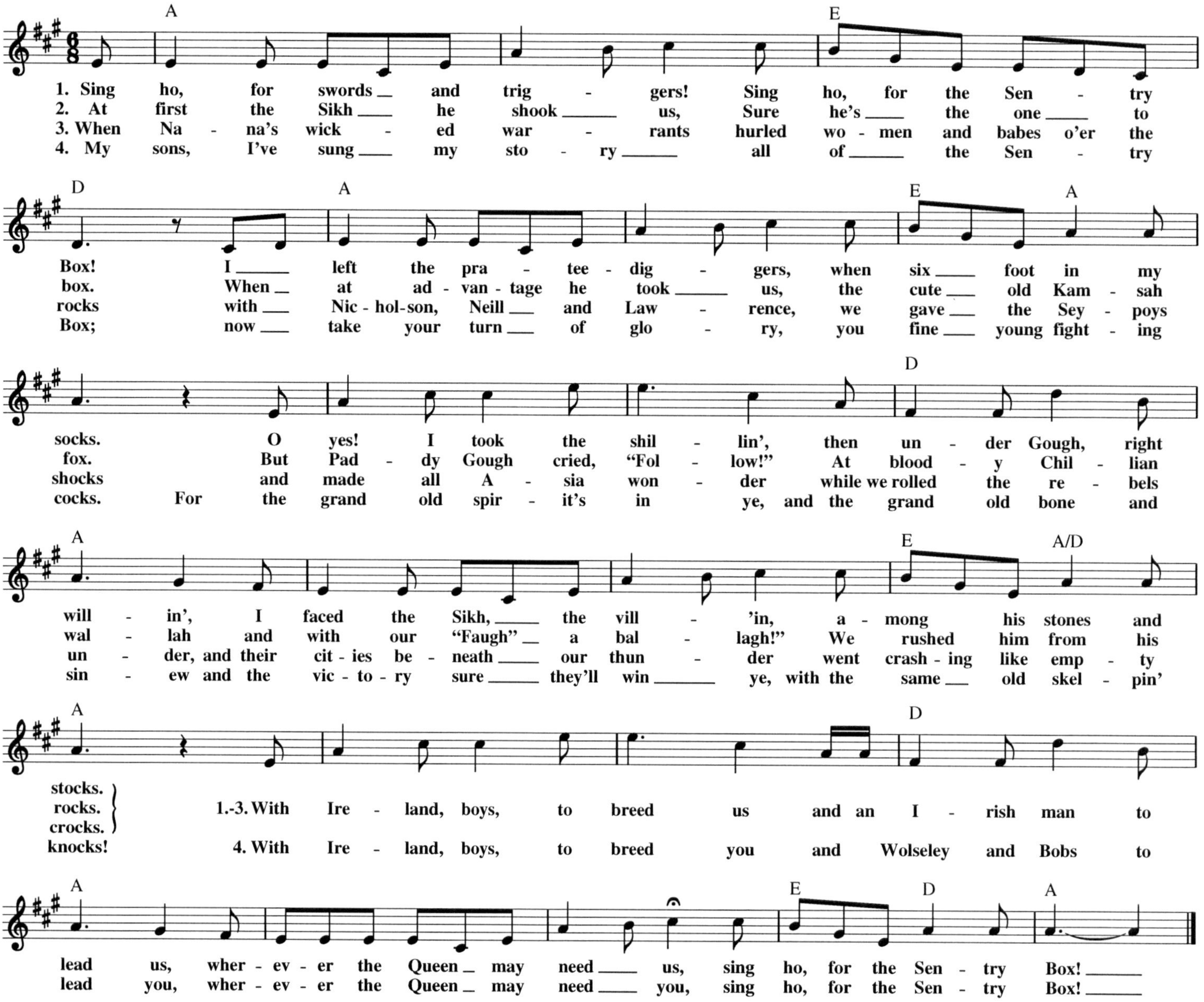

1. Sing ho, for swords and trig - gers! Sing ho, for the Sen - try
2. At first the Sikh he shook us, Sure he's the one to
3. When Na - na's wick - ed war - rants hurled wo - men and babes o'er the
4. My sons, I've sung my sto - ry all of the Sen - try

Box! I left the pra - tee - dig - gers, when six foot in my
box. When at ad - van - tage he took us, the cute old Kam - sah
rocks with Nic - hol - son, Neill and Law - rence, we gave the Sey - poys
Box; now take your turn of glo - ry, you fine young fight - ing

socks. O yes! I took the shil - lin', then un - der Gough, right
fox. But Pad - dy Gough cried, "Fol - low!" At blood - y Chil - lian
shocks and made all A - sia won - der while we rolled the re - bels
cocks. For the grand old spir - it's in ye, and the grand old bone and

will - in', I faced the Sikh, the vill - 'in, a - mong his stones and
wal - lah and with our "Faugh" a bal - lagh!" We rushed him from his
un - der, and their cit - ies be - neath our thun - der went crash - ing like emp - ty
sin - ew and the vic - to - ry sure they'll win ye, with the same old skel - pin'

stocks. }
rocks. } 1.-3. With Ire - land, boys, to breed us and an I - rish man to
crocks. }
knocks! 4. With Ire - land, boys, to breed you and Wolseley and Bobs to

lead us, wher - ev - er the Queen may need us, sing ho, for the Sen - try Box!
lead you, wher - ev - er the Queen may need you, sing ho, for the Sen - try Box!

THE SEVEN IRISHMEN

Irish folksong

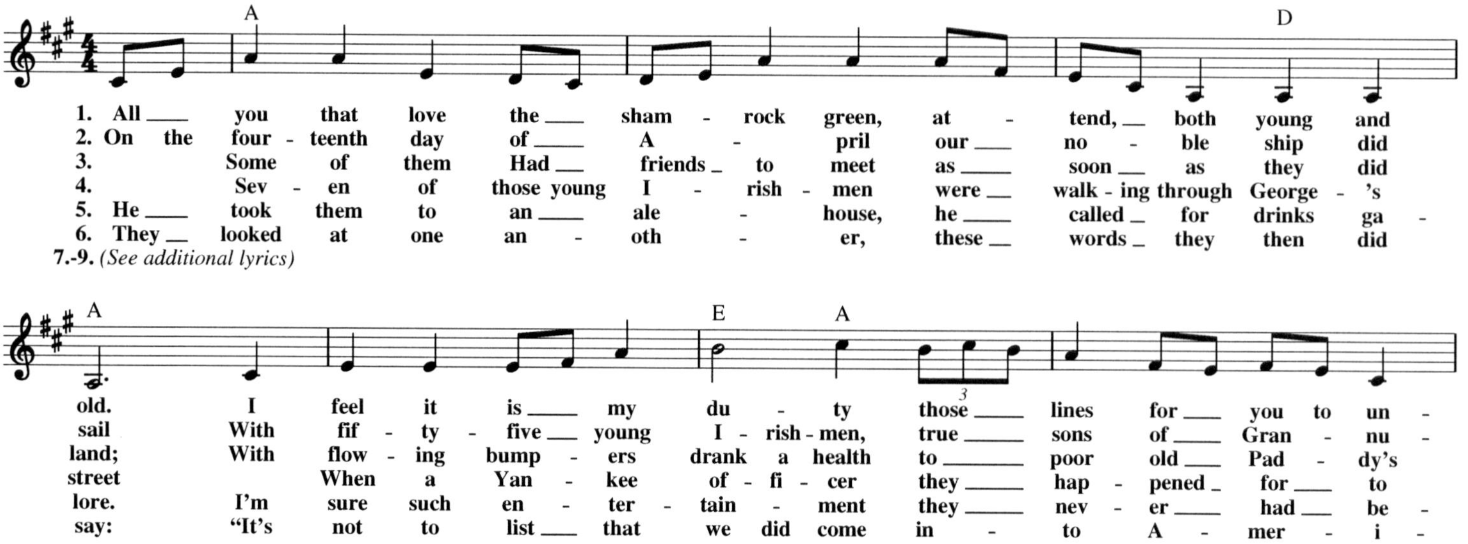

1. All you that love the sham - rock green, at - tend, both young and
2. On the four - teenth day of A - pril our no - ble ship did
3. Some of them Had friends to meet as soon as they did
4. Sev - en of those young I - rish - men were walk - ing through George - 's
5. He took them to an ale - house, he called for drinks ga -
6. They looked at one an - oth - er, these words they then did

7.-9. (See additional lyrics)

old. I feel it is my du - ty those lines for you to un -
sail With fif - ty - five young I - rish - men, true sons of Gran - nu -
land; With flow - ing bump - ers drank a health to poor old Pad - dy's
street When a Yan - kee of - fi - cer they hap - pened for to
lore. I'm sure such en - ter - tain - ment they nev - er had be -
say: "It's not to list that we did come in - to A - mer - i -

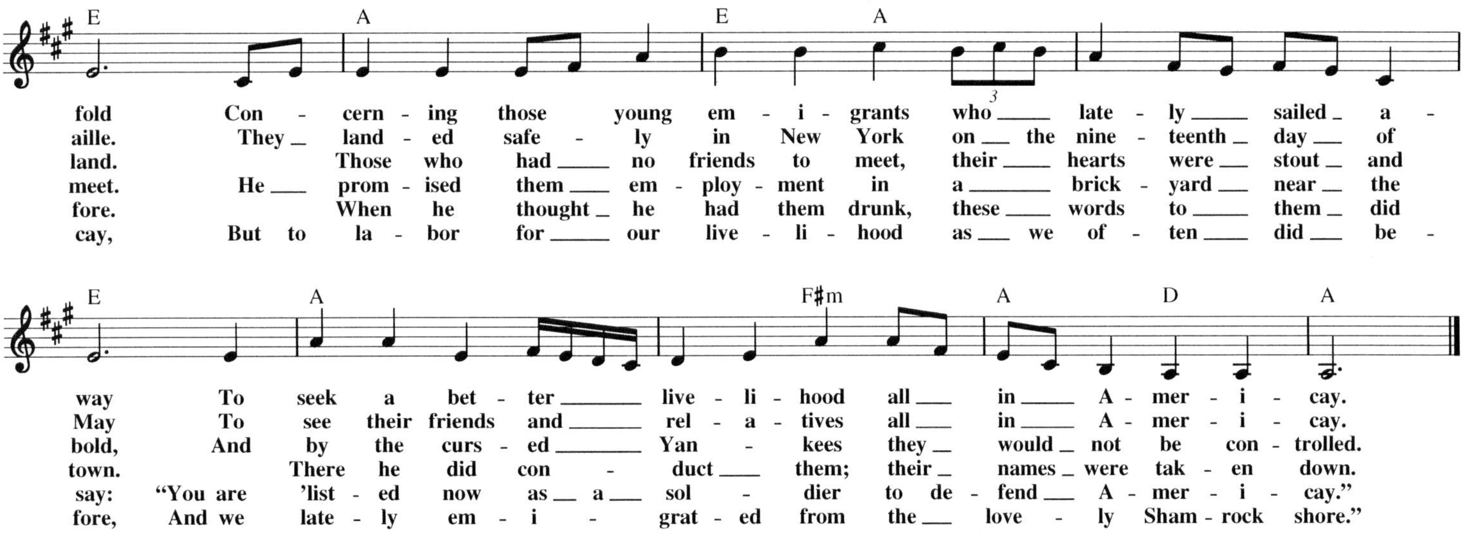

fold Con - cern - ing those young em - i - grants who _____ late - ly _____ sailed _ a -
aille. They _ land - ed safe - ly in New York on _ the nine - teenth _ day _ of
land. Those who had _____ no friends to meet, their _____ hearts were _ stout _ and
meet. He _ prom - ised them _____ em - ploy - ment in a _____ brick - yard _ near _ the
fore. When he thought _ he had them drunk, these _____ words to _____ them _ did
cay, But to la - bor for _____ our live - li - hood as _ we of - ten _____ did _ be -

way To seek a bet - ter _____ live - li - hood all _____ in _____ A - mer - i - cay.
May To see their friends and _____ rel - a - tives all _____ in _____ A - mer - i - cay.
bold, And by the curs - ed _____ Yan - kees they _ would _ not be con - trolled.
town. There he did con - duct _____ them; their _ names _ were tak - en down.
say: "You are 'list - ed now as _ a _ sol - dier to de - fend _____ A - mer - i - cay."
fore, And we late - ly em - i - grat - ed from the _____ love - ly Sham - rock shore."

Additional Lyrics

7. Twelve Yankees dressed as soldiers came in without delay.
They said, "My lads, you must prepare with us to come away.
You signed with one of our officers, so you cannot now refuse,
So prepare, my lads, to join our ranks, for you must pay your dues."

8. The Irish blood began to rise, one of those heroes said,
"We have one only life to lose, therefore we're not afraid.
Although we are from Ireland, this day we'll let you see,
We'll die like Sons of Grannuaille and keep our liberty."

9. The Irish boys got to their feet, it made the Yankees frown.
As fast as they could strike a blow, they knocked the soldiers down.
With bloody heads and broken bones, they left them in crimson gore,
And proved themselves St. Patrick's Day throughout Columbus' shore.

SHE MOVED THROUGH THE FAIR

Irish folksong
Words by Padraic Colum

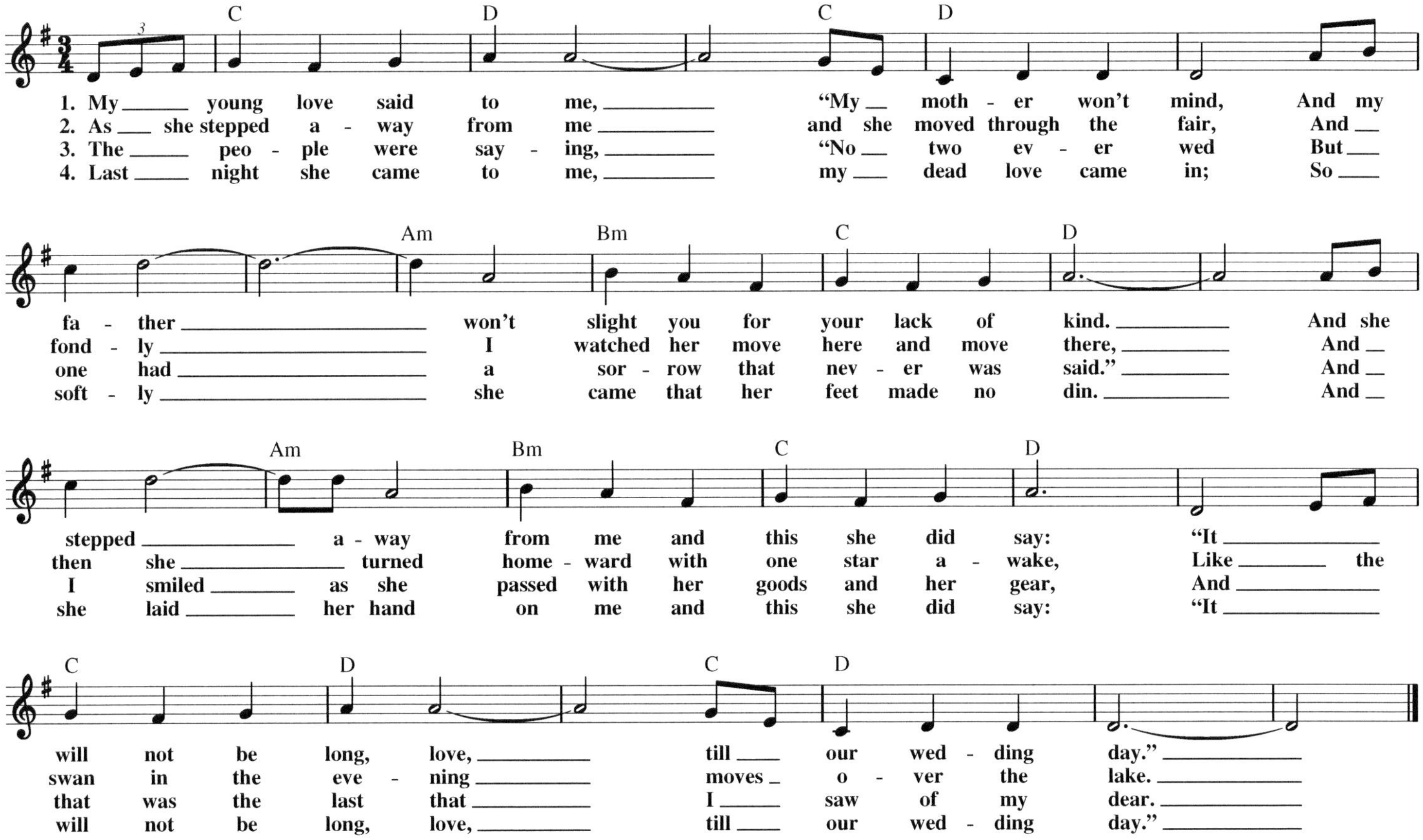

1. My _____ young love said to me, _____ "My _ moth - er won't mind, And my
2. As _ she stepped a - way from me _____ and she moved through the fair, And _
3. The _____ peo - ple were say - ing, _____ "No _ two ev - er wed But _
4. Last _____ night she came to me, _____ my _ dead love came in; So _

fa - ther _____ won't slight you for your lack of kind. _____ And she
fond - ly _____ I watched her move here and move there, _____ And _
one had _____ a sor - row that nev - er was said." _____ And _
soft - ly _____ she came that her feet made no din. _____ And _

stepped _____ a - way from me and this she did say: "It _____
then she _____ turned home - ward with one star a - wake, Like _____ the
I smiled _____ as she passed with her goods and her gear, And _____
she laid _____ her hand on me and this she did say: "It _____

will not be long, love, _____ till _ our wed - ding day." _____
swan in the eve - ning _____ moves _ o - ver the lake.
that was the last that _____ I _ saw of my dear.
will not be long, love, _____ till _ our wed - ding day." _____

THE SHAN VAN VOCHT

Irish folksong

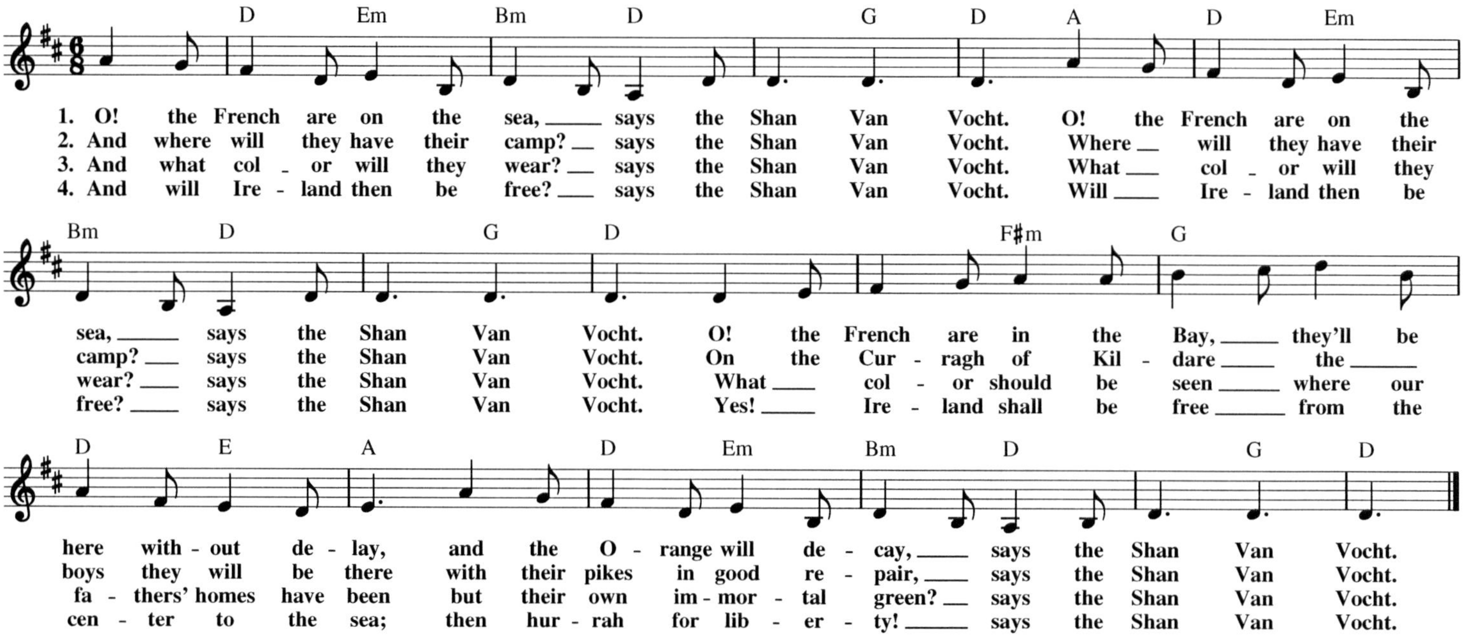

1. O! the French are on the sea, ____ says the Shan Van Vocht. O! the French are on the
2. And where will they have their camp? ____ says the Shan Van Vocht. Where ____ will they have their
3. And what col _ or will they wear? ____ says the Shan Van Vocht. What ____ col _ or will they
4. And will Ire _ land then be free? ____ says the Shan Van Vocht. Will ____ Ire _ land then be

sea, ____ says the Shan Van Vocht. O! the French are in the Bay, ____ they'll be
camp? ____ says the Shan Van Vocht. On the Cur _ ragh of Kil _ dare ____ the ____
wear? ____ says the Shan Van Vocht. What ____ col _ or should be seen ____ where our
free? ____ says the Shan Van Vocht. Yes! ____ Ire _ land shall be free ____ from the

here with - out de - lay, and the O - range will de - cay, ____ says the Shan Van Vocht.
boys they will be there with their pikes in good re - pair, ____ says the Shan Van Vocht.
fa - thers' homes have been but their own im - mor - tal green? ____ says the Shan Van Vocht.
cen - ter to the sea; then hur - rah for lib - er - ty! ____ says the Shan Van Vocht.

THE SHIP AT SEA
(Cuan ag eirigh)

Folksong from the Hebrides

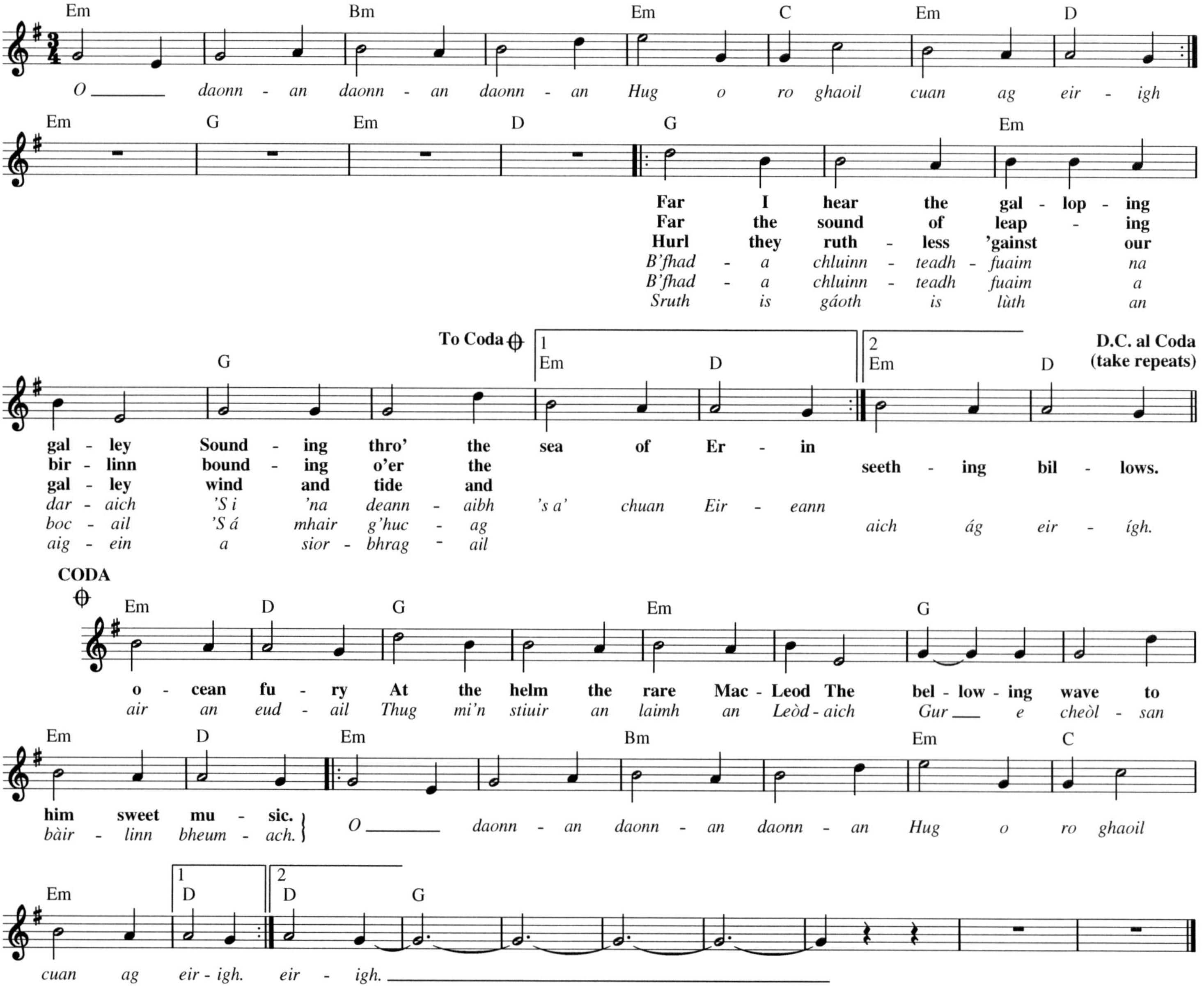

O ____ daonn - an daonn - an daonn - an Hug o ro ghaoil cuan ag eir - igh

Far I hear the gal - lop - ing
Far the sound of leap - ing
Hurl they ruth - less 'gainst our
B'fhad - a chluinn - teadh - fuaim na
B'fhad - a chluinn - teadh fuaim a
Sruth is gáoth is lùth an

To Coda
D.C. al Coda
(take repeats)

gal - ley Sound - ing thro' the sea of Er - in seeth - ing bil - lows.
bir - linn bound - ing o'er the seeth - ing bil - lows.
gal - ley wind and tide and
dar - aich 'S i 'na deann - aibh 's a' chuan Eir - eann
boc - ail 'S á mhair g'huc - ag aich ág eir - ígh.
aig - ein a sior - bhrag - ail

CODA

o - cean fu - ry At the helm the rare Mac - Leod The bel - low - ing wave to
air an eud - ail Thug mi'n stiuir an laimh an Leòd - aich Gur ____ e cheòl - san

him sweet mu - sic.} O ____ daonn - an daonn - an daonn - an Hug o ro ghaoil
bàir - linn bheum - ach.

cuan ag eir - igh. eir - igh. ____

THE SHORES OF AMERIKAY

Irish folksong

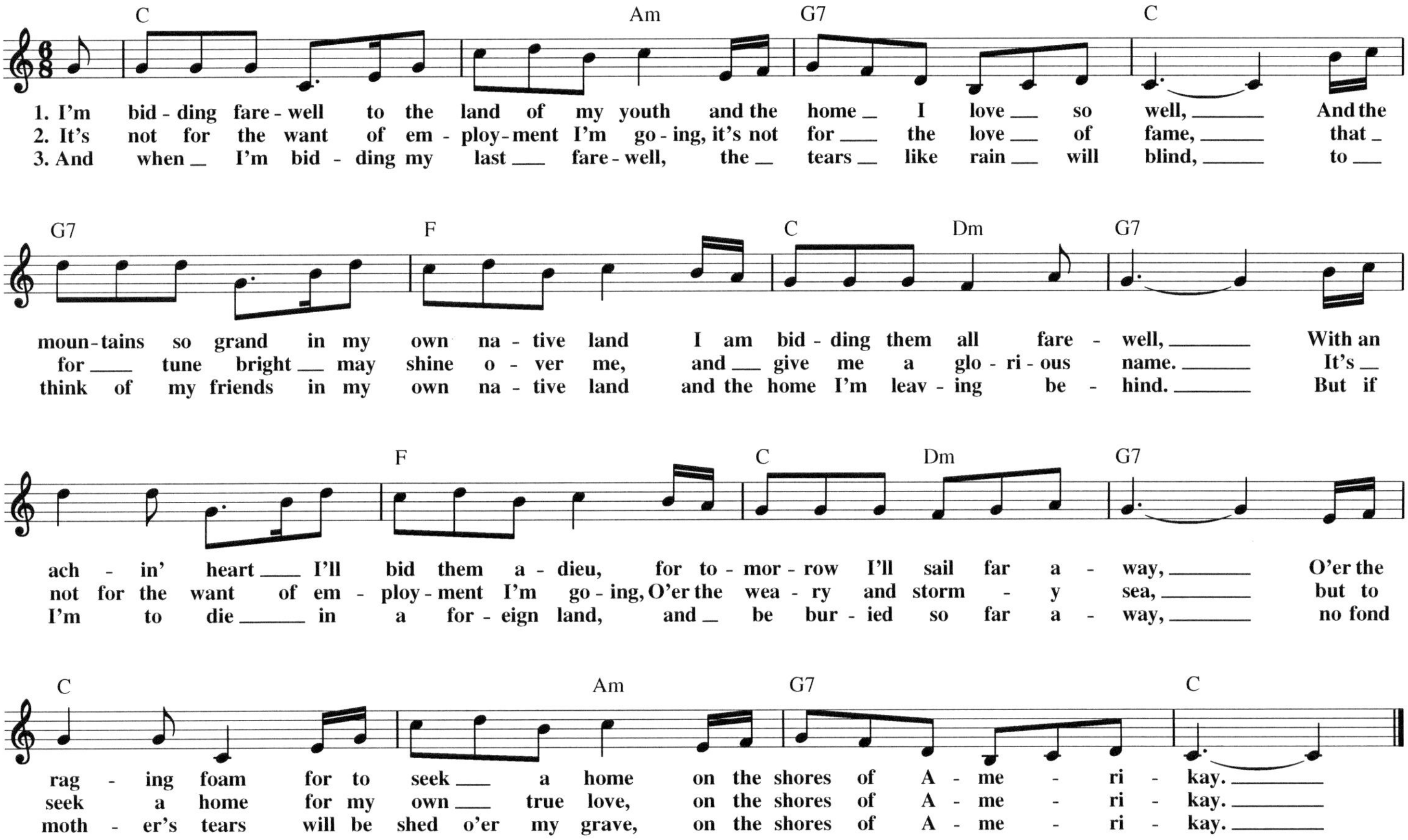

1. I'm bid-ding fare-well to the land of my youth and the home _ I love _ so well, _____ And the
2. It's not for the want of em-ploy-ment I'm go-ing, it's not for ___ the love _ of fame, _____ that _
3. And when _ I'm bid-ding my last ___ fare-well, the _ tears _ like rain _ will blind, _____ to ___

moun-tains so grand in my own na-tive land I am bid-ding them all fare-well, _____ With an
for ___ tune bright _ may shine o-ver me, and _ give me a glo-ri-ous name. _____ It's _
think of my friends in my own na-tive land and the home I'm leav-ing be-hind. _____ But if

ach-in' heart ___ I'll bid them a-dieu, for to-mor-row I'll sail far a-way, _____ O'er the
not for the want of em-ploy-ment I'm go-ing, O'er the wea-ry and storm-y sea, _____ but to
I'm to die _____ in a for-eign land, and _ be bur-ied so far a-way, _____ no fond

rag-ing foam for to seek ___ a home on the shores of A-me-ri-kay. _____
seek a home for my own ___ true love, on the shores of A-me-ri-kay. _____
moth-er's tears will be shed o'er my grave, on the shores of A-me-ri-kay. _____

SHULE AGRA

Irish folksong

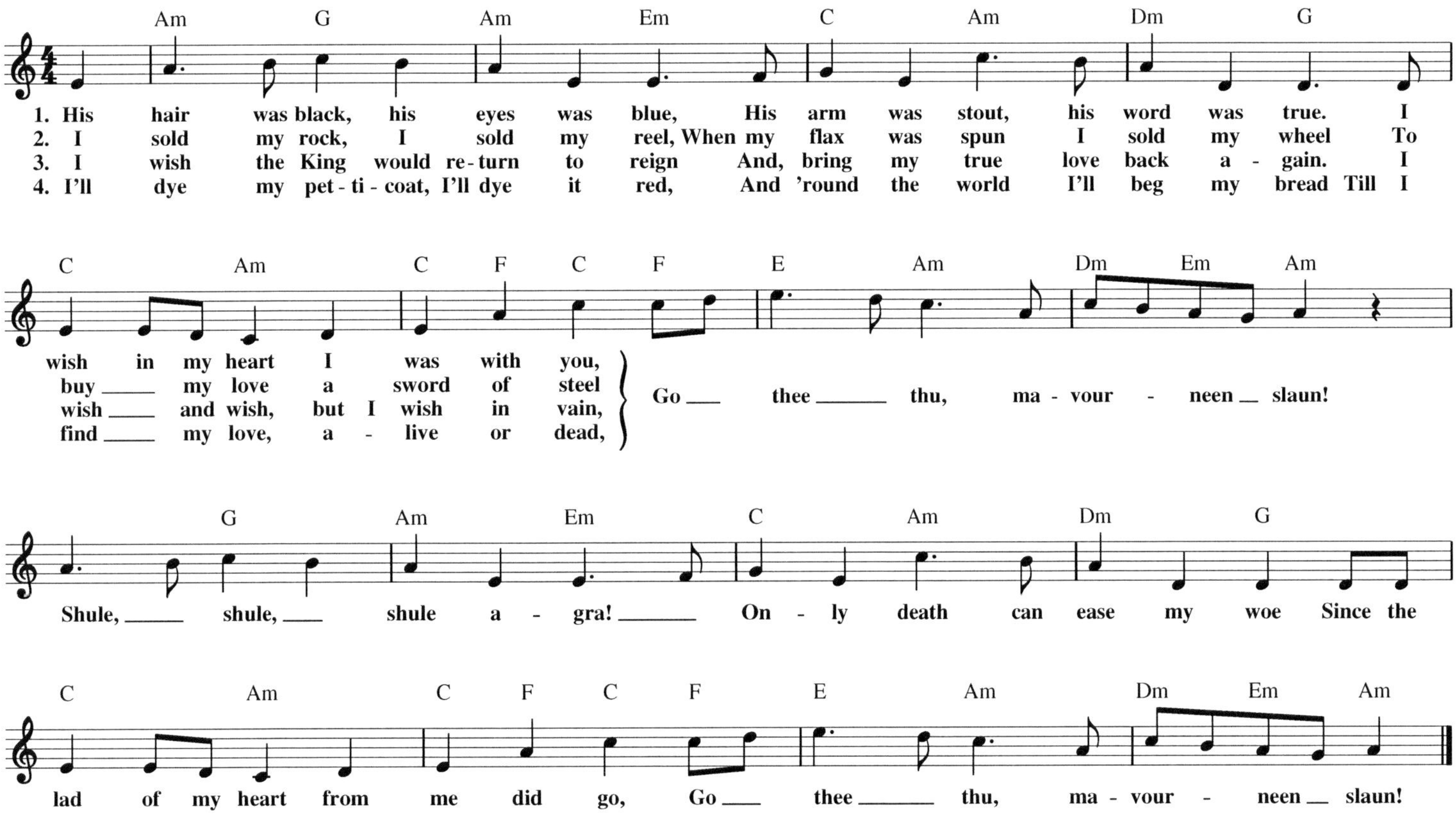

1. His hair was black, his eyes was blue, His arm was stout, his word was true. I
2. I sold my rock, I sold my reel, When my flax was spun I sold my wheel To
3. I wish the King would re-turn to reign And, bring my true love back a-gain. I
4. I'll dye my pet-ti-coat, I'll dye it red, And 'round the world I'll beg my bread Till I

wish in my heart I was with you,
buy ___ my love a sword of steel, } Go ___ thee _____ thu, ma-vour-neen _ slaun!
wish ___ and wish, but I wish in vain,
find ___ my love, a-live or dead, }

Shule, _____ shule, _____ shule a-gra! _____ On-ly death can ease my woe Since the

lad of my heart from me did go, Go ___ thee _____ thu, ma-vour-neen _ slaun!

SINCE I'VE BEEN IN THE ARMY

Irish folksong
Traditional Scottish Melody
("Wha'll Be King but Charlie?")

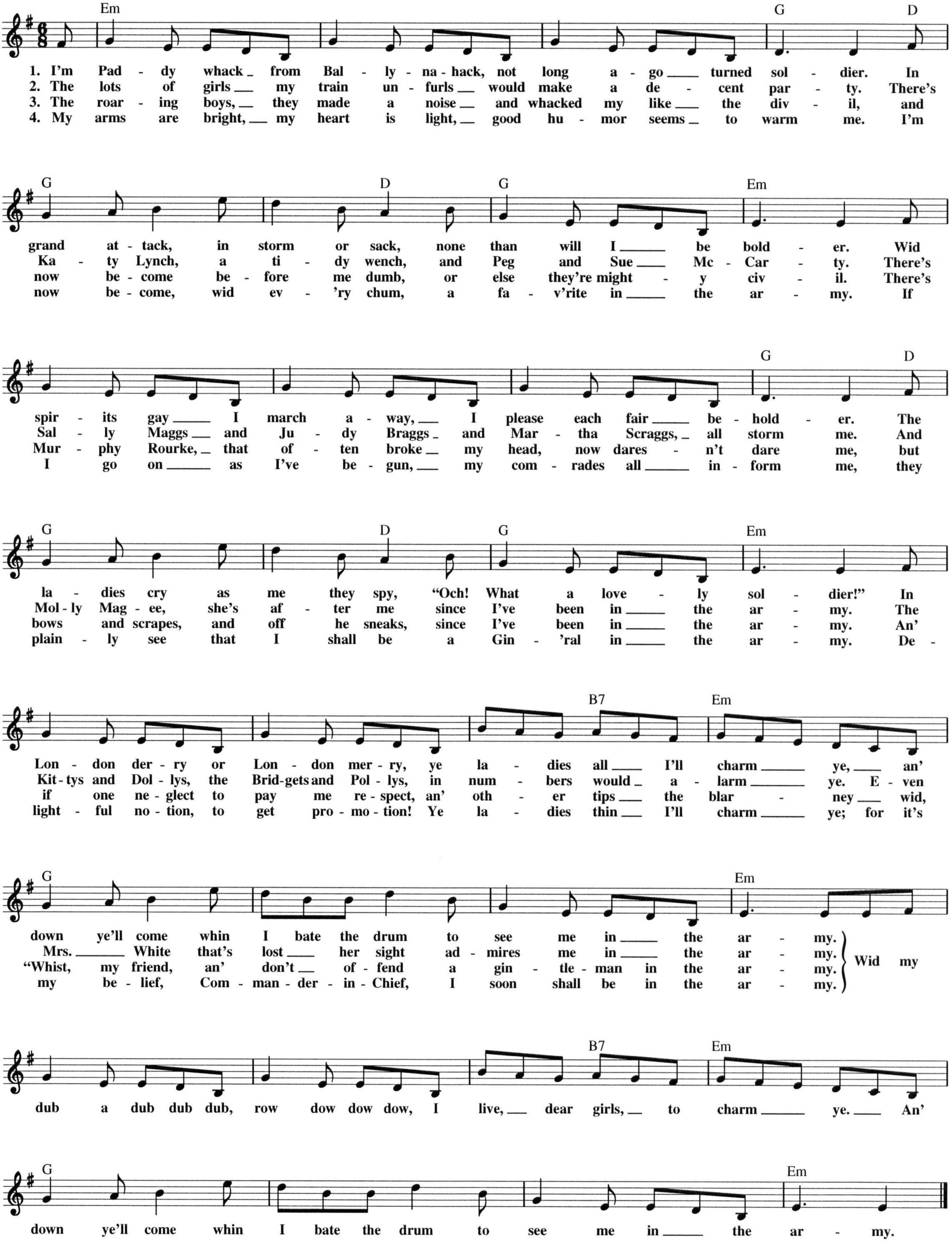

SILKIE

Scottish folksong

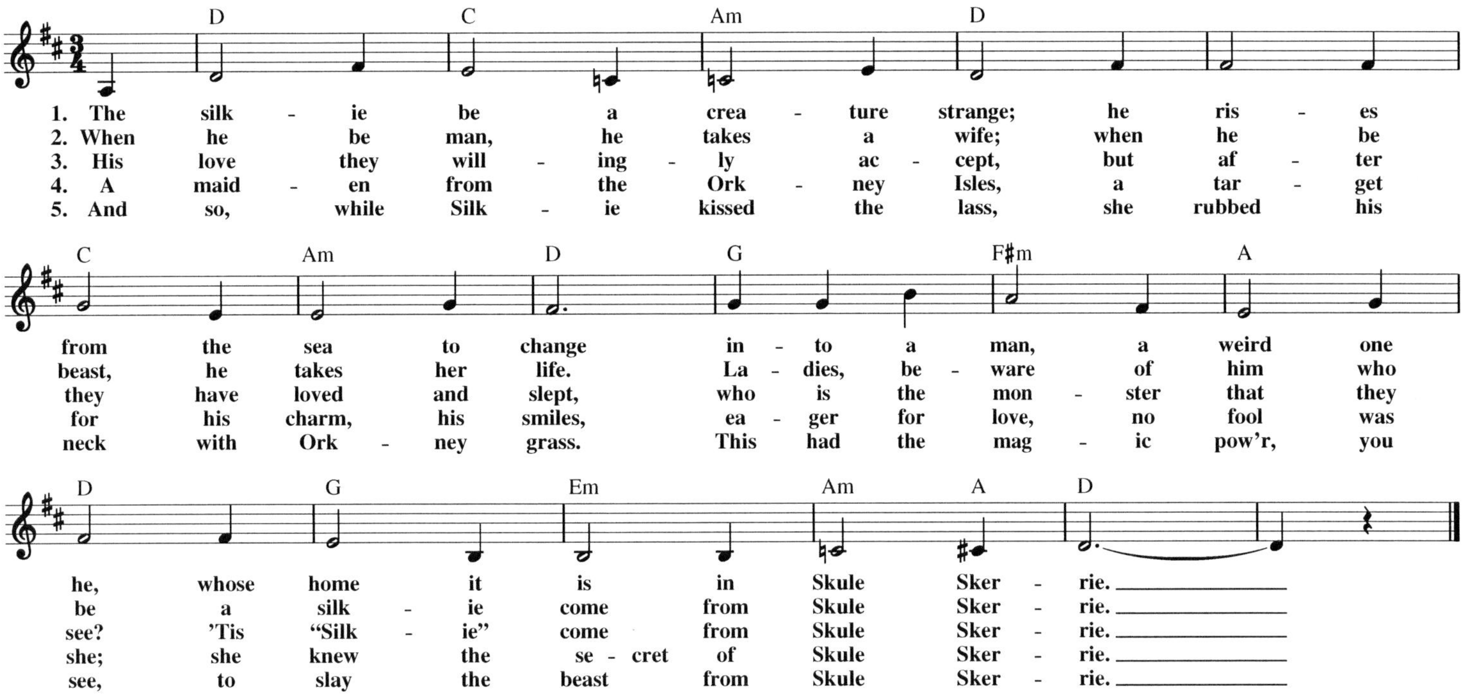

1. The silk - ie be a crea - ture strange; he ris - es from the sea to change in - to a man, a weird one he, whose home it is in Skule Sker - rie. _____
2. When he be man, he takes a wife; when he be beast, he takes her life. La - dies, be - ware of him who be a silk - ie come from Skule Sker - rie. _____
3. His love they will - ing - ly ac - cept, but af - ter they have loved and slept, who is the mon - ster that they see? 'Tis "Silk - ie" come from Skule Sker - rie. _____
4. A maid - en from the Ork - ney Isles, a tar - get for his charm, his smiles, ea - ger for love, no fool was she; she knew the se - cret of Skule Sker - rie. _____
5. And so, while Silk - ie kissed the lass, she rubbed his neck with Ork - ney grass. This had the mag - ic pow'r, you see, to slay the beast from Skule Sker - rie. _____

SINCE JAMES PUT ON HIGH COLLARS

Words and Music by
Joseph P. Skelly

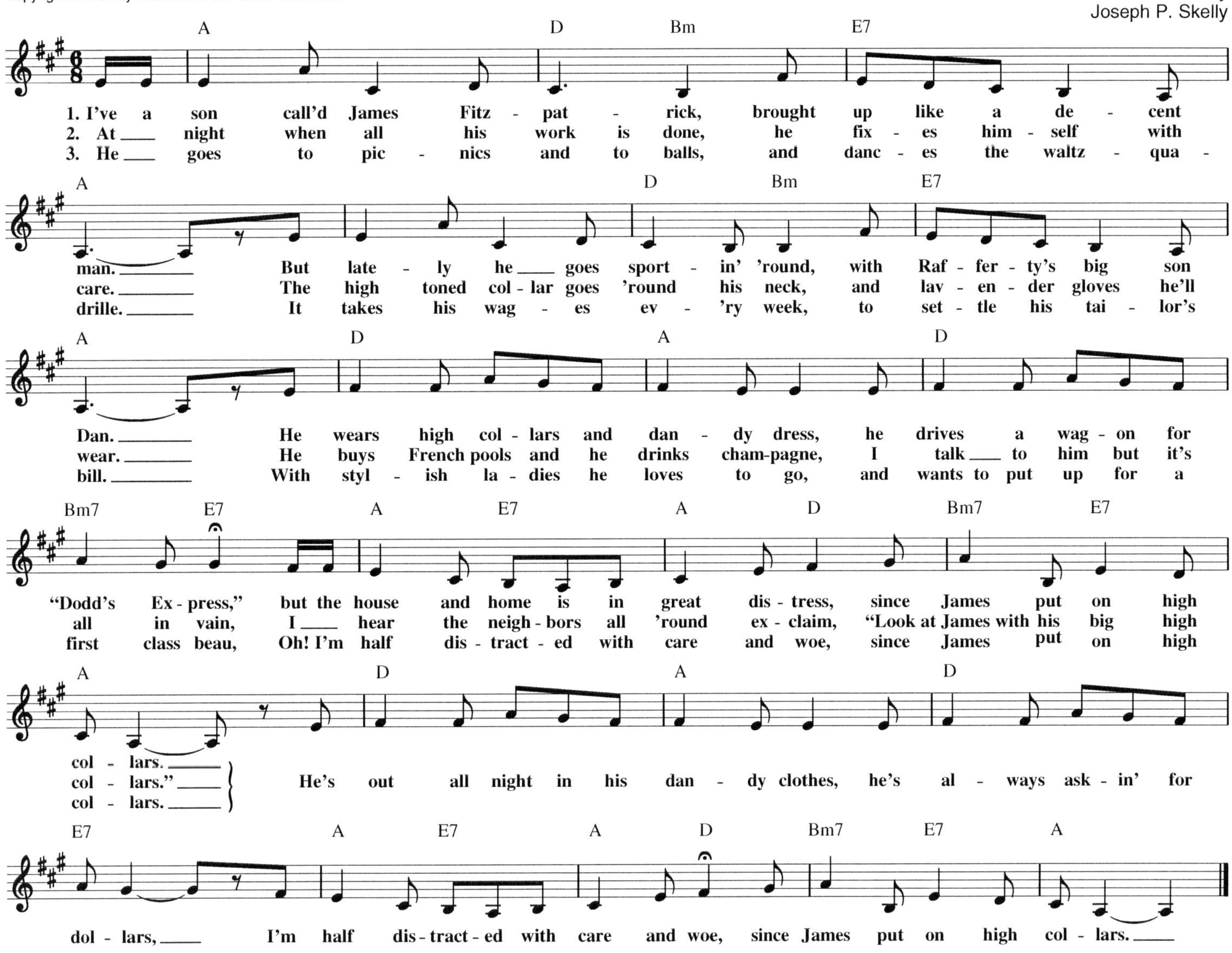

1. I've a son call'd James Fitz - pat - rick, brought up like a de - cent man. _____ But late - ly he _____ goes sport - in' 'round, with Raf - fer - ty's big son Dan. _____ He wears high col - lars and dan - dy dress, he drives a wag - on for "Dodd's Ex - press," but the house and home is in great dis - tress, since James put on high col - lars. _____ He's out all night in his dan - dy clothes, he's al - ways ask - in' for dol - lars, _____ I'm half dis - tract - ed with care and woe, since James put on high col - lars. _____

2. At _____ night when all his work is done, he fix - es him - self with care. _____ The high toned col - lar goes 'round his neck, and lav - en - der gloves he'll wear. _____ He buys French pools and he drinks cham - pagne, I talk _____ to him but it's all in vain, I _____ hear the neigh - bors all 'round ex - claim, "Look at James with his big high col - lars." ____

3. He _____ goes to pic - nics and to balls, and danc - es the waltz qua - drille. _____ It takes his wag - es ev - 'ry week, to set - tle his tai - lor's bill. _____ With styl - ish la - dies he loves to go, and wants to put up for a first class beau, Oh! I'm half dis - tract - ed with care and woe, since James put on high col - lars. _____

SINCE MAGGIE WENT AWAY

Irish folksong

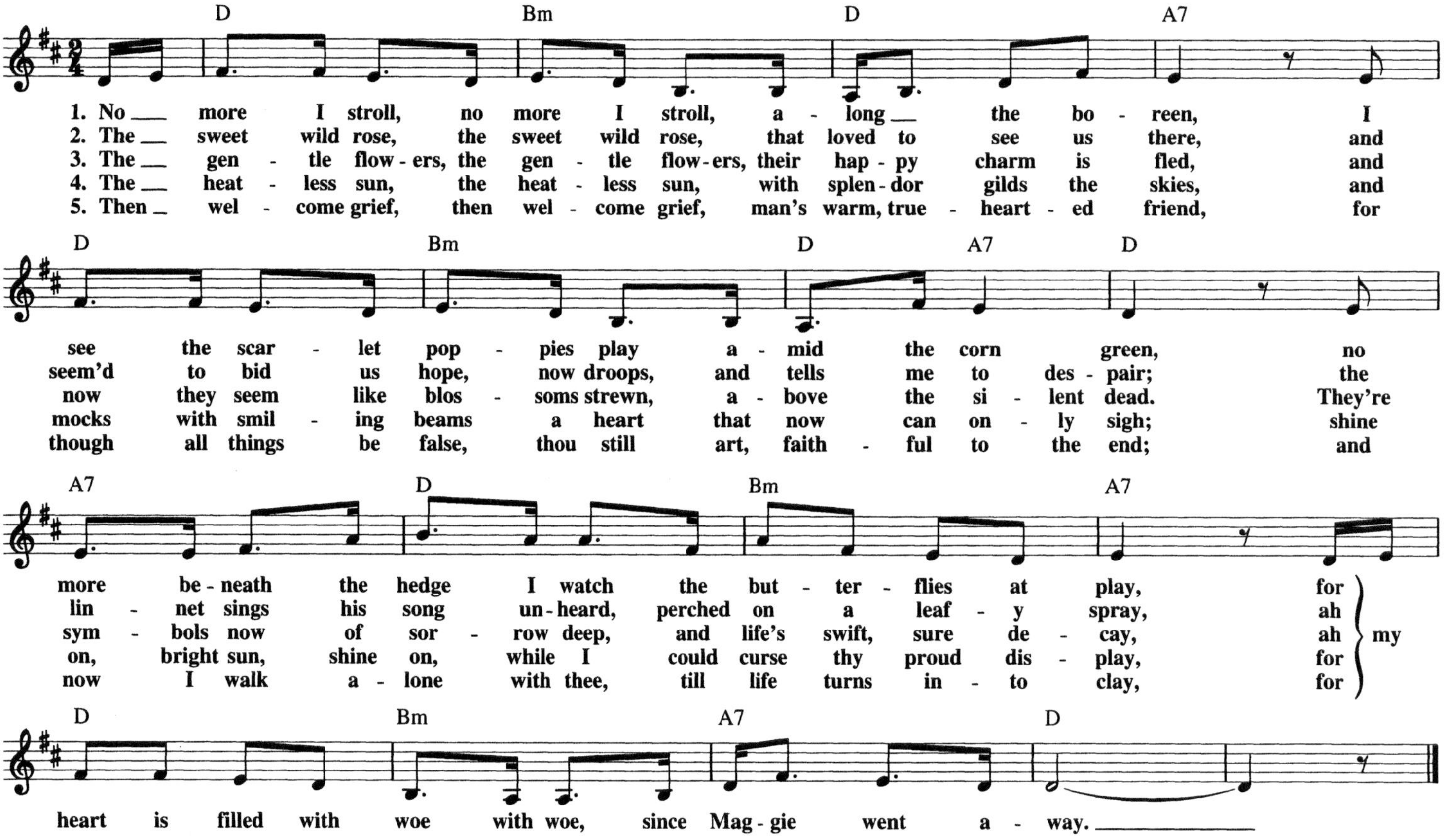

SKIBBEREEN

Irish folksong

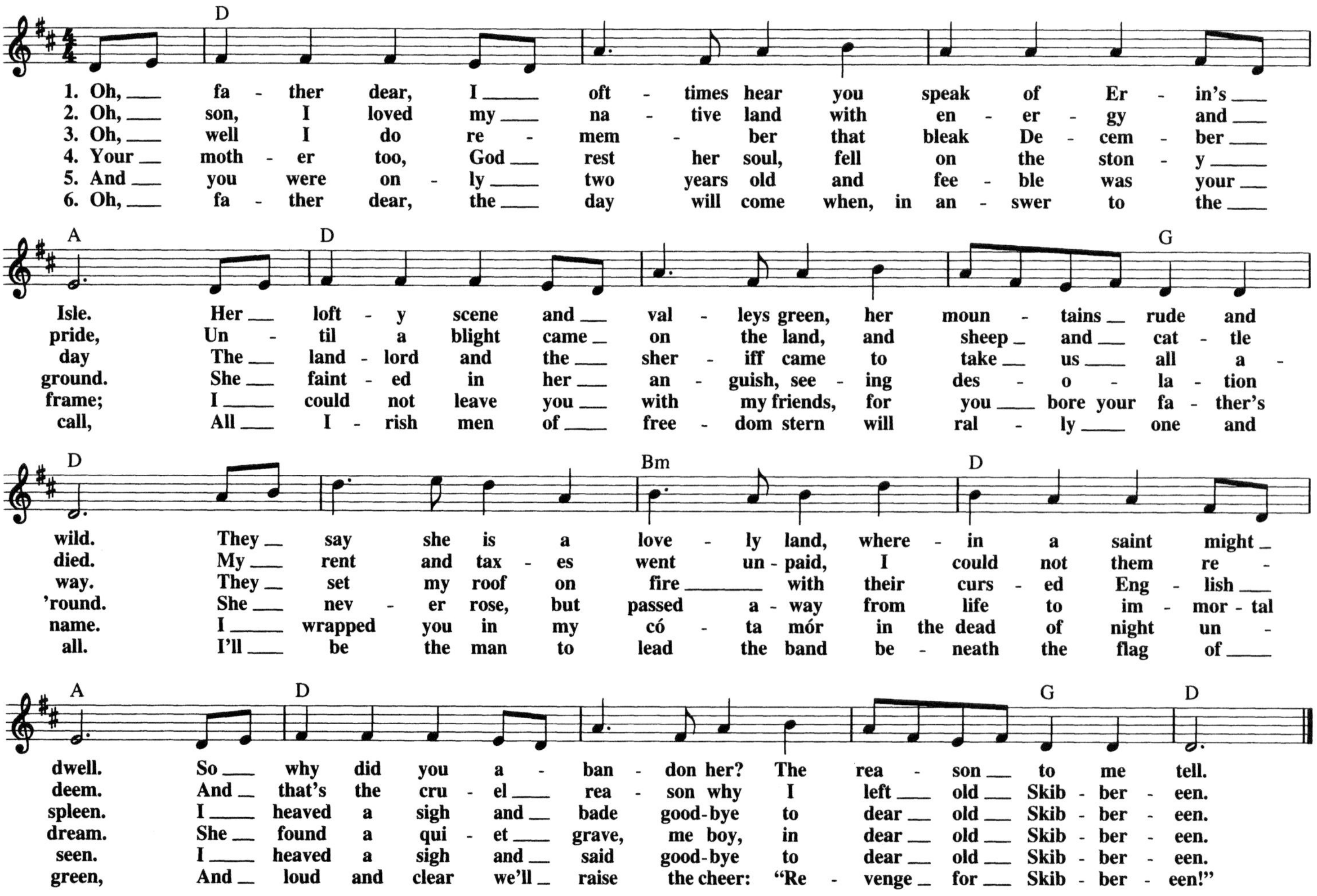

THE SKUA-GULLS
(Na Lochlinnich)

Folksong from the Hebrides

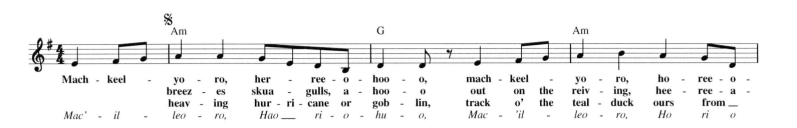

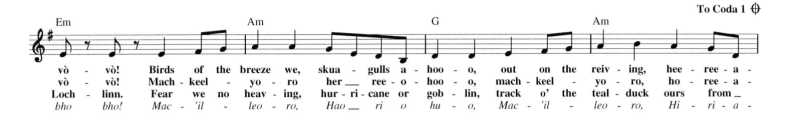

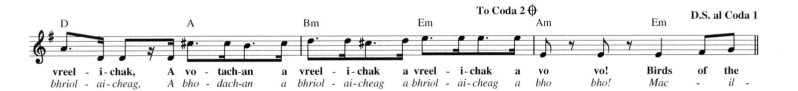

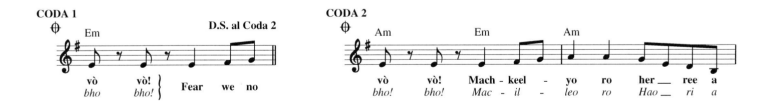

SKYE FISHER'S SONG
(Tir-nan-òg)

Folksong from the Hebrides

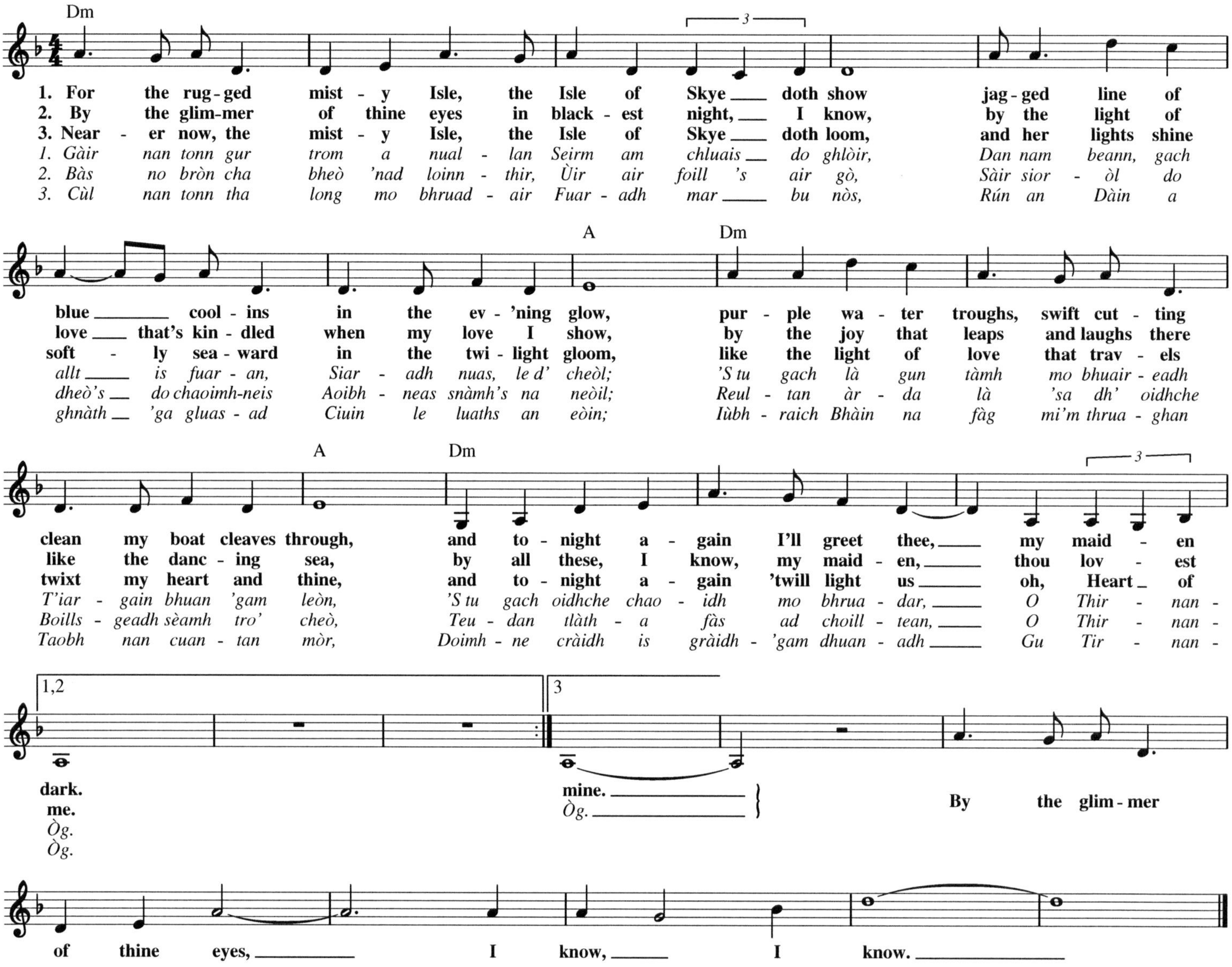

1. For the rug-ged mist-y Isle, the Isle of Skye doth show jag-ged line of
2. By the glim-mer of thine eyes in black-est night, I know, by the light of
3. Near-er now, the mist-y Isle, the Isle of Skye doth loom, and her lights shine

1. Gàir nan tonn gur trom a nual-lan Seirm am chluais do ghlòir, Dan nam beann, gach
2. Bàs no bròn cha bheò 'nad loinn-thir, Ùir air foill 's air gò, Sàir sior-òl do
3. Cùl nan tonn tha long mo bhruad-air Fuar-adh mar bu nòs, Rún an Dàin a

blue coolins in the ev-'ning glow, pur-ple wa-ter troughs, swift cut-ting
love that's kin-dled when my love I show, by the joy that leaps and laughs there
soft-ly sea-ward in the twi-light gloom, like the light of love that trav-els

allt is fuar-an, Siar-adh nuas, le d' cheòl; 'S tu gach là gun tàmh mo bhuair-eadh
dheò's do chaoimh-neis Aoibh-neas snàmh's na neòil; Reul-tan àr-da là 'sa dh' oidhche
ghnàth 'ga gluas-ad Ciuin le luaths an eòin; Iùbh-raich Bhàin na fàg mi'm thrua-ghan

clean my boat cleaves through, and to-night a-gain I'll greet thee, my maid-en
like the danc-ing sea, by all these, I know, my maid-en, thou lov-est
twixt my heart and thine, and to-night a-gain 'twill light us oh, Heart of

T'iar-gain bhuan 'gam leòn, 'S tu gach oidhche chao-idh mo bhrua-dar, O Thir-nan-
Boills-geadh sèamh tro' cheò, Teu-dan tlàth-a fàs ad choill-tean, O Thir-nan-
Taobh nan cuan-tan mòr, Doimh-ne cràidh is gràidh-'gam dhuan-adh Gu Tir-nan-

dark.
me.
Òg.
Òg.

mine. Òg.

By the glim-mer

of thine eyes, I know, I know.

THE SKYE STEERSMAN'S SONG
('S mo lamh air a stiuir)

Folksong from the Hebrides

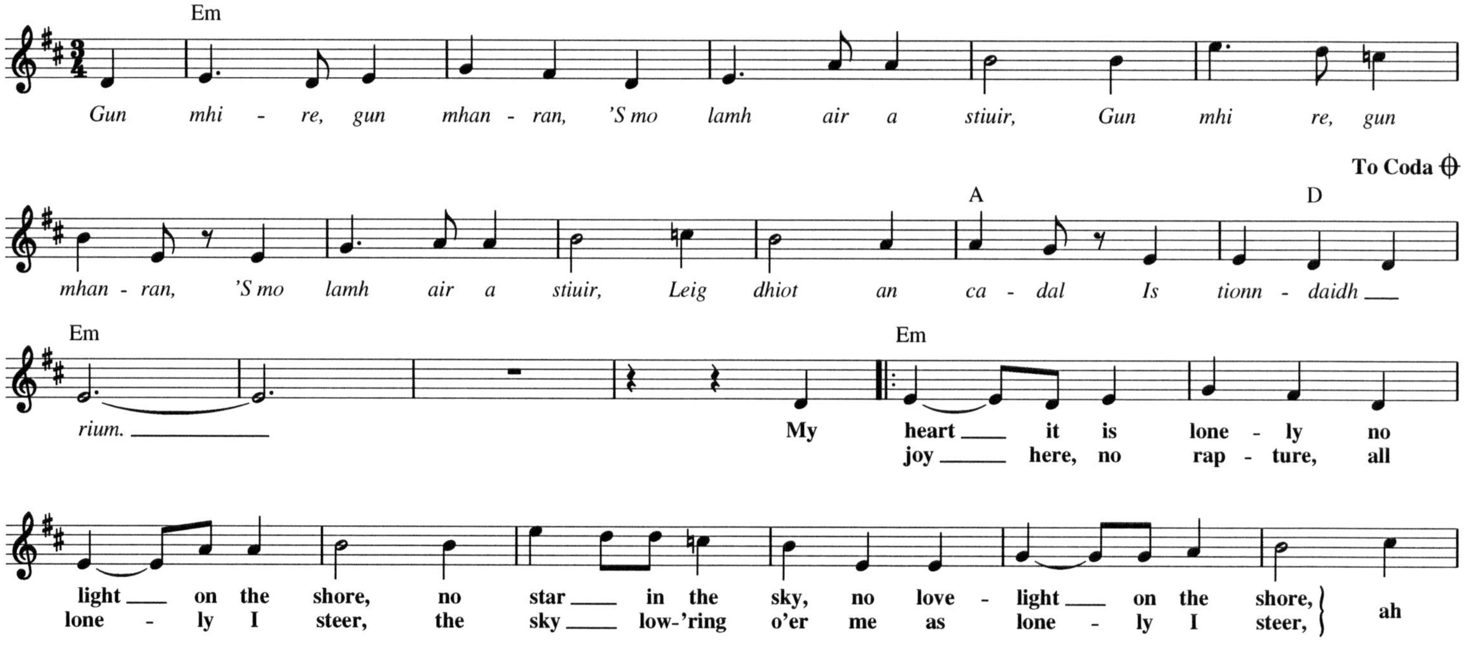

Gun mhi-re, gun mhan-ran, 'S mo lamh air a stiuir, Gun mhi re, gun

To Coda

mhan-ran, 'S mo lamh air a stiuir, Leig dhiot an ca-dal Is tionn-daidh

rium.

My heart it is lone-ly no
joy here, no rap-ture, all

light on the shore, no star in the sky, no love-light on the shore, ah
lone-ly I steer, the sky low-'ring o'er me as lone-ly I steer,

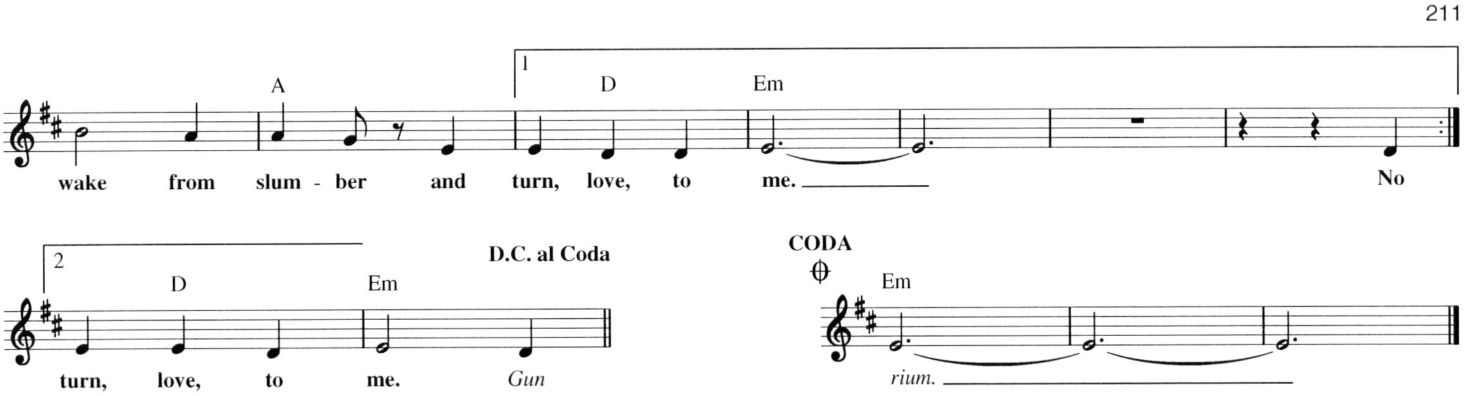

wake from slum - ber and turn, love, to me. _____ No

turn, love, to me. *Gun*

D.C. al Coda

CODA

rium. _____

SKYE WATER-KELPIE'S LULLABY

Folksong from the Hebrides

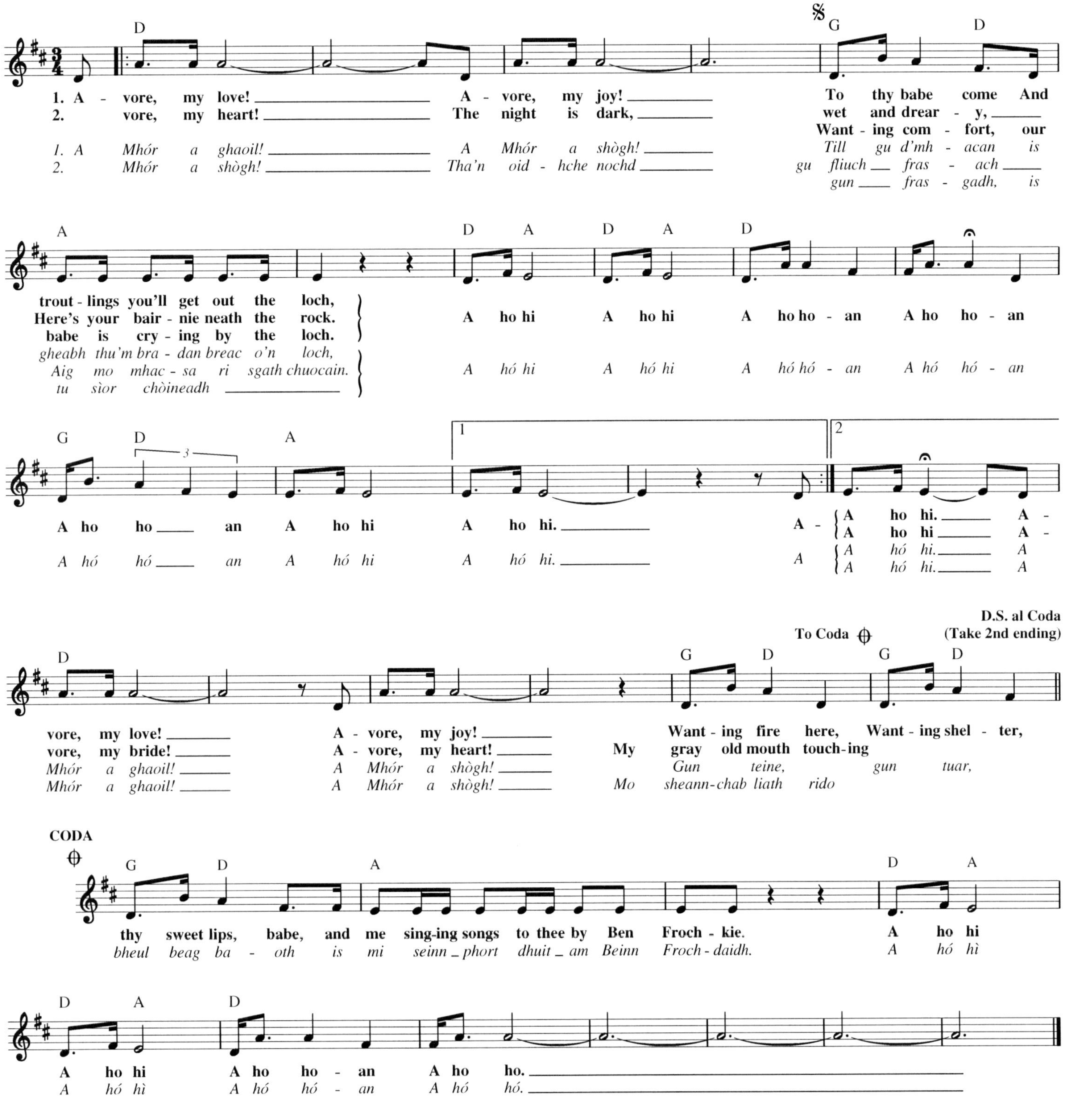

1. A - vore, my love! _____ A - vore, my joy! _____ To thy babe come And
2. vore, my heart! _____ The night is dark, _____ Want - ing com - fort, our

1. A Mhór a ghaoil! _____ A Mhór a shògh! _____ Till gu d'mh - acan is
2. Mhór a shògh! _____ Tha'n oid - hche nochd _____ gu fliuch _____ fras - ach _____
gun _____ fras - gadh, is

trout - lings you'll get out the loch,
Here's your bair - nie neath the rock.
babe is cry - ing by the loch.

gheabh thu'm bra - dan breac o'n loch,
Aig mo mhac - sa ri sgath chuocain.
tu sìor chòineadh _____

A ho hi A ho hi A ho ho - an A ho ho - an
A hó hi A hó hi A hó hó - an A hó hó - an

A ho ho _____ an A ho hi A ho hi. _____
A hó hó _____ an A hó hi A hó hi. _____

To Coda

D.S. al Coda
(Take 2nd ending)

A- { A ho hi. _____ A-
{ A ho hi _____ A-
A { A hó hi. _____ A
{ A hó hi. _____ A

vore, my love! _____ A - vore, my joy! _____ Want - ing fire here, Want - ing shel - ter,
vore, my bride! _____ A - vore, my heart! _____ My gray old mouth touch - ing

Mhór a ghaoil! _____ A Mhór a shògh! _____ Gun teine, gun tuar,
Mhór a ghaoil! _____ A Mhór a shògh! _____ Mo sheann - chab liath rido

CODA

thy sweet lips, babe, and me sing - ing songs to thee by Ben Froch - kie. A ho hi
bheul beag ba - oth is mi seinn _____ phort dhuit _____ am Beinn Froch - daidh. A hó hì

A ho hi A ho ho - an A ho ho. _____
A hó hì A hó hó - an A hó hó. _____

SLEEPS THE NOON IN THE DEEP BLUE SKY

Folksong from the Hebrides

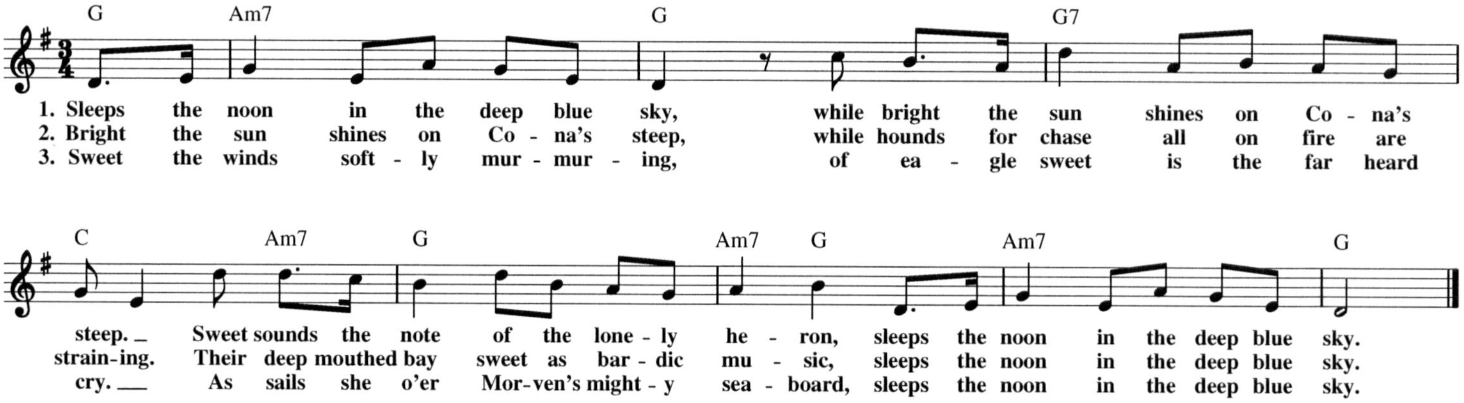

SLIEVENAMON

Irish folksong

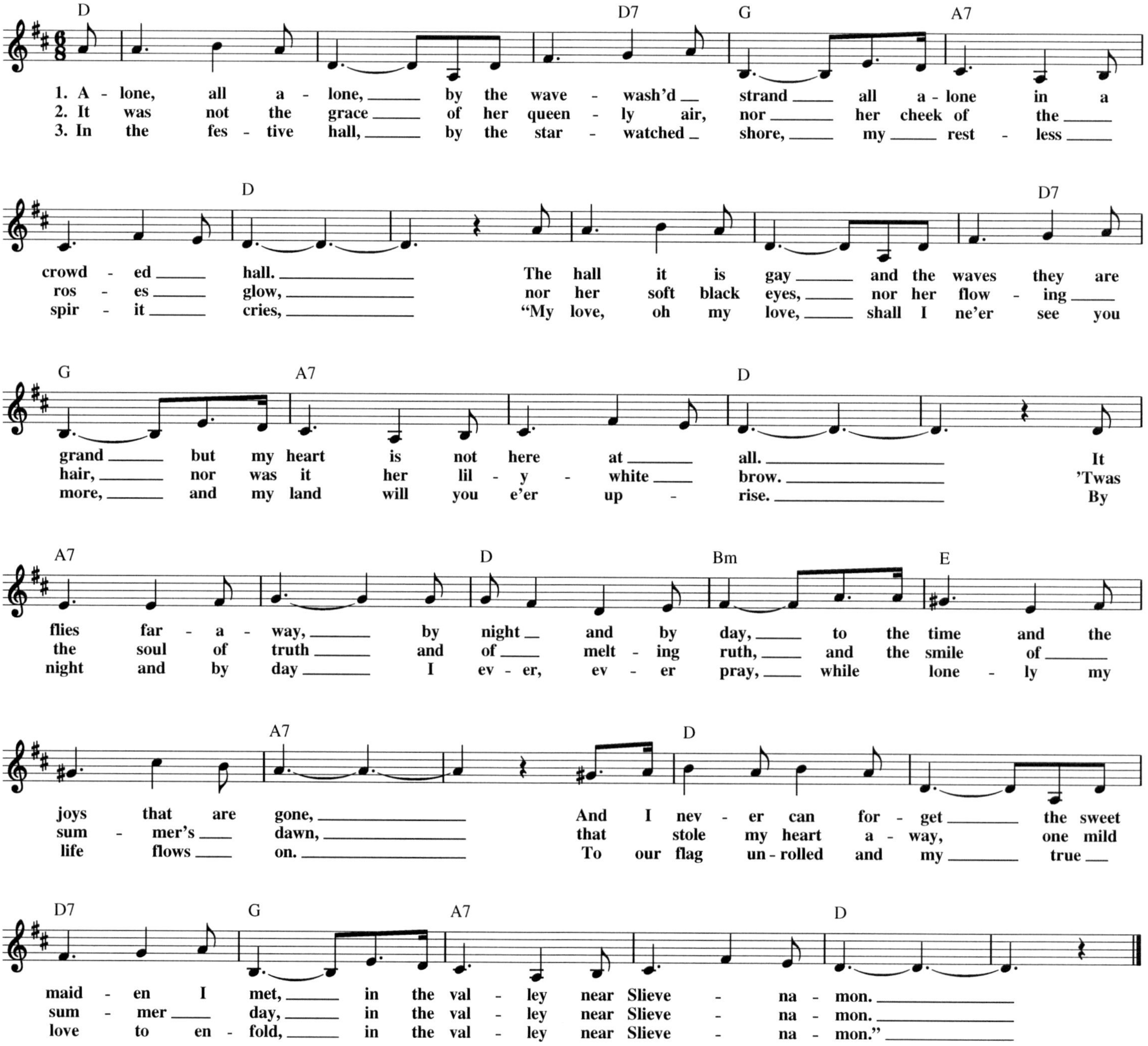

SLIEVE GALLEN BRAES

Copyright © 2001 by HAL LEONARD CORPORATION

Irish folksong

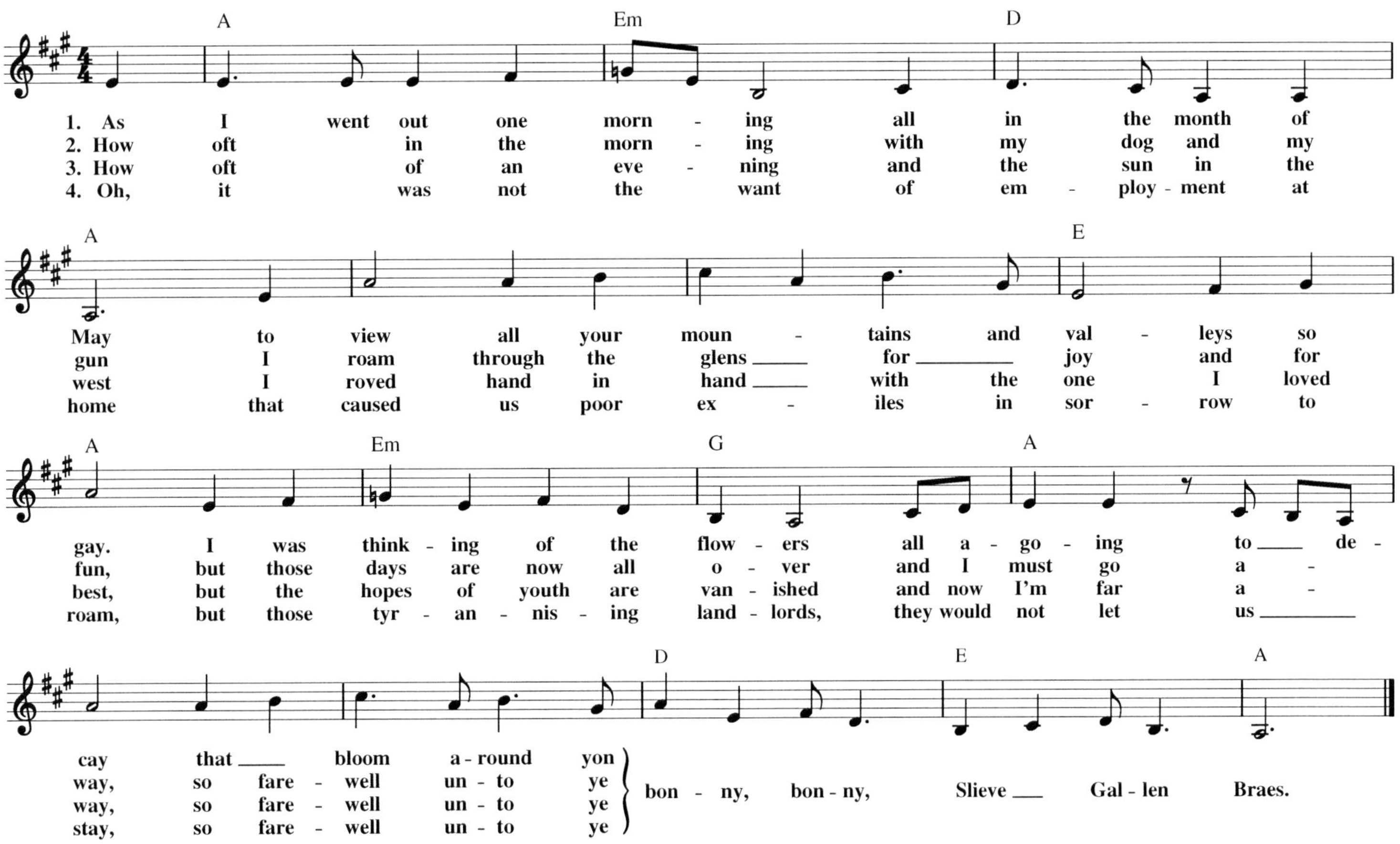

THE SONS OF LIBERTY

Copyright © 2000 by HAL LEONARD CORPORATION

Irish folksong

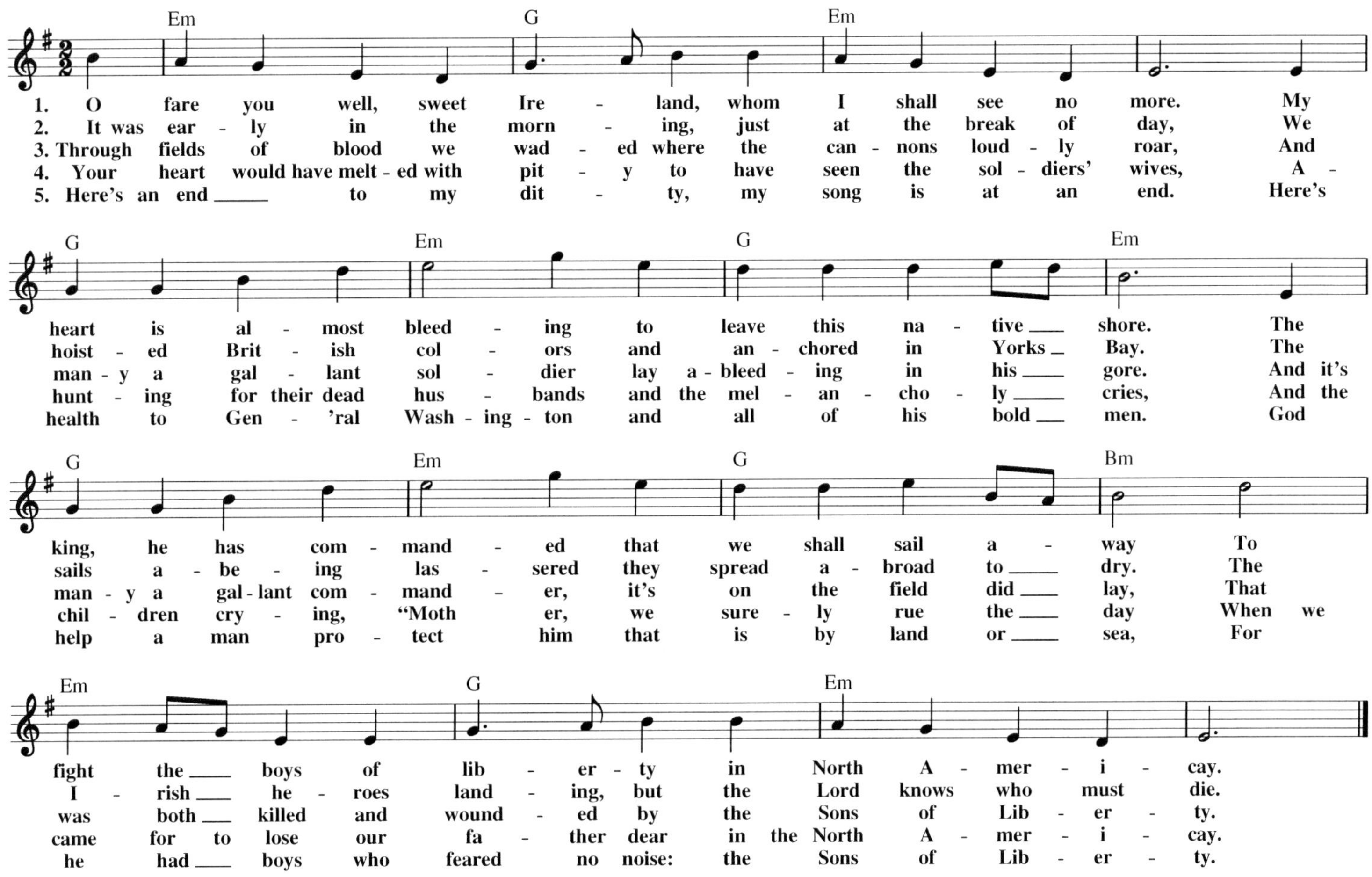

THE SNOWY-BREASTED PEARL
(Péarla An Bhrollaigh Bháin)

Irish folksong

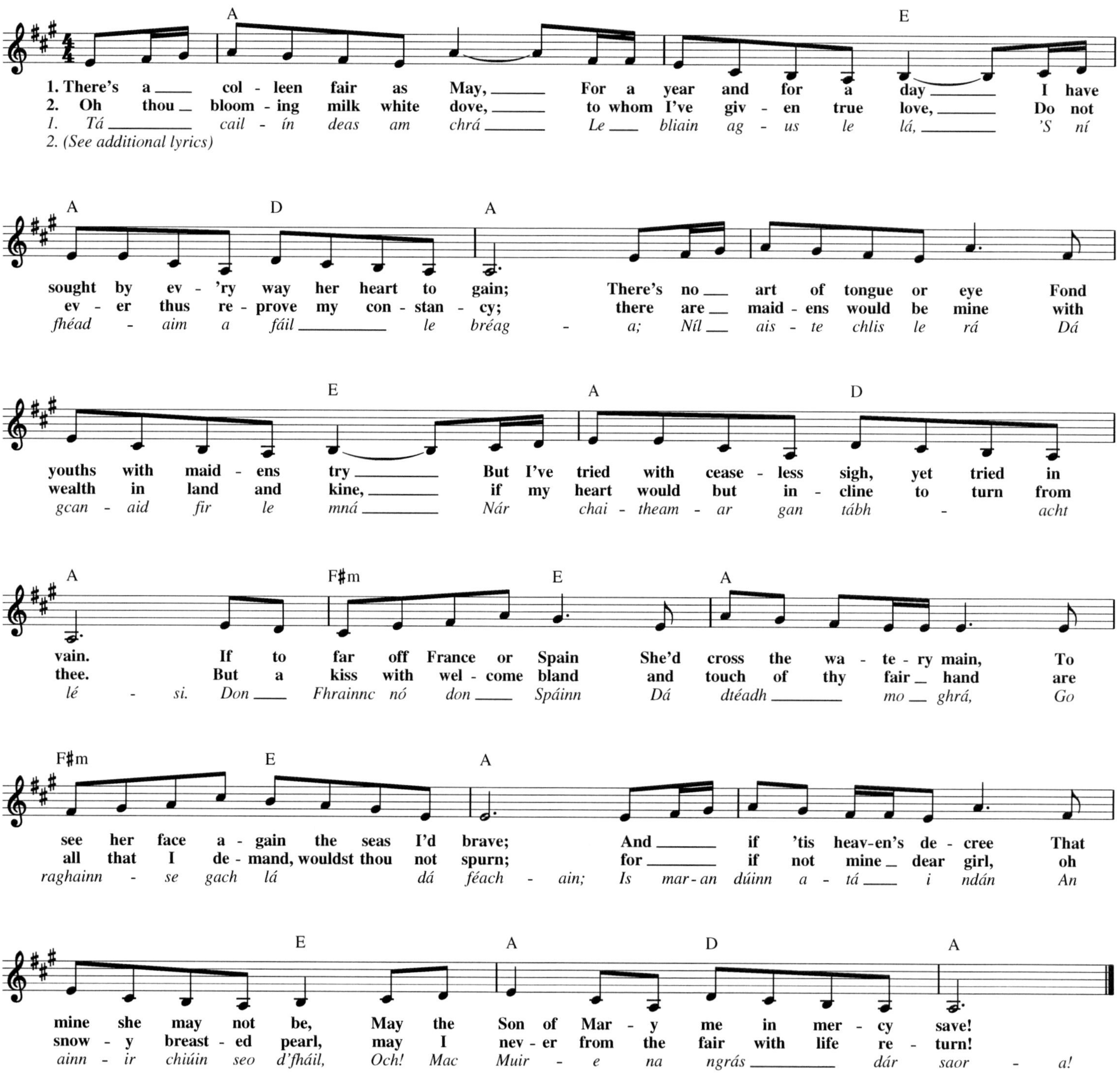

1. There's a ___ col - leen fair as May, ___ For a year and for a day ___ I have
2. Oh thou ___ bloom - ing milk white dove, ___ to whom I've giv - en true love, ___ Do not

1. Tá ___ cail - ín deas am chrá ___ Le ___ bliain ag - us le lá, ___ 'S ní
2. (See additional lyrics)

sought by ev - 'ry way her heart to gain; There's no ___ art of tongue or eye Fond
ev - er thus re - prove my con - stan - cy; there are ___ maid - ens would be mine with
fhéad - aim a fáil ___ le bréag - a; Níl ___ ais - te chlis le rá Dá

youths with maid - ens try ___ But I've tried with cease - less sigh, yet tried in
wealth in land and kine, ___ if my heart would but in - cline to turn from
gcan - aid fir le mná ___ Nár chai - theam - ar gan tábh - acht

vain. If to far off France or Spain She'd cross the wa - te - ry main, To
thee. But a kiss with wel - come bland and touch of thy fair ___ hand are
lé - si. Don ___ Fhrainnc nó don ___ Spáinn Dá dtéadh ___ mo ___ ghrá, Go

see her face a - gain the seas I'd brave; And ___ if 'tis heav - en's de - cree That
all that I de - mand, wouldst thou not spurn; for ___ if not mine ___ dear girl, oh
raghainn - se gach lá dá féach - ain; Is mar - an dúinn a - tá ___ i ndán An

mine she may not be, May the Son of Mar - y me in mer - cy save!
snow - y breast - ed pearl, may I nev - er from the fair with life re - turn!
ainn - ir chiúin seo d'fháil, Och! Mac Muir - e na ngrás ___ dár saor - a!

Additional Lyrics

2. *Is a chailín chailcee bhláith,*
   Dá dtugas searc is grá,
   Ná túir-se gach tráth dhom éara;
   'S a liacht ainnir mhín im dheáidh
   Le buaibh is maoin 'n-a láimh,
   Dá ngabhaimís it áit-se céile.
   Póg is míle fáilte
   Is barra geal do lámh
   'Sé 'n-iarrfainn-se go bráth mar spré leat;
   'S maran domh-sa taoi tú i ndán,
   A phéarla an bhrollaigh bháin,
   Nár thí mise slán ón aonach!

THE SOFT DEAL BOARD
(An Clár Bog Déil)

Irish folksong

1. I ____ would ____ wed you, dear, with - out gold or gear or ____ count - ed
2. Oh, ____ come ____ my bride, o'er the ____ wild hills' side, to the ____ val - ley
3. Love ____ ten - der, true I ____ gave to you, and ____ se - cret
4. In ____ church ____ at pray - er first I saw the fair, in glo - ri - ous
5. A ____ neck ____ of white has my ____ heart's de - light, and ____ breast like

kine, my ____ wealth you'd be, would your friends a - gree, and ____ you be
low, A ____ down - y bed for my love I'll spread, where ____ wa - ters ____
sighs, In ____ hope to see up - on you and me, one ____ hour a -
sheen, In man - tle flow - ing, with jew - els glow - ing, and ____ front - let ____
snow, and ____ flow - ing hair whose ____ ring - lets fair to ____ the ____ green grass ____

mine; my ____ grief, my gloom! that you do not come, my ____ heart's dear
flow; and ____ we shall stray where ____ stream - lets play, the ____ groves a -
rise when the ____ priest's blest voice would con - firm my choice, and ____ the ____ ring's strict
green, and robe ____ of white - ness whose fold of light - ness might ____ sweep the
flow, a - las ____ that I did not ____ ear - ly die be - fore the

hoard! To ____ Cash - el fair, though our couch were there but ____ a ____ soft deal board!
mong, where ____ ech - o tells to the list - 'ning dells the ____ black - birds song.
tie: if ____ wife you be, love, to one but me love, in ____ grief I'll die!
lea, oh, my ____ heart is bro - ken since tongues have spo - ken that ____ maid for me!
day that ____ saw me here, from my bos - om's dear far, ____ far a - way!

Gaelic Lyrics

1. *Do ghlacfainn tú gan ba, gan púint,*
   gan áireamh spré,
   A chuid 'en tsaol, le toil do mhuínntre,
   dá mb'ail leat mé.
   'Sé mo ghalar dúch gan mé gus tú.
   a dhian-ghrá mo chléibh,
   l gCaiseal Mumhan 's gan do leabaidh fúinn
   ach an clár bog déil!

2. *Siúil, a chogair, is tar a chodla*
   liom féin don ghleann,
   Gheó tú fosca, leabaidh fhlocais
   is aer cois abhann;
   Beidh na srotha a' gabháil thorainn
   faoi ghéagaibh crann,
   Beidh an londubh i n-ár bhfochair
   is an chéirseach ann.

3. *Searc mo chléibh do thug mé féin duit,*
   agus grá tré rún,
   Dá dtigeadh sé do chor sa' tsaol
   go mbéinn féin is tú,
   Ceangal cléireach eadrainn araon,
   's an fáinne dlúth—
   Is dá bhfeicinn féin mo shearc ag aon fhear
   gheóinn bás le cumha!

4. *Dia Domhnaigh nuair a chínn*
   ag an dteampoll í,
   Fallaing riabhach is ribín uaithne uirthi
   anún mar ghnaoi,
   Agus gúna do sguabfadh
   na gleannta fraoich:
   Och! 'sé mo bhuaire mar do luadh liom
   'n-a maighdin í!

5. *Tá úr-phíob ag mo mhúirnín,*
   is a bráid mar aol,
   A cúilin casta búclaidheach
   a' fás go féar;
   'Sé mo chumha nimhe nách san úir síos
   do fágadh mé
   Sara stiúiríodh mé i gcúigíbh
   is mo ghrá thar m'éis!

THE SON OF A GAMBOLIER

Irish folksong

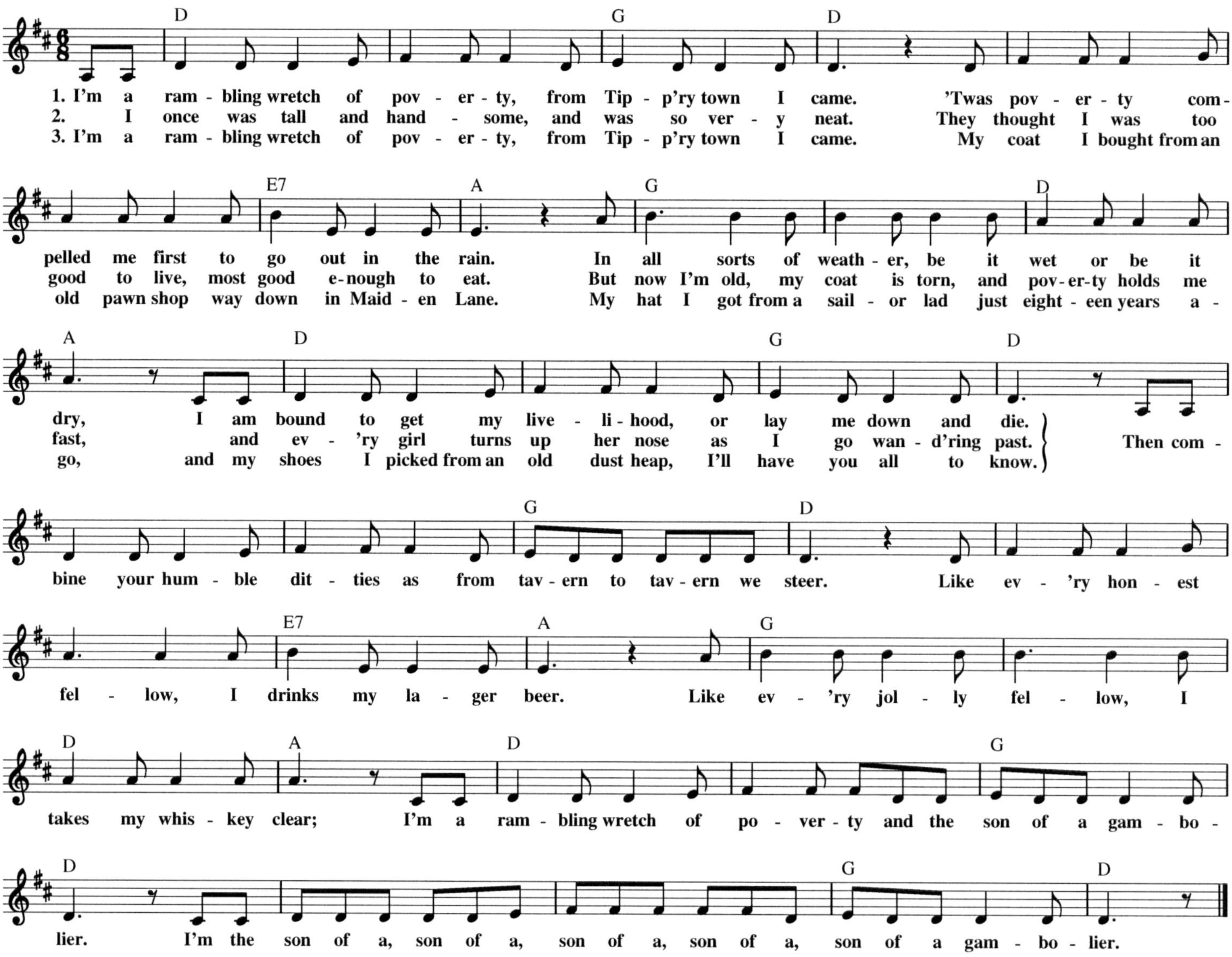

1. I'm a ram-bling wretch of pov-er-ty, from Tip-p'ry town I came. 'Twas pov-er-ty com-
2. I once was tall and hand-some, and was so ver-y neat. They thought I was too
3. I'm a ram-bling wretch of pov-er-ty, from Tip-p'ry town I came. My coat I bought from an

pelled me first to go out in the rain. In all sorts of weath-er, be it wet or be it
good to live, most good e-nough to eat. But now I'm old, my coat is torn, and pov-er-ty holds me
old pawn shop way down in Maid-en Lane. My hat I got from a sail-or lad just eight-een years a-

dry, I am bound to get my live-li-hood, or lay me down and die.
fast, and ev-'ry girl turns up her nose as I go wan-d'ring past. } Then com-
go, and my shoes I picked from an old dust heap, I'll have you all to know.

bine your hum-ble dit-ties as from tav-ern to tav-ern we steer. Like ev-'ry hon-est

fel-low, I drinks my la-ger beer. Like ev-'ry jol-ly fel-low, I

takes my whis-key clear; I'm a ram-bling wretch of po-ver-ty and the son of a gam-bo-

lier. I'm the son of a, son of a, son of a, son of a, son of a gam-bo-lier.

THE SONG OF NIAMH OF THE GOLDEN TRESSES

Irish folksong

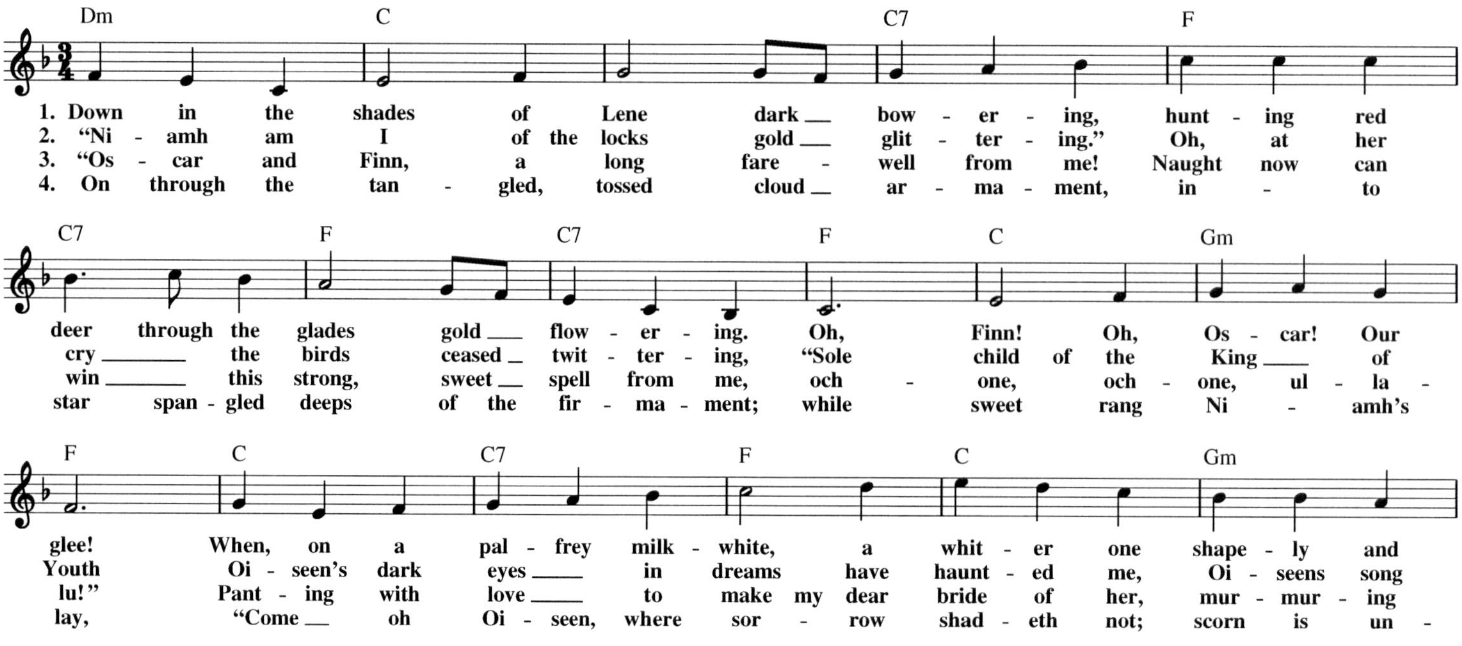

1. Down in the shades of Lene dark bow-er-ing, hunt-ing red
2. "Ni-amh am I of the locks gold glit-ter-ing." Oh, at her
3. "Os-car and Finn, a long fare-well from me! Naught now can
4. On through the tan-gled, tossed cloud ar-ma-ment, in-to

deer through the glades gold flow-er-ing. Oh, Finn! Oh, Os-car! Our
cry the birds ceased twit-ter-ing, "Sole child of the King of
win this strong, sweet spell from me, och-one, och-one, ul-la-
star span-gled deeps of the fir-ma-ment; while sweet rang Ni-amh's

glee! When, on a pal-frey milk-white, a whit-er one shape-ly and
Youth Oi-seen's dark eyes in dreams have haunt-ed me, Oi-seens song
lu!" Pant-ing with love to make my dear bride of her, mur-mur-ing
lay, "Come oh Oi-seen, where sor-row shad-eth not; scorn is un-

slight, ah, no shap - li - er, slight - er one! Waved her scep - tre star
streams __ all day have __ daunt - ed me, I, who scathe - less of
dove _____ I leaped to the side of her, forth a - bove, neigh - ing
seen _____ and an - ger up __ braid - eth, not; come with thy queen, ___ where

bright, the far bright - er one - waved, waved in sup - pli - ant plea.
love long have vaunt - ed me, ah, now know his search - ing truth."
thrice in his pride of her, forth, forth our white pal - frey flew!
beau - ty ___ fad - eth not, where youth and love are for aye!"

THE SONG OF THE WOODS

Irish folksong

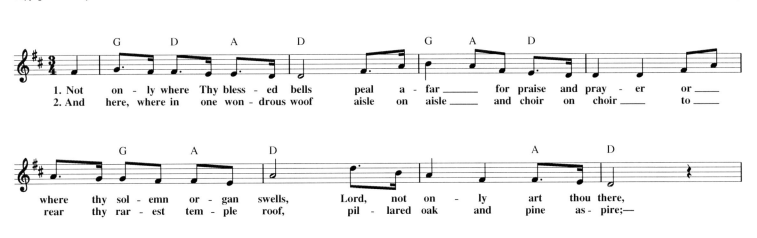

1. Not on - ly where Thy bless - ed bells peal a - far _____ for praise and pray - er or _____
2. And here, where in one won - drous woof aisle on aisle _____ and choir on choir ____ to ____

where thy sol - emn or - gan swells, Lord, not on - ly art thou there,
rear thy rar - est tem - ple roof, pil - lared oak and pine as - pire;—

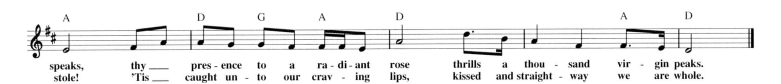

thy voice of man - y wa - ters from _____ out the o - cean com - fort __
life wear - y here __ we wan - der, when _____ lo, the sav - iour's gleam - ing __

speaks, thy __ pres - ence to a ra - di - ant rose thrills a thou - sand vir - gin peaks.
stole! 'Tis __ caught un - to our crav - ing lips, kissed and straight - way we are whole.

A SOOTHING CROON FROM EIGG

Folksong from the Hebrides

1. Ah, what my love ail - eth thee?
2. May - be thy heart ach - eth sore?
3. May - hap thy moth - er was wroth?
   Oh I __ know not, Nought can I eat to - night! _____

1. Ciod è a ghaoil a bhitheadh ort?
2. An è do cheann a bhi goirt?
3. An e do mhathair a ghabh ort?
   O cha 'n fhios a'm Ach cha'n ith mi mir an nochd! _____

THE SPANISH LADY

Irish folksong

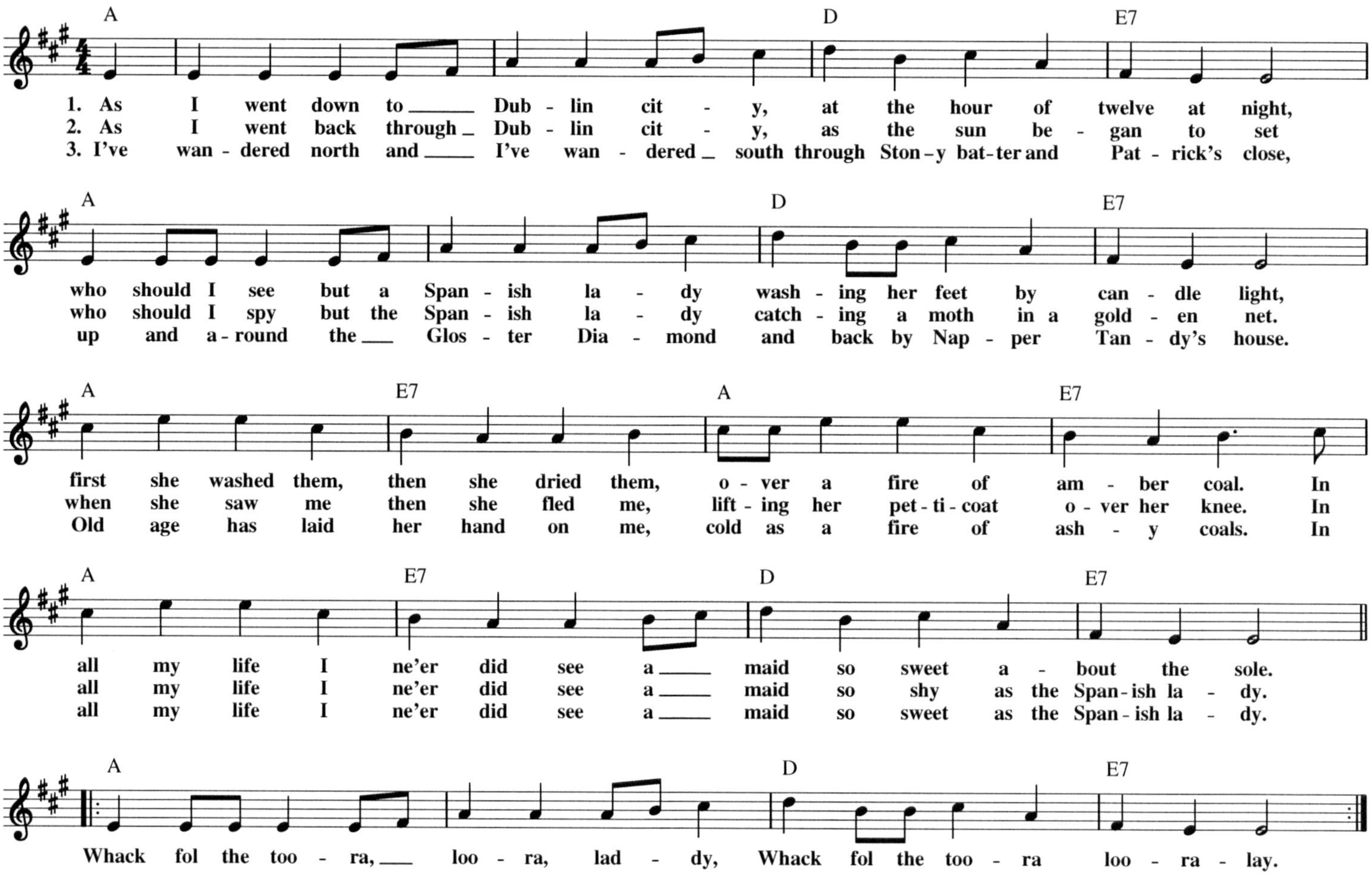

1. As I went down to _____ Dub-lin cit-y, at the hour of twelve at night,
2. As I went back through _ Dub-lin cit-y, as the sun be-gan to set
3. I've wan-dered north and _____ I've wan-dered _ south through Ston-y bat-ter and Pat-rick's close,

who should I see but a Span-ish la - dy wash - ing her feet by can - dle light,
who should I spy but the Span-ish la - dy catch - ing a moth in a gold - en net.
up and a-round the _ Glos-ter Dia-mond and back by Nap-per Tan-dy's house.

first she washed them, then she dried them, o - ver a fire of am - ber coal. In
when she saw me, then she fled me, lift - ing her pet - ti - coat o - ver her knee. In
Old age has laid her hand on me, cold as a fire of ash - y coals. In

all my life I ne'er did see a _____ maid so sweet a - bout the sole.
all my life I ne'er did see a _____ maid so shy as the Span-ish la - dy.
all my life I ne'er did see a _____ maid so sweet as the Span-ish la - dy.

Whack fol the too-ra, _____ loo-ra, lad - dy, Whack fol the too-ra loo - ra-lay.

SPINNING SONG

Folksong from the Hebrides

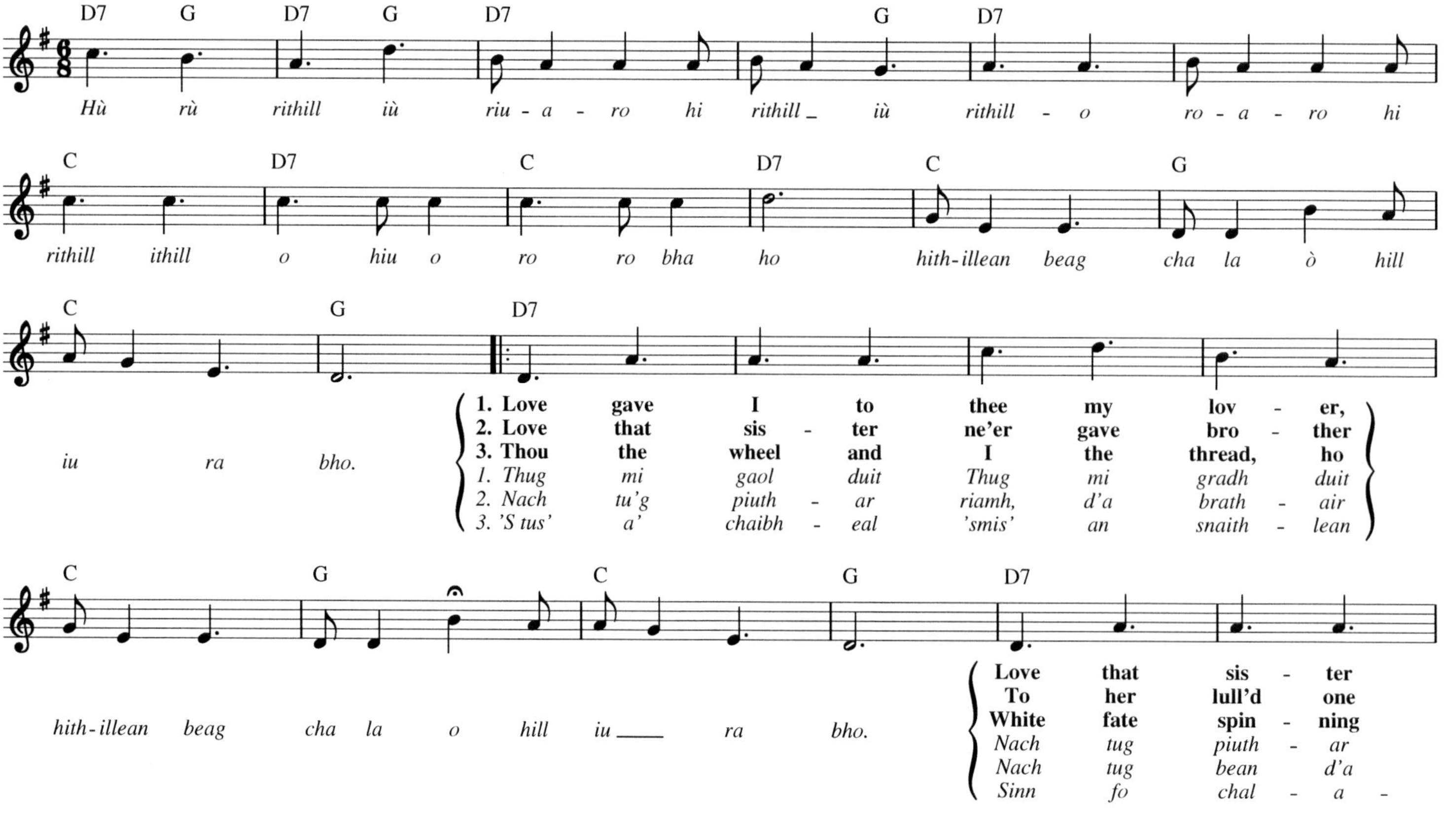

Hù rù rithill iù riu - a - ro hi rithill _ iù rithill - o ro-a - ro hi

rithill ithill o hiu o ro ro bha ho hith-illean beag cha la ò hill

iu ra bho.

1. Love gave I to thee my lov - er,
2. Love that sis - ter ne'er gave bro - ther
3. Thou the wheel and I the thread, ho
1. Thug mi gaol duit Thug mi gradh duit
2. Nach tu'g piuth - ar riamh, d'a brath - air
3. 'S tus' a' chaibh - eal 'smis' an snaith - lean

hith-illean beag cha la o hill iu _____ ra bho.

Love that sis - ter
To her lull'd one
White fate spin - ning
Nach tug piuth - ar
Nach tug bean d'a
Sinn fo chal - a -

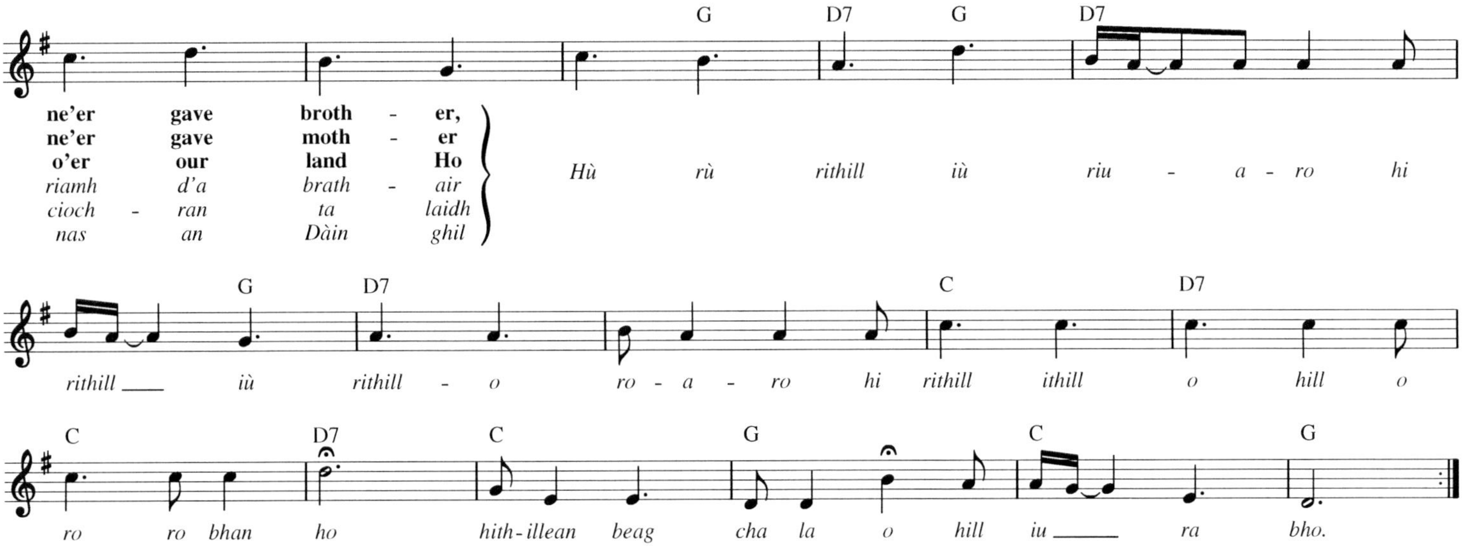

ne'er gave broth - er,
ne'er gave moth - er
o'er our land Ho
riamh d'a brath - air
cioch - ran ta laidh
nas an Dàin ghil

Hù rù rithill iù riu - a - ro hi

rithill ___ iù rithill - o ro - a - ro hi rithill ithill o hill o

ro ro bhan ho hith-illean beag cha la o hill iu ___ ra bho.

SPINNINGWHEEL SONG

Irish folksong

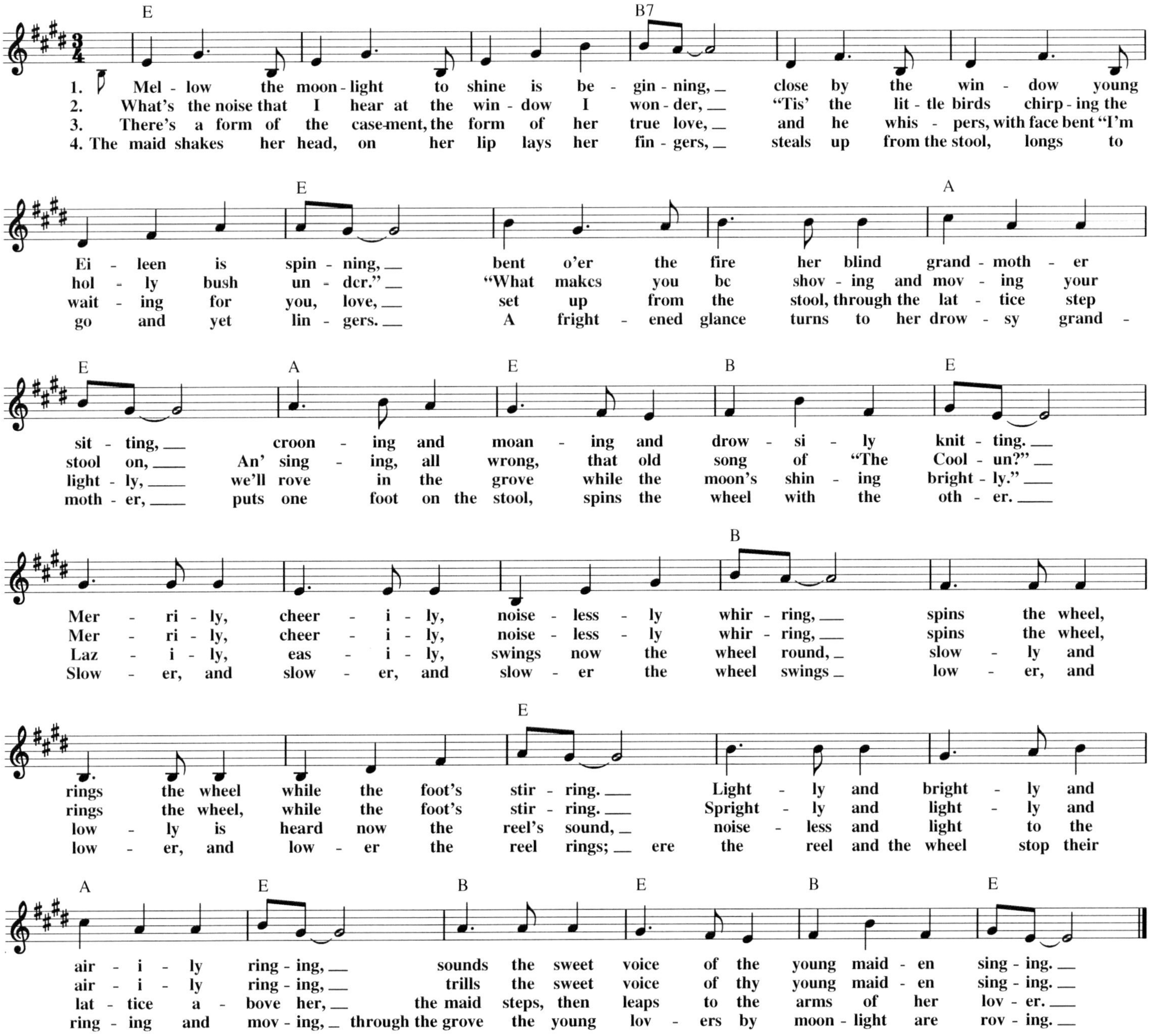

1. Mel - low the moon - light to shine is be - gin - ning, __ close by the win - dow young
2. What's the noise that I hear at the win - dow I won - der, __ "Tis' the lit - tle birds chirp - ing the
3. There's a form of the case-ment, the form of her true love, __ and he whis - pers, with face bent "I'm
4. The maid shakes her head, on her lip lays her fin - gers, __ steals up from the stool, longs to

Ei - leen is spin - ning, __ bent o'er the fire her blind grand - moth - er
hol - ly bush un - der." __ "What makes you be shov - ing and mov - ing your
wait - ing for you, love, __ set up from the stool, through the lat - tice step
go and yet lin - gers. __ A fright - ened glance turns to her drow - sy grand -

sit - ting, __ croon - ing and moan - ing and drow - si - ly knit - ting. __
stool on, __ An' sing - ing, all wrong, that old song of "The Cool - un?" __
light - ly, __ we'll rove in the grove while the moon's shin - ing bright - ly." __
moth - er, __ puts one foot on the stool, spins the wheel with the oth - er. __

Mer - ri - ly, cheer - i - ly, noise - less - ly whir - ring, __ spins the wheel,
Mer - ri - ly, cheer - i - ly, noise - less - ly whir - ring, __ spins the wheel,
Laz - i - ly, eas - i - ly, swings now the wheel round, __ slow - ly and
Slow - er, and slow - er, and slow - er the wheel swings __ low - er, and

rings the wheel while the foot's stir - ring. __ Light - ly and bright - ly and
rings the wheel, while the foot's stir - ring. __ Spright - ly and light - ly and
low - ly is heard now the reel's sound, __ noise - less and light to the
low - er, and low - er the reel rings; __ ere the reel and the wheel stop their

air - i - ly ring - ing, __ sounds the sweet voice of the young maid - en sing - ing. __
air - i - ly ring - ing, __ trills the sweet voice of thy young maid - en sing - ing. __
lat - tice a - bove her, __ through the lat - tice the maid steps, then leaps to the arms of her lov - er. __
ring - ing and mov - ing, __ through the grove the young lov - ers by moon - light are rov - ing. __

SPREADING THE SEA-WRACK

Folksong from the Hebrides

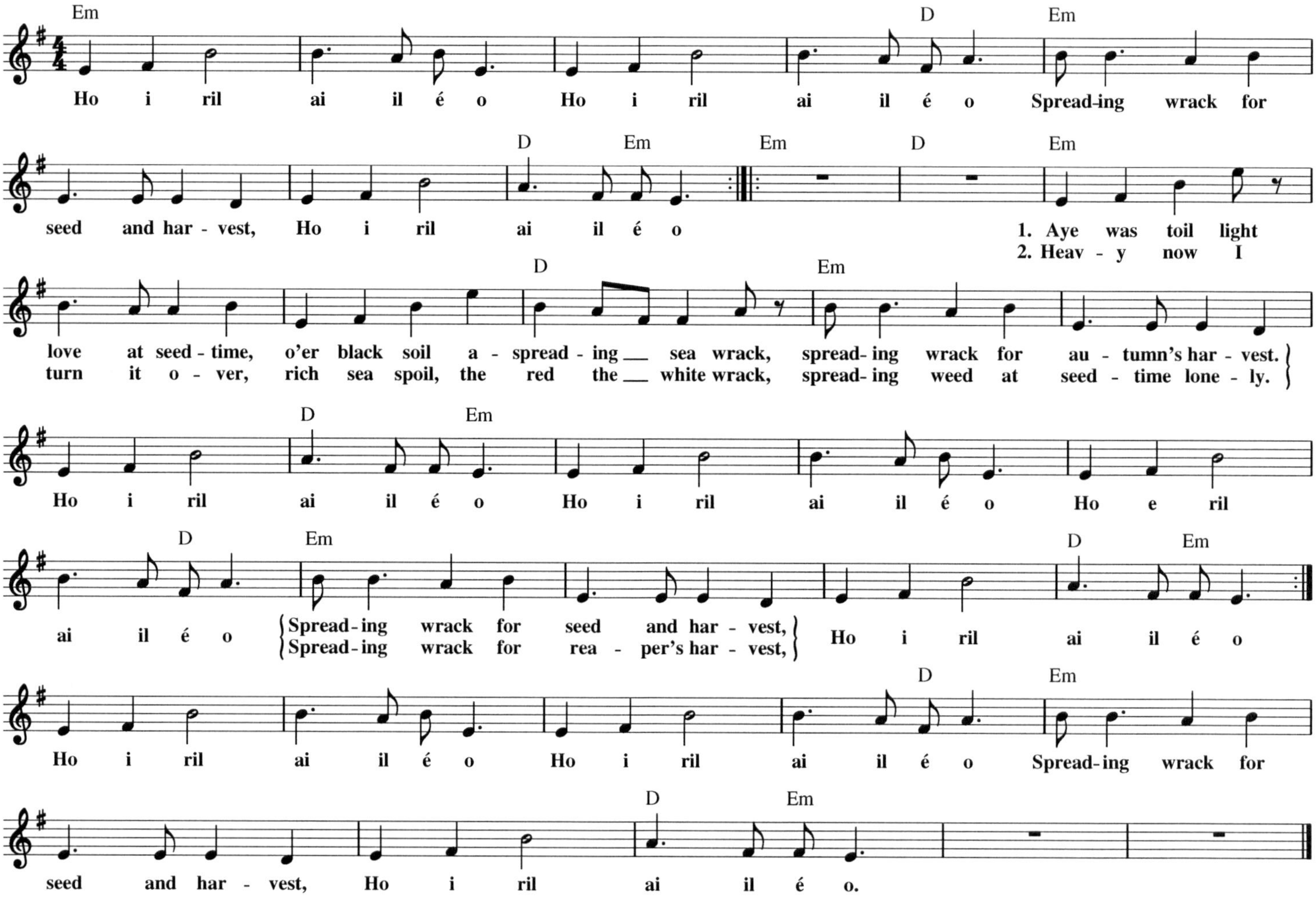

THE STAR OF COUNTY DOWN

Irish folksong

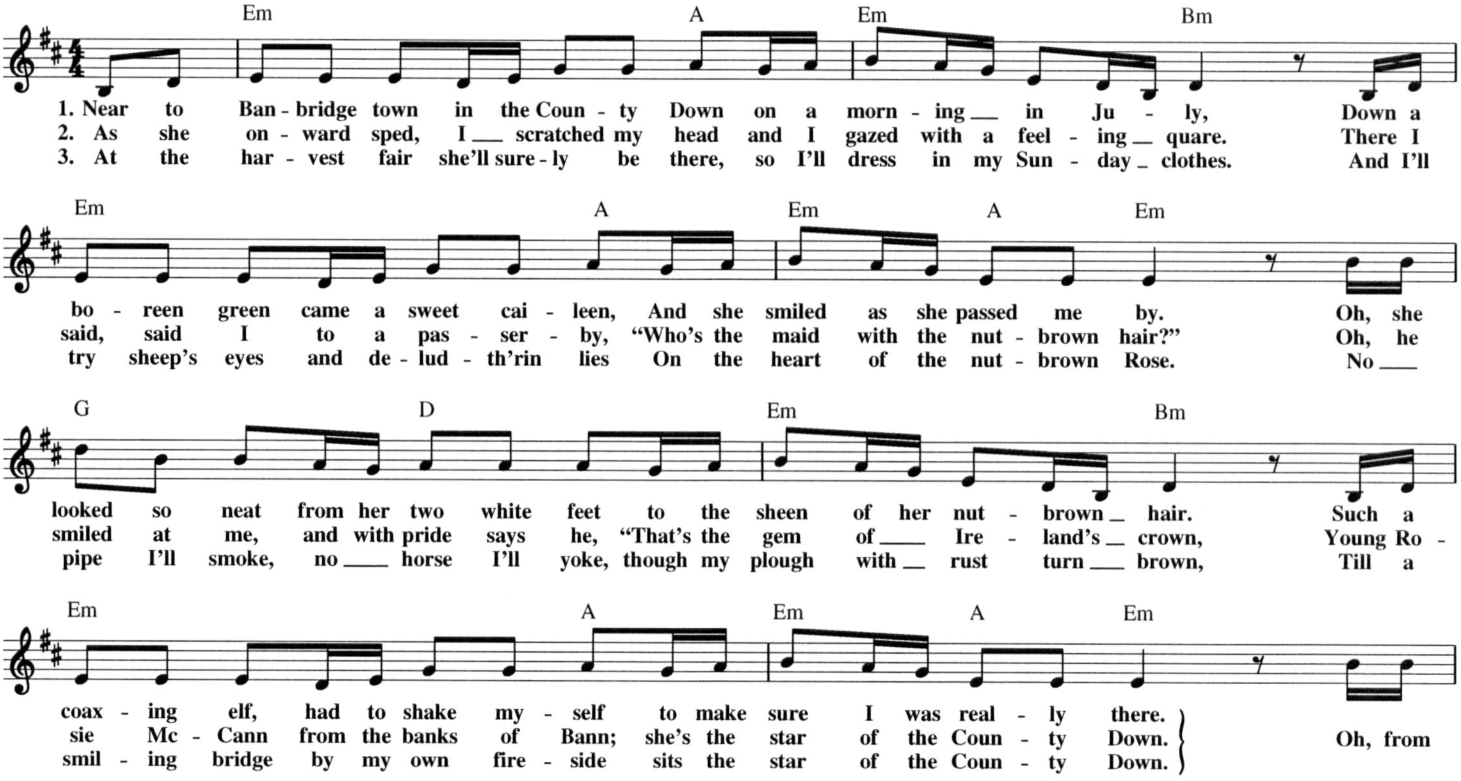

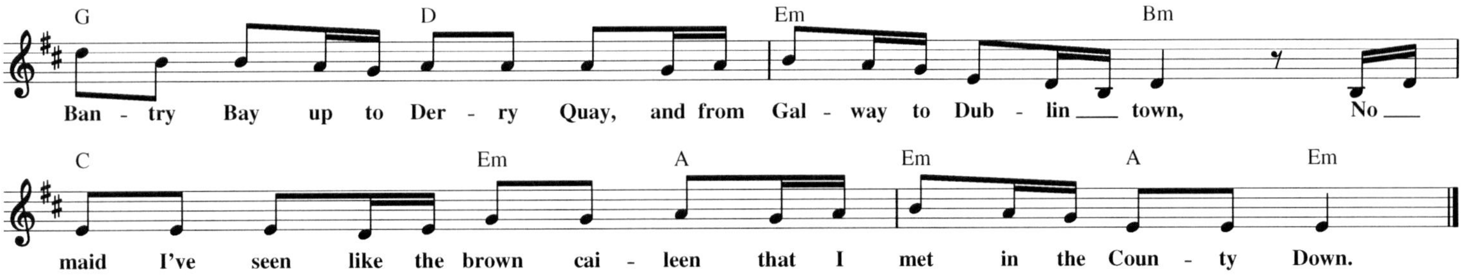

SWEET ROSIE O'GRADY

Words and Music by
Maud Nugent

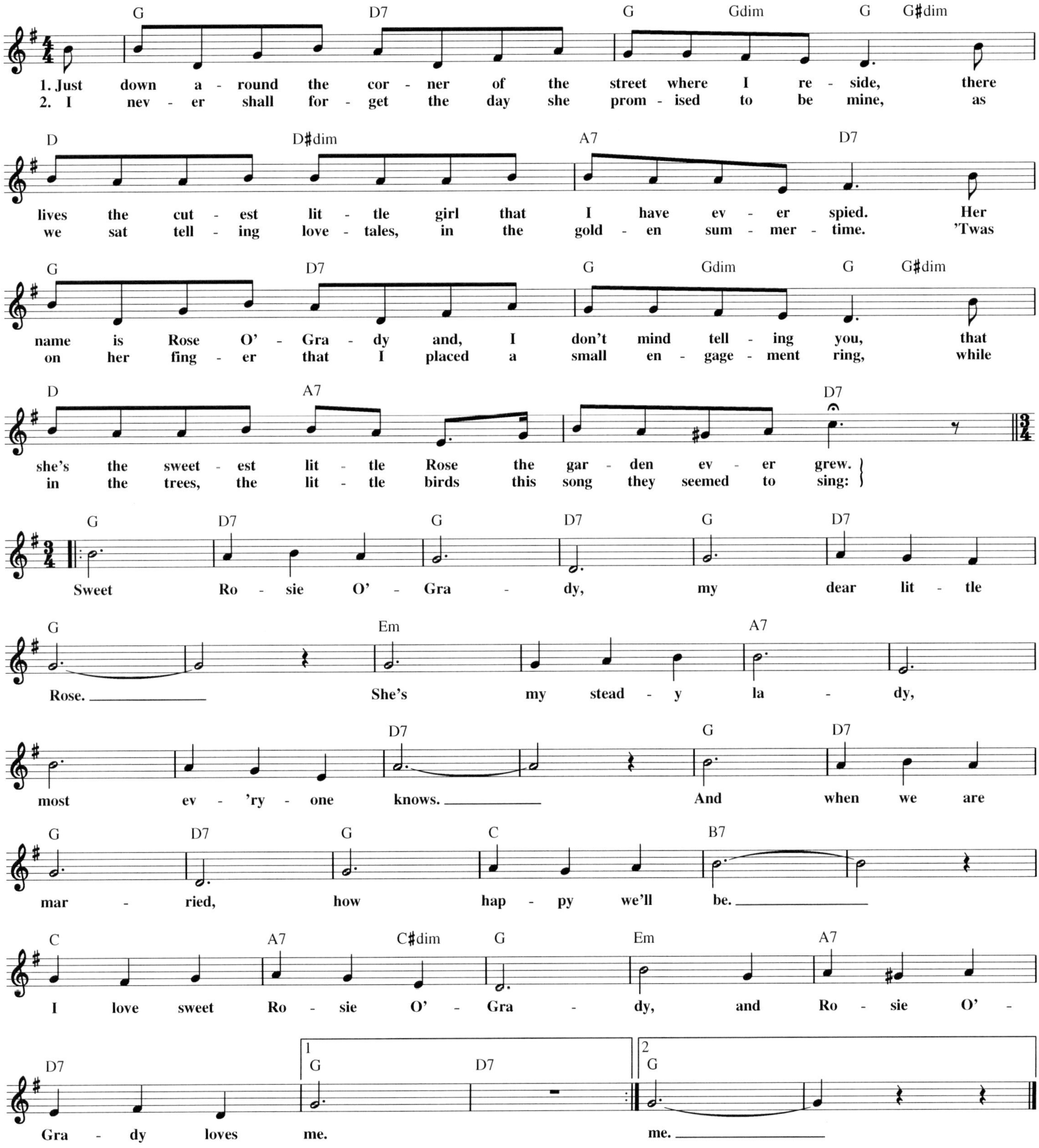

TAM PIERCE

Scottish folksong

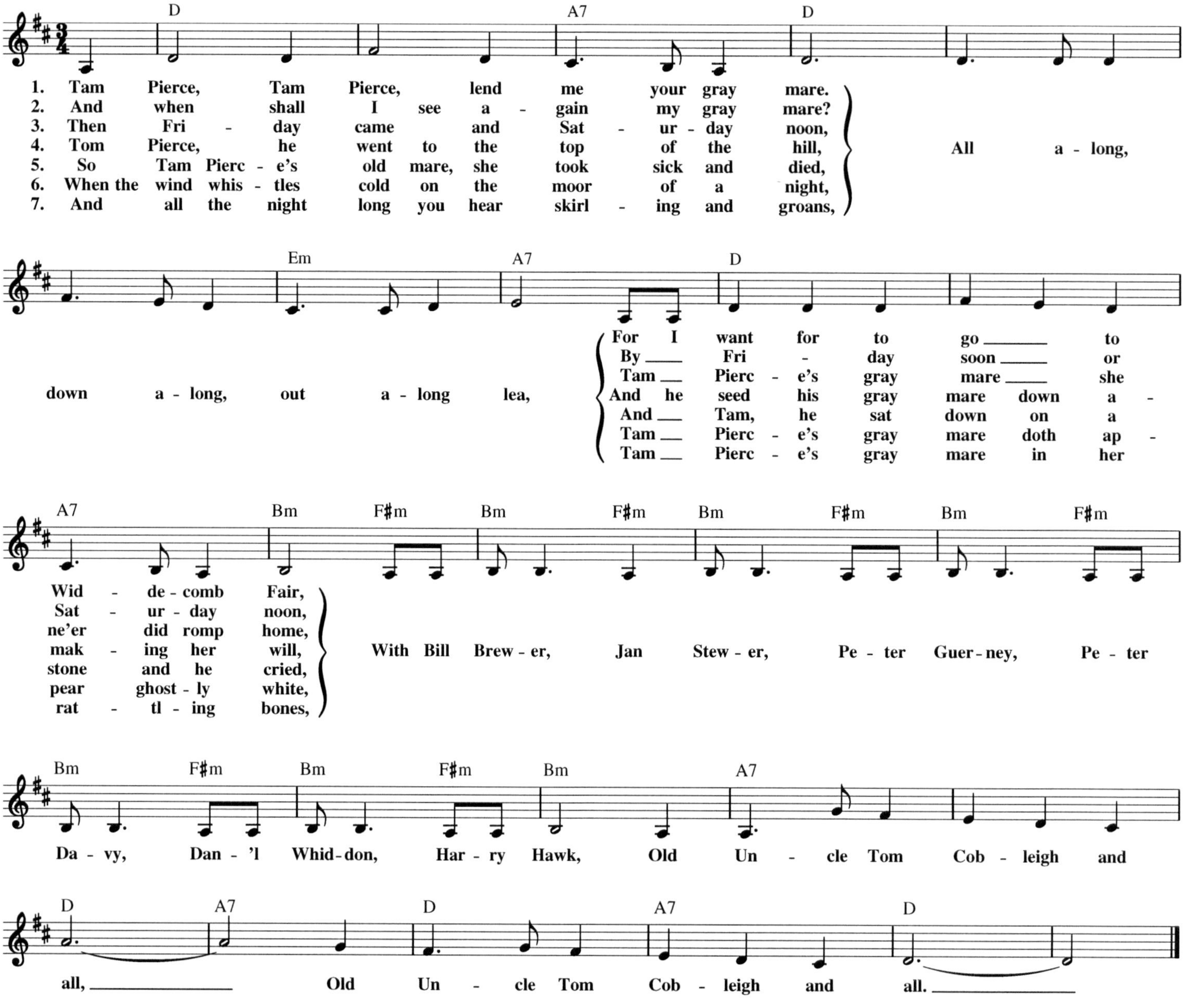

THE TANYARD SIDE

Irish folksong

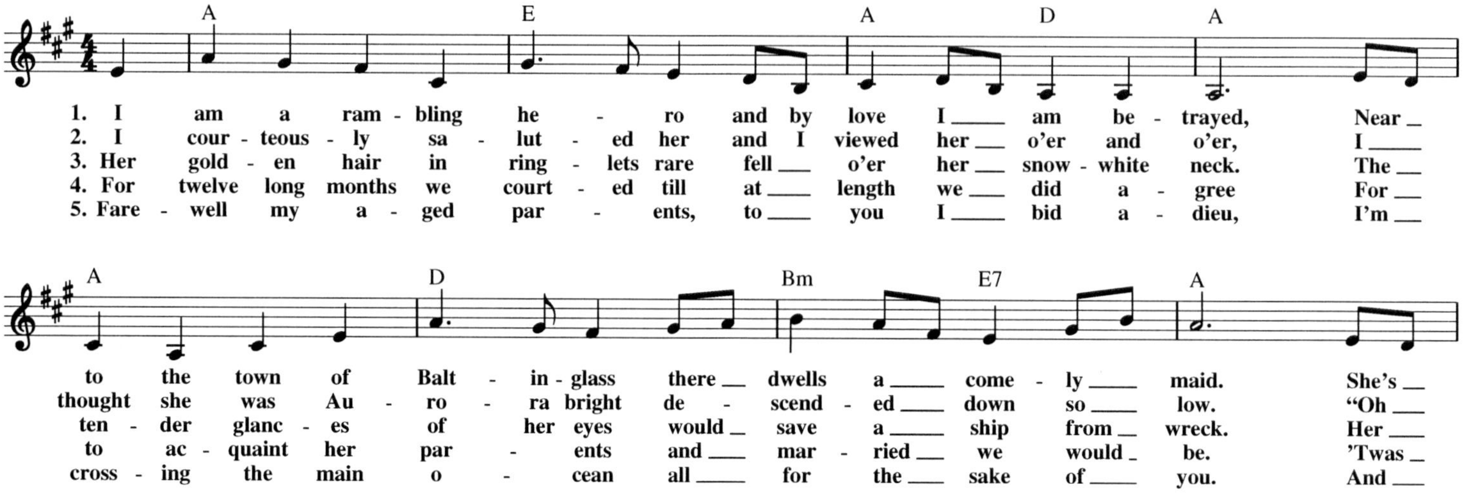

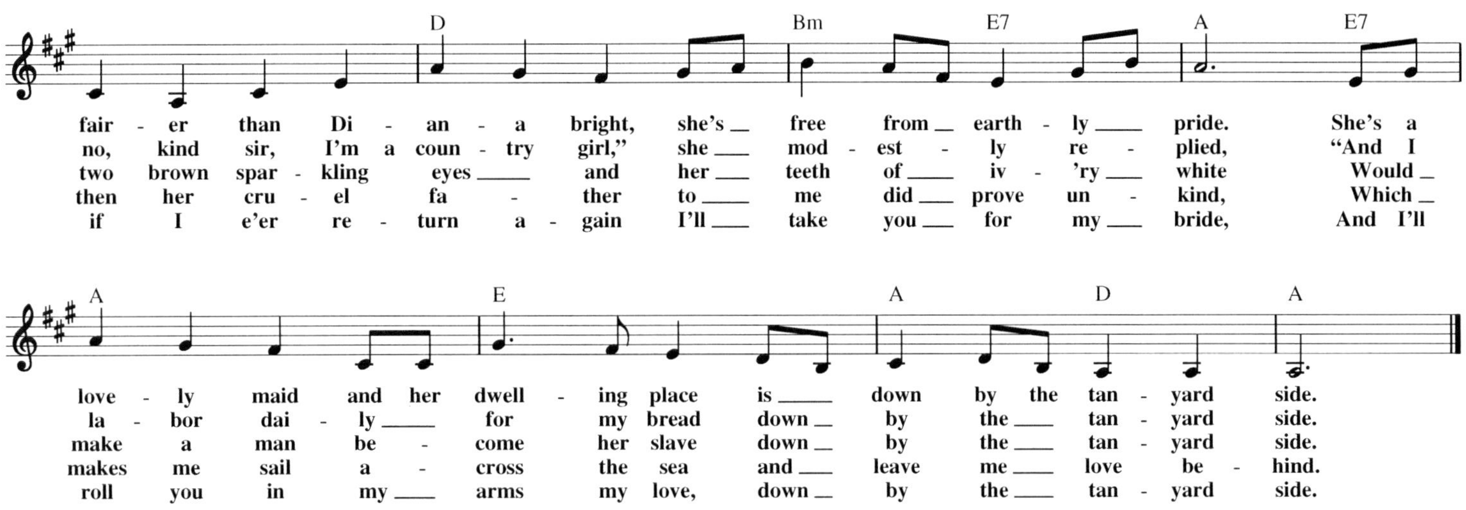

fair - er than Di - an - a bright, she's __ free from __ earth - ly __ pride. She's a
no, kind sir, I'm a coun - try girl," she __ mod - est - ly re - plied, "And I
two brown spar - kling eyes __ and her __ teeth of __ iv - 'ry __ white Would __
then her cru - el fa - ther to __ me did __ prove un - kind, Which __
if I e'er re - turn a - gain I'll __ take you __ for my __ bride, And I'll

love - ly maid and her dwell - ing place is __ down by the tan - yard side.
la - bor dai - ly __ for my bread down __ by the __ tan - yard side.
make a man be - come her slave down __ by the __ tan - yard side.
makes me sail a - cross the sea and __ leave me __ love be - hind.
roll you in my __ arms my love, down __ by the __ tan - yard side.

THAT TUMBLE-DOWN SHACK IN ATHLONE

Words by Richard W. Pascoe
Music by Monte Carlo and Alma M. Sanders

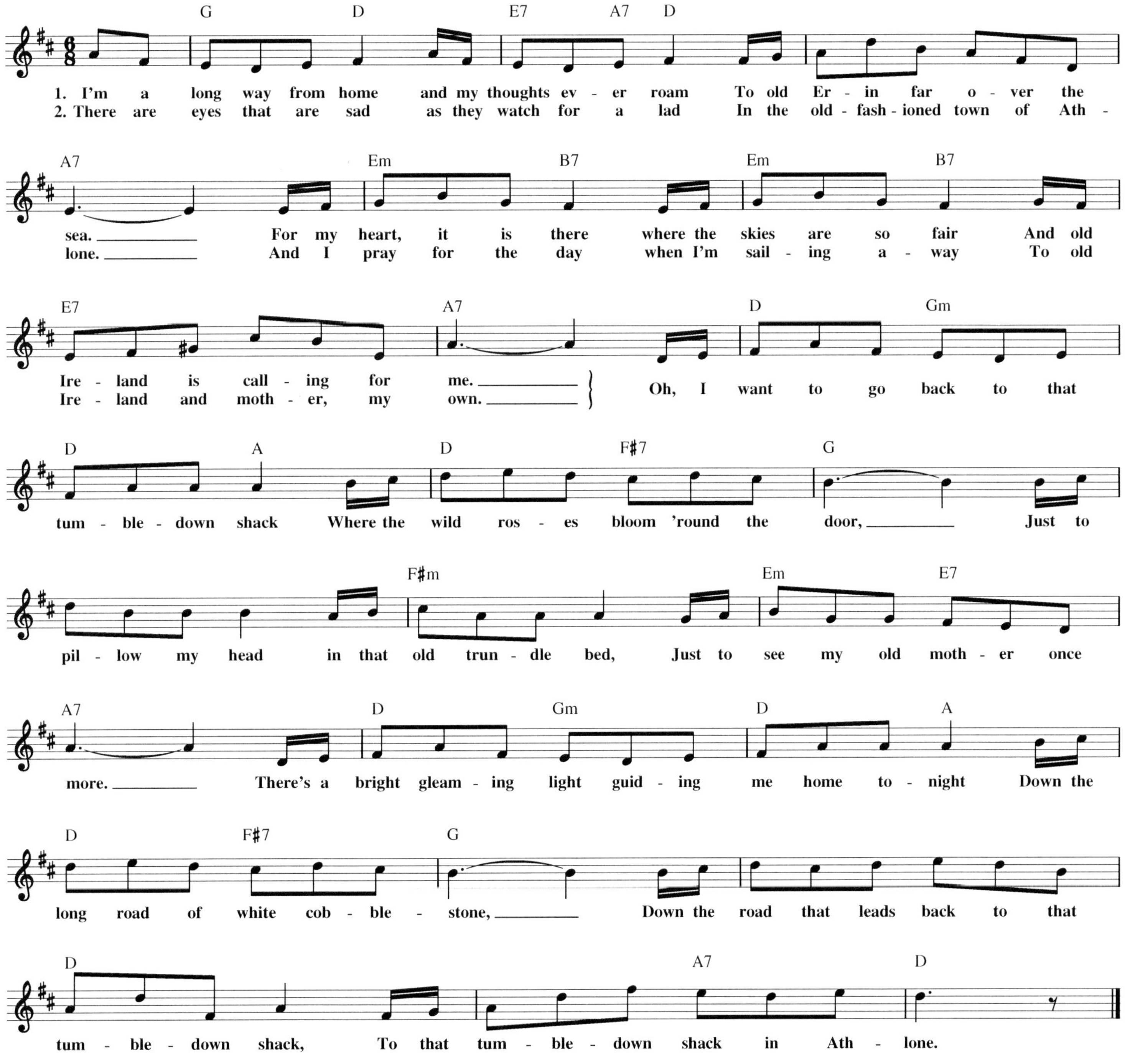

1. I'm a long way from home and my thoughts ev - er roam To old Er - in far o - ver the
2. There are eyes that are sad as they watch for a lad In the old - fash - ioned town of Ath -

sea. ____ For my heart, it is there where the skies are so fair And old
lone. ____ And I pray for the day when I'm sail - ing a - way To old

Ire - land is call - ing for me. ____
Ire - land and moth - er, my own. ____

Oh, I want to go back to that

tum - ble - down shack Where the wild ros - es bloom 'round the door, ____ Just to

pil - low my head in that old trun - dle bed, Just to see my old moth - er once

more. ____ There's a bright gleam - ing light guid - ing me home to - night Down the

long road of white cob - ble - stone, ____ Down the road that leads back to that

tum - ble - down shack, To that tum - ble - down shack in Ath - lone.

THEY KNOW NOT MY HEART

Irish folksong

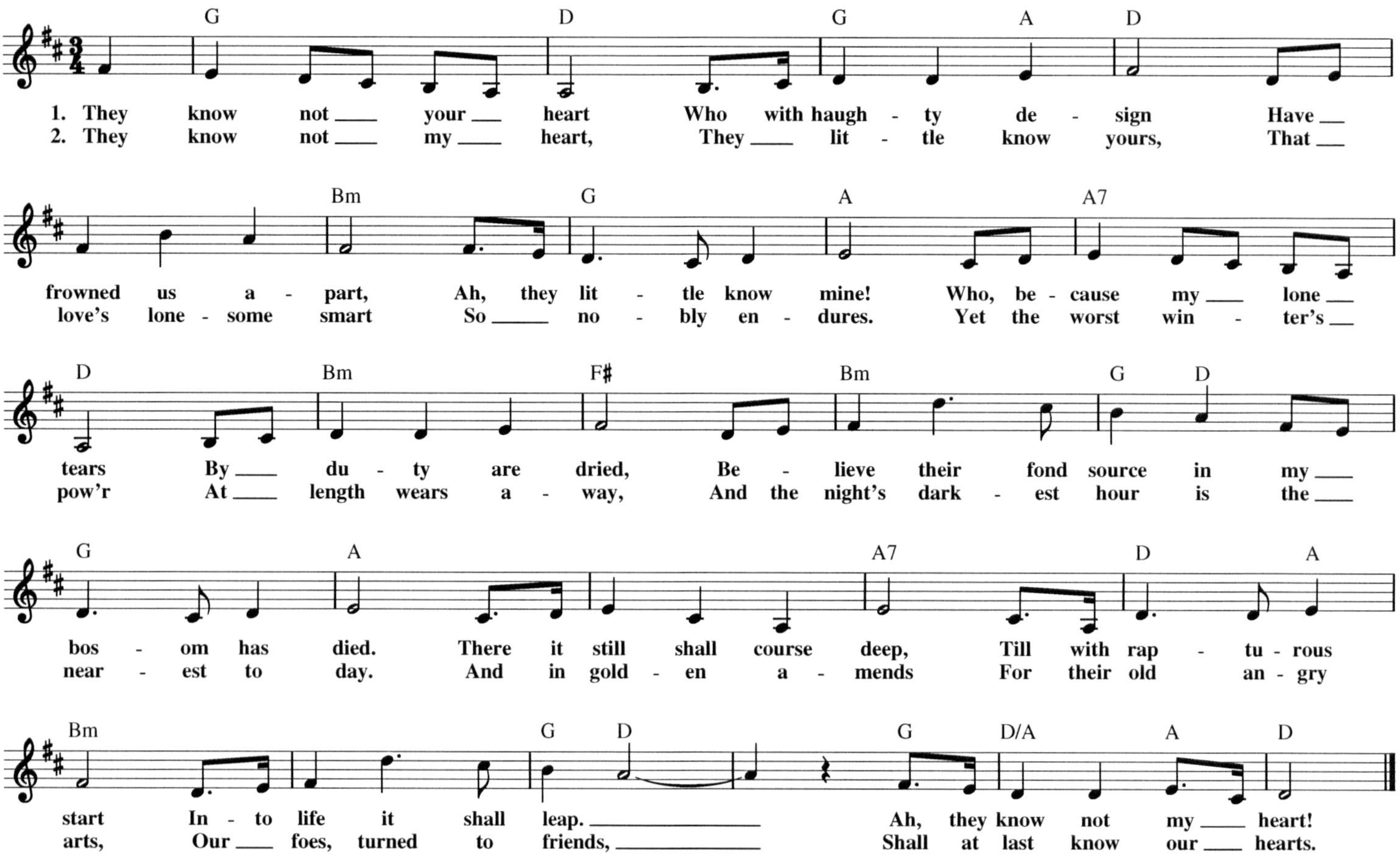

'TIS THE LAST ROSE OF SUMMER

Words by Thomas Moore
Music by Richard Alfred Milliken

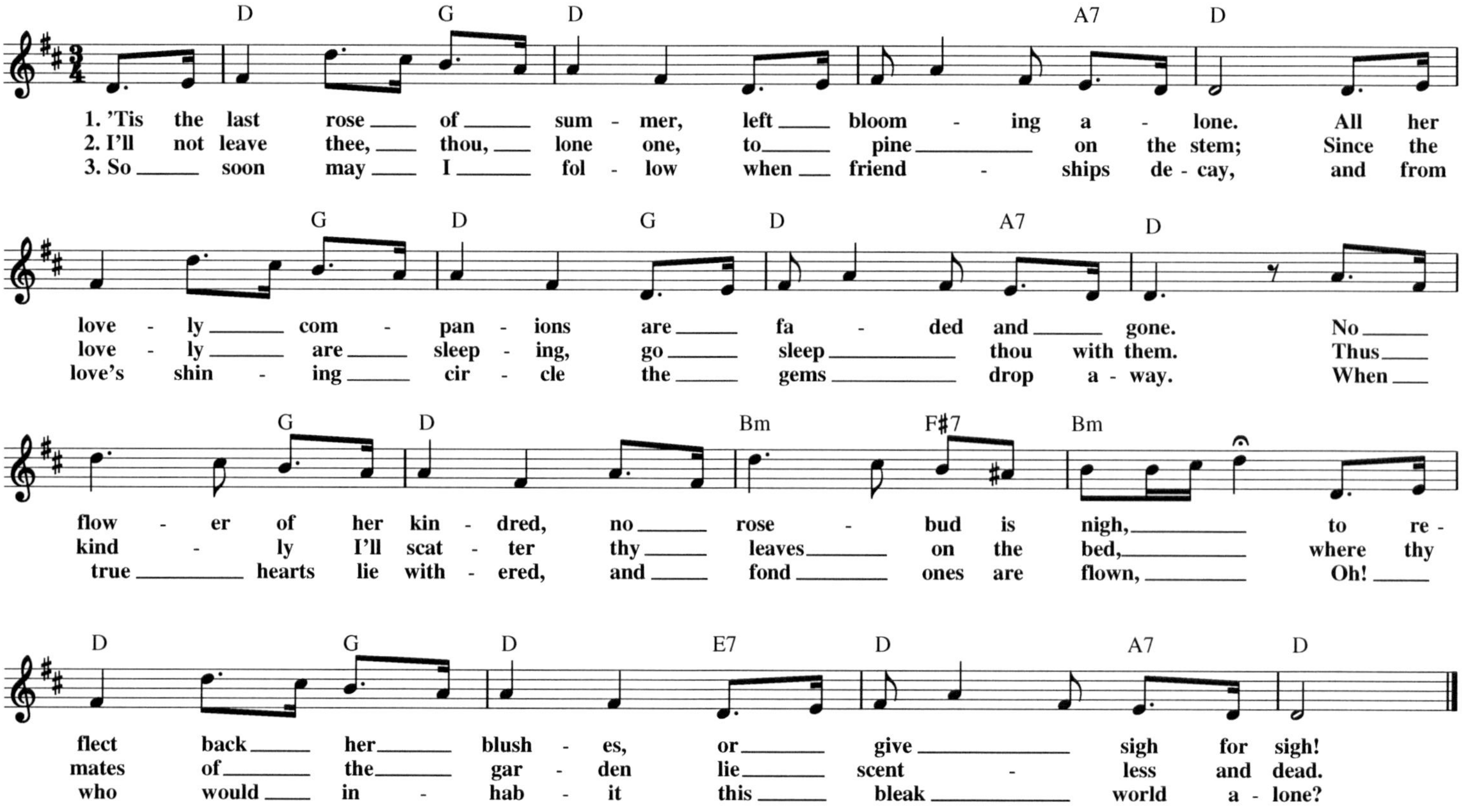

THROW HIM DOWN, McCLOSKEY

Words and Music by
John W. Kelly

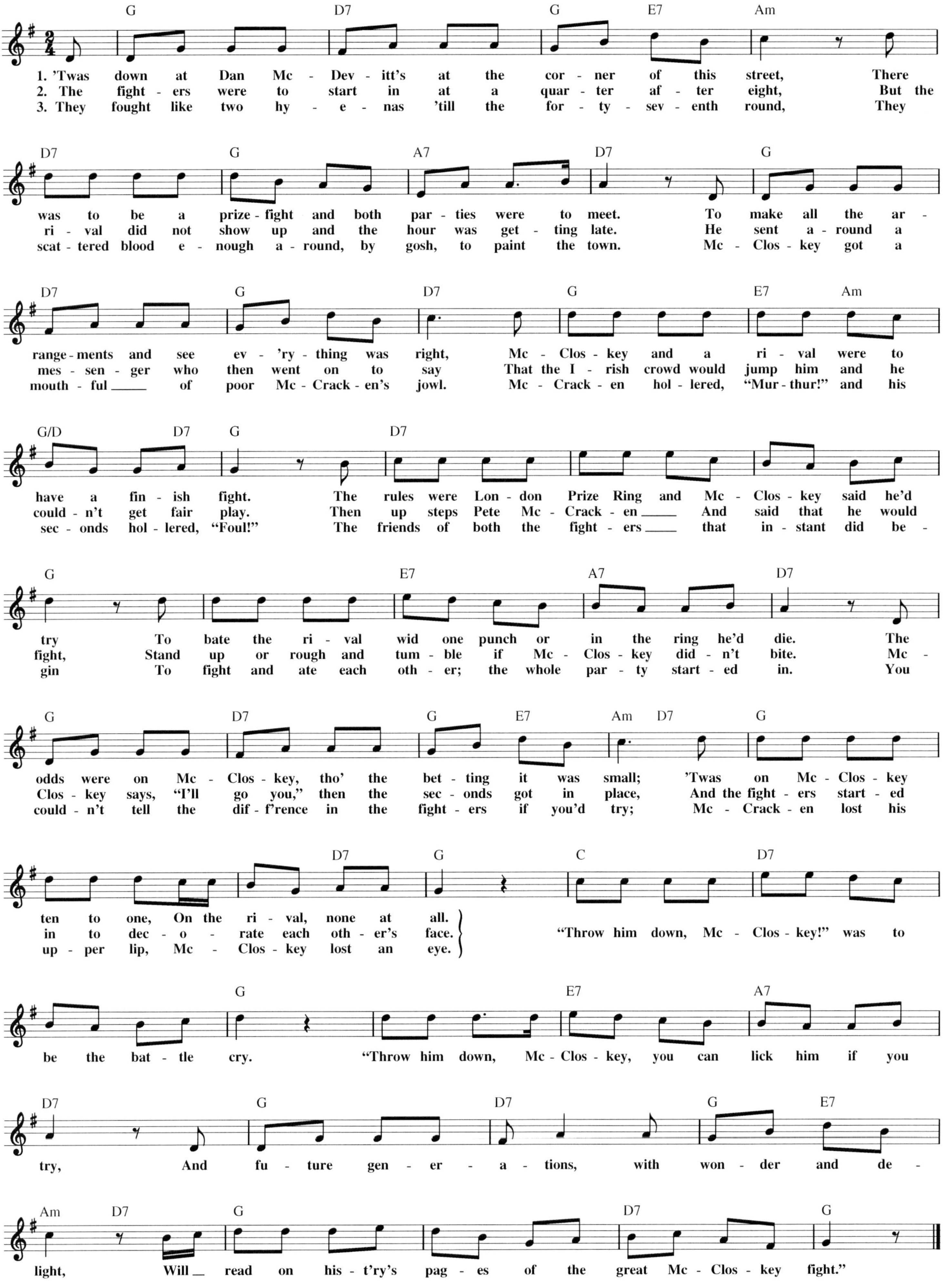

THAT'S AN IRISH LULLABY

Words and Music by
J.R. Shannon

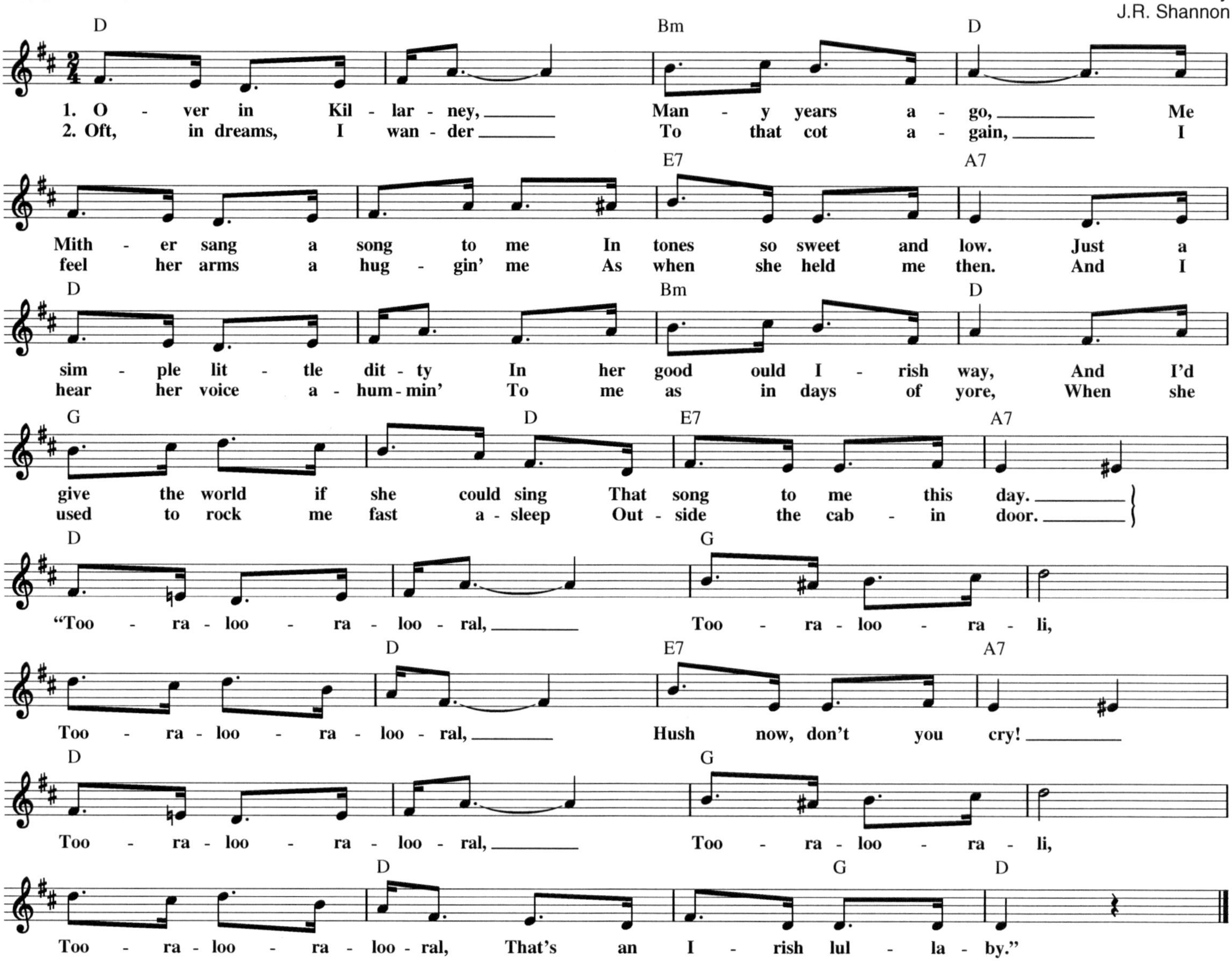

1. O - ver in Kil - lar - ney, _____ Man - y years a - go, _____ Me
2. Oft, in dreams, I wan - der _____ To that cot a - gain, _____ I

Mith - er sang a song to me In tones so sweet and low. Just a
feel her arms a hug - gin' me As when she held me then. And I

sim - ple lit - tle dit - ty In her good ould I - rish way, And I'd
hear her voice a - hum - min' To me as in days of yore, When she

give the world if she could sing That song to me this day. _____
used to rock me fast a - sleep Out - side the cab - in door. _____

"Too - ra - loo - ra - loo - ral, _____ Too - ra - loo - ra - li,

Too - ra - loo - ra - loo - ral, _____ Hush now, don't you cry! _____

Too - ra - loo - ra - loo - ral, _____ Too - ra - loo - ra - li,

Too - ra - loo - ra - loo - ral, That's an I - rish lul - la - by."

TIPPERARY RECRUITING SONG

Irish folksong

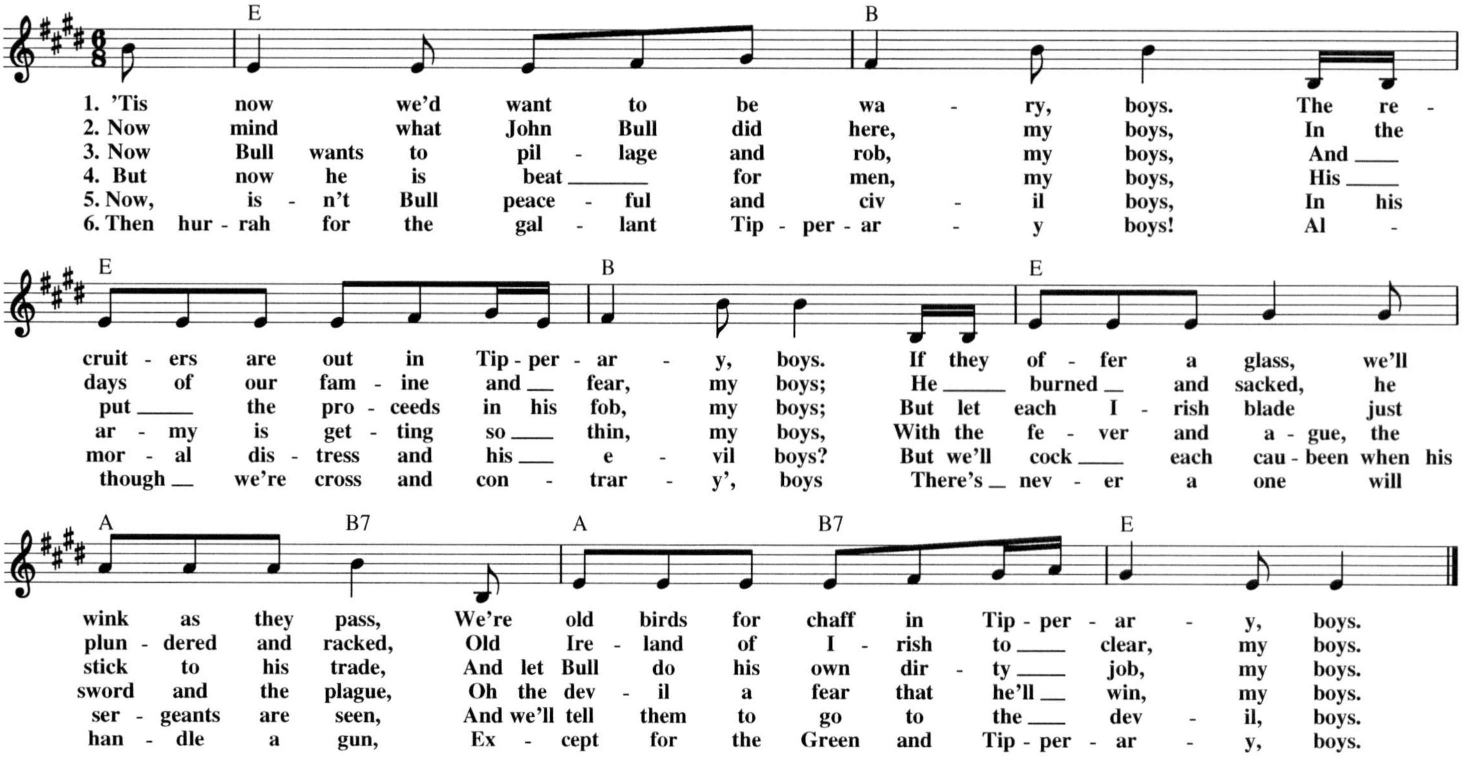

1. 'Tis now we'd want to be wa - ry, boys. The re -
2. Now mind what John Bull did here, my boys, In the
3. Now Bull wants to pil - lage and rob, my boys, And _____
4. But now he is beat _____ for men, my boys, His _____
5. Now, is - n't Bull peace - ful and civ - il boys, In his
6. Then hur - rah for the gal - lant Tip - per - ar - y boys! Al -

cruit - ers are out in Tip - per - ar - y, boys. If they of - fer a glass, we'll
days of our fam - ine and _____ fear, my boys; He _____ burned _____ and sacked, he
put _____ the pro - ceeds in his fob, my boys; But let each I - rish blade just
ar - my is get - ting so _____ thin, my boys, With the fe - ver and a - gue, the
mor - al dis - tress and his _____ e - vil boys? But we'll cock _____ each cau - been when his
though _____ we're cross and con - trar - y', boys There's _____ nev - er a one will

wink as they pass, We're old birds for chaff in Tip - per - ar - y, boys.
plun - dered and racked, Old Ire - land of I - rish to _____ clear, my boys.
stick to his trade, And let Bull do his own dir - ty _____ job, my boys.
sword and the plague, Oh the dev - il a fear that he'll _____ win, my boys.
ser - geants are seen, And we'll tell them to go to the _____ dev - il, boys.
han - dle a gun, Ex - cept for the Green and Tip - per - ar - y, boys.

THE T'READ ON THE TAIL O' ME COAT

Words and Music by
Patrick Ryan

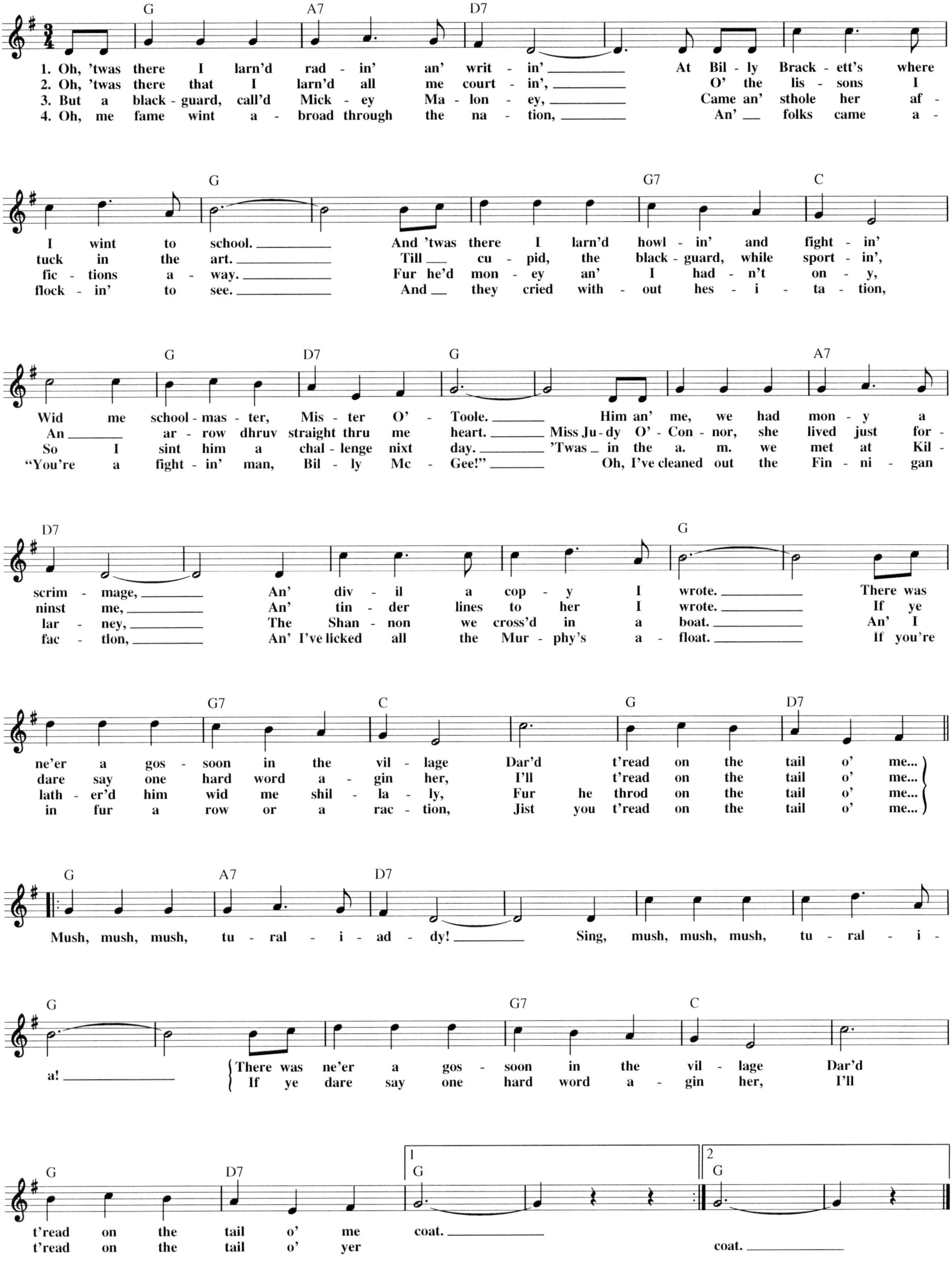

TOURELAY

Words and Music by
Dennis O'Shay

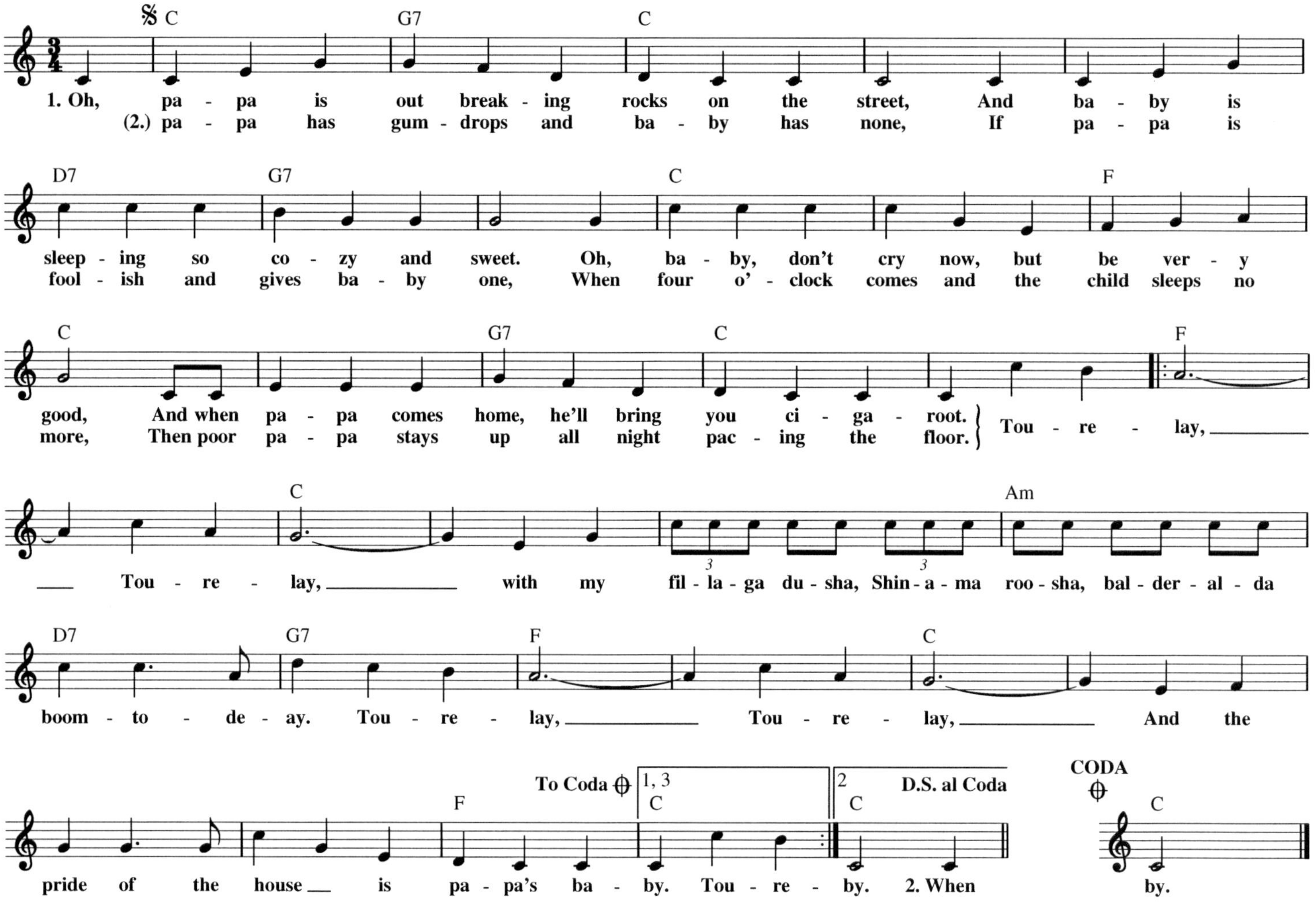

1. Oh, pa - pa is out break - ing rocks on the street, And ba - by is
(2.) pa - pa has gum - drops and ba - by has none, If pa - pa is

sleep - ing so co - zy and sweet. Oh, ba - by, don't cry now, but be ver - y
fool - ish and gives ba - by one, When four o' - clock comes and the child sleeps no

good, And when pa - pa comes home, he'll bring you ci - ga - root. } Tou - re - lay,
more, Then poor pa - pa stays up all night pac - ing the floor. }

Tou - re - lay, with my fil - la - ga du - sha, Shin - a - ma roo - sha, bal - der - al - da

boom - to - de - ay. Tou - re - lay, Tou - re - lay, And the

pride of the house is pa - pa's ba - by. Tou - re - by. 2. When by.

To Coda
1, 3 C
2 C D.S. al Coda
CODA
C

THE TROOPER AND THE MAID

Scottish folksong

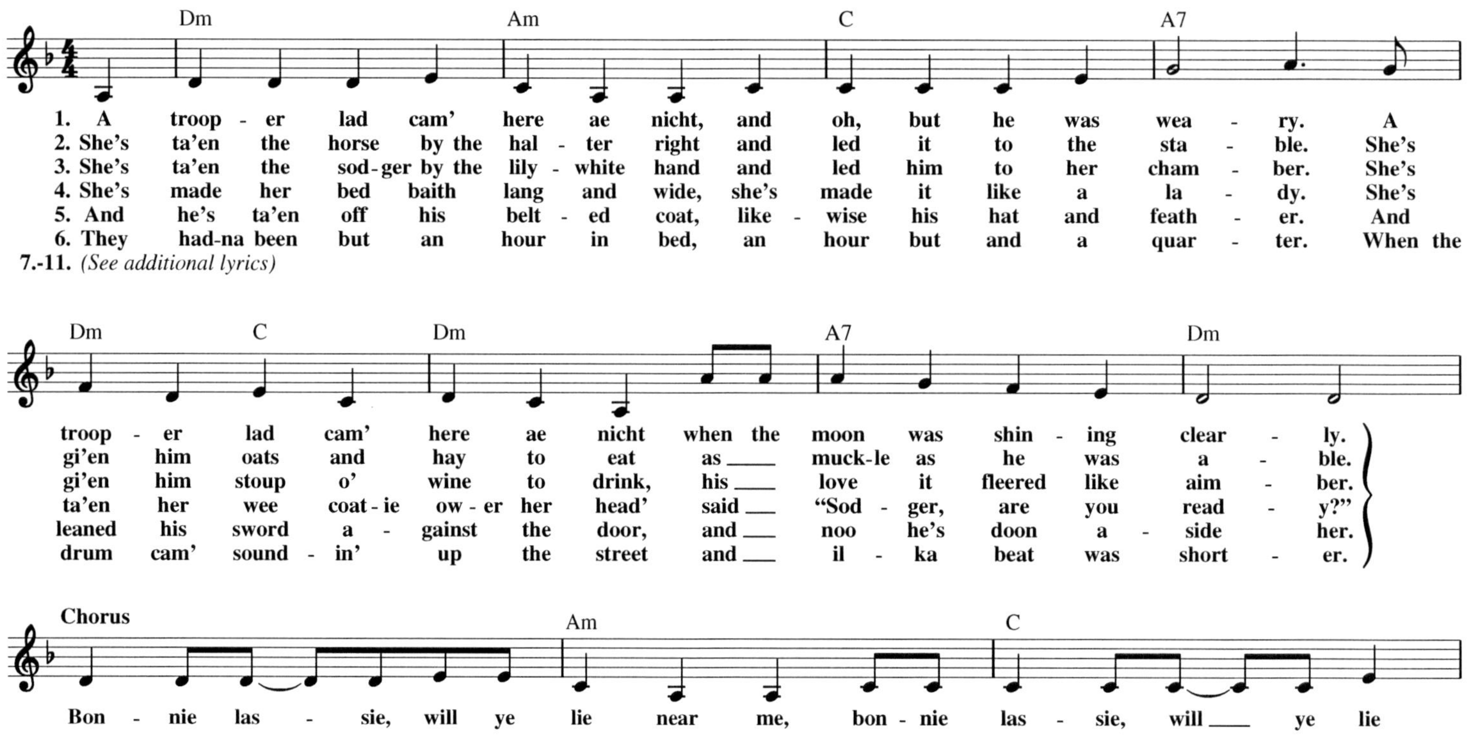

1. A troop - er lad cam' here ae nicht, and oh, but he was wea - ry. A
2. She's ta'en the horse by the hal - ter right and led it to the sta - ble. She's
3. She's ta'en the sod - ger by the lily - white hand and led him to her cham - ber. She's
4. She's made her bed baith lang and wide, she's made it like a la - dy. She's
5. And he's ta'en off his belt - ed coat, like - wise his hat and feath - er. And
6. They had - na been but an hour in bed, an hour but and a quar - ter. When the
7.-11. (See additional lyrics)

troop - er lad cam' here ae nicht when the moon was shin - ing clear - ly.
gi'en him oats and hay to eat as muck - le as he was a - ble.
gi'en him stoup o' wine to drink, his love it fleered like aim - ber.
ta'en her wee coat - ie ow - er her head' said "Sod - ger, are you read - y?"
leaned his sword a - gainst the door, and noo he's doon a - side her.
drum cam' sound - in' up the street and il - ka beat was short - er.

Chorus
Bon - nie las - sie, will ye lie near me, bon - nie las - sie, will ye lie

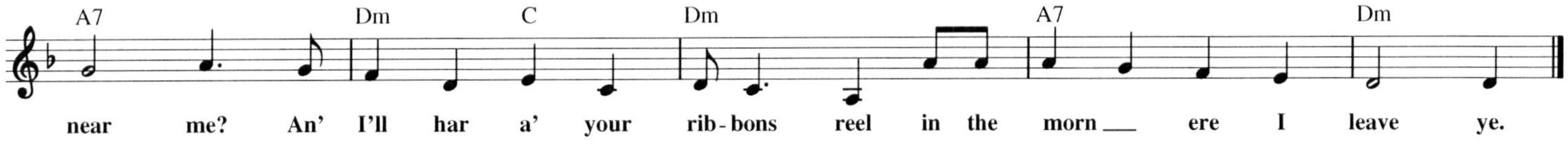

near me? An' I'll har a' your rib-bons reel in the morn ___ ere I leave ye.

Additional Lyrics

7. "It's up, up, up, and our colonel cries,
It's up, up, up and away then;
I maun sheathe my sword in its scabbard case,
For tomorrow's our battle day then."
Chorus

8. "And when will ye come back again,
My ain dear sodger laddie?
When will ye come back again,
And be your bairn's daddie?
Chorus

9. "O, haud your tongue, my bonnie wee lass,
Dinna let this pairtin' grieve ye:
When heather cowes grow ousen bows,
Bonnie lassie, I'll come and see ye."
Chorus

10. She's ta'en her wee coatie ower her heid,
And followed him up to Stirlin',
She's grown sae fu' that she couldna boo,
And he's left her in Dunfermline.
Chorus

11. It's breid and cheese for carles and dames,
And oats and hay for horses;
A cup of tea for auld maids,
And bonnie lads for lasses.
Chorus

THE 23RD OF JUNE

Irish folksong

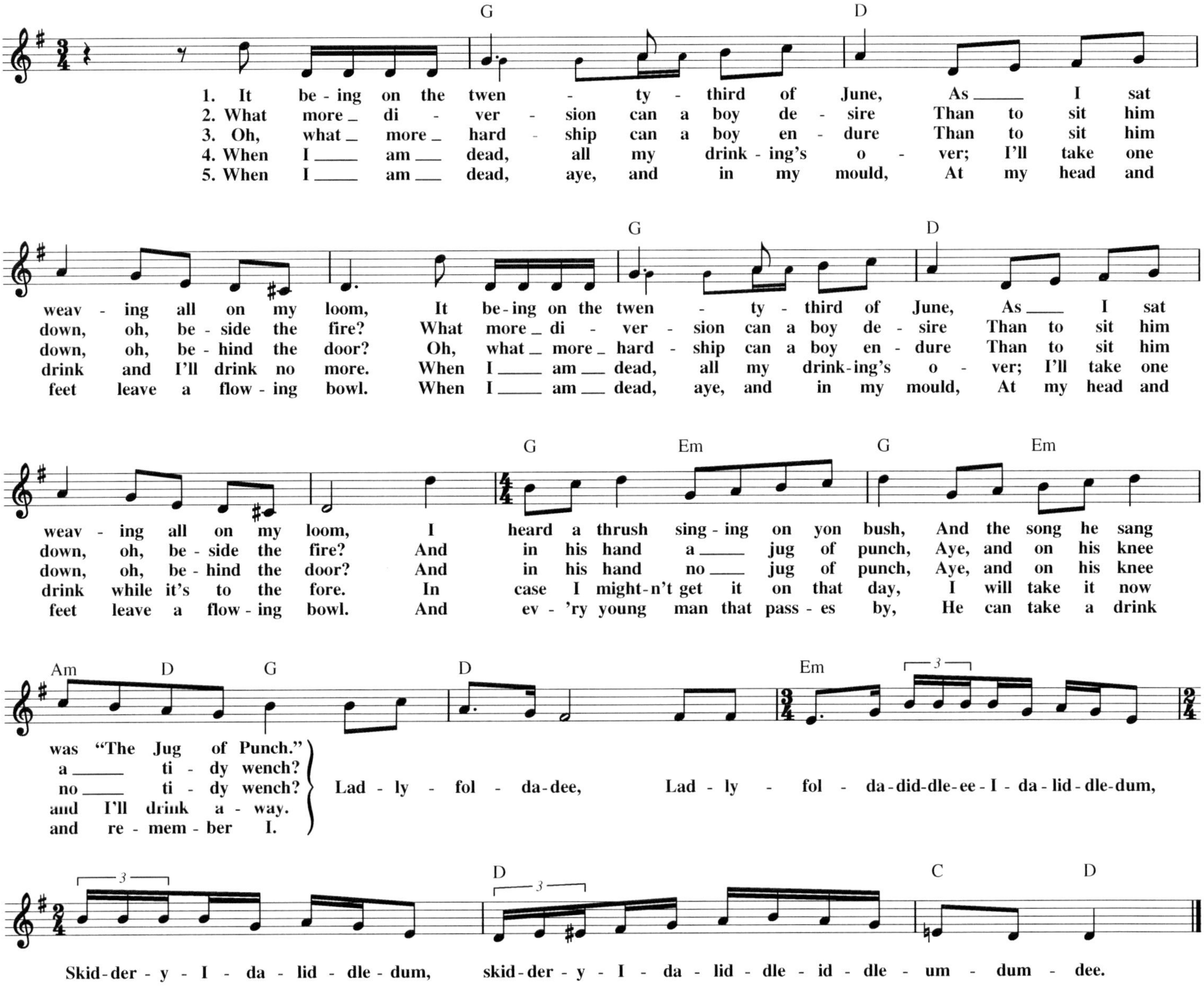

1. It be-ing on the twen - ty - third of June, As ___ I sat
2. What more _ di - ver - sion can a boy de - sire Than to sit him
3. Oh, what _ more _ hard - ship can a boy en - dure Than to sit him
4. When I ___ am ___ dead, all my drink-ing's o - ver; I'll take one
5. When I ___ am ___ dead, aye, and in my mould, At my head and

weav - ing all on my loom, It be-ing on the twen - ty - third of June, As ___ I sat
down, oh, be - side the fire? What more _ di - ver - sion can a boy de - sire Than to sit him
down, oh, be - hind the door? Oh, what _ more _ hard - ship can a boy en - dure Than to sit him
drink and I'll drink no more. When I ___ am ___ dead, all my drink-ing's o - ver; I'll take one
feet leave a flow-ing bowl. When I ___ am ___ dead, aye, and in my mould, At my head and

weav - ing all on my loom, I heard a thrush sing-ing on yon bush, And the song he sang
down, oh, be - side the fire? And in his hand a ___ jug of punch, Aye, and on his knee
down, oh, be - hind the door? And in his hand no ___ jug of punch, Aye, and on his knee
drink while it's to the fore. In case I might-n't get it on that day, I will take it now
feet leave a flow-ing bowl. And ev - 'ry young man that pass - es by, He can take a drink

was "The Jug of Punch."
a ___ ti - dy wench?
no ___ ti - dy wench? } Lad - ly - fol - da-dee, Lad - ly - fol - da-did-dle-ee - I - da-lid-dle-dum,
and I'll drink a - way.
and re - mem - ber I. }

Skid - der - y I - da - lid - dle - dum, skid - der - y I - da - lid - dle - id - dle - um - dum - dee.

UIST CATTLE CROON

Folksong from the Hebrides

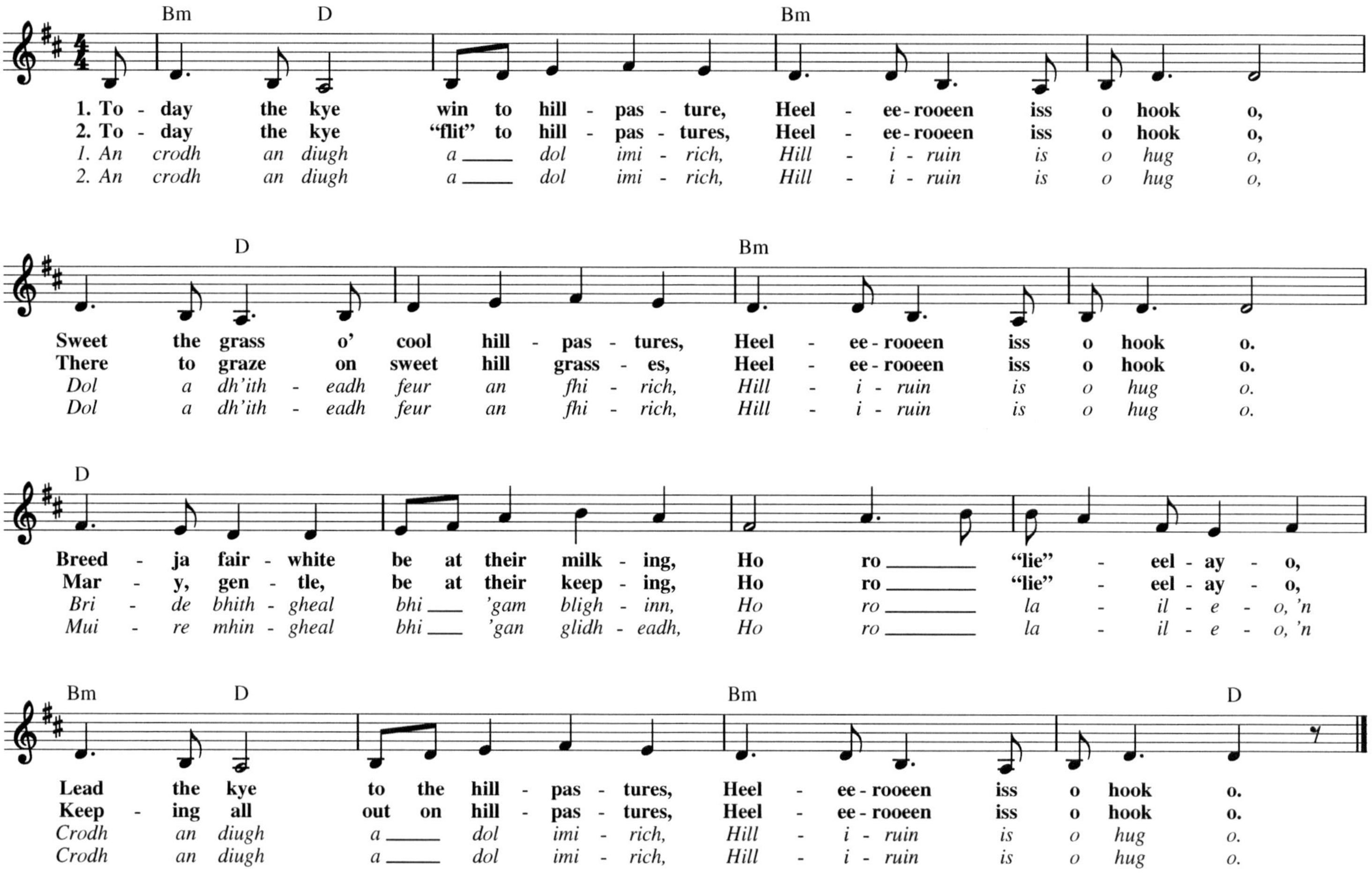

1. To - day the kye win to hill - pas - ture, Heel - ee - rooeen iss o hook o,
2. To - day the kye "flit" to hill - pas - tures, Heel - ee - rooeen iss o hook o,
1. *An crodh an diugh a____ dol imi - rich, Hill - i - ruin is o hug o,*
2. *An crodh an diugh a____ dol imi - rich, Hill - i - ruin is o hug o,*

Sweet the grass o' cool hill - pas - tures, Heel - ee - rooeen iss o hook o.
There to graze on sweet hill grass - es, Heel - ee - rooeen iss o hook o.
Dol a dh'ith - eadh feur an fhi - rich, Hill - i - ruin is o hug o.
Dol a dh'ith - eadh feur an fhi - rich, Hill - i - ruin is o hug o.

Breed - ja fair - white be at their milk - ing, Ho ro_____ "lie" - eel - ay - o,
Mar - y, gen - tle, be at their keep - ing, Ho ro_____ "lie" - eel - ay - o,
Bri - de bhith - gheal bhi____ 'gam bligh - inn, Ho ro_____ la - il - e - o, 'n
Mui - re mhin - gheal bhi____ 'gan glidh - eadh, Ho ro_____ la - il - e - o, 'n

Lead the kye to the hill - pas - tures, Heel - ee - rooeen iss o hook o.
Keep - ing all out on hill - pas - tures, Heel - ee - rooeen iss o hook o.
Crodh an diugh a____ dol imi - rich, Hill - i - ruin is o hug o.
Crodh an diugh a____ dol imi - rich, Hill - i - ruin is o hug o.

ULLAPOOL SAILOR'S SONG

Folksong from the Hebrides

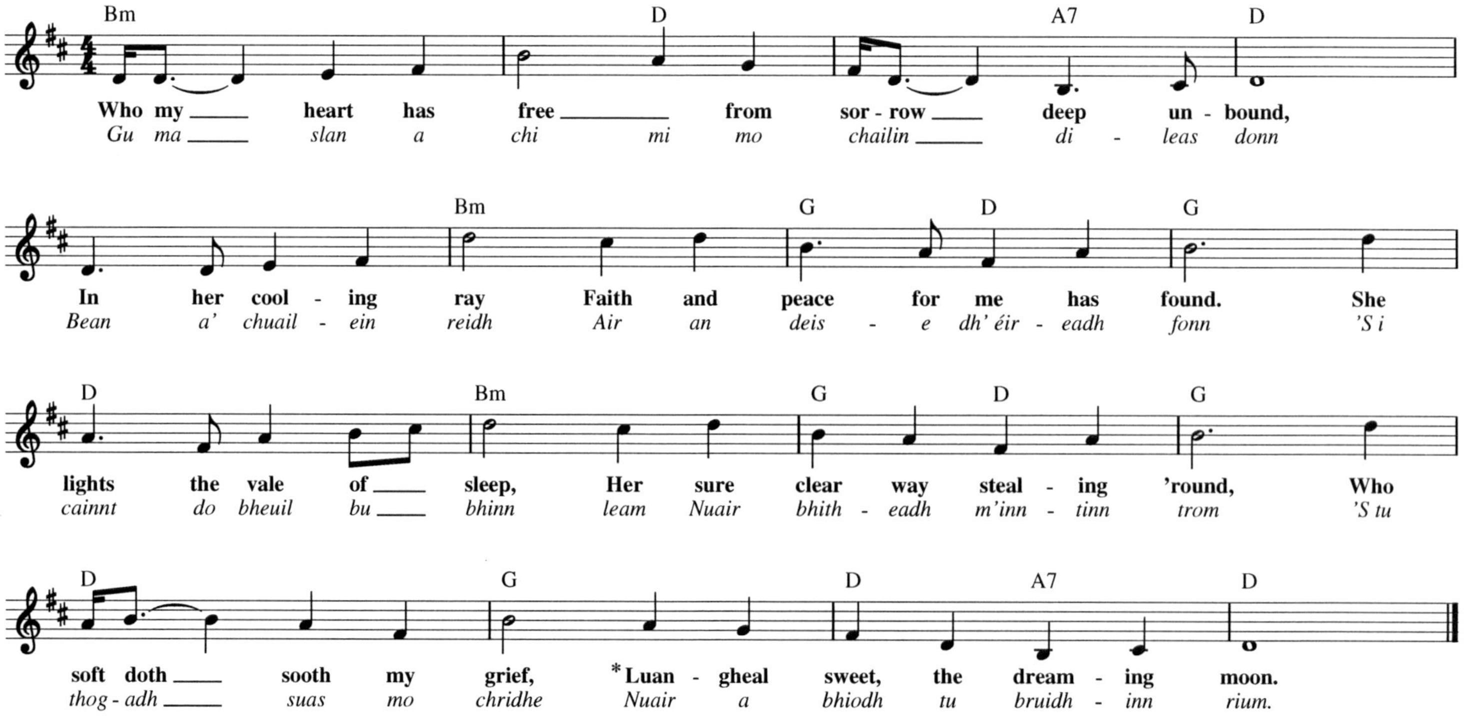

Who my____ heart has free_____ from sor - row____ deep un - bound,
Gu ma____ slan a chi mi mo chailin____ di - leas donn

In her cool - ing ray Faith and peace for me has found. She
Bean a' chuail - ein reidh Air an deis - e dh' éir - eadh fonn 'S i

lights the vale of____ sleep, Her sure clear way steal - ing 'round, Who
cainnt do bheuil bu____ bhinn leam Nuair bhith - eadh m'inn - tinn trom 'S tu

soft doth____ sooth my grief, *Luan - gheal sweet, the dream - ing moon.
thog - adh____ suas mo chridhe Nuair a bhiodh tu bruidh - inn rium.*

* *Luangheal = white moon*

VAN DIEMEN'S LAND

Irish folksong

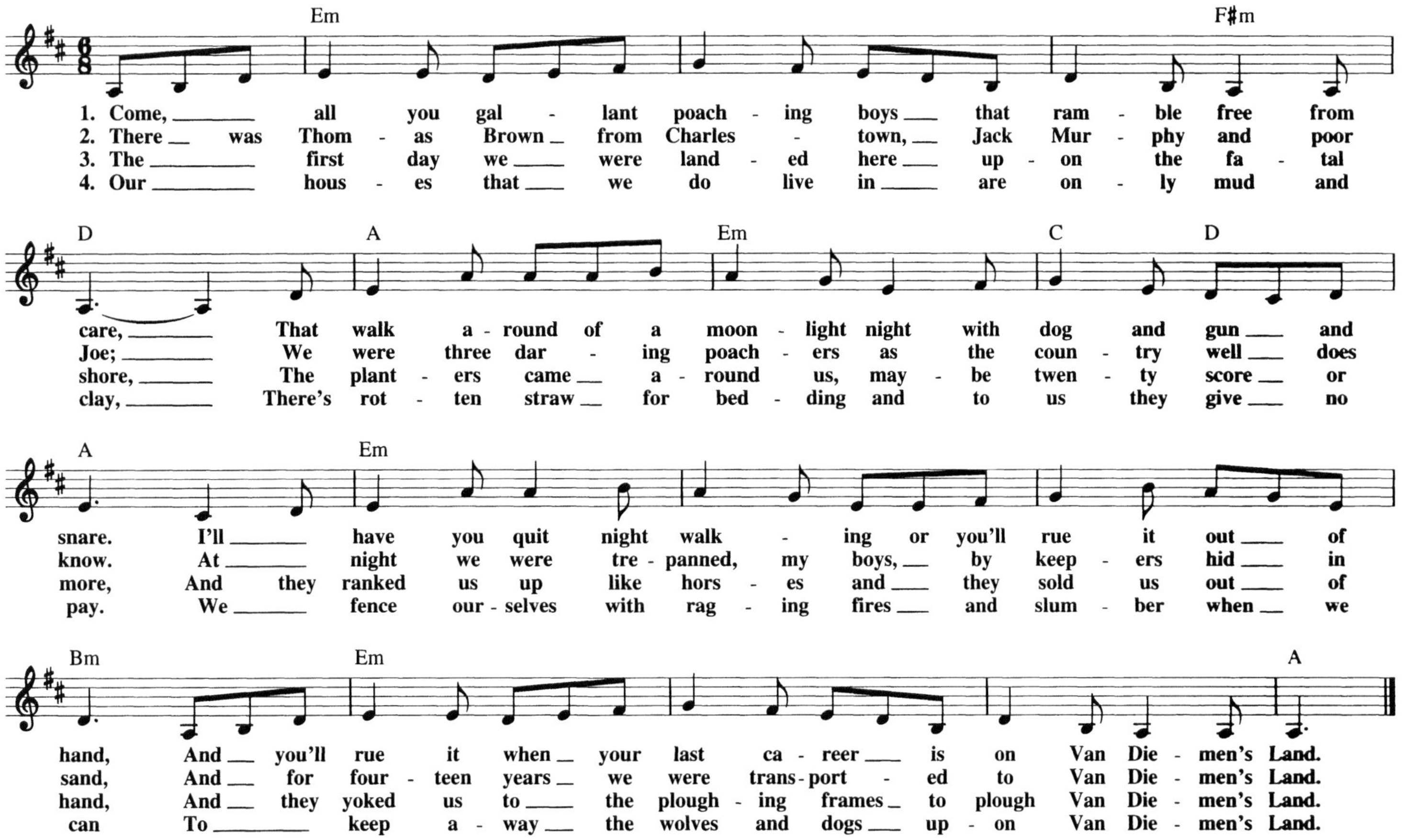

WAE'S ME FOR PRINCE CHARLIE

Scottish folksong
Words by William Glen

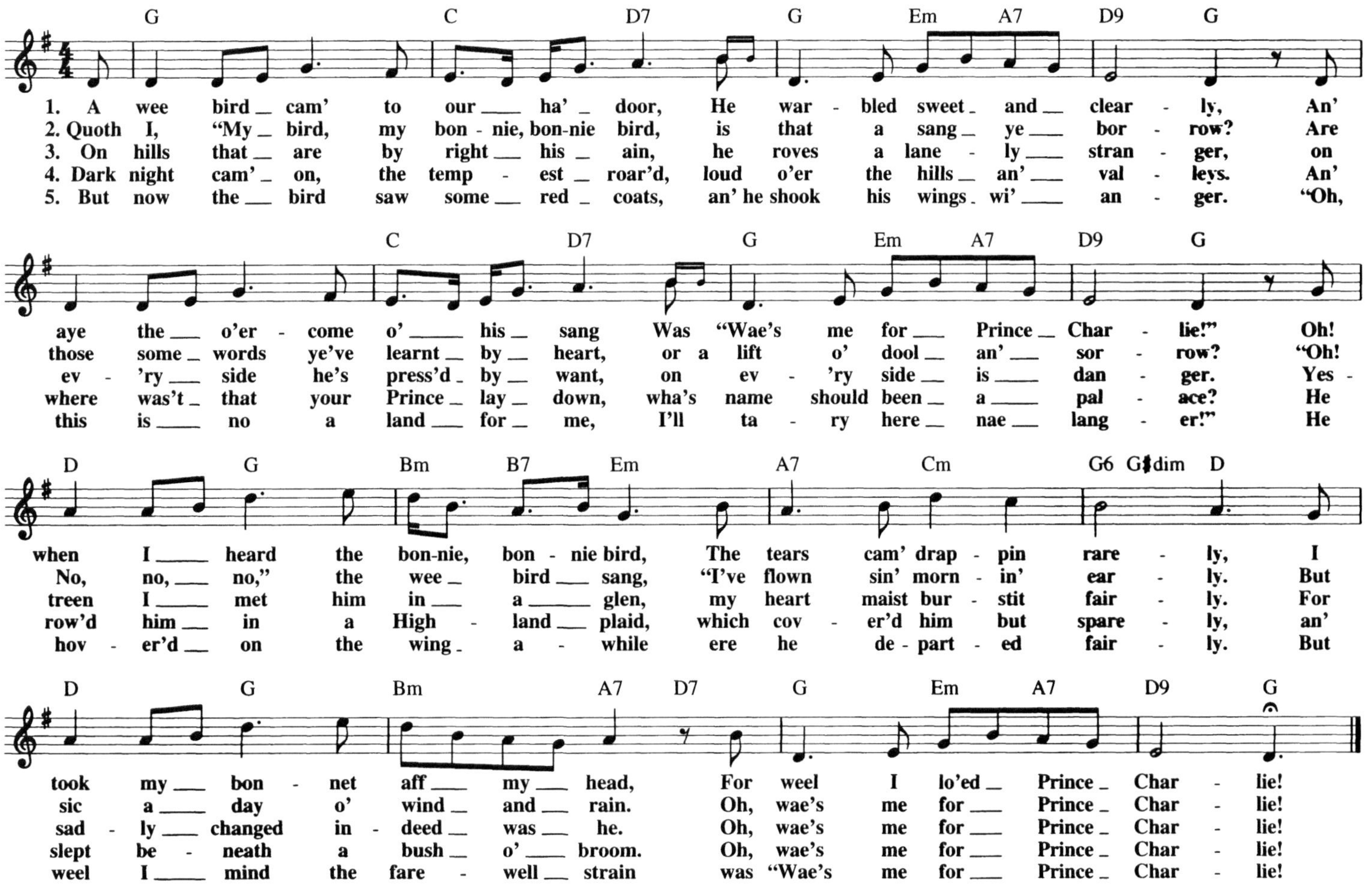

A WANDERING SHADE
(Faileas nam Beam)

Folksong from the Hebrides

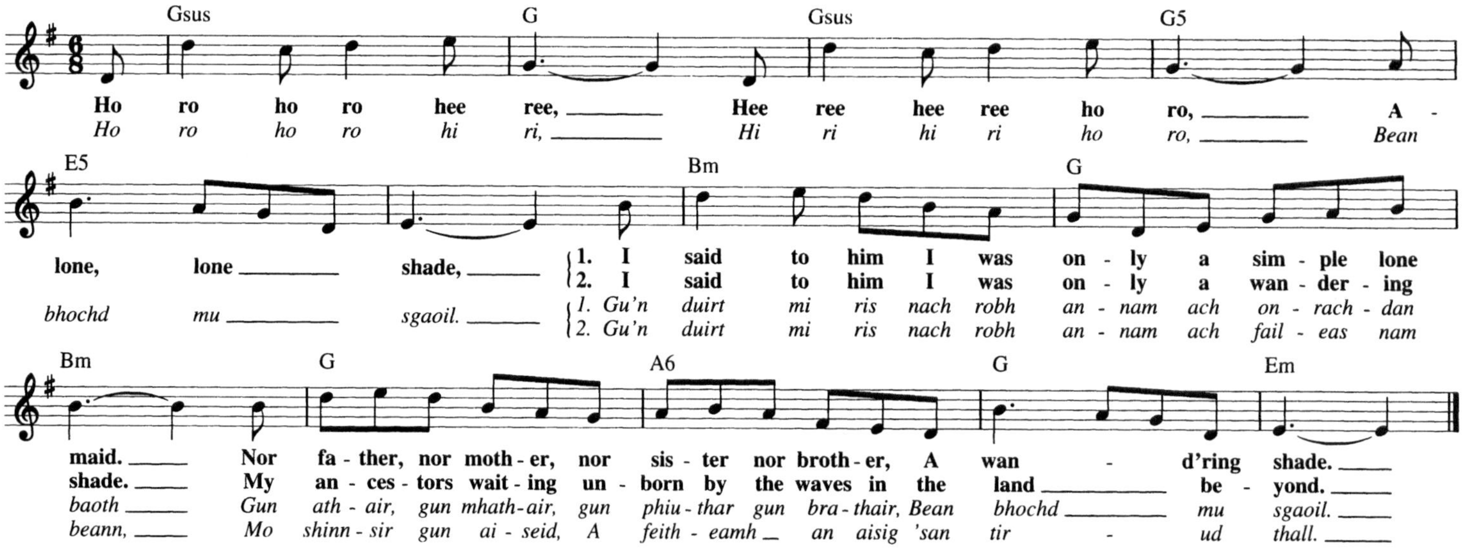

Ho ro ho ro hee ree, _____ Hee ree hee ree ho ro, _____ A-
Ho ro ho ro hi ri, _____ Hi ri hi ri ho ro, _____ Bean

lone, lone _____ shade, _____ 1. I said to him I was on-ly a sim-ple lone
2. I said to him I was on-ly a wan-der-ing
bhochd mu _____ sgaoil. _____ 1. Gu'n duirt mi ris nach robh an-nam ach on-rach-dan
2. Gu'n duirt mi ris nach robh an-nam ach fail-eas nam

maid. _____ Nor fa-ther, nor moth-er, nor sis-ter nor broth-er, A wan - d'ring shade. _____
shade. _____ My an-ces-tors wait-ing un-born by the waves in the land _____ be- yond. _____
baoth _____ Gun ath-air, gun mhath-air, gun phiu-thar gun bra-thair, Bean bhochd _____ mu sgaoil. _____
beann, _____ Mo shinn-sir gun ai-seid, A feith-eamh _ an aisig 'san tir - ud thall. _____

THE WEARING OF THE GREEN

Irish popular song
Words by Dion Boucicault

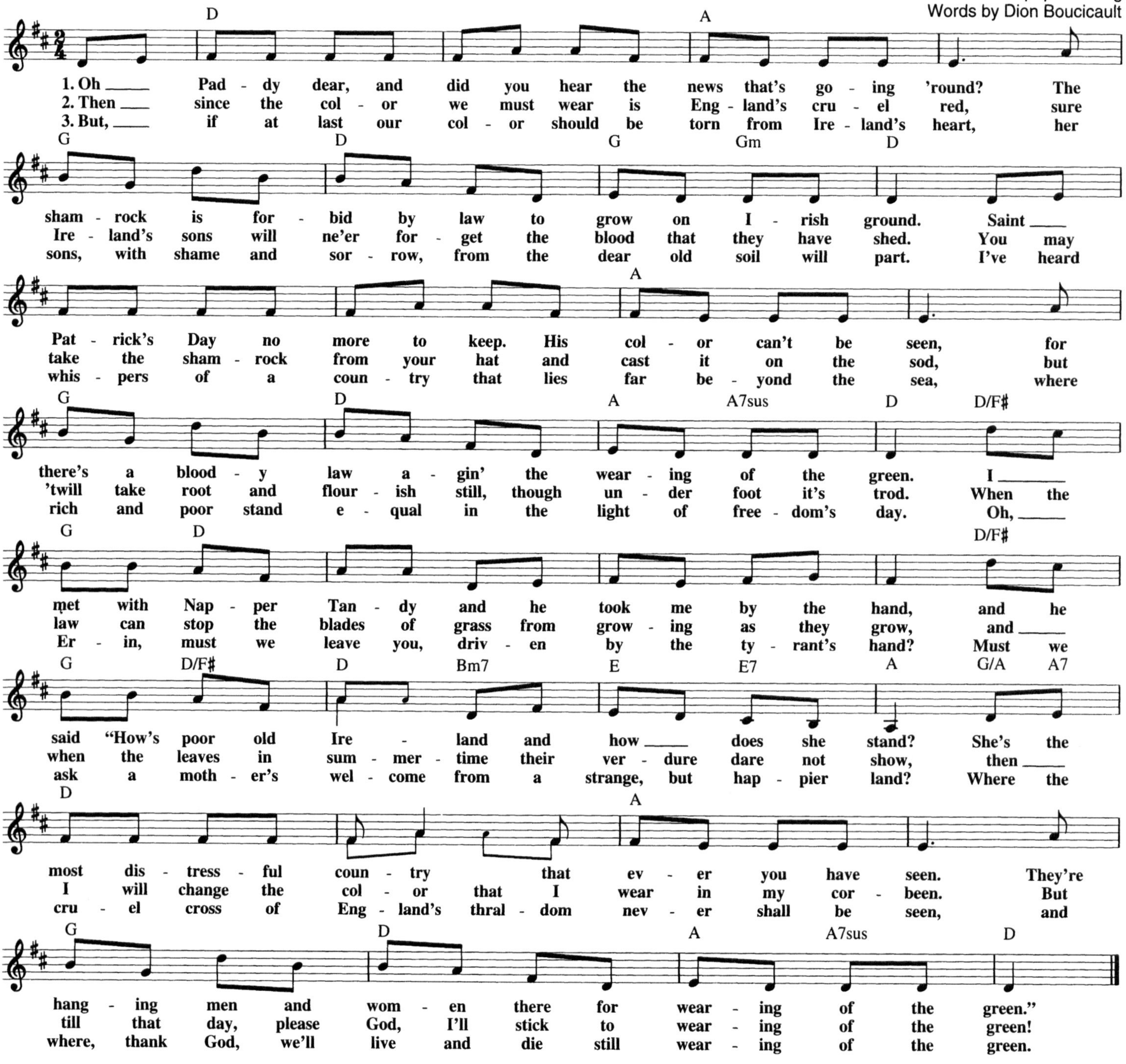

1. Oh _____ Pad-dy dear, and did you hear the news that's go-ing 'round? The
2. Then _____ since the col-or we must wear is Eng-land's cru-el red, sure
3. But, _____ if at last our col-or should be torn from Ire-land's heart, her

sham-rock is for-bid by law to grow on I-rish ground. Saint
Ire-land's sons will ne'er for-get the blood that they have shed. You may
sons, with shame and sor-row, from the dear old soil will part. I've heard

Pat-rick's Day no more to keep. His col-or can't be seen, for
take the sham-rock from your hat and cast it on the sod, but
whis-pers of a coun-try that lies far be-yond the sea, where

there's a blood-y law a-gin' the wear-ing of the green. I
'twill take root and flour-ish still, though un-der foot it's trod. When the
rich and poor stand e-qual in the light of free-dom's day. Oh, _____

met with Nap-per Tan-dy and he took me by the hand, and he
law can stop the blades of grass from grow-ing as they grow, and _____
Er-in, must we leave you, driv-en by the ty-rant's hand? Must we

said "How's poor old Ire - land and how _____ does she stand? She's the
when the leaves in sum-mer-time their ver-dure dare not show, then _____
ask a moth-er's wel-come from a strange, but hap-pier land? Where the

most dis-tress-ful coun-try that ev-er you have seen. They're
I will change the col-or that I wear in my cor-been. But
cru-el cross of Eng-land's thral-dom nev-er shall be seen, and

hang-ing men and wom-en there for wear-ing of the green."
till that day, please God, I'll stick to wear-ing of the green!
where, thank God, we'll live and die still wear-ing of the green.

WEELA WALLIA

Irish folksong

1. There was an old wom-an who lived in the wood,
2. She had a ba - by six months old,
3. She had a pen - knife three foot long,
4. She stuck the knife in the ba - by's head,
5. Three big knocks came a-knock - ing at the door,
6. "Are you the wom-an what killed the child?"

7.-9. (See additional lyrics)

Wee - la wee - la wal - lia.

There
She
She
The
"Are

was an old wom-an who lived in the wood,
had a ba - by six months old,
had a pen - knife three foot long,
more she stabbed it the more it bled,
Two po - lice - men and a man,
you the wom-an what killed the child?"

Down by the riv - er Sal - lia.

Additional Lyrics

7. "I am the woman what killed the child,"
Weela weela wallia.
"I am the woman what killed the child
Down by the river Sallia."

8. The rope got chucked and she got hung,
Weela weela wallia.
The rope got chucked and she got hung
Down by the river Sallia.

9. The moral of this story is,
Weela weela wallia,
Don't stick knives in babies' heads
Down by the river Sallia.

THE WEST'S AWAKE

Irish folksong

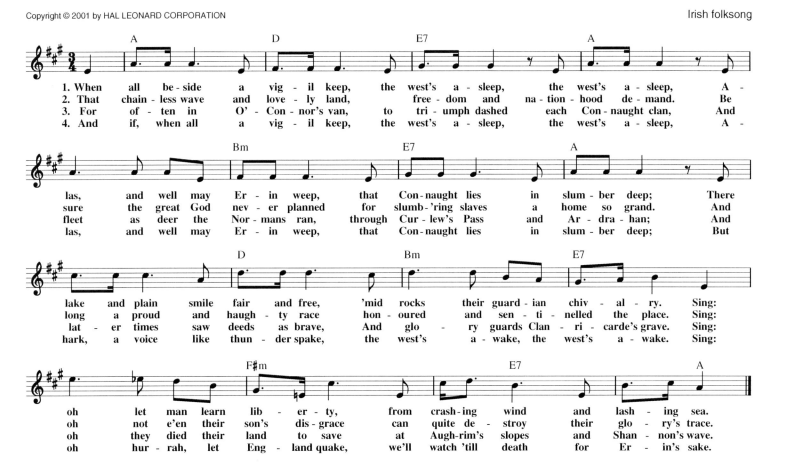

1. When all be - side a vig - il keep, the west's a - sleep, the west's a - sleep, A-
2. That chain - less wave and love - ly land, free - dom and na - tion - hood de - mand. Be
3. For of - ten in O' - Con - nor's van, to tri - umph dashed each Con - naught clan, And
4. And if, when all a vig - il keep, the west's a - sleep, the west's a - sleep, A-

las, and well may Er - in weep, that Con-naught lies in slum - ber deep; There
sure the great God nev - er planned for slumb-'ring slaves a home so grand. And
fleet as deer the Nor - mans ran, through Cur - lew's Pass and Ar - dra - han; And
las, and well may Er - in weep, that Con-naught lies in slum - ber deep; But

lake and plain smile fair and free, 'mid rocks their guard - ian chiv - al - ry. Sing:
long a proud and haugh - ty race hon - oured and sen - ti - nelled the place. Sing:
lat - er times saw deeds as brave, And glo - ry guards Clan - ri - carde's grave. Sing:
hark, a voice like thun - der spake, the west's a - wake, the west's a - wake. Sing:

oh let man learn lib - er - ty, from crash - ing wind and lash - ing sea.
oh not e'en their son's dis - grace can quite de - stroy their glo - ry's trace.
oh they died their land to save at Augh - rim's slopes and Shan - non's wave.
oh hur - rah, let Eng - land quake, we'll watch 'till death for Er - in's sake.

WEAVING LILT

Scottish folksong

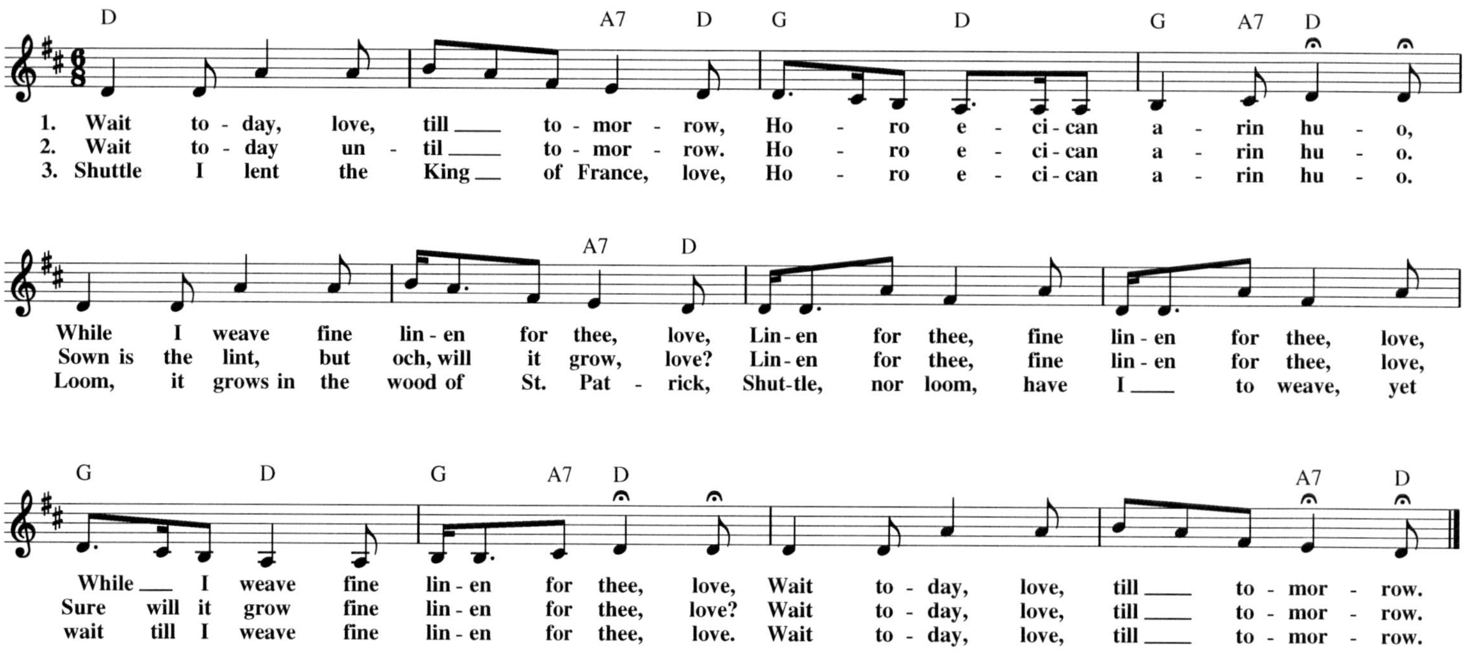

1. Wait to - day, love, till ___ to - mor - row, Ho - ro e - ci - can a - rin hu - o,
2. Wait to - day un - til ___ to - mor - row. Ho - ro e - ci - can a - rin hu - o.
3. Shuttle I lent the King ___ of France, love, Ho - ro e - ci - can a - rin hu - o.

While I weave fine lin - en for thee, love, Lin - en for thee, fine lin - en for thee, love,
Sown is the lint, but och, will it grow, love? Lin - en for thee, fine lin - en for thee, love,
Loom, it grows in the wood of St. Pat - rick, Shut-tle, nor loom, have I ___ to weave, yet

While ___ I weave fine lin - en for thee, love, Wait to - day, love, till ___ to - mor - row.
Sure will it grow fine lin - en for thee, love? Wait to - day, love, till ___ to - mor - row.
wait till I weave fine lin - en for thee, love. Wait to - day, love, till ___ to - mor - row.

WHAT WOULD YOU DO IF YOU MARRIED A SOLDIER?

Irish folksong

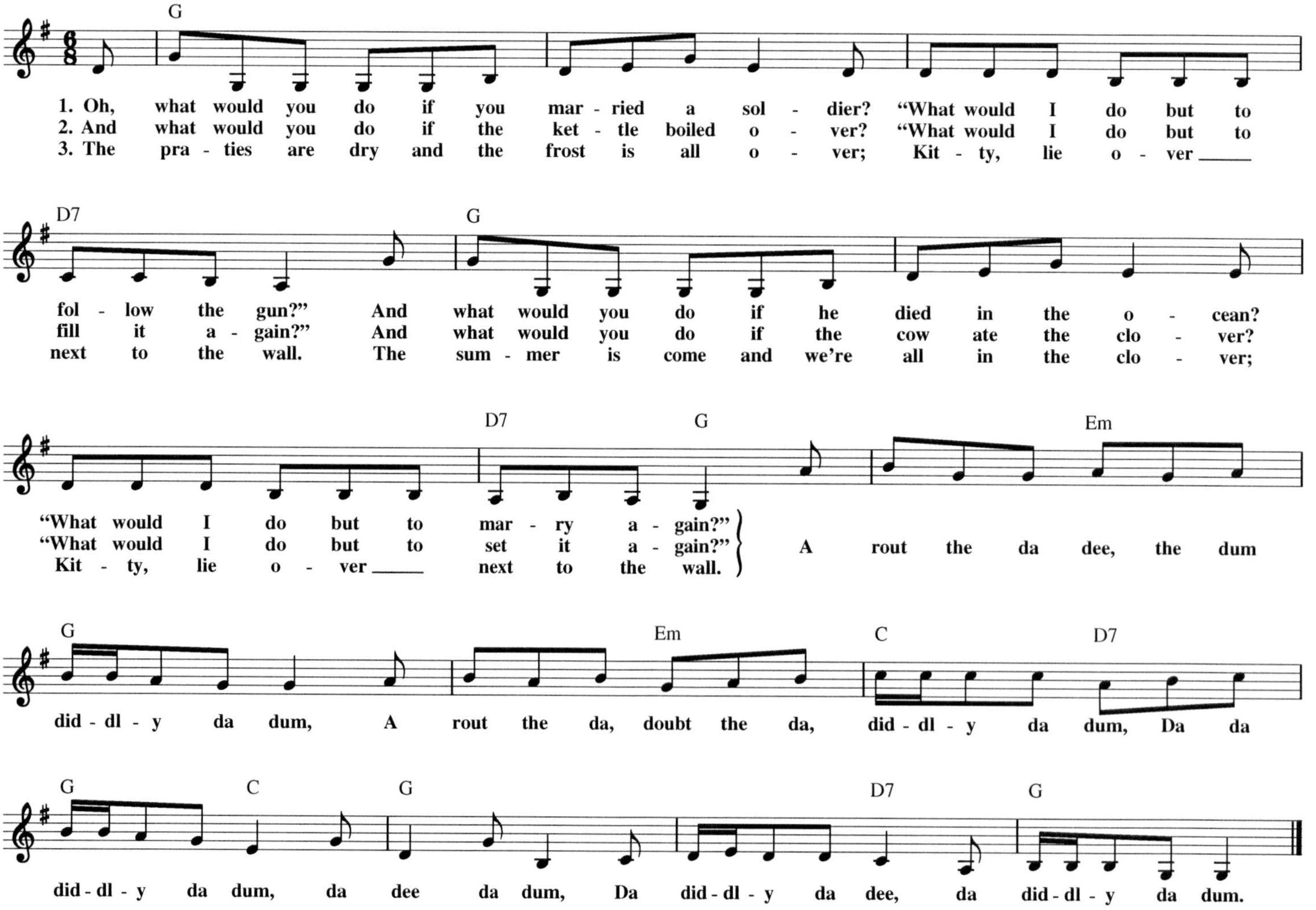

1. Oh, what would you do if you mar - ried a sol - dier? "What would I do but to
2. And what would you do if the ket - tle boiled o - ver? "What would I do but to
3. The pra - ties are dry and the frost is all o - ver; Kit - ty, lie o - ver ___

fol - low the gun?" And what would you do if he died in the o - cean?
fill it a - gain?" And what would you do if the cow ate the clo - ver?
next to the wall. The sum - mer is come and we're all in the clo - ver;

"What would I do but to mar - ry a - gain?"}
"What would I do but to set it a - gain?"} A rout the da dee, the dum
Kit - ty, lie o - ver ___ next to the wall.)

did - dl - y da dum, A rout the da, doubt the da, did - dl - y da dum, Da da

did - dl - y da dum, da dee da dum, Da did - dl - y da dee, da did - dl - y da dum.

WHEN IRISH EYES ARE SMILING

Lyric by Chauncey Olcott and Geo. Graff Jr.
Music by Ernest R. Ball

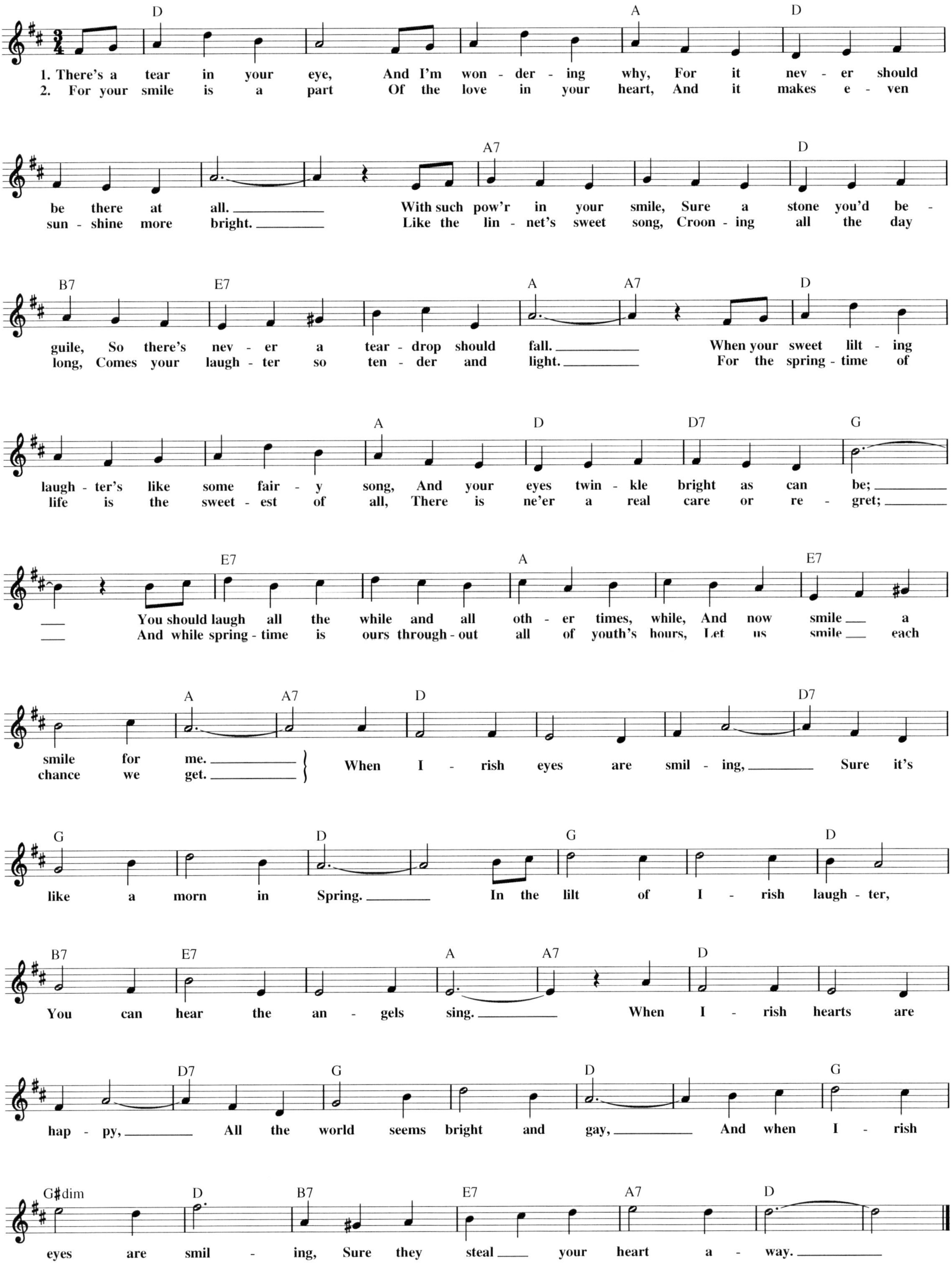

236

WHEN HE WHO ADORES THEE

Irish folksong

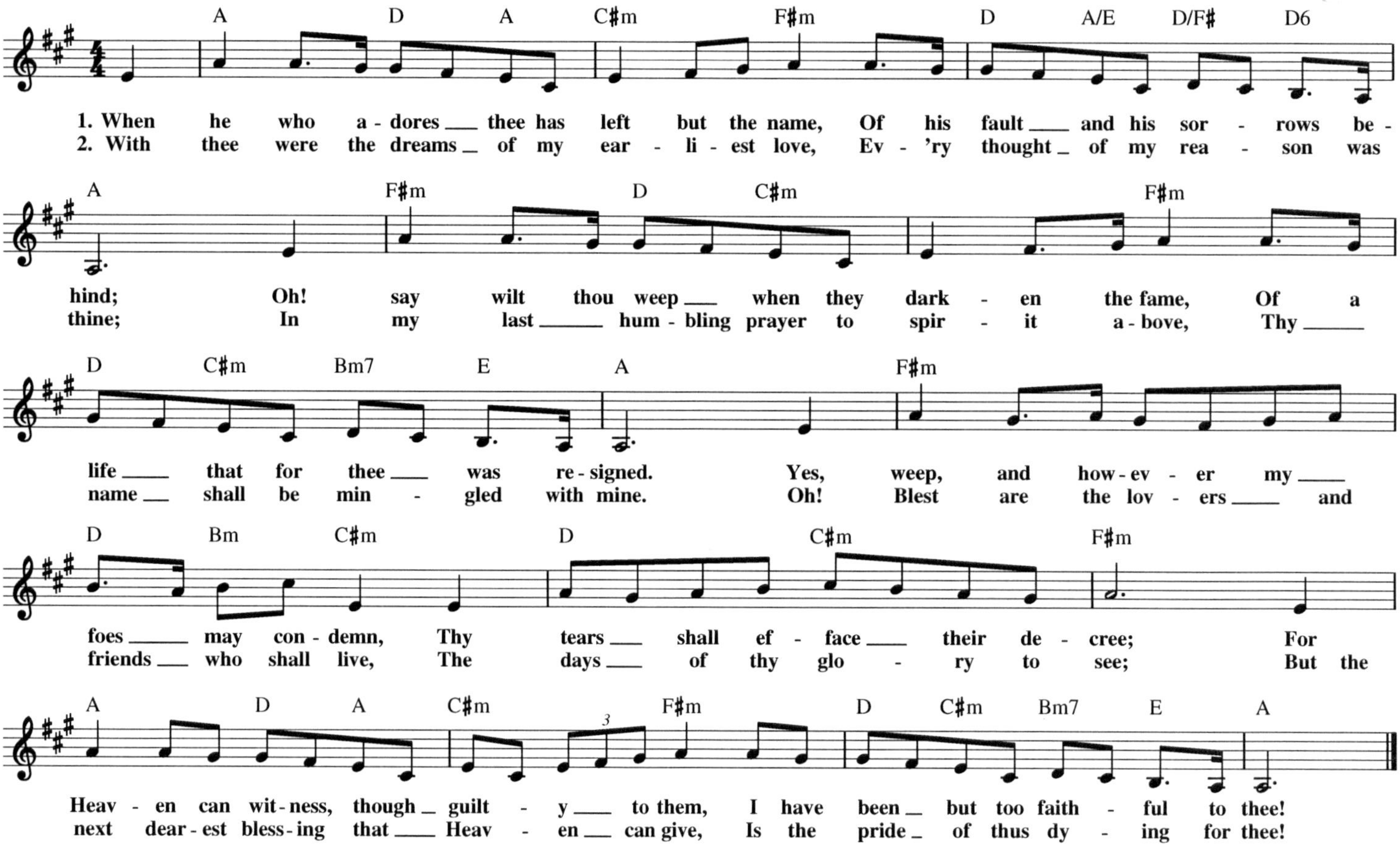

WHEN WE WERE BOY AND GIRL

Irish folksong

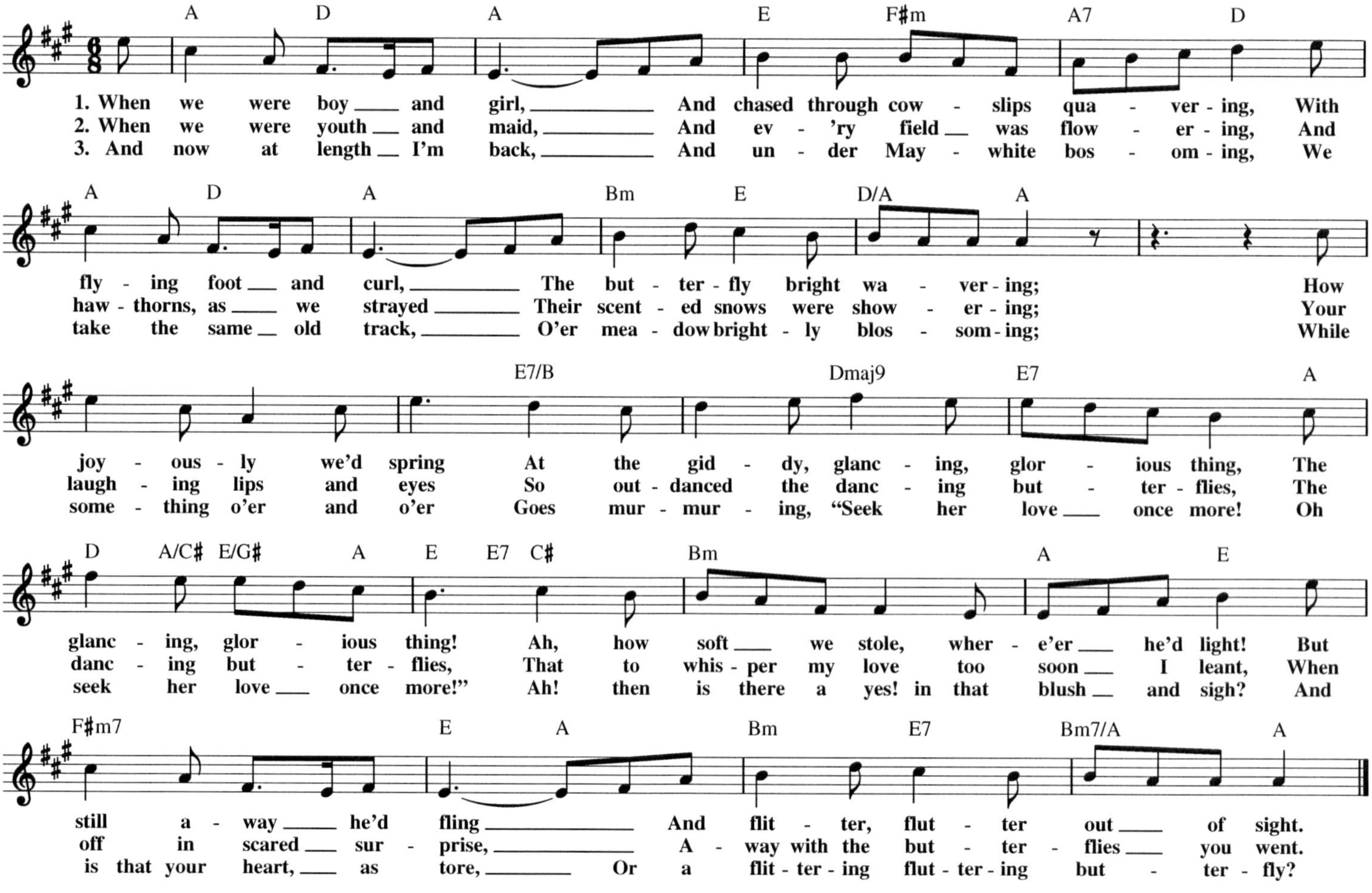

WHO THREW THE OVERALLS IN MISTRESS MURPHY'S CHOWDER

Words and Music by
George L. Geifer

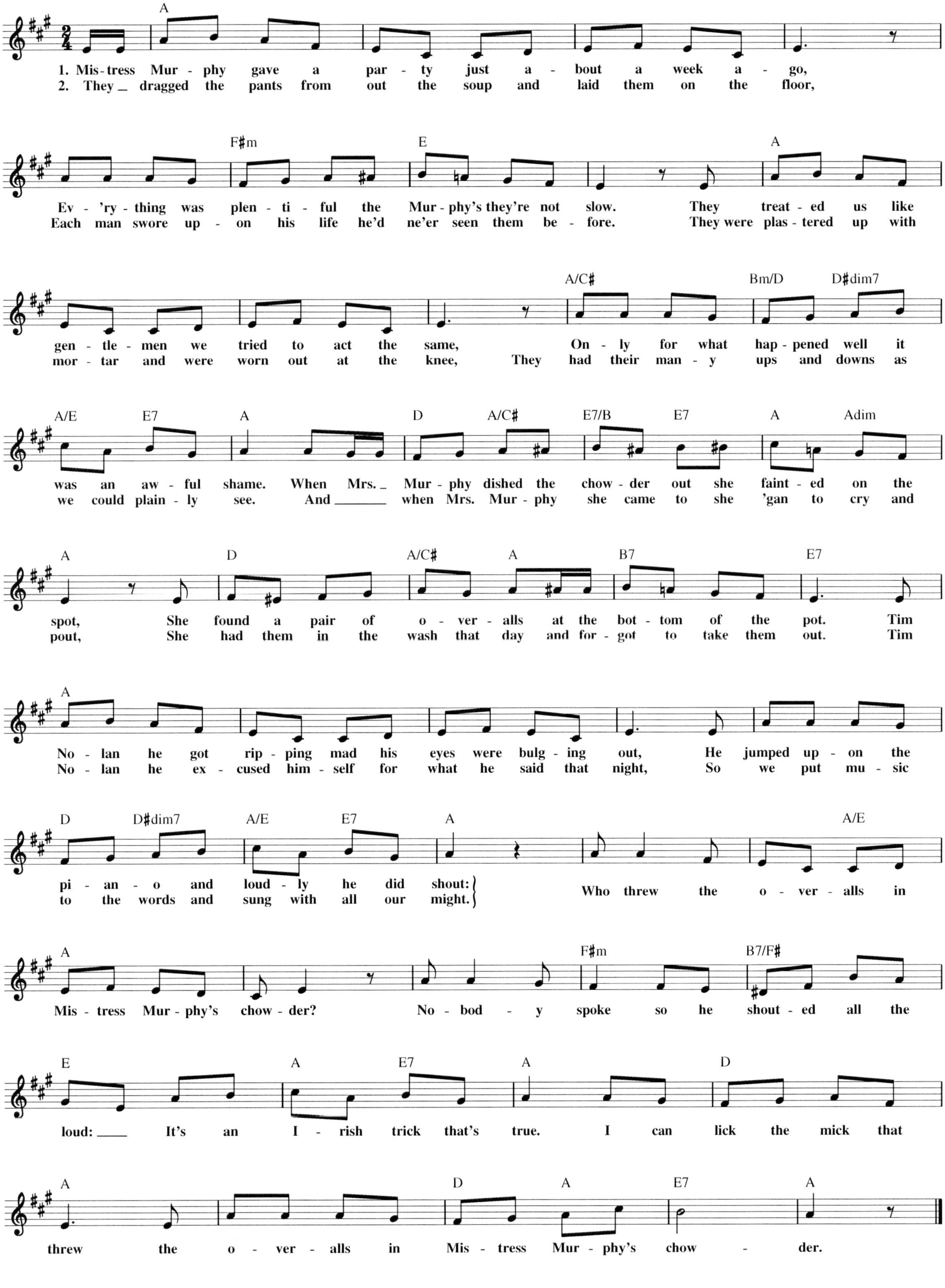

WHERE THE RIVER SHANNON FLOWS

Words and Music by
James I. Russell

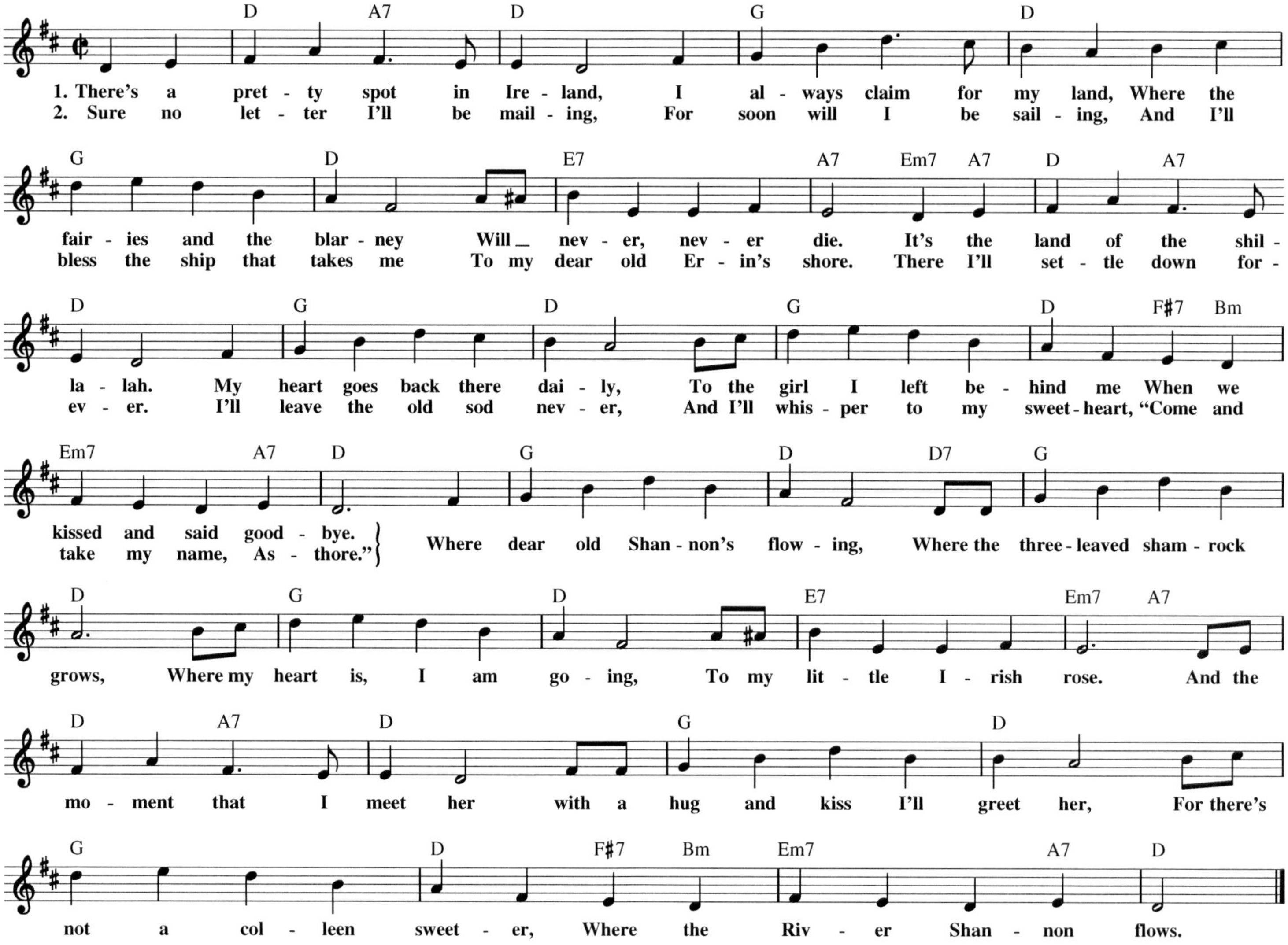

WHISKEY, YOU'RE THE DEVIL

Irish folksong

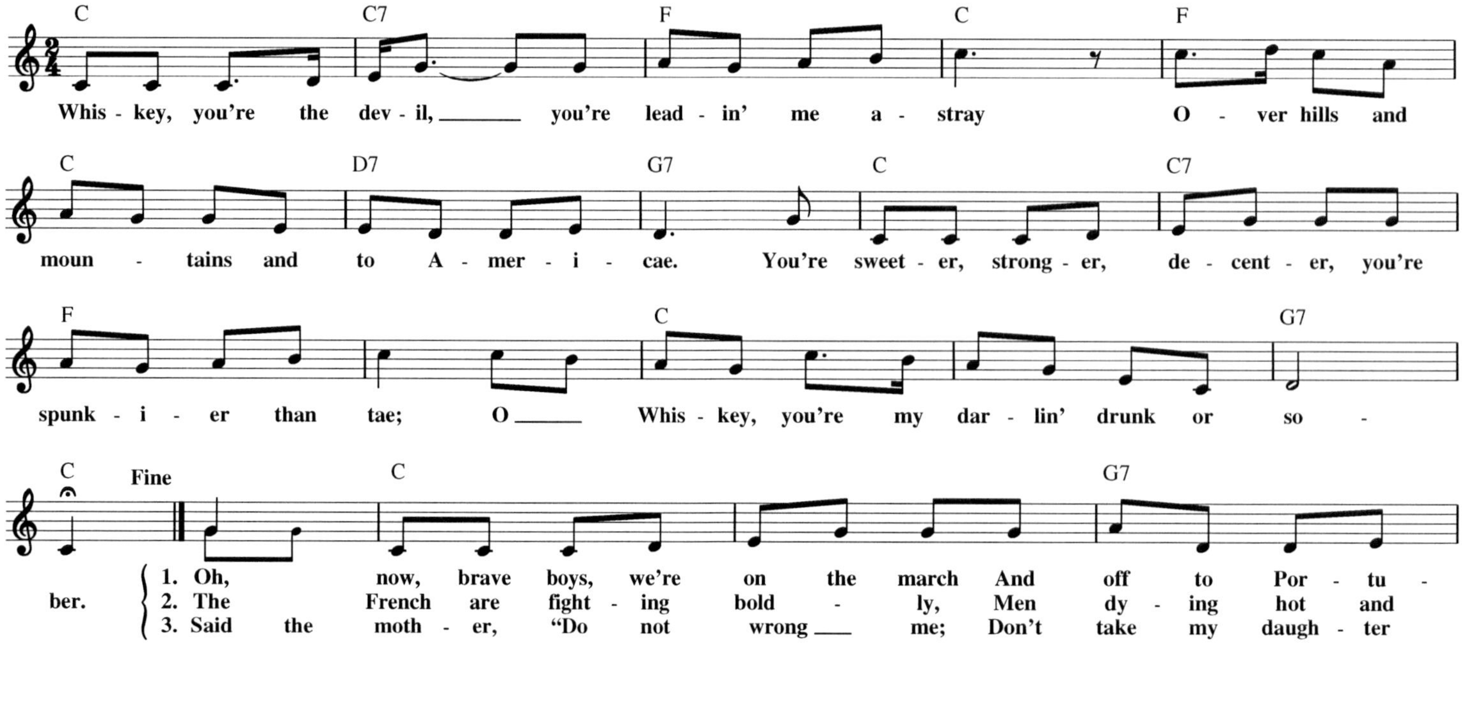

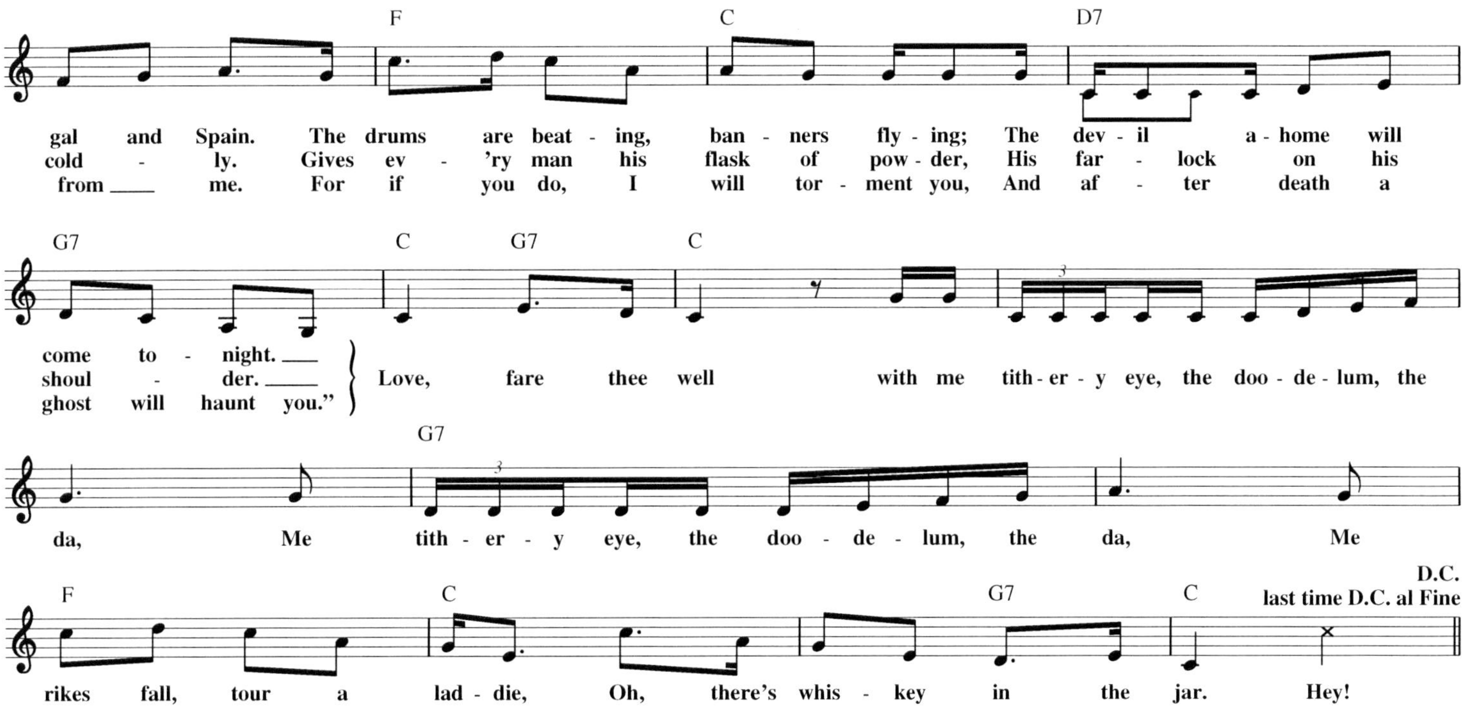

gal and Spain. The drums are beat - ing, ban - ners fly - ing; The dev - il a - home will
cold - ly. Gives ev - 'ry man his flask of pow - der, His far - lock on his
from ___ me. For if you do, I will tor - ment you, And af - ter death a

come to - night. ___
shoul - der. ___ } Love, fare thee well with me tith - er - y eye, the doo - de - lum, the
ghost will haunt you." }

da, Me tith - er - y eye, the doo - de - lum, the da, Me

rikes fall, tour a lad - die, Oh, there's whis - key in the jar. Hey!

D.C.
last time D.C. al Fine

THE WILD COLONIAL BOY

Irish folksong

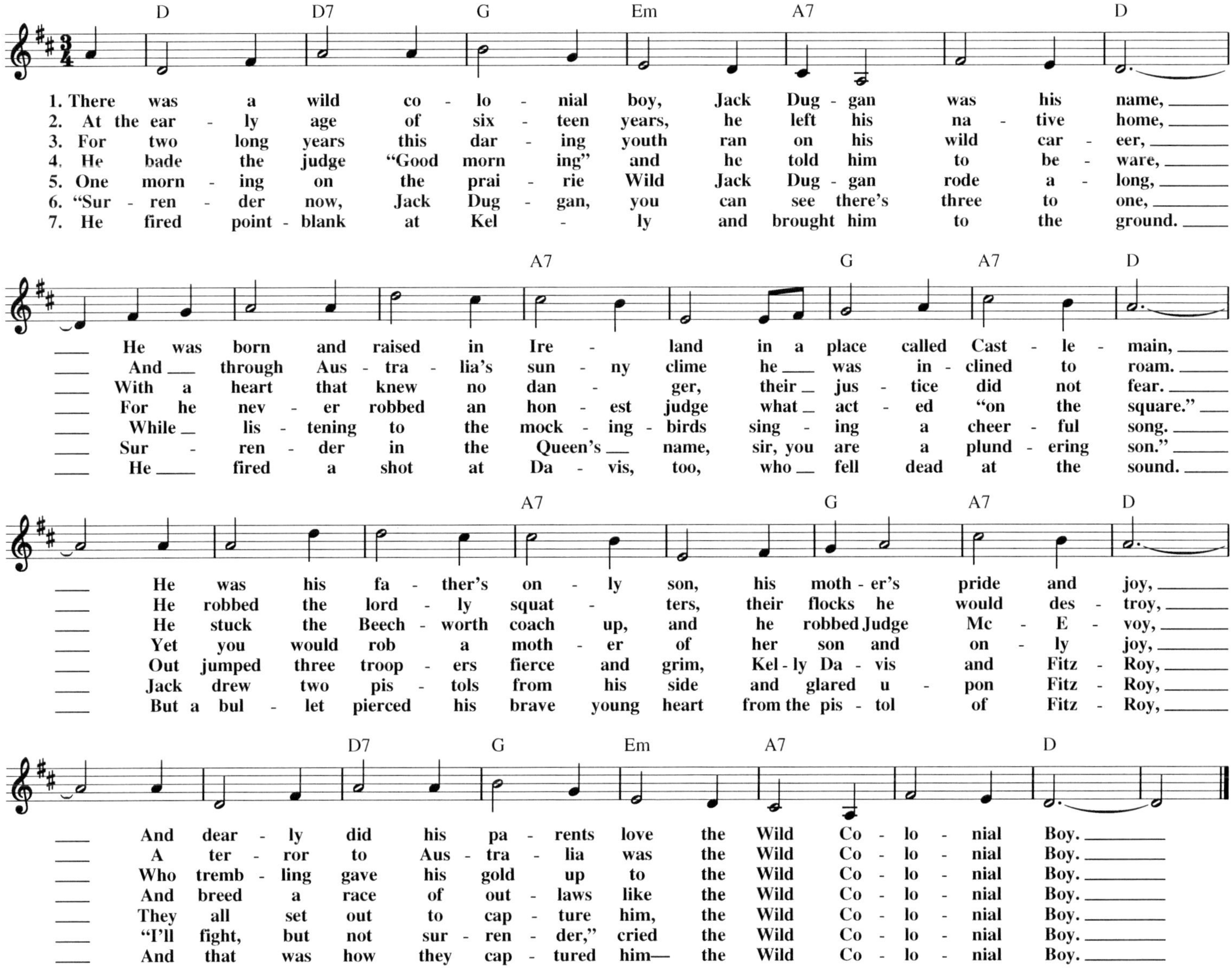

WHY, LIQUOR OF LIFE, DO I LOVE YOU SO?
(A Fhuisgí, Croí Na n-Anamann)

Irish folksong

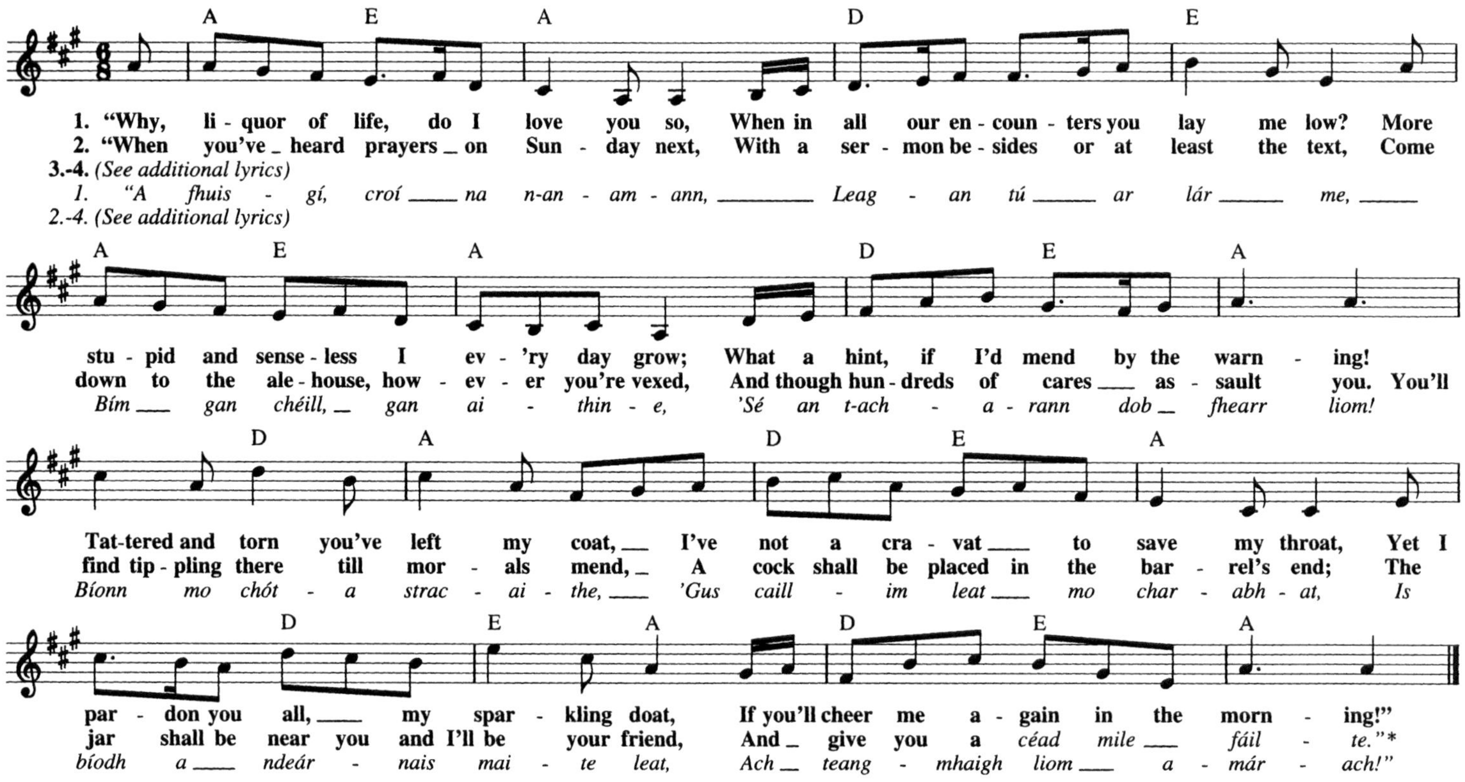

1. "Why, li - quor of life, do I love you so, When in all our en - coun - ters you lay me low? More
2. "When you've _ heard prayers _ on Sun - day next, With a ser - mon be - sides or at least the text, Come
3.-4. (See additional lyrics)
1. "A fhuis - gí, croí ____ na n-an - am - ann, ____ Leag - an tú ____ ar lár ____ me, ____
2.-4. (See additional lyrics)

stu - pid and sense - less I ev - 'ry day grow; What a hint, if I'd mend by the warn - ing!
down to the ale - house, how - ev - er you're vexed, And though hun - dreds of cares ___ as - sault you. You'll
Bím ___ gan chéill, _ gan ai - thin - e, 'Sé an t-ach - a - rann dob _ fhearr liom!

Tat-tered and torn you've left my coat, ___ I've not a cra - vat ___ to save my throat, Yet I
find tip - pling there till mor - als mend, _ A cock shall be placed in the bar - rel's end; The
Bíonn mo chót - a strac - ai - the, ___ 'Gus caill - im leat ___ mo char - abh - at, Is

par - don you all, ___ my spar - kling doat, If you'll cheer me a - gain in the morn - ing!"
jar shall be near you and I'll be your friend, And _ give you a céad mile ___ fáil - te."*
bíodh a ___ ndeár - nais mai - te leat, Ach _ teang - mhaigh liom ___ a - már - ach!"

Additional Lyrics

2. "Nuair cistfidh tusa an t-Aifreann
Is beidh do shailm ráite,
Déin-se ionad coinne liom
Is teangmhaigh liom i dtigh 'n táirne,
Mar a bhfeicfir cáirt is cnagaire,
Is coc i dtóin an bharraille,
Is bíodh an jar i n-aice leat,
Is rót-sa chuirfead fáilte!"

3. "You're my soul and my treasure without and within,
My sister, my cousin, and all of my kin;
'Tis unlucky to wed such a prodigal sin,
But all other enjoyment is vain, love!
My barley ricks all turn to you,
My tillage, my plough and my horses too;
My cows and my sheep have bid me adieu,
I care not while you remain love!"

4. "Many's the quarrel and fight we've had,
And many a time you have made me mad;
But while I've a heart it can never be sad,
When you smile at me full on the table!
For surely you are my wife and brother,
My only child, my father and mother;
My outside coat, I have no other,
Oh I'll stand by you while I'm able!"

3. "Och mo stór is mo charm thú,
Moshiúr agus mo bhrá thair,
Mo chúirt, mo thigh, mo thalamh thú,
Mo chruach agus mo stáca!
Mo threobha, mo chéacht, mo charpaill thú;
Mo bha's mo chaoire, geala thú,
Is targash ni dár thagaras,
Do chongaibh mise páitleat!"

4. Is lomdha bruion is acharann,
Bhiodh ead rainn le ráite;
Ach nifhanann brón im aigne,
Nuair liontar chúm archlár thúl
Mo bhean agus mo leanbh thú;
Mo m-háthair agus m'athair thú,
Mo chó tamôr is mo wrapper thú,
'S ni sgarfaidh mé go bráthleat.

*A hundred thousand welcomes

WILL YE GO, LASSIE?

Irish folksong

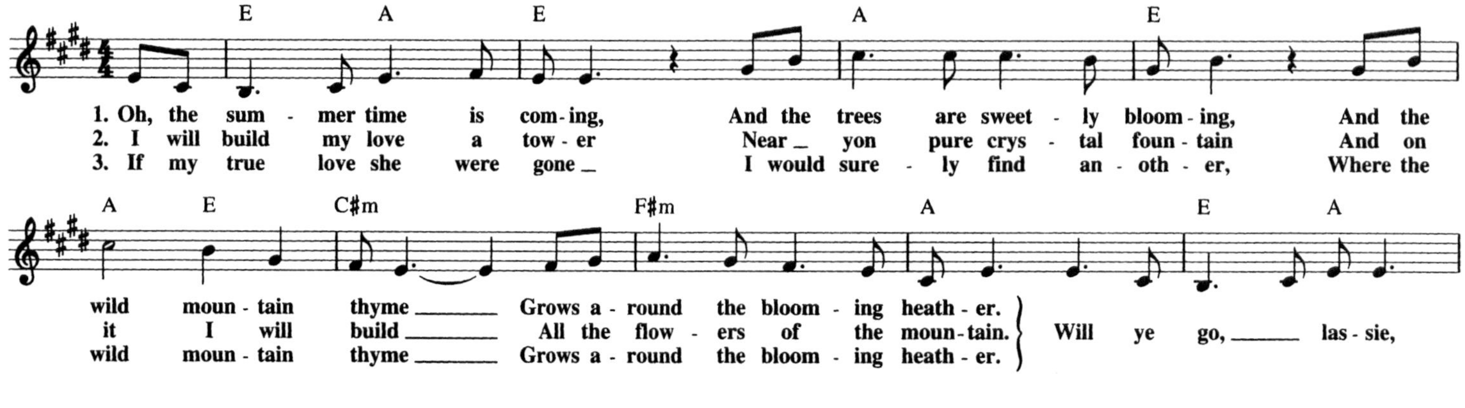

1. Oh, the sum - mer time is com - ing, And the trees are sweet - ly bloom - ing, And the
2. I will build my love a tow - er Near yon pure crys - tal foun - tain And on
3. If my true love she were gone _ I would sure - ly find an - oth - er, Where the

wild moun - tain thyme ____ Grows a - round the bloom - ing heath - er.
it I will build ____ All the flow - ers of the moun - tain.
wild moun - tain thyme ____ Grows a - round the bloom - ing heath - er.
Will ye go, ____ las - sie,

E A E A E
go? And we'll all go to - geth - er, To pluck wild moun - tain
C♯m F♯m A/B E A E
thyme, ___ All a - round the bloom - ing heath - er. Will ye go, ___ las - sie, go?

THE WILD ROVER

Irish folksong

G C
1. I've been a wild ro - ver for man - y a year, ___ And I've
2. I went in - to an ale - house I used to fre - quent, ___ And I
3. Then out of my pock - et I took sover - eigns bright, ___ And the
4. I'll go back to my par - ents, con - fess what I've done, ___ And ___
G D7 G
spent all my mon - ey on whis - key and beer. ___ But now I'm re -
told the land - la - dy my mon - ey was spent. ___ I asked for a
land - la - dy's eyes o - pened wide with de - light. ___ She said, "I have
ask them to par - don their pro - dig - al son. ___ And if they ca -
C G D7
turn - ing with gold in great store, ___ And I nev - er will play the wild
bot - tle; she an - swered me, "Nay, ___ Such a cus - tom as yours I can
whis - kies and wines of the best, ___ And the words that I said, sure, were
ress me as oft - times be - fore, ___ Then I nev - er will play the wild
G D
ro - ver no more.
get an - y day."
on - ly in jest."
ro - ver no more.
And it's no, nay, nev - er; ___
G C G
No, nay, nev - er no more ___ Will I play ___ the wild
C G D7 G
ro - ver, ___ No, nev - er ___ no more. ___

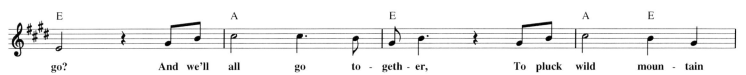

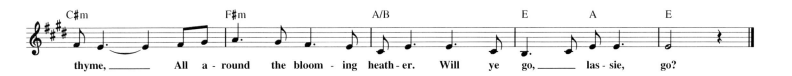

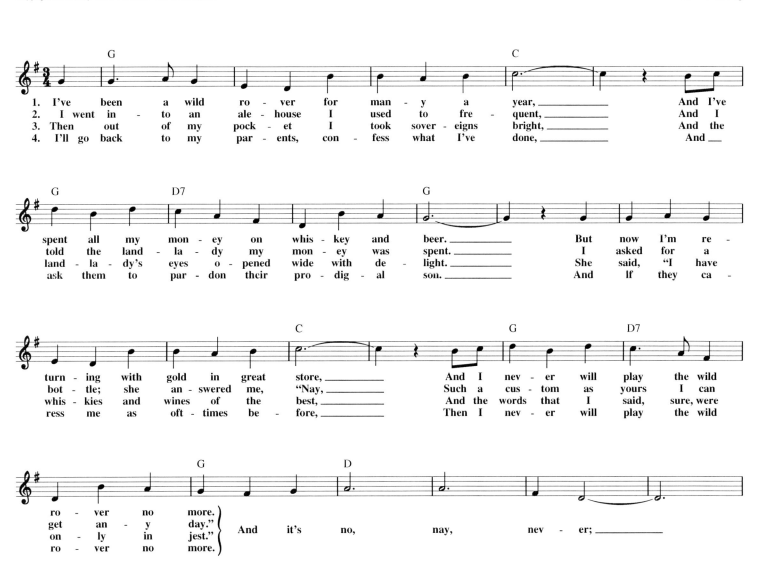

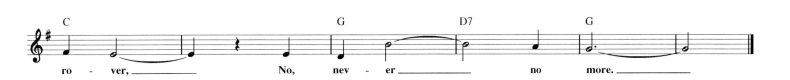

WILL YE NO' COME BACK AGAIN?

Scottish folksong

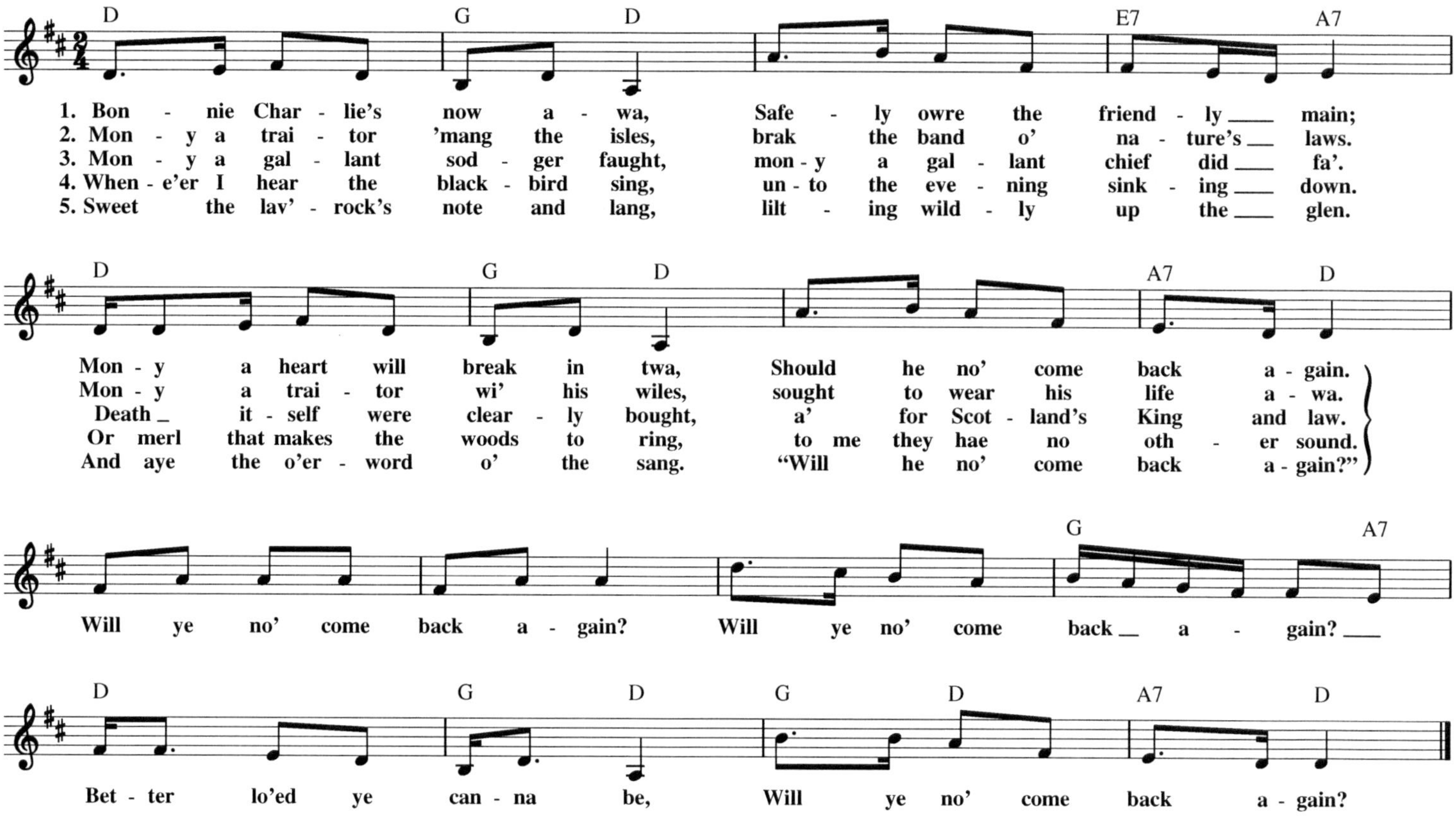

1. Bon - nie Char - lie's now a - wa, Safe - ly owre the friend - ly ___ main;
2. Mon - y a trai - tor 'mang the isles, brak the band o' na - ture's ___ laws.
3. Mon - y a gal - lant sod - ger faught, mon - y a gal - lant chief did ___ fa'.
4. When - e'er I hear the black - bird sing, un - to the eve - ning sink - ing ___ down.
5. Sweet the lav' - rock's note and lang, lilt - ing wild - ly up the ___ glen.

Mon - y a heart will break in twa, Should he no' come back a - gain.
Mon - y a trai - tor wi' his wiles, sought to wear his life a - wa.
Death _ it - self were clear - ly bought, a' for Scot - land's King and law.
Or merl that makes the woods to ring, to me they hae no oth - er sound.
And aye the o'er - word o' the sang, "Will he no' come back a - gain?"

Will ye no' come back a - gain? Will ye no' come back _ a - gain? ___

Bet - ter lo'ed ye can - na be, Will ye no' come back a - gain?

WILL YOU COME TO THE BOWER

Irish folksong

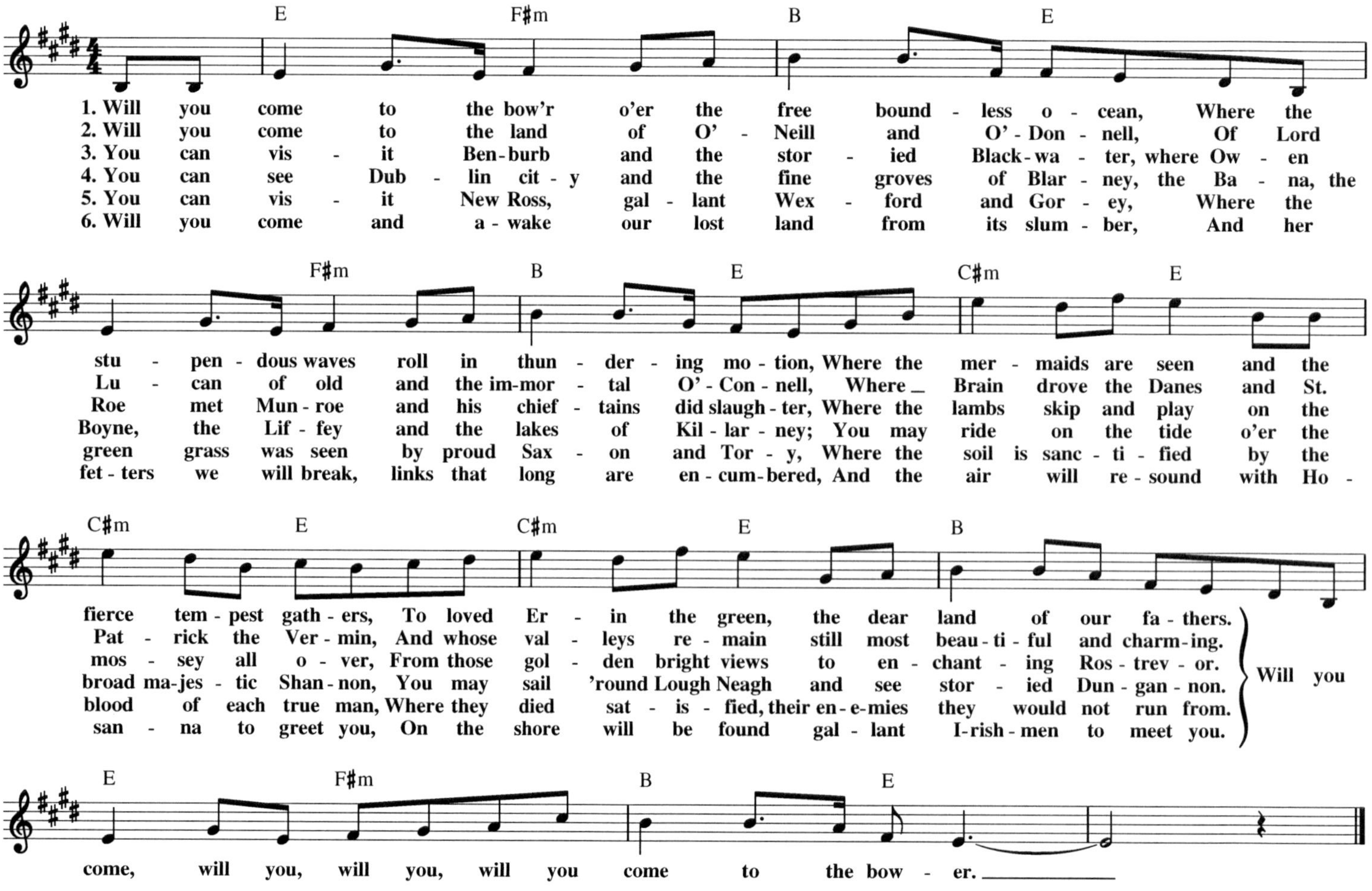

1. Will you come to the bow'r o'er the free bound - less o - cean, Where the
2. Will you come to the land of O' - Neill and O' - Don - nell, Of Lord
3. You can vis - it Ben - burb and the stor - ied Black - wa - ter, where Ow - en
4. You can see Dub - lin cit - y and the fine groves of Blar - ney, the Ba - na, the
5. You can vis - it New Ross, gal - lant Wex - ford and Gor - ey, Where the
6. Will you come and a - wake our lost land from its slum - ber, And her

stu - pen - dous waves roll in thun - der - ing mo - tion, Where the mer - maids are seen and the
Lu - can of old and the im - mor - tal O' - Con - nell, Where _ Brain drove the Danes and St.
Roe met Mun - roe and his chief - tains did slaugh - ter, Where the lambs skip and play on the
Boyne, the Lif - fey and the lakes of Kil - lar - ney; You may ride on the tide o'er the
green grass was seen by proud Sax - on and Tor - y, Where the soil is sanc - ti - fied by the
fet - ters we will break, links that long are en - cum - bered, And the air will re - sound with Ho -

fierce tem - pest gath - ers, To loved Er - in the green, the dear land of our fa - thers.
Pat - rick the Ver - min, And whose val - leys re - main still most beau - ti - ful and charm - ing.
Roe met Mun - roe and his chief - tains did slaugh - ter, Where the lambs skip and play on the
mos - sey all o - ver, From those gol - den bright views to en - chant - ing Ros - trev - or.
broad ma - jes - tic Shan - non, You may sail 'round Lough Neagh and see stor - ied Dun - gan - non.
blood of each true man, Where they died sat - is - fied, their en - e - mies they would not run from.
san - na to greet you, On the shore will be found gal - lant I - rish - men to meet you.

Will you

come, will you, will you, will you come to the bow - er. ___

THE WIND ON THE MOOR
(Null A Mhonadh E Nall A Mhonadh)

Folksong from the Hebrides

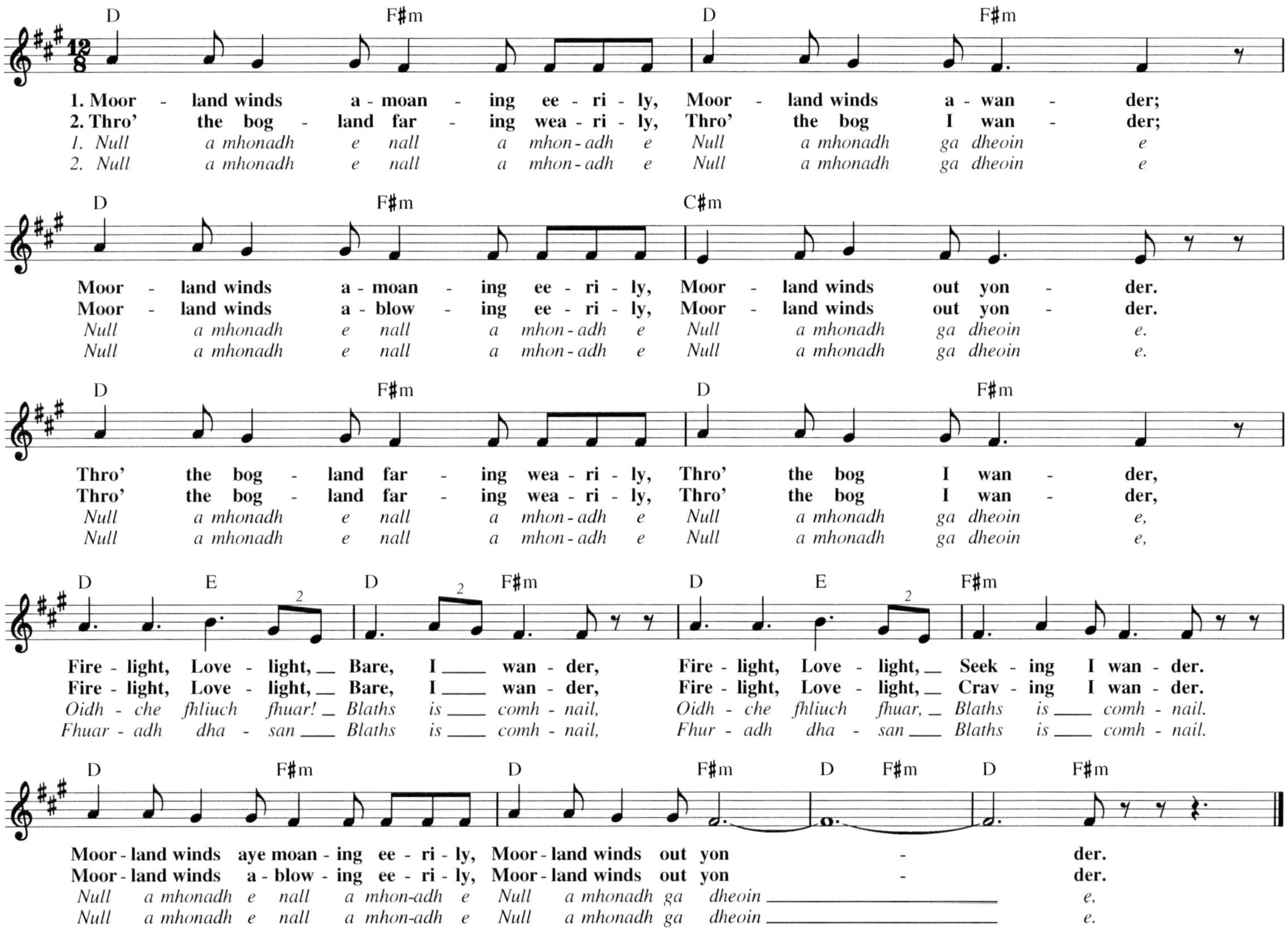

WITCHERY CANTRIPS
(Bòilich Nam Bana-Bhuidseach)

Folksong from the Hebrides

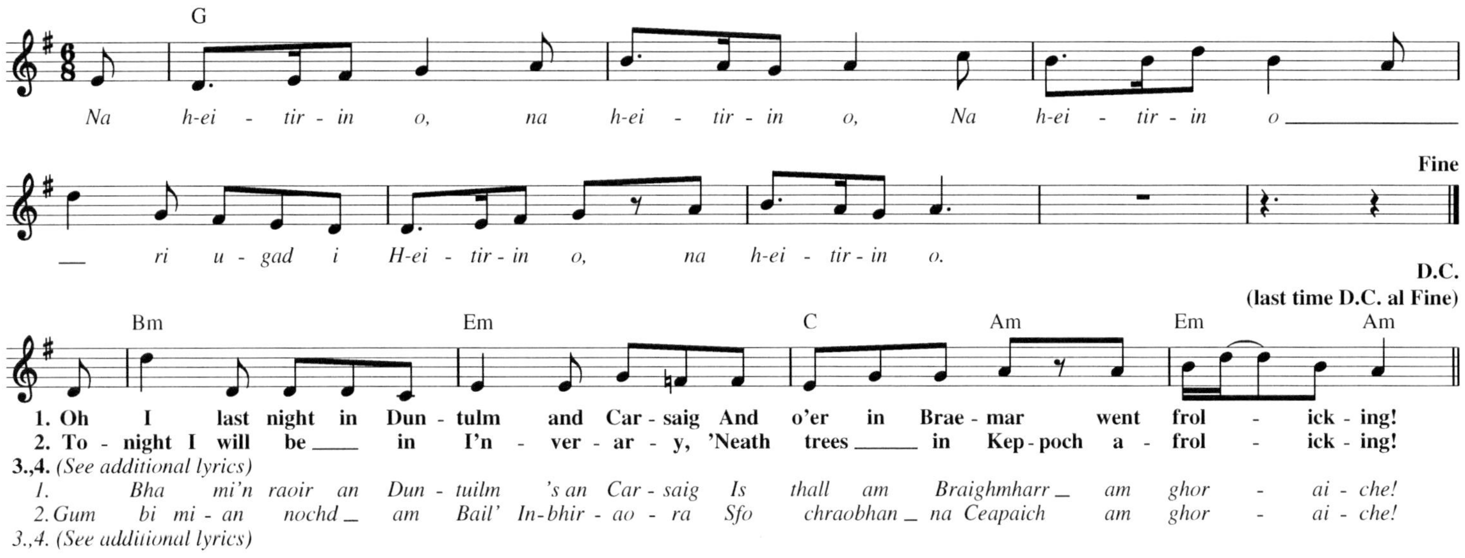

Additional Lyrics

3. **And I last night in Rannoch and Isla,**
   Iona and Canna went frolicking!

4. **Tonight I will be in Uist of shelldrakes,**
   And Kilchiaran strand a-frolicking!

3. *Bha mi'n raoir an Raineach 's an Ile,*
   An Canaidh 's an I am ghoraiche!

4. *Gum bi mi an nochd an Uibhist nam craghiadh,*
   Air traigh Cill-Chiaran am ghoraiche!

THE WIND THAT SHAKES THE BARLEY

Irish folksong

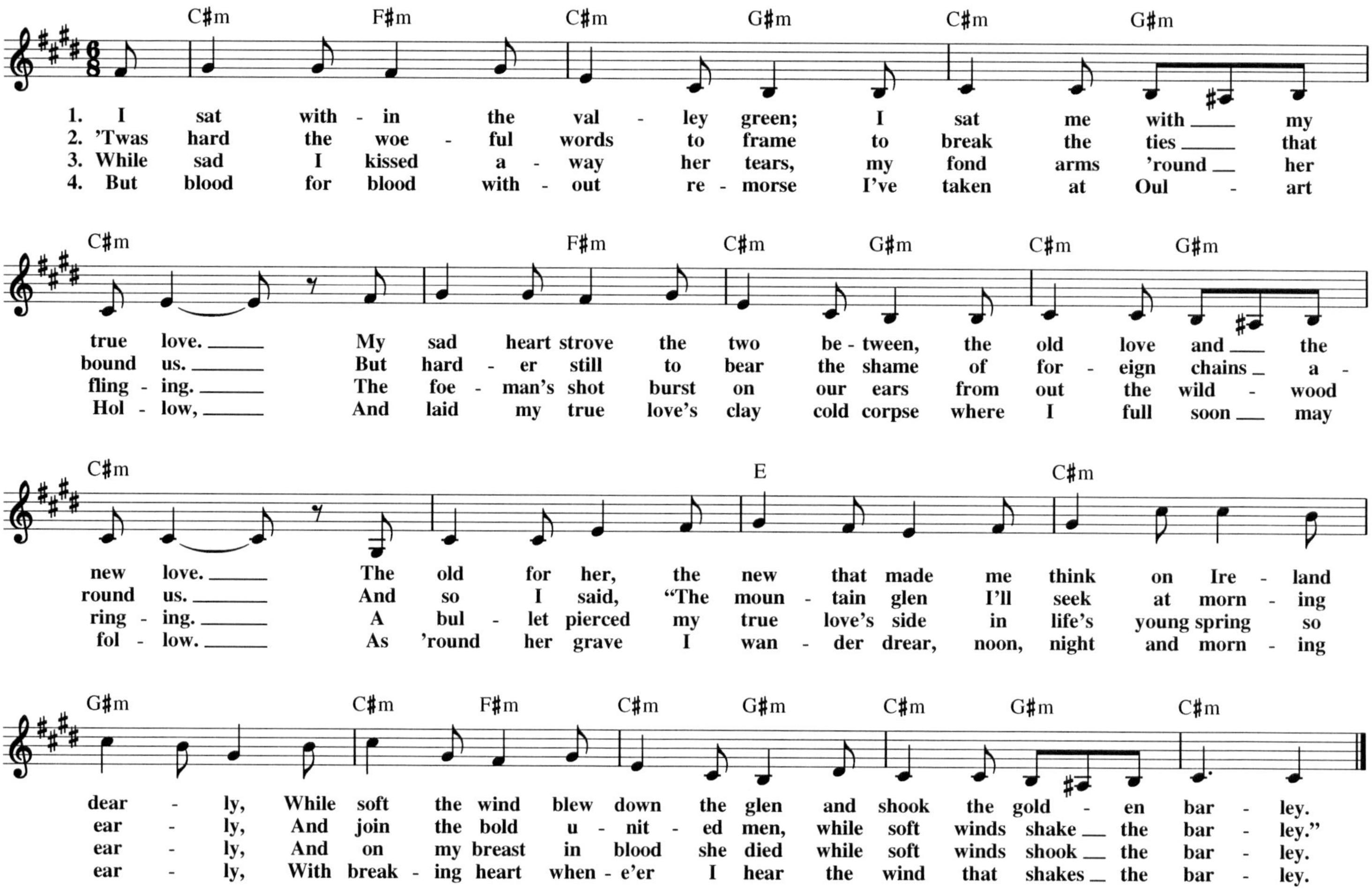

1. I sat with - in the val - ley green; I sat me with ____ my
2. 'Twas hard the woe - ful words to frame to break the ties ____ that
3. While sad I kissed a - way her tears, my fond arms 'round ____ her
4. But blood for blood with - out re - morse I've taken at Oul - art

true love. ____ My sad heart strove the two be - tween, the old love and ____ the
bound us. ____ But hard - er still to bear the shame of for - eign chains __ a -
fling - ing. ____ The foe - man's shot burst on our ears from out the wild - wood
Hol - low, ____ And laid my true love's clay cold corpse where I full soon ____ may

new love. ____ The old for her, the new that made me think on Ire - land
round us. ____ And so I said, "The moun - tain glen I'll seek at morn - ing
ring - ing. ____ A bul - let pierced my true love's side in life's young spring so
fol - low. ____ As 'round her grave I wan - der drear, noon, night and morn - ing

dear - ly, While soft the wind blew down the glen and shook the gold - en bar - ley.
ear - ly, And join the bold u - nit - ed men, while soft winds shake __ the bar - ley."
ear - ly, And on my breast in blood she died while soft winds shook __ the bar - ley.
ear - ly, With break - ing heart when - e'er I hear the wind that shakes __ the bar - ley.

WITCHERY CROON
(Fise Faise Fó)

Folksong from the Hebrides

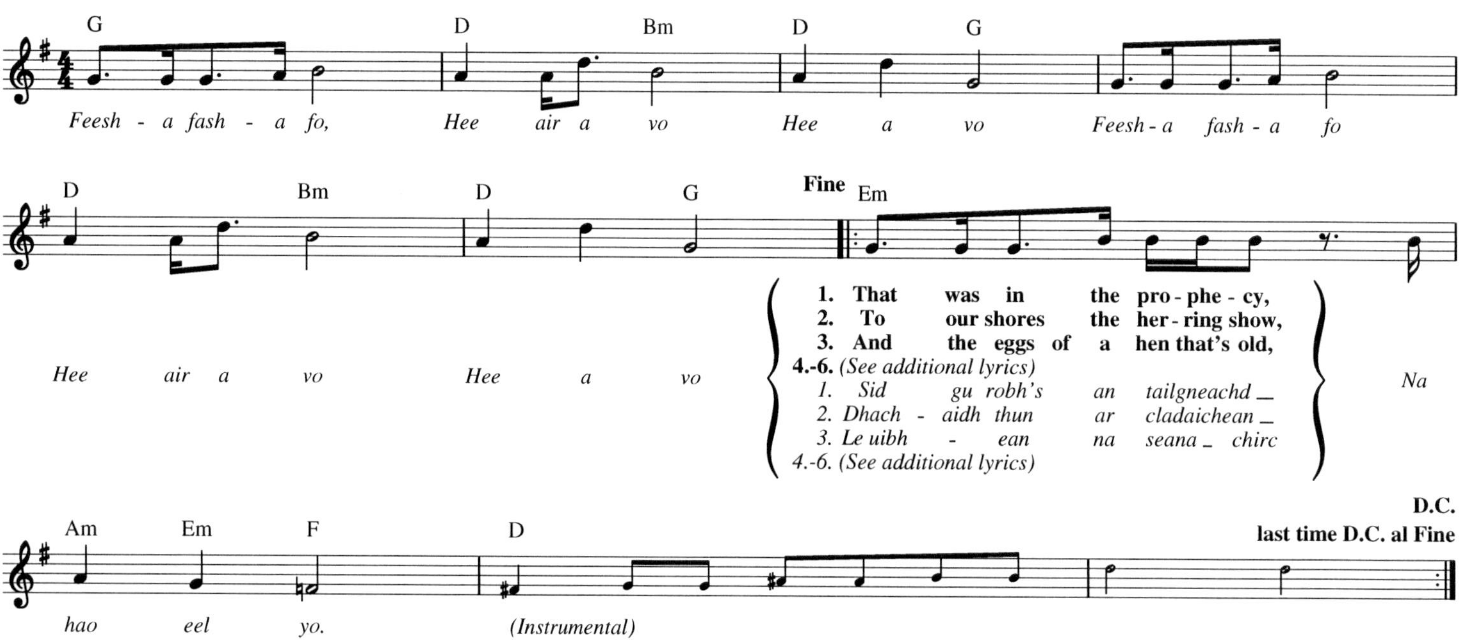

Feesh - a fash - a fo, Hee air a vo Hee a vo Feesh - a fash - a fo

Hee air a vo Hee a vo

1. That was in the pro - phe - cy,
2. To our shores the her - ring show,
3. And the eggs of a hen that's old,
4.-6. *(See additional lyrics)*
1. *Sid gu robh's an tailgneachd __*
2. *Dhach - aidh thun ar cladaichean __*
3. *Le uibh - ean na seana __ chirc*
4.-6. *(See additional lyrics)*

Na

D.C.
last time D.C. al Fine

hao eel yo. *(Instrumental)*

Additional Lyrics

4. Oft I brought by wizardry.
5. Thro' the minnows in cogue.
6. That was in the prophecy.

4. *'Stric a thug mi'n sgadanaich.*
5. *Leis a'mheudar gharbhan.*
6. *Sid gu robh's an tailgneachd.*

THE WITCHERY FATE SONG

Folksong from the Hebrides

WITCHERY GRACES
(Obaidh Na Cloinne)

Folksong from the Hebrides

THE WOMEN ARE WORSE THAN THE MEN

Irish folksong

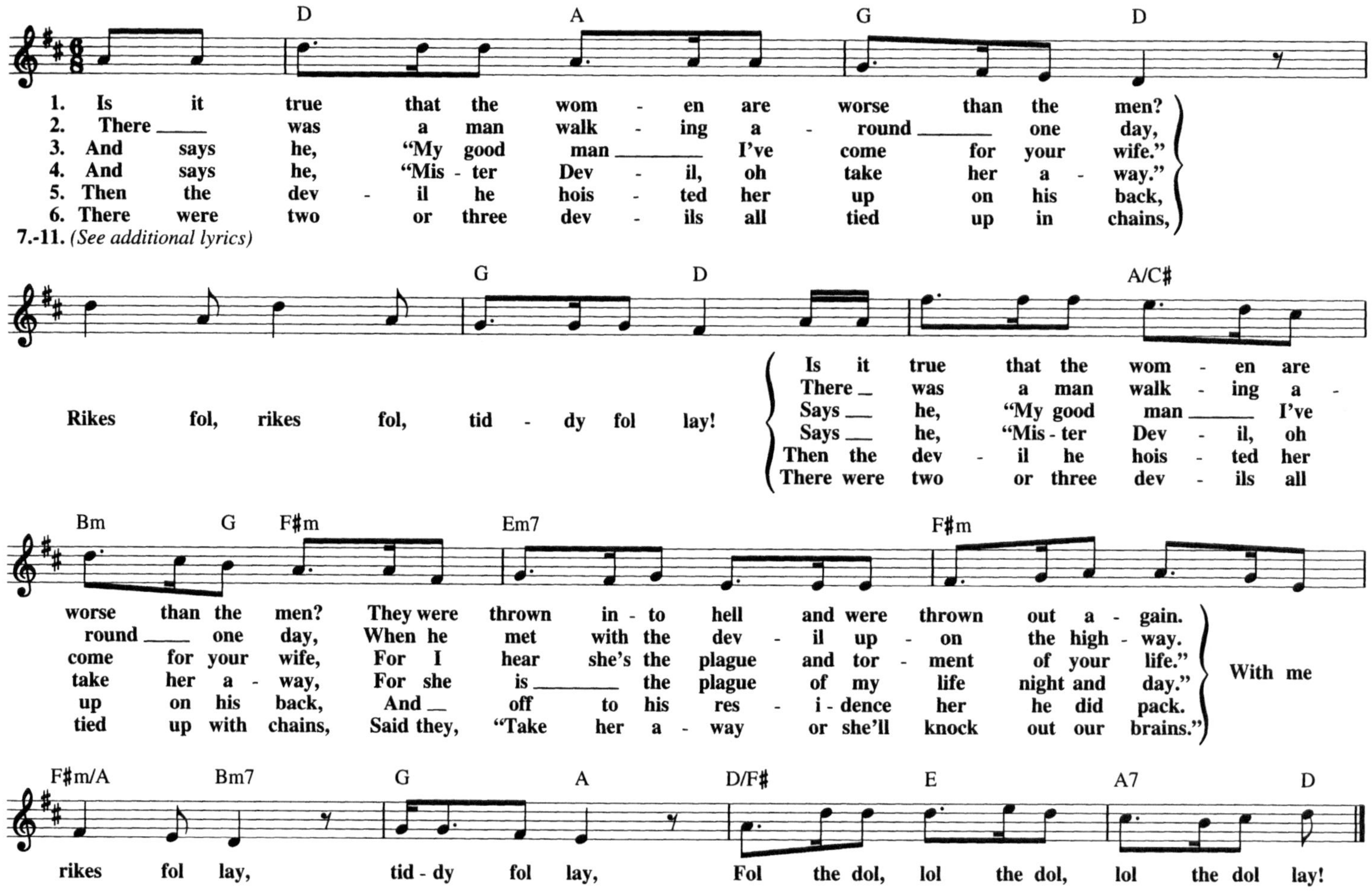

Additional Lyrics

7. And two other young devils were climbing the wall,
Rikes fol, rikes fol, tiddy fol lay!
And two other young devils were climbing the wall,
They said, "Take her away or she'll murder us all."

8. So the devil he hoisted her up on his back,
Rikes fol, rikes fol, tiddy fol lay!
So the devil he hoisted her up on his back
And back to her old fellow her he did pack.

9. And says he, "My good man, here's your wife back again,"
Rikes fol, rikes fol, tiddy fol lay!
And says he, "My good man, here's your wife back again,
For we couldn't put up with her in hell."

10. They were seven years going and nine coming back,
Rikes fol, rikes fol, tiddy fol lay!
They were seven years going and nine coming back
And she's called for the scrapin's she left in the pot.

11. So it's true that the women are worse than the men,
Rikes fol, rikes fol, tiddy fol lay!
So it's true that the women are worse than the men
For they went down to hell and were thrown out again.

THE WREN SONG

Irish folksong

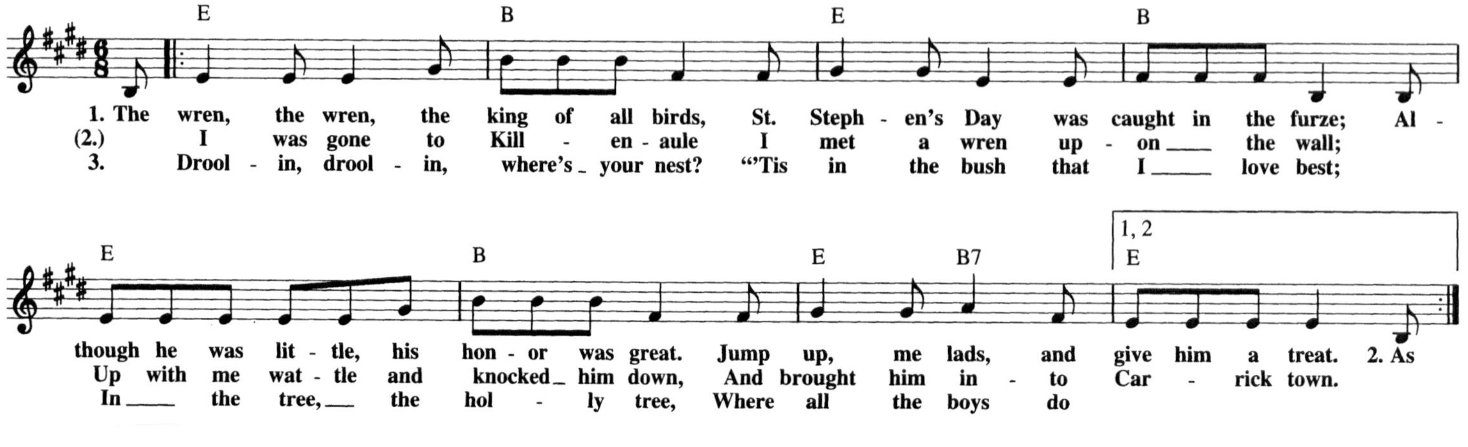

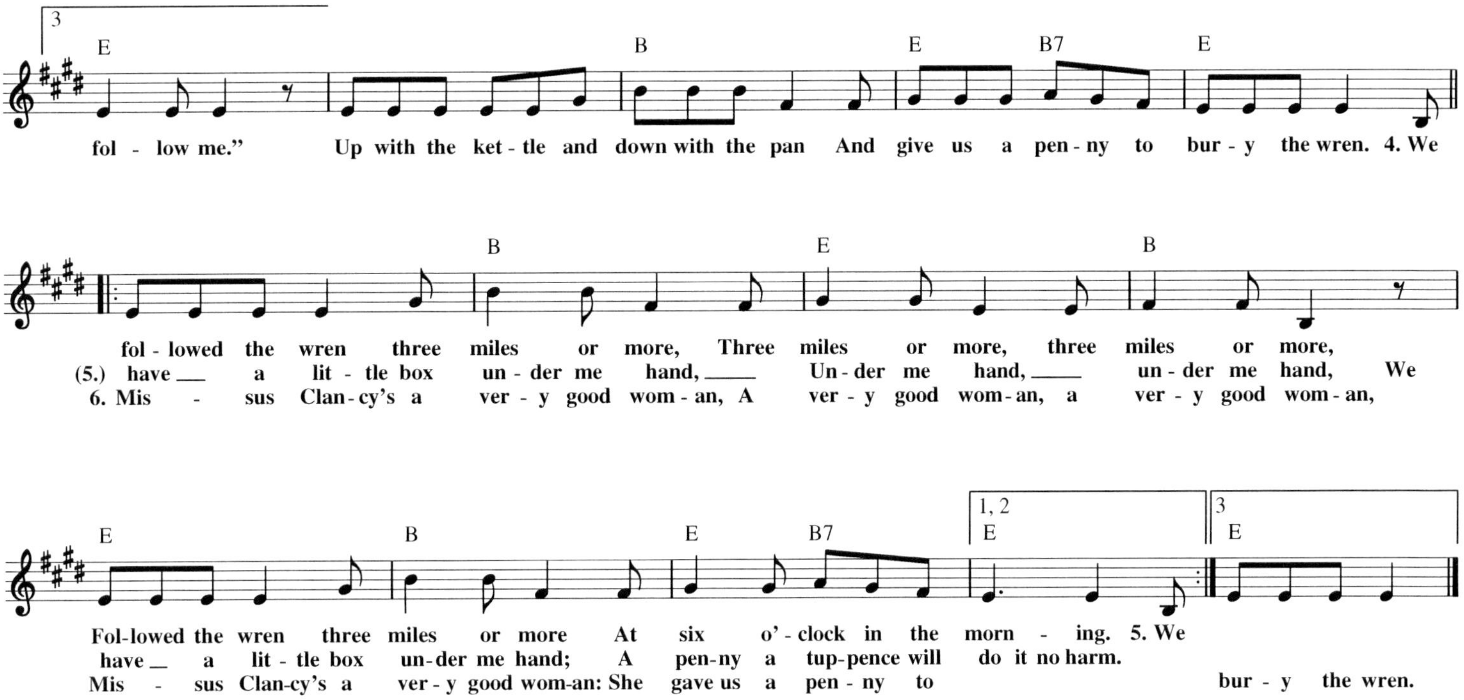

fol - low me." Up with the ket - tle and down with the pan And give us a pen - ny to bur - y the wren. 4. We

fol - lowed the wren three miles or more, Three miles or more, three miles or more,
(5.) have ___ a lit - tle box un - der me hand, ___ Un - der me hand, ___ un - der me hand, We
6. Mis - sus Clan-cy's a ver - y good wom-an, A ver - y good wom-an, a ver - y good wom-an,

Fol-lowed the wren three miles or more At six o' - clock in the morn - ing. 5. We
have ___ a lit - tle box un-der me hand; A pen - ny a tup-pence will do it no harm.
Mis - sus Clan-cy's a ver - y good wom-an: She gave us a pen - ny to bur - y the wren.

THE WORK OF THE WEAVERS

Scottish folksong

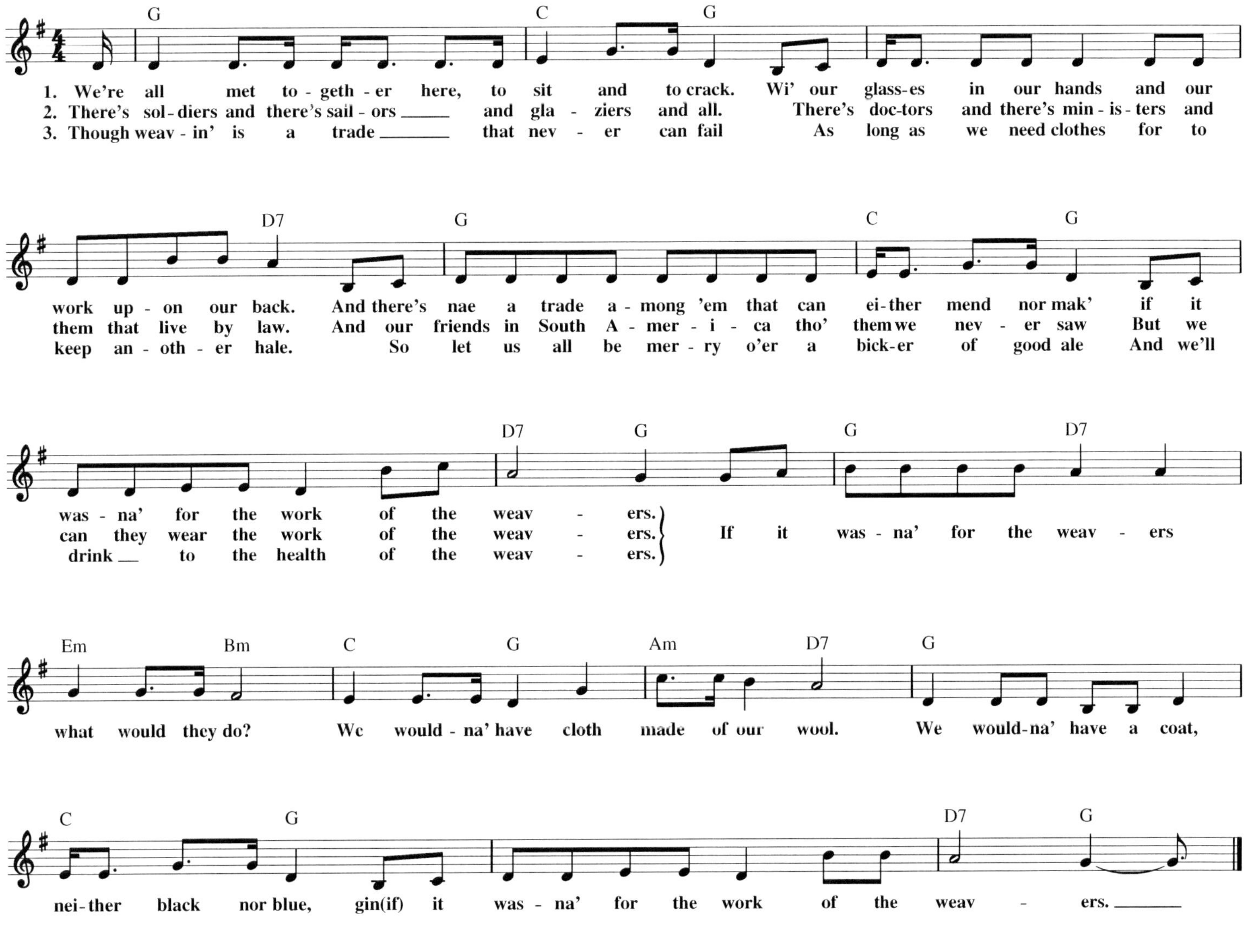

1. We're all met to - geth - er here, to sit and to crack. Wi' our glass - es in our hands and our
2. There's sol - diers and there's sail - ors ___ and gla - ziers and all. There's doc-tors and there's min - is - ters and
3. Though weav - in' is a trade ___ that nev - er can fail As long as we need clothes for to

work up - on our back. And there's nae a trade a - mong 'em that can ei - ther mend nor mak' if it
them that live by law. And our friends in South A - mer - i - ca tho' them we nev - er saw But we
keep an - oth - er hale. So let us all be mer - ry o'er a bick - er of good ale And we'll

was - na' for the work of the weav - ers.}
can they wear the work of the weav - ers.} If it was - na' for the weav - ers
drink ___ to the health of the weav - ers.}

what would they do? We would - na' have cloth made of our wool. We would-na' have a coat,

nei - ther black nor blue, gin(if) it was - na' for the work of the weav - ers. ___

THE WITCHERY MILKING CROON
(Obaidh Buaile)

Folksong from the Hebrides

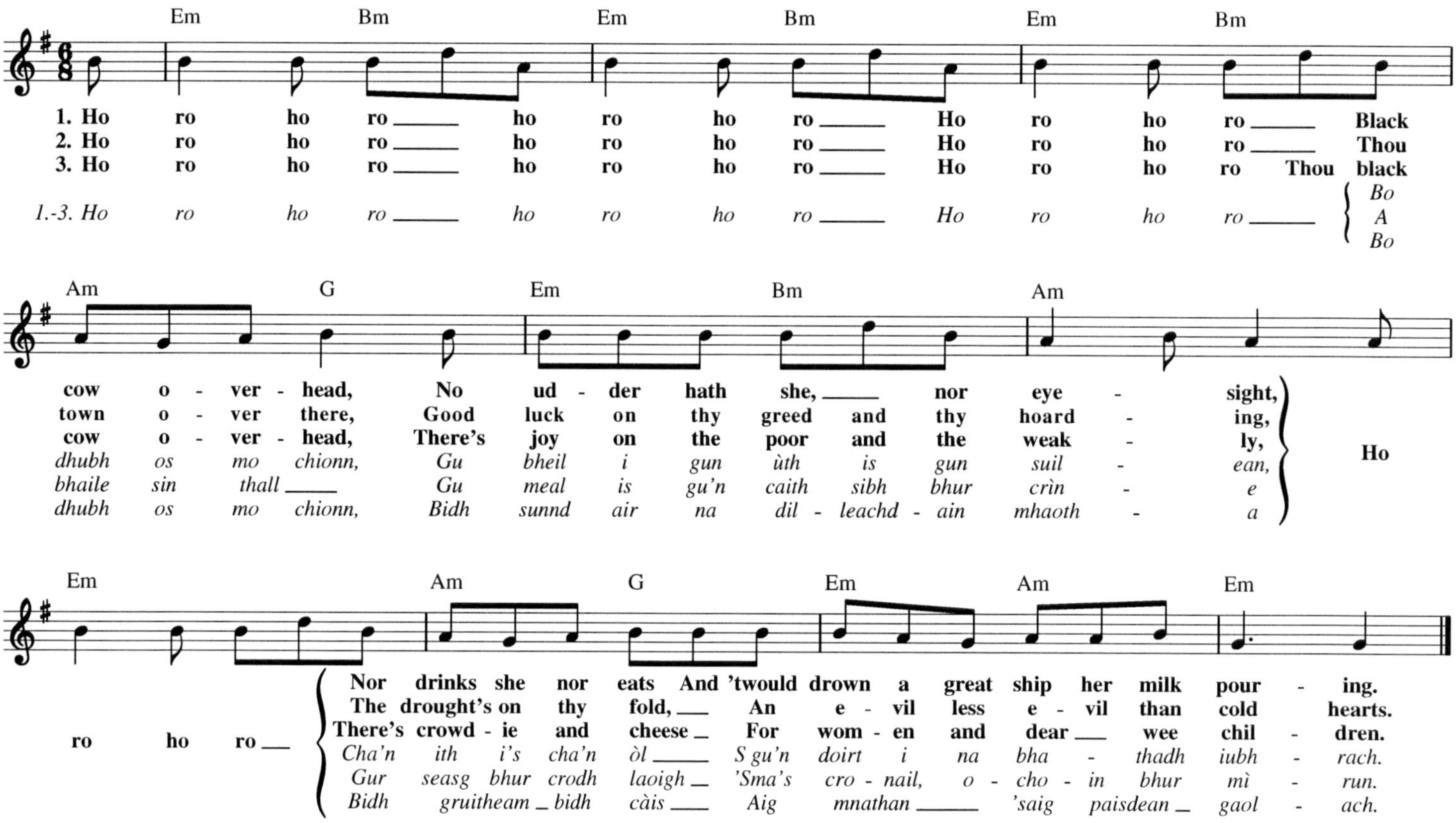

THE YELLOW PONEE
(An Póní Beag Buí)

Irish folksong

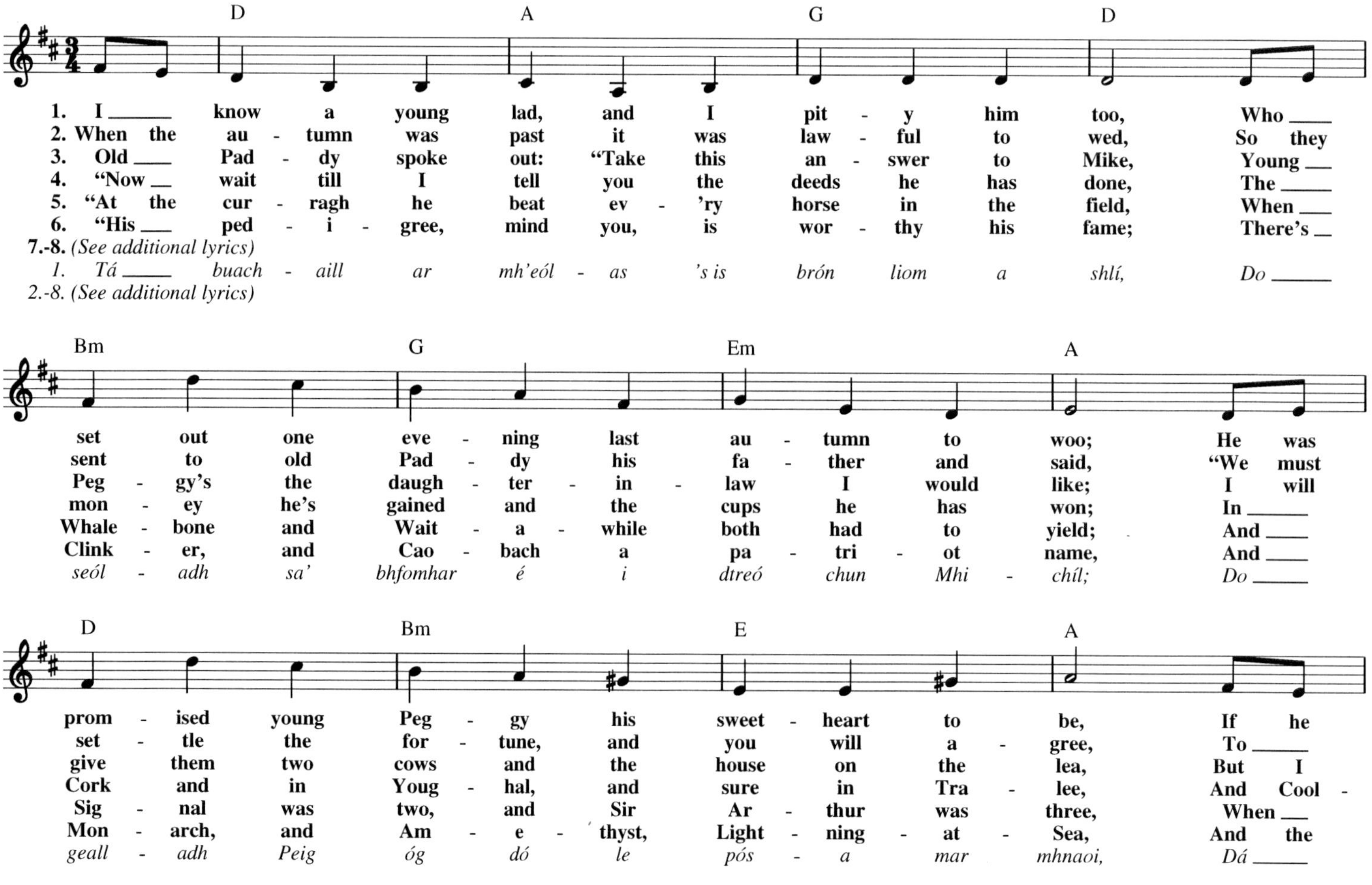

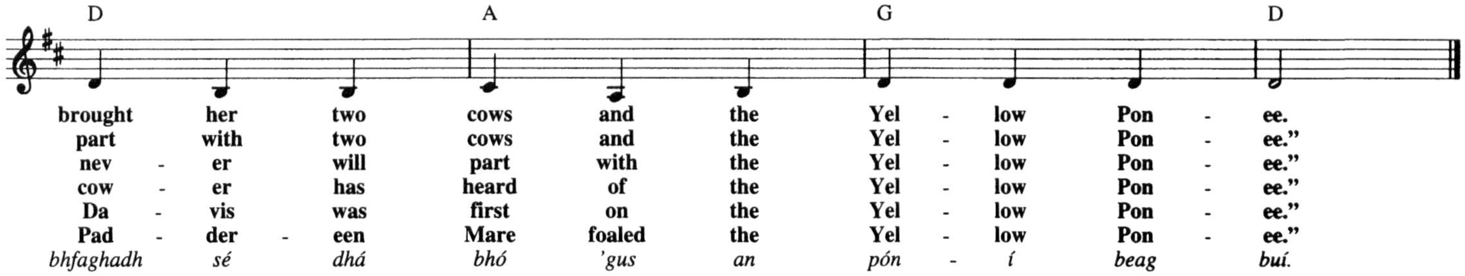

brought	her	two	cows	and	the	Yel	-	low	Pon	- ee.
part	with	two	cows	and	the	Yel	-	low	Pon	- ee."
nev	- er	will	part	with	the	Yel	-	low	Pon	- ee."
cow	- er	has	heard	of	the	Yel	-	low	Pon	- ee."
Da	- vis	was	first	on	the	Yel	-	low	Pon	- ee."
Pad	- der - een	Mare	foaled	the	Yel	-	low	Pon	- ee."
bhfaghadh	*sé*	*dhá*	*bhó*	*'gus*	*an*	*pón*	-	*í*	*beag*	*buí.*

Additional Lyrics

2. *Nuair imigh an fomhar bhí cead pósta ag an mnaoi*
Agus teachtaire seóladh chun seana-Phaidí,
Féachaint an dtúrfadh aon treó uaidh don óigfhear chun tis—
Cúbach is Cróinseach is an póní beag buí.

3. *Do fhreagair Paid Mór iad le glórthaibh a chinn:*
"Taithneann a sgeól liom 's an óigbhean mar mhnaoi;
Túrfad dhá bhó dhóibh 'gus tigh an Doirín,
Ach ni sgarfainn go deó leis an bpóní beag buí.

4. *"Eachtra 'neósfad ar mh'óig-each sa' tir,*
Gur i Malla do thóg sé mór-chuid cupaí,
I gCorcaigh, i n-Eóchaill is dar ndóigh i dTráilí,
'Gus ó Chúil Cabhair do fógradh mo phóní beag buí.

5. *"Ar an gCurrach 'n-a dhéidh sin do dhéin sé an gníomh*
Nuair a bhuaidh sé ar Whalebone *is ar* Wait-awhile *groí;*
Ar Signal *is ar* Sir Arthur *i rás Chonntae an Rí*
Do thóg Dávis *an Pláta le n-a phóní beag buí.*

6. *"Ó* Chlinker *le léaghadh dhíbh do théarnaigh a shíol,*
Ó Mhonarch, *ó* Eclipse *is ón gCaobaigh le maoiamh,*
Amethyst *tréitheach do b'fhearr laochas is gníomh,*
'Gus is í an Paidrín Mare *do rug an póní beag buí.*

7. "So Mickey, old friend and dear neighbor of mine,
Though I like your proposal, your terms I decline;
You may offer one daughter, or two or all three,
But I never will part with the Yellow Ponee."

8. Now I never would say a wrong word of old Pad,
But with gout and rheumatics he's terrible bad;
And next time he climbs upon the Yellow Ponee,
He must ride for a cure to the Spaat Tralee.

7. *"A Mhichil a chomharsa a stóraigh's a mhaoin,*
Taithneann do mheónlion, do ghnô is do chrich;
Ach dá dtúrfá Peig óg dó faoi dhô 'gus Caitlin,
Ni sgarfainn go deó leis an bpóní beag buí."

8. *Ni maith lion go bráth a cháil do rith sios,*
Tágútu ins gash cnúmh leis is fásga dathaighe;
Nuair a thigeann sé anáirde ar an rábaire bui,
Togann é den stair sin go Spáo thráili.

YE BANKS AND BRAES O' BONNIE DOON

Scottish folksong
Words by Robert Burns
Melody attributed to Charles Miller

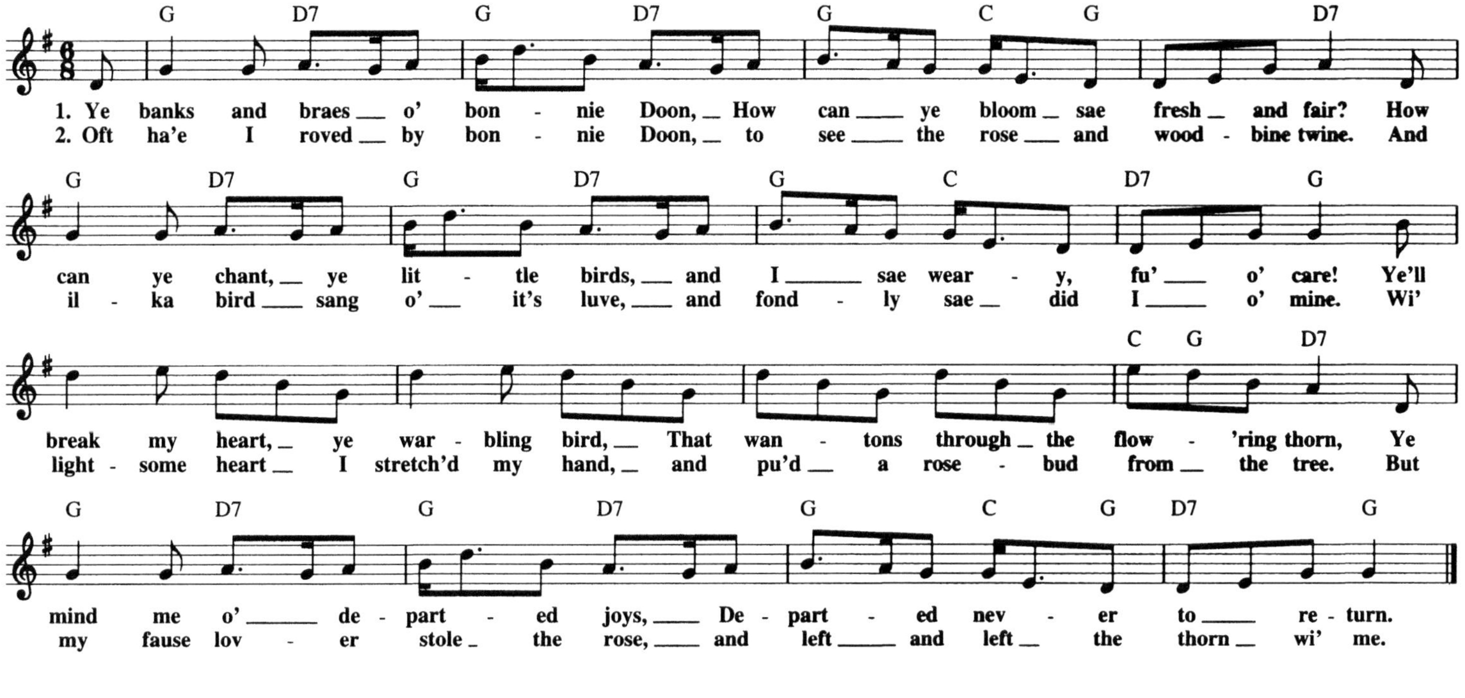

1. Ye banks and braes o' bon - nie Doon, How can ye bloom sae fresh and fair? How
2. Oft ha'e I roved by bon - nie Doon, to see the rose and wood - bine twine. And

can ye chant, ye lit - tle birds, and I sae wear - y, fu' o' care! Ye'll
il - ka bird sang o' it's luve, and fond - ly sae did I o' mine. Wi'

break my heart, ye war - bling bird, That wan - tons through the flow - 'ring thorn, Ye
light - some heart I stretch'd my hand, and pu'd a rose - bud from the tree. But

mind me o' de - part - ed joys, De - part - ed nev - er to re - turn.
my fause lov - er stole the rose, and left and left the thorn wi' me.

THE YELLOW BITTERN
(An Bunnán Buí)

Irish folksong

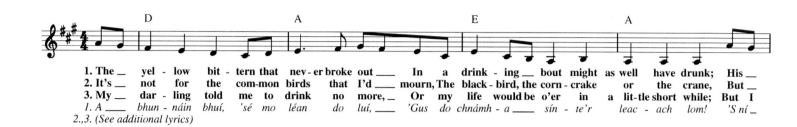

1. The __ yel - low bit - tern that nev - er broke out __ In a drink - ing __ bout might as well have drunk; His __
2. It's __ not for the com-mon birds that I'd __ mourn, The black - bird, the corn - crake or the crane, But __
3. My __ dar - ling told me to drink no more, __ Or my life would be o'er in a lit-tle short while; But I __

1. A __ bhun - náin bhuí, 'sé mo léan do luí, __ 'Gus do chnámh - a __ sín - te'r leac - ach lom! 'S ní __
2.,3. (See additional lyrics)

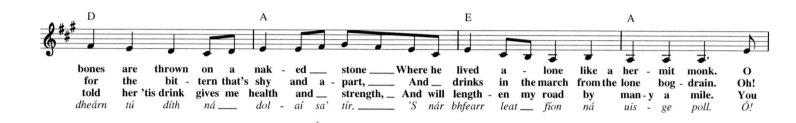

bones are thrown on a nak - ed __ stone __ Where he lived a - lone like a her - mit monk. O
for the bit - tern that's shy and a - part, __ And drinks in the march from the lone bog - drain. Oh!
told her 'tis drink gives me health and __ strength, __ And will length - en my road by man - y a mile. You

dheárn tú díth ná __ dol - aí sa' tír, _____ 'S nár bhfearr leat __ fíon ná uis - ge poll. Ó!

yel - low bit - tern! I pit - y your lot, Though they say that a sot like my - self is curst, I was
if I had known you were near your death, While my breath held __ out I'd __ run to you, 'Till a
see how the bird of the long smooth __ neck Could get his __ death from the thirst at last, Come __

bhí - theá 'síor - ól na _____ dighe, 'Gus deir siad go mbím ar an nós sin seal, 'S níl __

so - ber a - while, but I'll drink and be wise, __ For __ fear I should die in the end of thirst.
splash from the Lake of the Son of Bird, __ Your __ soul would have stirred and waked a - new.
son of my soul, and __ drink your cup, __ For you'll get no __ sup when your life is past.

braon dá bhfuíod nach __ leig - fead síos, __ Ar __ eag - la go bhfuinn féin bás don tart.

Additional Lyrics

2. *Ní h-iad bhur n-éanlaith 'tá mé 'éagcaoin*
   Nár chuir spéis ariamh sa' digh,
   Ach an bunnán léana bhíodh leis féin
   Ag ól go réidh ar na curraigh amuigh.
   Dá gcuirtheá sgéala fá mo dhéin
   Go raibh tú i bpéin, bhéinn in mo ruith
   Nó go mbaininn béim as Loch Mhic an Éin
   A fhliucfadh do bhéal is do chorp istigh.

3. *'Sé dúirt mo stór liom leigean don ól,*
   'S nach mbéinn-se beó ach seal beag gearr,
   Agus dúirt mé léithi gur chan si bréag,
   Gur bhfuide dom shaol an braon dighe 'fháil.
   Nach bhfeic tusa éan an phíobáin réidh,
   Go ndeacha sé dh'éag don tart ar ball?
   'S a dhaoine chléibh, Ó! fliuchaigí bhur mbéal,
   Ní bhfuí sibh braon i ndéidh bhur mbáis!

YOU CAN TELL THAT I'M IRISH

Words and Music by
George M. Cohan

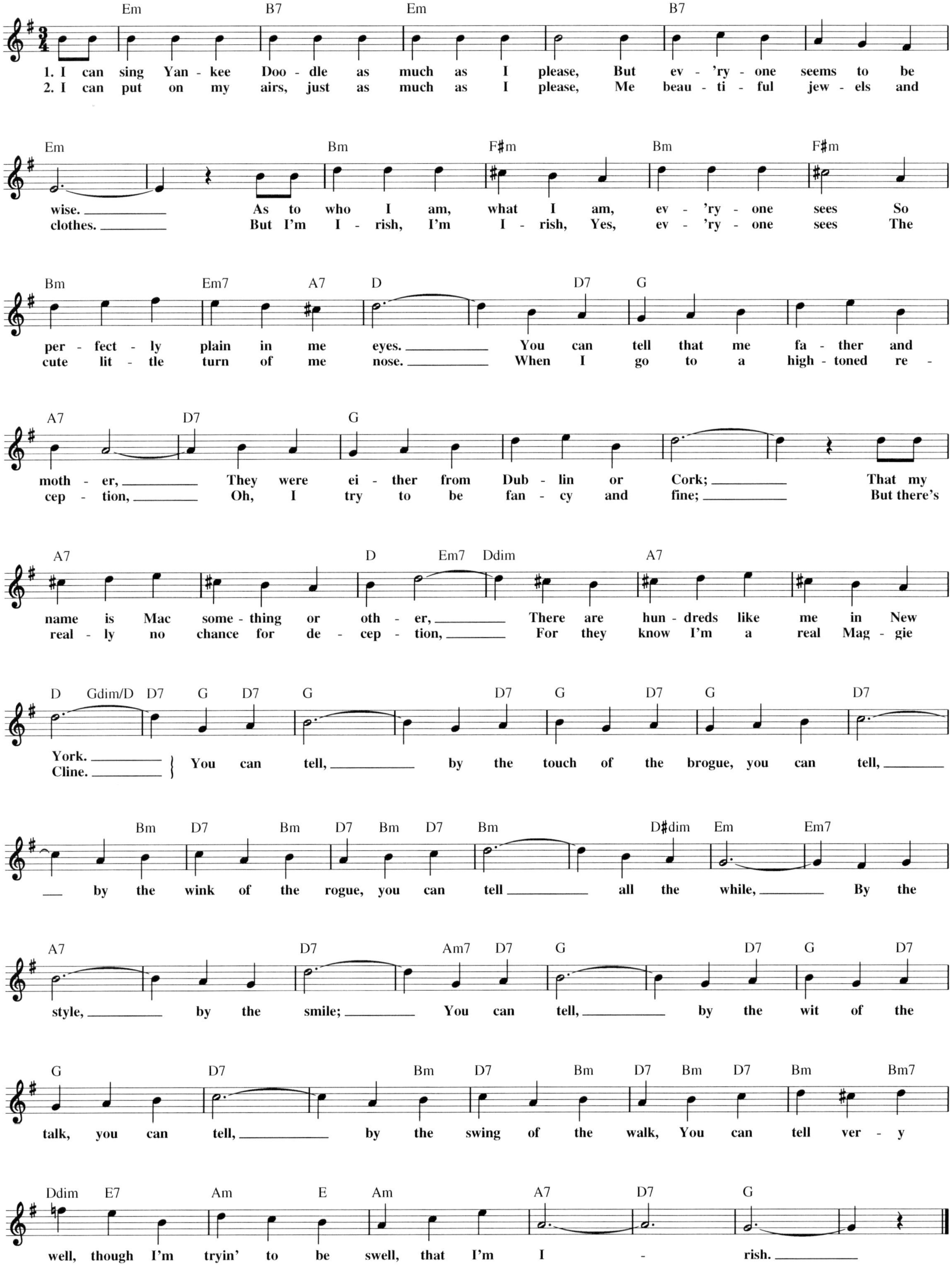

YOU CAN'T DENY YOU'RE IRISH

Words and Music by
George M. Cohan

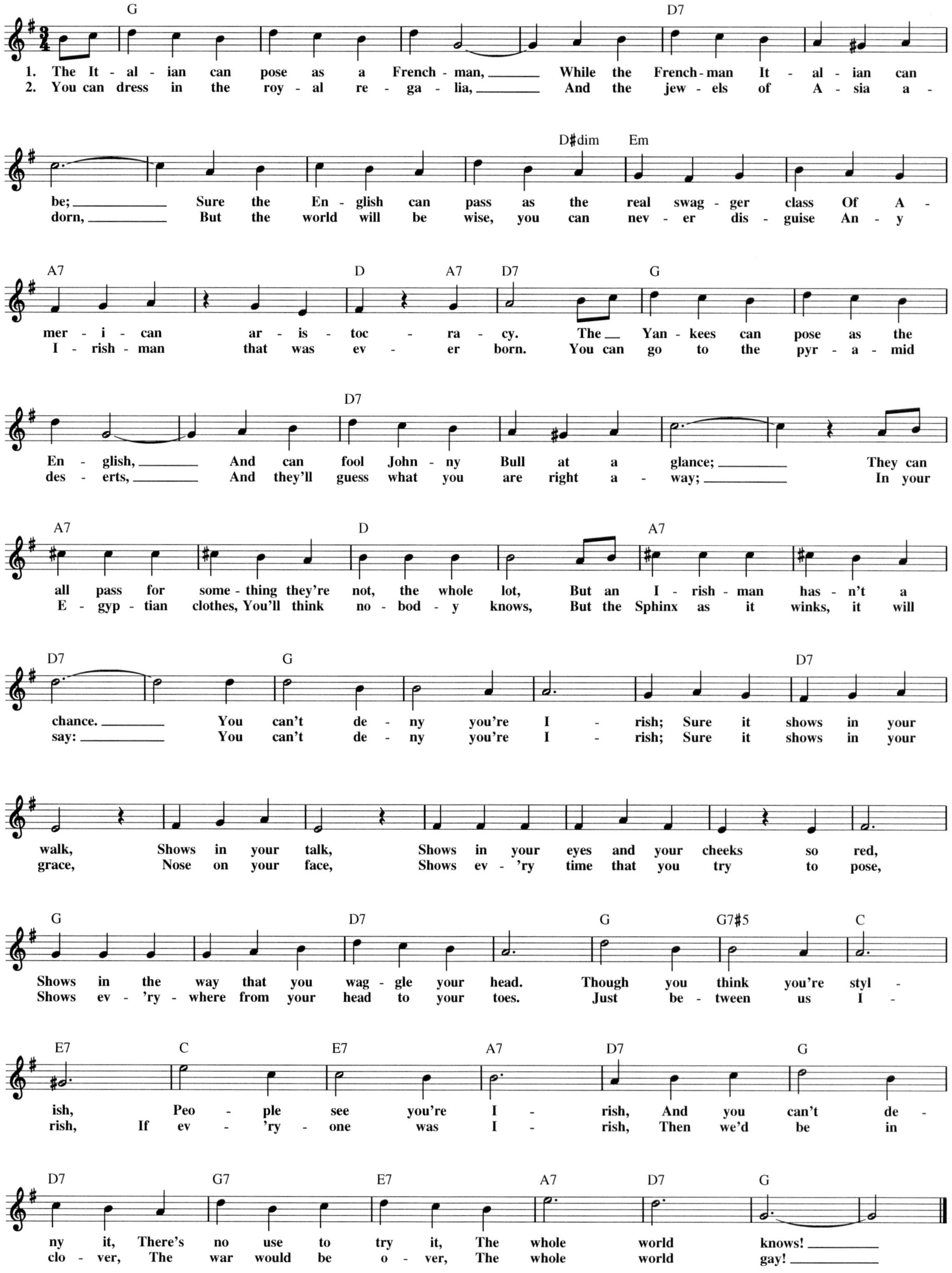

Guitar Chords

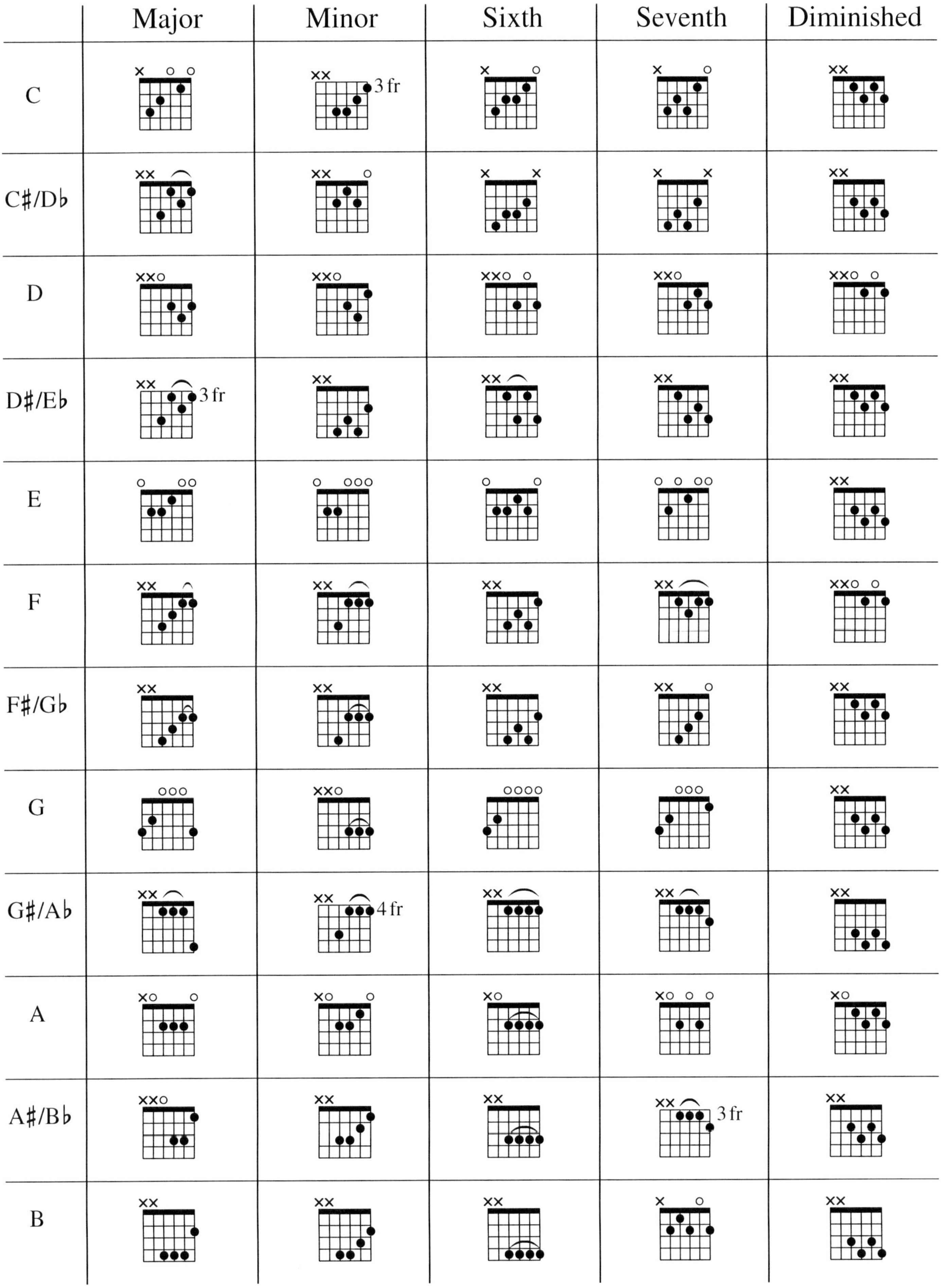

	Major	Minor	Sixth	Seventh	Diminished
C					
C#/Db					
D					
D#/Eb					
E					
F					
F#/Gb					
G					
G#/Ab					
A					
A#/Bb					
B					

THE ULTIMATE COLLECTION OF
FAKE BOOKS

The Ultimate Fake Book - 3rd Edition
Includes over 1,200 hits: Blue Skies • Body and Soul • Theme from Cheers • Endless Love • A Foggy Day • Isn't It Romantic? • Memory • Mona Lisa • Moon River • Operator • Piano Man • Roxanne • Satin Doll • Shout • Small World • Speak Softly, Love • Strawberry Fields Forever • Tears in Heaven • Unforgettable • hundreds more!

00240024 C Edition $45.00
00240026 B♭ Edition $45.00
00240025 E♭ Edition $45.00

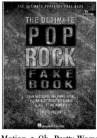

Best Fake Book Ever - 2nd Edition
More than 1000 songs from all styles of music, including: All My Loving • American Pie • At the Hop • Cabaret • Dust in the Wind • Fever • Free Bird • From a Distance • Hello, Dolly! • Hey Jude • King of the Road • Longer • Misty • Route 66 • Sentimental Journey • Somebody • Song Sung Blue • Spinning Wheel • Unchained Melody • We Will Rock You • What a Wonderful World • Wooly Bully • Y.M.C.A. • You're So Vain • and hundreds more.

00290239 C Edition $45.00
00240083 B♭ Edition $45.00
00240084 E♭ Edition $45.00

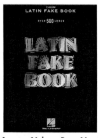

The Ultimate Pop/Rock Fake Book - 3rd Edition
Over 500 pop standards and contemporary hits, including: Addicted to Love • All Shook Up • Another One Bites the Dust • Crocodile Rock • Crying • Don't Know Much • Dust in the Wind • Earth Angel • Every Breath You Take • Hero • Hey Jude • Hold My Hand • Imagine • Layla • The Loco-Motion • Oh, Pretty Woman • On Broadway • Spinning Wheel • Stand by Me • Stayin' Alive • Tears in Heaven • True Colors • The Twist • Vision of Love • A Whole New World • Wild Thing • Wooly Bully • Yesterday • and many more!

00240099 $39.95

Latin Fake Book
Over 500 Latin songs in many styles, including mambos, sambas, cha cha chás, rhumbas, tangos, salsa, Latin pop and rock, and more. Songs include: Adiós • Água De Beber • Amapola • Antigua • Babalú • Bésame Mucho • Brazil • Cachita • Desafinado • Dindi • El Triste • Ella • Flamingo • Frenesí • The Girl from Ipanema • La Cucaracha • La Fiesta • Livin' La Vida Loca • Malagueña • Mambo No. 5 • Mambo No. 8 • Manteca • Maria Elena • One Note Samba • Poinciana • Similau • Spanish Eyes • Speak Low • St. Thomas • Tico Tico • Triste • Wave • more!

00240146 $35.00

The Ultimate Jazz Fake Book
Over 625 jazz classics spanning more than nine decades and representing all the styles of jazz. Includes: All of Me • All the Things You Are • Basin Street Blues • Birdland • Desafinado • A Foggy Day • I Concentrate on You • In the Mood • Take the "A" Train • Yardbird Suite • and many more!

00240079 C Edition $39.95
00240080 B♭ Edition $39.95
00240081 E♭ Edition $39.95

The Hal Leonard Real Jazz Book
A unique collection of jazz material in a wide variety of styles with no song duplication from *The Ultimate Jazz Fake Book!* Includes over 500 songs including a great deal of hard-to-find repertoire and a significant number of songs which have never before been printed.

00240097 C Edition $39.95
00240122 B♭ Edition $39.95
00240123 E♭ Edition $39.95

The Ultimate Broadway Fake Book - 4th Edition
More than 670 show-stoppers from over 200 shows! Includes: Ain't Misbehavin' • All I Ask of You • As If We Never Said Goodbye • Bewitched • Camelot • Memory • Don't Cry for Me Argentina • Edelweiss • I Dreamed a Dream • If I Were a Rich Man • Oklahoma • People • Seasons of Love • Send in the Clowns • Someone • What I Did for Love • and more.

00240046 $39.95

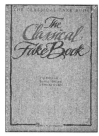

The Classical Fake Book
An unprecedented, amazingly comprehensive reference of over 650 classical themes and melodies for all classical music lovers. Includes everything from Renaissance music to Vivaldi and Mozart to Mendelssohn. Lyrics in the original language are included when appropriate.

00240044 $24.95

R&B Fake Book
This terrific fake book features more than 250 classic R&B hits: Baby Love • Best of My Love • Dancing in the Street • Easy • Get Ready • Heatwave • Here and Now • Just Once • Let's Get It On • The Loco-Motion • (You Make Me Feel Like) A Natural Woman • One Sweet Day • Papa Was a Rollin' Stone • Save the Best for Last • September • Sexual Healing • Shop Around • Smoke Gets in Your Eyes • Still • Tell It Like It Is • Up on the Roof • Walk on By • What's Going On • more!

00240107 C Edition $25.00

The Ultimate Country Fake Book - 4th Edition
This 4th edition includes even more of your favorite country hits – over 700 songs by country superstars of yesterday and today: Achy Breaky Heart (Don't Tell My Heart) • Always on My Mind • Are You Lonesome Tonight? • Boot Scootin' Boogie • Crazy • Daddy Sang Bass • Down at the Twist and Shout • Elvira • Forever and Ever, Amen • Friends in Low Places • The Gambler • Jambalaya • King of the Road • Rocky Top • Sixteen Tons • There's a Tear in My Beer • What's Forever For • Your Cheatin' Heart • and more.

00240049 $39.95

Wedding & Love Fake Book
Over 400 classic and contemporary songs, including: All for Love • All I Ask of You • Anniversary Song • Ave Maria • Can You Feel the Love Tonight • Endless Love • Forever and Ever, Amen • Forever in Love • I Wanna Be Loved • It Could Happen to You • Misty • My Heart Will Go On • So in Love • Through the Years • Vision of Love • and more.

00240041 $29.95

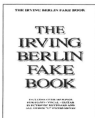

The Irving Berlin Fake Book
Over 150 Berlin songs, including: Alexander's Ragtime Band • Always • Blue Skies • Easter Parade • God Bless America • Happy Holiday • Heat Wave • I've Got My Love to Keep Me Warm • Puttin' on the Ritz • White Christmas • and more.

00240043 $19.95

Classic Rock Fake Book
This new fake book is a great compilation of more than 250 terrific songs of the rock era, arranged for piano, voice, guitar and all C instruments. Includes: All Right Now • American Woman • Birthday • Born to Be Wild • Brown Eyed Girl • Free Bird • Honesty • I Shot the Sheriff • I Want You to Want Me • Imagine • It's Still Rock and Roll to Me • Lay Down Sally • Layla • Magic Carpet Ride • My Generation • Rikki Don't Lose That Number • Rock and Roll All Nite • Spinning Wheel • Sweet Home Alabama • White Room • We Will Rock You • lots more!

00240108 $24.95

Gospel's Greatest Fake Book
An excellent resource for Gospel titles with over 450 songs, including: Amazing Grace • At the Cross • Behold the Lamb • Blessed Assurance • He Touched Me • Heavenly Sunlight • His Eye Is on the Sparrow • Holy Ground • How Great Thou Art • I Saw the Light • I'd Rather Have Jesus • In the Garden • Joshua (Fit the Battle of Jericho) • Just a Closer Walk with Thee • Lord, I'm Coming Home • Midnight Cry • Morning Has Broken • My Tribute • Near the Cross • The Old Rugged Cross • Precious Memories • Rock of Ages • Shall We Gather at the River? • What a Friend We Have in Jesus • and more.

00240136 $24.95

FOR MORE INFORMATION, SEE YOUR LOCAL MUSIC DEALER, OR WRITE TO:

HAL•LEONARD® CORPORATION
7777 W. BLUEMOUND RD. P.O. BOX 13819 MILWAUKEE, WI 53213

http://www.halleonard.com

Prices, contents and availabilty subject to change without notice

0700

HAL LEONARD presents

FAKE BOOKS FOR BEGINNERS

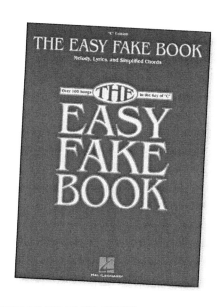

HOW TO PLAY FROM A FAKE BOOK

Faking your own arrangements from melodies and chords

by Blake Neely

Ever wondered how to create better accompaniments for the melodies in your favorite fake books? This "teach yourself" book introduces you to chord building, various rhythmic styles, and much more, so that you play the songs you like just the way you want them. Keyboard players with a basic understanding of notation and sight-reading will be on their way to more fun with fake books. The relaxed tone of the text and selection of fun songs keep *How to Play From a Fake Book* entertaining throughout – perfect for amateur musicians, or as a supplement for keyboard teachers and their students.

_____00220019 ....$10.95

YOUR FIRST FAKE BOOK

An entry-level fake book! This book features larger-than-most fake book notation with simplified harmonies and melodies – and all songs are in the key of C. An introduction addresses basic instruction in playing from a fake book. Includes over 100 songs, including: Ain't Misbehavin' • All the Things You Are • America the Beautiful • Beauty and the Beast • Bewitched • Blueberry Hill • Can't Help Falling in Love • Don't Get Around Much Anymore • Edelweiss • Getting to Know You • Heart and Soul • It Only Takes a Moment • Leaving on a Jet Plane • Let It Be • Love Me Tender • Maria • Mood Indigo • Satin Doll • Somewhere Out There • Try to Remember • When the Saints Go Marching In • Young at Heart • and more.

_____00240112 ....$19.95

THE EASY FAKE BOOK

This follow-up to the popular *Your First Fake Book* features over 100 more songs for even beginning-level musicians to enjoy. This volume features the same larger notation with simplified harmonies and melodies with all songs in the key of C. In addition, this edition features introductions for each song, adding a more finished sound to the arrangements! Songs include: Alfie • All I Ask of You • Always on My Mind • Angel • Autumn in New York • Blue Skies • Candle in the Wind • Fields of Gold • Grow Old With Me • Hey, Good Lookin' • I'll Be There • Imagine • Memory • Misty • My Heart Will Go On (Love Theme from *Titanic*) • People • Stand by Me • Star Dust • Tears in Heaven • Unchained Melody • What a Wonderful World • and more.

_____00240144...$19.95

FOR MORE INFORMATION, SEE YOUR LOCAL MUSIC DEALER,
OR WRITE TO:

HAL•LEONARD® CORPORATION
7777 W. BLUEMOUND RD. P.O. BOX 13819 MILWAUKEE, WI 53213

Visit Hal Leonard Online at www.halleonard.com

Prices, contents, and availability subject to change without notice